CW00808883

BP TANKERS
A Group Fleet History

The AFRA Suezmax 151,400 - sdwt *British Harrier*, launched in 1997 by Samsung Heavy Industries in Changwon, established a tank layout format which has served as a model for many future BP crude oil carriers. (*FotoFlite*)

BP TANKERS
A Group Fleet History

W J Harvey and Dr R J Solly

CHATHAM PUBLISHING
LONDON

MBI PUBLISHING COMPANY
MINNESOTA

First published in Great Britain in 2005 by
Chatham Publishing
Lionel Leventhal Ltd,
Park House, 1 Russell Gardens,
London NW11 9NN

Reprinted 2006

Distributed in the United States of America by
MBI Publishing Company
Galtier Plaza, Suite 200, 380 Jackson Street,
St Paul, MN 55101-3885, USA

British Library Cataloguing in Publication Data

Harvey, W. J.
BP tankers: a group fleet history
1. BP Shipping Limited — History 2. Tankers — History
I. Title II. Solly, Dr. Raymond
623. 8 245

ISBN 1 86176 251 8

Designed and Typeset by MRM Graphics, Winslow, Buckinghamshire
Printed and bound in China

Contents

Contents cont'd

Foreword

As a great grandson of Charles Greenway and current holder of the peerage he was awarded in 1927 on retirement from the Anglo-Persian Oil Company, I was delighted to be invited to write a foreword to this book which celebrates the 90th anniversary of the formation of the British Tanker Company.

Ships have been a ruling passion in my life since early childhood and I can well remember the excitement of a visit to Falmouth in 1950 when I first glimpsed the unmistakable red, white and green funnel markings of a number of BP tankers undergoing repair at the yard of Silley, Cox & Co.

Since then I have acquired many more BP tanker memories: the reassuring bulk of *British Hussar* (1962) looming out of the mist after a violent thunderstorm in a small yacht in the Western Channel; the French subsidiary's elegant *Azay-le Rideau* (1964) moored at bustling Port Said; the products tanker *British Hawthorn* (1964) threading her way through the Stockholm Archipelago and the smart red-hulled coastal tanker *BP Harrier* (1980) sweeping past Dungeness on a flood tide. Only this summer it was a joy to see *British Merlin* (2003), immaculate in the restored 1926 funnel colours, at the Trafalgar 200 International Naval Review, continuing a proud tradition begun with *British Fame* (1936) at the 1937 Coronation Naval Review. In the interim I was also privileged to witness the brand new *British Sailor* at our present Queen's Coronation Naval Review in 1953 and, a quarter of a century later, the imposing VLCC *British Respect* (1990) at her Silver Jubilee Review.

I never knew my great grandfather but he was by all accounts a notable personality in the oil business. Described in *The Times* obituary as a pioneer in empire trade, he was senior partner of the Indian trading house Shaw Wallace, which held the agency for marketing the Burmah Oil Company's products, when 'headhunted' in 1909 to be a director of the newly incorporated Anglo Persian Oil Company, becoming managing director the following year.

Mindful of the importance of keeping the vulnerable new company independent, he rebuffed the advances of the well-established Royal Dutch Shell group and worked closely with Winston Churchill and First Sea Lord 'Jackie' Fisher to secure in 1914 an important contract to supply fuel-oil to the Royal Navy in exchange for the Government purchasing a 51% stake for £2 million. This enabled him to set about transforming Anglo-Persian into a fully-fledged international oil company involved in exploration, refining, transportation and marketing, a task for which his sharp business acumen and dogged tenacity made him ideally suited.

Having assumed the additional role of chairman following the death of Lord Strathcona in 1914, he was quick to recognise the importance of transporting the company's products to a growing market in its own ships and was instrumental in setting up the BP Tanker Company in 1915. I was surprised a few years ago, when thumbing through a Lloyd's of London Confidential Register from the early 1920s, to find that the British Tanker fleet was listed under his name and it must indeed have been a proud moment when his wife launched the company's first motor tanker *British Aviator* in 1924. Had he lived an extra five years, I am sure he would have taken great pleasure from the fact that by 1939 the British Tanker fleet had grown to ninety-three ships and become a leading player in the British shipping industry, moreover one renowned for its high standards both technically and in the way it treated its employees.

Unlike in WW1, when it was largely spared, the company suffered heavily in WW2 losing half its fleet along with 657 crew members, necessitating an unprecedented post-war reconstruction programme. Tanker size rose rapidly and many of its new ships, which were fitted with spacious and comfortable crew accommodation, had a definite air of elegance about them.

The company has always been subject to the vicissitudes and setbacks that mark the international oil industry and it is sad that in the aftermath of the OPEC oil-price rises of the 1970s, which led to trade recession and overproduction, so many of the company's fine-looking turbine tankers went to the breakers prematurely, some after little more than a decade of service. Continuing uncertainty led to a huge increase in chartering activity and the use of outside crewing agencies, such that the owned and managed fleet steadily declined, reaching a nadir of around thirty ships in 1990.

Happily, the position has now improved and the star of BP Shipping, as it is now styled, is once again in the ascendant. Policy reversals have ensured greater emphasis once more on 'owned' tonnage, evidenced by the increasing number of new orders, and the re-employment where possible of British officers and crew - measures deemed necessary to maintain the highest standards in today's safety conscious world.

Throughout its existence the company has played a major part in British shipping history whilst at the same time making a significant contribution to the wellbeing of the country as a whole. The fact that it still performs these roles today when so many other British shipping companies are but memories is a justifiable matter of pride for its employees, past and present, and I have no doubt that it will continue to do so in the future, especially now that the fleet is climbing back towards something approaching its historic levels with eighty-five ships projected by its centenary year in 2015.

I wish the authors every success with this well researched book which not only lists the individual histories of the thousand or so ships owned by the BP group - ranging from giant VLCCs to bunkering barges and from gas tankers to offshore production ships - but which also provides a wealth of historical and contemporary information relating to the development and operation of tankers.

Ambrose Greenway
September 2005

Authors' Preface

The involvement of two authors in this book suggests it would be appropriate to explain the contributions made by each towards the project.

Bill Harvey started the work some 15 years ago with research into the fleet. As time marched on, so also did the size of the book, and it became apparent that ships were gradually being uncovered that belonged not only to the British Tanker Company, but also to numerous lesser-known subsidiary or associated operators. For example, the Petroleum Steamship Company, apart from some tankers, controlled also most of BP's smaller support craft, including tugs, barges, dredgers – and even at one time a refrigerated fish carrier. A diverse fleet was additionally discovered consisting of distribution and bunkering barges. Collectively, these held logistical roles in the Company and performed a task equally as important as the larger deep-sea and coastal tankers. Frequently, these subsidiary ships were owned on a world-wide basis under flags of many nations. The result has seen documentation of a fleet exceeding 1,100 vessels – but even this cannot hope to incorporate every single craft. It was originally intended that a detailed company history would be included, but further research determined that academic authors, in volumes of leviathan proportions, had already undertaken this task. These findings suggested that a shift in emphasis would be correct regarding the section covering detailed pre-fleet investigation. It was at this point about two years ago that a mutual friend introduced the two authors with the suggestion that each might complement the work of the other.

Ray Solly, with his seafaring background on tankers and knowledge of their operation, set about the task of revising Bill's outline introductory narrative. The inadvisability of avoiding mention of any BP Group history was quickly recognised. This was because BP shipping (under its various names) always operated purely as the Group's transport arm, such that fortunes of the latter affected inextricably successes of the former. It was decided therefore that historical coverage of the vast Group involvements would be restricted to those factors influencing directly management and operation of the various BP fleets. As any maritime history assumes chronological investigation into ships incorporated into that ownership it seemed essential to outline why and how oil tankers developed. Consequently, Part One was worked into an appreciation covering the technical development of BP's tankers as this was affected by international political, technical and local commercial considerations. This involved assessment of the proposed needs of readers. Academic researchers at post-graduate level would invariably seek information at depths different to the vast number of often highly-knowledgeable ship enthusiasts. Mariners with or without tanker experience may require information varying considerably from the diverse market requirements of readers with professional and business backgrounds. The factor of impossibility at mentioning every technical advance to which tankers of the BP Group fleet have been subject since 1916 conditioned the complex task of determining what should be included/excluded, and the scope at which to write. Much material is highly technical and does not easily translate into simple explanations within the allowance of a few lines. Inevitably, a compromise was made in the sincere hope that at least some requirements of each reader could be met.

W J (Bill) Harvey
Dr R J (Ray) Solly

Acknowledgements

Part One

Gratitude is expressed to many people and organisations who have contributed source material, photographs and information. Whilst it might be invidious to single out one at the expense of others, specific mention has to be made of *The Motor Ship* magazine and to John Barnes (Editor) and his PA Karen Tolley for allowing access to their archives and assisting numerous visits eliciting and checking information. Grateful thanks are extended also to *Lloyd's List*, especially Julian Bray and Mark Warner. We are very grateful also to AMVER; The British Library at Euston and Colindale; J K Byass; Concordia Maritime AB; Consilium Marine (UK); The Decca Company; Lawrence Dunn; *Fairplay Shipping* magazine; Fibromar Piping Systems; FotoFlite; FGI Systems and John Mills; Guildhall Library; P Harrington; Andrew Humphreys of World Ship Society; The Institute of Marine Engineering, Science and Technology; International Maritime Organisation; INTERTANKO of Norway; International Association of Classification Societies; Sir Joseph Isherwood Limited; Jahre Wallem Shipping Company; Jotun Paints (Europe); Judges of Hastings and Barry Oates; David Manning; Kockum Sonics (UK); The Marine Society; Oil Companies International Marine Forum; Racal-Decca Marine; SAAB Marine (UK); *Shipping* magazine; Shell International Shipping and Trading; *Shipping World and Shipbuilder* magazine; Sperry Marine; *Syren and Shipping* magazine; Strainstall Engineering Systems; *Tanker Times* magazine; *Tanker and Bulk Carrier* magazine; Tyne and Wear Archives Service; Paul Taylor.

Part Two

David Asprey for his knowledge and personal records of the vessels constructed for, and others operated by, the Army (including the Middle East), and his willingness to assist in the search for details of those vessels acquired by the Company after the First World War.

Rowan Hackman (now deceased) for delving into his shipbuilding records for obscure dates.

Lloyd's Register of Shipping, London – the Information Section, – Barbara Jones, Anne Cowne and Emma Haxhaj and the Maritime Information Publishing Group (now part of Lloyd's Register *Fairplay*, Redhill) – Leslie Spurling, Peter Brazier, Chris Cheetham and Richard Pryde.

Photographs

Ownership of copyright (where known) has been attributed in each photograph caption. Every effort has been made to trace all copyright owners but it has not been possible always to establish this correctly. Some photographs from 'unknown/untraceable' sources have been ascribed to suppliers. The authors' apologise for – and would be grateful of the opportunity to redress – such errors.

For the majority of the ship photographs, we have been extremely fortunate to be granted unrestricted access to the photographic and resource library of the World Ship Society Limited. (worldshipsociety.org) This enthusiasts' organisation was formed in 1947 as the Ship News Club and has since developed into a world-wide organisation with over 4,000 members and branches in many countries. The Society, apart from regular publication of books on merchant shipping company histories alongside naval subjects, has a vast archive of maritime reference works under numerous custodians available to answer members' questions. Many of the members have submitted articles to *Marine News*, the monthly journal of the Society. Others have collected shots of ships and, through their donations and bequests, the photograph library has expanded in print, slide and negative form. We are extremely grateful to the Chairman Dr Richard Osborne and his Executive Council for allowing us access, and to the custodian Mr Tony Smith, for extracting some 1,300 images. Without this collective assistance, our illustrations would have been reliant on commercial photographers and would have lacked the excellent variety of views and locations presented. A small number of these are of sub-standard quality, but their inclusion has been considered justified to provide wider photographic coverage.

PART ONE
THE HISTORY

Chapter One **Emergence of Giants**

Emergence of Giants

PLUTARCH, DISCUSSING FAMOUS people in his *Lives*, believed 'History repeats itself' and, whilst this might be debatable as an eternal truth, historical facts prove beyond argument that, when situations occur in life requiring men of special calibre to solve them, noteworthy people regularly appear at just the right moment. Equally as strange, they always seem to possess the necessary skills, vision and creative drive in just the right quantities to enforce change – often with an impact. These 'men of destiny' represent a unique band, even if sometimes they touch very closely that paper-thin membrane between genius and eccentricity.

William Knox D'Arcy was one such historical 'giant'. He was born in 1849 in Devon, and ten years later in Titusville, Pennsylvania, Colonel Drake discovered oil. With D'Arcy of such tender years, there clearly could be no contemporary link between these events, but this state of affairs was to change. D'Arcy trained as a solicitor and subsequently emigrated to Australia. He possessed an insatiable appetite for horse racing indicating by this very pursuit the character of a man with gambling spirit who was prepared to take risks. In the early 1880s he joined a prospecting syndicate planning to re-activate a defunct gold mine, investing £2,000 – a veritable fortune for those days – with a 50 per cent holding in the venture. A rich vein was eventually struck with the result that by 1886 D'Arcy and his fellow directors were millionaires. Developments in the wider world had continued during the intervening period. Oil had subsequently been discovered in Burma leading, also in 1886, to the founding by a group of Scottish merchants of the Burmah Oil Company. This developed as an extension of their existing trading interests and, consistent with many patterns of ownership during this period, the management of the company was in the United Kingdom through, in this case, headquarters in Glasgow.

William Knox D'Arcy
(Internet source)

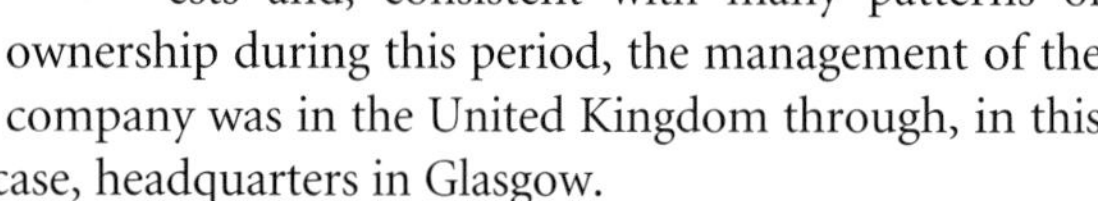

In 1890, reports began to filter back to England concerning the work of French geologists who were tentatively examining rock structures in Persia, comparing similar strata patterns that had proved so successful at producing oil in America and Burma. Ten years later, a Persian Government official who once served as Director of Customs named General Antoine Kitabgi, was invited to open the Persian Exhibition in Paris. His government had invested over ambitiously supporting oil exploration in their country, so Kitabgi's other function was to seek a major source of European investment to continue underwriting further work.

D'Arcy's speculative instincts remained strong and he formed many new syndicates during the intervening years. With his ear to the ground as ever, he heard about the prospects of Persian oil through the timely word of a retired British diplomat. Careful examination of all available details, including latest French reports, led him to regard this venture as 'just up his street' and the probability of repeating his Australian gold mining success encouraged him to lend support. Working through emissaries, D'Arcy eventually overcame a number of internal Persian objections as well as soothing rumbles emanating from the Russian government. Russia had long been a thorn in the side of both Persia and Britain. They had expansionist ideas of their own, which included the domination of India, and viewed the British-Persian negotiations with considerable concern. In May 1901, D'Arcy secured a 60-year concession giving him a lion's share of the investment. He guaranteed continued support of the Shah of Persia by giving him a large sum in cash and £2,000 worth of shares, along with the promise of 16 per cent from defined annual profits. D'Arcy's concession covered 75 per cent of Persia, from which he selected various promising sites in the north of the country for drilling exploratory boreholes. He tactfully excluded the remaining 25 per cent of Persia from his agreement, including the five northernmost states, in order to reduce tension with Russia who had their own plans for this region.

D'Arcy's Persian negotiations had already brought him into tentative involvements with the British government but in 1903, an imperceptible but more definite merging occurred between his ongoing plans and British politics. This launched the series of events that culminated, amongst other things, in the creation of British Petroleum (BP). The Admiralty, whilst continuing to use coal for major units of the Royal Navy, were becoming increasingly interested in changing their fuel supply to oil. Smaller ships within the fleet had been using refined crude as an experiment, achieving very successful results. Certain noteworthy chiefs of the naval staff were following with interest the emergence of diesel-powered river tankers, increasingly used to transport oil in Burma and America. There was a move therefore to expand consumption, but first they had to win round powerful opposing factions to this change from within their own ranks who continued advocating use of coal.

The intervening two years had strained D'Arcy's finances considerably. He had made unsuccessful appeals for British government support and, whilst two of his wells had produced some oil, this had since reduced to only a trickle. He was not completely beaten however, for forceful allies had been recruited from the Admiralty, including Admiral Fisher whom he had met in Bohemia when the latter was Second Sea Lord. They expressed mutually acceptable views on the potential of oil as the 'modern fuel' that would ultimately supersede coal. The Admiral was promoted First Sea Lord in 1904, an appointment he held until 1909, and again from 1914 to 1915.

Fisher, later to become Admiral of the Fleet Lord Fisher of Kilverstone, was another 'giant' who 'happened upon the scene' at the right moment. He possessed both a very strong personality and refined intellect. He not only firmly favoured oil to power the Fleet, but his shrewd insight into international affairs led him to foresee the possibility of war with a rapidly expanding German nation. The dallying that he saw from some fellow senior naval officers and a number of politicians filled him with controlled impatience, and enforced a sense of urgency. The Admiral was, however, in an awkward position. His role officially was as a professional sailor, but he found himself unexpectedly involved in wider international politics. He felt compelled to take some positive action that would help focus minds of both the Naval Staff and Members of Parliament onto the immediate situation. Unable to influence affairs directly, he went behind the scenes and pointed out to Burmah Oil company directors the potential benefits arising by funding D'Arcy's explorations in Persia. His encouragement held certain attractions because although oil production in Burma was already supplying the fuel used in small naval craft, the output was really quite meagre. Burmah additionally viewed the possibility of Persian oil production with some concern. The situation was still very much one of speculation, for the promised Persian wells had yet to produce substantial quantities, notwithstanding the considerable sums of money poured into this venture. The canny Scottish directors were not to be hurried, but suggested their financial support might be forthcoming if the government would agree to place the potential Persian oilfields under the safeguard of British control. The Foreign Office, whilst supporting the Admiralty and D'Arcy, suddenly found they had become directly involved with the quest for oil. Working with others behind the scenes, Fisher's strong support of Burmah Oil, coupled with governmental fears of Russian expansion in the Persian Gulf, finally encouraged both Houses of Parliament to concur. This resulted in the formation of a Persian Oil Concession Syndicate in 1905 – a director of which was William Knox D'Arcy. Burmah Oil became something of a special investor for, although their main contribution was financial, the company used their management technical expertise, consistent with D'Arcy's plans, to cap the existing wells and move operations further south into the Shardin area of Persia. Shifting the considerable quantity of equipment proved a monumental task that even involved the additional expense of building a road. The joint planning and machinations proved a shrewd move however for, in June 1908 just six months after commencing drilling and with both D'Arcy and Burmah Oil approaching financial desperation, oil eventually gushed from the ground at Masjid-I-Suleiman in south-west Persia.

Admiral of the Fleet, Lord Fisher of Kilverstone. *(Internet source)*

The momentum of developments required the founding of a brand new company so, once again, the need arose to find the most appropriate director for this formidable task. The person selected was Sir Charles Greenway who had been manager of a Scottish trading concern in India. He was a man in the Fisher mould: single-minded and possessing considerable force of character. Equally as important, he had wide experience trading in oil. In overcoming many obstacles confronting his new venture, Greenway required all his entrepreneurial and professional skills.

In January 1909, the Anglo-Persian Oil Company was incorporated with 97 per cent of its Ordinary Shares held by Burmah Oil. D'Arcy was appointed a director of the new organisation and given additionally a substantially valuable packet of shares. The following year saw Greenway as managing director of a new company employing around 2,500 people. Their headquarters was at Britannic House in Great Winchester Street, London, which remains the headquarters of BP International.

In 1911, concurrent with the completion of a pipeline between Masjid-I-Suleiman and a new refinery at Abadan, a political 'man of destiny' called Winston Churchill emerged. He was First Lord of the Admiralty and characteristically immediately began (even before his transfer from the Home Office) to take particular interest in the strength of the Royal Navy. Churchill possessed almost prophetic insight into international affairs and was quick to recognise the ever-growing threat from German naval expansion. In this, he matched the concerns of both Admiral Fisher and, by this time, certain other political leaders. Fisher had one more task to fulfil. His belief in the value of oil as the fuel for all units of the future Fleet, including the powerful Dreadnought battleships, remained unshakeable so, with the success of recent events adding support to his arguments, he gradually wooed a reluctant Churchill to his point of view.

Britannic House. *(Author's Collection)*

Around this time, another entrepreneur contributed to the wider scheme of 'things about to happen'. Sir Marcus Samuel, later Viscount Bearsted, had formed the Royal-Dutch Shell group as a Tanker Syndicate in 1893 which had subsequently gone from strength to strength. By the early 1900s, the company was heavily involved in the oil industry and operated a substantial fleet of tankers. Fisher and Samuels had met each other as long ago as 1899 when they found much in common over a range of professional interests and were united in bringing about the conversion of the Fleet from coal. The path was not easy – for Churchill and Samuels failed to find much common ground, and in fact some sources argue they disliked each other intensely. By 1912, Shell provided between 12 and 14 per cent of the oil then needed for warships, but another more politically serious problem existed. Shell was 60 per cent Dutch-controlled and the Dutch were at that time potentially open to influence from Germany.

1912 was to prove a watershed year. The Anglo-Persian Oil Company had signed a ten-year contract with Asiatic Oil – a trading arm of Royal-Dutch Shell – and secured their ever-growing markets by arranging for Shell to sell crude oil and refined products on their behalf. The Company needed additional trading capital and, because of their existing contract, now stood potentially in danger of a take-over by Shell. It was at this stage that Greenway made a decisive move and showed something of the mettle originally elevating him into office. Using the fact that his company was 100 per cent British-owned, even if struggling considerably, he approached the Admiralty offering a 25-year contract to provide fuel oil. He used as the main thrust of his argument the threat that Shell might swallow his company in a rescue bid. He had a ready advocate with Admiral Fisher and the Foreign Office – both of whom expressed fears that both company and Persian oilfields might well fall into foreign, and more especially perhaps, German hands. Oil supplies by 1912 were coming from a number of international sources, and concerns were expressed not only about the need to protect British interests in supply and storage, but also regarding the building of reserve stocks at various ports around the world. As if the situation was not sufficiently difficult, there existed an economic problem. The maritime and industrial world's increasing demands for oil had led to a considerable increase in price. This had in fact doubled during the first six months of 1913. Events culminated in June of that year when Churchill finally became convinced of the use of oil for all future military and industrial uses. Prime Minister Asquith, Admiral Fisher and the Foreign Office, each reinforced his recommendations. With the support of such 'big guns' an approach was made by Asquith to King George V. The result was for the Cabinet to appoint a fact-finding mission to go to Persia under the chair of Admiral Edmond Slade.

The Slade Report, submitted in January 1914, stressed the consequences arising from the Persian oil concession 'falling into the wrong hands'. By this time, Admiral Fisher was again First Sea Lord – the operational head of the Royal Navy – and was able to give powerful 'behind-the-scenes' support to the Commission's findings. Slade approved the Anglo-Persian Oil Company's operations to fulfil existing needs of the Royal Navy and, as soon as May 1914, an agreement was signed between company and politicians to provide oil for the Fleet. At a cost of £2.2 million, the British government eventually acquired a major shareholding in Anglo-Persian, with two directors on the Board, and the right to exercise a veto on all non-commercial matters relating to fuel contracts. Burmah Oil, the original founder and majority shareholder, unwisely perhaps in the face of such strong forces, opposed what it regarded as steam rolling methods used to rush the Bill through Parliament. Consequently, although continuing as shipowners in their own right, their role in the new concern was as only a minor partner. In August 1914, Royal Assent was received and Charles Greenway became Chairman of Anglo-Persian Oil.

Eleven days after parliamentary approval for Churchill's Bill to become an Act, Archduke Franz Ferdinand was assassinated; Germany violated Belgium's neutrality and the First World War commenced. A short while later Turkey entered the conflict on Germany's side, posing an immediate threat to Anglo-Persian oil operations and the oilfields themselves. British troops entered Basra and secured the refinery at Abadan, and spent the remainder of the war opposing incursions by Turkish forces to damage the pipeline. The presence of British forces on their back door protected the Amir of Kuwait, and other local rulers who were sympathetic to Britain, thus consolidating Allied interests in Middle East oil. At this time, production from Abadan was very slight – around 1 per cent of world output but, with stability in the region, this increased by 1918 to 18,000 barrels daily – about ten times that of 1912.

Sir Winston Churchill.
(Internet source)

The Persian production resources were in place and secured. All that remained now was to develop a fleet of ships. On 30 April 1915 the British Tanker Company Limited (BTC) was founded as a subsidiary of Anglo-Persian. The brief was simple: transporting oil to refineries in increasing and ever widening world markets. Initially the shipping company had no vessels, but this changed with the acquisition in June 1915 of the German prize *Furth*, renamed *Kerman*. Two months later Anglo-Persian transferred their tanker *Ferrara* and the company placed orders for their own new tonnage.

From actions of men with conviction, each appearing on the scene at the right moment yet operating across diverse motives, consequences became situations and gave birth to the British Tanker Company to operate alongside the coastal fleets of both the Anglo-Persian Oil Company Ltd, and British Petroleum Company Ltd.

Tanker Construction *Chapter Two*

When oil was discovered in America in 1859, another 'giant' emerged dragging in its wake not people but a number of totally unconsidered transportation difficulties. The immediate and rapidly increasing demand for oil to replace coal as the industrial world's major power source took everyone concerned by surprise. Initially, production matched demand, as by 1862 United States oilfields were producing 400,000 tons of crude per annum. Sailing ships still conveyed freight across the world, although steamers were rapidly taking a larger share of the trade. For centuries, liquid cargoes such as water, vegetable oils and wines had been carried satisfactorily in casks. It seemed a natural thing therefore to ship oil in the same way – accepting such traditional methods without further thought. It very soon became apparent that such means were not only impracticable, they were also extremely dangerous, and, as distances between points of production and world-wide markets increased, more attention became focussed on the task of conveying this new fuel.

The empty casks were heavy, often weighing as much as 20 per cent of their oil content. They were bulky, making them difficult to stow and, because they did not completely fill the holds, potential payload was wasted. A highly obnoxious smell also emanated from them. These disadvantages were least problems, except to officers and crew operating the ships. More dangerous was the leakage from barrels distorted in shape and split by storm force winds and rough seas. Before voyages were half-completed, some of the cargo had already been lost but even worse, a highly toxic and inflammable liquid along with its accompanying hydrocarbon gas had seeped into the lower holds. Much of this then settled into cellular double-bottoms, made its way into the propeller shaft tunnel and emerged in engine-room and accommodation, frequently with fatal results. There were additional problems of disposal because oil-contaminated casks proved difficult to re-circulate, and re-loading them for re-transporting hence further use was impracticable. Burning ashore seemed to be the answer, but this turned out both expensive and messy.

Over subsequent years, ingenious experiments occurred to improve safety and increase cargo capacity in what were still 'oil-carrying ships'. These included transporting filled crates of small cans, or converting dry cargo ships by placing within the hold a series of small rectangular or cylindrical tanks. Both methods afforded only a restricted payload in comparison to the tonnage capacity of the ship. The introduction of inboard tanks created an additional difficulty. Unlike vegetable oil or wine, crude oil and petroleum products varied in volume and contracted or expanded appreciably according to any changes in sea temperature experienced during international voyages. A method had to be found of coping with this difficulty. One way was to fill tanks to only 98 per cent capacity, but the enhanced 'free-surface area' effect so created introduced its own crop of additional risks. As soon as the ship encountered any kind of seaway, the 'slopping' effect from this 2 per cent 'Ullage' endangered stability by shifting the centre of gravity and meta-centric height. It also produced excess hydrocarbons. Piping, valves and pumping arrangements in these early oil-tank ships remained necessarily primitive but sufficiently effective.

There was an urgent need for a solution. In 1863, the sailing vessel *Atlantic* was built of iron by Rogerson's on the Tyne. She had an oil-tight centre longitudinal and three transverse bulkheads. The experiment although lasting until the loss of the craft some six years later was not very successful. The ship was too small and her hollow masts, whilst containing the effects of cargo expansion and gas emission, did little to solve the problems. Whilst other diverse and often ingenious ships were built along similar lines, it was not until three years later that an answer seemed to appear.

In 1886, Armstrong Mitchell's Newcastle shipbuilding yards received an order from the German-American Oil Company, owned by Wilhelm Riedemann, to construct partly from iron and partly steel, a ship specifically designed for the bulk carriage of oil at sea. The ship was called *Gluckauf* and she became the model, with considerable modifications, upon which all modern tankers are based. Mitchell's yard was later purchased by Swan, Hunter & Wigham Richardson, whilst GAOC became Esso A G Hamburg – a founding company of the Esso Group. *Gluckauf* was the brainchild of Colonel Henry Swan, a director of Armstrong Mitchell. She was a 310 by 37.3-foot motorised sailing ship of 2,307 gross registered tons (grt), 3,000 summer deadweight tons (sdwt) that permitted a laden draft of 24.5 feet on a moulded depth of 31.0 feet. When fully laden she sat quite low in the water. She was launched on 16 June 1886, completed successful trials on 10 July, and sailed almost immediately on her maiden voyage.

The ship was innovative in a number of ways. For the first time, the engine room was situated aft in a poop extending one-third the vessel's length that, for further strengthening, retained the cellular double-bottom. She was fitted with a triple expansion steam engine whose coal-fired boilers, at a steam pressure of 150lb – combined with a barquentine rig of sails – gave a service speed of some 10 knots. The ship carried 560 tons of bunker coal. Officers berthed aft, whilst the crew of ten sailors and ten firemen lived in port and starboard messes respectively up forward. A generous

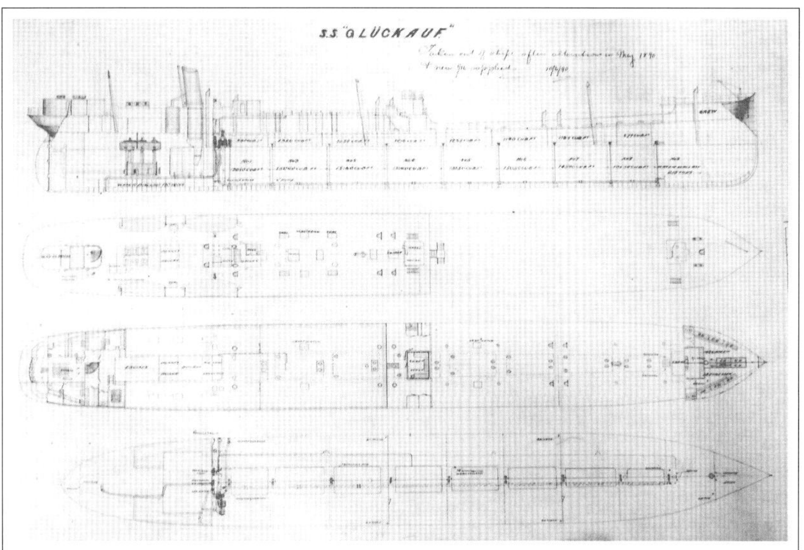

A plan view of *Gluckauf*. *(Tyne and Wear Archives Service)*

allowance of four large lifeboats was made. For the first time aboard ship, electric lighting was provided in accommodation, all appropriate working spaces and for navigation. With the bridge sited midships to assist ship handling, the vessel had a lengthy forward well deck, contributing to a rather clumsy appearance. Practical she may well have proved, but the tanker was far from attractive.

Below the open spar deck with its 12-inch camber, a continuous single-angled double-riveted oil-tight, centre-line longitudinal bulkhead ran from Number Nine tank aft of the short raised fo'c'sle head, to the oil-tight bulkhead at Number One tank forward of the engine-room. A cofferdam separated cargo space from the engine-room, preventing oil seepage into this vulnerable area, and served also as a pump room. The numbering of oil-tanks in this ship is interesting and opposed current practices which always today commence forward with Number One tank. Number Nine tank in this ship was designated for 325 tons of water ballast. The fo'c'sle head, partially above this tank, was fitted with ventilators serving the ratings' quarters, together with a derrick for raising the Admiralty-type anchors – still very much the norm for deep-sea ships.

For the first time in any ship, the double-bottom was eliminated in the cargo section of the hull and oil was loaded to the bottom of the tank next to the keel.

The midships' section. *(Tyne and Wear Archives Service)*

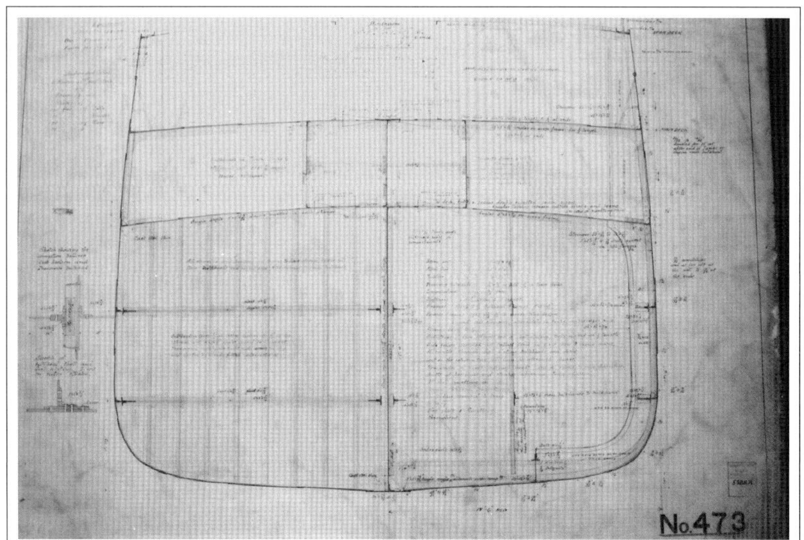

This solved the problem of in-board hydrocarbon gas leakage. The hull plating was constructed partly of steel and partly of iron and riveted throughout, providing compensatory strengthening. With the fitting of eight transversals, devoid of brackets, the carrying capacity of *Gluckauf* was stabilised over sixteen tanks. All stringers and keelsons in the tanks were fitted with strong knees at the bulkheads, although these were not carried through the bulkheads themselves. These were wider at the bottom (some half an inch) tapering to three-eighths of an inch at the top. Additional tank stiffening to compensate for the lack of a cellular double bottom was provided by a series of 4 × 3-inch angles spread 2 feet apart.

A fore-and-aft expansion trunk was constructed to each tank in a 'tween deck having a 7-foot opening with bulkheads on either side between the web frames of the shell plating. This permitted a full load to be carried in the main tanks with extra cargo capacity and helped to reduce considerably free-surface area 'sloshing' effects. The combination of sails with steam was not satisfactory and the ship was far from perfect, but she continued in service until 1893 when she ran aground off Fire Island just outside New York.

A novel type of ship had been created that, within the parameters of the time, carried crude oil quite effectively. It was not long before shippers of molasses, creosote, whale oil, turpentine and (traditional) vegetable oils took advantage of tankers to transport these commodities in bulk. The liquids varied considerably in specific gravity from around 0.7 to in excess of one, and their viscosity also was often high, but the ships proved quite adaptable at carrying such diverse loads.

Consistent with the entrepreneurial giants who developed the oil industry and created shipping companies another man emerged with equally good timing. He too possessed that enquiring type of mind which produces solutions from circumstances and, in his case, made such a significant contribution to oil-tanker construction that his name became a byword in this field. Sir Joseph William Isherwood was born in Hartlepool in 1870. A ship designer and naval architect he worked as a surveyor for Lloyd's Register of Shipping between 1896 and 1907, initially in Hartlepool and shortly afterwards in London. For much of his professional career he focussed on public concerns regarding ship safety and the sailing of more seaworthy ships. There was no shortage of material to occupy his mind and talents.

Samuel Plimsoll's strenuous efforts had resulted in 1875/6 Acts of Parliament introducing a load line on the sides of ships. However, the height of this was fixed 'at the discretion of owners of ships' and, as a safety device, was not proving very effective. In 1882, a disastrous watershed occurred in maritime history when 548 ships (over ten a week) were lost at sea – resulting in the deaths of a staggering 3,118 seamen. An article on International Load Lines written by J Foster King CBE in an April 1931 edition of the leading authoritative magazine *Syren & Shipping* directed the blame for this early tragedy precisely where it was deserved. King was an early designer of tankers whose transversal system of construction had met with some success. In his introduction, he explained bluntly how in the previous century 'Shipowners allowed their ships to go to sea over-laden or, at least, dangerously laden and in an utterly un-seaworthy condition'.

The outcry over this horrific statistic eventually drove Parliament to pass the Merchant Shipping (Load Line) Act of 1890. This legislation was to act as a catalyst because, over the years, it focussed attention to a range of potential areas ripe for improvement in safety and comfort for mariners – even if this was frequently to take considerable time before implementation.

Isherwood was plainly aware of the obligations shipbuilders, as well as shipowners, had towards those taking their ships to sea and began researching current designs. He left Lloyd's after 11 years' service to develop his own research. His findings led to an alternative method of building that used less iron and more steel, resulting in dry cargo vessels with stronger hulls. A more economically efficient ship emerged, carrying an enhanced payload, which appealed considerably to ship-owners. Encouraged by such positive conclusions, it was inevitable that Isherwood soon focussed his attention on the difficulties experienced in oil tanker construction.

Coincident with the discovery of oil in 1900 in Texas, and the subsequent establishment of additional oil wells world-wide, the demand for fuel became so insatiable that casks were completely inadequate. There was an urgent need for larger and wider 'tankers', as they were now commonly known, with increased bulk tonnage (hence payload) proportional to their length. Some builders were producing very strong ships, such as the *Iroquois,* launched from Harland & Wolff's Belfast yard in 1907 for Anglo-American Oil. She was a tanker of 11,800-sdwt, length 467.3 feet, beam 60.3 feet and moulded depth of 35.5 feet. This ship was exceptional: she was designed specifically to tow a tank barge, the *Navahoe*, across the Atlantic (a story in itself), and survived two world wars, giving sterling service until she was scrapped in 1947.

More generally, yards were sending tankers to sea with a disproportional length/depth ratio. These were built on the 'ordinary transversal system' of ship construction that had developed gradually from the innovative *Gluckauf*. The hull retained its single longitudinal bulkhead and transversals of previous years. A series of bottom brackets had been introduced, constructed between an interlocking system of longitudinal and transversal girders fitted with short vertical stiffeners, which strengthened internal tanks. Transversal frames extended from the hull shell plating of the ship's sides with horizontal stiffeners forming the expansion trunk. Two major problems plagued tankers built to this design. Emphasis had been placed on transversal strength – possibly to counteract potential racking and compressive stresses – at the expense of longitudinal stiffening. In adverse weather conditions, this structure exposed deficiencies in the areas of bracket construction at the oil-tight bulkheads and led to cargo seepage. With an increase in tanker size, this method of construction became archaic: it was simply 'not up to the job'.

Sir Joseph Isherwood, inventor of the modern tanker. *(Sir Joseph Isherwood Limited)*

Isherwood, answering questions after delivering a paper to the Society of Engineers in London in May 1918, highlighted this difficulty and explained how, in retrospect, his patent had worked towards overcoming it: 'Tankers built on the ordinary (transversal) system have constantly recurring trouble in the attachments of side stringers and bottom keels onto the transverse bulkheads – on account of the redundancy of parts and the system of inter-dependent girders.'

The magazine *Fairplay* regarded Isherwood's lecture of such significance to the shipbuilding industry that the editor allowed him to publish his work shortly after its delivery.

There was a second shortcoming in construction of transversal tankers. Existing methods to achieve the required enlarged tonnage frequently produced a considerable increase in the weight of materials used. Isherwood demonstrated that a 410 × 52 × 32 feet tanker, with a summer deadweight of 8,620 tons on a draft of 26 feet and a co-efficient of 0.76, would require 2,370 tons of iron and steel. A tanker built on his system, with an additional 10 per cent in length bringing this to 451 feet, would have summer deadweight of 9,720 tons on the same draft. This ship was 6.5 per cent stronger longitudinally than the shorter vessel. She could steam with similar engines and coal consumption at practically the same speed as the other tanker, whilst carrying some extra 1,000 tons deadweight at the expense of 75 tons of steel. The extra cubic capacity of the ship was introduced precisely where it would be most valuable – namely amidships. In the same paper, Isherwood explained: 'Vessels built on the ordinary transverse system of construction usually have not sufficient margin of longitudinal strength, or rather it might be advisable to say are lacking in direct longitudinal stiffening to prevent the plating from bending between the transverse supports. When exceptional conditions are met with, either in the case of severe weather or bad loading, or a combination of both, structural damage occurs with more or less serious results.'

A tanker built on the 'ordinary transversal system'. *(Fairplay)*

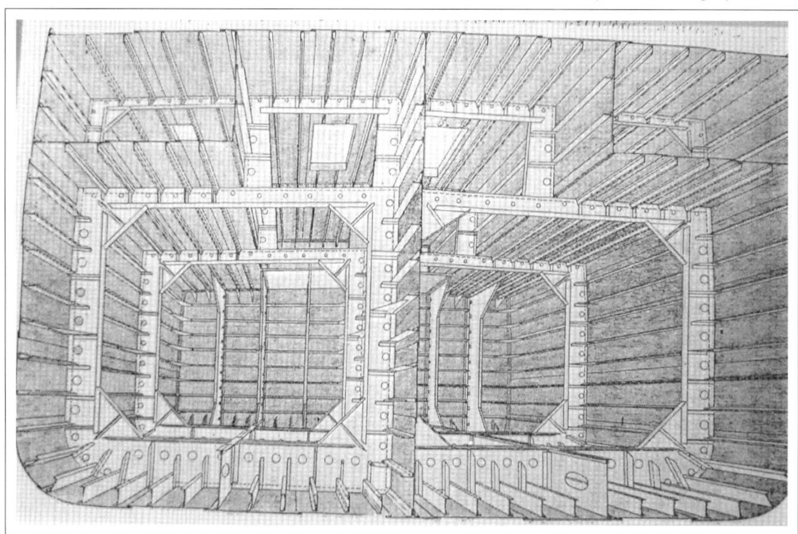

Isherwood's design was revolutionary. He reduced the number of transversal frames within each tank and introduced much stronger web plates, spacing these about 15 feet apart along the side shell plating, and reinforcing them with strong corner brackets. The webs worked thwartships across the keel interlocking with a series of longitudinal girders, placed about 3 feet apart, with additional web frames midships between each port and starboard tank. The longitudinal girders were extended along the side plating and under-deck expansion trunk areas. Additionally, across the two oil-tight transversals constituting each individual tank, the two web plates were fitted about 8 feet apart. This had the effect of distributing stresses more evenly around the periphery of tank bulkheads, whilst bracket connections were strengthened proportionally to the members to which they were attached. Near tank corners, for instance, very large brackets were fitted extending diagonally between lower ship's side and transverse webs to a distance of 8 feet. Following standard practices of the day, shell plating was 'clinker' built, but with overlapping strengthened plates. Tank lengths remained at a standard maximum of 30 feet, whilst the central expansion trunkway, to assist stability, was not permitted to exceed 60 per cent of the breadth of the tanker, with a height between 7 and 8 feet.

For its day, an extremely strong, stable and comparatively oil/gas-tight tanker resulted that would serve as a model for later development. There was room still for improvements. On ships fitted with a single pump room, for instance, this was often situated amidships causing considerable inconvenience to sleeping deck officers when colleagues working cargo had to enter their cabin to operate manual deck valves. This ceased to be humorous when the mate disturbed may well have to take a bridge navigating watch immediately the ship sailed, or turn-to for a routine cargo watch. In large tankers two pump rooms were fitted, spaced between the cargo tanks and dividing these into three groups. This facilitated the carriage of different grades – or 'parcels' – of oil without risk of contamination caused by seepage or an accidental turning of incorrect valves. There was a further advantage. By distributing stresses more evenly around the periphery of the bulkheads, and by making the bracket connections more consistent in strength with adjacent plating, a partial remedy emerged helping solve problems of oil leakage.

FLUCTUATIONS IN VALUES AND ISHERWOOD CONSTRUCTION.

It has now been proved by experience that by adopting the Isherwood System of Construction a stronger ship can be obtained, and an increased carrying capacity on the same dimensions. A 7,500-ton steamer, if built on the Isherwood system, would carry about 7,700 tons and cost no more to build, yet at the present time the latter vessel would fetch in the market £2,200 more than the former. In the running of the vessel the extra deadweight can be carried with no extra expense, so that at the freights recently current she would earn about £2,500 per annum more than the vessel built on the transverse system.

A steamer has, it is reported, just been fixed for six years at 7s. 6d. per ton per month. Such a vessel, if built on the Isherwood system and carrying 7,700 tons, would earn £5,400 more under this charter than if built on the ordinary system.

With the greatly increased cost of building, and in view of the necessity of providing for any depression in shipping in the future, it is more than ever imperative that owners should adopt that system which, while increasing their earning power during a boom, would also enable them to make a profit instead of a loss during a depression, and at the same time give them a stronger ship.

Since the commencement of the war no less than 345,994 tons of shipping have been ordered to be constructed on the Isherwood system.

Mr. Justice Dunlop, in dealing with the construction of the *Storstad*, which sank the *Empress of Ireland*, said that the *Storstad* was "built on the Isherwood System, *and consequently very strong.*"

Isherwood's marketing of his system - *(Fairplay)*

Isherwood concluded his paper by citing continued successes achieved by the very first tanker constructed using his longitudinal system of framing. This was the *Paul Paix*, built ten years previously in 1908 by Craggs of Middlesborough, at 6,600-sdwt; 355.2 × 49.4 × 28 feet moulded depth. She was fitted with two transversals between consecutive bulkheads, with a complete half frame on each side in sixteen tanks. Plating used at the oil-tight transversals was 0.437 inches thick, whilst that of her shell plating was 0.5 inches. The tanker was constructed initially for use in the motor spirit trade.

It was only a matter of time before the previously wasted open deck space each side of the expansion trunk was developed into cargo-carrying capacity by constructing it below the main deck. The tanks were of strong construction, using treble riveted lap joints, and can be seen clearly either side of the expansion tank in the plan. They extended across two sets of longitudinal tanks, and were often used to carry oil of a lighter specific gravity than the main cargo, sufficient in quantity to bring the tanker to *summer* draft marks appropriate for her voyage. On occasions, the tanks could also carry crude oil of the same grade as the main cargo. The tanks were discharged by opening drop valves, which allowed oil to flow into the main tanks, after these had been emptied. Summer tanks also contributed towards reducing free surface area within

Isherwood's longitudinal system of oil tanker construction. *(Fairplay)*

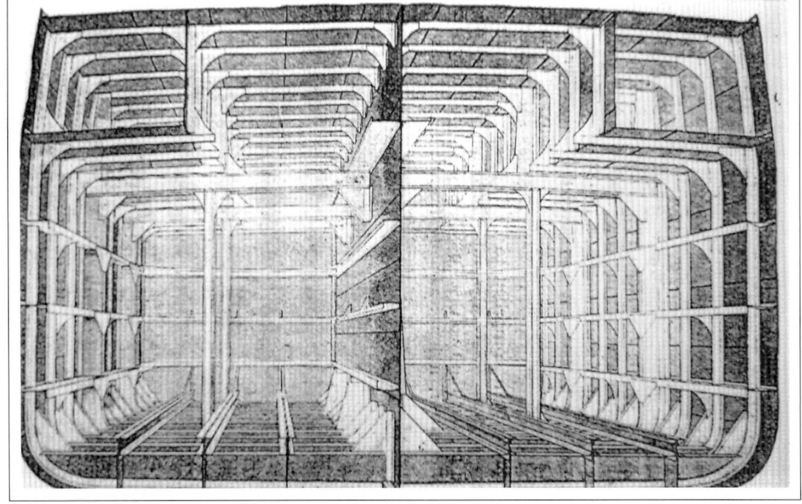

the 'tween decks.

It would be incorrect, however, to assume that pumping oil into summer tanks directly increased the deadweight of the ship. For instance, an 8,000-ton tanker fitted with summer tanks of around 1,000 tons capacity would rarely carry 9,000 tons of crude. The specific gravity of the bulk cargo, and voyage routing in terms of sea temperatures and likely weather severity anticipated, would determine the amount of extra oil transported. Crude loaded from the Persian Gulf always varied considerably between the areas of loading – it was either light or heavy, with specific gravities varying between 0.8398 and 0.8877 respectively.

The advertisement on the previous page was similar to many that appeared in most shipping journals over the following ten years extolling the undoubted success of Isherwood constructions. The collision between the *Empress of Ireland*, 14190grt/1906, and the Norwegian collier *Storstad*, 6028grt/1910, took place on 29 May 1914, whilst both ships were approaching the Quebec Pilot station in the River St. Lawrence. The area in the vicinity of any pilot station with a convergence of numerous ships, each manoeuvring to drop or pick-up a pilot, especially in poor visibility before the days of radar, was already potentially hazardous, requiring delicate ship-handling. It was unfortunate that it required a maritime casualty to reinforce virtues of the 'Isherwood Method of Construction' – a point emphasised in *Fairplay* some months later following the inquiry by Mr Justice Dunlop.

By 1915, as the British Tanker Company acquired its fleet, the world was well involved in war. Therefore, coincident with its growth, the company found itself directly involved in this carnage of the sea.

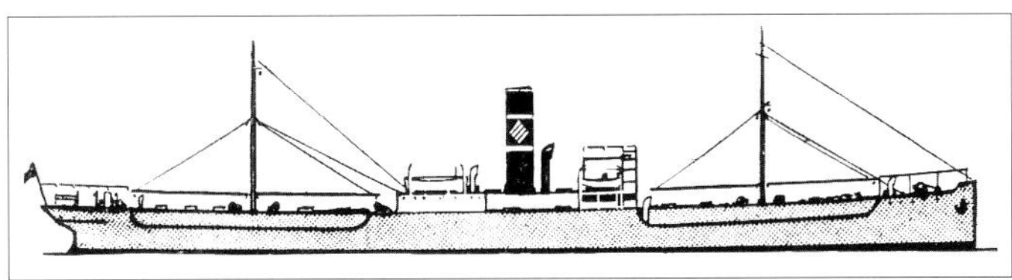

The 6,600-sdwt *Paul Paix* proved the efficiency of Isherwood's longitudinal system of tanker framing. She was built in 1908 by Craggs of Middlesborough and broken-up in the 1930s. *(Laurence Dunn)*

Chapter Three **Fleet Growth**

Fleet Growth

IN 1916, THE BRITISH TANKER COMPANY ordered the first seven of their own ships from British Tyneside yards. The *British Emperor* was the first launching from Armstrong Whitworth Company Limited in Newcastle-upon-Tyne.

Armstrong Whitworth's shipbuilding yard in 1921. The yard covered an area of 80 acres with a frontage on the Tyne of around 4,380 feet. The four-funnel liner is the Aquitania, built 1913 and in for a refit. *(Syren & Shipping)*

Since the success of the *Gluckauf* and Isherwood's work, tankers constructed on the patent of a single double-riveted oil-tight centre-line longitudinal bulkhead with a number of transversals had carried crude oil in bulk for many years. The *British Emperor* was of 5,500 summer deadweight tons (sdwt), 345 × 49.1 × 17.0 feet, with seven main port and starboard tanks, a summer tank and cargo hold forward, and equipped with one single triple expansion engine of 1900 hp. The ship sailed on her maiden voyage in September 1916. It had been agreed previously, for patriotic motives as much as acknowledgement to the British government for its financial backing, that all tankers of the new company would carry the prefix *British*. An announcement of her launch appeared in *Lloyd's List* for 7 June 1916.

The first of many launches for BTC to be published in *Lloyd's List*.

LAUNCHES.

The following details of vessels launched have been received during the week ended June 5, 1916.

Vessel.	Flag.	Gross Tons.	Where Built.	Builders.	Owners.
British Emperor	Br	3636	Walker-on-Tyne	Sir W. G. Armstrong, Whitworth & Co., Ltd.	The British Tanker Co., Ltd.
Conneaut	Am	4810	Ecorse (Mich.)	Great Lakes Engineering Works	Wyandotte Transportation Co., Michigan.
Yselhaven	Du	3551	Rotterdam	Rotterdamsche Droogdok Maatschappij	Gebr. van Uden, Rotterdam.
Hirose	Br	244*	Middlesbrough	Smith's Dock Co., Ltd.	Neale & West, Ltd., Cardiff.
Muira	Br	244*	Middlesbrough	Smith's Dock Co., Ltd.	Neale & West, Ltd., Cardiff.
Munisla	Am	1815	Ecorse (Mich.)	Great Lakes Engineering Works	Munson Steamship Line, Ltd., New York.
D. G. Kerr	Am	—	Lorain (O.)	American Shipbuilding Co.	——
Standard Arrow	Am	7750	Camden (N.J.)	New York Shipbuilding Co.	Standard Transportation Co.
Lady Borden	Br	—	Montreal	Canadian Vickers Co.	Canadian Government.
Tribesman	Br	71	Yarmouth (Nor.)	Crabtree & Co., Ltd.	T. Gray & Co., Hull.
Seddon (steam trawler)	Br	—	Beverley	Cook, Welton & Gemmel, Ltd.	Standard Steam Fishing Co., Ltd., Grimsby.
Sabreur (steam trawler)	Br	—	Beverley	Cook, Welton & Gemmel, Ltd.	A. Black, Grimsby.
Niceto de Larrinaga	Br	5560	Port Glasgow	Russel & Co.	Larrinaga & Co., Ltd., Liverpool.
Rijn	Du	3000†	Capelle a/d Yssel	A. Vuijk & Zonen	Naamlooze Vennootschap Houtvaart, Rotterdam.
Ysseldijk	Du	10350†	Rotterdam	Maatschappij voor Scheeps en Werktuigbouw "Fyenoord"	Nederlandsch-Amerikaansche Stoomvaart Maatschappij, Rotterdam.
Anders	Du	2200†	Krimpen a/d Yssel	C. Van der Giessen & Zonen	Gebr. van Uden, Rotterdam.
Ameland	Du	6200†	Rotterdam	Rotterdamsche Droogdok Maatschappij	Stoomvaart Maatschappij Triton Rotterdam.

† Deadweight. * Under Deck.

The remaining six ships were delivered during 1917: the *British*-named *Princess*, *Sovereign*, *Ensign* and *Isles* came from Armstrong Whitworth's, with engines made by the North-Eastern Marine Engineering Company of Newcastle. The *British Empress* and *Admiral* came from the yards of Swan, Hunter & Wigham Richardson who built also the engines. Swan, Hunter's was destined to become the foremost builder of tankers for the BP Group, a working relationship that lasted until 1983.

In 1917, the British Tanker Company acquired additional ships. The first group was bought from The Prince Line of London. Originally formed by James Knott, N Shields and later Newcastle, Prince Line had been a pioneer tanker operator, until its recent acquisition by Furness, Withy, in London. They had indicated their intention in the future to operate only dry cargo ships and offered for sale their remaining fleet of four tankers.

Mexican Prince was not in the end renamed, but continued on charter until sold in November 1919. Virtually simultaneously, Lane and McAndrew who were London ship-owners and brokers, decided to concentrate purely on ship management rather than ownership. They owned the Petroleum Steamship Company which was purchased by Anglo-Persian Oil, so adding a further nine tankers to the Group fleet. Towards the end of that year, the company owned twenty-two deep-sea tankers of varying ages.

A number of 'behind-the-scenes' machinations took place in the shipping world around this time which coincided with needs for additional tankers world-wide, and for improved distribution resources. With the outbreak of war, the assets of the deceptively-named British Petroleum Company (BPC) had been taken-over by the British Government and placed with Anglo-Persian Oil. The BPC was a largely German-controlled distribution network of enormous proportions and competency. By acquiring this 'up and running' enterprise, Anglo-Persian had equipped itself with a complete marketing arm for its own products.

In February 1917, the German government announced their policy of unrestricted submarine warfare with immediate devastating effects for British and Allied shipping. Compared to other companies, BTC suffered lightly and lost only two ships in the First World War, both in 1918. These were the *British Viscount*, torpedoed by *U-91* off the Skerries on 23 February and the *Eupion*, sunk by *U-123* near the

River Shannon on 3 October. The latter tanker had been transferred to BTC from Anglo-Persian Oil in 1917 and retained her own name. Three other Company tankers were torpedoed in 1918: the *British Princess* on 4 March and the *British Star* on 26 March. This latter ship was struck immediately after leaving the Tyne on her first voyage. The *British Major* was torpedoed on 26 July but (like the other two casualties) was eventually repaired and restored to service.

John Straughan was serving aboard the *British Princess* as third engineer and, in his own words: 'I was perched on spars above the bridge repairing a Morse lamp and vividly recall seeing the white streak of the torpedo before it struck the midships pump-room killing the Chinese pump man.' John was typical of many mariners who served the Group conscientiously on long service contracts and regarded them as 'first-class employers'. Coincidentally, he joined the *British Star* upon her return to service following repairs. He survived both world wars and remained with BP for 41 years in seagoing and then senior management posts ashore, until his retirement in 1958. He recalled, in the very early days, having to provide his own straw mattress – 'the donkey's breakfast' – along with bedding, pillow and towels.

In 1919, with hostilities over, BTC acquired seven surplus Government-owned tankers from the Shipping Controller and the Admiralty.

The Company had for some years operated these Royal Fleet Auxiliary ships on behalf of the Admiralty which had served in various guises including, as the individual history of each ship outlines in Part Two, the *British Vine* that found herself emulating a dummy warship for a brief period.

1919 also saw the French government recognise their own increasing needs for oil. Following lengthy and at times rather aggressive negotiations at the Paris Peace Conference that year, agreement was reached in 1920 with the British government, allowing the French 25 per cent of oil production from Mesopotamian fields that had become a British Mandate under the League of Nations. The operator for this was The Turkish Petroleum Company in which Anglo-Persian Oil had a substantial shareholding. By 1921, the Association Petroliere in France became established and the new building *British Industry* was transferred and renamed *St. Jerome.*

British Soldier and company tug **St. Athan.** *(World Ship Society Photograph Library)*

Georgian Prince	acquired 31.1.1918.	and 21.5.1918 renamed	*British General.*
Mexican Prince	acquired 6.2.1918.	and proposed to rename	*British Commander.*
Roumanian Prince	acquired 6.2.1918.	and 18.5.1918 renamed	*British Major.*
Russian Prince	acquired 6.3.1918.	and 21.5.1918 renamed	*British Marshal.*

The current situation concerning the varied companies associated with and owned by the BP Group in 1920 stood as follows:

Anglo-Persian Oil Company Limited – would remain the governing body responsible for financing and exploration, amongst other responsibilities, and operate a fleet of service craft around the world in conjunction with the establishment of new ventures in marketing.

British Tanker Company Limited: to retain responsibility for operating long-haul tankers and managing vessels on behalf of others, inside or outside the group.

Petroleum Steamship Company Limited – would operate the numerous service craft such as tugs, barges and dredgers – as well as their few existing tankers.

British Petroleum Company Limited: with an expanded fleet to continue United Kingdom marketing.

British Oil Bunkering Company, Limited – would operate bunkering craft around the United Kingdom, supplementing those of British Petroleum Company Limited.

* * *

During the early to mid-1920s Anglo-Persian accepted a five-year management contract on behalf of Tankers Ltd., (formerly Scottish-American Oil & Transport Company), for their small fleet of 'Scottish-prefixed' ships, some still under construction. They ventured also into many areas of Continental Europe as well as expanding oil markets and marketing prospects world-wide. Anglo-Persian began also building a network of international marine bunkering stations and substantiated plans for oil refineries in Wales, Scotland and Australia. Imperceptibly, working directly and through its associates, BP was becoming a very big name in the oil industry.

Birchleaf	8.9.1919	and was subsequently renamed	*British Birch.*
Hollyleaf	8.9.1919	and was subsequently renamed	*British Holly.*
War Sikh	4.10.1919	and was subsequently renamed	*British Soldier.*
Mapleleaf	4.10.1919	and was subsequently renamed	*British Maple.*
Vineleaf	4.10.1919	and was subsequently renamed	*British Vine.*
Roseleaf	5.1.1920	and was subsequently renamed	*British Rose.*
Fernleaf	9.2.1920	and was subsequently renamed	*British Fern.*

With the infrastructure in place by 1920, amidst a world suddenly enjoying peace, an ambitious programme of tanker construction commenced. BTC placed orders around various British shipyards for the delivery of thirty-nine deep-sea tankers over the following five years. Many of these were to be powered by steam turbine or steam reciprocating engines. Additionally, orders were placed for a considerable number of barges and smaller estuarial craft over the three ship owning companies.

The launching party of the *British Merchant*. The group includes Mr A J Campbell of Dalmuir Works, Mrs Greenlees, performing the launching, and Lord Invernairn. *(Syren & Shipping)*

Twenty-three tankers were delivered between 1921 and 1923. They ranged in tonnage from the *British Commerce* at 6,089-sdwt to the *British Architect,* launched from Blythswood's yard in Glasgow at just over 11,000-sdwt. Many of the coastal craft were also launched; including the *British Scout* from Swan, Hunter's at 2,210-sdwt. *Syren & Shipping* in the edition for 6 September 1922 acknowledged the debt owed to British shipbuilding by this ambitious spate of orders: 'The work of the British Tanker Company, Limited, of London, has meant a good deal to the United Kingdom shipyards within the past year, and it will mean something substantial for a year or so to come, if not longer.' Typical of these tankers was the *British Merchant.* She was the only ship ordered from Beardmore's of Glasgow on this occasion, but was the fifth order for tankers this yard had received from BTC. She was completed in November 1922 and was 10,792-sdwt at 440.7 × 57.2 × 34.1 feet. The ship was fitted with double-reduction HP and LP steam turbines of the Rateau type capable of developing 3700 ihp. These were manufactured by Metropolitan-Vickers Electrical Company of Manchester. This tanker was designed particularly for the carriage of oil at low specific gravity over twenty compartments, with expansion trunks and summer tanks. Cargo was discharged by two duplex oil pumps each with a capacity, once worked up, of 300 tons per hour, through two main lines of 14-inch wrought-iron pipe.

The launching of the *British Merchant*. *(Syren & Shipping).*

Tankers owned by BTC were not exempt from the vicissitudes suffered by all ships. The unwritten 'rules of the sea' dictated that embarking on a maritime career invariably placed officers and crew in situations which at times could be extremely dangerous and many a loss of life at sea has been witnessed, or even an accident occurring to terminate a promising career permanently. We saw something of these potential dangers recorded by John Straughan. One such incident occurred with the *British General.* She was completed by Palmer's Shipbuilding and Iron Company of Jarrow in 1922 and, on her maiden voyage from the Persian Gulf bound 'Land's End for Orders' on 22 October of that year, sent a wireless message informing she had hit an uncharted pinnacle rock in way of Numbers One to Five tanks and was made fast. The pump room became flooded, the deck pipelines were broken and an ingress of water taken forward. HMS *Cyclamen* was standing by the vessel rendering assistance, but the situation was so serious, it was thought that little chance existed of saving the tanker and the Navy requested an indemnity from BTC that they would be compensated for any damage suffered whilst attempting to tow off their ship. The oil was 'sucked out' of the *British General,* and she was towed to shallow water and beached. Local repairs were effected by the officers and crew aboard (no mean feat) and, in the absence of any suitable dry dock in the Gulf, they navigated her to Bombay in a voyage described by *Syren & Shipping,* through an article in their 10 January 1923 edition, as ' . . . a feat of plucky and resourceful seamanship which is worthy of a high place in the records of the British Mercantile Marine. . . . The difficulty of the task and the amount of courage required to bring

Turbines and gears of a typical steam-turbine engine in the erecting shops of Metropolitan-Vickers of Manchester. This particular engine was constructed for the *British Lord* of 9,517-sdwt built by Thompson's of Sunderland also completed in November 1922. *(Syren & Shipping).*

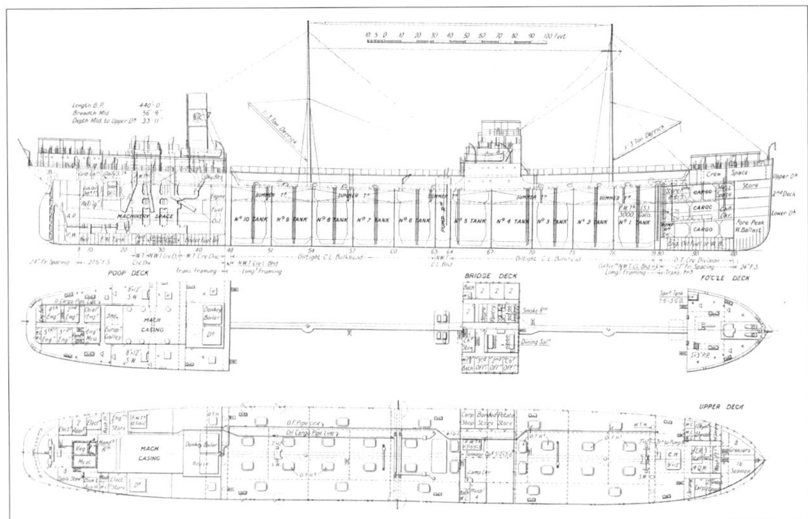

The general arrangement plan of the *British Chancellor* indicates the tank layout and shows how the bridge-deck accommodation was distributed. *(World Ship Society Photograph Library)*

the vessel in this state across the Indian Ocean is quite evident.'

The magazine also included a tribute to Palmers for their part in constructing such a strong ship, recording that the owners and underwriters 'must be gratified that so valuable a vessel should have been salved from a position, which was at one time considered hopeless'. The tanker spent five months in dry dock undergoing extensive repairs to severely damaged keel plating, extending from forward, to Number Six tank.

By 1924, Anglo-Persian Oil, working with its allied company National Oil Refineries Limited, saw Queen's Dock at Swansea successfully operational. On 1 July 1923 the entire dock complex, built by the Harbour Trust, had been acquired by the Great Western Railway Company and, by the end of that year, was importing 650,000 tons and exporting nearly half-a-million tons of oil. Queen's Dock was the largest on the Bristol Channel and its system of storage tanks, pipelines and refinery enabled it to accept the maximum capacity tankers then afloat. The largest liners also could bunker from the adjacent King's Dock at any state of tide. Swansea docks complex included over 100 cranes for general cargo and twenty-seven hoists that served its principal export of coal (4.5 million tons in 1923). The port also boasted seven dry docks under the auspices of Palmer's Repair yards, helping make Swansea a major port on the Welsh coast.

By 1920, considerable technical advances had been made in tanker propulsion. Experiments over the years had not surprisingly turned thoughts towards adapting oil to fuel the tankers that carried this commodity. If anything was surprising, it was that coal had remained for so long the main source of fuel, particularly with the impetus provided by the Royal Navy. Experiments had been carried out successfully in the United States embracing marine diesels which had examined the advantages and otherwise of adapting this oil-fired internal combustion engine for seagoing purposes. The advantages were enormous: a cleaner engine that took far less time to start being amongst the most obvious. It helped also towards a cleaner environment both on board and ashore. Coaling ship was a filthy job entailing dust permeating everywhere as coal was loaded into the narrow hatch opening of the bunker hold. Trimmers were required to bring barrowloads to firemen serving the furnaces and, with the ship pitching and rolling, both jobs could be very dangerous. Of course, there were problems to overcome with diesel engines (as with any new technology).

Some of the issues taking up so much engineers' time on both sides of the Atlantic were concerned apparently with determining how regular combustion might be maintained at slow speeds, and whether or not salt or fresh water could be adapted as an engine coolant instead of air pressure. A diesel engine would also be heavier than a steam one of similar dimensions and power, and cost more money to install. Even if the ship could be propelled by oil, there remained a need for steam auxiliary machinery, which would have to be run from boilers. Steam was required for a variety of purposes: to operate the cargo pumping plant, to supply the heating coils fitted in tank bottoms often necessary to retain certain heavy crude oils at the correct temperature, as well as for bunker compartments and settling tanks. The operation of much deck machinery such as winches, windlass for the anchor and steering gear equipment, also relied heavily on steam. Inevitably, like all difficulties, these were eventually overcome. Oil-fired boilers,

The *British General* in Bombay shows evidence of the crews' efforts to effect temporary repairs before navigating her to Bombay Dry Dock. *(Syren & Shipping).*

British Tanker Company oil tankers in Queen's Dock, Swansea. *(Syren & Shipping).*

powered by electricity, were fitted to diesel tankers so, within a few years, these became the norm with many owners abandoning steam as the favoured method of tanker propulsion.

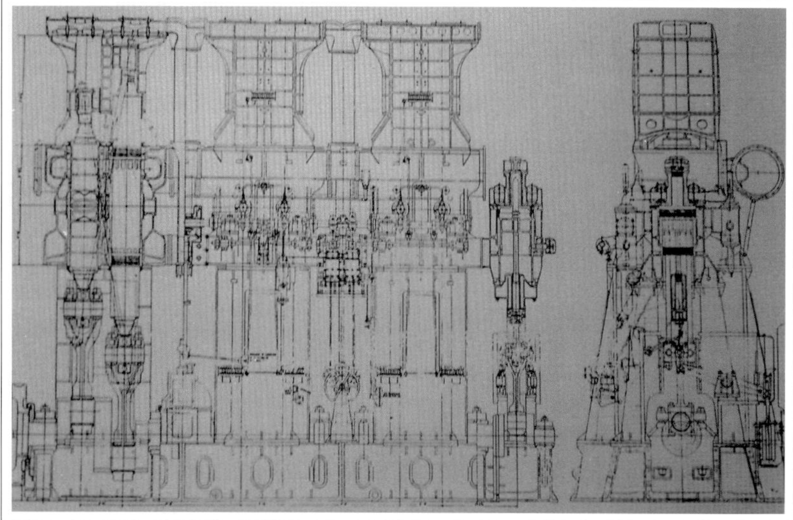

The engine plan of the *British Aviator* (above) and her steam reciprocating triple expansion engine (below). *(Syren & Shipping)*

Engine-room plans of the *British Aviator*. *(The Motor Ship)*

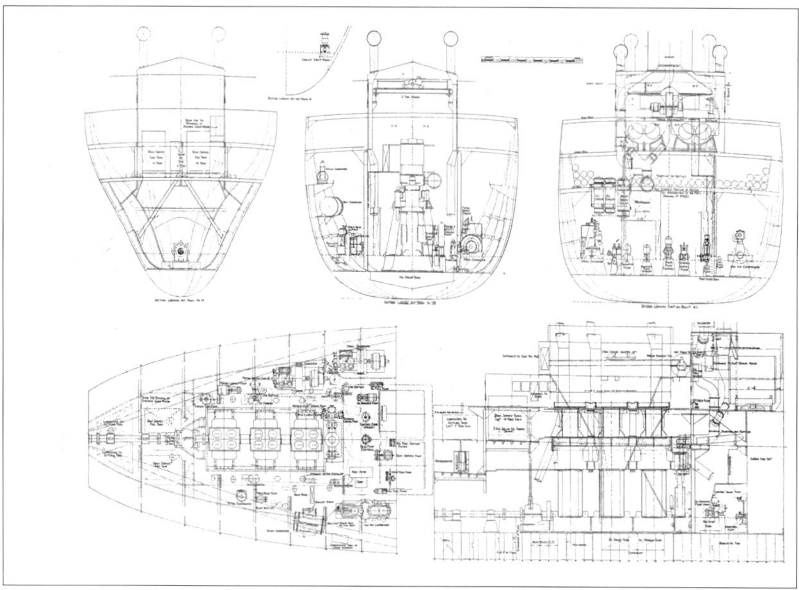

1924 was a significant year for the British Tanker Company. It heralded the entering into service of their first motor-ship. This was the *British Aviator*, built by Palmer's shipyard in Newcastle. The ship was typical of this class of around 10,000-sdwt tankers being built from 1924. She was 10,762-sdwt, 439.8 × 57.1 × 33.8 feet, giving a laden draught of 26.5 feet, launched on 20 May and completed the following August. The engine which made this ship unique was a high-powered six-cylinder Palmer-Fullagar marine diesel. In both the plan and the photograph of the engine on its test bed in Palmer's Yard, the cylinders in their housing are plainly visible. The output of the motor was 3,000 bhp at 90 rpm, geared to a single propeller shaft, which gave a speed of 11.7 knots at 2,950 bhp, with a fuel consumption of 0.408 lb per bhp-hour. A service speed was eventually calculated for this ship of 10.58 knots at 72.8 rpm and a fuel consumption of 0.404 lb per bhp-hour, under 'normal steaming conditions'. This delightfully nautical euphemism refers to conditions in which the weather was only roughly moderate, without too many Force Ten storms and above, and that she was correctly loaded or ballasted at the commencement of each voyage. The engine was cooled by fresh water from a pump with an output of 200 tons per hour. A total of 622 tons of bunker fuel was carried, together with 188 tons of oil for the boilers. The capacity of the lubricating oil tanks was 31 tons. All fuel was supplied (not surprisingly) by the Anglo-Persian Oil Company.

The engine-room plan shows an interesting aspect of the propulsion area. The section drawings indicate how the engine was mounted, and shows plainly the solid frames of the supporting cellular double-bottom. There was rarely wasted space anywhere aboard ship so, apart from the cofferdam below the double-bottom, this area would have stored engine fuel, feed or fresh-water tanks. The drive for the single propeller, and the shaft on its liners, is clearly shown. An oil transfer line was channelled within a steel pipe along the main deck to the reserve bunker tank at the lower part of the fo'c'sle head. The pump serving this was situated forward, along with a ballast pump.

The engine was fitted with comparatively few moving parts so any running and maintenance problems were well within the capacity of company engineering officers – even if their ingenuity was to be strained with some early models. This ship together with another in the class was re-fitted in February 1930 with a more powerful Doxford four-cylinder, 3,980 bhp engines.

The ship was, other than the engine, very much a traditional building for the company. Constructed on the Isherwood system, she had one oil-tight centreline longitudinal bulkhead and transversals sufficient to provide twenty cargo tanks port and starboard across ten sets, with five summer tanks. She was fitted with the by now mandatory two cofferdams fore and aft, together with one pump room amidships, abaft Number Five Tank, and clear of accommodation areas. There were two cargo pumps each with a capacity of 325 tons per hour. The engine-room and general arrangement plans indicate how tanker development in 1924 had progressed since days of the *Gluckauf*.

Electric auxiliary pump of the *British Aviator*. *(The Motor Ship)*

The construction visible above the wheelhouse, after part and fo'c'sle head represented a series of spars designed to support canvas awnings. These were rigged during extremes of heat frequently experienced in the Persian Gulf where temperatures could often reach in excess of 120°F. It was extremely uncomfortable at times doing essential work on deck, whilst the officers and crew in the engine-room laboured under nightmare conditions. Additional to the two 3-ton storing derricks, there was a smaller derrick in way of the manifolds to support the flexible pipes during loading/discharging operations for, were these permitted to rest on the steel rails with cargo flowing, a very real danger existed of an explosion in tanks partially filled with mixtures of hydrocarbons and oxygen due to a build-up of static electricity

The main cargo manifolds leading thwartships are in the foreground of this view. The raised catwalk remains a Classification Society regulation mandatory aboard all registered tankers facilitating safe crew movement when the ship is fully loaded with low freeboard – often of less than 10 feet – during which green seas were shipped across the main deck areas, fore and aft. This meant that European ratings or Asian crew from Hong Kong or India/Pakistan doubtless stoically endured a sometimes spray-soaked walk to and from work, especially when the tanker was loaded to her marks. The watertight square tank tops allowed entry for tank cleaning and inspection purposes and were fitted in the centre with small Ullage caps enabling oil samples, temperature and clearance between tank top and oil level to be recorded. A dry cargo colleague on one occasion humorously referred to an Ullage as 'the amount of oil which is not in the tank' – a comment fundamentally correct, but perhaps rather technically deficient. These early tank tops were made fast with a number of wing nuts. The coaming was only a foot or so in height, requiring surrounding metal rails not only to help access, but also prevented unwary crewmen from tripping over the tank top when working. They were particularly heavy to lift and equally awkward to lower.

The array of 'wheels' in the foreground are manual deck valves serving cargo manifolds, summer tanks and port side cargo tanks. A ready-rigged gangway can be seen on the port side placed near the bulwark by Number Seven tank. The pipe inboard of the man was the fuel oil transfer, mentioned previously, leading from forward to the engine-room. The mast step can just be seen aft below the catwalk and close to the docking winch by Number Nine tank. The docking winches and windlass aboard this ship remained powered by steam, served by two lines (not clearly visible) one for high-pressure steam input and another to provide water drainage. The main drums would serve operating power to the 3-ton derrick, with drum ends used to handle mooring ropes and later wires during

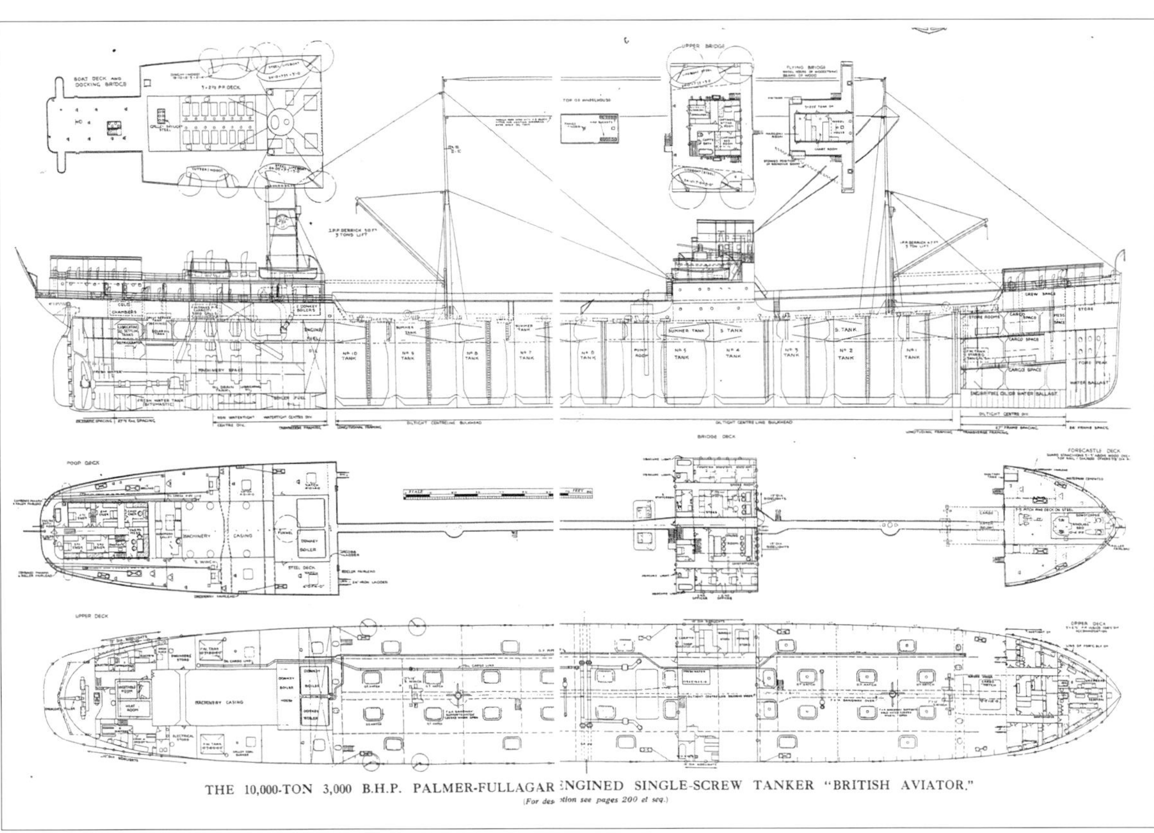

General arrangement plan of the *British Aviator*. *(The Motor Ship)*

View of the main deck of *British Aviator* looking aft. (*The Motor Ship*)

berthing. The boiler room on the plan is forward of the internal aft accommodation. This was fitted with two Scotch boilers 11 feet 6 inches in diameter and the same measurement in length. Both were oil-fired with one fitted to take exhaust from the engine.

The carriage of a spare propeller was, at that time, an essential safety Rule for all deep-sea ships, not only oil tankers. The *British Aviator* carried spare blades that were bolted and bracketed near the catwalk aft of the same docking winch (in the previous photograph) between the summer access tanks port and starboard, of the main mast. A spare anchor, shown in the general arrangement plan, was fitted on the fo'c'sle head abaft the anchor windlass – not a particularly convenient place when the crew were involved in intricacies that sometimes arose during a berthing stand-by with wires and ropes leading from bitts to fairleads ashore. In the event of need for either propeller or anchor, these would have to be fitted in a dry dock due to lack of handling facilities, as much as weight. The anchor alone on a ship of this size would probably have weighed in the region of 7 tons.

A view from aft, looking forward towards the midships accommodation on *British Aviator*. (*The Motor Ship*)

The *British Motorist* was another diesel oil powered tanker built for BTC at Swan, Hunter's Tyneside yard in August 1924. She also was of 10,772-sdwt, 440.2 feet in length, of 57.0 feet beam and 33.8 feet moulded depth. She was not a sister ship to the *British Aviator*, but was of similar type. Her engine was also constructed and fitted at Swan, Hunter's. The following set of photographs give a closer indication of the engine aboard this class of ship, together with captions that offer a simple non-engineering explanation of the starboard lower side of the main engine, together with its manoeuvring controls. This also was built by Swan, Hunter's, but was eight-cylinder, instead of six, of 3,980 bhp. The extra two cylinders, providing almost an extra 1,000 horsepower.

By the end of 1924, the British Tanker Company owned, including coasters, sixty tankers in excess of half a million tons deadweight capacity. The *British Petrol* was built in 1925 as a near sister ship to the *British Motorist*. The *Petrol*'s gross registered tonnage for instance was 6,906 compared to 6,891 of the former tanker. This variation between ships from the same yard and constructed to the same specification appears unusual, but is accounted for in slight quality differences found in materials used. For instance, a delivery of shell plating might vary fractionally from different batches previously supplied from the same manufacturers, not to such an extent that it would fail to reach agreed specifications, but just slightly so that over the use of a range in the hull the total gross ton-

***British Motorist*: starboard side of the main engine showing a new type of lubricator. On the left is an auxiliary Polar Diesel set.** (*The Motor Ship*)

Engine controls of *British Motorist*. The large handwheel is for going astern, and the two small levers below for starting. (*The Motor Ship*)

The *British Motorist* on her maiden voyage. *(The Motor Ship)*

nage would be slightly reduced or increased. The following photograph gives a different view of what were becoming standard diesel oil engines fitted aboard BTC tankers. The engine aboard *British Petrol* was built and installed by Swan, Hunter's and the eight cylinder-heads are easily counted in this photograph of the valve gear fitted to this diesel.

With the expiry of Isherwood's 'Longitudinal Oil Tanker Construction' patent, the door was open for him to rectify what he clearly regarded as 'some irritating faults'. Over the intervening years he had been continuously refining his invention seeking more optimum methods of improving efficiency. 1,492 ships of all types aggregating in excess of 12·5 million tons deadweight carrying capacity had been constructed according to his system. Of this phenomenal figure, 696 were bulk oil carriers at almost 6.75 million summer deadweight tons. That the 'Isherwood' system was universally accepted is unquestionable. It had been adopted by Lloyd's Register of Shipping and incorporated into their Rules for Oil Tanker Construction. The years between Isherwood's initial patent and its expiry proved he had found a satisfactory solution to problems of longitudinal strengthening in tankers of the existing tonnage. There still existed, however, some difficulties of leakage at the bulkhead bracket connections. Isherwood examined these and found they were largely ones of detail rather than indications of more serious structural deficiencies.

Valve gear of the Neptune Marine Oil Engine. *(Syren & Shipping)*

This photograph clearly shows the large number of brackets connecting the longitudinal members at deck, sides and bottom to the bulkheads, as well as the brackets connecting the horizontal stiffeners of the middle line bulkhead to the tank ends, providing points of rigidity by binding the entire structure of longitudinals, shell and deck plating. Isherwood examined the various stress loads involved and found that tankers, in any kind of seaway, were prone to longitudinal rigidity at the point of their bulkhead brackets. In other words, the leakage occurred because there was insufficient flexibility in the hull. This created stress on fittings at the transversals enabling oil seepage to occur. His problem was how to overcome this but still produce a tanker of sufficient strength that would be acceptable to Lloyd's Register. He explained in an article in *Syren & Shipping*, dated 6 January 1926, how this problem was overcome: 'My aim has been to remove this maximum point of stress on the longitudinal member away from the bulkhead . . . by fitting the deep transverse frames in closer comparative proximity to the bulkheads than hitherto, ie: instead of either having an equidistant spacing of deep transverses between the bulkheads or of having the transverses at a greater distance from the bulkheads than the equal spacing, the transverses are at less distance from the bulkheads than the distance between them'.

In fundamental terms, he eliminated the entire system of horizontal and vertical bulkhead brackets where these were fitted at the top, sides and bottom of the transversal separating individual sets of tanks, including areas of the expansion trunk. In the 'Bracketless' system, as he now referred to the tank construction of his modified tanker, two transverses only existed in each individual tank. These were spaced, in a tank (still 30 feet in length) from forward bulkhead to adjacent transverse 8 feet 9 inches – from transverse to transverse 12 feet 6 inches – and from transverse to aft bulkhead 8 feet 9 inches. He increased the strength of the longitudinal between bulkheads and adjacent transversals, which helped reduce stress loads to a minimum and retained integrity of the hull. He fitted also shell doublings – or wide liners – near

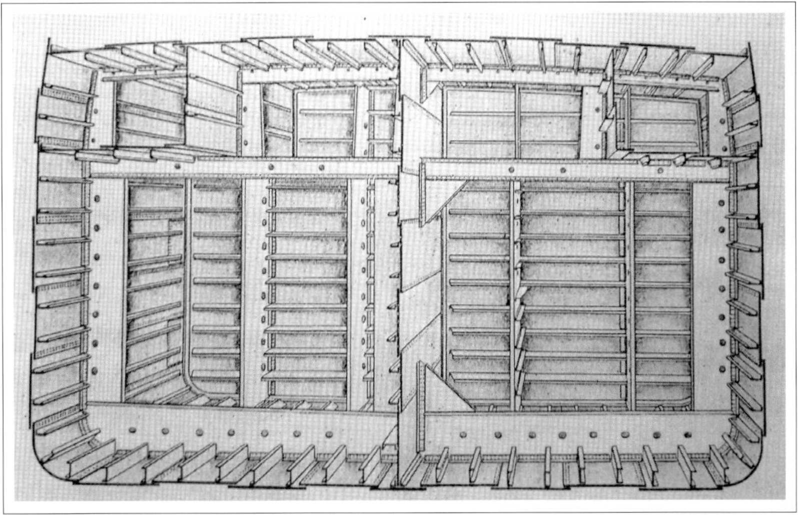

Perspective drawing by Isherwood indicating 'caulking' brackets stiffening the oil-tight transversal bulkhead at the shell plating in his 'established' tanker. *(Syren & Shipping).*

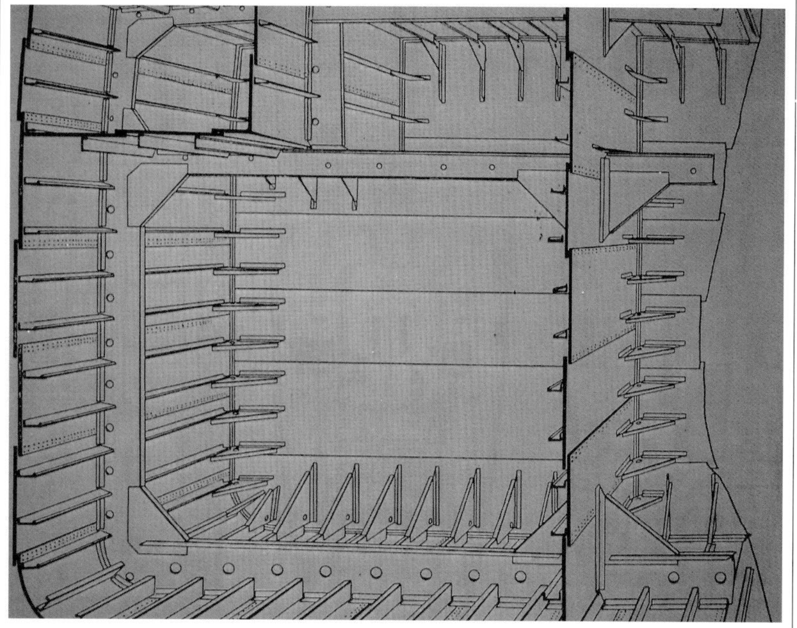

The Isherwood 'Bracketless' tank construction. *(Syren & Shipping).*

the end of the bulkheads, with alternate strakes at the sides of the ship and deck.

The advantages and strength of Isherwood's new system were considerable and soon led to its adoption by Lloyd's Register. In practical terms, he had produced a tanker experiencing less vibration: with a modest saving in weight (hence permitting marginally enhanced payload); reductions in costs of upkeep, damage repairs and tank cleaning, and a ship that was easier and cheaper to build. He also eliminated problems of oil seepage. Inevitably most British, and many foreign, tanker owners gave orders to shipbuilders for tankers to be constructed on Isherwood's 'Bracketless' system. The British Tanker Company saw their first tanker constructed to this specification launched on the 11 May 1926. This was the *British Inventor.*

BTC have always been prominent in encouraging experimentation that would help discover the 'optimum ship' to meet the operating circumstances and conditions of the time. Their *British Diplomat* was launched in April 1926 by John Brown's Clydebank yards. She was of 9,151-sdwt and diesel powered. The ship was unique to the fleet in that it was their first tanker fitted with twin propellers in efforts to increase manoeuvrability. It was not a qualified success. Two 8-cylinder diesel engines totalling 7760 bhp were required, at additional cost. There was a further disadvantage for those serving at sea who were accustomed to 'traditional' methods of propulsion. A captain handling a 10,000-deadweight ton tanker and placing the ship precisely where he wanted her to go, often without tugs and coping with adverse cross-winds or tide, could sometimes be presented with a difficult task. On such occasions, the 'propeller thrust' of a single screw frequently facilitated operations such as coming alongside a jetty, and similar close-quarter ship handling. This kind of in-built assistance was not so readily available with twin-screw ships, but the issue remained largely academic, as BP was not to fit twin propellers in any future ships.

In 1927, to boost the relationship being developed between BTC and Persian interests the funnel colours of BTC throughout the fleet were altered to reflect these new trends. These removed the 'BTC' logo, retained the red in a different position, and incorporated the Persian colours of green and white. The new funnel was to remain a hallmark of the Company until it was again changed some twenty-five years later, in 1955.

Pre 1927 funnel colours and flag.

Post 1927 funnel colours and flag.

New Challenges *Chapter Four*

During the dark years of the 'Great Depression' that hit all levels of British industry so hard, competitive marketing together with some support from the government ensured that no BTC tankers were laid-up. 1928 saw a world-wide glut of oil that led to fluctuating prices and a number of previously-unexpected mergers and company alliances. It was during this year that Anglo-Persian and Shell became equal partners in an oil distribution organisation known as Consolidated Petroleum Company. The worst year for the Group was 1932 when Anglo-Persian revised operations in efforts to combat effects of the Depression. Shell-Mex and BP merged to co-ordinate distribution of both partners' refined products in the United Kingdom. All areas of the Company were hit including shareholders, general company expenditure, crewing levels, and even the Shah of Persia. The latter, however, with many interests at stake concerning oil concessions, was eager to re-negotiate a new contract the following year. For officers and crew employed and retained by the Company the years of good fortune diminished slightly. Many were lucky in remaining at sea, but a very bleak time indeed followed for their colleagues – as had been the case for seafarers' elsewhere in the Merchant Navy for many years. Fully-qualified Masters with certificates of rank and extensive experience were forced to ship away as deck hands – and considered themselves fortunate in finding a ship with Articles to sign. Newly qualified officers found they were unable to obtain sea-going posts and had to turn their hand to a variety of jobs ashore, if these were obtainable. The bitterness and frustration they expressed remain understandable. The situation was marginally improved for engineers, whose maritime skills were more readily transferable, but even these officers experienced some very lean times.

Throughout the 1920s and 1930s BTC continued their building programme of tankers that were constructed and distributed around British yards to maintain the fleet and assist allied industries. 1928 saw the final batch of thirteen 10,000-sdwt tankers, marking the termination of ships ordered within this Class. Probably with the economic situation in mind, the company spread their net extremely widely for six different British yards were used, with three ships each coming from Swan, Hunter's and Palmers' yards. The thirteen diesels used included three different types of oil engine ordered from six different makers. Doxford Marine provided two directly. They also permitted the building of a further three under licence by Richardsons Westgarth of Sunderland. Other engines were built – four by Burmeister & Wain/Kincaid, and two by Sulzer. Overall, the final batch of tankers represented an extremely mixed bag of constructors yet proved of very sound quality. Internally, as far as hull construction, tank arrangements and piping were concerned, comparison of the General Arrangement plans indicates this class differed little from the earlier 1924 tankers: each retained the single centre-line with ten port/starboard and summer tanks.

One ship of this class was the *British Glory* that had been built at Sir John Laing's Yard (Number 701) in 1928, although the 3,210 bhp diesel engine was by Harland & Wolff in Glasgow. In April 1940, the *Motor Ship* was able to report in retrospect some voyage statistics of this tanker. She had steamed over 417,000 nautical miles in eleven years to the end of 1939. In 1938 alone, she steamed 40,903 miles transporting crude oil from the Gulf regions to UK and Continental ports. The magazine remarked: 'The most remarkable consistency is shown in the matter of speeds, both loaded on the homeward run and in ballast, outward-bound. . . . There are no occasions where the six-monthly figures for the ship loaded have differed by so much as half a knot in speed . . . 10.4 loaded and 11.04 in ballast.'

In 1931, on her loaded voyages throughout the year, she averaged 10 knots with minute fluctuations in the speed across the 12-month period. Whilst her speed in ballast ranged between 10.9 and 11.09 knots. This margin may probably be accounted for in adverse winds and tides experienced because, when only partially loaded with ballast, a large expanse of comparatively light ship is available which is subjected to these external forces. The highest speed this tanker recorded was during a voyage in 1932 when she reached 11.43 knots. In the light of such impressive sailing figures, it is interesting to see a cover of the Agreement document for her building which started turning the 'wheels of her construction', as it were.

The magazine paid considerable tribute to the workforces' both of Laing's for the solid tankers constructed, and to Doxford's for the quality of their engine. Incidentally, this tanker sustained torpedo damage in October 1941, but was repaired and continued in service until she was scrapped in 1954.

BTC have always been recognised for their fleet of deep-sea tankers, but they operated also an impressive fleet of smaller ships designed for the coastal trade. The *British Pluck* (see Photograph BT99 in Part Two), was launched in April 1928 by Swan, Hunter & Wigham Richardson at their Tyneside Neptune Works. Of 1,087-sdwt she was 240.0 feet length overall, with a beam of 32.6 feet and, fully laden, a draught of 12 feet. Following the practice of many smaller tankers, the bridge and officers' accommodation was aft, leaving an open foredeck hampered only by an apparently impressive array of foredeck vertical wires for such a modest ship. These were used to hoist wind sails and assist clearing gas from the

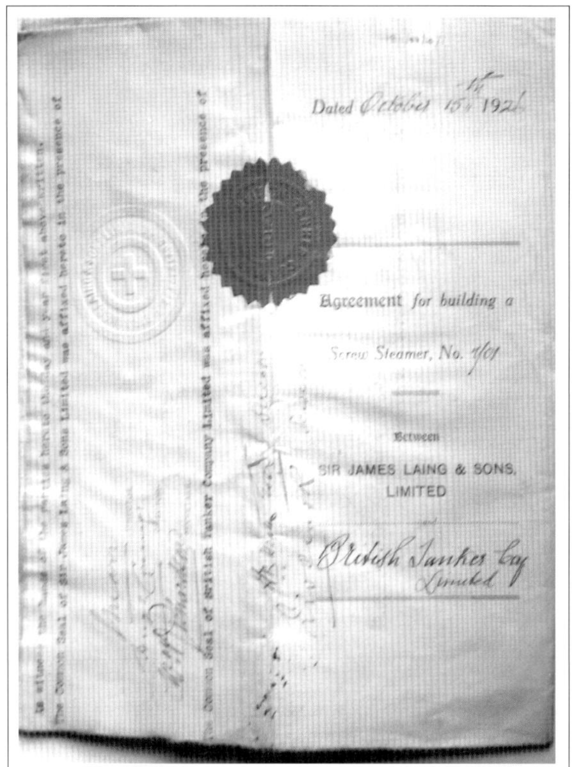
Dated October 15th 1921

Agreement for building a Screw Steamer, No. 701

Between

SIR JAMES LAING & SONS, LIMITED

British Tanker Coy Limited

The 'Sealed' Agreement between the British Tanker Company and Sir James Laing and Sons for the construction of Screw Steamer No 701 – ***British Glory.*** *(Tyne and Wear Maritime Museum and Archive)*

tanks in days before portable or fixed gas freeing fans became compulsory fittings. Accommodation for seamen and greasers was in the fo'c'sle head. A dry cargo hold was fitted forward served by a 2-ton safe working load (swl) derrick off the fore mast and sometimes used, for example, to ship bulk consignments of lubricating oil drums.

The expansion trunk fitted above the harbour deck is clearly visible in the photograph. For many of her voyages, refined petroleum products were carried in seven sets of double tanks, with traditional centre-line longitudinal, separated from the engine-room by an after cofferdam and pump room. She carried two × 200-ton 70 bhp cargo pumps driven by two-cylinder Atlas diesel engines representing a very powerful tanker for her size and period. Steam was used to operate deck equipment, the two capstans fore and aft, steering gear and heating in the accommodation. The engine was the latest design from Neptune-Polar and

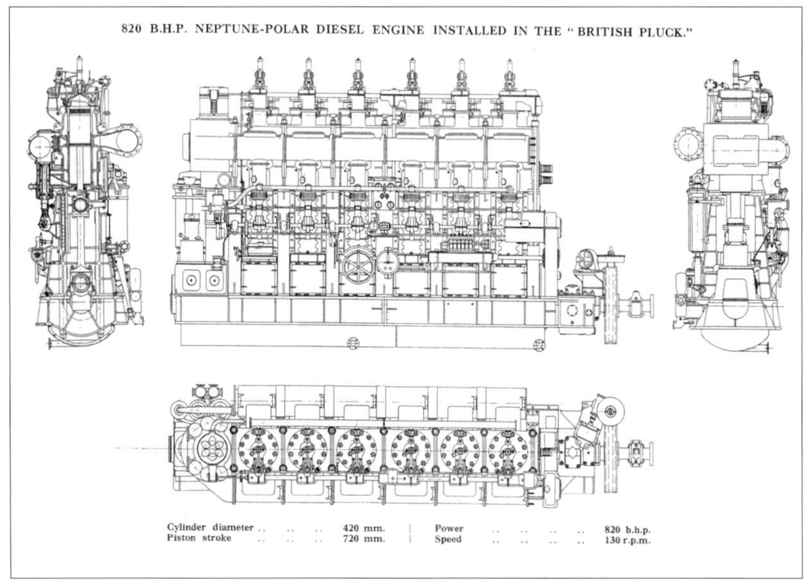

820 bhp Neptune-Polar Diesel Engine installed in the *British Pluck.* *(The Motor Ship).*

was built by Swan, Hunter's. The 820 bhp, six-cylinder diesel had been constructed under licence from Atlas and, on her trials, gave a maximum speed of almost 11 knots. It is sad to relate that this fine vessel hit a mine in September 1940 and subsequently sank.

Anglo-Persian had been exploring for oil in Kuwait for some time, as also had the American Gulf Oil Company, but both failed to find any significant quantity. Direct talks with Gulf Oil were opened in the belief that their only way forward was the establishment of a 50:50 company to apply for the concession. By December 1933 agreement had been reached and the Kuwait Oil Company Limited, was founded. The Foreign Office however was fearful of American influence increasing in the area and insisted that operations on the ground should be under British control. This led to further talks between the Government and the Kuwait Oil Company. In March 1934 agreement was reached where, despite Gulf's 50 per cent stake, all development activities within Kuwait would be British dominated. The approach and negotiations with the Amir was entrusted to Frank Holmes for Gulf and Archibald Chisholm for the Anglo-Persian Oil Company. The Amir had been thwarted in his game of playing one against another but had versed himself well in the knowledge of the political developments and concession terms in Iraq, Persia and Saudi Arabia and had on occasions proved a tough negotiator. Despite his displeasure at London's insistence on British dominance in the project he approved a deal on 23 December 1934. The agreement gave a 75-year concession in return for an up-front payment of £35,700 ($179,000) and a minimum annual payment of £7,150 ($36,000) until oil was found. Depending on volumes found he would then receive a minimum of £18,800 ($94,000) annually. Holmes was appointed to Kuwait Oil Company, as representative of the Amir in London, until his death in 1947. Seismic work was initiated in the Burgan area of south-east Kuwait in 1936 and on 23 February 1938 an extremely large flow was struck.

During 1935 the Medway Oil & Storage Company Ltd., established during 1928 by Power Petroleum Company Ltd., London became associated with the Anglo-Persian Oil Company. The latter took shares in their operation as security for the charter of *British Thrift* after which she was renamed *Thriftie* to fall in line with their naming system. In June 1935, Anglo-Persian was renamed the Anglo-Iranian Oil Company and increased its interest in Medway Oil & Storage Company Limited, acquiring control by 1936. *Thriftie* and *Energie* were operated within the Shell-Mex & BP network. During 1942 for rationalisation purposes the Anglo-Iranian Oil Company interests in Medway Oil were transferred to Shell-Mex & BP until their total absorption into the latter during 1956. Refineries, petroleum harbours and jetties continued to expand. For reasons of safety as much as security these were often placed in sparsely populated areas, which might explain perhaps why tankers sometimes lacked that same kind of appeal for 'average ship enthusiasts' held by liners, tugs or dry cargo ships. They could physically see and come close to ships of the latter classes and even obtain company permits to go aboard them, but could rarely come equally as close to tankers. The Dingle oil jetty in the River Mersey was typical of the type of oil jetty found anywhere in the world.

A major development occurred off the Mersey in 1933 when Stanlow Oil Dock was opened under auspices of the Manchester Ship Canal Company. The dock measured 600 feet in length by 180 feet wide with a uniform depth of 30 feet. It had accommodation then for two tankers and could cope with the largest in BTC's fleet. There was also a 600-foot lay-by berth constructed on the south side of the canal capable of discharging grades of oil that did not flash below 73°F. This was used also by both deep-sea and coastal tankers for transhipping by-products. A BTC ship was the first commercial tanker to enter the new dock and its arrival was greeted with that customary acclaim which often heralds any major maritime event in this country. The *British Duchess* found herself accompanied by a fleet of pleasure and sundry craft, including the Alexandra Towing Company's tug *Ryde* which on this occasion carried dignitaries involved in the opening ceremony. Cargo at Stanlow was handled ashore by derricks supporting the delivery ship's pump by using flexible pipes slung in specially-constructed cradles to prevent pipes touching rails during operations.

A Company tanker discharging crude oil at the Dingle Bank jetty near Liverpool. *(Syren & Shipping)*

***British Duchess*, accompanied by pleasure craft, was the first tanker to enter and use Manchester's Stanlow Dock.** *(Syren & Shipping)*

The main discharge pipe was channelled in a subway constructed under the canal, through a conduit some 466 feet in length, which terminated in a pipe manifold connected with installations provided by several oil companies. An extensive area was reserved and earmarked for future development of this important dock.

In the mid-1930s a major contribution to tank safety and development occurred following research by William Millar (amongst others) into oil tanker construction. The technical ramifications were complex and detailed, but further development of the ideas led eventually to the building of tankers with two longitudinal oil-tight bulkheads replacing the single centre-line that had been the main feature of previous constructions. These revolutionary findings produced tankers with increased longitudinal, bottom and under-deck strength; smaller transversal dimensions (which reduced weight and free-surface area), elimination of the expansion trunk, an increase in the length of oil tanks, and a marked reduction in shearing stresses. Centre tanks could be available for water ballast and would offer smaller corrosive surfaces. The double longitudinal system was used in all future tanker buildings following acceptance by the classification societies, and became integrated into future Isherwood systems.

Until the outbreak of the Second World War, BTC consistently ordered a number of deep-sea tankers from various British yards, plus a further assortment of coastal craft. The ships represented a range of different tonnages, from the *British Venture* of 1930 at 6,922-sdwt, through classes of around 11,000-sdwt, to the twenty-one larger capacity 12,000-sdwt tankers built from 1936 to 1939. The latter ships were constructed to take advantage of the 1930 Load Line Rule which permitted tankers of this deadweight to load 15 inches below the previous summer load line, with a considerable increase in payload. This was something American tanker owners had been allowed

The *British Duchess* alongside Stanlow Dock discharges the first cargo of crude oil to be received in that port. The flexible hose connections between tanker and pipe lines are clearly visible. *(Shipping)*

to do for some years and had acted to the detriment of the British tanker trades.

The *British Endurance* represented a ship of the new 12,000-sdwt class tankers. She followed the *British Fame* that had also been launched by Swan, Hunter's on 19 June 1936. Both ships were 481 feet length overall, and 464 feet $2\frac{1}{2}$ inches between perpendiculars, with a moulded beam of 61 feet 9 inches and a moulded depth of 34 feet $0\frac{1}{2}$ inches. They had a draught of 27 feet 6 inches at their summer load line, on a deadweight of 12,250 tons. It is interesting to note, following an earlier comment, that their respective gross tonnages vary by some 400 tons. *British Fame* was of 8,303 grt compared to 8,406 of her sister-ship. This class were each fitted with a slightly raked stem and cruiser stern – the latter being more dynamically efficient than the old counter stern of the *British Aviator* (and later *Duchess*).

Using the *British Endurance* as a representative tanker, she was launched on 19 August 1936 and was completed the following October. She presented a number of interesting features. Asian crew continued to be berthed forward, with British officers aft and midships. It was a common feature of BTC tankers that they often carried accommodation midships in excess to requirements of normal operating purposes. This gave their ships a very squat, solid yet distinctive silhouette that provided instant identification of a company deep-sea tanker when seen through binoculars from the wheelhouse. Occasionally, a cabin was used by a pilot taken aboard for a run – for instance, picked up in Rotterdam and carried to the UK, who would take over his duties perhaps on (or even slightly before) sighting Trinity Buoy off Harwich. Company directors or transit officers for other ships might also be carried in days before flying across the world to join or leave ships became the norm. The spare propeller remained aft whilst the statutory spare anchor, although not shown, would almost certainly be on the main deck below the fo'c'sle head. Other ships with less generous cabin allowance would carry 'passengers' either in a spare cadet berth or a pilot cabin provided for the purpose.

The engines were built by Doxford's, with 3,435 bhp giving a service speed of around 12 knots. The steering gear was two-ram and operated from a Telemotor on the Bridge. As with the earlier *British Aviator* class, a considerable amount of steam was required to drive cargo and ballast pumps, windlass, winches and, aboard this tanker, two warping capstans port and starboard aft. Again, this was provided by two boilers in a casing forward of the main engine.

A forced air draught system was also fitted to this class of tankers. Thermo-tank units drew clean air from cowls fitted with filters situated in areas on deck known to be free from oil fumes. This was then distributed throughout the accommodation via a series of ducts and a cabin controlled system of *punka louvres*. The air produced was not temperature-controlled, but produced a welcome blast of filtered air providing at least a measure of comfort to cabins, particularly during sandstorms in the Suez Canal and elsewhere in the Persian Gulf.

The midships and general arrangement plans show this tanker was constructed on the still comparatively novel system of two longitudinals previously described. There were twenty-seven individual tanks divided into nine sets of three. A separate ballast pump was again run from forward enabling certain designated tanks (usually centres) to be used as necessary for seawater ballast. Two pump rooms were fitted, one forward on the port side and the other midships, allowing the tanker to trade in products as well as transporting perhaps two or more different grades of crude. There were four cargo pumps fitted, each with a capacity of 230 tons per hour, so that when fully worked-up *British Endurance* could discharge an impressive 920 tons of oil per hour.

The disposition of pipelines can be seen from the elevation drawing. The two main cargo operations aboard tankers remain loading and discharging. In many respects, these work from different practices even though pipes common to both are used. The chief officer would draw up a loading plan and discuss this with the Master and shore superintendents. This would cover the specific gravity of the cargo to be lifted and give estimated tonnages, temperatures and final Ullages to be expected upon completion. The destination was rarely fixed at this stage in the voyage but, if travelling from the Persian Gulf towards Europe would usually be entered in the Mate's Rough Log as 'Bound Persian Gulf towards LEFO [Land's End for Orders]'.

Loading would be from shore-side pumps working through the main manifolds where deck officers would direct the cargo into the required tanks through the piping system. There were a number of alternative arrange-

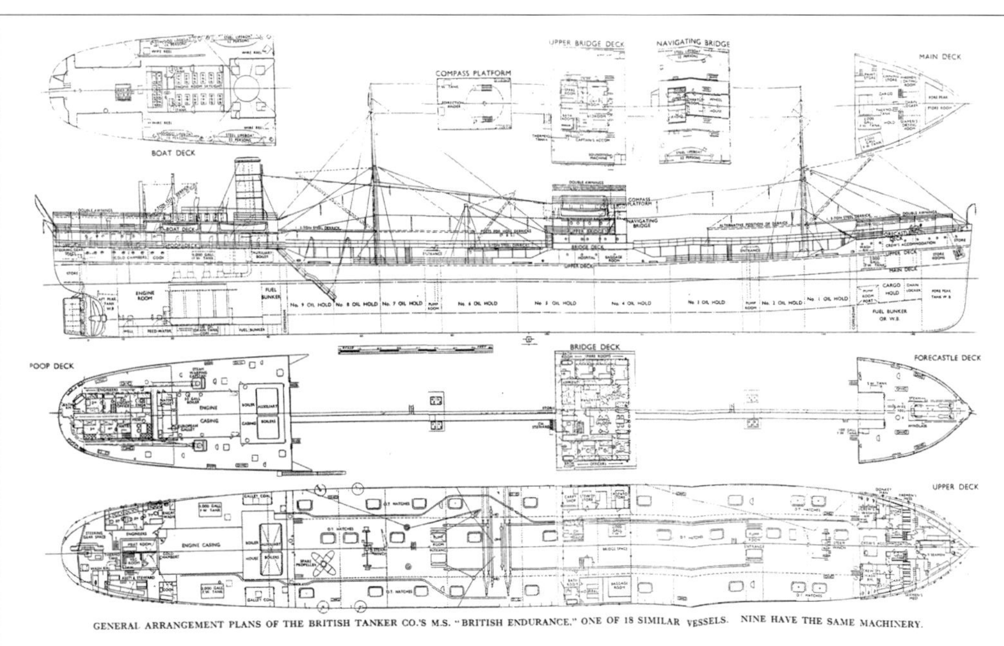

GENERAL ARRANGEMENT PLANS OF THE BRITISH TANKER CO.'S M.S. "BRITISH ENDURANCE." ONE OF 18 SIMILAR VESSELS. NINE HAVE THE SAME MACHINERY.

General arrangement plan of the *British Endurance*. *(The Motor Ship).*

ments existing, but the one illustrated is a variation of many modifications to the 'Ring System'. Briefly, this used a series of tank, master and crossover valves to direct cargo oil along one side of the appropriate set of tanks, across the other side, and eventually into its designated tank for the voyage. The ship's pumps during loading would of course be isolated.

The *Motor Ship* said of this ship: 'The owners are to be congratulated on the standard of accommodation which has been arranged on the *British Endurance* and her sister ships . . . The Thermo-tank installation is probably the most comprehensive yet fitted in a tanker . . . [This ship] is, throughout, a typical example of up-to-date tanker construction and of the thoroughness with which her owners' technical department carry out their work.'

The tanker survived the Second World War, and countless subsequent potential marine dangers, and was scrapped after 25 years service at MacLellan's of Bo'ness yard in 1959.

The *British Genius* was 12,416-sdwt and completed by William Doxford's Sunderland yard in January 1939. An interesting feature occurs upon the comple-

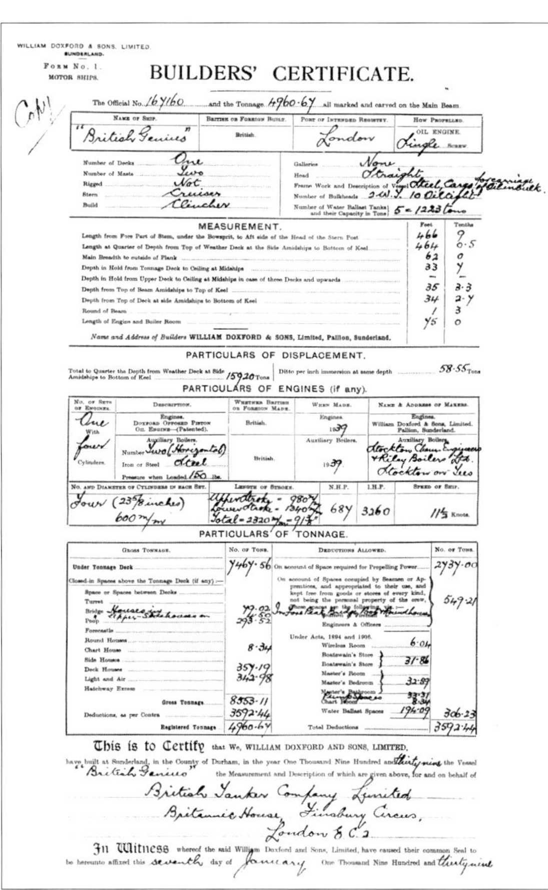

WILLIAM DOXFORD & SONS, LIMITED
SUNDERLAND.

FORM No. 1.
MOTOR SHIPS.

BUILDERS' CERTIFICATE.

Copy

The Official No. 164160 and the Tonnage 4960·64 all marked and carved on the Main Beam.

Name of Ship.	British or Foreign Built.	Port of Intended Registry.	How Propelled.
"British Genius"	British.	London	OIL ENGINE. Single Screw

Number of Decks: One
Number of Masts: Two
Rigged: Not
Stern: Cruiser
Build: Clincher
Galleries: None
Head: Straight
Frame Work and Description of Vessel: Steel, Cargo [illegible]
Number of Bulkheads: 2 W.T. 10 Oiltight
Number of Water Ballast Tanks and their Capacity in Tons: 5 = 1223 tons

MEASUREMENT.

	Feet	Tenths
Length from Fore Part of Stem, under the Bowsprit, to Aft side of the Head of the Stern Post	466	9
Length at Quarter of Depth from Top of Weather Deck at the Side Amidships to Bottom of Keel	464	0·5
Main Breadth to outside of Plank	62	0
Depth in Hold from Tonnage Deck to Ceiling at Midships	33	4
Depth in Hold from Upper Deck to Ceiling at Midships in case of three Decks and upwards	—	—
Depth from Top of Beam Amidships to Top of Keel	35	3·3
Depth from Top of Deck at side Amidships to Bottom of Keel	34	2·4
Round of Beam	1	3
Length of Engine and Boiler Room	45	0

Name and Address of Builders WILLIAM DOXFORD & SONS, Limited, Pallion, Sunderland.

PARTICULARS OF DISPLACEMENT.

Total to Quarter the Depth from Weather Deck at Side Amidships to Bottom of Keel 15920 Tons | Ditto per inch immersion at same depth 58·55 Tons

PARTICULARS OF ENGINES (if any).

No. of Sets of Engines.	Description.	Whether British or Foreign Made.	When Made.	Name & Address of Makers.
One With four Cylinders.	Engines. Doxford Opposed Piston Oil Engine—(Patented).	British.	Engines. 1939	Engines. William Doxford & Sons, Limited. Pallion, Sunderland.
	Auxiliary Boilers. Number Two (Horizontal) Iron or Steel Steel Pressure when Loaded 150 lbs.	British.	Auxiliary Boilers. 1939.	Auxiliary Boilers. Stockton Chem. Engineers + Riley Boilers Ltd. Stockton on Tees

No. and Diameter of Cylinders in each Set.	Length of Stroke.	N.H.P.	I.H.P.	Speed of Ship.
Four (23⅝ inches) 600 m/m	Upper Stroke = 980 m/m Lower Stroke = 1340 m/m Total = 2320 m/m = 91⅜"	684	3260	11½ Knots.

PARTICULARS OF TONNAGE.

Gross Tonnage.	No. of Tons.	Deductions Allowed.	No. of Tons.
Under Tonnage Deck	7464·56	On account of Space required for Propelling Power	2734·00
Closed-in Spaces above the Tonnage Deck (if any):—		On account of Spaces occupied by Seamen or Apprentices, and appropriated to their use, and kept free from goods or stores of every kind, not being the personal property of the crew. These spaces are the following, viz.:— In Fore Peak, Bridge, Poop & Roundhouse	549·21
Space or Spaces between Decks		Engineers & Officers	
Turret		Under Acts, 1894 and 1906.	
Bridge Houses in upper	79·02	Wireless Room	6·04
Skylights on	4·50	Boatswain's Store / Boatswain's Store	31·86
Poop	293·52	Master's Room / Master's Bedroom / Master's Bathroom	32·89
Forecastle		Pump Spaces	33·31
Round Houses		Chart Room	8·34
Chart House	8·34	Water Ballast Spaces	194·09
Side Houses			306·23
Deck Houses	354·19		
Light and Air	342·98		
Hatchway Excess			
Gross Tonnage	8553·11		
Deductions, as per Contra	3592·44		
Registered Tonnage	4960·64	Total Deductions	3592·44

This is to Certify that We, WILLIAM DOXFORD AND SONS, LIMITED, have built at Sunderland, in the County of Durham, in the year One Thousand Nine Hundred and thirty nine the Vessel "British Genius" the Measurement and Description of which are given above, for and on behalf of British Tanker Company Limited Britannic House, Finsbury Circus, London E.C.2

In Witness whereof the said William Doxford and Sons, Limited, have caused their common Seal to be hereunto affixed this seventh day of January One Thousand Nine Hundred and thirty nine.

Doxford's Builder's Certificate covering completion of the *British Genius*. *(Tyne and Wear Archives Service)*

tion of any ship. A builder's certificate is issued giving about it a brief but precise statement outlining particulars of hull measurements, particulars of displacement, engines and tonnage. That covering the *British Genius* is shown from which can be seen the emphasis placed upon tonnage and its method of compilation.

In its broadest terms, ship tonnage remained based on the Merchant Shipping Act of 1854 (Revised in

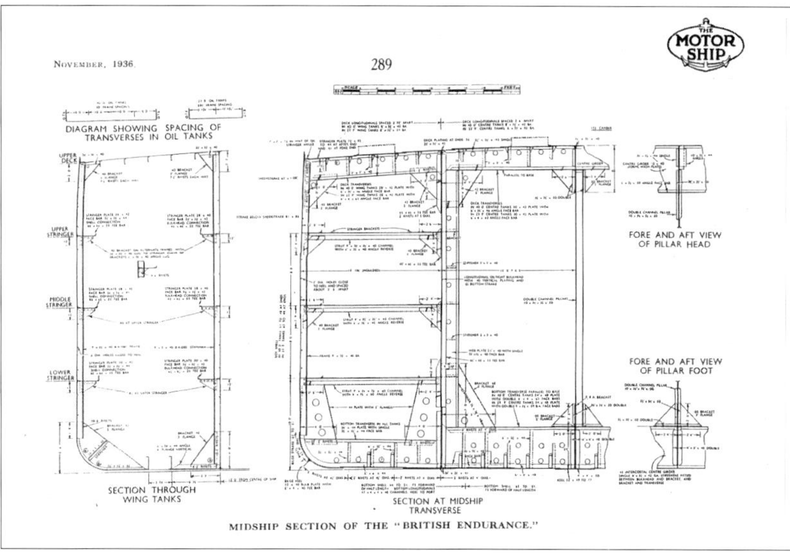

The midships section of *British Endurance*. *(The Motor Ship).*

1894), where the Gross Registered Tonnage (grt) of any ship was expressed in terms of her moulded volume, where 100 cubic feet of permanently enclosed space became the equivalent of one ton. Net tonnage (nrt) represented the revenue earning capacity of the ship or cargo space available. It was calculated from the gross tonnage of the tanker with deductions made for enclosed non-earning spaces such as accommodation, engine-room space, ballast and domestic water tanks etc. Dock charges remain based on net tonnage. The summer deadweight tonnage, against which all references to tanker tonnage should be made, is based on the weight carried by the ship to bring her down to her summer draught mark. This includes crew and personal effects, stewards' stores, cargo, fuel and ballast, so deductions had to be made for the latter when deducing how much cargo might be loaded. The shipowner however was more concerned with volume than weight as far as tankers were concerned for, as it has been shown, the actual tonnage loaded could vary considerably in volume with temperature fluctuations that might be experienced during the voyage.

The clouds of war were gathering not only over Europe, but throughout the world, encouraging the British government to take interim steps protecting fuel supplies for the Admiralty. During 1937, six tankers under construction for BTC were taken over on the stocks and completed under Company supervision. They were all allocated names ending with 'Dale'. Simultaneously, four ships with '*British*' names man-

Arrangement of cargo oil suctions and discharges in the *British Endurance*. *(The Motor Ship)*

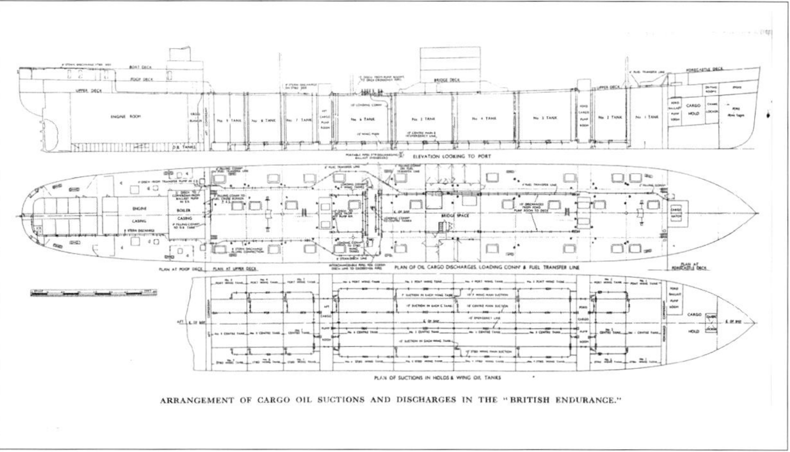

THE SIX VESSELS SOLD TO THE ADMIRALTY WHILST UNDER CONSTRUCTION.
NO PROPOSED BRITISH TANKER NAMES WERE LOCATED.

ABBEYDALE
O.N. 165409. 8,299g. 4,926n. 466.3 × 61.9 × 33.9 feet.
4-cyl. 2 S.C.S.A. (23-5/9″ × 91-5/16″) oil engine manufactured by Wm.Doxford & Sons Ltd., Sunderland. 3,435 bhp.
28.12.1936: Launched by Swan, Hunter & Wigham, Richardson Company Ltd., Newcastle (Yard No.1506), for the Admiralty. 3.1937: Completed. 4.9.1960: T.W.Ward Ltd., Barrow for demolition.

ARNDALE
O.N. 165578. 8,503g. 5,011n. 466.3 × 61.9 × 33.9 feet.
4-cyl. 2 S.C.S.A. (23-5/9″ × 91-5/16″) oil engine manufactured by Wm.Doxford & Sons Ltd., Sunderland. 3,435 bhp.
5.8.1937: Launched by Swan, Hunter & Wigham, Richardson Company Ltd., Newcastle (Yard No.1516), for the Admiralty. 9.1937: Completed. 12.4.1960: Sold to Belgian shipbreakers.

ALDERSDALE
O.N. 165572. 8,402g. 4,926n. 464.3 × 61.9 × 33.9 feet.
4-cyl. 2 S.C.S.A. (23-5/9″ × 91-5/16″) oil engine manufactured by Wm.Doxford & Sons Ltd., Sunderland. 3,435 bhp.
7.7.1937: Launched by Cammell, Laird Shipbuilders Ltd., Birkenhead (Yard No.1025), for the Admiralty. 9.1937: Completed. 26.5.1942: Sunk by aircraft in the Barents Sea.

BISHOPDALE
O.N. 165468. 8,406. 4,925n. 467.6 × 61.7 × 33.9 feet.
6-cyl. 4 S.C.S.A. (29-1/8″ × 59-1/16″) B&W type oil engine manufactured by J.G.Kincaid & Company Ltd., Greenock. 2,450 bhp.
31.3.1937: Launched by Lithgows Ltd., Glasgow (Yard No. 887), for the Admiralty. 6.1937: Completed. 28.1.1970: Sold.

BOARDALE
O.N. 165489. 8,562g. 5,001n. 467.8 × 61.7 × 33.8 feet.
6-cyl. 4 S.C.S.A. (29-1/8″ × 59-1/16″) B&W type oil engine manufactured by the shipbuilder. 2,450 bhp.
22.4.1937: Launched by Harland & Wolff Ltd., Govan (Yard No.971g), for the Admiralty. 7.6.1937: Completed. 30.4.1940: Sunk whilst grounded at Narvik.

BROOMDALE
O.N. 165594. 8,562g. 5,001n. 467.8 × 61.7 × 33.8 feet.
6-cyl. 4 S.C.S.A. (29-1/8″ × 59-1/16″) B&W type oil engine manufactured by the shipbuilder. 2,450 bhp.
2.9.1937: Launched by Harland & Wolff Ltd., Govan (Yard No.973g), for the Admiralty. 3.11.1937: Completed. 1.1960: Sold to Belgian shipbreakers.

The six tankers sold to the Admiralty by BTC whilst under construction.

aged by BTC on behalf of the Admiralty were given names beginning '*Ol . . .*' and removed from Company management. The British Tanker Company entered the war with a fleet of ninety-three tankers – most of which were diesel-powered – the last to be constructed being the *British Influence,* which was completed in May 1939.

Ravages of War *Chapter Five*

BY SEPTEMBER 1939, CHANGES in British industry meant demand for oil had increased significantly. On the domestic front consumption was appreciable, but not that heavy, because the use of oil was unsophisticated compared with today. Gas and coal remained major household fuels, horse-drawn traffic was still common, and one car per street (let alone two a family) in many parts of the country was still unusual. It nevertheless became apparent that oil production and supply would be major issues in the forthcoming war.

The painful horror and unbelievable loss of life caused by the conflict at sea from the first day of war until the very last is, in 2005, well documented. The many accounts relate stories of unique personal trauma. Collectively, they obviate the necessity to quote further incidents even though the not doing so in no way diminishes attempts to convey the enormity of this conflict. Over 36,000 merchant seamen died: a staggering figure which no subsequent book, film or play could ever hope to rationalise or allow effective comprehension. Further evidence of that which poetry calls 'the glorious sacrifice', is evident when standing in front of the Merchant Navy Memorial, Tower Hill in London. The sheer enormity of the bronze rolls, commemorating each individual life and ship lost, leaves any sensitive observer in deeply reflective mood.

The British Tanker Company shared in this loss at a level totally unforeseen by the Company's experiences in the First War. BTC commenced the conflict with a massive fleet of ninety-three deep-sea and coastal tankers that totalled around 1 million summer-deadweight tons. They employed a staff of thousands ashore and afloat. During the Second World War, the Company had forty-four tankers sunk (plus a further six of the Company's managed ships), twenty-two damaged, and 657 seagoing staff killed. There are, of course, the majority of BTC seafarers who experienced the Second World War and survived – those who suffered direct attack, who saw ships sunk around them, had their own ship sunk underneath them, and who witnessed the death of fellow seafarers. What is not recorded on Tower Hill Memorial, of course, are the effects of permanent physical injuries and mental scars, carried to this day, of those whom Fate deemed should survive. This sobering thought cannot fail to result in deeper appreciation of the debt owed to those officers and ratings who served in the Merchant Navy during the Second World War. Speaking to such merchant mariners is a moving experience even after the passage of so many years because, once reminiscence begins, beneath the thin veneers of casual indifference is clear evidence of a haunting by painful memories. The sad rheumy eyes of John Straughan, for instance, spoke more than could ever have been verbalised.

The first tanker to be lost was, by one of those peculiar quirks of fate, the last ship launched before the outbreak of war. Completed in May 1939, the *British Influence* was homeward bound for Hull from Abadan when she was surprised off the coast of south-west Ireland by the German submarine *U-29* on 14 September of that year. The U-Boat surfaced and allowed the crew to abandon ship before sinking the tanker with a torpedo and gunfire.

A radio officer serving aboard the *British Dominion* wrote of his experiences in North Atlantic convoys for the *Seafarer,* the magazine of the Marine Society or, as the organisation was called then, 'The Seafarers' Education Service'. Ships in convoy maintained radio silence, enabling 'Sparks' to share Bridge watches with the navigating officers and assist by looking after visual communications via flag and Aldis lamp with escorts and convoy commodore. Radio Officer Grieve won first prize with his essay in the 1941–2 competitions and captured adequately the constant pressure under which everyone aboard lived, especially ship's engineers: 'Down below, amid the heat and grime of the engine-room, the fourth Engineer left the telephone, and manipulated the controls, watching the revolution counter as he did so. He sometimes wondered what weird movements of the convoy necessitated so many changes in speed; but he seldom complained, and hardly ever did the thought of danger enter his head. The favourite spot for an enemy torpedo was the engine-room, and when the weapon found its mark, there was not much chance for the engineers on watch. The Fourth did not often think on these things. His was to obey, and to trust in those who could see and hear the turn of events in the outer world.' Grieve made the point that more ships arrived at their destination when in convoy than when going solo, and he captured also the atmosphere of ever-present unrelieved tension of 'what *might* happen'; occasional incidents of humour, but most of all the boredom. He concluded: 'the advantages of a convoy lies in its comparative safety and it is this which is the most important point to remember when the advantages and disadvantages of a convoy are disputed.'

As it was obvious from the very beginning that tankers would prove prime targets for the Navies of all

British Bombardier **seen at Cape Town with her funnel placed amidships that having been replaced with twin funnels aft disguised as kingposts.** *(World Ship Society Photograph Library)*

nations, attempts were made to camouflage these extra-valuable ships. The *Empire Bombardier*, for example – later to serve as the *British Bombardier* – was rigged-up with a dummy funnel midships and attempts made to convert her engine exhaust to look like a kingpost aft, complete with cargo runners.

Realistically of course, the thought remains that such efforts were more for the psychological comfort of those aboard than for practical effect because in a time (once again) of unrestricted submarine warfare, any Allied ship was all too obviously a target for Axis warships or aircraft.

In the early and mid-1940s the situation concerning escort vessels for convoys was desperate because there were simply insufficient warships available. A problem existed for which a solution had to be found. The result was a typically British compromise when it was discovered that the catwalk and comparatively unhindered foredeck of tankers (and certain dry bulk carriers) would make them a natural choice for conversion into temporary aircraft carriers. As a result, the Merchant Aircraft Carrier – or MAC ship – was born.

The Merchant Aircraft Carrier (MAC) tanker *Empire Mackay.* *(World Ship Society Photograph Library).*

The acoustic boom fitted to *British Vigour.* *(The Motor Ship)*

The tanker could continue carrying its cargo yet also provide aircraft for convoy escort duty. Initially, the scheme was positively dangerous for only one aircraft was then carried, with the pilot ditching into the sea and awaiting recovery by the nearest available ship once his flight was finished. Later, with sophisticated techniques learnt by experience, additional aircraft could be carried and, on these tankers, a team of regular RN ratings supported pilots and aircraft. Contrary to some popular beliefs, both Service crews intermingled under a Merchant Navy captain of the tanker with very few difficulties. The taking-off and landing of aircraft on an unstable flight deck by the usually RNVR/RNR pilots of the Swordfish aircraft used created far more tension, but the experiment proved a great success and, in the two years of their operations, few convoys escorted by MAC ships experienced serious submarine assault. The Ministry of War Transport selected three British Tanker Company ships under construction and commandeered these for conversion, but retained them under BTC management. These were the *British Caution* (launched as *Empire Maccoll*), the *British Virtue* which became *Empire Maccabe*, and *British Wisdom* which became the *Empire Mackay*. The three survived the war and in 1946 were each purchased by BTC and re-named respectively *British Pilot*, *Escort* and *Swordfish* – names which reflected something of the debt owed to these ships for their operations with the convoys.

Replenishment at Sea (RAS) has, for many years, been provided for the Royal Navy by the Royal Fleet Auxiliary (the RFA), which remains manned by Merchant Navy personnel. During the Second World War the task was too great for the RFA to handle on its own and a number of merchant ships had to be coopted. From 1942, the British Tanker Company provided three tankers – the *British Valour*, *Chivalry* and *Glory* – each of which served with distinction in this role.

During most years of the Second World War, BTC continued a modest new building programme. No ships were built in either 1940 or 1944, but two were constructed in 1941 – the *British Harmony* and *Character*. 1942 and 1943 each saw five ships completed and, during 1945, eight were delivered. The 1942 buildings were about 12,300-sdwt, apart from the *British Merit* at 4,755-sdwt. The 1943 tankers were three of around 12,000-sdwt and two of 8,400-sdwt. The twenty tankers aggregated around 227,000-sdwt.

The *British Vigour* was fitted with an acoustic boom erected around the fo'c'sle head that was allowed to hit the water with sufficient force to explode any nearby mines. It was then raised by a tackle system worked from the drum ends of the anchor windlass.

Following the *Titanic* disaster of 1912, lifeboats increased in size, meeting improved Classification Society Rules which stipulated that aboard tankers sufficient lifeboats had to be carried, midships and aft port and starboard, of such size they could carry the entire crew between each two sets. This allowed for safe evacuation from either part of the ship in the event of fire or even the ship splitting apart. Eventually it became essential for a number of spare lifejackets to

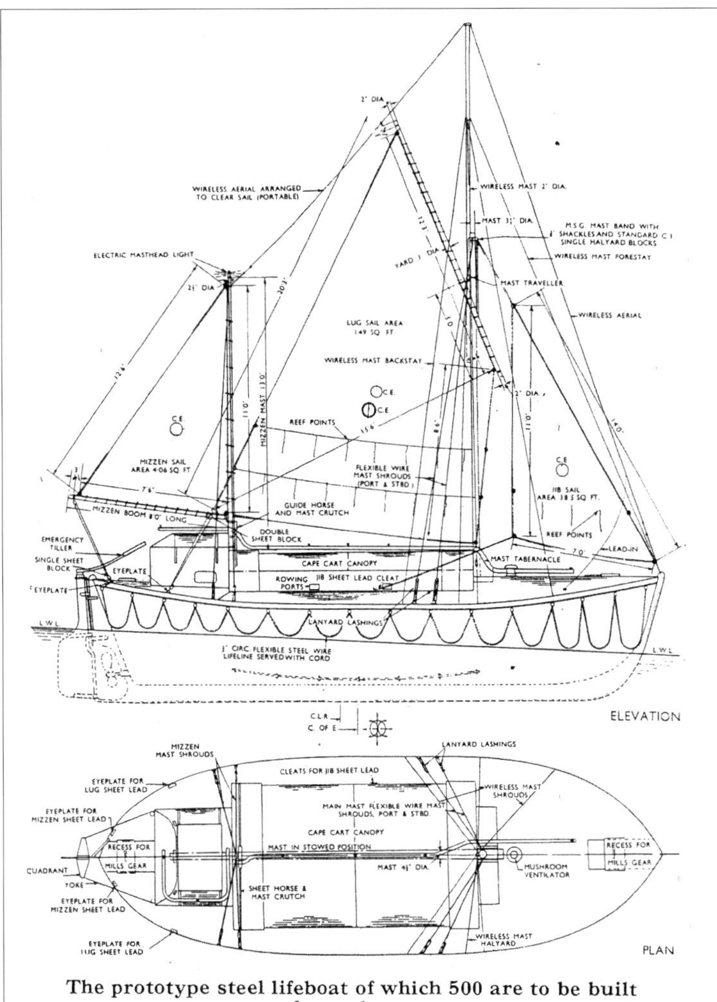

The prototype steel lifeboat of which 500 are to be built

A prototype steel lifeboat made available for tanker use by the Ministry of War Transport. *(Motor Ship).*

be carried forward in the Bosun's Store locker so any personnel trapped there could at least take to the water before being picked up by the boats.

In the autumn of 1943, the Ministry of War Transport patented all-steel lifeboats specifically for tankers to replace the existing wooden or composite boats carried aboard most ships. The idea of steel lifeboats was not new. They had first been used aboard merchant ships in 1900 when the Seamless Lifeboat Company of Sheffield patented their 28-foot boat fitted with a 15 bhp motor. In 1933, developments by Marconi were leading to new levels of efficiency in the use of ship-borne radio (as wireless sets were becoming increasingly called), so it was inevitable that experiments should follow examining the feasibility of using radio aboard lifeboats.

The magazine *Shipping* reflected much of the enthusiasm for this new device: 'With a lifeboat fully equipped with a small radio transmitter, there is always communication possible after the parent ship has left. Nowadays these lifeboat sets are extremely efficient installations. The power for the transmitter is obtained from an accumulator battery (which is kept in good condition as part of the wireless men's routine) and considering the very limited space for the complete installation, the range is undeniably good.' The magazine cited reported instances where the rescuing ships were only a few miles away from a lifeboat lost in mid-ocean following the foundering of its parent ship whose crew would otherwise have been rescued more quickly if their boat had been so equipped. This soon became a mandatory fitting to lifeboats aboard merchant ships.

Five hundred of the new lifeboats were ordered by the Ministry of War Transport specifically for tankers, based on a prototype prepared by the Tanker Planning Committee of the Petroleum Board, and made available to those ship owners who wished to fit them to their tankers. Two-thirds of the new boats were propelled by diesel engines or electric motors, with the remainder using Fleming gear – a system of crew-operated hand levers geared to the propeller shaft and situated midships. Later developments led to the construction of hand-held rods that ran along the centre of the lifeboat so that, by sitting facing in-board and turning these, the crew again provided their own motive power. The device proved quite effective and remained a standard fitting aboard a selected number of prescribed lifeboats aboard most merchant ships for a number of years. Under Classification Rules, the number of boats carried aboard any merchant ship had to include at least one propelled by machinery.

The new lifeboats were launched from an experimental gravity davit by flexible steel-wire falls attached to a quick-release gear in the boat. The boats retained the original 28-foot length, which was 26 feet on the waterline, and had a seating capacity of thirty-three. A 10 bhp Victor oil engine provided a speed of around 5.5 knots and, fully laden with equipment and personnel, it weighed just over 7 tons. A lugsail, jib and mizzen were also provided. In-built buoyancy tanks

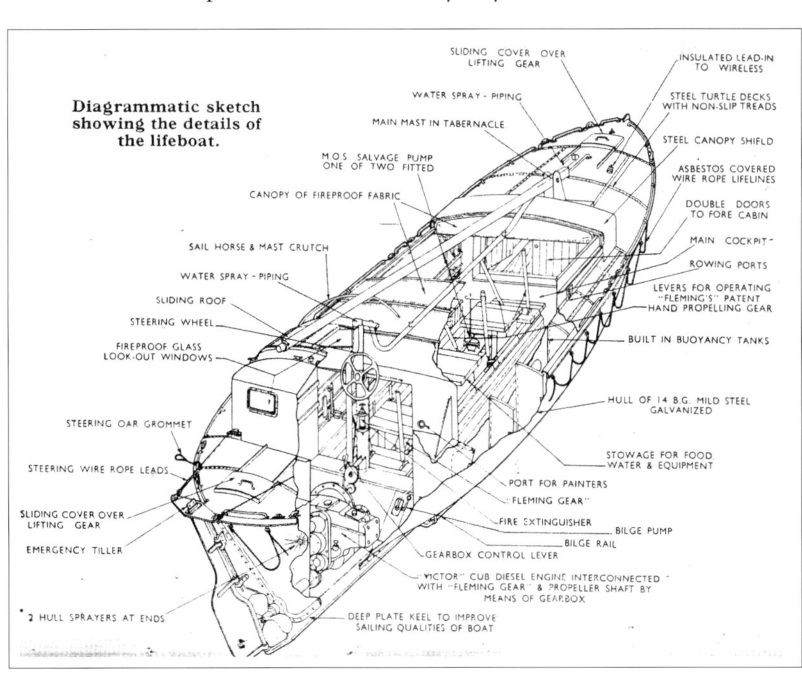

were fitted giving a good stability base, along with water sprayers capable of discharging 30 gallons per minute. The boat was fitted with a raised shelter deck forward and aft with a fireproof sliding canopy of double-thickness asbestos cloth over the cockpit. During tests, this protection was proved when a boat passed satisfactorily through burning oil.

Four BTC tankers were involved in the epic of D-Day from 6 June 1944. Five ships were originally directed, but *British Engineer* struck a mine midships on the starboard side on 12 June. It must have been something of a glancing blow – probably whilst manoeuvring in Convoy EBC7 from Barry in south Wales – because the tanker, although fully laden with parcels of petrol and diesel oil, did not explode and was successfully off-loaded and eventually repaired. The coastal tanker *British Scout* of 2,210-sdwt was built in 1922 and made a number of trips transporting assorted parcels of fuel oils to the Mulberry Harbour at Arromanches. The *British Statesman* served as a fresh-water carrier, initially off Omaha Beach, until contamination by petrol was discovered when (not surprisingly) she was withdrawn and reverted to ordinary service. *British Princess* also transported fresh water and was based as part of the Eastern Task Force Area in the Solent. *British Renown* was part of Convoy EBC20W during which she worked off Utah Beach.

The last Company tanker sunk in the Second World War was the *British Freedom* that had been requisitioned by the Admiralty. She was sailing in Convoy BX141 when, shortly after commencing a voyage from Halifax to the United Kingdom, was torpedoed and sunk by *U-1232* on 14 January 1945. Sadly, one seafarer lost his life. The contribution made by the British Tanker Company to the war effort was enormous for, during the six-year duration, company tankers transported over 46 million tons of crude oil and assorted products. Mariners serving with BTC across all ranks and nationalities earned over 210 decorations, distinctions and bravery awards.

When the war in Europe ended on 6 May 1945, the thoughts of the British Tanker Company directors turned towards the enormous job of taking stock and re-building their decimated fleet. Their task was not helped by the inexorable link existing between BTC ships and the shifting sands of Middle Eastern politics, especially as these affected the various plans of the parent Anglo-Iranian Oil Company. The political situation in the Gulf, never completely stable, became one of increasing unrest during and after the Second World War. Abadan had been a major port for oil companies, providing millions of gallons of aviation fuel for the Allied cause, and meeting increasing demands for other products as the war continued. With the cessation of hostilities and the reconstruction of Europe, particularly as post-war Britain began the slow process of industrial and domestic recovery, a totally unexpected and unprecedented demand existed for all grades of oil. This developed at a time when the Shah of Iran faced dangerous opposition from extremists within his own government. These were factions hostile to European influences, especially those of Britain and Anglo-Iranian Oil, regarding them as 'western capitalists milking their country dry'. Whilst the internal conflict bubbled uneasily over the following few years, Anglo-Iranian introduced a significant expansion programme in the Persian Gulf. This resulted in the Company becoming one of the top oil producers in the region. Inevitably, BTC became a central part of this new drive.

A casualty of war: The *British Premier* was built in 1922 and was torpoed by *U65* in Dcember 1940, off Monrovia, with the loss of 32 lives, 13 members of the crew survived. (*World Ship Society Photograph Library*)

Recovery *Chapter Six*

OF NINETEEN NEW BUILDINGS for the British Tanker Company between 1941 and 1945, *British Vigilance* had been sunk in 1943, whilst three others had been seriously damaged, although these were later repaired. Additionally, a number of ships had been acquired from the Admiralty in 1946. These included eight ex-*Empire* tankers, which were re-named the *British Bugler*, *Commando*, *Drummer*, *Fusilier* and *Piper*. This figure included the 'three sisters' (as they were colloquially and affectionately called in seafaring circles) which had served as MAC ships. Even so, the state of the fleet in 1946 was not particularly healthy. Many tankers were old and war-weary, some with rushed repairs and dry dockings and often 'essentials only' carried out just sufficiently to complete an Annual Survey, and obtain the next Certificate of Seaworthiness, so the tanker could be sent back to work.

The situation was eased considerably with the lifting of wartime restrictions imposed by the Admiralty concerning tanker construction. This left the naval architects of BTC free to design a new class of ship to their own specification. However, they faced a tonnage limitation outside governmental or owners' control. Tankers were required that would transport a substantial payload yet remain within the depth parameters of the Suez Canal. This very significant factor had been ignored, to their chagrin, by some shipbuilders in the United States who had ploughed ahead with tankers in excess of 18,000-sdwt only to find they were too large to make the Canal transit. BTC therefore contracted for an ambitious new-building programme based in the main around the efficient 12,000-sdwt class of 1936. Orders were placed with British yards for fifty-seven of these tankers (again whose careers are given in Part Two) with Harland & Wolff receiving contracts for twelve ships. The first of this new class was the *British Success*. She was built at the Blythswood Shipbuilding Company in Glasgow, launched on 7 November 1945 and completed in February 1946. Additionally, orders were placed for eleven tankers around 8,000-sdwt and a number of smaller coastal craft.

The *British Marquis* was the fourth tanker in the 12,000-sdwt class built, and the second ship in the fleet to bear this name. Carrying names forward had become a practice common to many shipping companies. She was launched by Doxford's on 3 April 1946 and completed the following month. The tanker was of 12,310-sdwt on a laden summer draught of 27.7 feet, with an overall length of 469.6 feet. Like the rest of the new class she was diesel-powered, had a raked stem and cruiser stern, and was fitted with telescopic masts to facilitate passing under the bridges of the Manchester Ship Canal. Cargo was carried in nine oil-tanks subdivided by two longitudinal and transversal bulkheads on the now well-established Isherwood system of tanker frame construction.

Hull frame spacing is particularly significant on tankers with distances prescribed by Classification Society Rules. The distances aft within the vicinity of the engine-room were comparatively narrow for obvious reasons. A greater distance between frames serving cargo tanks space was consistent to contain stresses within these areas. The narrowness of frames, at 24- and 17-inch spacing below the fuel bunker space and forepeak tank forward of the cofferdam separating them from Number One cargo tanks, was perhaps not quite so apparent. When in ballast, tankers rode high out of the water with a large freeboard, leaving areas forward prone to a series of longitudinal stresses. As the peak plunged into rough seas, a tendency existed for a series of slamming forces to pound the forepart of a tanker. This would not only have damaged the bottom plating but, in extreme instances, could have resulted in a 'corrugation' effect. This occurred when the bottom plating became racked and buckled which, if unchecked, could have resulted in cracks appearing at the tops of displaced plates. If corrugation extended into areas of Number One tank before this had been cleaned and aired then there was risk of an explosion.

Although the design was virtually the same as the 1936 *British Endurance*, whose specifications were examined in the last chapter, tankers of the new 12,000-sdwt class did have significant differences. *British Marquis* and her sisters were fitted with the latest navigational equipment. Considerable advances had been made to adapt electronic developments as these had passed beyond the experimental stage over the previous decades. It was in February 1926 that MacTaggart, Scott and Company, Limited of Edinburgh had patented their safety steering motor

British Marquis general arrangement plan. *(The Motor Ship)*

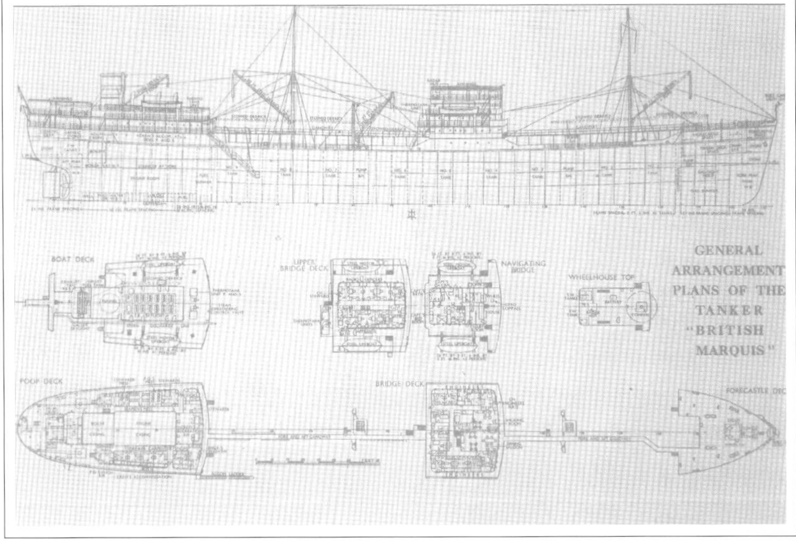

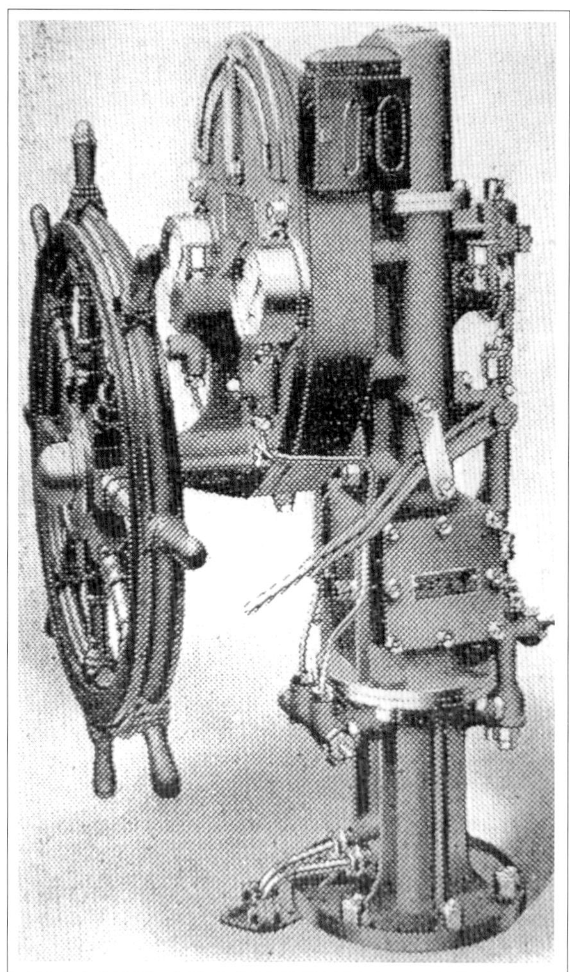

The MacTaggart Scott Steering Telemotor. *(Fairplay).*

which soon became a standard fitting aboard BTC tankers.

This became an instant success due to its ease of movement and comparative lack of maintenance required. The latter factor was of particular importance to deep-sea tankers – more perhaps than dry-cargo ships – for they were frequently away for lengthy periods and in port only for as long as it took to load or discharge. With the standard 10,000-sdwt BTC tanker loaded to her marks and everything working to maximum efficiency (more often the case than not) her turn-round period could be as little as 20 hours. This limitation allowed only a small period of time for fitters to come aboard to effect any repairs. A number of other factors had to be considered because prolonged shore-side maintenance to any shipboard gear could necessitate delays on the berth. This meant not only lost revenue to owners from payload, but also interfered with berthing plans for refineries, as it was not always possible to shift the tanker to anchorage, especially when engine-room equipment was involved.

The Sperry Gyro Pilot fitted on the monkey island of the Cunard liner *Laconia*. *(Syren & Shipping)*

Advances had taken place in the field of automated steering. Experiments had been made in December 1923 aboard the Cunard liner *Laconia,* initially during an Atlantic crossing between Liverpool and New York, and later on a round-the-world cruise. The results were extremely encouraging and it was only a matter of time before BTC carried the equipment in the enclosed wheelhouse of their tankers. An article in *Syren & Shipping* for 2 January 1924 offered the editor's enthusiastically professional assessment of what he termed this 'ingenious equipment': 'The apparatus is of a simple and rugged nature, although it is sufficiently sensitive to apply the requisite helm immediately the ship's head departs one-sixth of a degree from the required course. It will be seen therefore that far less helm is required, and consequently a better course is steered, resulting in a saving of distance from point to point.'

Steering equipment in the wheelhouse of the *British Marquis.* *(The Motor Ship)*

There were added advantages facilitating making ordinary ocean-going passages. With manual steering, three members of the crew were needed for each four-hour bridge watch. One to steer, another to act as lookout reporting lights and 'anything of a potential navigational interest' to the mate on duty, and a third to act a 'stand-by man'. It was quite demanding to concentrate effectively on manual steering, especially with the ship in any kind of seaway, and it was gener-

The cheese-shaped radar scanner fitted aboard the *British Marquis*. *(The Motor Ship)*

ally recognised that the efficiency of the AB delegated to this task could be impaired after about an hours' trick on the helm. Auto-pilots did away with the need for two of these men per watch (retaining the look-out), although various situations still required the occasional shift from automatic steering to manual.

When the Master considered this necessary, an AB was turned-to from the watch below and put onto the wheel. Such occasions occurred whilst entering or leaving harbour or during certain heavy weather situations when human instincts from a good quartermaster allowed more sensitive assessment of sea conditions than inanimate equipment. The photograph on page 30 indicates the modern contemporary equipment carried aboard most BTC tankers.

The wheel is run through the standard magnetic compass binnacle to the Telemotor, so that the quartermaster could also steer magnetic courses. The magnetic compass still remains a legal fitting aboard all registered merchant ships. The Brown gyrocompass is seen by the wheelhouse window. The latest radar was fitted aboard this tanker. This was luxury indeed for navigating officers on most post-war ships – especially when training courses became a mandatory part of certificates of competency, enabling effective use to be made of the set. The wooden rigging is to support the awnings rigged in hot weather conditions and often the only method of attempting to cool the wheelhouse.

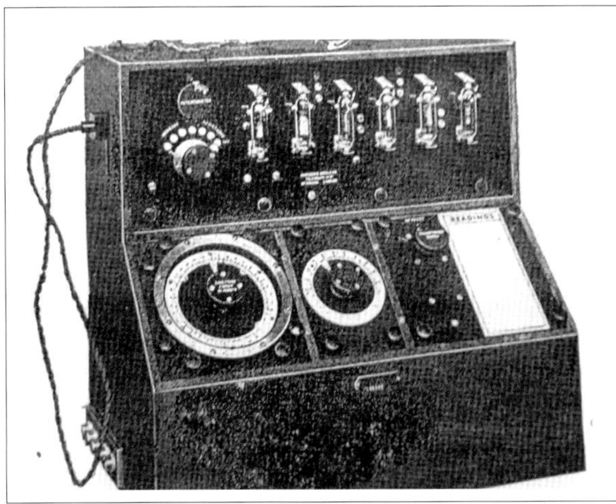

Marconi Wireless Direction Finder. *(Syren & Shipping)*

The Radio Communication Company's aerial was a standard fitting on the monkey island above the wheelhouse of over 500 British merchant ships. *(Shipping)*

Apart from developments in lifeboat and radio-communication, there was at least another positive result from the *Titanic* disaster. Marconi lost little time in extending his experiments to examine how radio could be used to determine direction finding at sea. His invention appeared in 1920 and this too became a mandatory fitting aboard merchant ships. The equipment worked by using a series of search coils that detected radio transmissions from either ships or land stations that gave a bearing line received from two aerials fitted at ninety degrees to each other. The accuracy of this early set was initially questionable, but sufficiently reliable results were obtained to encourage further research. Marconi explained an outline of the theory upon which his set worked in the *Syren & Shipping* magazine for 20 October 1920: 'The direction of the sending station can be ascertained by rotating search coils until the signals are of maximum or minimum strength and noting its position. In practice the minimum is used since it is more sharply defined'.

The Radio Communication Company, with offices in the Strand, London, made considerable improvements over the basic theories innovated by Marconi so that, by the end of the 1920s, their apparatus had been installed aboard almost 500 British ships totalling over 3 million tons – a figure that included most BTC

The radio direction finding aerial aboard the *British Marquis*, also showing the magnetic compass on the monkey island. *(The Motor Ship)*

tankers. Their improvements were not just in the basic receiving set, but also in aerial configurations. An extensive network of radio beacon stations around the United Kingdom coastline supported a system that was providing extremely accurate facilities for reliable direction finding in all weathers. By 1946, stations were transmitting around the world, providing international coverage that offered a series of strong and reliable signals. Improvements had occurred in aerial design approaching an optimum, leading to few design changes in those used aboard ship until they were finally superseded in the 1990s.

The British Tanker Company placed considerable emphasis on crew comfort in the new class of tankers. Ratings were transferred from what had become the traditional fo'c'sle head cabins and messes to be accommodated aft. Engineering officers were placed amidships on the Bridge Deck, below the deck officers on the Upper Bridge or Boat Deck, whilst the Master's suite was aft on the Navigating Bridge abaft the wheelhouse and chartroom. This contributed to making the squat midships accommodation block even more so but of more importance were the novel efforts made to alleviate intense heat whilst working ship in the Suez, Persian Gulf and Red Sea regions. As the magazine *Motor Ship* commented in July 1946, following their inspection of the *British Marquis* immediately after the tanker's launch: 'We gained the impression of roominess and comfort, which has been the owners' aim in housing the officers and crew. Mechanical ventilation and heating are installed throughout the ship, and in the European hospital, which is on the Bridge Deck, the full air-conditioning system installed allows a lower temperature to be maintained than in other parts of the vessel . . . the crew have a large, well-furnished and upholstered recreation room on the poop deck . . . These are some of the points which reflect the great care that the owners have bestowed on advancing the standard of living on board.'

British Earl. *(World Ship Society Photograph Library)*

It was this sort of concern that made BTC a solid company for which to work. This was particularly true when compared with conditions experienced by many seafarers' working aboard some contemporary merchant naval tramping companies that (even in the 1960s) often remained comparatively appalling. Such concerns contributed to the high standard of officers employed who invariably sought company contract employment and, like John Straughan, made their career with BTC. On a more prosaic note (and speaking merely as a navigating officer), however good the company's intentions were, the experiment of moving engineering officers midships away from the engine-room might not have proved very practical. Whenever an emergency occurred below, necessitating urgent and immediate attendance of additional and often senior staff, time would have been lost and inconvenience incurred covering a comparatively long distance – often during bad weather.

Although the majority of these approximately 12,000-sdwt tankers served the Company well, it was inevitable with such large numbers that some of the ships, in merchant naval jargon, unashamedly taking the lines of a popular period song, were either 'bewitched, bothered or bewildered'. The *British Builder*, 12,270-sdwt, served only from 1951 to September 1963 when sent for scrap in Belgium. She had experienced a breakdown during a voyage in 1954 whilst trading in Australasian waters that necessitated a long-haul tow to the United Kingdom, in two stages, undertaken by two different company tankers. The task must have appeared daunting to put things mildly and I can well imagine the initial consternation caused in both smoke-rooms upon hearing such glad tidings from the 'Kremlin', or head office. The intervening oceans are invariably rough, unpredictable and certainly not renowned for suffering fools gladly. Tankers are not designed to tow fellow deep-sea ships with ease and, although obviously feasible, success would have depended considerably on the ingenuity of the masters, chief officers and chief engineers of the ships involved – the *British Merit* and *British Baron*. For such magnificent feats they, their junior officers, and ratings are worthy indeed to receive a salute.

The circumstances concerning the *British Earl* (12,250-sdwt) bear describing in some detail. She had been built by Swan, Hunter's and completed in January 1947 and had embarked upon her maiden voyage with a cargo of 11,140 tons of Grade 5F Furnace Oil bound Abadan for Stockholm. Whilst proceeding along the swept NEMEDRI (North Europe and Mediterranean Routing Instructions) channel off the Danish coast she struck a 'floater' – as drifting mines were referred to colloquially. The bow contacted in way of Number One starboard wing tank, forward hold and cofferdam.

Isherwood tankers of the period were designed to withstand the enormous shearing forces created when some tanks are filled around 98 per cent capacity and others are empty. In this case, the shock of the explosion resulted in a rapid loss of oil from the starboard wing tank. Considerable ingress of water was experienced that flooded the fore-hold, pump room and cofferdam. The stress effects were felt along the hull in way of Number Seven tank where the ship split on the bottom from bilge to bilge. The shell plating was buckled and the tanker 'hogged' by an incredible thirty degrees. Fortunately, there was no loss of life or injury. The crew had little time to assimilate their considerable shock because quick action was called for. The tanker was settling rapidly by the head and listing steadily to starboard. It speaks volumes for Isherwood's patents, and the ship's designers and builders that *British Earl* did not immediately split in half and sink. Her master, Captain O E Evans, ordered the tanker to be run aground in the nearest and safest area of shallows. This was off Spodsbjaerg on the island of Langeland. An American steamer, the *James Kerney,* following international maritime codes of practice, stood by rendering assistance until relieved by the Danish salvage tug *Aegir.* Salvage operations were begun at once and even though the seas began freezing around the assisting ships, 9,500 tons of oil were safely transhipped to another tanker. The cargo tanks were then cleaned and gas-freed, temporary repairs were undertaken – all duties carried out by the crew – and three months' later, on 12 April, as soon as the ice had cleared and the weather became favourable, she sailed under her own power to the Burmeister and Wain dry-dock in Copenhagen. There, temporary repairs were effected by welding deep girders to the decks, eight heavy channel bars to the bottom, port and starboard sides in way of Numbers Six, Seven and Eight tanks, abaft the midships accommodation. The *British Earl* then returned to the Tyne for permanent repairs, which necessitated considerable replacement of the forward and after cargo tanks – including the ballasting by cement of the after part of the ship to keep this section steady whilst the tanker's keel was re-aligned. It proved a formidable repair job lasting many months. The hogging of this tanker may well have caused a permanent residue strain for, during her next voyage to the Persian Gulf, she broke her crankshaft and once again the services of a fellow BTC tanker, the long-suffering *British Baron*, were enlisted to tow her back to North Shields for additional repair. Laid up in Falmouth in July 1957, the tanker remained idle until July 1961, when she was towed to Inverkeithing for demolition.

By July 1948, the *Motor Ship* was again able to report on the state of the Company's development, but on this occasion with a note of caution: 'The British Tanker Co has the largest number of vessels under contract among all the ship-owners of the world. The war losses however were so heavy and the prospective increase in oil production . . . so large that even when the new tonnage is completed in the next two or three years, it is probable that all demands will not be met.'

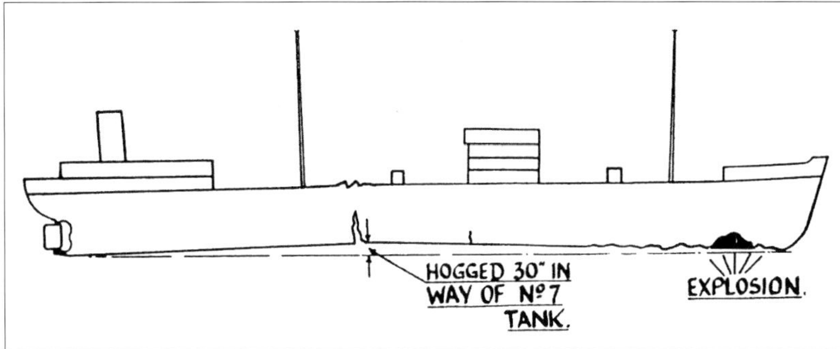

Damage sustained to the *British Earl.* *(World Ship Society Photograph Library Resources)*

In justification of this forecast, the new-building programme indeed remained inadequate at meeting the continually increasing demand for crude oil. This led BTC to purchase ten T2 tankers of around 16,400-sdwt from American sources. Half of these had been built between the Kaiser Company at Portland, Oregon, and the Alabama Dry-Dock Company at Mobile. Engines for all ten were manufactured by the General Electric Company of Lynn, and each had two steam turbines of 7,240 shp. The tankers had been built under the mass construction programme of 1944, were 506.5 feet length overall, with a beam of 68.2 feet and moulded depth of 39.2 feet. The ships retained their own, often-exotic names – such as *Smoky Hill, Beecher Island, Chisholm Trail, Cottonwood Creek* and *Rogue River* – but bore BP funnel colours.

With the inclusion of these tankers, the British Tanker Company flagged nearly 120 deep-sea ships, of which seventy-five were motor powered, ranging in tonnage from 8,400-sdwt to the US 16,400-sdwt. In the same month, BTC had orders placed for an additional 51 tankers, approaching nearly 650,000-sdwt, each powered by single-propeller diesel engines. There were eight 8,400-sdwt, thirty-five 12,000-sdwt and, following the success of the Company with the American T2s, new orders had been placed for eight 16,000-sdwt tankers to be built also in British yards. The new tankers only of 8,500-sdwt and 12,000-sdwt tankers were built to previous class specifications.

The first of the new eight 16,000-sdwt tankers was launched in April 1948 by Blythswood's of Glasgow. This was the *British Chivalry* at 16,847-sdwt, completed in January 1949. She was the second tanker to carry this name. The new ships were longer and marginally wider in extreme beam and moulded depth to accommodate the extra tonnage, yet keep within Suez Canal operating limits. The *British Chivalry* was 515 feet length bp (between perpendiculars) and 547 feet length oa (overall) with a moulded beam of 69 feet 10 inches and depth 37 feet 6 inches. The ship had a summer draught of around 30 feet with a freeboard of about 7½ feet. These measurements compared favourably with those of the T2 tankers. The design of this class followed the traditional single-deck type with poop, bridge and forecastle, with twenty-seven cargo tanks, and two pump rooms situated between Numbers Two/Three and Six/Seven tanks. The cargo pumps each held a capacity of 500 tons per hour working through 12-inch diameter manifolds. A 6-inch vapour line was fitted fore and aft, with PV (pressure

The Steering Gear fitted aboard the 1924 ***British Motorist*** **. . . compared with the 1949** ***British Chivalry.*** *(The Motor Ship)*

vacuum) relief valves in way of each tank, by way of mast-led outlets. These ships, in keeping with the earlier *British Marquis* class, were also fitted with a stern-line discharge/loading pipe to cater for the increasingly new areas in which tankers had recently been trading. These were often situated in remote places possessing facilities that restricted alongside jetties, but retained sufficient depth of water for stern manoeuvring using local tugs and pilotage. One such port was Falconara, on the east coast of Italy that received crude oil and exported refined products. Ancona Bay serving this port could accept tankers drawing up to eight fathoms (48 feet).

British Chivalry was powered by a six-cylinder Doxford diesel, of 6,450 bhp, allowing a service speed of around 14 knots fully laden. Bunker capacity allowed a holding of around 1,000 tons with a daily consumption of between 22 and 24 tons. This gave the tanker a range of 12,000 nautical miles, permitting a generous 15 per cent safety margin – 5 per cent above the universal trading norm of most merchant ships. Since the days when ships increased in size making chain steering gears not only impracticable but illegal, technical developments had enabled all ships to be fitted with power-operated steering motors. These were fitted directly above the rudder-pintle enabling this to be turned by hydraulic methods. Many of the steering gears fitted to tankers at this time were built by Clarke-Chapman Marine of Tyne and Wear. This company had innovated also a wide range of deck equipment including windlasses and winches. Their 'Donkin' range served all classes of ships and, although changing in appearance with modern developments, invariably proved reliable and efficient. The type fitted to the contemporary size of tankers was usually two-ram, but four-ram devices were also used. To conform with Classification Society regulations the system had to be capable of turning the ship's rudder from hard a port to hard a starboard – a maximum of 35 degrees either side – in around 30 seconds. The size of the gear that is fitted aboard any ship is determined by comparing the rudder area with the square of the speed of the tanker.

In 1950, the Company launched sixteen deep-sea tankers. These included two of 8,420-sdwt, ten around 12,200-sdwt and three approaching 16,800-sdwt, along with a number of subsidiary craft. The *British Defender* of 8,420-sdwt was completed July 1950 by Doxford's yard in Sunderland. The Hull Specification of this ship makes interesting reading, extending knowledge of further 'behind-the-scenes' paperwork discussed between shipowners and builders resulting in the ultimate birth of any vessel. The specification was all-inclusive, covering everything concerned with the tanker ranging from accommodation and cabin fittings: boilers and bollards, cargo room and chain locker – masts, pump room and potato locker, vapour pipes and radio room.

The illustration, for example, mainly concerns the Wash Deck Line and gives clear instructions regarding all aspects of the construction of this pipe. Hull Specifications end with this all-embracing paragraph: 'Finally, the vessel to be completed and made ready for sea in accordance with this specification and the usual requirements for a first-class vessel of this type and size . . . Vessel to have all gear properly stowed and handed over after satisfactory sea trial'.

In 1951, the cauldron bubbling away in the Persian Gulf finally boiled over. Anglo-Iranian Oil discovered the Iranian Government had nationalised the considerable assets held by the company. This caused a major world-wide oil crisis plus total collapse of the company's operations in Iran. The action led to the development of alternative oil sources from a number of

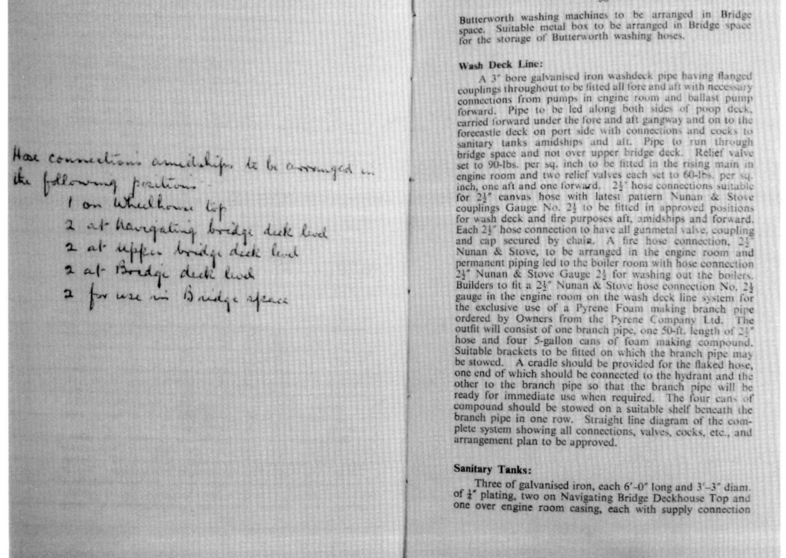

Hose connections amidships to be arranged in the following positions
1 on Wheelhouse top
2 at Navigating bridge deck level
2 at upper bridge deck level
2 at Bridge deck level
2 for use in Bridge space

50

Butterworth washing machines to be arranged in Bridge space. Suitable metal box to be arranged in Bridge space for the storage of Butterworth washing hoses.

Wash Deck Line:

A 3" bore galvanised iron washdeck pipe having flanged couplings throughout to be fitted all fore and aft with necessary connections from pumps in engine room and ballast pump forward. Pipe to be led along both sides of poop deck, carried forward under the fore and aft gangway and on to the forecastle deck on port side with connections and cocks to sanitary tanks amidships and aft. Pipe to run through bridge space and not over upper bridge deck. Relief valve set to 90-lbs. per sq. inch to be fitted in the rising main in engine room and two relief valves each set to 60-lbs. per sq. inch, one aft and one forward. 2½" hose connections suitable for 2½" canvas hose with latest pattern Nunan & Stove couplings Gauge No. 2½ to be fitted in approved positions for wash deck and fire purposes aft, amidships and forward. Each 2½" hose connection to have all gunmetal valve, coupling and cap secured by chain. A fire hose connection, 2½" Nunan & Stove, to be arranged in the engine room and permanent piping led to the boiler room with hose connection 2½" Nunan & Stove Gauge 2½ for washing out the boilers. Builders to fit a 2½" Nunan & Stove hose connection No. 2½ gauge in the engine room on the wash deck line system for the exclusive use of a Pyrene Foam making branch pipe ordered by Owners from the Pyrene Company Ltd. The outfit will consist of one branch pipe, one 50-ft. length of 2½" hose and four 5-gallon cans of foam making compound. Suitable brackets to be fitted on which the branch pipe may be stowed. A cradle should be provided for the flaked hose, one end of which should be connected to the hydrant and the other to the branch pipe so that the branch pipe will be ready for immediate use when required. The four cans of compound should be stowed on a suitable shelf beneath the branch pipe in one row. Straight line diagram of the complete system showing all connections, valves, cocks, etc., and arrangement plan to be approved.

Sanitary Tanks:

Three of galvanised iron, each 6'-0" long and 3'-3" diam. of ¼" plating, two on Navigating Bridge Deckhouse Top and one over engine room casing, each with supply connection

Extract from 'Hull Specification Book' covering building of the ***British Defender*** **in 1950.** *(Tyne and Wear Archives Service)*

The *British Bulldog* is launched from Swan, Hunter & Wigham Richardson's Newcastle Shipyard. The impressive 81.2-foot beam is shown to advantage as the tanker hit the water from her slipway. *(Courtesy Tyne and Wear Archives Service)*

countries creating, over ensuing years, a massive network of international refineries covering a vast range of oil by-products. Elsewhere in the Persian Gulf, Britain still held considerable influence and retained pre-Second World War loyalties. The loss of Abadan was obviously a major blow, but access to crude oil was available still from Kuwait, especially with developments at the port of Mina al Ahmadi, and Bahrain.

Notwithstanding the knocks taken by its parent company, the transport arm of BP Tankers continued unabashed. 1951 saw completion of a further sixteen ships plus a number of smaller craft. The fleet was becoming one of considerable size, and continuing to grow. It was during this year that a new class of tanker appeared heralding a term that – initially – became used almost hesitatingly, yet one deemed to become a by-word in shipping nomenclature. The ship was the *British Adventurer* and the term was 'Supertanker'. Launched by Vickers-Armstrong at Barrow-in-Furness on 12 December 1950, the tanker was completed on 1 June 1951 and was the first in a class of nine 'Supertankers' launched that year. She was 30,128-sdwt – virtually double the capacity of any other tanker in the fleet – on a summer-laden draught of 28 feet, at 619.5 feet length (bp) with 81.3 feet beam and 44.7 feet moulded depth. Two steam turbine engines, geared to a single propeller powered the ship, giving her a laden cruising speed of 15 knots, making her the fastest ship owned by the Company. She was of the traditional 'three-island' deck design and was followed a month later by the *British Bulldog* from Swan, Hunter's, with engine built by the Wallsend Slipway Company.

The *British Envoy* was launched in 1953. It seems appropriate to the significance of this event that the start of a ship's career is accompanied by ceremony and celebration. There is invariably a party hosted by the shipbuilders for the launching principals – usually followed by further celebrations at the handing over ceremony. This was a much quieter celebration that occurred after successful completion of sea trials when she had been formally received into the fleet by the operating company.

In 1954, following three years' intensive negotiations, a consortium of oil companies succeeded in restarting Iran's oil industry with the effect that Abadan again became a viable port. Considering the events which had transpired it was no longer considered appropriate for the Company to operate under the title Anglo-Iranian Oil Company Limited and the name was changed in December that year to the British Petroleum Company Limited thus uniting (at least on paper) the oil production and transport arms. The new concern was not exactly 'left out in the cold' following talks because the new Company held a 40 per cent share in the consortium. The first BTC tanker to re-use the facilities was *British Advocate* which loaded 8,500 tons of crude oil for Ceylon.

The launch of the *British Envoy* at Newcastle in 1953. *(Courtesy Tyne and Wear Archives Service)*

Amongst the nineteen deep-sea tankers completed between 1952 and 1954 was the *British Vision*. She was based on the traditional 16,000-sdwt class previously owned; retained similar dimensions although slightly larger and deeper in hull at the expense of beam, but differed in a number of details. The steel lifeboats were replaced by aluminium for greater durability, with a slightly increased capacity. The class retained also the

At the celebration party for the *British Envoy* at Newcastle in 1953, Mrs A Aitken receives a present from the Chairman of the Yard, sharing the moment with the ship's Master, the Chairman's wife and other dignitaries. *(Courtesy Tyne and Wear Archives Service)*

Foredeck of *British Vision*. *(The Motor Ship)*

very heavy Triatic Stay between the masts, supporting radio aerials and signal halyards, and permitting the hoisting of wind sails to assist with tank ventilation following cleaning operations by the crew at sea.

Tank tops were modernised and fitted with the latest rounded design for easier manoeuvrability. The opened hatch in the photograph served as ventilation for the forward pump room. It is interesting to see lined into the plan for a first time that internal ladders to each tank showed the horizontal rest built into their construction to aid 'tank diving' – as entering cargo tanks to clean or inspect is called. This broke down the 30-feet deep haul to (and especially from) the tank bottom. For crew amenity, a swimming pool was placed on the port side of the funnel. Prior to such permanent fittings, temporary alternatives had sometimes been constructed by the ship's carpenter assuming sufficient quantities of timber and canvas could be appropriated from a range of alternative sources. This was an important and much appreciated asset. Tanker life was hard, with often-long voyages, and even if the ship ventured to 'exotic' ports – such as bunkering around South Seas islands – there was rarely much opportunity for shore leave. The parcels delivered to each were often around the 300/500-ton mark (delivering fuel for generators, perhaps) and took very little time to discharge before the tanker was heading for the next port. Oil berths in larger ports were usually miles from civilisation restricting considerably shore leave. Tanker philosophy invariably imbibed an attitude – 'once on board, stay on board'. Officers sailing with BP in those days were very fortunate indeed if relieved within six months and voyages in excess of a year were not unheard of.

In January 1955, the Company experienced a further change to funnel design when the BP shield joined their existing colours. A number of minor changes were made also to the Company house-flag. The *British Soldier*, built in October 1954, was the first tanker to receive new funnel markings and colours. Two new buildings were completed for BP the following year, the *British Officer* at 15,893-sdwt from Hamilton's of Port Glasgow, and the *British Victory* from Vickers-Armstrong at 34,118-sdwt.

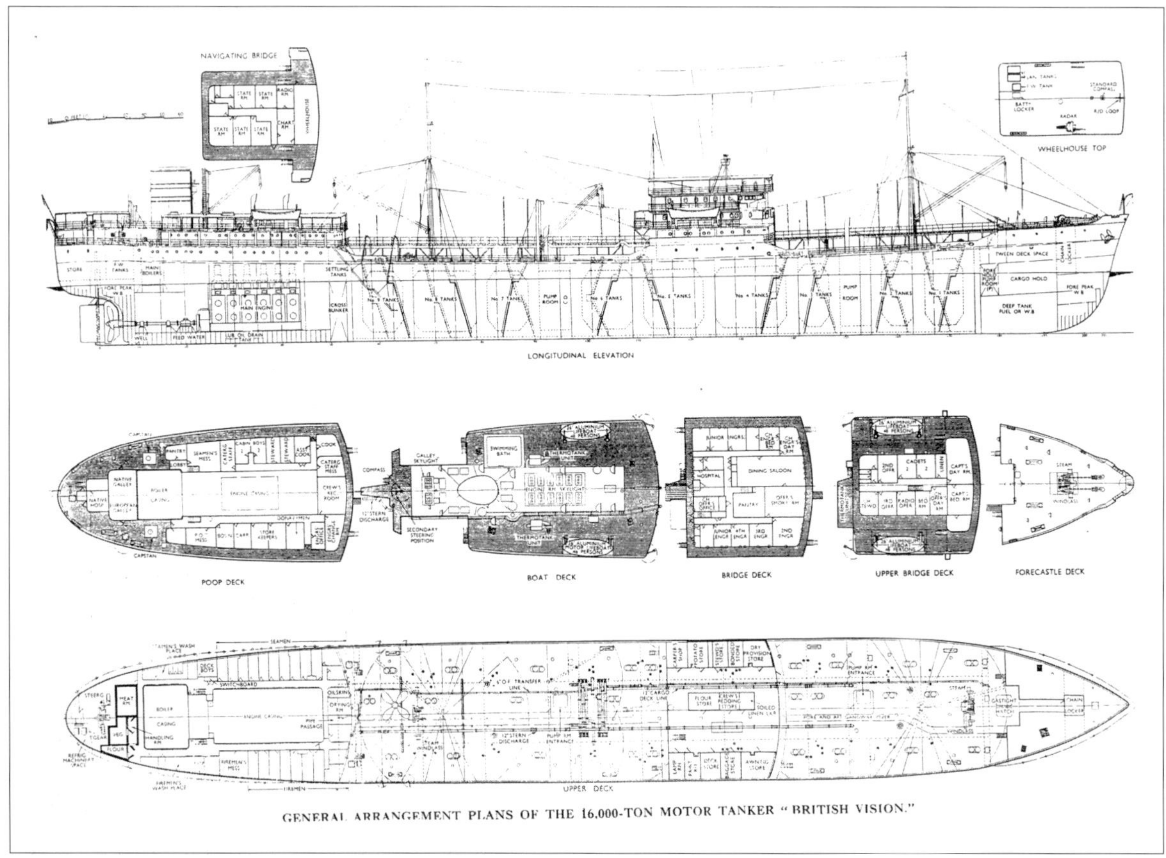

General arrangement plan of the *British vision*, launched 1954. *(The Motor Ship)*

Prospering *Chapter Seven*

In 1956, THE FORTUNES of the BP fleet again became entangled with international politics when the Suez Canal was closed to all shipping. For tankers preceding on the round trip from UK to the Gulf this was bad news in terms of bunkering and extended voyages. A round voyage from Coryton to Mina al Ahmadi, for example, is roughly 13,000 nautical miles via Suez, but 22,200 nautical miles rounding Agulhas Point, South Africa – virtually double the steaming distance. The outcomes were inevitable and twofold. Of direct consequence, a 10 per cent cut in consumption was imposed in Britain leading to a prolonged spate of petrol rationing at the pumps, whilst indirectly, a scheme of company mergers was planned for later implementation.

The significant event directly affecting the history of the fleet in 1956 was the re-styling of the company as the BP Tanker Company Limited. The following year saw the opening of the Canal again, but a further effect of the 'Suez Incident' was to focus the directors' minds on ship size. The effects of any future closure were clearly in their thoughts. The 16,000-sdwt tanker had proved its versatility: it was a handy-sized vessel, with easy manoeuvrability, making it useful for trading into the range of varied deep-sea ports and coastal petroleum harbours in which BP operated. The tanker possessed sufficient deadweight capacity to transport a worthwhile payload in all 'dirty and clean' trades, ranging from transporting crude around the Cape to a variety of oil by-products. It remains easy to speak of 'deadweight tonnage' without always appreciating perhaps the implications of the term in practice: of understanding what, for example, '16,000 deadweight tons of crude oil' actually represented. The figures were variable depending on Specific Gravity and temperature, but in realistic terms – visualised at the pumps where most people in practice met the commodity – 16,000 tons of crude oil, at 60°F of SG 0·8, represented then something like 4.2 million gallons (subject of course to refining processes) – a formidable figure and one difficult to visualise.

Whilst the earlier 30,000-tonners had cemented the idea of one ship transporting virtually double (or even perhaps more) the capacity of this handy sized tanker (a theoretical 8·4 million gallons), plans were already being prepared for ships of larger sized tonnage. The problem facing the directors' was financial, because forecast long-term planning had not provided for a sudden outlay covering the provision of ships with such enhanced capacity.

A number of both long and short-term partnerships were arranged. In January 1957, Tanker Charter Company Ltd., was specifically established by Ship Mortgages Ltd (50:50 A C Lenton and Robert Fleming), to assist British Petroleum Company Ltd with the financing of its fleet rebuilding programme. The basic principle was that when completed, vessels were taken over on lease to BP with an option to repurchase 'at par' after 22 years. In some cases, tankers were accepted before completion. The initial batch of ships were the *British Courage*, *Glory*, *Industry*, *Renown*, *Trader*, *Valour* and *Vigilance*, each around 32,000-sdwt. Also in 1957, six BP tankers were transferred to new external managers: the *British Confidence*, *Fortitude* and *Diligence* were placed under Common Brothers of Newcastle management, becoming *Anglian Confidence* etc. Common Brothers were also involved in Lowland Tankers – a consortium comprising of BP with a 50 per cent shareholding, and Common Brothers and Matheson's of London jointly holding 50 per cent shares, and The *British Integrity*, *Fidelity* and *Destiny* were placed with Denholm's of Glasgow, to become the *Gaelic Integrity* etc. In 1958, two tankers around 33,000-sdwt were completed, along with one 36,000-sdwt, two at 37,000-sdwt and two of 44,000-sdwt, one of the latter classes being the *British Ambassador* of 44,929-sdwt.

1959 saw the Clyde Charter Company formed, in similar fashion to the Tanker Charter Company, this time by a group of Scottish financiers, again with the intention of providing funds for continuing fleet renewal. Further partnerships were cemented with the Danish A/S Det Ostasiatiske Kompagni (EAC) and the British Houlder Brothers Limited, who both agreed to operate two of the contracts ordered in 1956 and run these under conditions similar to those currently agreed with other principals. To fulfil those agreements both Nordic Tankships A/S and Warwick Tankers Limited, were created, respectively. This meant that, during the rather turbulent years from 1956–8, whilst numerous world-wide political machinations raged about them, the BP Tanker Company

The wheelhouse/chartroom of the *British Destiny* represented the best available navigational equipment in 1959. *(Tyne and Wear Archives Service)*

Kent 'Clear View' screen mounted in a wheelhouse window. *(Syren & Shipping)*

experienced a hiatus during which all but one of their ordered tankers were transferred.

The tankers were equipped with the latest innovations in propulsion, cargo handling and navigation. Amongst them, the 1959-built *British Destiny,* of 44,902-sdwt, from Swan, Hunter's was transferred upon completion to the Clyde Charter Company. Her combined wheelhouse and chartroom represented the epitome of maritime technology at the time (see photograph on page 37).

The dials above the wheelhouse windows forward are indicators of engine revolutions ahead or astern, and the helm indicator, enabling these two essential aids to close quarter manoeuvring to be seen at a glance. The circular disc on the wheelhouse window is a Kent 'Clear View' screen. Introduced in 1920, it had proved an immediate success with officers-of-the-watch.

An article in *Syren & Shipping* described how this 'ingenious device eliminates the difficulties of using binoculars during wet or stormy weather at sea'. Like so many useful devices, the screen was of quite simple design. A circular disc, operated by a small motor, rotated at such high speed that it immediately threw aside the heaviest rain or snow on contact to allow unhindered lookout duty. The difference in telegraphs is also notable where the older Chadburn Ship Telegraph illustrated above proved unduly complicated even for its time. The magazine *Syren and Shipping* referred to it in 1933, with tongue somewhat in cheek, as a design which worked 'through a system of gongs, wires, chains and sprocket wheels'. The single handle at the top of each instrument indicates it is fitted to a single-screw ship. The roomy chart-table, with the attendant drawers for various voyage folio's, contains the glass cabinet housing two chronometers essential to accurate timing of sextant observations – one serving as a check for the other. Above this is the latest design of echo sounder.

Ships approaching the coast from deep-sea (especially deeply-laden tankers) have always been at risk. In fact, two different philosophical approaches between coastal and ocean watch keeping remain towards navigation and collision avoidance. The British Admiralty had long before patented their echo sounder and made this readily available commercially in the wider interests of safety at sea.

The advantage of this early 1930s model was its ability to record depths received which provided a contour of the seabed over which the ship was travelling. This proved of immense value to the navigator, equipping him in conditions of restricted visibility with a trace that could be compared with the navigating chart of the area. It was valuable also in confirming positions fixed by radio direction-finding, particularly when navigating in unfamiliar waters or again during conditions of heavily restricted visibility. *Syren & Shipping* commented on the basic operating principle: 'The recording gear comprises a drum, over which a paper is passed after being damped with a suitable chemical solution. The drum is the positive pole of a microphone circuit, whilst the pen which passes across the moist paper is the negative one. Thus, the variation of current created by the echo reaching the microphone causes a discoloration of the paper at the echo point'.

The British Admiralty Echo Sounder (Type 752) fitted with recorder. *(Syren & Shipping)*

It is particularly interesting that the magazine showed a far-reaching perspicacity regarding the technological advances made in navigational aids by 1930 – some 60 years in advance of its time – when it commented that any ship equipped with radio and direction-finding apparatus together with 'recording gear attached to echo sounder and a course-recorder on the automatic "metal Mike" or gyro-compass is as nearly automatically controlled as it is possible to imagine.' Technology had most certainly come to sea, bringing devices that cut across traditional methods in new and exciting ways. These instruments were not 'woolly toys'. Each piece represented equipment essential to the safe navigation of ships that was fast becoming mandatory. The 'black box' projecting from the bulkhead is the Mark 12 Decca Navigator based on a system of transmitting Master and receiving Slave stations providing generally very accurate electronic position fixes – even if the quality of signals fluctuated considerably within the refractive conditions of the Persian Gulf.

A number of significant tankers were included amongst the ships completed during 1959. The *British Fulmar* was the first of a new series of fourteen similar 15,500-sdwt tankers ordered from various British shipyards. This ship was launched in September 1958 for the BP Tanker Company, and completed February 1959 for Clyde Charter. She was designed to carry her 15,500 tons deadweight on a draft of 29 feet 4$^{5}/_{8}$ inches at a speed of 14.5 knots with a daily consumption of 30 tons of fuel oil, and about 1 ton of diesel for the generators. The ship was very attractively designed, of single-deck construction with a raked funnel, clipper stem and cruiser stern. She had a high-extended 'topgallant' foc's'le – conforming to Classification Society Tanker Rules – and rather lengthy midships superstructure giving the by now distinctive streamlined British Tanker Company style. This was emphasised by the angled stanchions and large open bridge that helped breakdown the previously 'solid squatness' of traditional buildings.

British Fulmar was planned specifically for multi-grade cargoes of refined products. Longitudinal framing was arranged throughout the cargo spaces, fitted with horizontal stiffeners supported by webs, whilst transverse bulkheads had vertical stiffeners fixed at the top and bottom by plate brackets and supported by horizontal girders. The resulting ship proved strong and practical. Sub-division of the hull gave a reinforced forepeak, forward deep-tanks for fuel, a cofferdam, and two longitudinal bulkheads resulting in twenty-seven cargo compartments. Consistent with developing current practices, the cargo tanks were protected against corrosion by being shot-blasted and coated to a depth of 3 feet – allowing for 98 per cent loading. Two pump rooms were installed at the ends of the ship, clear of cargo spaces, and were fitted with steam-driven cargo pumps each of 500 tons/hour capacity. There was four main 12-inch cargo lines plus stern loading/discharging.

British Fulmar. (J K Byass)

This tanker was the first post-war BP vessel to be fitted with a turbo-charged Sulzer engine designed to run on low-grade fuel oil. The engine-room plan shows clearly the spacious, well laid-out design along with the spacing at floor-plate level of the generators, pumps and ancillary machinery. The tanker was fitted with accommodation for seventy-five crew that incorporated facilities for Indian ratings across all departments. The officers' dining room and smoke room were fitted to very high standards with Marinite incombustible bulkhead linings that had been attractively faced with wood veneers on plywood.

The smoke-room was midships, fitted with double doors leading onto the after deck, whilst the spacious dining saloon was on the poop deck. The ratings also had a very high standard of accommodation. A special galley was provided for the deck and engine-room *Bhandarys* (or Indian cooks) together with other appropriate amenities. The crew mess was fitted with

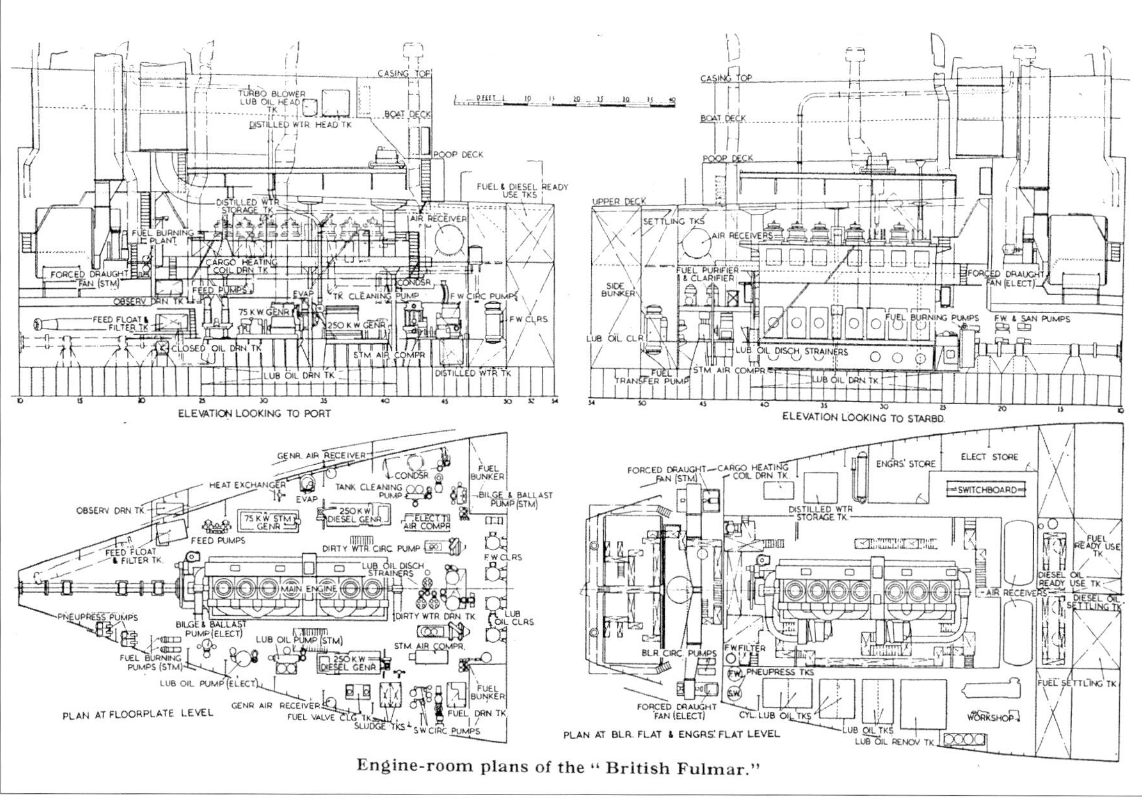

Engine-room plans of the *British Fulmar*. *(The Motor Ship).*

The officers' dining room and smoke room (above) and crew mess room (below) aboard the *British Fulmar*. *(The Motor Ship)*

plastic-faced walls, washable fabrics and tubular steel furniture. A considerable amount of thought had been given to all areas of accommodation: all ratings (apart from boys) were berthed in single-cabins, each fitted with the same incombustible facings as provided for the officers, but of brightly-coloured and serviceable plastics.

The *British Queen* was of 49,967-sdwt and was built by John Brown's yard on the Clyde – the first of a new class of twelve ordered from various British yards. The magazine *Tanker Times* in March 1960 commented on the plans for ship delivery of BP Tanker Company: 'Altogether this company has over 1mn.Tons deadweight of tankers on order in Britain, including seven 65,000-tonners. It is not likely that any of these bigger ships will be ready to surpass the 50,000-tonners before 1962.' Her keel had been laid on 31 October 1957. She was launched by Her Majesty the Queen Mother in September 1959 and transferred to Tanker Charter Company three months' later. At the time of her launching, she was the largest ship under the Red Ensign and the biggest ship launched on the Clyde since the *Queen Mary,* some 21 years previously. By the time of her launching, her fitting-out was well under way – a very unusual advancement for any new building – so that she had completed sea trials by 18 December. It is interesting to note *British Queen* was planned originally as a 42,000-sdwt tanker but, with a number of other vessels of this capacity, BP subsequently decided an increase in size. She was 760 feet overall (725 feet between perpendiculars) by 97 feet moulded breadth, with 54 feet moulded depth. Her laden draught was 40.6 feet and she was designed for the crude oil trades outward by way of Suez and home via the Cape. This was because the Suez Canal permitted summer deadweight of only around 40,000 tons. The geared steam turbine propelling machinery developed a maximum 17,600 shp giving a laden speed of around 15.5 knots – even though on trials she achieved nearly 17 knots.

The cargo space was divided into thirty-six tanks with three wing tanks port and starboard amidships designated for permanent water ballast. The three cargo pumps each had a capacity of 1,250 tons per hour, the water ballast pump, 750 tons/hour, and the two stripping pumps each of 250 tons/hour. She was a very powerful ship permitting, under optimum conditions, loading in around 13 hours and cargo discharge in about 15 hours. The accommodation was superb – air-conditioned throughout and single cabins for all seventy-six officers and ratings except cadets and boys who retained traditional double bunking. Protection was provided in the cargo tanks by means of 30 tons of magnesium anodes and all ballast tanks were coated against corrosion. The engineering officers were transferred back to the boat deck aft and a lift was fitted running from there to the engine-room. The latest 16-inch display radar was provided fitted with the newest reflection plotter enabling collision avoidance triangles to be drawn onto the PPI with chinagraph pencil. The lifeboats were of fibreglass – one motor and the other three fitted with Fleming gear.

In 1960, the Organisation of Petroleum Exporting

Companies (OPEC) was formed, firing a warning shot across the bows for all oil-importing countries. Notwithstanding such political implications, this same year saw a considerable number of tankers built for the BP fleet, many of which were transferred to managing companies upon completion. A significant construction for The Lowland Tanker Company, managed by Common Brothers of Newcastle in whom BP had 50 per cent shareholding, was the *Border Shepherd.* Lowland's already owned ten 16,000-sdwt tankers, and this was the first of five motor-ships ordered by them, and the first BP tanker to have her navigating bridge and all accommodation placed aft. She was built by Lithgow's of Glasgow, launched in March 1960 and completed the following July. She was 19,750-sdwt on 572 feet length oa (540 bp) × 72.92 feet moulded breadth and 40 feet depth, carrying her loaded deadweight on a draft of 31 feet 7 1/2 inches.

This tanker was the first BP ship to be fitted with one oil-hose davit mounted on the centre-line serving both sides of the ship. It had been designed and built by Schat Davits of Colney in Hertfordshire, England and replaced the conventional derrick and Samson post powered by warping winches, normally carried on each side of a tanker. The safe working load of the davit was five tons and it possessed a radial outreach ranging from 14 feet 0 inches minimum to 43 feet 6 inches maximum, the latter measurement coping well with the 36 feet 0 inches moulded breadth of the ship from the centre-line. The maximum height of the lifting hook above the base was 14 feet 9 inches and its slewing and luffing movements were controlled by air-motors. The advantages were considerable.

Under normal conditions, it could take a crew of three or four men around one hour to rig conventional derricks before they were ready to receive the hose. Taking the hose on board and connecting this to the manifolds, often using a number of reducing pieces to compensate for differences in pipe sizes, could take also around the same amount of time. Two men could bring on board the hose and connect the manifolds using the davit in around 30 minutes. There would also have been the advantage of more delicate handing of the hose, more positive control of the operation generally, and a simplified handling of the accommodation ladder immediately the ship had made the main wires fast alongside. The were four other davits fitted aboard the *Border Shepherd* – two of 1-ton swl on each side aft, for storing ship, and two of 1.5 tons each side forward used for bosun's stores and any bulk general cargo lifts.

* * *

In October 1960, *British Statesman* brought her first cargo of 39,000 tons of Iranian crude to BP's new jetty at Angle Bay, Milford Haven. This was a £6.25 million development with a pier extending 1,350 feet and with a jetty head of 2,300 feet leading to the edge of the deep-water dredged channel. The 55-foot depth of water, even at low tide, made the facility capable of berthing the largest tankers afloat. A gantry served each of the two berths fitted with four chiksans with 12-inch arms for handling crude oil and two 8-inch for bunkering purposes. The crude was discharged by pipeline to an oil farm just under 2 miles away.

A further event of significance in 1960 was the Amendments introduced by Lloyd's Register leading to extensive revisions of the Rules for Oil Tanker Construction that came into force on 7 July. The previous revisions of any consequence to the tanker trades had been around 1930 and in 1949, which took into

General arrangement plan of the *Border Shepherd.* *(Tanker Times).*

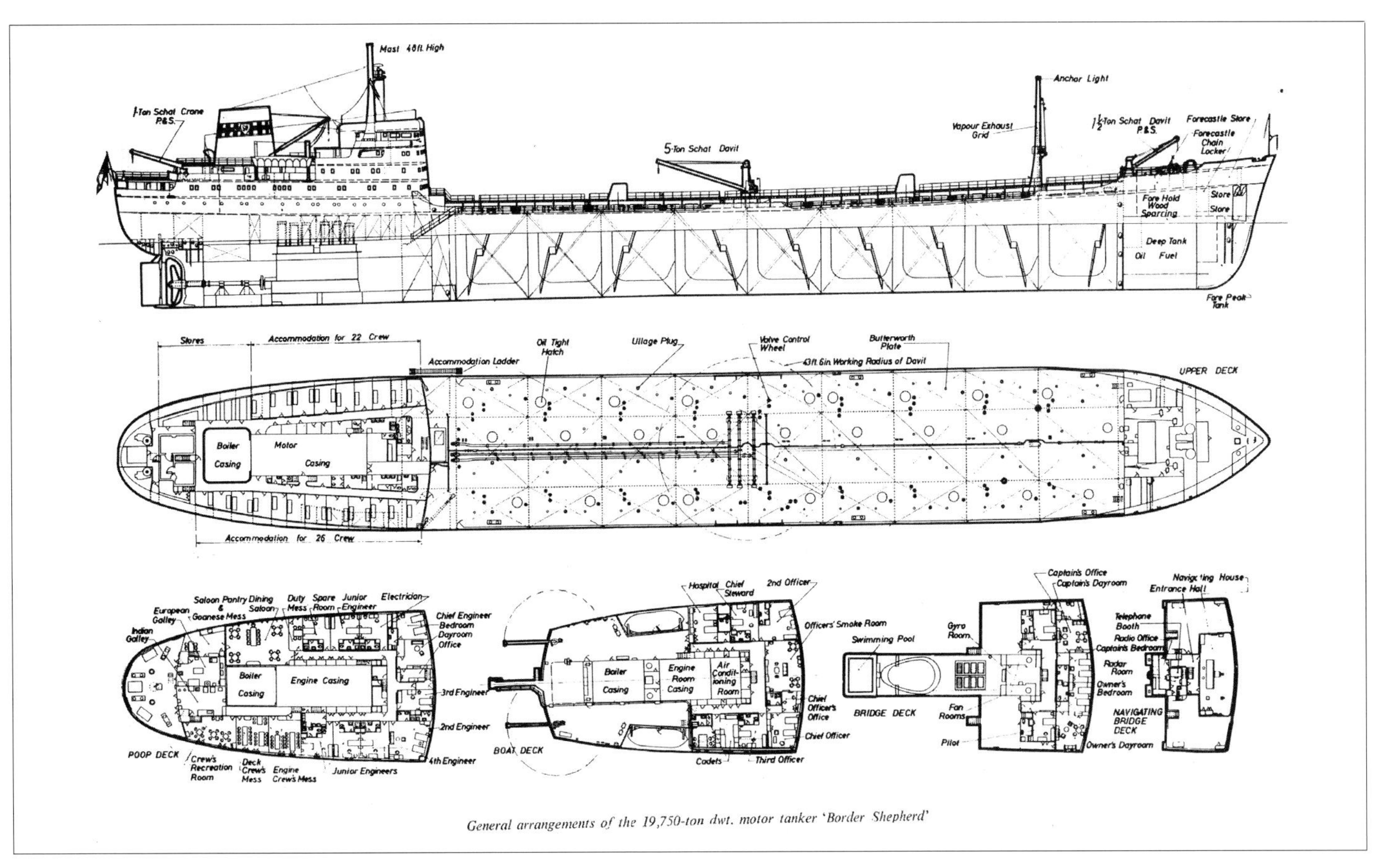

General arrangements of the 19,750-ton dwt. motor tanker 'Border Shepherd'

SAMPLE OF LAY-UP PERIODS AND LOCATIONS OF OLDER VESSELS.

Falmouth.

British Marshal 9.7.1957 – 3.11.1961 thence demolition.
British Supremacy 11.7.1957 – 21.9.1961 thence demolition.
British Earl 15.7.1957 – 18.7.1961 thence demolition.
British Success 22.9.1957 – 27.8.1961 thence demolition.
British Marquis 22.9.1957 - 21.9.1961 thence demolition.
British Harmony 23.9.1957 – 29.9.1960 thence Cardiff.
British Gratitude – 10.5.1959 thence demolition.
British Restraint 31.12.1957 – 5.1959 thence demolition.
British Wisdom 10.2.1958 – 8.9.1960 thence Cardiff.
British Fern 7.2.1959 – 30.8.1961 thence demolition.
British Knight 3.3.1959 – 4.10.1961 thence demolition.
British Major 5.5.1959 – 28.9.1961 thence Cardiff.
British Admiral 6.5.1959 – 26.9.1961 thence demolition.
British Enterprise 15.7.1959 – 17.6.1961 thence demolition.
British Rose 25.4.1959 – 14.6.1961 thence demolition.
British Commerce 1.10.1960 – 10.6.1961 thence demolition.
British Baron 7.10.1960 – 6.1.1962 thence demolition.

Portland.

British Merit 3.7.1958 – 8.12.1960 thence Cardiff.
British Tradition 2.9.1958 – 28.10.1960 thence Cardiff.

Methil.

British Promise 31.1.1958 – 23.2.1959 thence demolition.
British Ensign 24.2.1959 – 29.8.1961 thence demolition.
British Empress 29.3.1959 – 31.7.1961 thence demolition.

Barry.

British Virtue 18.6.1958 – 16.7.1961 thence Cardiff.
British Caution 16.8.1959 – 10.12.1961 thence demolition.

Swansea.

British Princess 22.4.1959 – 17.2.1962 thence demolition.

Devonport.

British Bombardier 28.5.1958 – 1.1959 thence demolition.

Cardiff.

The vessels listed as transferring to Cardiff did so to be prepared for sale and / or made safe for demolition.

The old must give way to the new. The above table gives a snapshot of lay-ups and disposals as the fleet renewal programme gathered momentum.

account the increase in average tanker size before and after the Second World War. Since then of course tankers had increased considerably in deadweight, with the size of many doubling over the previous ten years since 1950. New methods were introduced for determining the all-important main longitudinal scantlings. Under the 1949 Rules, the scantlings were derived from the main dimensions of tankers and their draft, with an upper limit in length of 620 feet overall. By 1960, tankers had increased internationally to over 900 feet, a length that exceeded parameters of bending moments to which such large ships were subjected. The new rules applied to tankers of all sizes. The significant change was the elimination of tables determining characteristics of tankers and the implementation of findings, based purely on formulae, which included ships up to 1,000 feet in length. The revised sections referred to the main hull girder of the ship, its frames and internal structure, and declared minimum stress loads to which members used in construction should be subjected. The rules allowed longer cargo tanks to be built that enabled tankers not only to save weight by reducing the number of transversal oil-tight bulkheads, but also to simplify piping arrangements. Commenting on the new rules, the authoritative magazine *Tanker Times* for that month was moved to conclude: 'These rules reflect not only the great experience of the society derived from reports of surveys of tankers over a long period, but also mathematical investigations and experimental work done on components of the structure. It is felt that the new rules are a great advance on those which they will supersede and will be of benefit to owners and builders.' To which of course they could have added the officers and crews responsible for operating and sailing the tankers.

An innovative tanker completed in 1962 for BP Tanker Company was the *British Kestrel.* She was similar in many respects to the *British Fulmar* – the first of the new 'bird class' series of 15,500-sdwt ships partially described above. She was 15,922-sdwt, 525 feet 3 inches × 69 feet 4 inches × 29 feet 4$^{1}/_{4}$ inches from William Hamilton's Port Glasgow yard and was fitted with a 7,600 bhp diesel engine built by Kincaid and Company. For some years previously, BP had been making considerable efforts to improve overall engine efficiency aboard tankers of their fleet, seeking ways of reducing costly routine maintenance work. Their own engineering staff, working with the Senior Economiser Company of London, had together developed what the *Motor Ship* described as 'the most advanced heat-recovery system yet installed in a Diesel-engined vessel'. In elementary terms, using a combined low pressure/high pressure steam system, the BP plant installed aboard this tanker extracted the maximum possible heat from exhaust gases that would otherwise have been expended into the atmosphere. The success of the system was far-reaching for it was to be integrated into all future Company shipbuilding.

At the other end of the telegraph, as it were, the *British Kestrel* proved innovative in her wheelhouse design. For many years, BP had adopted a combined wheelhouse and chartroom into their bridge designs. Aboard many tankers and general cargo ships within a wider merchant navy, the wheelhouse was still a separate cabin. It had long been a bone of contention that every time the navigating officer wished to plot the ship's position, after taking visual bearings on the bridge gyro-repeater and invariably crossing these with radar and Decca Navigator fixes, he had to go into a separate chart-room and leave his all-important duty of 'keeping an effective look-out'. Invariably, it was easy to become side tracked by measuring distances travelled, and the like, until a lengthy period could elapse before returning to the wheelhouse. A combined layout made it easier for the officer to maintain his effective lookout yet still perform essential and legislative chart-work. The success of the combined wheelhouse/chartroom fitted aboard *British Kestrel* encouraged BP to adopt this layout as standard fitting aboard all their new buildings.

The first thing of note was the spaciousness in the new design. The wheelhouse aboard many ships was to remain for many years – in fact, well into the late 1970s – considerably cramped with plenty of scope, until their positions had become familiar, of bumping into things and falling over them during the initial period

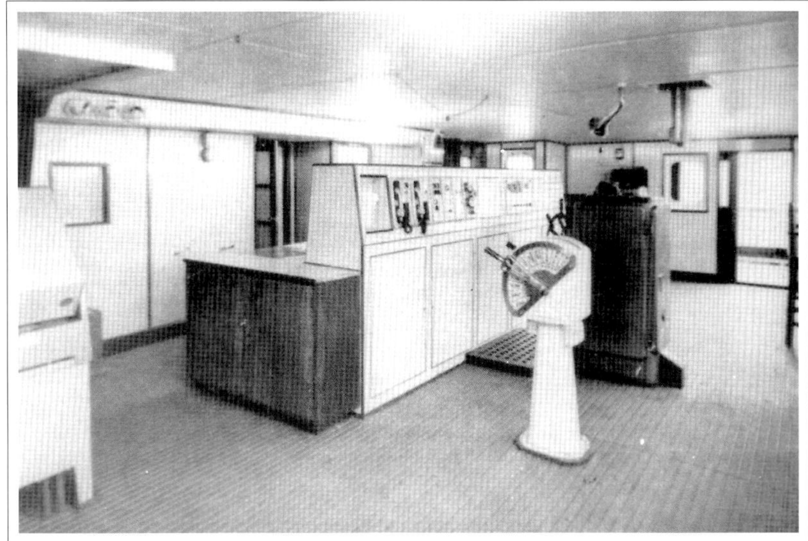

The combined wheelhouse/chartroom aboard the *British Kestrel*. *(The Motor Ship)*

of darkness whilst taking-over a watch. The non-slip decking was a marked safety feature when quick movements were required to answer say, the strident ringing of a telephone, when the deck was wet. The removal of the duplicated magnetic compass from the wheelhouse, into a universal fitting (on all ships) of a periscope tube below the standard compass on the monkey island was welcomed. This was perfectly acceptable as virtually all tankers were by this time using gyrocompass for course keeping. The modern telegraph situated close to the quartermaster's steering position at the Arma-Brown steering console, and adjacent to the telephones, facilitated the duties of the officer-on-watch during manoeuvring operations considerably.

The *British Venture* was completed in April 1963 for, and was managed and run by the BP Tanker Company. This was the first tanker powered by large-bore engine, and one of the first to have all accommodation aft. Of 36,300-sdwt she was designed specifically for the crude oil trade, with a length oa of 678 feet, 86 feet breadth and 50 feet moulded depth on a working loaded draft of 37 feet 6 inches and a speed of 15.5 knots. Ten main tanks were divided to provide thirty cargo compartments, with Numbers Four and Five Wings being arranged for clean ballast only. Full zinc cathodic protection was fitted into the remaining tanks that could be used for seawater ballast – namely, Numbers One, Three and Seven Centre, and Two, Three, Six and Eight Wings. Whessoe automatic Ullage gauges were fitted inside tanks for the first time aboard a BP tanker. The pump room was located forward of the engine-room transverse bulkhead and was equipped with three 1000 ton/hour Drysdale turbine-driven pumps and a 7-inch diameter stripping pump. A 5-ton electro-hydraulic Schat davit was fitted midships, together with a davit of 1-ton swl aft.

BP's deep-sea tanker fleet was not being developed at the expense of the smaller distribution vessels. The *Hamble*, launched in February 1964 at Henry Robb's Leith yard was a coastal tanker jointly owned by Shell-Mex & BP, and represented the first in what was to prove a modest fleet of modern coastal ships.

Of 1,480-sdwt, 214 feet 9 inches length oa, beam of 36 feet 11 inches and depth 15 feet 6 inches, she drew 14 feet 0 1/2 inches fully laden. She was propelled by a British Polar 6-cylinder diesel engine, which gave a service speed of 11 knots. She had five main cargo compartments divided into pairs by a longitudinal bulkhead under a trunk, each coated with epoxy resin. Cofferdams were fitted fore and aft and the cargo pump room contained three displacement pumps each with an output varying from 166 tons/hour when handling petroleum spirit, to 259 tons/hour for cargoes of heavy fuel oil. The crew of fourteen were berthed in accommodation of a very high standard for the coastal trades – a note of envy to visiting crews from other tankers berthed near-by whose own companies were not always exactly renowned for providing comfort. The navigation gear was standard for this class of ship, consisting of a Decca Navigator, radar, echo sounder, vhf radio and a domestic W/T receiver.

1965 proved a monumental year in the fleet history of a tanker company that was breaking new ground in the development of both ships and equipment. The modifications already introduced by BP were innovative and essentially practical with many being adopted by other national and international ship and tanker-owners. Two new classes of tanker appeared during 1965. The *British Fern* was around 20,000-sdwt and the fourth in a series of thirteen similar tankers ordered from British and – in a move unprecedented

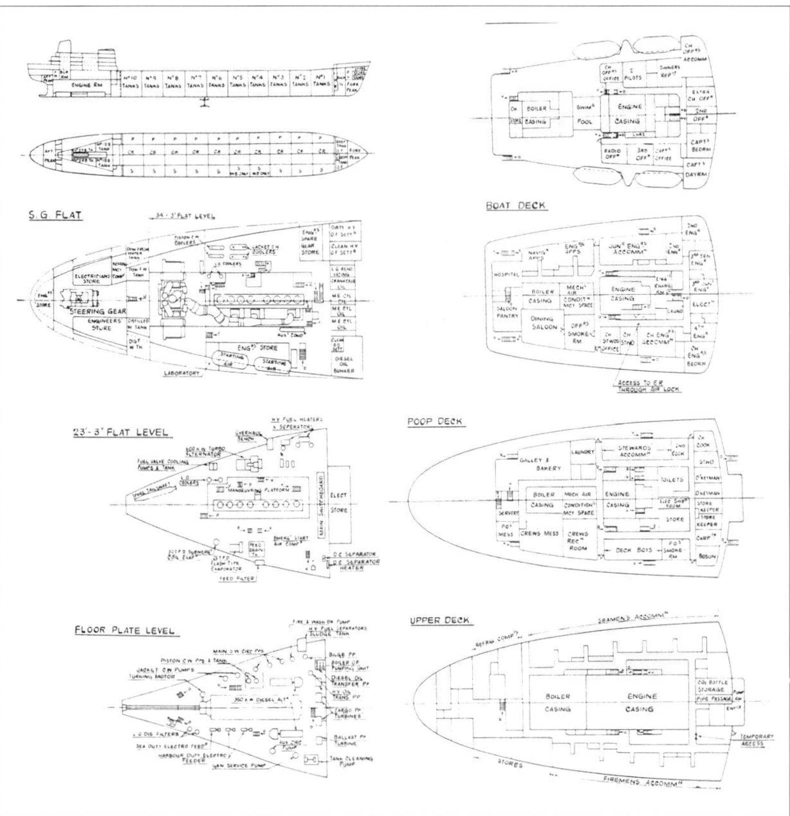

***British Venture* general arrangement and engine-room plans.** *(Tanker Times)*

The 1,480-sdwt *Hamble* on the Mersey inward-bound for Stanlow on the Manchester Ship Canal. *(World Ship Society Photograph Library)*

in Company history – Australian and Swedish yards. Three of the class were ordered from Eriksberg's, complete with engines, and two from the Australian State Dockyard. She was the first tanker fitted with a semi-automatic cargo-pump control system for discharging the refined products for which she had been designed. She was fitted also with vertical corrugated transversal bulkheads dividing the cargo carrying capacity into thirty-three tanks, eleven centre and twenty-two wing. This facilitated considerably the task of tank cleaning between cargoes. The complement of fifty-five mariners included double-banked cabins for eight cadets – four each for the deck and engine departments – emphasising the seriousness with which the company undertook their responsibilities for encouraging qualified and competent officers to man tankers of their future fleet.

The galley aboard ships of this class was modern and well-equipped. It proved a considerable improvement over ranges fitted aboard the early tankers. The standard fitting aboard many BP ships introduced in 1921, for instance, was rudimentary. The 1921 galley was oil-fired where the oil was atomised by steam or compressed air, depending upon the model, at low pressure through burners fitted with regulating and stop valves that permitted use of any burner individually. The company stressed, reassuringly, how 'all elements of the combustion process are under complete control'. The advantages over previous models provided a quick rising in temperature, and its easy regulation, plus the provision of a steady uniform heat, with economy of fuel. Comparison with the modern galley fitted aboard ships of the BP fleet indicates that it was not only in the field of professional maritime technology that the Company took their responsibility for crew welfare seriously.

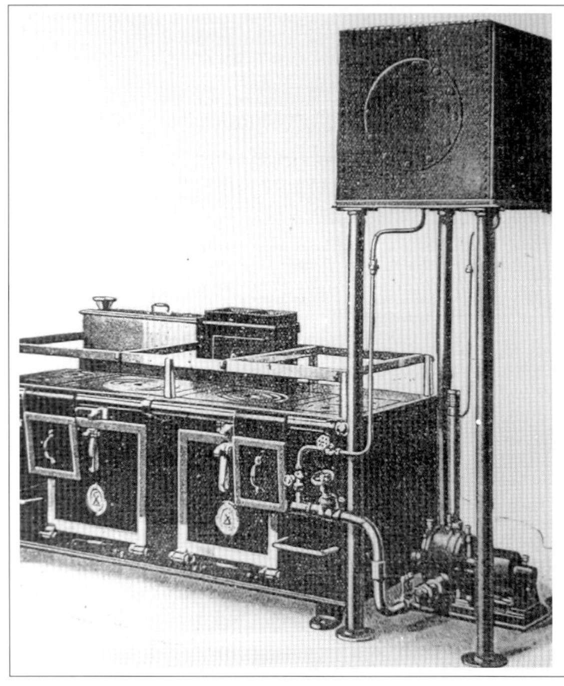

Carron's Works of Stirlingshire introduced their oil-fired galley range in 1921 for fitting aboard many BP tankers. *(Fairplay Supplement)*

In the history of any fleet a ship is launched which proves to be a milestone. For The BP Tanker Company such an event was marked in the launch of *British Admiral.* This tanker coincided with the fiftieth anniversary celebration of the founding of the transport arm of Anglo-Persian Oil – and, rightly, the Company celebrated in appropriate style. There was something unique in passing the 100,000-sdwt barrier, especially as this Supertanker represented the largest merchant ship completed in Europe, and the largest owned by BP. She was 111,274-sdwt on an overall length of 917 feet 6 inches, beam 128 feet and depth 66 feet with a draft of 49 feet and service speed around 15.5 knots. Her engineering facilities were described by *Tanker and Bulk Carrier* magazine for August 1965 as 'undoubtedly the most advanced vessel in the BP fleet, the complexity of her control systems being reflected in the composition of her 43-man complement, nearly 50 per cent of which are officers.'

Her Majesty Queen Elizabeth II launched this impressive ship on 17 March 1965 at Vickers Yard in Barrow-in-Furness. The Company built also the two steam turbine engines, developing a maximum of 25,000 shp geared to a single shaft. She was fitted with a generating capacity higher than that installed in any previous British merchant ship through two generator sets. The Company and builders took advantage of the revised Rules for Oil Tanker Construction by reducing the number of cargo tanks to seven sets of three. Of the twenty-one tanks, four were designed for water ballast, and the single pump room contained four cargo pumps each with the capacity of 1,860 tons/hour. The cargo control aboard this ship was fully automated and the first of its kind in the world. It was an early example of effective computerisation at sea. Designed in Japan for one-man control, all valves were push-button operated, worked around the insertion of a predetermined programming card punched by the chief officer based around loading, discharging and any inter-voyage cargo transfer operations that occasionally prove necessary. Amongst the advantages claimed for the cargo control system was the elimination of possible spillage or overflow of crude oil by the use of valves that closed automatically once cargo had reached the programmed level. A move had been made away from the Ring pipeline system with these large tankers into one called the 'Free-flow system'. This used hydraulic-actuated pipelines and bulkhead valves fitted into the transverse and longitudinal bulkheads that allowed the free flow of cargo into the aftermost tank so that it could be pumped ashore. The scope for introducing stresses along the hull and across frames, leading to hogging or sagging, was considerable aboard these large tankers and necessitated the use of a computer for all cargo operations.

Deck equipment included a 100-ton steam windlass and eight steam-mooring winches. The windlass alone was formidable. It stood 9 feet high, 40 feet over the warp ends, and was capable of an anchor breakout pull of 110 tons when using both steam engines positioned below the fo'c'sle head.

The warping duty was 21 tons at 120 feet/minute. The winches were fitted with speed change gear capable of pulling 19 tons at 100 feet/minute in slow speed. The Supertanker was fully air-conditioned and equipped with the latest designs in all navigational, catering and radio facilities.

In the light of universal increases in tanker length, the hitherto traditional echo sounder proved to be inadequate. It remained very much an effective instrument aboard smaller ships but, it indicated depths only immediately under the keel beneath the bridge in which it was sited. These larger tankers required more accurate information of water depths in the all-important forward area. Draught was indicated both forward and aft. The equipment was fitted additionally with a specific gravity indication. This was useful when assessing draught experienced when berthed or operating at the mouth of rivers as fresh water flowing over the sensors could affect appreciably the accuracy obtained in draught reading. The draught indication box was versatile in that it could be sited anywhere aboard the ship, although the most useful place for it was in the wheelhouse.

The *British Admiral* was commanded by Commodore Henney OBE, who had joined BTC as a junior officer in 1928. He had been appointed Master in 1940. His wartime service included two tankers sunk underneath him by torpedo. The chief engineering officer was Mr J Sutton who had joined the Company in 1941 as a junior engineer. His first ship (the *British Strength*) was sunk by enemy action one month after he joined her, resulting in his detention as a prisoner-of-war until 1945.

The magazine *Tanker and Bulk Carrier* for June 1965 commented on the status held within the shipping industry by the Company: 'Today, as owners of one of the world's largest tanker fleets, the company looks back upon half a century of progress and development that has reflected and matched the rapid growth of the oil industry itself. The BP Tanker fleet now consists of more than 100 ships, aggregating 2,700,000 tons dwt and there are a further 28 ships totalling 700,000 tons dwt operated under associated company house flags. In addition, ships totalling 3,400,000 tons dwt are long-term chartered from independent tramp owners, not to mention other vessels which are chartered on a voyage basis.'

The galley aboard the *British Willow* completed for BP Tankers in May 1965. *(Tyne and Wear Archives Service)*

Fo'c'sle head of the *British Admiral*. *(The Motor Ship).*

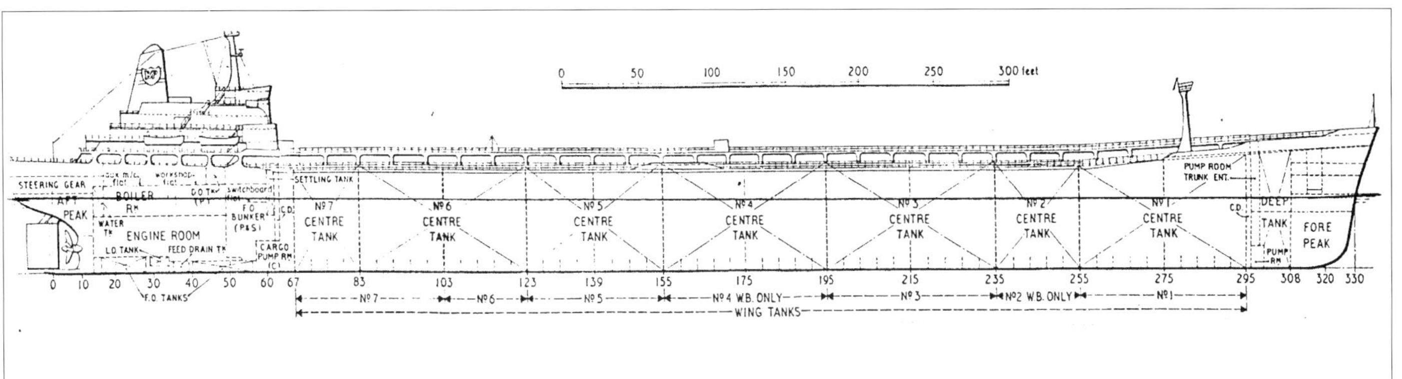

Side elevation plan of *British Admiral*. *(World Ship Society Photograph Library)*

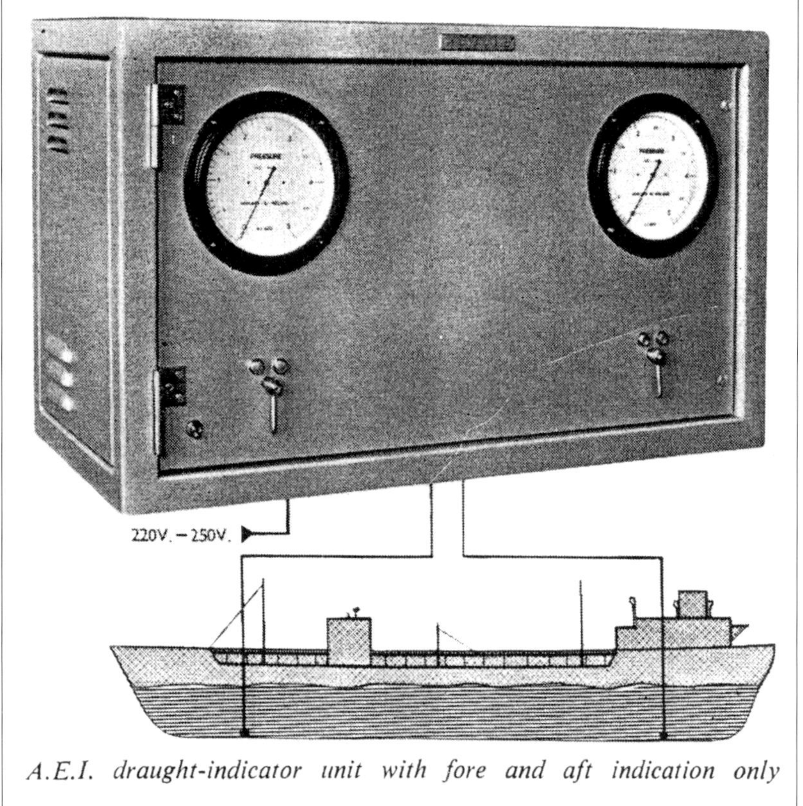

A.E.I. draught-indicator unit with fore and aft indication only

Associated Electrical Instrument Ltd, of London devised a system of draught indication that was widely adopted aboard the larger BP tankers. *(Tanker Times)*

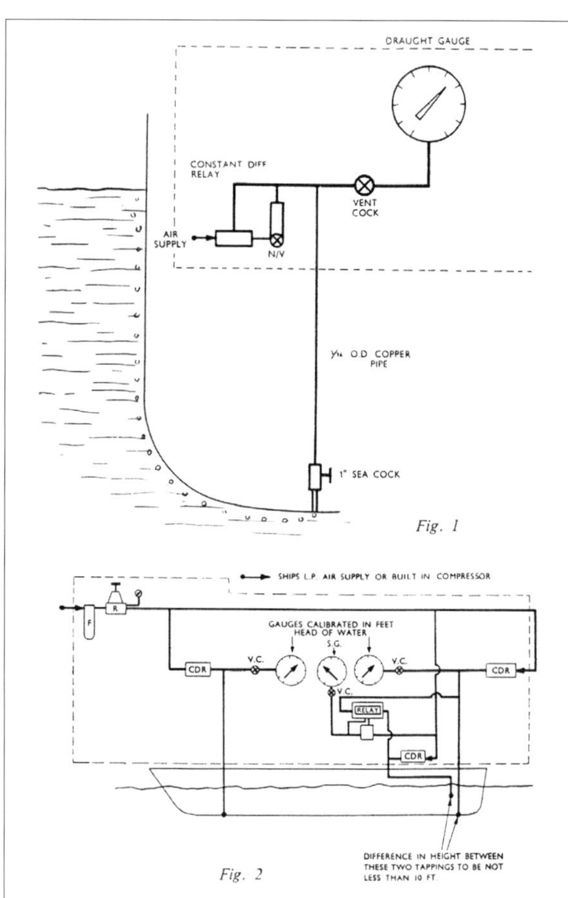

The principle of the Associated Instruments Draught Indicator. *(Tanker Times)*

It is perhaps the latter part of this statement which reinforces the extent to which BP had world-wide involvements in the oil and shipping industry – often rarely publicised facts – but very much in keeping with tacit traditions of 'quietly getting on with things' regardless of external pressures and events nationally and internationally occurring around them. A positive attitude very much the hallmark of Company development reflected so far throughout this fleet history.

Continued Progress *Chapter Eight*

The launching and completion of the *British Argosy* in June 1966 for the BP Tanker Company from Swan, Hunter's yard really endorsed the term 'Supertanker' in the eyes of the professional maritime world. Following so soon after the *British Admiral*, this new 112,786-sdwt tanker marked a decisive change in management attitude, particularly with the experience of a years successful trading by the 'fore-runner in the fleet'. Like her near-sister ship, the *Argosy* was fitted also with a breakwater forward of the manifolds protecting this vulnerable area from sea-storm ravages when fully laden with a freeboard of around 12 feet.

It was from May 1967 that fortunes of the British Petroleum fleet again became caught up in world politics. Justifying earlier fears of BP directors, the Suez Canal was once more closed on 5 June when Colonel Nasser ejected United Nations observers from his country and sent troops into Sinai in an attempt to block Israeli communications through the Gulf of Aquaba. He was backed by most Arab countries, together with Libya and Algeria, who collectively imposed an oil embargo on all countries trading with Israel – which of course included Britain and America. The ensuing chaos to industrial markets was obvious. Aristotle Onassis, the Greek tanker owner, rose to the occasion. He cancelled his existing agreements and proposed to BP's chartering manager – Mr P I Walters, during a weekend telephone call to his home – the hire of his entire fleet at double the existing rate BP was already paying. An immediate decision had to be made. Mr Walters (in the mould of the many 'people of destiny' already encountered) rose to the occasion and agreed to Onassis' terms. The wisdom of his decision was proved two days' later the following Monday when charter rates internationally increased by 40 per cent and continued rising. His decision saved his employers several million pounds.

On 5 June Israel launched a surprise attack on Egypt and by 8 June had reached the Suez Canal, destroying 80 per cent of Egypt's military capacity. By then, Arabian oil production was down 40 per cent whilst the oilfields in Saudi Arabia and Libya had closed completely. Iraqi marine pilots had already left the Shat Al Arab waterway, an action that effectively closed the port of Abadan, and forced a previously reluctant Iran into the conflict. On 11 June Israel, with her borders secured, declared the 'Six Day War' ended, but the Suez Canal was totally blocked by sunken ships and was to remain so for a number of years. The Persian Gulf did not immediately resume oil supplies, but other sources in Indonesia and Venezuela increased existing production. Nigeria however experienced civil unrest that closed down her oil fields exacerbating an already serious situation. BP, in keeping with all other oil transport companies, was forced again to use the Cape route for all supplies to Europe and the United States, and to re-assess the size of individual tankers within their fleet. It was not until September 1967 the Arabian oil producers realised they were losing considerable sums of money and had failed to prevent supplies reaching the West. They reluctantly resumed production and re-opened their oil fields to foreign trade and shipping.

In the face of such diverse political interventions, the fleet of BP tankers continued to grow – although initially with ships of more modest dimensions. During 1967, three 67,500+-sdwt tankers were launched for BP Tankers and transferred upon completion to Tanker Charter Company. These were the *British: Commodore, Centaur* and *Captain.* It was this year also that the *BP Endeavour* of 19,500-sdwt was

***British Argosy* before and after launch.** *(both Tyne and Wear Archives Service)*

launched and completed from Australian yards for BP Tankers Australia Pty, a company formed in 1964, which was followed in 1968 by *BP Enterprise* of similar tonnage. Also in 1968, three tankers were launched from Swedish yards. The *British: Liberty, Loyalty* and *Security* were around 20,000-sdwt ton capacity. That British Petroleum had become a thriving international organisation by this time is clear from the confident tones of a press advertisement.

V.L.C.C's

Yard No.	*Shipbuilder*	*Name*	*For delivery*
847.	Mitsui S.B.& E., Chiba	*British Pioneer*	1971
872.	——0——	*British Surveyor*	1972
1133.	Kawasaki Dockyard, Kobe	*British Scientist*	1971
1674.	Mitsubishi H.I.Ltd., Nagasaki	*British Navigator*	1971
1675.	——0——	*British Prospector*	1971
C.25.	Ch.del'Atlantique, St.Nazaire	*British Pride*	1973
288.	Ch.Navale La Ciotat, La Ciotat	*Beaugency*	1973
303.	——0——	*Brissac*	1976
845.	Nederlandsche Dok, Amsterdam	*British Progress*	1973
846.	——0——	*British Purpose*	1974
850.	Verolme Dok, Rosenburg	*British Promise*	1974
851.	——0——	*British Patience*	1974

In 1969, oil was discovered by BP in Alaska and, the following year, this was consolidated by a leasing agreement with the Standard Oil Company of Ohio thus merging two major oil companies. 1970 proved a year of considerable advancement for the Company when they discovered oil in the North Sea. The 112,000-sdwt class tankers had proved the value of their investment and the fleet stood around 108 tankers of varied capacity. The situations regarding both shipping and construction were quite serious. Tanker charter rates had tripled from those in 1967 by this time and continued again to rise whilst, simultaneously, the demand for oil increased considerably. By 1970, numerous ship-owners world-wide had seen the advantages of ordering larger tonnage ships. Universe Tankships Incorporated of America, for instance, had launched their 122,876-sdwt *Universe Apollo* as long ago as 1959, following this in 1968 with *Universe Ireland* of a then staggering 326,585-sdwt. BP management had to think and act fast in order to secure yard space to beat what was becoming an almost undignified rush for larger tonnage.

Some initial moves had already been made by BP Tanker Company who had registered the BP Medway Tanker Company Limited in 1967 following this move, with customary perspicacity, by placing orders for a series of fifteen tankers exceeding 200,000-sdwt from a mixture of European and Far Eastern shipyards. This was then the first move away from British shipbuilders that must have fired more than a warning shot across their individual bows.

The shipbuilding orders of the late 1960s were crowned in 1969 with another change in funnel markings. The colours adopted in 1955 (left) were swept aside for the simplified design (right). This was coupled with a very upbeat advertising spree.

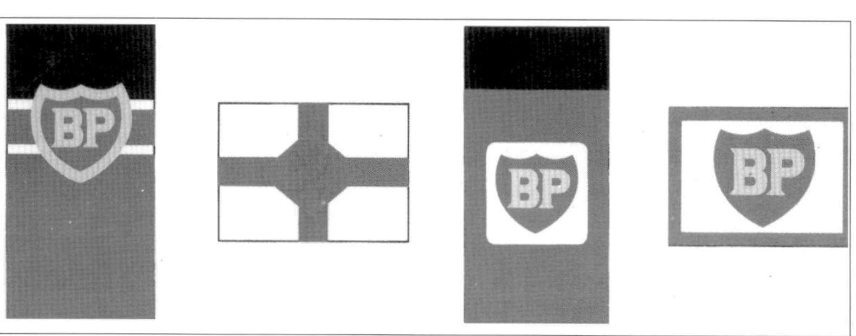

Funnel and flag introduced in 1955 *(left).* **Funnel and flag further simplified in 1969** *(right).*

By April 1969, the first of the new 'Very Large Crude Carriers' (VLCCs) had been launched for BP Tankers and was transferred to Medway Tankers upon completion in April 1970.

This was the *British Explorer* of 215,603-sdwt at 1,069.7 feet between perpendiculars, and a moulded breadth of 160 feet and depth 62 feet. She was launched by the Mitsubishi Heavy Industries Yard at Nagasaki and was followed, three months later, by the *British Inventor* of similar dimensions from the same builders. The 239,708-sdwt Supertanker *Blois* had also entered service after her launch in April 1970 for French BP.

The remaining twelve similar-sized VLCCs were ordered for the British and French fleets as a mixture of owned and leased ships with the last scheduled for delivery in 1976.

Also in the early 1970s, a further fifteen VLCCs (also for varied operated and managed BP British and

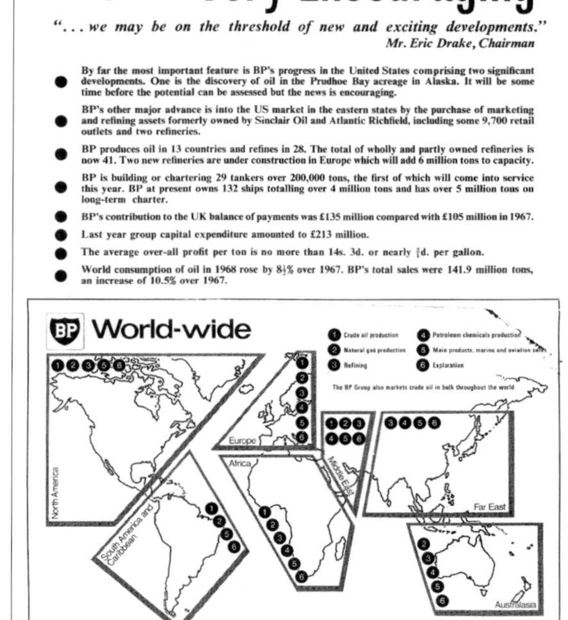

A BP press advertisement from 1969. *(Shipping World and Shipbuilder)*

French fleets) were ordered mainly from Mitsubishi. These numbered ten of the British 'R' class, and five French 'C' class with delivery spread over a number of years. It is not a vital issue, but one perhaps of some conjecture why BP never undertook delivery of Supertankers in the ULCC class. The largest capacity tanker they ever owned or managed in the 1970s and 1980s was the *British Respect,* at 277,746-sdwt. She was ordered from the Kawasaki Heavy Industry Yard, for BP Tanker Company as managers, due for completion in September 1974.

It had been 20 years previously, in 1954, that London freight brokers working through their Average Freight Rate Assessment Panel (AFRA) determined future professional, business and commercial maritime nomenclature. They divided tankers into a number of fixed statistical categories based upon their freight-carrying capacity, various routes and trades. AFRA used a 'key-stem size' of 400,000 barrels for the economic trading of crude oil and, in early 1974, faced with ships in excess of 300,000-sdwt, they integrated with the word Supertanker the term 'VLCC' – 'Very Large Crude Carrier' – to indicate a vessel between 159,999-sdwt and 319,999-sdwt involved in transporting a minimum of two million barrels. The following May, they devised the expression 'Ultra Large Crude Carriers' (ULCCs) for those behemoths exceeding 320,000-sdwt and carrying over three million barrels. They based the carrying of crude products around much smaller stem sizes. The 'General Purpose' tanker was between 10,000 and 24,999-sdwt – the 'Medium Range' 25,000 to 44,999-sdwt and 'Large Range' covered tankers of capacity between 45,000 and 159,000-sdwt. The London Tanker Brokers' Panel, owning the rights of AFRA, became a registered company in 1983, since when a more flexible market scale has been introduced to work alongside the continuing Fixed Scale.

The most significant and blatantly obvious point to make concerning the new class of tanker concerned their size. A few comparisons helped deepen appreciation of this remark at the time. Canterbury Cathedral remains a prominent building certainly familiar to most people.

The cathedral is 157.6 metres long, 21.3 metres wide and the Nave stands 24.3 metres high. The *British Reliance* was 338.6 (oa) × 53.68 in beam × 26.4 metres moulded depth.

British Petroleum's Supertanker exceeded twice the length of the cathedral, twice the width, and from keel to main deck was only about 3.6 metres short of the height of the nave. The largest tanker ever constructed, the ULCC *Jahre Viking* (now *Knock Nevis*) of 564,739-sdwt of 458 × 68.8 × 29.8 metres – when compared is nearly three times the length and three times the width of the cathedral and would tower over the Nave by some 4.5 metres.

***British Navigator* was typical of this class of Supertanker. Launched in March 1971 for BP Medway, she was completed the following June.** *(The Motor Ship).*

Canterbury Cathedral. (Bill Oates and Judges Cards of Hastings)

British Reliance's cargo capacity was divided into five centre cargo tanks and four wing tanks, with Number Five being the Slop Tank for 'Load on Top' cargo. Both sets of wing tanks were sub-divided into A and B tanks such that Number Two tank consisted of a centre tank equal in capacity to the sum of the wings on either side. Number Two was slightly the largest tank at 62.76 metres in length. When fully laden at the

The ULCC *Jahre Viking* – the largest moving object created by man. The hull effect, on the submerged laden area, is an indication of the successful effect of tin-free hull coatings. (Jotun Paints – Europe)

V.L.C.C's

Yard No.	Shipbuilder	Name	For delivery
1703.	Mitsubishi H.I. Ltd., Nagasaki	*British Renown*	1974
1704.	——0——	*British Resolution*	1974
1705.	——0——	*British Rover*	1973
1706.	——0——	*British Ruler*	1974
1707.	——0——	*Cheverny*	1975
1736.	——0——	*Chambord*	1974
1737.	——0——	*Chinon*	1974
1738.	——0——	*British Resource*	1975
1739.	——0——	*British Reliance*	1975
1740.	——0——	*British Ranger*	1975
1757.	——0——	*Chenonceaux*	1976
1758.	——0——	*Chaumont*	1976
1767.	——0——	*British Realm*	canc
1768.	——0——	*British Restraint*	canc

summer draught mark the freeboard of this Supertanker was 5.7 metres. The fo'c'sle including bulbous bow extended 27.4 metres.

Viewed from the monkey island above the wheelhouse the deck space of any Supertanker was an impressive sight.

The pipes leading fore and aft are the main cargo lines and service pipes, including water and foam lines serving the red-painted fire monitors, diesel and fuel pipes, steam lines and stripping pipes, electrical conduit and exhaust returns. The length of a Supertanker could increase by a surprising half-metre in the Persian Gulf due to temperature increases. To prevent certain lines bursting under this strain a number of pipes were moulded away from the norm in what were called 'Omega' bends. Often expansion joints were fitted into pipe joins as alternatives. Vapour control valves for gas tight Ullage tapes appeared as thin black vertical pipes near the coloured safe walkways on the main deck. The familiar tank top accesses are clearly visible.

The manifold connections to the shore were subject to strict IMCO regulations ensuring safety. VLCCs were Category 'D' tankers within the various statutory codes meaning that a number of reducing pieces were usually necessary to provide oil-tight integrity at connections between main flanges at the manifold points and chiksans leading ashore.

The main deck of any early VLCC always appeared cluttered by an apparent maze of different sized pipes. (Author's Collection).

Modern ship/shore connections make an interesting contrast with those of the *British Duchess* at Stanlow, some 60 years earlier (see page 21) and incorporate today connections for fuel, diesel and lubricating oils.

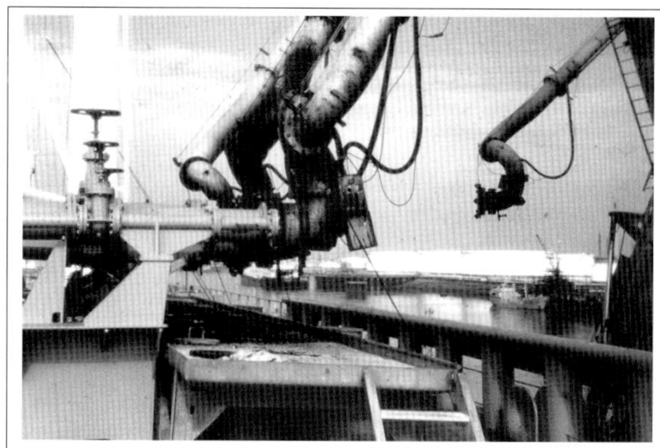

Oil was transferred between ship and shore through cargo manifolds on board and chiksans ashore. (Author's Collection).

The years 1973 and 1974 proved of considerable importance for the international oil markets, the BP Group fleet, and tanker safety. From the 'Oil in Navigable Waters Act' passed by the British government in 1922, to the 1954 London Convention (with its 1962 Amendments), preventing pollution at sea had become a major concern. For example, Zones were established in which it was illegal for tankers to discharge the oily-waste that resulted from cleaning tanks in between cargoes. Unfortunately, the Conventions had not received complete international coverage, but a way forward had already become established that was to prove crucial. In 1948, under United Nations Convention a major organisation, the International Maritime Consultative Organisation (IMCO), had been instituted to improve safety at sea. This organisation imposed regulations introducing far-reaching safety, operational and design measures, to which was added a brief directed at preventing marine oil pollution. Collectively these rules became known as MARPOL73 Protocols – which were revised in the light of experience five years later, accepted eventually by member countries internationally, and referred to colloquially as 'MARPOL73/78'. The 1973 implementation had immediate and far-reaching effects on the tanker industry by making mandatory a series of anti-pollution – and further amendments to the Safety of Life at Sea (or SOLAS) regulations established originally in 1914 following the *Titanic* disaster. Water used for tank-washing is collected in Slop Tanks and when settled is discharged to sea. Oil-water separators monitored the first trace of oil appearing in the discharged ballast, at which stage the operation was stopped. Dirty ballast water was discharged on reaching the loading port, again stopping before oil is seen, the remainder being pumped to the Slop Tanks. The new cargo was then 'loaded on top' of the remains. There was little possibility of pollution between grades of oil because the amounts retained were comparatively small. MARPOL concerns however were not restricted to pollution of the world's oceans from tank cleaning. In December 1969, three explosions had occurred in less than two weeks aboard Supertankers, which subsequent enquiries attributed to the ignition, by a build-up of static electricity, of highly toxic and inflammable hydrocarbon gases within tanks. Loss of life and serious damage had been caused, and in one case one of these large vessels had been sunk.

Two essential Protocols were generally accepted without too much concern – at least by reputable shipowners. Oil companies themselves – headed by BP – had for some years previously investigated the whole process of tank cleaning and then produced arrangements acceptable to MARPOL. The first of these was Crude Oil Washing (COW) in which crude oil from the cargo was used as an agent to clean the tanks themselves, instead of the previous all-water wash. The result was for cleaner tanks and a marked reduction in 'sludge' – or residue remaining at the bottom and sides of tanks following water washing. The second Protocol concerned the use of what was called an 'Inert Gas System' (IGS). The Technical Association of Lloyd's Register, working with shipping companies, had been conducting intensive research since the early 1950s into tank-cleaning processes aboard ship (as opposed to shoreside installations), examining how flue gas from the uptake in a ship's boilers might be used as a neutralising agent for the hydrocarbons remaining in recently cleaned cargo tanks. The safety level was determined by the amount of oxygen permitted to enter any tank so, briefly, a system was needed that would reduce this to a mixture between what was termed a 'lower and upper limit of flammability'. For crude oil, this was between 1 per cent and 9.5 per cent hydrocarbons. BP had played an integral role also in these investigations and introduced an IGS that fulfilled all requirements.

Very briefly, the operation had two major components: to use plant in the engine-room to clean and purify the neutralising agent in non-hazardous conditions, and secondly, to regulate this for distribution in perfect safety to the tanks. For the first part, a remotely operated butterfly valve was fitted to a flue pipe at the base of the funnel that drew off hot exhaust. The flue gases were also wet, dirty, and full of particles of soot and other matter, which required cooling and purifying, so they

The Scrubbing Tower remains an essential component in cleaning flue gases from the boiler before distributing inert gas to the cargo tanks. (FGI Systems Ltd and John Mills - Photographer)

Deck water sea, forward of the accommodation on a VLCC. (Author's Collection)

were led into what was called a Scrubbing Tower.

The water was often seawater taken from an uptake valve in the engine-room. In some systems, a dry seal was used. The inert gas was put under slight pressure and distributed to the tanks by an isolated Inert Gas piping system.

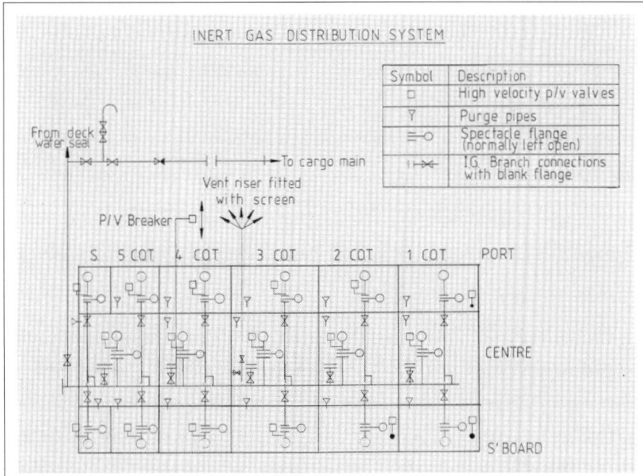

Flow diagram of an Inert Gas System aboard tankers. (Author's Collection, drawn by Paul Taylor)

The refined gas was then led into a fan blower to keep it constant and stable during its onward flow. It was then ready for the more hazardous part of the operation. First, it entered a water deck seal forward of the accommodation whose function was to prevent any back-flow of hydrocarbons from the tanks into the boiler system.

High Velocity Pressure Vacuum Valves fitted to cargo tanks aboard a large tanker. (Author's Collection)

There was an ever-present risk that tanks could become over-pressured and, in order to prevent this, a liquid-filled pressure breaker was introduced aboard large tankers.

The expended inert gas was expelled through purge pipes and exited via a PV (pressure vacuum valve) fitted either on deck, or fed to a vent riser attached to a mast-top. The system was regulated from the cargo

An operational Inert Gas control panel in the cargo office of a large tanker. (Author's collection)

control room and could be monitored from panels in the engine room and wheelhouse. To a lesser extent, IGS helped also to preserve the steel integrity within tanks. Most tankers ran a special IGS generator to provide a 'top-up' supply.

The Inert Gas System proved undoubtedly one of the greatest contributions to tanker safety ever invented and was a regular fitting aboard all BP tankers long before it became mandatory under International Maritime Regulations. Until then some tanker companies merely thought about retrofitting this powerful safety device. Not all ships however were able to conform to these important Protocols due to age or smaller size. To do so would have required major modifications that would have been very expensive and taken up space in already over-subscribed yards.

An Inert Gas monitoring panel in the wheelhouse of a large tanker. (Author's collection)

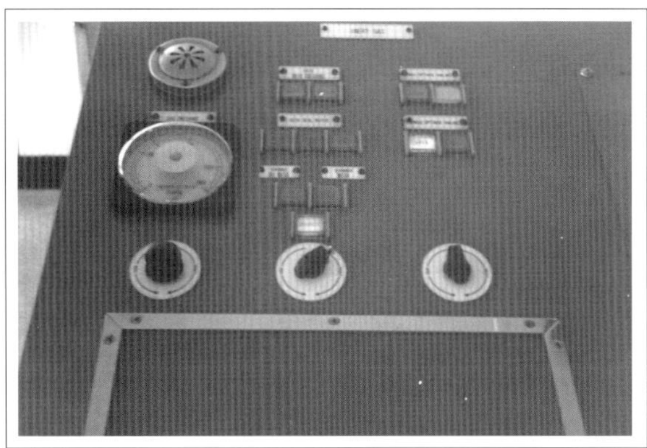

With the establishment of their crude oil fleet replacement BP turned attention to updating their clean-product carriers. This fleet was becoming aged and in need of replacement. A series of sixteen tankers of around 25,000-sdwt were ordered from a range of British and overseas yards, each named after rivers in Great Britain.

The *British Tay* was a typical example of this class of product carriers. She was the third tanker in the series to be completed following the *British Dart* in 1972 and the *British Test* in 1973. Completed by June 1973 from Swedish builders for The BP Tanker Company, she was of 25,650-sdwt, and 171.46 × 25.05 × 9.56 metres. The vessel was fitted with a 'V' or ram bulb to the stem, raked fo'c'sle and transom stern and, with her streamlined accommodation and funnel, she impressed as a trim smart tanker – an effect that was enhanced by the introduction of a conning section projecting forward from the wheelhouse front. *British Humber* completed in 1973 was something of an oddity and was to cause some confusion. Although graced with a river name she was not of the class, but had a superstructure similar to the *British Integrity* type.

Bridge controls are placed within easy reach of the navigating officer. *(The Motor Ship).*

The hull was divided into six Centre tanks comprising unusually two long and four shorter cargo spaces, and sixteen Wings. The pump room was located forward of the engine-room and was fitted with four steam turbine cargo pumps, each with capacity of 750 tonnes/hour. The wheelhouse was fitted with cen-

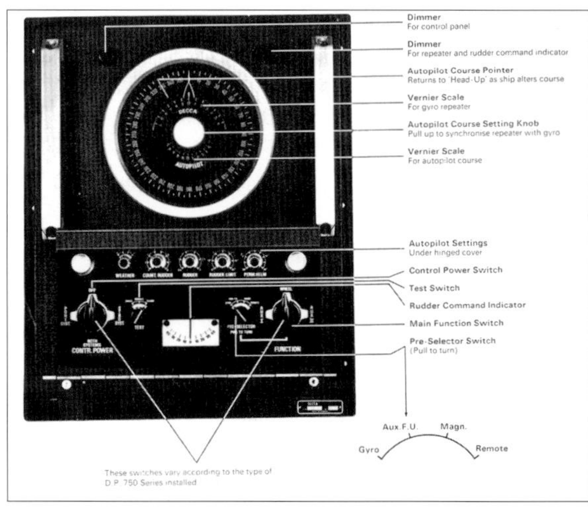

The Decca Arkas 750 range of Automatic Pilot Control aboard the *British Tay* was a standard fitting aboard many BP tankers. (Decca Company)

'RIVER' CLASS REFINED PRODUCTS CARRIERS

Yard No.	*Shipbuilder*	*Name*	*Due*
658	Eriksbergs AB, Gothenburg	*British Dart*	1972
659	——0——	*British Test*	1973
660	——0——	*British Tay*	1973
661	——0——	*British Trent*	1973
675	——0——	*British Wye*	1974
676	——0——	*British Fal*	1974
869	Cockerill Yards, Hoboken	*British Neath*	1974
870	——0——	*British Severn*	1974
724	Scott's S.B.Company, Greenock	*British Avon*	1972
725	——0——	*British Kennet*	1973
726	——0——	*British Tweed*	1973
727	——0——	*British Forth*	1973
1469	Boelwerf, Tamise	*British Tamar*	1973
1470	——0——	*British Esk*	1973
1187	Lithgows Ltd., Port Glasgow	*British Spey*	1974

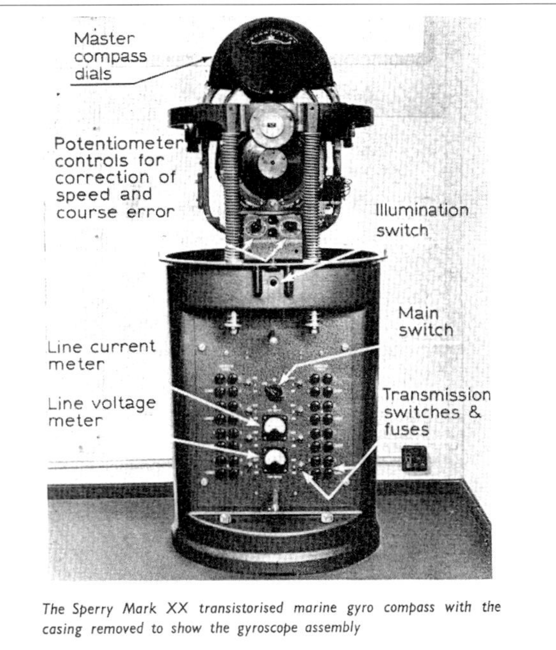

The Sperry Mark XX transistorised marine gyro compass with the casing removed to show the gyroscope assembly

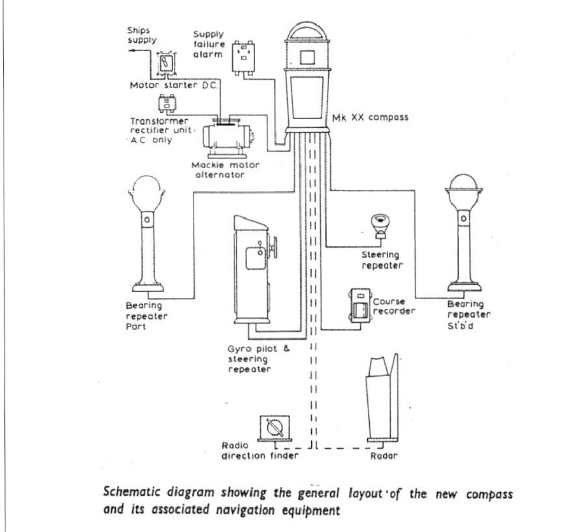

Schematic diagram showing the general layout of the new compass and its associated navigation equipment

The Sperry Mk XX Gyro-System was a popular fitting aboard many tankers in the 1960s. *(Tanker Times)*

tralised bridge equipment placing all controls within easy reach of the navigating officer on watch.

The Decca Company of London provided much of the navigating equipment. Their True Motion TM1629 and Relative Motion RM425 radars served numerous ships of all classes with efficiency and reliability and many others vessels were equipped with their Navigator Mark 12 (and later Mark 21) plus Arkas 750 series automatic pilot that were additional fittings. This latter device enabled the tanker to maintain courses to within a quarter-degree accuracy in conditions often of quite severe weather. It was fitted with an adjustable off-course alarm that emitted a strident ring if the parameters set were exceeded.

Similar models were extensively fitted even to the largest VLCCs in the fleet. The autopilot enabled hand steering to be used when necessary, but permitted minor alterations of course by moving the Autopilot Course Setting Knob to port or starboard as required. It was astounding to realise that a Supertanker exceeding 1,000 feet in length could be steered merely by moving a small button.

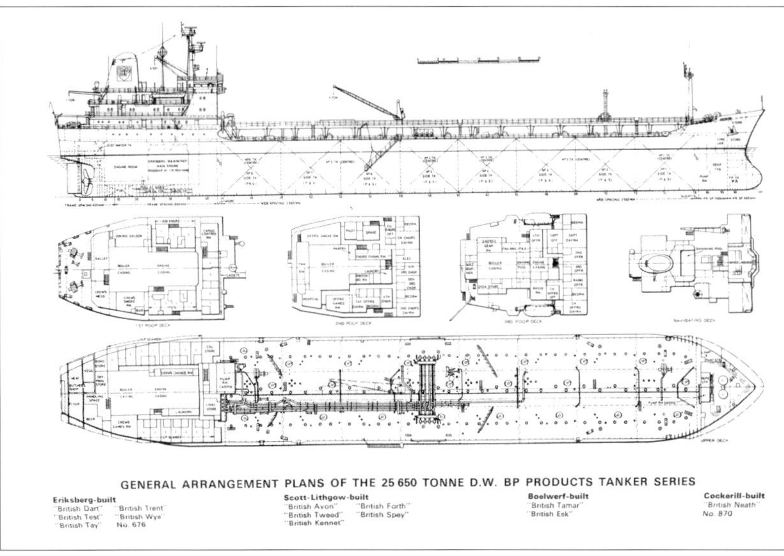

General arrangement plan of the *British Tay*. *(The Motor Ship)*

In an advance that was still comparatively rare aboard ships at the time, the main engine was controlled directly from the telegraph lever. Control changeover switches and engine-room alarms with an engineer call-out system were also available. The steering gear fitted was a Hastie four-ram electro-hydraulic type. A Walker speed log and Marconi Lodestone 11D direction finder completed a navigating area second to none for a ship of this classification. The Kent screen had been replaced by high-powered windscreen wipers aboard this class of tanker.

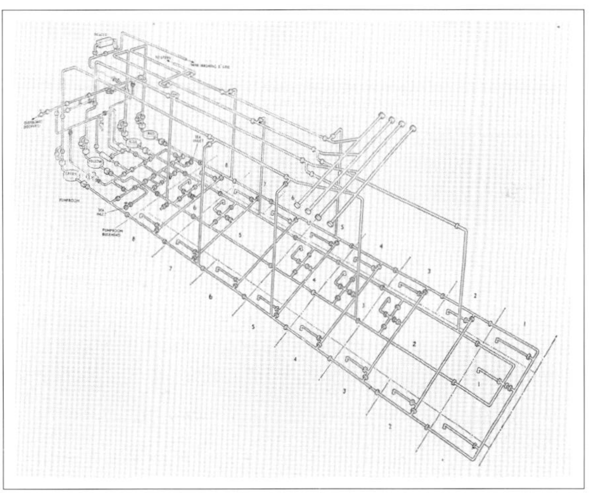

The cargo-piping diagram of the *British Tay*. *(The Motor Ship).*

The cargo control system aboard the *British Tay* was fitted with hydraulic valves operated from a console that housed stop/start and speed controls for cargo pumps. The stripping system used to drain the final drops of the cargo from low fitting suctions at the tank bottom was independently controlled. The main cargo lines were 12-inch diameter for loading and a mixture of 14-inch diameter ring mains, having 12-inch suctions and 14-inch crossover and isolating valves for discharging. A mimic diagram in the Cargo Control Office showed the state of all controls and valves aboard the ship and was fitted with malfunction alarms. Cargo piping was of the modified ring system previously encountered with this design incorporating the double ring suction with centre and stern discharge lines.

It was standard BP company practice by this time

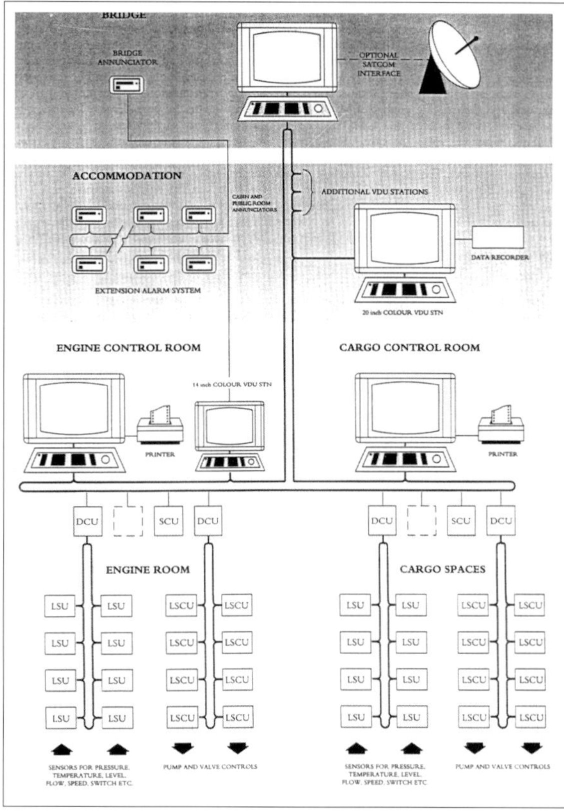

Typical configuration in the ISIS 300 Alarm and Monitoring System. (Racal-Decca)

that each cargo pump and its associated suction and discharge lines were identified by a colour code system. All valves and lines were painted in red, blue, green or yellow as required. The idea proved extremely useful during cargo operations when all assistance was acceptable. It was particularly helpful in relieving stress on the duty officers during 'stepping down tanks' toward the end of loading or discharging.

The engine-room aboard the *British Tay* was equipped with a low-powered Swedish diesel engine of six-cylinders developing 9,000 bhp at 119 rpm giving a service speed of 14 knots. The control station was air-conditioned and soundproofed and fitted with a Racal-Decca ISIS 300 monitoring and alarm system covering 140 points.

Such comprehensive coverage was offered through separate loops, each with its own data capture unit (DCU) that governed the area under surveillance. An additional sequence control unit (SCU) monitored the operation of the DCUs and provided a series of specialised functions including running hours of the machine concerned, blackout recovery, tank content calculations and tasks. A channelled alarm unit (LSCU) collected data via the loop concerned and sent this to the workstation involved. ISIS 300 represented a highly sophisticated alarm and monitoring system.

A Brotherhood Company steam turbine coupled to an alternating current generator met electrical power requirements aboard *British Tay*. The diesel propulsion machinery utilised waste heat for power generation, assisting greater operating economy. *Motor Ship* magazine complimented the owners for providing officer and crew quarters of a very high standard: 'Accommodation for the master, radio officer and four deck officers is provided on the third poop deck with the master and first officer each having a separate suite of four rooms comprising, bedroom, dayroom, bathroom and an office. All accommodation in the vessel is attractively furnished and air-conditioned and most of the rooms are carpeted. Cabins for engineering officers (including a four-room suite for the chief engineer and a three-roomed suite for the second) are located on the second poop deck.' The four cadets carried were accommodated on the second poop deck near the Cargo Control Room. Unusual in those days, they were given the untold luxury of individual cabins, their own toilet and wash area, and a large study. The modern galley and the swimming pool contributed towards crew welfare.

A 'mimic' diagram in the Cargo Control Room shows the relative position of all cargo and ballast valves, together with tank pressures and controls. (*Author's collection*)

Periods of Difficulty *Chapter Nine*

British Norness. (Airfoto Malacca)

IN JUNE 1973, OPEC raised the price of crude oil to unprecedented levels. The increase from US$2.90 to US$11.65 a barrel was completely unexpected and caught the western world by surprise. At a time when the demand for oil was also unexpectedly high this move was a devastating blow. The immediate effect was a massive increase in oil prices covering existing power contracts and at the pumps, which inevitably led to an initial sharp reduction in demand. A severe international economic depression ensued that affected directly every company engaged in oil transportation throughout the world.

By this time, BP was well advanced with their new construction programme. The 'River' class product carriers were coming into service as scheduled, but the proposed fleet of Supertankers experienced profoundly adverse effects. The existing fleet was gradually laid-up, whilst others went from completion into redundancy. The largest BP VLCC, for example, the *British Respect* went immediately following delivery, in September 1974, to Brunei Bay where within four years a further five company Supertankers were mothballed. The *British Resolution* was used as a storage vessel, whilst a number of smaller dirty-trade tankers saw lay-up periods in various UK Rivers and ports.

With so much at stake, moves were initiated to try to re-negotiate the fourteen VLCC contracts with Mitsubishi Heavy Industries. Unfortunately there was little success in agreeing cancellation terms, without incurring major financial penalties. The one success however was the sale of the contract for Yard No. 1707 (*Cheverny*) at an early stage of construction to other French buyers who renamed her *Onyx*. Talks were then opened with several other financial and shipping organisations that proved more fruitful. The end result was that the contracts for Yard Numbers 1705 and 1706 proposed as *British Rover* and *British Ruler*, were completed as *British Norness* and *British Trident* respectively, and taken on a 15-year back-charter from P&O.

The building of 1705 was given precedence over 1703 and 1704 whose constructions were slowed permitting a delay in stage payments to the builder. Another four orders were transferred to newly formed single-ship operating companies that reduced the overall capital burden. Airlease International Nominees, the new contract owners for Yard Numbers 1767 and 1768, proposed as *British Realm* and *British Restraint*, had discussed with the company concerning whether or not they would actually require them and as a result approached Mitsubishi H.I. with a package proposal. Having reached an 'agreement in principle', with the Liverpool based Ocean Transport & Trading Company Limited; Airlease International negotiated the conversion of the two VLCCs into four smaller contracts for a series of multi-purpose combination cargo ships (Combo's) for lease to the Blue Funnel Line. The agreement was ratified by all parties and the ships were built with the traditional names of *Memnon*, *Menestheus*, *Menelaus* and *Melampus*.

The situation concerning the world's tanker fleets soon became one of devastation. By 1975, brokers estimated some 466 tankers representing 37 million tons were laid-up. Rafts of Supertankers belonging to owners world-wide, lashed alongside each other bow to stern, became a common sight in deep-water sheltered anchorages across the globe, whilst orders covering 174 tankers of 41 million tons received notices of cancellation. A further 219 tankers of 6.2 million tons were scrapped which at least had the effect of 'weeding out' some of the older tonnage. All classes and ranges of AFRA tanker-tonnage became affected.

This period represented very much a black time in the Company's fortunes that was not helped by a decision from the Kuwaiti Government to commandeer 60 per cent of the Kuwait Oil Company in 1973 – returning for the remaining 40 per cent the following year. Initially, they refused to pay BP compensation but eventually in December 1975, following 'tentative negotiations', $50 million was paid to BP and the other

***Menestheus* in the Straits of Malacca – one of four sister-ships operated by Blue Funnel Line of Liverpool, and built in lieu of two BP 'R' class VLCCs.** (World Ship Society Photograph Library)

IRANO – BRITISH SHIPPING COMPANY LTD.
(Irano – British Ship Service Company Ltd., managers)

V.L.C.C's.

British Explorer	1976 -1981 then sold for demolition.
British Pioneer	1976 -1981 then sold for further trading.
*British Prospector**	1976 -1979 then sold for further trading.
*British Inventor**	1976 -1981 then sold for demolition.
Susangird	ex *British Pride* 76
Sivand	ex *British Navigator* 76(*Semnan* proposed name)
Shoush	ex *British Surveyor* 76
Sanandaj	ex *British Promise* 76

* It had also been planned that *British Prospector* and *British Inventor* would both be sold to the National Iranian Tanker Company, and to have been renamed *Shadgan* and *Geshm* respectively, but this part of the transaction was not concluded.

River Class clean-product tankers.

British Dart	removed from management 1979.
British Test	removed from management 1979.
British Wye	removed from management 1979.
Minab	ex *British Fal* 76
Mokkran	ex *British Neath* 76
Marun	ex *British Severn* 76

Chartered units

V.L.C.C's

British Renown
British Trident

River Class

British Trent
British Tay

company involved, Gulf Oil Corporation. Inevitably, BP directors were forced once more into making hard decisions at a time when clear-minded planning could have been hindered by the turmoil.

The end of December 1975 saw the fruits of management deliberations that resulted in a major restructuring of the Company fleet. Tankers were to be segregated into three sectors:

The crude oil fleet would consist of twenty-nine vessels.

The clean products fleet of thirty-five tankers – and –

A third part, referred to as 'The 'I' Fleet', would consist of up to sixteen tankers equally divided between crude and clean vessels.

Between twenty and twenty-five older tankers were appointed for demolition. The management of Lowland Tankers was taken over from Common Brothers, whilst Shell-Mex & BP Limited managing most coastal tankers was dissolved and the ships either distributed between the two companies or sold. Those coasters taken-over by BP were allocated to BP Oil Limited. The company also disposed of some Norwegian interests to their government for £27 million, although this did not include BP's investment in the Norwegian sector of the North Sea.

British Dart at Rotterdam October 1975 wearing Irano-British Shipping Company funnel. (World Ship Society Photograph Library)

BP management has to be complimented on its directors' perspicacity before and during this difficult period. Since the mid-1960s, the company had been forecasting future developments across a range of alternative industries and, without possessing 'second sight' or 'divine inspiration', had consolidated some attractive investments. By the end of the 1970s interests had been acquired in the rapidly expanding information technology industry; the Company were the second largest chemicals organisation in the world, including other expanding interests of plastics and solvents; had diversified into animal breeding, animal feed, and consumer goods, as well as entering the minerals and coal businesses. A further investment also paid dividends in 1975 when their explorations of five years previously in the North Sea oil business came to fruition with the first production from the Forties Field. At its peak, Forties would produce 500,000 barrels a day and meet around 25 per cent of the UK's daily oil demands. As output from the field stabilised this was to have a profound international effect. BP became a major oil producer denting considerably the company's independence upon OPEC oil.

The Suez Canal was re-opened around 1975/6 but now restrictions existed as it had the capacity only for smaller draught ships due to the on-going processes of wreck removal. Plans were also implemented to deepen and widen this important waterway facilitating larger capacity ships of all trading classes. The potential implementation of this move led to a modest revival in tanker trading for AFRA-class general and some medium range sizes.

At about the same time as the Kuwaiti nationalisation, the Iranian government was examining also the viability of flexing its muscles. They had recently formed the National Iranian Tanker Company (NITCO).

A co-operative agreement was quickly negotiated that resulted in the Irano-British Shipping Company Limited becoming a 50:50 concern between BP and Iran. Irano-British would operate tankers on behalf of the two owners accounting for the third (or 'I fleet') part of the Company's earlier restructuring plans. A number of additional BP ships would also be chartered to the new owners. However, following applied pressures a number of the BP tankers designated to the I-fleet were sold to NITCO and re-named, with even more BP vessels operating within the pool-fleet, wearing new funnel markings.

The BP tanker fleet was by this time reduced to around fifty-seven owned and managed tankers.

Another aspect of transportation developed with the advent of Supertankers. It was impossible for some ports to accept deeper draught vessels. Very often the approaches to major European oil refineries necessitated navigation of the Dover Strait, which had shallow water restrictions to fully-laden tankers drawing perhaps in excess of 80 feet. Some tankers off-loaded part cargo to fixed Single Buoy Moorings (SBM) situated in sheltered places such as Sete in the Gulf of Lyon, or partially discharged at Cap D'Antifer, but frequently some crude was off-loaded into a smaller tanker. The process was known as a 'lightening operation' and frequently occurred in a sheltered anchorage, such as Lyme Bay, off Berry head, in the United Kingdom. The process was conducted under the close supervision of IMO Regulations to ensure safe transfer, reducing risks of pollution and random sparking, and was of necessity taken at a leisurely pace. Both ships were initially under way on parallel courses and low speeds of around 4 knots – determined beforehand by radio communication. The smaller tanker (2) with her superior manoeuvrability came alongside the VLCC (1) and they both made fast, after which the Supertanker anchored. From initial VHF contact, until both tankers were in position and alongside, could take around three hours.

BP Shipping converted *British Dragoon* specifically for this operation by fitting her with four Swettenham fenders along her port side. These were foam filled and measured approximately 4.5 metres in length and 3.3 metres diameter, suspended on specially constructed davits, but lowered and raised in a manner similar to lifeboats. The pipeline of the off-lightening tanker was connected to runners of the VLCC to keep pipes off the rails purely to prevent damage, as the ships would be operating inert gas systems. The Supertanker's pumps were used and, after gradual working-up, ran at around 5,000 tons/hour. Once commenced, the operation could take a further 11 hours to complete.

1979 was another year heralding deeper involvements between BP and international world affairs. Ayatollah Khomeini inspired the Iranian Revolution, which was followed by the Iran-Iraq Gulf War of 1980. This further strained the still tenuous relationships between BP and the recently-formed shipping companies. The agreement was finally dissolved in 1981 following which the remaining three BP-owned VLCCs were scrapped. Meanwhile in Africa, Nigeria unilaterally nationalised the extensive BP holdings in their country allegedly in retaliation for BP's sale of oil to South Africa. These two events effectively resulted in a reduction of BP's oil supply by around 40 per cent. This inevitably meant a cut by BP in deliveries to their customers resulting in a further international oil crisis.

1981 was another significant year in which BP company history directly affected their tanker fleet. Mr P I Walters who had taken the initiative so effectively at the beginning of the 1967 Suez crisis was appointed Chairman of BP. He had subsequently been instrumental in a number of successful policy decisions and, with his overview of the Company's fortunes, decided a de-centralisation would better serve their wider interests. Accordingly, he re-organised BP into a number of self-supporting and self-financing companies that would be more flexible in responding to market trends. The BP Tanker Company Limited was renamed BP Shipping Limited, with the fleet retaining the house-flag and funnel colours held since 1967. The company would have responsibilities other than for their by now reduced fleet of fifty-two owned and managed turbine and diesel-powered tankers.

British Test (above) and _British Wye_ (below) arriving at Portsmouth 12 July 1986 both wearing Irano-British Shipping Company funnel. (Both World Ship Society Photograph Library)

Policies of financial independence led to a closer study of all aspects of maritime operations. Ship and engine performances, for instance, resulted in investigations that led to a series of minor design changes. The July 1981 issue of *Motor Ship* explained some of the savings BP deemed achievable: 'At a recent seminar organised by the City of London Polytechnic on aspects of bunkering conservation, officials from the company's fleet operations division told how a 70,000-sdwt motor tanker could save 700 tonnes of bunkers annually for an initial outlay of £23,000, or how a 225,000-sdwt VLCC could reduce its annual bunker consumption by 2,740 tonnes for an initial expenditure of £58,000'. It was a programme containing some eye-opening practical statistics. Turning off the main engine-room lighting during periods of unmanned operation could save £3,450 per annum; turning the galley cooking range off instead of down, and reducing wastage from lights left on in unoccupied storerooms and cabins could save around £1,785 annually. Other savings were also investigated including the prevention of compressed air and steam leakage, especially along deck lines and steam traps. Simultaneously, developments were reviewed arising from an experiment 10 years previously in which glass reinforced plastic (GRP) pipes had been fitted in the cargo lines of the 1969, 25,000-sdwt products tanker *British Fidelity*.

These had been designed by Redland Reinforced Plastics near Poole in Dorset and had proved so successful that this specially designed marine pipe was

British Dragoon after conversion. (World Ship Society Photograph Library)

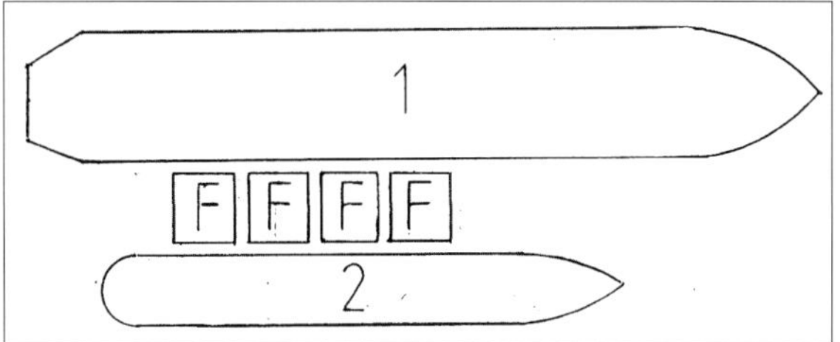

Both tankers in position to take moorings and commence lightening . . . using derricks of both ships for safety. (Paul Taylor and Author's Collection).

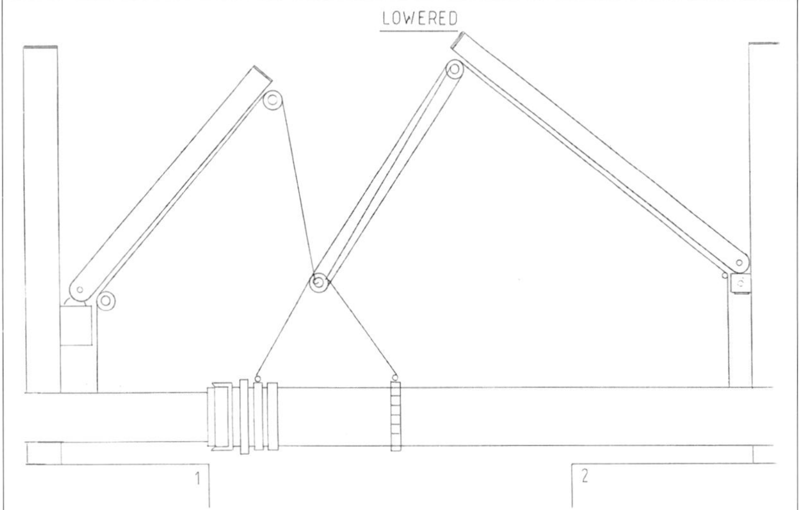

Glass Reinforced Plastic (GRP) water ballast piping fitted aboard the *British Fidelity*. *(The Motor Ship).*

retrofitted to five more BP products carriers of the 'River' class, as well as the VLCCs *British Promise* and *British Explorer.* Three former BP tankers owned now by National Iranian Tankers, the *Marun*, *Sivand* and *Shoush* had also been similarly equipped with 'Fibamar Pipes' – to use the term under which these were marketed. Lloyd's Register, amongst other classification societies, had approved the use of GRP for both cargo and ballast pipes. The *Motor Ship* commented: 'Fibamar pipes will easily outlast steel or iron pipe work, particularly since their corrosion resistant properties are first-class.' In the light of this latter comment, it was only to be a matter of time before pipes used in IG systems were integrated. Survey and test results were, however, regarded by some officers in the company with a certain foreboding. The wider moves were seen as very much 'the thin end of a financial wedge' that indicated portends of future policies in which accountants might become more directly involved in the practicalities of taking tankers to sea.

A far greater and more realistic threat to BP's continuity of fleet operations occurred in 1982 with Argentina's invasion of the Falkland Islands, launching the greatest invasion fleet since 1944. Ironically, the English Tourist Board had designated this particular year 'Maritime England 1982' in celebration of Britain's nautical history. The ramifications for BP Shipping were profound. The government still retained a large shareholding in the company and called for a lion's share of their fleet of product carriers to support the conflict. In the name of 'national emergency', existing commitments were overridden and most of the 'River' class tankers were chartered for service upon completion of their respective voyages. The following table indicates the dates and places from where commercial voyages were terminated:

Requisitioning effectively reduced the company's fleet but as often happens in 'the affairs of men', the move coincided with a lull in market demand for oil so did not prove too commercially or ethically disastrous. Some tankers such as the *British Dart* transported high-octane aviation fuel, but many of the tankers were used to carry oil and lubricants.

Tankers requisitioned for Operational Military Use in the Falklands War

British Tay	5.4.1982	Swansea
British Tamar	7.4.1982	Grangemouth
British Esk	7.4.1982	Hamburg
British Dart	9.4.1982	Gibraltar
British Test	9.4.1982	Gibraltar
British Trent	12.4.1982	Enroute to Lavera, France
British Avon	17.4.1982	Puerto Foxi, Mediterranean
British Wye	19.4.1982	Cristobal
British Forth	25.6.1982	Tyneside
British Vine	1.7.1982	Swansea

British Ivy, *British Fern* } were both voyage chartered for the U.K.coastwise movement of fuel

The *British Trent* had recently served with the Fleet on a NATO exercise in the North Atlantic, acting as a RAS tanker to the Royal Navy, so was already appropriately equipped to continue serving in this role. Company tankers served with considerable distinction throughout this campaign, and Masters were awarded commendations from admirals serving as chiefs-of-staff together with appropriate plaques.

Crews were awarded the South Atlantic campaign medal. The Falklands deployment was to last for a number of years after the Islands had been liberated. This was largely as a 'holding operation', but one continuing to require much logistical support.

Meanwhile, the international situation affecting oil transportation was again experiencing a number of external influences. The Iran-Iraq conflict in the Gulf continued unabated. Israel invaded the Lebanon also in June 1982, but efforts of OPEC to impose a further embargo were not sustained largely due to fears of falling oil sales. To exacerbate the situation, the Soviet Union was exporting oil at prices that undercut all other suppliers – including BP. There were, however, a few hopeful signs, for exports from the British Sector of the North Sea in that year exceeded the combined output of Algeria, Libya and Nigeria. Collectively, these moves from outside the Gulf forced OPEC into making further substantial price reductions, even though Saudi Arabia held their own independent brief. By the end of 1983, the Company had lost 40 per cent of its guaranteed supply since Nigerian nationalisation and the Gulf conflict, additional to losses in Kuwait, Iraq and Libya.

BP had two VLCCs damaged during the latter stages of the Iran-Iraq War. In July 1984, the Supertanker *British Renown* experienced a rocket attack by aircraft, although the damage was negligible – after a fire forward was extinguished. *British Respect* was also attacked, again by Iraqi aircraft, in December 1987 but with little structural or tank damage. A number of Supertankers and product carriers transferred to the National Iranian tanker company also suffered varying degrees of damage.

October 1984 finally saw full implementation of Protocols under MARPOL73/78 Regulations briefly examined in the previous chapter. That it had taken so long arose from a number of reasons. The various Definitions, Annexes, Protocols and Regulations were extremely complicated and, because legislation was involved at every stage, thorough examination was essential. A few problems arose in obtaining international agreement to all measures between individual member nations of IMCO. Member tanker owners had to be given sufficient interval to convert or retrofit their existing vessels with the IG or COW systems, and to prepare plans for new-buildings, which incorporated the various Regulations within ANNEX One concerned with preventing pollution of the world's seas by oil. As a shipboard safety measure existing tankers exceeding 70,000-sdwt, for instance, had to be fitted with IGS by 1 May 1983 at the latest. An examination of the pipe diagrams shown in earlier chapters indicates that ballast had to be pumped into designated cargo tanks using cargo lines. MARPOL 73/78 altered this system by insisting that segregated ballast pumps, valves and lines had to be installed aboard crude oil vessels exceeding 20,000-sdwt and product carriers over 30,000-sdwt. Agencies associated with tanker operation also required time to implement those areas of MARPOL relevant to their operation. Shore installations, for instance, had to build and generate facilities necessary to receive dirty ballast water from the Slop tanks of tankers.

In December 1984, the Sullom Voe oil terminal in the Shetland Isles commenced operations. It had been commissioned just one year previously and the 100-acre site was built and operated by BP at a cost of £1,175 million. It received through the Brent and Ninian pipelines the production of eleven oilfields in the east Shetlands and served as a base for loading the 1.41 million barrel daily output into tankers of the 100,000-sdwt range. Working from the Companies control and experimental centre at Sunbury-on-Thames, great efforts had been made to ensure Sullom Voe was environmentally friendly. From their vast resources the Company created an oil pollution response unit, which more than justified its financial expense when the 85,000-sdwt *Braer* stranded in February 1993. On that occasion BP provided a technical support team that assisted the Shetland Islands Council and local Coastguard units.

The main BP shipping fleet during 1983 saw delivery of two tankers, followed by a third the following year. All three had been ordered originally by BP Thames Tanker Company and were transferred upon completion. An additional vessel of similar class, the *BP Achiever* had been launched previously in March 1983 for Thames Tankers from Swan, Hunter's yard. Upon completion, she was handed over to Associated Steamships of Australia for management. This tanker was the last construction ordered from this famous British yard for BP Shipping. The move broke a tradition that had commenced in 1917 with the launch of *British Empress* and *British Admiral.* The two new ships were medium class tankers, around 127,800-sdwt – that represented 109,000-sdwt on a 15.25-metre draught. They were designed for crude oil carriage as well as refined products – particularly naptha and heating oils. The second vessel to be delivered was *British Skill,* a second ship to bear this name. She was 261 metres length overall (250 metres bp) 39.60 metres beam and 23.10 metres depth. During trials, she achieved 15 knots, but her service speed was 13.7 knots. She came from Harland & Wolff's Belfast yard, who supplied also her 16,250 bhp engine. Her maiden voyage was to carry crude oil from Sullom Voe to Wilhelmshaven after which she entered BP's Arabian Gulf/Australian service. She was of all-welded construction with a raked stem, ram bow and mariner-type stern.

British Skill was representative of the new class built to MARPOL specifications. She therefore incorporated a number of refinements in design new to the BP fleet. A close study of her general arrangement plan depicts many of the previously examined technical

General arrangement plan of the *British Skill.* *(The Motor Ship).*

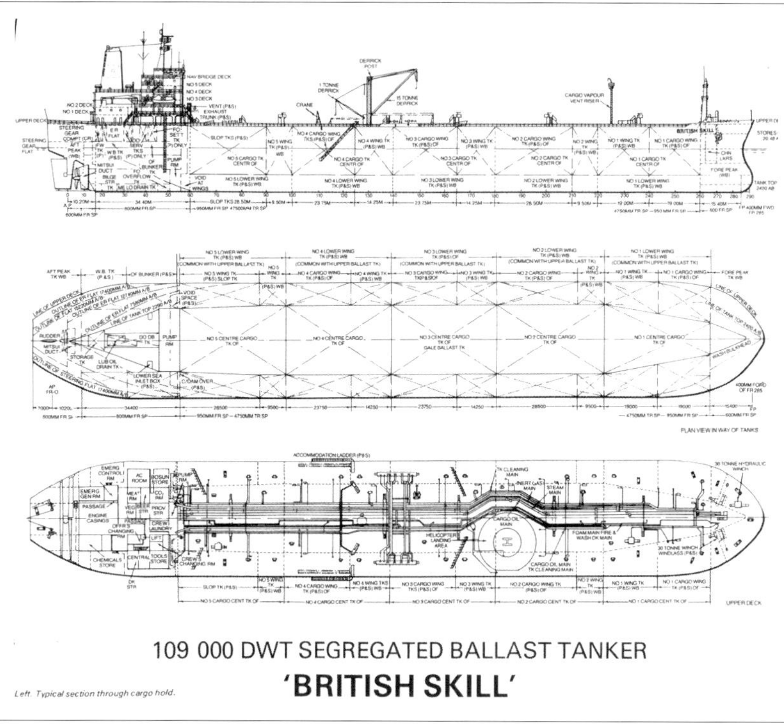

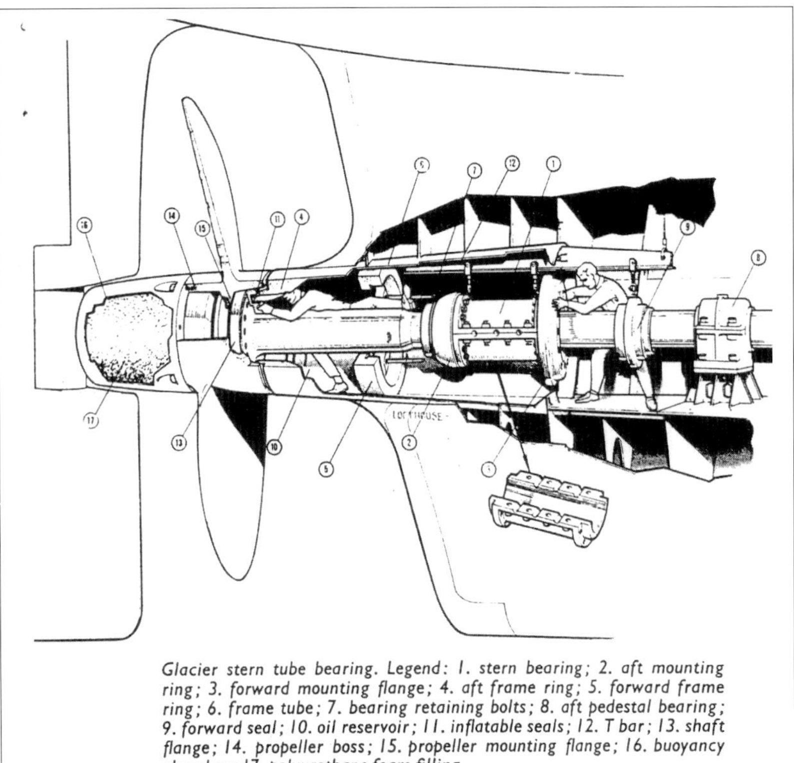

Glacier stern tube bearing. Legend: 1. stern bearing; 2. aft mounting ring; 3. forward mounting flange; 4. aft frame ring; 5. forward frame ring; 6. frame tube; 7. bearing retaining bolts; 8. aft pedestal bearing; 9. forward seal; 10. oil reservoir; 11. inflatable seals; 12. T bar; 13. shaft flange; 14. propeller boss; 15. propeller mounting flange; 16. buoyancy chamber; 17. polyurethane foam filling

The diagram showing propeller arrangements, propeller-shaft maintenance and packing. *(Tanker Times)*

functions incorporated within BP tanker development, as innovations and improvements were implemented over previous years. These show a few service deck pipes but, more importantly, indications of arrangements of the IG lines and risers – to name just two. Structurally, the two longitudinal bulkheads were extended through the engine-room to form wing fuel and ballast tanks. A member of the *Motor Ship*'s technical staff invited to inspect this ship prior to launching commented: 'Water ballast is carried in five lower port and starboard wing tanks and five L shaped tanks, built to a patented BP design; the latter are similar to cofferdams between each cargo tank.'

For the first time, cargo was carried only in part of each wing tank, whilst the remaining section was reserved for water ballast. The ballast tanks were served by their own pipe, pump and valve system complying with Segregated Ballast Tank (SBT) rulings. Ballast remains essential for a number of reasons. Any ship without cargo is light in the water causing her to bounce along the top of the waves. Seawater is an obvious choice for bringing her down around the boot-topping mark along the lower hull and submerging her propeller and bulb of the bow. This helps the ship to slice through the waves, making handling easier and, equally as importantly, to reduce hull stress. In exceptionally heavy weather, it is always advisable to lower the centre of gravity. With this in mind, Number Three centre tank on the *British Skill* was capable of being flooded to act as an additional ballast tank on those occasions when the Master deemed such a drastic move necessary.

The propulsion of this tanker also incorporated some original designs. She was the first British tanker to have a Mitsui integrated propeller duct to enhance propulsion, fitted slightly forward of the propeller. The Mitsui duct increased propulsive efficiency considerably. As *Motor Ship* commented: 'Fuel savings amounting to 5–6 per cent have been claimed for the duct, and BP is monitoring its performance to judge whether retro fitting on other vessels would be economically beneficial.'

A typical pump room. Graphic monitoring and valve operating board fitted aboard many large tankers of this period. (Author's collection).

Stern arrangements of *British Skill* showing the Mitsui duct forward of the propeller and part of the spade rudder. *(The Motor Ship)*

Amongst other details of interest, this tanker was fitted with Redland's GRP pipes on cargo and ballast lines, with hydraulic deck valves supplementing cargo control room pumps and pump-room valves.

Japanese manufacturers also supplied centrifugal pumps – four covering cargo control, two for ballast, and one serving the stripping line. Above a mariner type stern frame, a semi-balanced rudder was fitted that was powered by a Hastie steering gear. The helicopter landing area on the foredeck followed from experiments undertaken as long ago as September 1968 when operations involving the *British Guardsman*, off the UK coast, proved the efficacy of this method to land stores and personnel. Helicopters were to play a major part in supplying all classes of BP tankers off Cape Town and transferring pilots at Europoort and other anchorages. The *British Comet* was the first BP tanker to receive mail and stores whilst on passage off Cape Town the same year.

It was in 1986 that the Company 'flagged out' the fleet. Effectively, they ceased to directly employ officers and ratings, but recruited them instead through a system of offshore agencies. To their ex-employees the decision in practical terms meant, in the early years, end of a previously established career pattern with regular contracts of employment, implying termination of their jobs when Ship's Articles were closed. The move, perhaps not surprisingly, led to an immediate feeling of insecurity on the part of loyal sea staff that was accompanied by a sense that their Company had let them down very badly.

In the commercial and political fields, a number of events occurred during the 1980s that influenced ownership and management of the fleet. The Conservative government of Margaret Thatcher began an extensive programme of privatisation of major nationalised industries. The Government sold their shares in BP over two batches, the first in 1986 and the second a year later, effectively terminating a holding that had existed since the formation of the company in 1915. For some who regarded BP, railways, heavy industry, coal, steel, shipbuilding and railways as major assets, it was a black period for the country. BP continued to trade in areas other than oil, buying and selling a range of commodities. In the oil industry during 1987 the company purchased the remaining 45 per cent share they had held for some years in Standard Oil of Ohio. This created BP America, making the Group the third largest oil company in the world. They also acquired BRITOIL plc – formerly the British National Oil Corporation – heavily involved in exploration and production of resources, particularly in the North Sea, strengthening the Company's position as a dominant gas and oil producer. In 1989, BP Oil Ltd launched a new corporate identity that had extensive repercussions world-wide. The new company was termed BP Oil UK Ltd incorporating an internationally logo on service stations, other holdings and, particularly, the colours of the fleet. A new design of BP Shield was the central theme:

BP was now a privatised independent enterprise that was expanding globally.

A major event occurred in 1989 that was nothing at all to do with BP, but whose ramifications were to have profound influence on future ship construction and affect the world's tanker fleet. The *Exxon Valdez*, a VLCC of 211,470-sdwt built in 1986, had loaded a full cargo of crude oil from the refinery in Prince William Sound, Alaska on 24 March.

She then grounded on Bligh Reef after dropping the pilot, and ruptured her Number One centre and starboard wing tanks. Some 50,000 tonnes, or around a quarter-of-a-million barrels, of oil escaped into the sea and whilst this represented less than fifth of her cargo the resulting slick was some 40 miles in length and about half-a-mile wide. The oil contaminated around 10,000 square miles of sea and coastline causing considerable environment damage. Tough and compulsory legislation was rightly introduced by the United States government that resulted in August of the following year (an amazingly prompt and decisive response less than nine months after the incident) which led to the Oil Pollution Act 1990, known throughout the shipping industry as 'OPA90'. The legal intricacies of this legislation were extremely complex and very wide ranging. Rules 9.3 and 9.4 made it mandatory that all tankers who wished to trade oil with the United States had to be hull protected against spillage due to collision or grounding. Briefly, any tanker ordered after 30 June 1990, or delivered after 1 January 1994, had to be constructed with double-bottoms and sides. The legislation was non-discriminatory, leading Mr A G Gavin, Principal Surveyor with Lloyd's Register and an internationally respected authority on matters pertaining to VLCCs, to point out in a technical paper published during 1994/5: 'The new legislation for double hulled tankers does not take account of the tanker operator with a high safety and maintenance record. All owners/operators will be bracketed together and forced to comply if their ships trade with the US.'

The VLCC *Exxon Valdez* under the name *Exxon Mediterranean* – (World Ship Society Photograph Library)

Working groups were instituted by the International Maritime Organisation (IMO) that included ship-owners of all maritime nations, together with all of the major professional organisations, whose collective findings largely supported IMO. In March 1992, new Amendments 13E, 13F and 13G were made to Annex 1 of MARPOL73/78. These Rulings insisted that all tankers exceeding 600-sdwt had to be constructed with a double hull. The ramifications did not stop there for, shortly afterwards, an 'Exxon Drug and Alcohol Clause' began to appear in Charter Party Agreements. The IMO Amendments relating to ship construction were very relevant, leading ship-owners to plan a new class of vessel. This was initiated from guidelines published by the Oil Companies International Maritime Forum (OCIMF) in 1991. The outcome, for marine personnel, led virtually all ship-owners (including BP) to screen officers and crews for drug and alcohol abuse.

Three tankers joined the main fleet after a five-year void between 1985 and 1990 during which there were no new buildings. These were around 40,000-sdwt class vessels ordered from Mitsubishi: the *BP Admiral* and *BP Adventurer,*

Funnel and House flag 1988 to 1992.

launched in February and April 1990 respectively and completed in September and December of that year. The following year *BP Argosy* followed from the same Japanese yard. The state of the fleet in 1990 consisted of 30 tankers owned or managed by the BP Group including six 'River' class registered in Bermuda, and six 'R' class VLCCs. The three tankers were designed specifically for the products trade (although of course fully adaptable for carrying crude) and represented by far the most financially and technically sophisticated tankers ever ordered by the Company. They were fabricated completely from mild steel with no high tensile steel components being used. The six-cylinder engine developed 7,000 bhp at 90 rpm at maximum rating, and 6,300 bhp at 87 rpm, with a fuel consumption of 21 tonnes at 14.3 knots – or 19 tonnes at 14 knots. The ship had a specially adapted under water hull form and was fitted with a fin near her propeller that improved propulsive efficiency. Fully-segregated water ballast tanks included the forepeak, ten wings and two slop tanks, with heavier scantlings than those prescribed as minimum by the classification society. Virtually complete collision protection was provided for the eight cargo tanks, which were separated by two longitudinal bulkheads. Two-valve segregation between the pipelines facilitated carriage of up to four grades of oil. Cargo control was of the latest design incorporating a computer controlled automatic pump system that improved port turn-round time and reduced workloads for the officers on board. The four steam-driven centrifugal cargo pumps each had capacity of 800 m^3 at 150 tonnes/hour. Each ship in the class could carry 40,000-sdwt (scantling) at 11.5 metres draught, or 33,000-sdwt design draught of 10 metres. Fully computerised navigational and bridge-engine control and alarm systems meant that a crew of nine officers and ten Filipino ratings could operate the ship. This compared favourably with the eleven officers and sixteen ratings carried aboard the 'River' class tankers of some seventeen years previously.

As BP became increasingly involved in oil exploration, their new company BP Petroleum Development – managed by BP Shipping – invested with Harland & Wolff on a 50:50 share basis in a purpose-built vessel to undertake with greater efficiency oil exploration as and where required. The vessel was the Single Well Oil Production Ship (SWOPS) *Seillean* – named perhaps appropriately after the Gaelic name for a bee. Originally, a converted tanker hull had been used, but as dynamic positioning and production plant became increasingly sophisticated the need for a specialised craft was essential to hold station accurately in dynamic positioning mode (DPM) immediately above an oil well-head. *Seillean* was based upon a tanker hull format. The result was the construction of an amazing ship containing a range of highly complex and 'state of art' technology. She was completed in April 1990, of 249.7 metres (bp) with moulded beam and depth of 37 metres and 20.5 metres respectively. The ship was 45,000-sdwt tonnage with a design draught of 11m and a service speed of 9 knots. Extensive trials occurred for a month between October and November 1989 off various parts of the Irish coast, and upon satisfactory completion *Seillean* returned to Harland's yard for final stages of fitting-out.

Seillean operating principles. *(The Motor Ship)*

The well was marked by seabed transducers and a system of highly-accurate radio beacons. Once this unique ship arrived on station, her function was to lower a pipe connected to the seabed wellhead and pump oil from this into shipboard tanks. To achieve this, the ship sat stern-to the weather allowing the flare of the bow to sit downwind. A series of electrically powered thrusters kept her in position, two of which acted also as propulsion for a craft that was not fitted with conventional propeller and rudder. The connection was made by use of a Riser Connection Package (RCP) suspended from a derrick through a 'moonpool' and lowered through the hull of the ship. The fix was obtained by flexible pipe, permitting relative movement of the ship in her sea environment, using hydraulic signals transmitted between the RCP and wellhead. A second smaller moonpool was fitted with a camera and light platform, and equipped with manipulator arms to operate wellhead connections. The entire process could be monitored on board by video camera at the dynamic positioning console in the wheelhouse. The well fluids were separated into oil, water and gas. Each element was processed through a treatment package after which water was returned clean to the sea, gas burned off, and oil

The SWOPS ship *Seillean* fitting out in Harland & Wolff's Belfast Yard. *(The Motor Ship)*

pumped into the tanks. She had a cargo capacity of around 300,000 barrels – the equivalent of 20 days production – before returning to port for discharging.

Notwithstanding legislation, BP retains an international reputation for ship maintenance and in 1990 the Company planned a 'Mid Life Refurbishment' (MLR) programme designed to cover all ships in the fleet and scheduled initially to operate between 1991 and 1993. The tasks were far from routine and arose from certain equipment reaching the end of its economic life but, equally as importantly, included retrofitting equipment with more recent models. Navigation and communications equipment for instance had improved considerably even in the previous decade. It was in 1968 that a ship-borne satellite navigation system using a PDP8 computer and accessories had been placed upon the *Queen Elizabeth II.* In the 1970s, IMO had reviewed the SOLAS74 Convention regulating ship's communications at sea, resulting in the implementing of a Global Maritime Distress and Safety System (GMDSS) based upon satellite technology. This increased both range and efficiency of communications between ship and shore and made considerable advances regulating action to be taken concerning distress situations. GMDSS was eventually to declare radio officers at sea redundant, as well as direction finding equipment. In 1979, the United Kingdom based International Maritime Satellite Organisation (INMARSAT) had been created to provide mobile communications world-wide for commercial, distress and safety purposes – a system that was adopted by IMO. The three 1990/1 'A' class tankers were the first to be fitted with GMDSS and eventually sail without a radio officer.

In the field of navigation, Global Positioning Systems (GPS) were to be standard equipment aboard BP tankers, assisting more accurate and near-continuous position fixing. Developments had also taken place in radar technology that incorporated computerised, coloured screens with daylight viewing. This equipment had a number of advantages over older sets. The 'nearest approach and time' of a target together with details of her course and speed represented essential information when assessing collision avoidance and any proposed action necessary. Such information was now immediately available in windows at the lower part of the screen, together with forecasts concerning how any proposed action of 'own ship' might alter the situation. The open view permitted any number of navigating officers to examine available information and share experience concerning potential developments. This was a valuable aid between senior and junior officers confronting multi-ship situations and invaluable in training cadets. Much of the retrofitting programme was completed whilst tankers were dry-docked for statutory surveys but, where feasible, some was undertaken whilst ships were on passage.

Changing operational radar systems without interfering with 'the keeping of a proper look-out' was a physical task clearly not to be taken lightly and required skill, understanding and co-operation between the Master, his navigating officers, and the contractors performing the conversion. Work had been carried out aboard two of the 'River' class tankers – the *British Esk* and *British Trent* in 1991 and the following year a start was made on the VLCC fleet, beginning with *British Ranger* in 1992. The *British Reliance* was fitted in April while the *Resource* and *Resolution* received attention in 1993. Further tankers of the 'River' class were also included in the programme. All ships had their navigation and communication systems aligned with latest IMO legislation, and tank coatings inspected and re-worked as necessary.

Daylight viewing radar technology popular from the early 1990s represented a typical installation aboard BP tankers. (Consilium Marine)

Supertankers additionally had COW – IGS – and Cargo/Ballast pipes, lines and valves completely overhauled and modified. These ships were fitted also with a computerised system that monitored closely structural stresses, especially longitudinal Bending Moments during cargo work, superseding the older LODEMASTER equipment that had served tankers – especially VLCCs – faithfully and reliably. Advances had taken place also in calculating slamming and pitching stresses experienced when under way.

Strainstall's STRESSALERT 11 monitoring system was a popular fitting aboard many tankers, including the BP fleet, giving indications of longitudinal stresses experienced measured against pre-determined levels approved by the classification society. A number of long baseline deck mounted strain gauges consisting of a 2-metre rod, along with beam type bow pressure transducers scaled for a deflection of $\pm 2g$, were connected to display monitoring screens fitted usually in the wheelhouse. Basically, the system compared wave frequency against the natural pitching frequency of the ship. Invariably it was appropriate to reduce speed but, on occasions when close similarity was indicated, an *increase* in speed might sometimes prove the best action.

If computerisation drastically affected operating practices in the engine-room and in matters of practi-

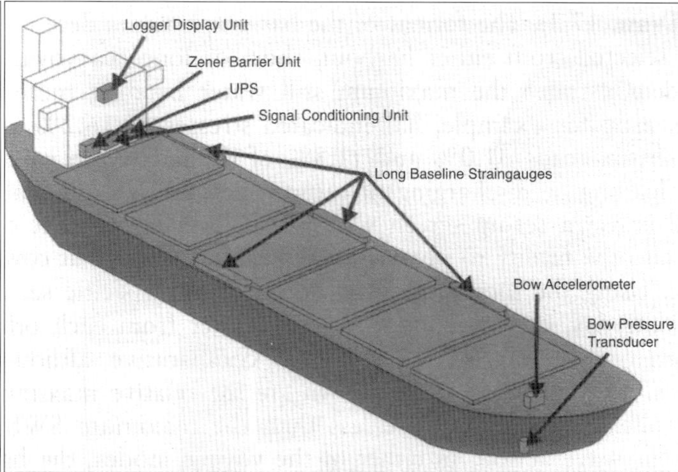

Stress monitor fitted to the main deck of a 1990s Supertanker, with plan diagram showing the monitoring of this equipment in the wheelhouse of a bulk-carrier. (Strainstall Engineering Company)

cal navigation and seamanship, then an equally marked effect was experienced monitoring and operating cargo operations aboard tankers of all sizes. As part of BP's MLR programme ships were overhauled or where necessary retrofitted. These reduced considerably maintenance costs and provided highly accurate measuring of temperatures, volumes and Ullages within tanks. A number of systems were offered the industry each making considerable contributions towards safety and efficiency. An early tank gauge was the SENTRY 11 of Consilium Marine Ab of Sweden that incorporated a stainless steel tape sensor suspended from the tank top sensor housing, with digital displays in the wheelhouse. This system was later superseded by their more sensitive VANGUARD, which interfaced with the loading computer indicating levels in cargo and ballast tanks. An alternative to the strip was a radar-based device projecting a concentrated narrow beam – completely harmless – through a conical or parabolic reflector with antenna feeder. The equipment was transmitted through a Zener

Flow diagram indicating how cargo monitoring and control functions inter-related. (Saab Marine Electronics)

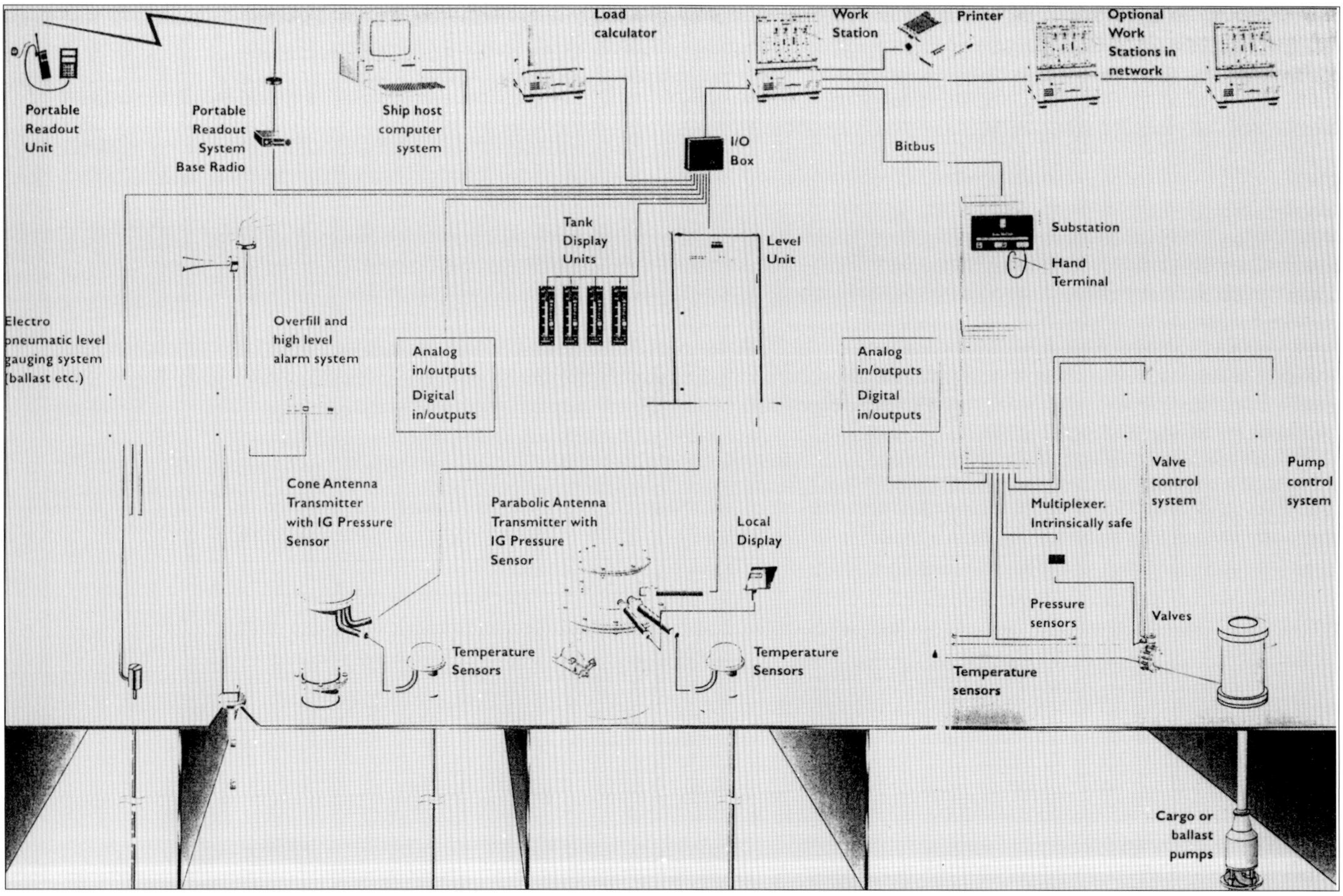

The rate of the pump serving Number Two cargo tank regulated by the touch of a light pen on the screen. ***(Saab Marine Electronics)***

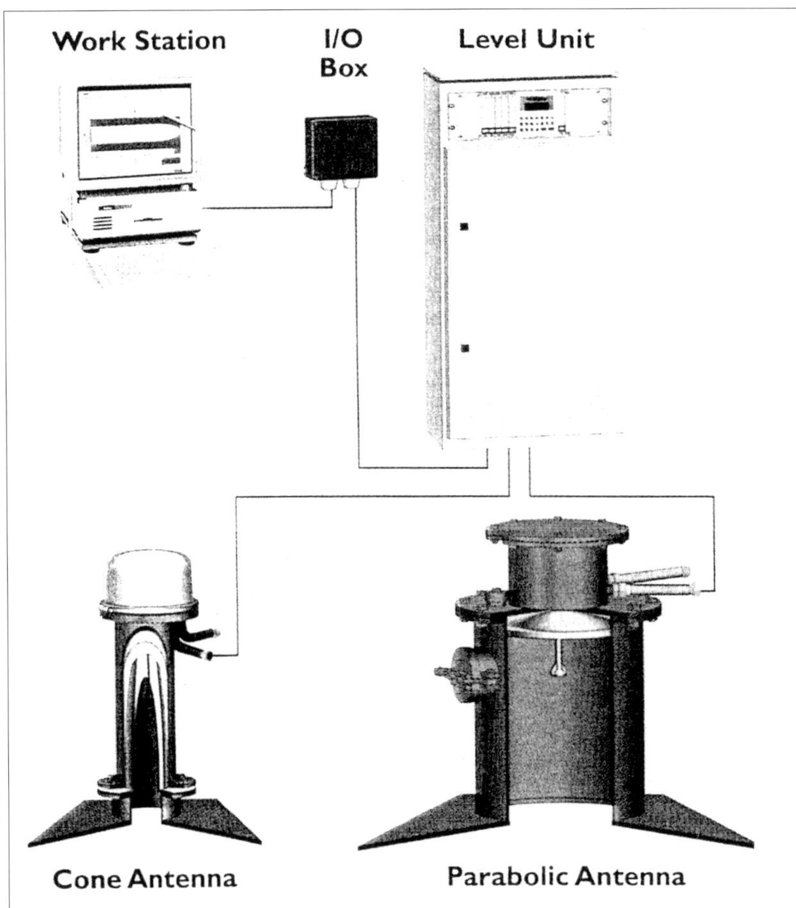

The three main features of the SAAB TANKRADAR G3. (Saab Marine Electronics)

Barrier Board that isolated a potentially dangerous deck area from the operating electronics. Computerised sensors led into a workstation situated anywhere aboard the tanker, but fitted invariably in the cargo control room or wheelhouse. The overall situation regarding state of tanks, pump-discharging rates etc was easily obtainable by using a light pen on the screen, a device used additionally to open or close valves, and regulate completely any cargo operation. A mimic board enabled the current loading or discharging situation to be seen at a glance.

In 1992, the Company changed funnel and houseflag. Use of the BP shield was discontinued and replaced on the flag by the original red lion rampart of 1955 surmounted on a green diamond. The funnel colours reverted to those originally used from 1926 until 1955 and, from this time until June 2005, both style and colours remain the same.

The twenty-year period from 1973 was a time of some unease in the fortunes of BP. It had entailed survival against considerable influences that, under different management structures, might well have seen, not demise of the company, but at least a diminishing from its position as a world leader. If the Company looked to the past regarding motifs, it was certainly looking forward concerning management involvements that were to have profound influence upon development of the fleet.

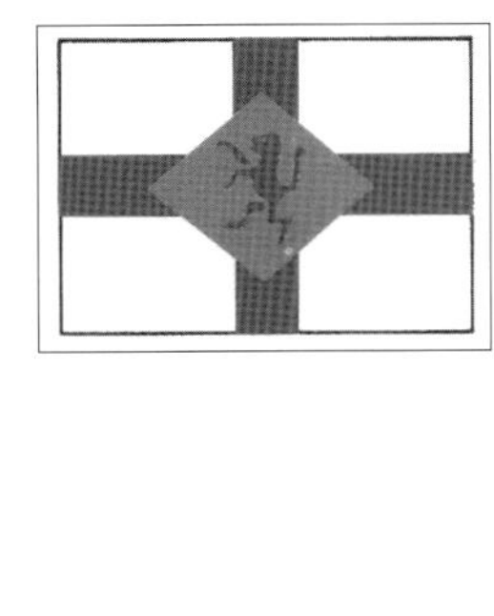

Current funnel and house flag.

Chapter Ten Revaluation

THE YEARS BETWEEN THE mid-1980s and 1993 were in some respects something of a hiatus during which BP recovered from a number of blows and needed time to re-assess a variety of situations – as hinted in the last chapter. Much time during this period however had been devoted largely to 'behind the scenes' planning – determining, as far as circumstances permitted, the correction of a few past mistakes and ensuring forecasts would be as accurate as humanly possible. The first positive moves were two-pronged: a review of the existing fleet – and expansion plans for its future.

If a renewed fleet were to be a reality then a correspondingly enhanced sense of loyalty would be an essential ingredient on the part of officers, petty officers and ratings operating the tankers. High standards of ship management 'at the sharp end', as it were, would require continuation of the thing which had been such a company asset in the past – namely motivated and competent men and women who could be encouraged to remain with the Company as 'career personnel' – officers in the mould of John Straughan, and thousands similar. BP Shipping needed more dedicated officers capable of advancing from cadetship through junior and senior officer ranks who would remain with the fleet to become superintendents and operations directors' of the future. The Company faced two problems. From the mid-1980s most British ship-owners had ceased cadet recruitment. This short-sighted move meant that the top calibre of intelligent well-educated youngsters (whom every employer loves to recruit) looked elsewhere for career opportunities. BP re-commenced cadet recruitment around 1988, some years before many other ship-owners, and re-employed those of their ninety cadets who still needed a couple of years to complete 'their time'. By 1993, the company employed the encouraging number of 120 cadets. Amongst the wider Merchant Navy however – over the next *20* years – many new recruitment overtures designed to woo this group of young men and women towards a career at sea would receive a guarded reception.

Far more important than cadet training was an on-going situation concerning the Company's serving certificated and experienced officers. The move to manning agencies employing officers on 'off-shore contracts' had not proved successful and, in retrospect, Management recognised these decisions to 'flag out' the fleet were now inconsistent with current plans. In this, they were undoubtedly correct. Views gained from those serving with BP during this difficult period exhibited more a sense of incomprehension than anger – although of course that commodity bubbled below the surface. Although they still regarded themselves as 'BP Men', they felt let down by the company – with a resulting loss of morale. Officers sent by the agencies from dry-cargo trading were not always suitable for the peculiarities of tanker life and found difficulty settling. They also needed 'on-the-job-training' to supplement shore-side courses prior to joining a ship. Others with tanker experience were sometimes not really 'up to the mark' and carrying them placed unfair burdens upon their fellow officers. No ship has spare navigators or engineers stashed away in the stores locker. Inevitably, a gulf existed between BP mariners and senior shore-staff. Of course, Group tankers continued to function efficiently and the name 'BP' amongst officers' still indicated reliable owners of seaworthy tankers – and a career-path – even if with some, the latter ideal was accompanied by a certain lack of conviction. As years progressed from 1988, the company introduced training grants for officers and ratings to improve statutory qualifications, and subsidised repatriation when crews left ships in ports abroad. There were however deficiencies in the existing situation. BP Shipping needed to regain greater control over its seagoing personnel. To achieve these ends, they began a number of progressive initiatives. In 1991, they held the first of a series of forums and workshops informing sea-staff about unfolding policies and reassuring them concerning their future role in Company plans. They reflagged certain tankers under the Red Ensign and created a marine personnel subsidiary in Bermuda to employ officers. They also renegotiated a dialogue with the officers' union NUMAST and actively encouraged all navigators and engineers to become members. For key senior officers – masters and chief engineers – the company introduced a novel 'back-to-back' manning policy. In this, two officers of each senior rank were assigned to every ship so that one of the team could become involved in projects and policy-making decisions in head office. Additionally the company discussed with the RMT, the ratings union, employment conditions for petty officers, Filipino and Sierra Leone seamen.

Implementation of the new policies began around 1994, signifying an era of renewed credibility in company-crew relationships. There was little doubt of the success of these moves amongst BP's 420 officers. A further incentive of a more subtle kind was made by company announcements of its commitment to recruit British and Irish officers – *where this proved possible.* In 1993, BP Shipping employed indirectly 390 British and Irish officers with the remaining 30 coming largely from Poland. The free exchange of the former combination had operated in the Merchant Navy for generations without problem and, indeed, foreign nationals had also served successfully for years aboard British ships, without cultural or language differences creating too many problems.

There were concerns also within BP management, arising from OPA90 and the implementation of double-hulled tankers, which led to the creation of new policies. Things had been moving quickly over this intervening period. The idea of double-sided tankers (and bulk ore carriers) was not new for many companies (including BP) already owned some constructions of this type. 1992 had seen the first of a new breed of completely double-hulled VLCCs entering service, where the 'outer skin' extended below the keel. The first from European yards was the 300,000-sdwt *Eleo Maersk* from the Lindo yard in Odense, Denmark for Maersk Tankers. This was followed a year later by the first from a Japanese yard, Hitachi Zosen, which was the 300,000-sdwt *Arosa,* ordered by Lykiardopolu of London on behalf of overseas clients. It was not possible for double hulls to be retrofitted. The task would have been impracticable and extremely costly – even if a yard could be found willing to undertake the work.

It must not be assumed, however, that all single-hulled tankers were unsafe. The tragedy of the *Exxon Valdez* was the *last* Supertanker – up to June 2005 – to be involved in any kind of environmental incident. Other tanker accidents between 1990 and 2005 have all involved ships out of AFRA's Supertanker category. One of the reasons ensuring single-hulled Supertanker safety was the implementation of Hydrostatically Balanced Loading (HBL). This had been approved by IMO in 1994, as an alternative to Regulation 13G, using the principle of density difference between crude oil and seawater. It was found that cargo tanks could be partially loaded below the 98 per cent Ullage, allowing for a corresponding loss of some cargo capacity, to a level consistent with the payload of the ship and specific gravity of the oil. If this were combined with an increased pressure of inert gas then, in the event of a tank being breached, a difference would be created so that the internal pressure of the oil would be less than that of the sea outside. Seawater would tend to flood into the tank rather than crude oil escape into the sea.

Even in rough seas – or if the VLCC happened to ground on an ebb tide – the theory proposed there would still be no escape of crude oil. The difficulty (perversely) was that this new system, however well ratified and received, had never actually been put to the test, something which produced its own crop of potential concerns over ensuing years. Probably the fear existed that if the tanker was carrying only a partial load – perhaps close to the water level (as often happens) – and the hull was breached near or below the waterline, oil might still flow out rather than seawater come in.

The first BP tanker to benefit from management's new resolve was one also chosen to implement a continued policy of major modification and refurbishment within the wider fleet. The *British Tamar*, of 25,094-sdwt completed in 1973, was reflagged in April 1994 and employed mainly on the UK coastal heavy fuel oil trades. She had six wing tanks converted to segregated seawater ballast, but retained the ability to load up to 24,500-sdwt on her maximum draught. The separate pump and pipelines enabled ballast to be handled concurrently with cargo operations resulting in quicker turn-round times. Additionally, the tanker had a major engine overhaul whilst in Falmouth together with deck and external accommodation paint renewal. The navigational equipment was also upgraded with latest ARPA (computerised anti-collision radar plotting aids), two of the most modern design gyrocompasses and three independent satellite navigation and communication systems.

At about the same time a near sister-ship, the *British Esk* was the first BP tanker fitted with a Voyage Event Recorder, or 'orange box', intended to retain information. A number of microphones were installed on the Bridge, cargo control room and in the engine-room to record conversations. Computer storing of electronic information was made also from bridge and engine-room, along with a widespread selection of data useful collectively to assist in determining causes during any investigations arising from a casualty. Some officers in both departments were concerned initially that casual conversation could be open to later examination, and needed some reassurance that the VER system was in existence purely in the event of an incident.

The Supertanker fleet was not neglected in the Company's replenishment programmes. The policy of sandwiching a voluntary survey in between the statutory five-year dry-dockings was re-instated as the age increased of these VLCCs. This was encouraged in the light of successful trials to remove Tributyl Tin Oxides (TBTs) from hull coatings that protected the steel from corrosive effects of sea immersion without harming the oceans in which ships sailed. In 1990/1, as part of this on-going environmental protection policy, the hulls of all BP's VLCC fleet had been given a trial of this new treatment. Vegetable and marine growths, such as various types of barnacle and weed, proliferated on the slow moving hulls of VLCCs amassing to an extent that slowed even more the speed of the ship. Previous treatments had used toxins upon which the growths fed until they died. Unfortunately, the process simultaneously released tin poisons into the ocean. A new method was devised that shot-blasted the underwater hull to Swedish Standard SA2.5 which was then coated with coal tar epoxy followed, in these cases, by

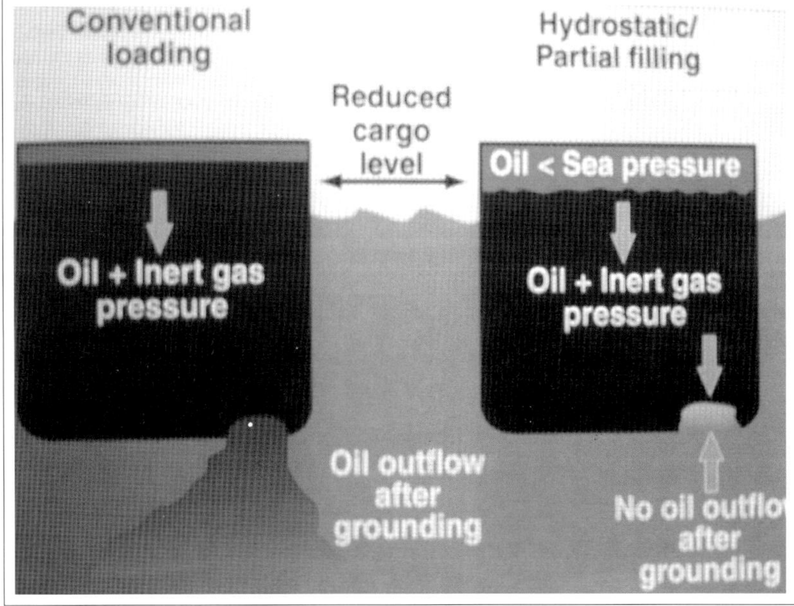

The Principle of Hydrostatic Balanced Loading. *(The Motor Ship)*

The *British Resolution* in dry-dock after being treated three years previously with new tin-free anti-fouling. (Jotun Paints - Europe)

a couple of coats of, perhaps, Jotun Paints (Europe)'s *Seaguardian* tin-free anti-fouling paint. The *British Resolution* was one of the first BP Supertankers treated during the ship's routine third-year survey dry-docking. When the VLCC was again dry-docked in 1993 at Sembawang Shipyard, Singapore for implementation of new Enhanced Survey rules, the hull was discovered to be completely free of marine growths – attained without causing any harmful environmental effects.

Following continued care and maintenance, this VLCC underwent successfully five 5-year surveys and remained in service until 1999 when she was scrapped in Alang. Trials with other Supertankers in the fleet were equally as successful and, as experiments continued, a paint was designed which allowed the tin-free coating to be applied without the cost involved of shot blasting.

New buildings within the Group in 1994/5 included a number of liquefied natural gas (LNG) carriers. Introducing LNGs into the fleet was a natural extension to earlier company involvements in the gas industry extending to their consultancy role through BP Exploration twenty-five years previously. The Group had owned a liquid petroleum gas (LPG) tanker in 1980 – the 53,500-sdwt *GAS Enterprise,* which had remained in the fleet until 1992 when she was sold for further service with Furness, Withy Group under the name *Darwin.* BP also at varying times chartered gas tankers.

Al Khaznah was the first of four 75,500-sdwt LNG tankers built between 1994/5 by Mitsui's yard in Japan. She was crewed by BP Shipping. The operating manager for all four ships was National Gas Shipping Company (NGSC) of Abu Dhabi, and they were owned by single-ship companies registered in Liberia. She was followed the same year by the *Shahama.* The tankers were each of 293 length (bp) × 45.84 × 19.95 metres. The latter experienced major vibration problems and underwent dry-docking in Dubai. The bridge structure was supported by struts under the wings and she was fitted with a fin to reduce vibration effects by re-shaping the water flow around rudder and propeller. The radar equipment also required renewal from cracks induced by metal fatigue.

Preparations to provide a fin to the *Shahama* in Dubai dry-dock. The grey pipe extending across the foreground of this shot is probably an air supply pipe for welding operations. (P Harrington)

1995 saw delivery of the remaining two LNG tankers, the *Ghasha* and *Ish.* Each was fitted with two steam turbine engines geared to a single propeller shaft of around 35,100 shp and capable of powering the ships at about 19.5 knots.

The inclusion of LNG tankers within the fleet, and the placing of BP Group orders for four LPG carriers between 2007/8 with *British*-prefixed names, indicate a necessarily brief inclusion concerning the carriage of gas by sea although, as mentioned in the Authors' Preface, inevitably much is highly technical and well outside the scope of this book. It has been seen that hydrocarbon gas remains an inherent component in oilfields that is released once the field is tapped. It has always been divided into two categories for the purpose of conveyance as a tanker cargo: LNG is often referred to as methane, while LPG includes butane used in heating or cooking, and propane and butadiene that have industrial uses. All petroleum gases are carried as a liquid under pressure in special cylinders, bottles or tanks.

Traditionally, in situations where they could easily be transported, gases were burned off and, as was shown with the *Seillean* operations, this is the safest option. Methane is the major constituent in natural gas and can represent as much as two thirds of the total volume of hydrocarbons. LNG carriers have been designed to transport liquid gas keeping it below boiling point, which is -258.7°F. If it rises above this temperature it transforms again into gas expanding to about 250 times its original volume. Because no refrigeration plant exists on board and it has to be transported at very low temperatures, around -260°F, it is carried in specially insulated tanks. In liquid form, it is highly flammable with a flashpoint of about 80°F or below, around the same category as aviation gas or jet fuel. LNG is a very hazardous cargo to carry that has led to the introduction of a unique classification within the categories of tankers at sea. Research in LNG technology emanated largely between United States, Norwegian, French and British manufacturers, the appropriate Classification Societies and ship-owners. MARPOL73/78 designated an Annex dealing specifically with the construction of LNG/LPG tankers, whilst in 1979 the Society of International Gas Tanker and Terminal Operators (SIGTTO) based in London was formed. Their brief was very comprehensive. The Society was to examine safe and reliable operation of this new breed of tanker, consulting with technical maritime associated organisations (including

IMO, the International Chamber of Shipping and Oil Companies International Maritime Forum, OCIMF, amongst others) so that all areas and aspects of transportation were covered including terminals for loading and discharge. SIGGTO have produced a number of authoritative publications covering training of all personnel involved, ashore and afloat, operating practices and the design of all supporting equipment. Their Model Code is mandatory in the UK and provides for a series of rigorous safety measures controlling all aspects of LNG/LPG operations. Rulings have also been ratified into a series of world-wide protocols and incorporated within IMO Regulations. The legislation has resulted in an impressive safety record when transporting gas by sea.

Aboard *Ish*, the five giant aluminium alloy spheres along the main deck extend below, cushioned from the ship's sides by one metre or so of insulation fitted as a cylindrical skirt around their equator. The tanks are unsupported in the lower part of the sphere to reduce surface area of heat transference that helps keep the tank as cold as possible. A drip tray equipped with a level alarm is fitted above the reinforced double-bottom. Amongst a number of technical advantages of spheres is the minimising of punctured tanks in the event of collision and strengthening of internal methods concerned with gas pressures under various circumstances. In the following photograph, the one-way vent risers and tank tops are clearly visible.

A view along the tank tops showing insulated pipes, catwalk and fire-fighting equipment boxes, aboard the *Ish*. (P Harrington)

The main steam turbine engine of the *Ghasha*. The gearbox can be seen in the foreground, whilst the propeller shaft is just visible in the extreme lower centre. (P Harrington)

Inert gas systems are essential requirements in carrying LNG. Unlike a crude oil tanker, the gas needs to have a very high level of purity and to be extremely dry. This is to prevent cargo contamination and it is achieved by having a separate IGS generator on board fuelled by diesel or heavy fuel oil, which uses nitrogen gas in excess of 95 per cent purity. The cargo is not kept cold entirely by insulation alone. It has a natural 'boil off' of around 0.15 per cent volume per day that is used in the engine-room to assist powering the main engine. As the gas 'boils off', the evaporation reduces the average temperature within the tank helping keep the cargo in liquid form. There are ten cargo pumps fitted aboard the *Ish*, two per tank each electrically driven at around 1,000 m^3/hr. Electrical cables are well insulated, and tracked along the bottom of the tank. Valves are operated remotely from Cargo Control or Engine-room. LNG is loaded/discharged by flow booms with a vapour boom connected that serves as a vent line between the shore installations and ship. In order to assist keeping tanks at a cold temperature some of the cargo is retained onboard. This is very much contrary to practices aboard the crude oil tanker where stripping pumps, and a special MARPOL line for finer clearing, determine as much as possible is discharged. The only occasion when tanks are completely cleared and cleaned is for statutory dry-docking. They often have a diameter of around 36.5 metres with a capacity of 135,000 cubic metres on a laden draft of 11 metres.

Below decks, it is interesting to compare the clean, well-lit engine-room aboard this tanker with non-slip decking and lack of residue oils and greases adhering to pump controls and other engine parts that were so much part of earlier working spaces below. The following photographs illustrate progressive advances in other areas aboard this class of tanker and offer interesting comparisons with shots of earlier company vessels. The engine-room control panel in surmounted by a mimic board equipped with major alarms covering pressure and temperatures of various components in

The main engine control panel in air-conditioned setting shows mimic boards and computer-controlled buttons. (P Harrington)

Connections of the two-ram steering gear with the rudder are clearly shown in this shot. (P Harrington)

the main engine, and including supporting machinery such as the steam turbine generators, fuel systems for boilers, condensers etc. The lower part consists of controls covering all areas of engine-room, main engine and cargo tanks – including all start and stop functions, burners in the boilers and diesel motors.

Dining saloons on all BP tankers each display a photograph of Her Majesty the Queen, and are well designed, modern and spacious – compared with those of even a few years previously. They have subdued lighting, curtained windows and pot plants, all of which collectively create a homely atmosphere conducive to relaxation, and far removed from working areas within the ship. The reduced seating reflects reductions in numbers carried. Aboard this class of tanker there are eleven officers: the Master – chief officer, second and two third officers. In the engineering department, a chief engineer is assisted by a second, third and fourth as watch-keepers, plus a junior. A cargo control engineer is carried who has the equivalent rank of third engineering officer and is on day-work alongside the Mate.

British Petroleum Shipping Company's fleet inevitably did not remain immune from disasters, but was involved in accidents similar to those previously chronicled. Amongst a few minor entanglements, three major events occurred in the early 1990s, including the much publicised collision in June 1993 between the *British Trent* and *Western Winner*. This happened whilst both ships were manoeuvring during thick fog – with visibility around one cable, or 200 metres – off Flushing pilot station. It will be recalled, mention was made in Chapter Two of the vulnerability of ships whilst taking aboard or dropping a pilot. During this accident nine crewmembers aboard the BP tanker were killed, whilst others were injured, and all sustained considerable shock. The tanker had virtually lost all way when the other vessel scraped along her port side, puncturing a cargo tank, and releasing part of her unleaded gas oil that ignited and burned off as it escaped from the ship. In 1995, the *British Esk* was struck on the starboard bow by the bulk carrier *Ipanema* whilst at anchor off Vlissingen. Although there were no casualties the latter vessel subsequently sank, and extensive damage was sustained to the BP tanker, with the loss of 150 tonnes of naptha. The recently-fitted VER proved useful in the ensuing enquiry. On both occasions, swift action by the crew, the Company's emergency procedures programme, and satellite communications with head office proved effectively constructive. A serious explosion happened aboard the *British Adventure* whilst she was undergoing her first special survey in Jurong dry dock at Singapore. This was in February 1994 during welding operations in the steering flat. Eight dockworkers killed and a further three badly injured.

The spacious dining room aboard *Ish*. (P Harrington)

Three significant events occurred in 1996 that directly affected the BP fleet. In April, a major step forward concerning international safety at sea was made when BP Shipping directors' decided all tankers in the fleet should become members of AMVER. This remains the United States Coast Guard Automated Mutual-Assistance Vessel Rescue System that uses updated modern satellite technology to co-ordinate distress information between potential rescue vessels and those hampered. The system operates from West Virginia at C-GHQ where it had been created in mid-1950. In 1990, some forty years on, AMVER held a registry of around 12,000 ships – or 40 per cent of the world's merchant fleets. The voyages of 2,700 merchant ships around the world were plotted continuously on a computer system that could be integrated with a display offering relevant information concerning any vessel that might be near a transmitted distress message from any craft. The new GMDSS deadline for all ships to be registered by 1 January 1999 was fast approaching, replacing the now obsolete Morse code, by which time AMVER complemented GMDSS for global shipping safety. *British Tamar* was one of the first BP tankers to be integrated into the new system.

It was in 1996 also that the giants BP and Mobil examined viability of combining their refining and marketing operations in Europe. The joint venture eventually agreed gave BP a 79 per cent share in the fuel side of the partnership and 49 per cent in lubricants. The move coincided with the closure or selling of some European and United States refineries that were producing low profit yield, and investment in others that showed more promise. Two years later a merger occurred – that was acclaimed as the largest industrial amalgamation in the world – with the

Company re-named from BP Shipping to BP-Amoco.

The final event of 1996, saw BP Shipping actively involved in a Seminar held at Warsash Maritime Centre designed specifically to investigate steps the industry might take to improve the image of the British Merchant Navy in secondary schools, and encourage more young men and women to embark upon a career at sea as navigating and engineer officer cadets. Certainly, there was a trickle of youngsters expressing interest but comparatively few (even amongst these numbers) actually presented themselves for training – with even fewer making it through to gain their first certificates of competency. It looked as if the forecast made by BP that they would have to look at other countries for officers might well become a reality. The problem itself had not altered appreciably. Youngsters with good GCSE results were encouraged to remain at school for 'A' levels – still then very much the academic 'gold standard' – whilst those with good passes in mathematics, physics and perhaps chemistry at Advanced level were being wooed by more attractive offers – especially from traditional universities, commerce, industry and the professions. The Royal Navy was also experiencing a flow of applicants for Dartmouth that threatened the trickle coming into the Merchant Navy. An enhanced recruiting campaign was a positive result of the Seminar's labour, but the issue would remain a matter of concern for years to come.

The first of a series of new ships entered company service in 1997 when two VLCCs were bare-boat chartered from the Maersk Line of Denmark, renamed and painted in BP colours. These were the *British Valour* and *British Vigilance* the first double-hulled tankers to enter the fleet. Both Supertankers were 210,575-sdwt, 343.7 (bp) × 56.44 × 21.58 metres. In July 1997, orders were placed with Samsung Heavy Industries in Korea for four VLCCs in excess of two million barrels capacity, or around 300,000-sdwt.

This order followed delivery in the same year of three AFRA Suezmax 'H' class tankers – the *British Harrier*, *Hawk* and *Hunter*, each around 151,400-sdwt – from the same yard for Nordic American Tanker Shipping as owners. The *British Harrier* as a representative of the class was 274.10 (length bp) ×46.04 × 23.6 metres. The grt was 80,187 tonnes, with Segregated Ballast Tank reduction of 63,421 grt. Laden to her summer load line at 151,458.6-sdwt she drew 17.020 metres, giving a freeboard of 3.121 metres.

In the photograph, the tanker was well out of the water with two officers on the port bridge wing watching the returning ship's lifeboat. The ship carried a complement of twenty-two, which included accommodation for four deck and engineering cadets. Three steam centrifugal cargo pumps delivered 3,700 m^3/hr, with two cargo eductors each of 600 m^3/hr. The steam reciprocating stripping pump was 300 m^3/hr and each of the two electrically driven centrifugal ballast pumps were 2,400 m^3/hr, whilst the ballast eductor was 400 m^3/hr. The three tankers were each powered by a six-cylinder B&W diesel engine manufactured by the builders at Changwon, of 20,685 bhp giving a laden service speed of around 14.5 knots. They had bunker capacity of around 3,000 tonnes, with a consumption of fuel oil of 65 tonnes per day, giving these tankers a substantial range for their size.

Cargo tanks on most BP tankers were generally inspected once per year according to planned maintenance programmes and, on rotation. *British Harrier* continued Company fleet policy of being dry-docked around the 2½-year period. For a while, the tanker was engaged loading in the Argentine and proceeding to United States ports – calling at Long Beach or Cherry Point for discharge, and often calling in at Valpariso for bunkers. The nature of crude loaded meant that heating coils were used to raise slightly the temperature of the oil. The cargo pipeline system followed that described previously when considering equipment aboard the *British Tay* using a colour code unique to BP. On this ship the port Slop tank and Numbers One, Four and Six were served by the 'red coloured' line, the starboard Slop and Numbers Two and Five by the 'yellow' – with 'black' serving Number Three tanks. There was also a Residue tank fitted, that was separate from the cargo lines, and used to store engine-room Slops.

The turn-round time for this class of tanker was around the 20-hour mark – dependant upon a number of variables including the type of crude carried, for often lighter grades made tank COW considerably quicker.

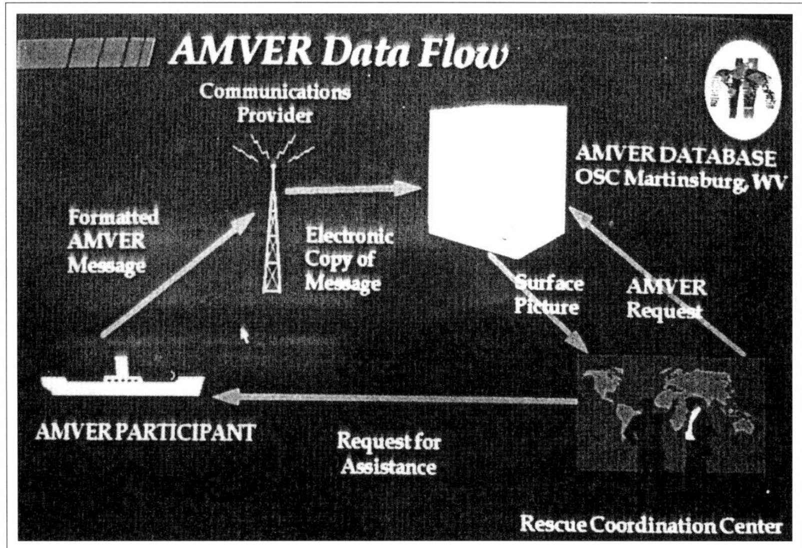

Flow diagram indicating AMVER's co-ordinating role in search and rescue. (AMVER)

The *British Harrier* seen from the port quarter. (P Harrington)

The main engine of the *British Hawk* showing the cylinder heads. In the background are two of the three diesel generators, with a turbocharger on the left hand side. (P Harrington)

The trio were fitted with state-of-the-art technology both in the engine-room and on the bridge. Navigating and engineering equipment had developed considerably from that used a decade or two previously, with the computerised technology hinted at in previous chapters now very much the norm. For the former, Integrated Navigation Systems (INS) was being installed aboard many tankers and general merchant ships. Many were similar in design to the VISION2100 Voyage Management System of Sperry Maritime. This linked inputs from a wide range of sensors to provide officers in the wheelhouse with an overall monitoring of the alarms covering all aspects of ship control.

The equipment represented a fully comprehensive navigational aid. 10cm and 3cm radars were incorporated, each fitted with computerised collision avoidance information, and linked to electronic charts. The idea of placing computerised charts aboard ships, as part of a wider navigational service, had been pursued by the United Kingdom Hydrographic Office in Taunton, working since the mid-1980s with interested commercial organisations.

As a result, by the late 1990s, a range of systems were in use with varying degrees of success (and not a little confusion) resulting from a range of 'teething problems' which, in 2005, are still not totally resolved.

There are two common electronic chart systems – the Admiralty Raster and the commercial Vector methods, each possessing technical ramifications outside the scope of this book. Suffice it to say, electronic charts are the way forward to navigation in the future but, currently, IMO Regulations determine that whatever system is favoured by whom, a complete set of

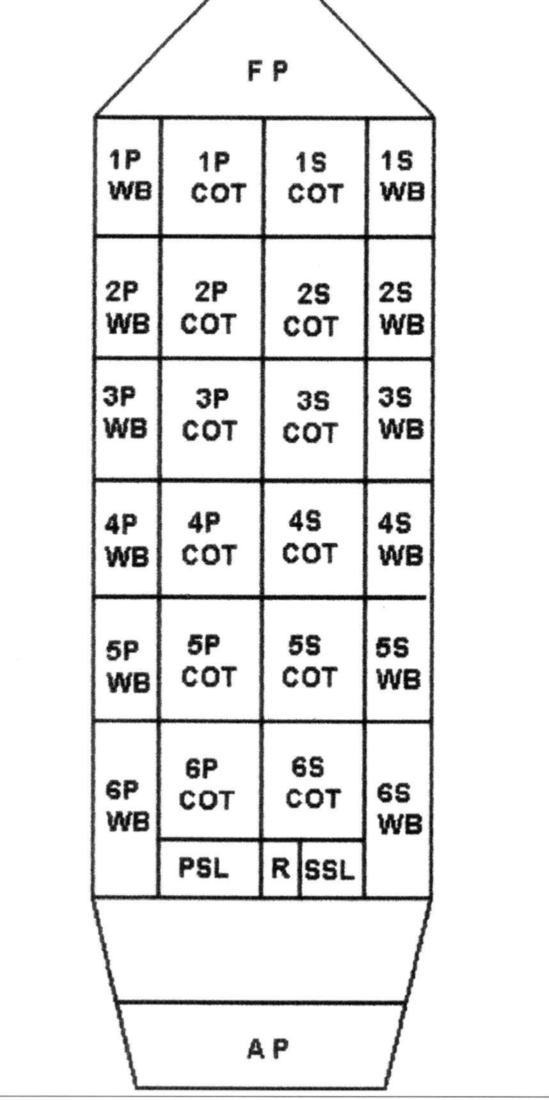

The diagram above gives an impression of the tank layout aboard 'H' class of vessels. (P Harrington)

The VISION 2100 VMS prepared in showrooms ashore indicating a range of essential monitoring and operational components. (Sperry Marine)

Screen shot of Racal-Decca's CHARTMASTER electronic chart system. (Racal-Decca).

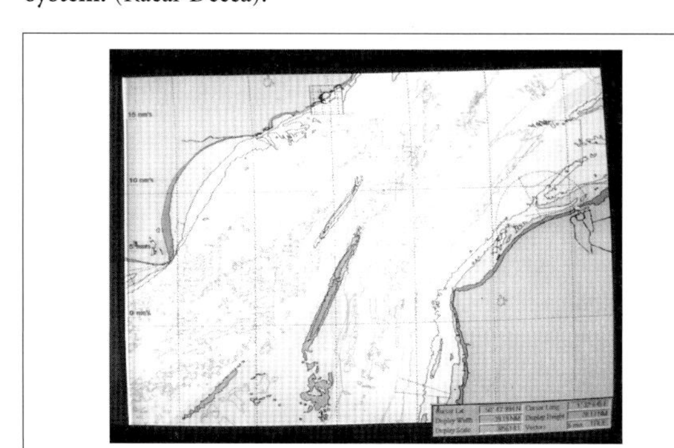

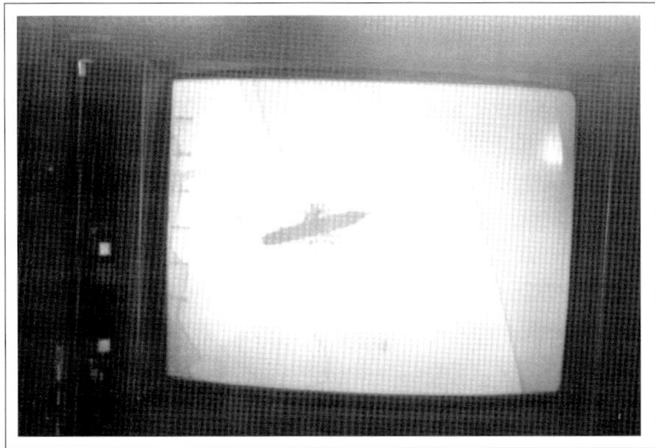

Close-up definition allows progress of the ship to be monitored as she approaches alongside her berth. (Racal-Decca).

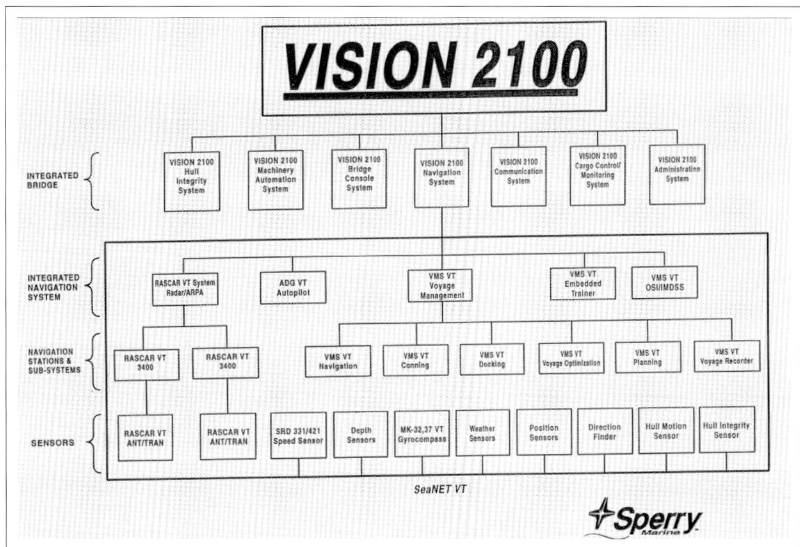

The VISION 2100 Voyage Management System. (Sperry Marine)

paper charts has to be used on board all ships, and these have to be up-dated regularly as part of the traditional duties of the second officer.

In the photograph, the Dover Strait is shown, with land coloured yellow and area of shallows, such as the Varne Bank and adjacent sandbanks in the centre, coloured blue. Drying areas appear as green. The absence of buoyage, depths of water or navigational marks indicate that this is a large-scale vector chart in which the 'layers' containing this particular information have been temporarily suppressed. Advantages of electronic-charting is the use to which systems may be put in conditions, for example, of reduced visibility when with the aid of Doppler-type docking radars, an image of the ship and jetty may be projected upon a screen for use of the Master and pilot.

The system on board the 'H' class tankers was Kelvin Hughes NINAS900 that was similar in design and covered all main features essential to consistent monitoring. This gear was inter-switched with NUCLEUS ARPA radars and the latest development in electronic charts. The H-class were the first BP tankers to be fitted with Integrated Navigation Systems.

1998 saw the *Loch Rannoch* handed over by Maersk to BP Exploration on a long-term bare-boat charter. She was managed by BP Shipping for an initial period of seven years, following delivery from South Korea's Okpo yard at Changwon, in less than eleven months following cutting of her first steel plate. This 130,000-sdwt tanker was destined to serve on the shuttle service transferring crude from the Harland & Wolff built FPSO *Schiehallion* to terminals at Sullom Voe. (A FPSO vessel was nomenclature for a Floating Production Storage and Offloading ship – generally of VLCC capacity – and still perfectly sound, but approaching the end of useful deep-sea trading.) She was constructed specifically to withstand North Sea storm conditions by having increased scantlings, beyond Lloyd's Register's usual requirements, and her two longitudinal bulkheads were extended into engine-room spaces. The hull girder strength was 10 per cent in excess of maximum computer generated hogging and sagging assessments. She had eighteen cargo spaces with extended Centre Tanks with twin fore and aft bulkheads. A two-stroke MAN B&W engine delivered around 27,160 bhp to twin variable pitch propellers offering a laden speed of around 14 knots dependant upon sea conditions.

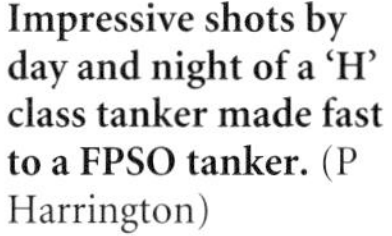

Impressive shots by day and night of a 'H' class tanker made fast to a FPSO tanker. (P Harrington)

Chapter Eleven Unprecedented Expansion

IN 2000 CONSIDERABLE CONCERN was being expressed amongst reputable ship-owners world-wide, including BP-Amoco, regarding the continued trading of some single-hulled tanker tonnage. Many of these vessels constructed in the mid-1970s were approaching their 25-year survey and, whilst some had been well maintained and still had a few years reliable service ahead of them, others did not inspire similar confidence. Even those tankers employing HBL remained suspect in the eyes of some owners – especially where chartering of these same tankers was concerned. BP-Amoco insisted that older tankers being considered for charter would have to conform to standards specified within the Condition Assessment Programme (CAP2) from an acceptable Classification Society. Fundamentally, the assessment insisted that older tankers would have to be of the same acceptable standard as if they were just 10 years old.

BP-Amoco had already sent two of their surviving 'R' class tankers for demolition in China, and planned to despatch the remaining two as soon as delivery had been made of new 'P' class VLCCs. The international situation was not entirely 'gloom and doom' with this older tonnage for, even as late as 2004, the life of the then 27-year-old *Jahre Viking* was extended for a further three years. This permitted her to serve as a FPSO vessel with Maersk Oil Qatar, whilst First-Olsen Tankers provided crew and other services. The contract included possible option of a further two years' service, working initially from June 2004 in the Al Shaheen field off Qatar.

In mid-January 2000, the *British Pioneer* delivered her first cargo of Saudi Arabian crude to Coryton on the River Thames. She had been completed in November 1999 by Samsung's for Abbey National December Leasing and was managed and crewed by BP-Amoco Shipping. Three further Supertankers of the same class were delivered later in 2000 – the *British*

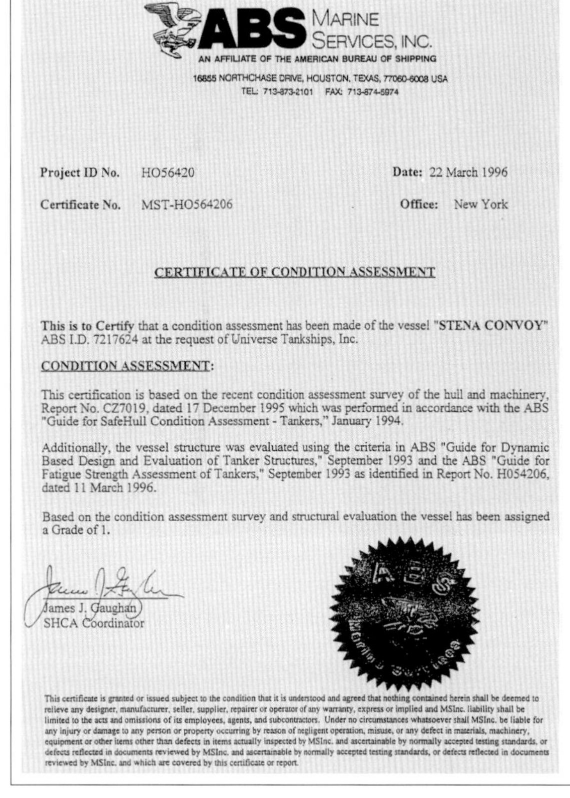
ABS MARINE SERVICES, INC.
AN AFFILIATE OF THE AMERICAN BUREAU OF SHIPPING
16855 NORTHCHASE DRIVE, HOUSTON, TEXAS, 77060-6008 USA
TEL: 713-873-2101 FAX: 713-874-5974

Project ID No. HO56420 **Date:** 22 March 1996

Certificate No. MST-HO564206 **Office:** New York

CERTIFICATE OF CONDITION ASSESSMENT

This is to Certify that a condition assessment has been made of the vessel **"STENA CONVOY"** ABS I.D. 7217624 at the request of Universe Tankships, Inc.

CONDITION ASSESSMENT:

This certification is based on the recent condition assessment survey of the hull and machinery, Report No. CZ7019, dated 17 December 1995 which was performed in accordance with the ABS "Guide for SafeHull Condition Assessment - Tankers," January 1994.

Additionally, the vessel structure was evaluated using the criteria in ABS "Guide for Dynamic Based Design and Evaluation of Tanker Structures," September 1993 and the ABS "Guide for Fatigue Strength Assessment of Tankers," September 1993 as identified in Report No. H054206, dated 11 March 1996.

Based on the condition assessment survey and structural evaluation the vessel has been assigned a Grade of 1.

James J. Gaughan
SHCA Coordinator

This certificate is granted or issued subject to the condition that it is understood and agreed that nothing contained herein shall be deemed to relieve any designer, manufacturer, seller, supplier, repairer or operator of any warranty, express or implied and MSInc. liability shall be limited to the acts and omissions of its employees, agents, and subcontractors. Under no circumstances whatsoever shall MSInc. be liable for any injury or damage to any person or property occurring by reason of negligent operation, misuse, or any defect in materials, machinery, equipment or other items other than defects in items actually inspected by MSInc. and ascertainable by normally accepted testing standards, or defects reflected in documents reviewed by MSInc. and ascertainable by normally accepted testing standards, or defects reflected in documents reviewed by MSInc. and which are covered by this certificate or report.

A Condition Assessment Programme Certificate issued by the American Bureau of Shipping Marine Services Agency covering the Supertanker *Stena Convoy*. (Concordia Maritime)

Progress, *Purpose* and *Pride*. The four Supertankers were sister-ships each around 306,000-sdwt, of 334 (bp) × 58.04 × 22.520 metres.

The conditions experienced in the adjacent photograph are not unusual, but indicate the enormous structural stresses to which all tankers are regularly subjected. The double-hull, with two longitudinal bulkheads, ensures that such massive Supertankers – when properly handled – are well able to encounter such powerful seas and heavy swell with perfect safety – and no risks of polluting their environment.

The hull structure and cargo tanks, built around the pattern of three sets by six of the 'P' class, were similar in design to those of the 155,000-sdwt 'H' Suezmax (but with of course considerably larger dimensions). Cargo pumps were three in number, steam turbine driven, and capable of a discharge rate of 5,600 m^3/hr. The tank-cleaning pump was around 60/70 per cent of the cargo pumps, whilst the single stripping pump was steam reciprocating at a maximum of 200 m^3/hr.

Two ballast pumps were fitted to the ships that were electrically driven at 3,500 m^3/hr each. The main deck pipe cranes were of standard dimensions for this class of VLCC, each of 20-tonne swl and having a radius of 17.45 metres. Whilst scantlings differed in double-hulled Supertankers, plate thicknesses at the bottom

Shipping green seas, and with heavy spraying forward extending over a third of her overall length, *British Pioneer* heads into Storm Force Ten seas off Cape D'Antifer. (P Harrington)

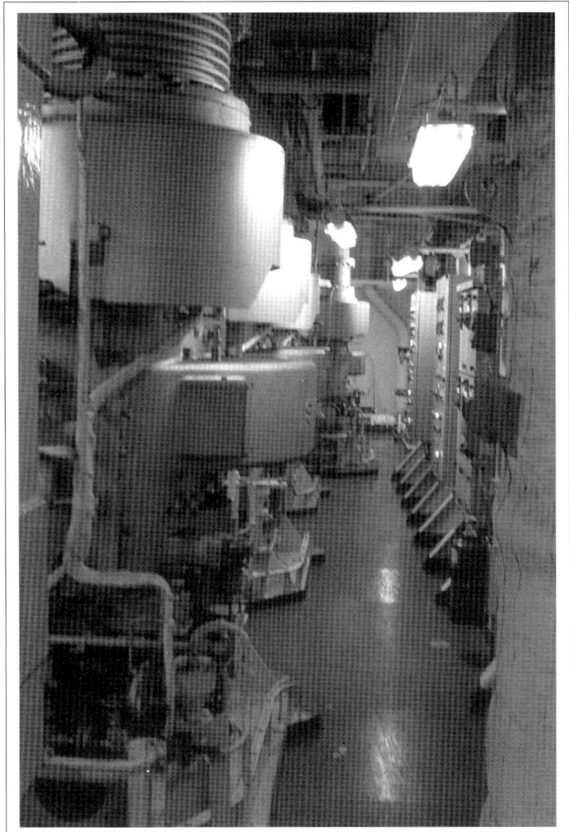

The three cargo pump turbines on a 'P' class VLCC, with the tank-cleaning pump in the background . (P Harrington)

plating were invariably around 18/20mm on the inner hull and 20/22mm on the outer. Side plating around the outer hull would have been approximately 18mm thick.

All large double-hulled VLCCs were constructed in a comparatively short period. With the *Arosa*, for example, a super-tanker of similar dimensions to *British Pioneer,* the first plate was laid down at the end of March 1992, the first blocks laid in dry-dock in August with construction well underway a few months later.

This particular VLCC was completed and had undergone trials by the following November and was carrying her first cargo in January 1993. The 650-tonne accommodation block being lowered into position by Hitachi Zosen's gantry crane indicates an idea of construction logistics involved in building modern VLCCs. The ship took 520,000 man-hours from start to completion – a time that varies favourably with the building of the same-sized BP Supertankers.

The bulbous bow of *British Pioneer* extended some

A description of the double-hulled VLCC showing construction details and offering nomenclature used. (Tanker Structure Co-Operative Forum)

The first plate is cut, the first completed blocks are placed and centre and wing tanks aft completed very quickly. The man crouching by the ladder, in the port side of the centre tank on the top photograph, offers an idea of dimensions. (David Manning)

20 metres in height and was designed to be submerged to a level at optimum depth to the forward draught so enabling a secondary pressure system to occur that would be out of phase with the wave motion generated by the forward motion of the Supertanker whilst under way. It has already been shown how this structure was reinforced to withstand considerable stresses.

A stern view of this class of VLCC indicates the 9.8-metre four-bladed propeller. This was solid cast Nickel aluminium bronze alloy and it makes interesting comparison with the Phosphorus Bronze type fitted to earlier ships. Propellers may weigh up to 60 tonnes, and often represent the most expensive single item aboard ship. By now, modern constructions were regularly adopting a variation of the Spade-type rudder which compared with the balanced rudder with either shaft or heel pintle design of previous generations of smaller tankers. Either way, they were invariably constructed of high-grade steel plating interfaced with a network of vertical and horizontal web frames.

Ships of this class were powered by MAN B&W seven-cylinder engines of 34,624 bhp giving a service speed laden around 15 knots. The bunker capacity of fuel oil was around 7,650 m^3/H, and 98 per cent laden consumption was to the order of 100 metric tonnes per day, with the main engine producing 79 rpm. This would give a service speed of some 16 knots under ideal weather conditions. *British Pioneer* was chartered for a while on the run from Arabian Gulf ports, via Suez, to the Louisiana Offshore Oil Port (LOOP). This is situated some 34 miles off the coast of Louisiana and is geared to handle any draft of Supertanker in fully-laden condition. Additionally, she was often diverted to the west coast of the United States, rounding Cape Horn and discharging at Long Beach, south of Los Angeles.

The BP-Amoco VLCC delivery was closely followed in 2000 by the £3 billion acquisition of Burmah Castrol Limited again without change of title. This act reinstated the earlier loss of lubricant products following the Mobil divorce. Burmah-Castrol was stated, during 1999, to have made a £284 million profit on a £3 billion turnover

On 1 May 2001, the Parent Group, now the second-largest oil conglomerate in the world, became restyled simply as BP, whilst the fleet remained as BP Shipping Limited. The same year saw delivery of a new class of 36,000-sdwt clean oil carriers, the *British Energy*, *Enterprise*, *Endeavour* and *Endurance* – (names familiar by now) joined the fleet the following year. A further two tankers, each of 106,500-sdwt and 75,109-sdwt – the *British Laurel* and *Trader* respectively came also into service.

In June 2002, BP Shipping announced a new management structure to increase expertise in the light of proposed company and fleet developments. A recent deal had been signed also with Frontline in which the Norwegian company would gradually fully employ between ten and twelve of their VLCC class vessels per year conveying BP oil cargoes. The aim of BP Shipping remained unequivocal – to possess a fleet that was modern: that conformed to all safety and environmental protection standards, and one that would continue the by now established policy of up dating, refurbish-

A new meaning to 'flying bridge' as a 650-tonne accommodation block is lowered into position on a Supertanker of comparable size to BP's 'P' class. (David Manning).

The rudder and propeller of the *British Pioneer*. (P Harrington)

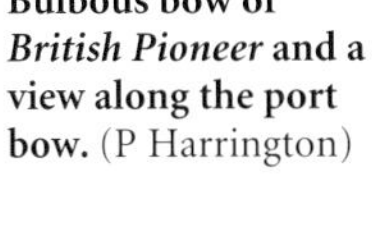

Bulbous bow of *British Pioneer* and a view along the port bow. (P Harrington)

ing and retrofitting, consistent with latest technological developments. Since the introduction of new manning policies, well before the turn of the millennium, the name 'BP' had re-acquired their reputation in the eyes of mariners as a first-class tanker employer offering a structured career programme, good salaries, assistance with enhanced professional qualifications and regular reliable voyage relief from virtually anywhere in the world upon termination of Agreements. These were the messages being exchanged (and heard) in nautical colleges where officers met for courses and exchanged views about their current employing companies based upon experience – a source equally as often of recruitment. The same year saw a veritable 'mini-fleet' of twelve tankers being delivered.

From around the late 1990s, BP have invested in excess of £3 billion in a massive new building policy. In this ambitiously controlled expansion programme, orders had already been placed for twelve Aframax tankers (under AFRA's alternative flexible market structure) between 80,000–120,000-sdwt, and twelve 46,000-product carriers from Far Eastern yards. Four 106,000-sdwt Aframaxes were due for delivery from the Tsuneishi yard in Japan by the end of 1994. Additionally, the North America Tanker Company, under contract with BP, had ordered four 185,000-sdwt crude oil tankers for the Alaskan crude trade. By July 2003, the British fleet run from Hemel-Hempstead – and later, Sunbury-on-Thames – owned and operated thirty-five tankers, with three single-hulled vessels due for sale. These included nine Handymax (around 46,000-sdwt), nine Aframax, four VLCCs, eight LNG carriers, and one shuttle tanker. The Company operated also four smaller coastal vessels that were up for sale, with replacements already ordered.

By March 2004, BP Shipping had twenty-three tankers on order, with a further forty-five planned – representing the largest extent of new building in the history of the Group. With typical foresight, a number of the proposed vessels were to be hull-toughened, so meeting Finnish-Swedish Ice Class rules enabling them to trade more widely in the Baltic Sea and north-west Europe. The orders included four Aframax and three 46,000-sdwt product tankers. The Group by October 2004 had extensive world-wide investments in liquid natural gas, including the Atlantic Basin, and this was reflected in orders being placed that month for four 155,000m^3 LNG carriers with Hyundai Heavy Industries to be fitted with dual-fuel diesel electric engines. The ships are due for delivery in 2007/8 and represent the largest LNG tankers yet ordered – with the Company having an option for a further four similar ships. The vessels will join the eight LNG carriers already in service with BP Shipping.

It was also in 2004 that the Company announced they would need in future to expand their horizons regarding officer employment. An insufficient number of British officers were being recruited to meet demands from an enlarging fleet. This led the company to fulfil the veiled hint – given ten years previously in 1994 – that if this were to happen they would be forced to look for human resources from other countries to meet the demand for professional navigators and engineers. Plans were well under way regarding the employment of Filipino ratings across the fleet – and six Aframax tankers were already manned entirely by Indian officers and ratings.

The main engine of 'P' class VLCCs seen from forward and showing the seven cylinder heads with three Wartsila diesel generators in the background. (P Harrington)

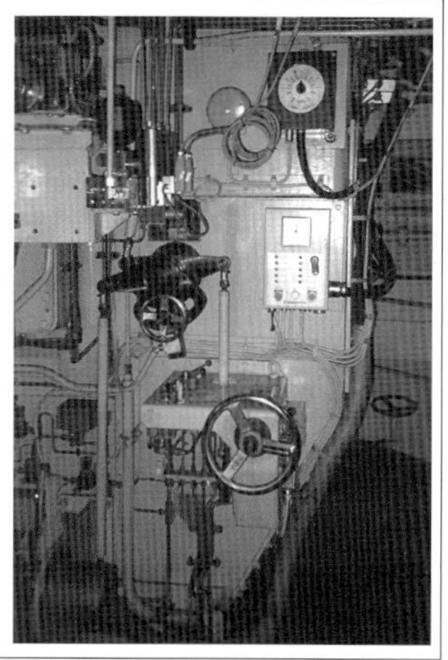

The local engine control station aboard *British Pioneer*. The bridge telegraph repeater, revolution counter and basic alarm panel are visible. (P Harrington)

Conclusion

This book was never intended to represent a history of the BP Group. It has been possible only to hint therefore and show, since the Company's formation in 1915 – 90 years ago – how a sequence of largely unexpected external thrusts have created moments of crisis amidst alternating positive periods. These distinctly cyclical patterns have occurred in *every* decade of the Group's existence and affected directly BP Shipping – their maritime transport arm – and subject of this research. On each occasion, the Group emerged stronger. This resulted entirely from levels of stability exercised by a measured calibre of unique senior leadership during those potentially difficult times. Judicious recruitment of personnel from 'corridors of power' ashore, and senior officers afloat, invariably ensured (without cliché) a flow in 'men of destiny'. Once selected, they were carefully nurtured to develop their existing entrepreneurial skills and experience grooming them for key top management posts in all areas of the Group. Such diverse men served 'the present moment' and were gifted additionally with temperaments of calm clarity, yet sufficient flexibility, to enable a forging of the most advantageous way forward for the Organisation as a whole. Plutarch *was* partially correct: shadowing this development of the BP Group has indicated, 'History (in some senses) does indeed repeat itself.'

The effects of such shore-based 'management realism' on BP Shipping resulted in the consistent development of a tanker fleet that adopted structural advances and was fitted with up-to-date technical developments as these came onto the market. It ensured also that professionally qualified and competent crews possessing appropriate Certificates of Competency, expertise and loyalty, always operated Company-owned ships.

Notwithstanding BP's considerable international involvements as a Group industry BP Shipping, representing still the maritime transport company, is in June 2005 undoubtedly a world leader whose fortunes remain inevitably inter-locked with successful management of the whole. Today, the present fleet growth continues to reflect similar progressive attitudes from men and women operating a 'no nonsense' senior executive strategy of planning, discussing, and then unobtrusively 'getting on with things' – in a seamanlike manner. They may well be running a fleet – but are doing so with feet firmly on the ground. As a result, BP Shipping has over 200 quality ships at sea – owned, managed or chartered – and they employ a shore staff in excess of 250, plus over 1,000 Merchant Navy officers. This Company continues a supportive yet intensive cadet-training programme for their 130 young men and women hoping to become navigating and engineering officers. By such continuum, a new embryo cyclical pattern of management emerges into creation where essential seagoing experience complements professionalism of colleagues recruited ashore. We believe William Knox D'Arcy would have approved unequivocally.

By 2015, BP Shipping will own eighty-five tankers of varying tonnage representing the largest, most modern and regularly serviced tanker fleet in the world, updated with latest technology. A truly new 'golden age' of British shipping has been achieved – one clearly designed to flourish well into a future financially sound and competently led – ashore and afloat. Perhaps that year represents also a time to review this chronicle of quietly confident success.

The *British Harmony* is a chemical/products carrier of 46,803-sdwt from Hyundai's Ulsan shipyard in July 2005. Seen underway on her maiden voyage she represents BP's latest launching. (Internet source)

PART TWO
THE FLEETS

NOTES ON THE SHIP HISTORIES

The first line contains the relevant fleet chronology number, ship name, the number of vessels that have carried the name in the fleet, the period in the relevant fleet section.

The seven-digit number displayed above the name in later vessels is the International Maritime Organisation (IMO) Identity No. That remains with the vessel for life and now must be displayed prominently on the vessel exterior. Examples seen thus far have been on the stern near to the name and port of registry

The second line contains the **O. N.** = Official Number (where known) **g.** = gross and **n.** = net tonnages and in later years **d.** = deadweight, followed by the dimensions between perpendiculars for earlier vessels given in feet and tenths of feet. From 1956 overall dimensions were given in feet and inches and from 1974 in metres. BB shows a bulbous bow is included.

The next section contains the number of engines (if more than one), followed by either steam turbines, or **C.**= compound; **T.**= Triple expansion, followed by the number of cylinders, for steam reciprocating machinery.
For motor machinery the number of cylinders is followed by **S. C**= stroke cycle and **S. A.**= single acting or **D. A.**= double acting.
Both types are succeeded by cylinder sizes x stroke length (where known) then by machinery type (where known) and the manufacturer thereof, followed by the figure and whichever of the following denominators that is applicable:-
HP = horsepower, **IHP** = indicated horsepower, **RHP** = registered horsepower, **NHP** = nominal horsepower, **SHP**= shaft horsepower, **BHP** = brake horsepower. (e.g. 2,500 ihp)
That is then followed by the vessel speed (where known) and any supplementary propulsion units (on later vessels), and finally the material (wood, iron if not steel) and type of vessel.

The final section contains the ship history commencing with keel laying, launch or completion dates (whichever are known), the shipbuilder (Yard No.) etc., followed by the vessel's career.

ADDITIONAL INFORMATION TO CLARIFY SOME ASPECTS OF THE FLEET INFORMATION PROVIDED.

For the numerous small craft owned by the various group owners, we have taken a conscious decision, due to the difficulty of locating accurate and complete details, to limit the extent of our research, so it is not surprising to find their histories as being 'far from complete'. The vessels in question, are identified at the end of the entry by the statement '*Due to small size and type of this vessel no further details have been recorded by the authors.*' or '*Due to type of this vessel no further details have been recorded by the authors.*'.

Section One # Wholly Owned Fleets

The Anglo-Persian Oil Company Ltd.
1936 – restyled as
The Anglo-Iranian Oil Company Ltd.
1955 – restyled as
The British Petroleum Company Ltd. (2)

AP. 1. FERRARA (1912–1915)

see ship No. BT. 4 in main fleet.

AP. 2. SIRDAR-I-NAPHTE (1913–1915)

O.N. 109958. 138g. 6n. 94.2 × 21.1 × 11.6 feet.
C.2-cyl. (19″ & 42″ × 24″) engine manufactured by J. G. Kincaid & Company, Greenock. 98 nhp.
Tug.

8.1898: Completed as EMPRESS OF INDIA by Carmichael, MacLean & Company, Greenock, for J. Constant, London. 1903: Sold to Sir John Jackson Ltd., London. 1907: Sold to the Florence Tugboat & Salvage Company Ltd. (W. H. Crosthwaite, manager), Middlesbrough. 30.6.1909: Sold to The Tees Tug Company Ltd. (same manager). 8.7.1913: Sold to the Anglo-Persian Oil Company Ltd. (J. Hamilton, Glasgow, manager), and renamed SIRDAR-I-NAPHTE. 31.10.1914: Requisitioned as an armed tug at the outbreak of war with Turkey (one 12-pounder and one Maxim machine gun). 7.11.1914: Commissioned in Royal Navy. 13.12.1914: Paid off. 19.3.1915: Whilst on a voyage from Abadan to Bombay, foundered off Bushire, in the Persian Gulf.

AP. 3. EUPION (1917–1918)

see ship No. BT. 13 in main fleet.

AP. 4. NAFTUN (1919–1921)

O.N. 147629. 58g. 7n. 81.7 × 16.5 × 4.5 feet.
C.2-cyl. horizontal (14″ & 28″ × 48″) engine manufactured by Campbell & Calderwood, Paisley. 190 ihp.
Paddle steamer.

1916: Completed by Alley & McLellan, Glasgow, for the War Office, Inland Waterway Transport Department, London, for Mesopotamian service, possibly with an 'S'-prefix name. 1919: Sold to the Anglo-Persian Oil Company Ltd., and renamed NAFTUN. 1921: Transferred to the Petroleum Steamship Company Ltd. 1924: Registered at London. 29.5.1925: Burnt at Salamad, upper Karun River.

AP. 5. THEGON (1920–1922)

O.N. 129319. 170g. 115n. 110.5 × 21.0 × 10.9 feet.
Post 1924: 174g. 0n. 110.5 × 21.7 × 10.5 feet.
Two, C.2-cyl. (13¹/₄″ & 32″ × 22″) engines manufactured by J. G. Kincaid & Company Ltd., Greenock. 160 nhp
Twin screw tug.

1915: Completed by P. McGregor & Sons, Kirkintilloch, for the Burmah Oil Company Ltd., Glasgow. 1916: Requisitioned by the War Office as the sea-going tug ST 13. 1920: Purchased by the Anglo-Persian Oil Company Ltd. 1922: Transferred to the Petroleum Steam Ship Company Ltd. 1951: Seized by the Iranian Government. No further details located.

AP. 6. NAFTAK (1920–1921)

O.N. 136324. 224g. 192n. 132.1 × 32.0 × 5.3 feet.
C.2-cyl. horizontal (15″ & 27″ × 54″) engine manufactured by the shipbuilder. 32 hp.
Stern ¹/₄ paddle steamer.

1914: Completed as PIMA by Yarrow Shipbuilders, Scotstoun (Yard No. 1357?), for the Irrawaddy Flotilla Company, Rangoon. 1915: Requisitioned by the War Office, Inland Waterway Transport Department, London, and renamed S. 02., for Mesopotamian service. 1920: Sold to the Anglo-Persian Oil Company Ltd., and renamed NAFTAK. 1921: Transferred to the Petroleum Steamship Company Ltd. 1947: Dismantled at Abadan.

AP. 7. Unknown (1) (1920–1921)

O.N. ? . 224g. 192n. 132.1 × 32.0 × 5.3 feet.
C.2-cyl. horizontal (15″ & 27″ × 54″) engine by an unspecified manufacturer. 32 hp.
Stern ¹/₄ paddle steamer.

1914: Built for the Irrawaddy Flotilla Company, Rangoon. 1915: Requisitioned by the War Office, Inland Waterway Transport Department, London, and renamed S.12., for Mesopotamian service. 1917: Converted into the hospital ship HS 12. 1920: Sold to the Anglo-Persian Oil Company Ltd. 1921: Transferred to the Petroleum Steamship Company Ltd. Details of original and subsequent war names have not been located.

AP. 8. DIYALA (1920–1921)

O.N. 147626. 60g. 9n. 81.7 × 16.5 × 4.5 feet.
C.2-cyl. (11″ & 22″ × 16″) engine manufactured by Plenty & Son, Newbury. 250 ihp.
Tug.

1917: Completed as T.38 by Rennie, Forrestt Ship Building, Engineering & Dry Dock Company, Wivenhoe (Yard No. 1305), for the War Office, Inland Waterway Transport Department, London, for Mesopotamian service. 1920: Sold to the Anglo-Persian Oil Company Ltd., and renamed DIYALA. 1921: Transferred to the Petroleum Steamship Company Ltd. 1951: Seized by the Iranian Government. No further details located.

AP. 9. CHARDINE (1920–1921)

O.N. 147630. 251g. 221n. 132.0 × 31.0 × 4.8 feet.
C.2-cyl. horizontal (15″ & 27″ × 54″) engine manufactured by the shipbuilder. 200 ihp.
Stern ¹/₄ paddle steamer.

1916: Completed as S.11 by Yarrow Shipbuilders, Scotstoun (Yard No. 1407), for the War Office, Inland Waterway Transport Department, London, for Mesopotamian service. 10.1916: Re-assembled at Abadan, for the Admiralty and commissioned as a floating workshop HMS SCOTSTOUN. 4.1920: Sold at Basrah to the Anglo-Persian Oil Company Ltd., and renamed CHARDINE. 1921: Transferred to the Petroleum Steamship Company Ltd. 1936: Collided with sternwheeler NUSRAT near Dorquain and damaged beyond economical repair. 10.1936: Sold for demolition. 1937: Dismantled at Abadan.

AP. 10. AMINIYEH (1920–1921)

O.N. 147674. 96g. 63n. 89.8 × 21.5 × 4.0 feet.
C.2-cyl. horizontal (14″ & 28″ × 48″) engine manufactured by Campbell & Calderwood, Paisley. 190 ihp.
Stern ¹/₄ paddle steamer.

1916: Completed as S.31 by Alley & McLellan, Glasgow (Yard No. 541), for the War Office, Inland Waterway Transport Department, London, for Mesopotamian service. 1917: Re-assembled at Mohammerah. 1920: Sold at Basrah to the Anglo-Persian Oil Company Ltd., and renamed AMINIYEH. 1921: Transferred to the Petroleum Steamship Company Ltd. 1951: Seized by the Iranian Government. No further details located.

AP. 11. EUPHRATES (1920–1921)

O.N. 147627. 58g. 5n. 81.7 × 16.5 × 4.5 feet.
Post 1928: 60g. 9n.
Two, C.2 -cyl. (9″ & 18″ × 12″) engines manufactured by McKie & Baxter, Glasgow. 250 ihp.
Post 1933: two, 4-cyl. 2 S.C.S.A. (9″ × 11″) oil engines manufactured by Norris, Henty & Gardner, Manchester. 192 bhp.
Tug.

1917: Completed as T 66 by Murdoch & Murray, Port Glasgow for the War Office, Inland Waterway Transport Department, London, for Mesopotamian service. 1920: Sold to the Anglo-Persian Oil Company Ltd., and renamed EUPHRATES. 1921: Transferred to the Petroleum Steamship Company Ltd. 1933: Converted to motor-engine. 1951: Seized by the Iranian Government. No further details located.

AP. 12. MAMATAIN (1920–1921)

O.N. 147628. 110g. 76n. 90.1 × 21.5 × 4.3 feet.
C.2-cyl. horizontal (14″ & 28″ × 48″) engine manufactured by Campbell & Calderwood, Paisley. 190 ihp.
Stern ¹/₄ paddle steamer.

1916: Completed as S.30 by Alley & McLellan, Glasgow (Yard No. 540), for the War Office, Inland Waterway Transport Department, London, for Mesopotamian service. 1917: Re-assembled at Mohammerah. 1920: Sold to the Anglo-Persian Oil Company Ltd., and renamed MAMATAIN. 1921: Transferred to the Petroleum Steamship Company Ltd. 31.12.1932: Sold for demolition at Abadan.

AP. 13. TIB (1920–1921)

O.N. 147625. 52g. 7n. 81.7 × 16.5 × 4.5 feet.
Two, C. 2-cyl. (9″ & 18″ × 12″) engines manufactured by the shipbuilder. 250 ihp.
Tug.

1916: Completed as T.27 by Wm. Simons & Company Ltd., Renfrew (Yard No. 576), for the War Office, Inland Waterway Transport

Department, London, for Mesopotamian service. 1920: Sold to the Anglo-Persian Oil Company Ltd., and renamed TIB. 1921: Transferred to the Petroleum Steamship Company Ltd. 1951: Seized by the Iranian Government. No further details located.

AP. 14. TIGRIS (1920–1921)

O.N. 147624. 52g. 7n. 81.7 × 16.5 × 4.5 feet.
Two, C. 2-cyl. (9″ & 18″ × 12″) engines manufactured by the shipbuilder. 250 ihp.
Tug.

1917: Completed as T.82 by Wm. Simons & Company Ltd., Renfrew (Yard No. 605), for the War Office, Inland Waterway Transport Department, London, for Mesopotamian service. 1920: Sold to the Anglo-Persian Oil Company Ltd., and renamed TIGRIS. 1921: Transferred to the Petroleum Steamship Company Ltd. 1951: Seized by the Iranian Government. No further details located.

AP. 15. Unknown (2) (1920–1921)

O.N. ?. 58g. 7n. 81.7 × 16.5 × 4.5 feet.
Two, C. 2-cyl. (9″ & 18″ × 12″) engines manufactured by the shipbuilder. 250 ihp.
Tug.

1917: Completed as T.70 by Bow, MacLachlan & Company Ltd., Renfrew (Yard No. ?), for the War Office, Inland Waterway Transport Department, London, for Mesopotamian service. 1920: Sold to Karun and Shatt-al-Arab Flotilla Company, but sale was not concluded. 1921: Sold to the Anglo-Persian Oil Company Ltd. 1921: Transferred to the Petroleum Steamship Company Ltd. Name and remaining details unlocated.

AP. 16. ST. PATRICE (1) (1922)

see ship No. BT. 44 in main fleet.

AP. 17. A. P. O. C. 10 (1923–1924)

see ship No. BP.18 in BP section.

AP. 18. A. P. O. C. 11 (1923–1924)

O.N. 130107. 205g. 123n. 100.0 × 24.0 × 10.1 feet.
Dumb tank barge.

2.1923: Completed by Hoare & Company, Colombo (Yard No. 5), for the Anglo-Persian Oil Company Ltd. 1924: Transferred to the British Oil Bunkering Company Ltd. 1928: Transferred to the Anglo-Persian Oil Company (Ceylon) Ltd. 1936: Owners restyled as the Anglo-Iranian Oil Company (Ceylon) Ltd. *Due to small size and type of this vessel no further details have been recorded by the authors.*

AP. 19. A. P. O. C. 12 (1923–1924)

O.N. 130108. 205g. 123n. 100.0 × 24.0 × 10.1 feet.
Dumb tank barge.

8.1923: Completed by Hoare & Company, Colombo (Yard No. 6), for the Anglo-Persian Oil Company Ltd. 1924: Transferred to the British Oil Bunkering Company Ltd. 1928: Transferred to the Anglo-Persian Oil Company (Ceylon) Ltd. 1936: Owners restyled as the Anglo-Iranian Oil Company (Ceylon) Ltd. *Due to small size and type of this vessel no further details have been recorded by the authors.*

AP. 20. BIBIAN (1923)

O.N. 147632. 96g. 67n. 89.8 × 21.5 × 4.2 feet.
C.2-cyl. horizontal (14″ & 28″ × 48″) engine manufactured by Campbell & Calderwood, Paisley. 190 ihp.
Stern 1/4 paddle steamer.

1916: Completed as S.32 by Ritchie, Graham & Milne, Whiteinch, Glasgow (Yard No. ?), for the War Office, Inland Waterway Transport Department, London, for Mesopotamian service. 1917: Re-assembled at Mohemmerah. 1923: Sold to the Anglo-Persian Oil Company Ltd., and renamed BIBIAN. 1923: Transferred to the Petroleum Steamship Company Ltd. 1951: Seized by the Iranian Government. No further details located.

AP. 21. KALGAH (1924)

O.N. 148562. 293g. 149n. 150.0 × 33.0 × 5.8 feet.
Two C.2-cyl. (13″ & 28″ × 48″) engines, 150 ihp, manufactured by unspecified manufacturers.
Stern 1/4 paddle steamer.

1917: Completed as S.52 by George Brown & Company Ltd., Greenock (Yard No. 104), for the War Office, Inland Waterway Transport Department, London. 1924: Sold to the Anglo-Persian Oil Company Ltd., and renamed KALGAH. 1924: Transferred to the Petroleum Steamship Company Ltd. 24.9.1942: Burnt out at a position 40 miles below Ahwaz, Karun River.

AP. 22. A. P. O. C. 13 (1924)

O.N. 147597. 224g. 208n. 94.6 × 27.0 × 11.0 feet.
Dumb tank barge.

3.1924: Completed by the Amble Shipbuilding Company Ltd., Amble (Yard No. 37), for the Anglo-Persian Oil Company Ltd. 1924: Transferred to the British Oil Bunkering Company Ltd. 1925: Reverted to the Anglo-Persian Oil Company Ltd. 1936: Owners restyled as the Anglo-Iranian Oil Company Ltd. 1949: Renamed ANGLIRAN 13. 1956: Transferred to BP (Aden) Ltd., and renamed BP MAALA. 1960: Entry removed from Lloyd's Register at owner's request. No further details located.

AP. 23. PANDO (1) (1924–1932)

O.N. 146165. 309g. 197n. 125.0 × 25.6 × 11.6 feet.
4-cyl. 2 S.C.S.A. (13 3/16″ × 13 3/4″) oil engine manufactured by Day, Summers & Company Ltd., Southampton. 615 bhp.
Post 1951: C.2-cyl. (11 1/4″ & 25″ × 18″) engine manufactured by Amos & Smith Ltd., Hull. 300 hp.
Powered tank barge.

24.6.1921: Launched by J. S. White & Company Ltd., Cowes (Yard No. 1557), for the British Oil Bunkering Company Ltd. (The British Tanker Company Ltd., managers), London. 10.1921: Completed. 1924: Transferred to Anglo-Persian Oil Company Ltd. 1932: Sold to Shell-Mex & BP Ltd., London. 1951: Converted into a steamship. 1967: Sold to T. W. Ward Ltd., Sheffield, for demolition at their Grays, Essex facility. 1.1968: Laying at Grays, Essex, awaiting demolition.

Pando. (World Ship Society Photograph Library)

AP. 24. PERSO (1) (1924–1932)

O.N. 145259. 309g. 197n. 125.0 × 25.6 × 11.6 feet.
4-cyl. 2 S.C.S.A. (13 3/16″ × 13 3/4″) oil engine manufactured by Day, Summers & Company Ltd., Southampton. 615 bhp.
Post 1951: C.2-cyl. (11 1/4″ & 25″ × 18″) engine manufactured by Amos & Smith Ltd., Hull. 290 hp.
Powered tank barge.

6.1921: Completed by J. S. White & Company Ltd., Cowes (Yard No. 1556), for the British Oil Bunkering Company Ltd. (The British Tanker Company Ltd., managers), London. 1924: Transferred to the Anglo-Persian Oil Company Ltd. 1932: Sold to Shell-Mex & BP Ltd., London. 1951: Converted into a steamship. 1967: Sold to the West of Scotland Shipbreaking Company Ltd. 21.2.1968: Arrived, in tow at Troon for demolition.

AP. 25. PETRO (1) /PHERO (1924–1932)

O.N. 146191. 337g. 206n. 140.4 × 24.0 × 12.2 feet.
4-cyl. 2 S.C.S.A. (13 3/16″ × 13 3/4″) oil engine manufactured by Plenty & Son Ltd., Newbury. 615 bhp.
Post 1951: C.2-cyl. (11 1/4″ & 25″ × 18″) engine manufactured by Amos & Smith Ltd., Hull. 290 hp.
Powered tank barge.

8.6.1921: Launched as PETRO by the Kings Lynn Shipbuilding Company Ltd., Kings Lynn (Yard No. 175), for the British Oil Bunkering Company Ltd. (The British Tanker Company Ltd., managers), London. 9.1921: Completed as PHERO. 1924: Transferred to the Anglo-Persian Oil Company Ltd. 1932: Sold to Shell-Mex & BP Ltd., London. 1951: Converted into a steamship. 1967: Sold to T. W. Ward Ltd., Sheffield, for demolition at their Grays, Essex facility. 1.1968: Laying at Grays, Essex, awaiting demolition.

AP. 26. PHILO (1924–1932)

O.N. 146199. 332g. 209n. 140.6 × 24.1 × 12.2 feet.

Perso. (World Ship Society Photograph Library)

Phero. (World Ship Society Photograph Library)

4-cyl. 2 S.C.S.A. (13³/16″ × 13³/4″) oil engine manufactured by Plenty & Son Ltd., Newbury. 615 bhp.
Post 1951: C.2-cyl. (11³/4″ & 25″ × 18″) engine manufactured by Amos & Smith Ltd., Hull. 300 hp.
Powered tank barge.

1.11.1921: Launched by Camper & Nicholson Ltd., Gosport (Yard No. 299), for the British Oil Bunkering Company Ltd. (The British Tanker Company Ltd., managers), London. 1924: Transferred to Anglo-Persian Oil Company Ltd. 1932: Sold to Shell-Mex & BP Ltd., London. 1951: Converted into a steamship. 1967: Sold to T. W. Ward Ltd., Sheffield, for demolition at their Grays, Essex facility. 1.1968: Laying at Grays, Essex, awaiting demolition.

AP. 27. POILO (1) (1924–1932)

O.N. 146166. 307g. 191n. 125.0 × 25.6 × 11.6 feet.
4-cyl. 2 S.C.S.A. (13³/16″ × 13³/4″) oil engine manufactured by Day, Summers & Company Ltd., Southampton. 615 bhp.
Post 1951: C.2-cyl. (11¹/4″ & 25″ × 18″) engine manufactured by Amos & Smith Ltd., Hull. 300 hp.
Powered tank barge.

22.6.1921: Launched by J. S. White & Company Ltd., Cowes (Yard No. 1558), for the British Oil Bunkering Company Ltd. (The British Tanker Company Ltd., managers), London. 10.1921: Completed. 1924: Transferred to Anglo-Persian Oil Company Ltd. 1932: Sold to Shell-Mex & BP Ltd., London. 1951: Converted into a steamship. 17.8.1967: Arrived in tow at Troon for demolition by West of Scotland Shipbreaking Company Ltd.

AP. 28. LIGER (1924–1930)

O.N. 147923. 1,576g. 638n. 254.0 × 43.1 × 16.9 feet.
Two, T.3-cyl. (15″, 24¹/2″ & 40″ × 24″) engines manufactured by the shipbuilder. 654nhp/1600ihp.
Hopper dredger.

10.1924: Completed by W. Simons & Company Ltd., Renfrew (Yard No. 667), for the Anglo-Persian Oil Company Ltd. 1930: Sold to the Government of Iraq (Directorate of Ports). 1958: Renamed KERBALA. 1963: Owners restyled Government of Iraq (Directorate General of Ports and Navigation). 1975: Owners restyled as Government of Iraq (Iraqi Ports Administration). 1976: Owners restyled as State Organisation of Iraqi Ports. 1978: Owners restyled as Government of Iraq (State Organisation of Iraqi Ports). 1979: Owners restyled as Government of the Republic of Iraq (State Organisation of Iraqi Ports). 1.8.1980: Lloyd's classification withdrawn. Still listed in Lloyd's Register 2003/2004.

AP. 29. TIGON (1924–1930)

O.N. 147940. 2,223g. 953n. 285.0 × 47.1 × 10.0 feet.
Two, T.3-cyl. (18″, 28″ & 48″ × 27″) engines manufactured by the shipbuilder. 850 nhp.
Hopper dredger.

12.1924: Completed by W. Simons & Company Ltd., Renfrew (Yard No. 668), for the Anglo-Persian Oil Company Ltd. 1930: Sold to the Government of Iraq (Directorate of Ports). 1958: Renamed KIRKUK. 1963: Owners restyled Government of Iraq (Directorate General of Ports and Navigation). 1975: Owners restyled as Government of Iraq (Iraqi Ports Administration). 6.1975: Damaged by fire. 1976: Owners restyled as State Organisation of Iraqi Ports. 1978: Owners restyled as Government of Iraq (State Organisation of Iraqi Ports). 1979: Owners restyled as Government of the Republic of Iraq (State Organisation of Iraqi Ports). 1980: Lloyd's Register entry deleted – 'Reported as being converted into a floating restaurant'.

AP. 30. A. P. O. C. 10 (1925 – 19??)

see ship No. BP.18 in BP section .

AP. 31. A. P. O. C. 13 (1925–1949)

see ship No. AP.22 above.

AP. 32. BRITISH SPINNER (1933–1940)

see ship No. BP.14 in BP section.

AP. 33. NO. 554 (1939–)

223g. 150.0 × 27.0 × 6.5 feet.
Dumb tank barge.

5.1939: Completed by B. R. Herman & Mohatta Ltd., Karachi, for the Anglo-Iranian Oil Company Ltd. *Due to small size and type of this vessel no further details have been recorded by the authors.*

AP. 34. NO. 555 (1939–)

223g. 150.0 × 27.0 × 6.5 feet.
Dumb tank barge.

5.1939: Completed by B. R. Herman & Mohatta Ltd., Karachi, for the Anglo-Iranian Oil Company Ltd. *Due to small size and type of this vessel no further details have been recorded by the authors.*

AP. 35. LARUBI (1945–)

100g. 74.0 × 22.0 × 7.0 feet.
Dumb land-reclamation dredger.

27.9.1945: Launched by Fleming & Ferguson Ltd., Paisley (Yard No. 733), for the Anglo-Iranian Oil Company Ltd. 12.1945: Completed. *Due to small size and type of this vessel no further details have been recorded by the authors.*

AP. 36. EMPIRE PHYLLIS (1947–1948)

O.N. 169190. 257g. 105.9 × 30.1 × 12.4 feet.
T.3-cyl. (16¹/2″, 27″ & 46″ × 30″) engine manufactured by the North Eastern Marine Engineering Company (1938) Ltd., Sunderland.
Tug.

2.12.1944: Launched as EMPIRE PHYLLIS by J. Crown & Sons Ltd., Sunderland (Yard No.218), for the Ministry of War Transport. 24.1.1945: Completed. 20.1.1947: Sold to the Anglo–Iranian Oil Company Ltd. (Kuwait Oil Company Ltd., managers). 1948: Transferred to the Kuwait Oil Company Ltd., and subsequently renamed HAYAT. 1961: Sold to Imprese Marittime Augustea S.p.A., Italy, and renamed BRUCOLI. 1982: Sold to the Italian Navy but never commissioned and was sold for demolition.

AP. 37. LOUTFY PASHA (1948–1949)

O.N. 183100. 50g. 60.0 × 14.5 × 7.7 feet.
8-cyl. 4 S.C.S.A. (5¹/2″ × 7³/4″) oil engine manufactured by L. Gardner & Sons Ltd., Manchester.
Tug.

8.1948: Completed by the Port Said Engineering Works, Port Said, for the Anglo-Iranian Oil Company Ltd. 1949: Renamed RANT. 1957: Transferred to BP (Aden) Ltd. *Due to small size and type of this vessel no further details have been recorded by the authors.*

AP. 38. ANGLIRAN 20 (1) (1948)

see ship No. BT. 224 in main fleet.

AP. 39. ANGLIRAN 17 (1948–1953)

O.N. 182882. 442g. 285n. 217.0 × 27.2 × 8.2 feet.
Two, 6-cyl. 4 S.C.S.A. (11″ × 15¾″) oil engines manufactured by D. & V. Boot, Alphen a/d Rijn.
Tanker.

1944: Completed as ALLER by N. V. Haarlemsche Scheepsbouw Maatschappij, Haarlem, for unspecified owners. 1948: Sold to the Anglo-Iranian Oil Company Ltd., and renamed ANGLIRAN 17. 1953: Transferred to BP Trading Ltd., and renamed BP ANTWERP. 1960: Entry removed from Lloyd's Register – for harbour service only.

AP. 40. ANGLIRAN 18 (1948–1955)

O.N. 182874. 442g. 285n. 217.0 × 27.2 × 8.2 feet.
Two, 6-cyl. 4 S.C.S.A. (11″ × 15¾″) oil engines manufactured by D. & V. Boot, Alphen a/d Rijn.
Tanker.

1944: Completed as WERRA by N. V. Haarlemsche Scheepsbouw Maatschappij, Haarlem, for unspecified owners. 1949: Sold to the Anglo-Iranian Oil Company Ltd., and renamed ANGLIRAN 18. 1955: Transferred to BP Trading Ltd., and renamed BP ELBE. 1960: Entry removed from Lloyd's Register – for harbour service only. No further details located.

AP. 41. ANGLIRAN 19 (1948–1953)

O.N. 182838. 442g. 285n. 217.0 × 27.2 × 8.2 feet.
Two, 6-cyl. 4 S.C.S.A. (9 7/16″ × 15¾″) oil engines manufactured by Kloeckner-Humboldt Deutz A. G., Koln/Deutz.
Tanker.

1941: Completed as LUHE by Ewald Berninghaus, Duisburg, for unspecified owners. 1948: Sold to the Anglo-Iranian Oil Company Ltd., and renamed ANGLIRAN 19. 1953: Transferred to BP Trading Ltd., and renamed BP ROTTERDAM. 1962: Sold to Louis De Koninck, Ghent, and renamed TINNY. Entry removed from Lloyd's Register – for river service only.

AP. 42. ANGLIRAN 20 (2) (1948–1956)

O.N. 182913. 214g. 143n. 179.5 × 16.6 × 7.8 feet.
5-cyl. 2 S.C.S.A. (9 13/16″ × 13″) oil engine manufactured by Sulzer Bros.Ltd., Winterthur.
Tanker.

1935: Completed as IBIS by Jos Boel and Fils, Tamise/Temse unspecified owners. 1948: Sold to the Anglo-Iranian Oil Company Ltd., and renamed ANGLIRAN 20. 1956: Sold to BP Trading Ltd., and renamed BP SHIPBUILDER. 1961: Sold to L. Cook, London. 18.10.1961: Whilst in tow from S. Shields to Terneuzen, encountered a severe gale and parted the tow. 23.10.1961: Located in two pieces at Bempton Cliff. 24.10.1961: Completely wrecked.

AP. 43. ANGLIRAN 13 (1949–1956)

see ship No. AP. 22 above.

AP. 44. RANT (1949–1957)

see ship No. AP. 37 above.

AP. 45. A. I. O. C. No. 26 (1949–1957)

75g. 80.0 × 19.0 × 6.6 feet.
Dumb tank barge.

12.1949: Completed by Mechans Ltd., Scotstoun, for the Anglo-Iranian Oil Company Ltd., and registered at Aden. 1957: Transferred to the British Petroleum Company Ltd., and renamed BP 21. 1960: Transferred to BP (Aden) Ltd. *Due to small size and type of this vessel no further details have been recorded by the authors.*

AP. 46. A. I. O. C. No. 29 (1950–1957)

30g. 80.0 × 19.0 × 6.6 feet.
Dumb tank barge.

5.1950: Completed by Mechans Ltd., Scotstoun, for the Anglo-Iranian Oil Company Ltd., and registered at Aden. 1957: Transferred to the British Petroleum Company Ltd., and renamed BP 24. 1960: Transferred to BP (Aden) Ltd. 1961: Renamed BP 106. *Due to small size and type of this vessel no further details have been recorded by the authors.*

AP. 47. A. I. O. C. No. 30 (1950–1957)

45d. 56.0 × 18.0 × 5.0 feet.
Dumb tank barge.

10.1950: Completed by Millen Brothers Ltd., Paisley, for the Anglo-Iranian Oil Company Ltd., and registered at Aden. 1957: Transferred to the British Petroleum Company Ltd., and renamed BP 27. 1960: Transferred to BP (Aden) Ltd. *Due to small size and type of this vessel no further details have been recorded by the authors.*

AP. 48. A. I. O. C. No. 31 (1950–1957)

45d. 56.0 × 18.0 × 5.0 feet.
Dumb tank barge.

10.1950: Completed by Millen Brothers Ltd., Paisley, for the Anglo-Iranian Oil Company Ltd., and registered at Aden. 1957: Transferred to the British Petroleum Company Ltd., and renamed BP 28. 1960: Transferred to BP (Aden) Ltd. *Due to small size and type of this vessel no further details have been recorded by the authors.*

AP. 49. A. I. O. C. No. 32 (1951–1957)

45d. 56.0 × 18.0 × 5.0 feet.
Dumb tank barge.

3.1951: Completed by Millen Brothers Ltd., Paisley, for the Anglo-Iranian Oil Company Ltd., and registered at Aden. 1957: Transferred to the British Petroleum Company Ltd., and renamed BP 29. 1960: Transferred to BP (Aden) Ltd. *Due to small size and type of this vessel no further details have been recorded by the authors.*

AP. 50. A. I. O. C. No. 33 (1951–1957)

45d. 56.0 × 18.0 × 5.0 feet.
Dumb tank barge.

3.1951: Completed by Millen Brothers Ltd., Paisley, for the Anglo-Iranian Oil Company Ltd., and registered at Aden. 1957: Transferred to the British Petroleum Company Ltd., and renamed BP 30. 1960: Transferred to BP (Aden) Ltd. *Due to small size and type of this vessel no further details have been recorded by the authors.*

AP. 51. A. I. O. C. 141 (1951–)

No details were located for this vessel.

AP. 52. A. I. O. C. 142 (1951–)

No details were located for this vessel.

AP. 53. IERLAND (1952–)

O.N. 185905. 80g. 20n. 73.4 × 18.8 × 6.8 feet.
500bhp, oil engine.
Tug.

1944: Completed at Martinshoek, Holland, for unlocated owners. 1952: Acquired by the Anglo-Iranian Oil Company Ltd., for use at Aden by C. Wimpey & Company during construction of a new refinery. 24.6.1953: Sailed from London en route to Aden. *Due to small size and type of this vessel no further details have been recorded by the authors.*

AP. 54. WRANGLER (1953–1955)

O.N. 182303. 457g. 289n. 184.5 × 30.1 × 6.2 feet.
Two, 12-cyl. 4 S.C.S.A. (7″ × 7½″) oil engines manufactured by Davey, Paxman & Company (Colchester) Ltd., Colchester.
Beach landing craft.

1944: Completed by Redpath, Brown & Company Ltd., Glasgow, for Marine Contractors Ltd., Southampton. 1953: Sold to the Anglo-Iranian Oil Company Ltd. 17.1.1954: Departed in tow as dead-ship, from Southampton. 21.3.1954: Arrived at Dar-es-Salaam, for use as a ferry for food and stores between the mainland and Mafia Island. 1955: Transferred to D'arcy-Shell Petroleum Company of Tangyanika Ltd. 1956: Owners restyled as BP-Shell Petroleum Company of Tangyanika Ltd. 1957: Transferred to BP Exploration Company Ltd. 1966: Sold to Belcon Shipping & Trading Company Ltd., London. 1967: Sold to Beira Transit Ltd., Portugal, and renamed TRIDENTE. 1.1967: Foundered.

AP. 55. BP No. 36 (1955–1957)

45d. 57′ 2″ × 18′ 4″ × 3′ 6″.
Dumb tank barge.

7.1955: Completed by Cory Brothers & Company Ltd., Aden, for the British Petroleum Company Ltd. 1957: Transferred to BP (Aden) Ltd., and renamed BP 31. *Due to small size and type of this vessel no further details have been recorded by the authors.*

AP. 56. BP No. 37 (1955–1957)

45d. 57′ 2″ × 18′ 4″ × 3′ 6″.
Dumb tank barge.

10.1955: Completed by Cory Brothers & Company Ltd., Aden, for the British Petroleum Company Ltd. 1957: Transferred to BP (Aden) Ltd., and renamed BP 32. *Due to small size and type of this vessel no further details have been recorded by the authors.*

AP. 57. BP 21 (1957–1960)

see ship No. AP. 45 above.

AP. 50. BP 24 (1957–1961)

see ship No. AP. 46 above.

AP. 59. BP 27 (1) (1957–1960)

see ship No. AP. 47 above.

AP. 60. BP 28 (1) (1957–1960)

see ship No. AP. 48 above.

AP. 61. BP 29 (1957–1960)

see ship No. AP. 49 above.

AP. 62. BP 30 (1957–1960)

see ship No. AP. 50 above.

AP. 63. BP 37 (1959–)

70g. 61′ 1″ × 23′ 11″ × 4′ 0″
Dumb tank barge.

24.12.1958: Launched by Clelands (Successors) Ltd., Wallsend (Yard No. 240), for the British Petroleum Company Ltd. 15.3.1959: Completed. *Due to small size and type of this vessel no further details have been recorded by the authors.*

AP. 64. BP 38 (1959–)

70g. 61′ 1″ × 23′ 11″ × 4′ 0″
Dumb tank barge.

24.12.1958: Launched by Clelands (Successors) Ltd., Wallsend (Yard No. 241), for the British Petroleum Company Ltd. 15.3.1959: Completed. *Due to small size and type of this vessel no further details have been recorded by the authors.*

British Petroleum Company Ltd. (1)

German principles created 1906.
Entered shipowning 1909.
1912: First entry in LCI steamers.
1914: Company title and assets seized by the British Government upon the outbreak of war.

1915: Assets entrusted to the Anglo-Persian Oil Company Ltd.
1917: Assets Purchased by the Anglo-Persian Oil Company Ltd.
1932: Restyled as Shell-Mex & BP Ltd.

BP. 1. PETROLEA (1909–1920)

see ship No. BT. 32 in main fleet.

BP. 2. QUEEN OF THE AVON (1909–1914)

O.N. 28862. 162g. 101.4 × 20.1 × 12.3 feet.
Iron Snow.

1856: Completed as GUDRUN by J. Vernon, Newcastle, for unknown owners. 1874: Sold to W. Lilley, London. 1879: Sold to A. Scott, Dundee. 1881: Sold to R. Swainson, Newcastle. 1889: Sold to the Tyne Wherry Company Ltd., Newcastle. 1890: Sold to the Anglo-American Oil Company Ltd., London. 1909: Purchased by the British Petroleum Company Ltd. 1914: Company title and assets seized by the British Government. 1914: Sold for demolition.

BP. 3. WHITE MAY (1910–1932)

O.N. 129176. 79g. 61n. 101.7 × 17.6 × 5.6 feet.
76hp, oil engine.
Powered tank barge.

1910: Completed at Amsterdam for the British Petroleum Company Ltd. 1911: Registered at London. 1914: Company title and assets seized by the British Government. 1915: Assets allocated to the Anglo-Persian Oil Company Ltd., without name change. 1932: Transferred to Shell-Mex & BP Ltd. 1936: Sold to E. L. Wilson & Company. 1938: Sold to John J. Bradley, London. *Due to small size and type of this vessel no further details have been recorded by the authors.*

BP. 4. HOME LIGHT (1911–1932)

O.N. 119588. 50g. 21n. 70.0 × 14.5 × 6.0 feet.

Scandinavia. (World Ship Society Photograph Library)

85 hp, oil engine.
Powered tank barge.

1904: Completed at Wivenhoe for unspecified owners. 1911: Purchased by British Petroleum Company Ltd. 1914: Company title and assets seized by the British Government. 1915: Assets allocated to the Anglo-Persian Oil Company Ltd., without name change. 1932: Transferred to Shell-Mex & BP Ltd. 1933: Sold to the New Medway Steam Packet Company Ltd. *Due to small size and type of this vessel no further details have been recorded by the authors.*

BP. 5. ROYAL STANDARD (1911–1932)

O.N. 129195. 75g. 43n. 100.5 × 17.1 × 5.8 feet.
70 bhp, oil engine.
Powered tank barge.

1911: Completed at Southampton, for the British Petroleum Company Ltd., registered at London. 1914: Company title and assets seized by the British Government. 1915: Assets allocated to the Anglo-Persian Oil Company Ltd., without name change. 1932: Transferred to Shell-Mex & BP Ltd. *Due to small size and type of this vessel no further details have been recorded by the authors.*

BP. 6. SCANDINAVIA (1912–1920)

see ship No. BT. 33 in main fleet.

BP. 7. BRITISH TOILER (1916–1932)

O.N. 146645. 131g. 101n. 105.6 × 21.1 × 7.3 feet.
As built: Oil engine manufactured by J. & C. G. Bolinders, Skarhamn.
Post 1938: 4-cyl. 2 S.C.S.A. (7" x 9") oil engine manufactured by Crossley Bros. Ltd., Manchester.
Powered tank barge.

Source 1 =1915: Completed as X100 by Dobson, Newcastle, for the Admiralty, London.
Source 2 = 1916: Completed as BRITISH TOILER by Pollock, Son & Company, Faversham (Yard No. 714), for the British Petroleum Company Ltd. 1932: Transferred to Shell-Mex & BP Ltd., London. 1938: Re-engined. 1975: Sold to Shell U.K. Ltd., London. 1981: Sold to Bowker & King Ltd., London. 11.1987: Romamet Ltd., commenced demolition at Rochester.

BP. 8. BRITISH EMPEROR (1917–1920)

see ship No. BT. 5 in the main fleet.

BP. 9. BRITISH EMPRESS (1) (1917–1920)

see ship No. BT. 6 in the main fleet.

BP. 10 BRITISH PRINCESS (1) (1917–1920)

see ship No. BT. 7 in the main fleet.

BP. 11. BRITISH ADMIRAL (1) (1917–1920)

see ship No. BT. 8 in the main fleet.

BP. 12. BRITISH SOVEREIGN (1) (1917–1920)

see ship No. BT. 9 in the main fleet.

BP. 13. BRITISH ENSIGN (1) (1917–1920)

see ship No. BT. 10 in the main fleet.

BP. 14. BRITISH SPINNER (1921–1932)

O.N. 135374. 41g. 23n. 66.6 × 14.3 × 5.8 feet.
C.2-cyl. (13 13/16″ × 13 3/4″) engine manufactured by Day, Summers & Company Ltd., Southampton. 26 nhp.
Powered tank barge.

7.7.1921: Launched by Rennie, Ritchie & Newport, Rutherglen, Glasgow (Yard No. 227), for the British Petroleum Company Ltd. 9.1921: Completed. 1932: Transferred to Shell-Mex & BP Ltd., London. 1933: Transferred to the Anglo-Persian Oil Company Ltd. 1936: Owners restyled as the Anglo-Iranian Oil Company Ltd. 1940: Declared a 'war loss' having fallen into German hands whilst operating in Belgium's inland waterways.

BP. 15. BRITISH FLAME (1921–1932)

O.N. 183117. 96g. ?n. ? × ? × ? feet.
Dumb tank barge.

1921: Built by J. S. White & Company Ltd., Cowes, for the British Petroleum Company Ltd. 1932: Transferred to Shell-Mex & BP Ltd., London. *Due to small size and type of this vessel no further details have been recorded by the authors.*

BP. 15. BRITISH LUSTRE (1922–1932)

O.N. 146838. 41g. 18n. 68.0 × 14.1 × 4.8 feet.
4-cyl. 2 S.C.S.A. (6 1/2″ × 7 1/2″) paraffin oil engine manufactured by L. Gardner & Sons Ltd., Manchester. 14 nhp.
Powered tank barge.

13.12.1922: Launched by J. S. White & Company Ltd., Cowes (Yard No. 1593), for the British Petroleum Company Ltd. 12.1922: Completed. 1932: Transferred to Shell-Mex & BP Ltd., London. 1950: Sold to J. E. Fisher thence to Hull Waterboats Company Ltd., Hull, and renamed WATERBOAT No. 8. *Due to small size and type of this vessel no further details have been recorded by the authors.*

BP. 16. BRITISH SPARK (1922–1932)

O.N. 146839. 41g. 18n. 68.0 × 14.1 × 4.8 feet.
4-cyl. 2 S.C.S.A. (6½″ × 7½″) paraffin oil engine manufactured by L. Gardner & Sons Ltd., Manchester. 14 nhp.
Powered tank barge.

8.12.1922: Launched by J. S. White & Company Ltd., Cowes (Yard No. 1592), for the British Petroleum Company Ltd. 12.1922: Completed. 1932: Transferred to Shell-Mex & BP Ltd., London. *Due to small size and type of this vessel no further details have been recorded by the authors.*

BP. 17. BRITISH TORCH (1922–1932)

O.N. 146840. 41g. 18n. 68.0 × 14.1 × 4.8 feet.
4-cyl. 2 S.C.S.A. (6½″ × 7½″) paraffin oil engine manufactured by L. Gardner & Sons Ltd., Manchester. 14 nhp.
Post 1949: 5-cyl. 2 S.C.S.A. (205 x 275mm) oil engine manufactured by Ruston & Hornsby, Lincoln.
Powered tank barge.

11.12.1922: Launched by J. S. White & Company Ltd., Cowes (Yard No. 1591), for the British Petroleum Company Ltd. 12.1922: Completed. 1932: Transferred to Shell-Mex & BP Ltd., London. 1949: Re-engined. *Due to small size and type of this vessel no further details have been recorded by the authors.*

BP. 18. A. P. O. C. 10 (1922–1923)

O.N. 130106. 205g. 123n. 100.0 × 24.0 × 10.1 feet.
Dumb tank barge.

10.1922: Completed by Hoare & Company, Colombo (Yard No. 4), for the British Petroleum Company Ltd., London. 1923: Transferred to the Anglo-Persian Oil Company Ltd. 1924: Transferred to the British Oil Bunkering Company Ltd. 1925: Reverted to the Anglo-Persian Oil Company Ltd. 1928: Transferred to the Anglo-Persian Oil Company (Ceylon) Ltd. 1936: Owners restyled as the Anglo-Iranian Oil Company (Ceylon) Ltd. *Due to small size and type of this vessel no further details have been recorded by the authors.*

BP. 19. BRITISH BEAGLE (1924–1932)

O.N. 181840. 30g. 5n. 82d. 78.6 × 17.7 × 5.1 feet.
Dumb tank barge.

25.4.1924: Launched by J. Pollock, Sons & Company Ltd., Faversham (Yard No. 1088), for the British Petroleum Company Ltd. 4.1924: Completed. 1932: Transferred to Shell-Mex & BP Ltd., London. *Due to small size and type of this vessel no further details have been recorded by the authors.*

BP. 20. BRITISH MAIDEN (1924–1932)

O.N. 147661. 102g. 55n. 90.1 × 19.4 × 7.1 feet.
4-cyl. 2 S.C.S.A. (11½″ × 12½″) paraffin oil engine manufactured by L. Gardner & Sons Ltd., Manchester. 40 nhp.
Powered tank barge.

5.5.1924: Launched by J. Pollock, Sons & Company Ltd., Faversham (Yard No. 1087), for the British Petroleum Company Ltd. 6.1924: Completed. 1932: Transferred to Shell-Mex & BP Ltd., London. *Due to small size and type of this vessel no further details have been recorded by the authors.*

British Maiden (World Ship Society Photograph Library)

BP. 21. BRITISH BOY (1926–1932)

O.N. 147413. 31g. 30n. 66.3 × 13.9 × 4.5 feet.
Dumb tank barge.

4.1926: Launched by J. Pollock, Sons & Company Ltd., Faversham (Yard No. 1221), for the British Petroleum Company Ltd. 6.1926: Completed. 1932: Transferred to Shell-Mex & BP Ltd., London. *Due to small size and type of this vessel no further details have been recorded by the authors.*

BP. 22. BRITISH GIRL (1927–1932)

O.N. 147419. 31g. 30n. 66.3 × 13.9 × 4.5 feet.
Dumb tank barge.

12.1927: Completed by W. H. Yarwood, & Sons Ltd., Northwich (Yard No. ?), for the British Petroleum Company Ltd. 1932: Transferred to Shell-Mex & BP Ltd., London. *Due to small size and type of this vessel no further details have been recorded by the authors.*

BP. 23. BRITISH YOUTH (1929–1932)

O.N. 147424. 45g. 24n. 72.0 × 14.4 × 4.4 feet.
3-cyl. 4 S.C.S.A. (8″ × 9″) paraffin oil engine manufactured by L. Gardner & Sons Ltd., Manchester. 16 nhp.
Powered tank barge.

27.12.1928: Launched by G. Brown & Company, Greenock (Yard No. 166), for the British Petroleum Company Ltd. 1.1929: Completed. 1932: Transferred to Shell-Mex & BP Ltd., London. 1955: Sold to H. E. Butler (Southsea) Ltd. 8.1957: Register closed upon sale to Holland.

The British Tanker Company Ltd.
1955 restyled as
The BP Tanker Company Ltd.
1981 restyled as
BP Shipping Ltd.
1999 restyled as
BP Amoco Shipping Ltd.
2001 restyled as
BP Shipping Ltd.

BT. 1. FÜRTH/KERMAN (1915–1920)

O.N. 136777. 4,397g. 2,758n. 389.0 × 51.0 × 25.2 feet.
T.3-cyl. (27¾″, 46¼″ & 76″ × 48″) engine manufactured by the shipbuilder. 2,365 hp.
Dry cargo vessel – used for cased oil transportation.

8.1907: Completed as FÜRTH by Flensburger Schiffsbouw Ges., Flensburg (Yard No. 273), for Deutsche-Australische Dampfschiff Ges., Germany. 1914: Captured by the Royal Navy off Colombo. 29.6.1915: Sold to the British Tanker Company Ltd., London. 3.8.1915: Renamed KERMAN. 14.6.1920: Sold to the Persian Gulf Steam Navigation Company Ltd., and renamed SULTANIA. 1933: Sold for demolition.

BT. 2. LADY CURZON (1915–1921)

O.N. 114903. 241g. 12n. 120.2 × 25.1 × 12.0 feet.
Two. C.2-cyl. (18″ & 38″ × 24″) engines manufactured by the shipbuilder. 138 nhp.
Twin screw tug.

12.1904: Completed by J. P. Rennoldson & Sons Ltd., S. Shields (Yard No.223), for Dover Harbour Board. 1912: Sold to S. Pearson & Son Ltd., London. 1913: Sold to General Works Construction Company Ltd., London. 1915: Purchased by the British Tanker Company Ltd. (D. Garrow, manager). 1921: Transferred to the Petroleum Steam Ship Company Ltd. 1953: Sold to Hanna El Sheik River Transport Company, Iraq. 1955: Entry removed from Lloyd's Register. No further details located.

BT. 3. FRIESLAND (1915–1922)

O.N. 139095. 1,169g. 1,087n. 215.4 × 40.2 × 13.3 feet.
Steel tank barge.

11.1908: Completed by Nederlandsche Scheepsbouw Maatschappij, Amsterdam (Yard No. 94), for the Nederlands Indische Tankstoomboot Maatschappij (Bataafische Petroleum Maatschappij, managers), Dutch East Indies. 1915: Sold to the British Tanker Company Ltd. 1922: Transferred to the Petroleum Steam Ship Company Ltd. 1955: Entry removed from Lloyd's Register. No further details located.

BT. 4. FERRARA (1915–1922)

O.N. 82009. 1,175g. 718n. 248.3 × 33.2 × 17.0 ft
C.2-cyl. (30″ & 52″ × 36″) engine manufactured by the shipbuilder. 135 nhp.
Dry cargo vessel – used for cased oil transportation.

8.1880: Completed by R. Steele & Company, Greenock (Yard No. 112), for J. Currie & Company, Leith. 1891: Transferred to Leith, Hull & Hamburg Steam Packet Company Ltd. (J. Currie & Company, managers). 23.5.1912: Sold to the Anglo-Persian Oil Company Ltd. 3.8.1915: Transferred to the British Tanker Company Ltd. 1922: Transferred to the Petroleum Steam Ship Company Ltd. 2.6.1923: Sold to Hajee M. H. Nemazee, Bombay. 7.1923: Gutted by fire and sank.

BT. 5. BRITISH EMPEROR (1916–1917)

O.N. 139156. 3,637g. 2,182n. 345.0 × 49.1 × 25.6 feet.
T.3-cyl. (23″, 38″ & 62″ × 42″) engine manufactured by the North Eastern Marine Engineering Company Ltd., Newcastle. 1,900 hp.
Ocean-going tanker.

18.2.1916: Launched by Armstrong, Whitworth & Company Ltd., Newcastle (Yard No. 887), for the British Tanker Company Ltd. 8.1916: Completed. 20.12.1917: Transferred to the British Petroleum Company Ltd. 10.12.1920: Transferred to the British Tanker Company Ltd. 7.5.1941: Whilst on a voyage from Durban to Abadan was captured and sunk by the German raider PINGUIN at a position 300 miles S.S.E. of Socotra.

BT. 6. BRITISH EMPRESS (1) (1917)

O.N. 140297. 6,847g. 4,253n. 10,738d. 430.1 × 57.0 × 33.1 feet.
T.3-cyl. (27″, 45″ & 74″ × 54″) engine manufactured by the shipbuilder. 3,100 hp.
Ocean-going tanker.

5.5.1917: Completed by Swan, Hunter & Wigham, Richardson Ltd., Wallsend (Yard No. 998), for the British Tanker Company Ltd. 20.12.1917: Transferred to the British

British Princess. (World Ship Society Photograph Library)

Petroleum Company Ltd. 10.12.1920: Transferred to the British Tanker Company Ltd. 1936: Sold, for £11,250, to Van Heyghen Freres, for demolition at Ghent. 31.12.1936: Delivered at Falmouth.

BT. 7. BRITISH PRINCESS (1) (1917)

O.N. 140298. 7,034g. 4,382n. 10,880d.
430.0 × 57.0 × 33.7 feet.
T.3-cyl. (27″, 45″ & 74″ × 54″) engine manufactured by the North Eastern Marine Engineering Company Ltd., Newcastle. 3,090 hp.
Ocean-going tanker.

17.5.1917: Completed by Armstrong, Whitworth & Company Ltd., Newcastle (Yard No. 891), for the British Tanker Company Ltd. 20.12.1917: Transferred to the British Petroleum Company Ltd. 4.3.1918: Whilst on a voyage from New York to Liverpool, was damaged by a torpedo fired by the German submarine U-92, at a position 16 miles N. W. from Lough Swilly, N. W. Ireland. Subsequently repaired and returned to service. 10.12.1920: Transferred to the British Tanker Company Ltd. 24.4.1946: Renamed BRITISH VETERAN, for subsequent use as a depot ship at Antwerp. 23.12.1948: Sold for demolition at Antwerp.

BT. 8. BRITISH ADMIRAL (1) (1917)

O.N. 140315. 6,842g. 4,213n. 10,738d.
430.1 × 57.0 × 33.1 feet.
T.3-cyl. (27″, 45″ & 74″ × 54″) engine manufactured by the shipbuilder. 3,100 hp.
Ocean-going tanker.

19.5.1917: Launched by Swan, Hunter & Wigham, Richardson Ltd., Newcastle (Yard No. 997), for the British Tanker Company Ltd. 6.1917: Completed. 20.12.1917: Transferred to the British Petroleum Company Ltd. 10.12.1920: Transferred to the British Tanker Company Ltd. 1936: Sold for demolition at Rotterdam.

BT. 9. BRITISH SOVEREIGN (1) (1917)

O.N. 140319. 3,657g. 2,176n. 5,796d.
345.2 × 49.1 × 25.6 feet.
T.3-cyl. (23″, 38″ & 62″ × 42″) engine manufactured by the North Eastern Marine Engineering Company Ltd., Newcastle. 1,900 hp.
Ocean-going tanker.

7.1917: Completed by Armstrong, Whitworth & Company Ltd., Newcastle (Yard No. 892), for the British Tanker Company Ltd. 20.12.1917: Transferred to the British Petroleum Company Ltd. 10.12.1920: Transferred to the British Tanker Company Ltd. 1951: Sold for demolition. 11.7.1951: Arrived in tow at Blyth, for demolition.

British Admiral wearing the original funnel markings. (World Ship Society Photograph Library)

BT. 10. BRITISH ENSIGN (1) (1917)

O.N. 140353. 7,048g. 4,390n. 10,860d.
430.1 × 57.0 × 33.7 feet.
T.3-cyl. (27″, 45″ & 74″ × 54″) engine manufactured by the North Eastern Marine Engineering Company Ltd., Newcastle. 3,090 hp.
Ocean-going tanker.

9.1917: Completed by Armstrong, Whitworth & Company Ltd., Newcastle (Yard No. 893), for the British Tanker Company Ltd. 20.12.1917: Transferred to the British Petroleum Company Ltd. 10.12.1920: Transferred to the British Tanker Company Ltd. 1937: Sold for demolition.

BT. 11. BRITISH ISLES (1) (1917–1938)

O.N. 140406. 7,108g. 4,427n. 10,240d.
430.2 × 57.0 × 33.7 feet.
T.3-cyl. (27″, 45″ & 74″ × 54″) engine manufactured by the North Eastern Marine Engineering Company Ltd., Newcastle. 3,090 hp.
Ocean-going tanker.

28.8.1917: Launched by Armstrong, Whitworth & Company Ltd., Newcastle (Yard No. 894), for the British Tanker Company Ltd. 11.1917: Completed. 1938: Sold for demolition.

BT. 12. BRITISH VISCOUNT (1) (1917–1918)

O.N. 95548. 3,287g. 2,074n. 312.0 × 40.4 × 21.1 feet.
T.3-cyl. (22$^1/_2$″, 37″ & 61″ × 39″) engine manufactured by the shipbuilder. 1,355 hp.
Ocean-going tanker.

19.12.1888: Launched as ROCK LIGHT by Oswald, Mordaunt & Company, Southampton (Yard No. 251), for Shell Transport & Trading Company Ltd. (M. Samuel & Company, managers), London. 4.1889: Completed. 29.9.1906: Sold to Lane & MacAndrew. 11.2.1907: Transferred to the Petroleum Steam Ship Company Ltd. (Lane & MacAndrew, managers). 1916: Managers restyled as a limited company. 6.1917: Purchased by the British Tanker Company Ltd., and renamed BRITISH VISCOUNT. 23.2.1918: Whilst on a voyage from Liverpool to Queenstown, was sunk by a torpedo from the German submarine U-91, at a position 12 miles N. by W. $^1/_2$ W. from the Skerries.

BT. 13. EUPION (1918)

O.N. 135320. 3,575g. 2,201n. 325.3 × 44.7 × 28.2 feet.
T.3-cyl. (23$^1/_2$″, 39″ & 66″ × 45″) engine manufactured by the North Eastern Marine Engineering Company Ltd., Newcastle. 401 nhp.
Ocean-going tanker.

2.1914: Completed by Mackay Bros., Alloa (Yard No. 21), for Eupion Steam Ship Company Ltd. (Howard Houlder & Partners Ltd., managers), London. 1917: Purchased by the Anglo-Persian Oil Company Ltd. 1918:

British Empress. (World Ship Society Photograph Library)

British Ensign wearing the original funnel markings. (World Ship Society Photograph Library)

Transferred to the British Tanker Company Ltd. 3.10.1918: Whilst on a voyage from Philadelphia to Limerick, was sunk by a torpedo from the German submarine UB-123, at a position 10 miles west of Loop Head, entrance to the River Shannon.

BT. 14. BRITISH GENERAL (1) (1918–1921)

O.N. 101840. 3,245g. 2,078n. 4,500d.
328.0 × 42.0 × 20.1 feet.
T.3-cyl. (24″ . 40″ & 65″ × 42″) engine manufactured by Blair & Company Ltd., Stockton. 1,410 hp.
Ocean-going tanker.

23.9.1893: Launched as GEORGIAN PRINCE by Armstrong, Mitchell & Company Ltd., Newcastle (Yard No. 611), for J. Knott, Newcastle. 11.1893: Completed. 1898: Transferred to the Prince Line Ltd. (J. Knott, manager). 1917: Owners sold to Furness, Withy & Company Ltd., London, who henceforth took over management. 31.1.1918: Purchased by the British Tanker Company Ltd., and renamed BRITISH GENERAL. 1921: Sold to Cia. Vasco Valenciana de Nav. S. A., Spain, and renamed EBROS. 1929: Converted into a depot ship. 1940: Sold for demolition.

BT. 15. MEXICAN PRINCE (1918–1919)

O.N. 101835. 3,028g. 1,933n. 4,330d.
328.3 × 41.0 × 19.5 feet.
T.3-cyl. (23″, 38″ & 62$^{1}/_{2}$″ × 42″) engine manufactured by Blair & Company Ltd., Stockton. 1,250 hp.
Ocean-going tanker.

9.1893: Completed by C. S. Swan & Hunter, Wallsend (Yard No. 183), J. Knott, Newcastle. 1898: Transferred to the Prince Line Ltd. (J. Knott, manager). 1917: Owners sold to Furness, Withy & Company Ltd., London, who henceforth took over management. 6.2.1918: Purchased by the British Tanker Company Ltd. (It was proposed to rename to BRITISH COMMANDER.) 6.11.1919: Sold to the Southern Whaling & Sealing Company Ltd. (N. C. Watt, manager), and renamed SOUTHERN ISLES. 1930: Sold to Cia. de Combustives de Lobito, Portugal, converted into a fuel hulk and renamed SILVA PORTO. 6.1937: Sold to T. W. Ward Ltd., Sheffield for demolition at their Pembroke Dock facility. 1.1938: Delivered at Pembroke Dock.

BT. 16. BRITISH MAJOR (1) (1918–1929)

O.N. 133526. 4,147g. 2,577n. 5,700d.
357.3 × 48.2 × 28.2 feet.
T.3-cyl. (25″, 42″ & 68″ × 48″) engine manufactured by the Wallsend Slipway Company Ltd., Wallsend. 1,810 hp.
Ocean-going tanker.

7.1.1913: Launched as ROUMANIAN PRINCE by the Tyne Iron Shipbuilding Company Ltd., Willington Quay on Tyne (Yard No. 185), for the Prince Line Ltd. (J. Knott, manager). 2.1913: Completed. 1917: Owners sold to Furness, Withy & Company Ltd., London, who henceforth took over management. 6.2.1918: Purchased by the British Tanker Company Ltd., and renamed BRITISH MAJOR. 26.7.1918: Attacked by U-140. 1929: Sold to Cie. Generale Armamento Societa Anonima, Italy, and renamed RIVA SICULA. 20.4.1933: Whilst on a voyage from Constantza to Dakar, grounded on Almadi Reef, Dakar. 24.5.1933: Refloated but subsequently sank in port.

BT. 17. BRITISH MARSHAL (1) (1918–1929)

O.N. 133513. 4,158g. 2,548n. 6,000d.
357.2 × 48.2 × 28.2 feet.
T.3-cyl. (25″, 42″ & 68″ × 48″) engine manufactured by the Wallsend Slipway Company Ltd., Wallsend. 1,810 hp.
Ocean-going tanker.

2.7.1912: Launched as RUSSIAN PRINCE by the Tyne Iron Shipbuilding Company Ltd., Willington Quay on Tyne (Yard No. 183), for Prince Line Ltd. (J. Knott, manager). 9.1912: Completed. 1917: Owners sold to Furness, Withy & Company Ltd., London, who henceforth took over management. 6.3.1918: Purchased by the British Tanker Company Ltd., and renamed BRITISH MARSHAL. 1929: Sold to Societa Italiana Transporti Petroliferi, Italy, and renamed TRITONE. 7.3.1933: Whilst on a voyage from Algiers to Constantza, grounded on Tenedos Island. 5.1933: Sold for demolition.

British Marshal. (World Ship Society Photograph Library)

BT. 18. BRITISH BIRCH (1) (1919–1931)

O.N. 139174. 5,873g. 3,555n. 9,000d.
405.3 × 52.0 × 31.5 feet.
T.3-cyl. (27$^{1}/_{2}$″, 45″ & 75″ × 48″) engine manufactured by J. Dickinson & Sons Ltd., Sunderland. 2,325 hp.
Ocean-going tanker.

1916: Laid down as OLDBURY by Short Brothers Ltd., Sunderland (Yard No. 391), for unspecified owners. 19.8.1916: Launched as BIRCHLEAF for the Shipping Controller (Lane & MacAndrew Ltd., managers). 12.1916: Completed. 8.9.1919: Purchased by the British Tanker Company Ltd., and renamed BRITISH BIRCH. 1931: Sold to Smith & Houston Ltd., for demolition at Port Glasgow.

BT. 19. BRITISH HOLLY (1) (1919–1931)

O.N. 140257. 5,162g. 3,191n. 7,480d.
397.1 × 50.0 × 27.2 feet.
T.3-cyl. (25$^{1}/_{2}$″, 42″ & 70″ × 48″) engine manufactured by D. Rowan & Company Ltd., Glasgow. 2,355 hp.
Ocean-going tanker.

3.1917: Completed as HOLLYLEAF by Wm. Hamilton & Company Ltd., Port Glasgow

British Major (World Ship Society Photograph Library)

British Soldier. (World Ship Society Photograph Library)

(Yard No. 302), for the Shipping Controller (Lane & MacAndrew Ltd., managers). 8.9.1919: Purchased by the British Tanker Company Ltd., and renamed BRITISH HOLLY. 1931: Sold for demolition.

BT. 20. BRITISH SOLDIER (1) (1919–1952)

O.N. 142707. 5,564g. 3,503n. 8,160d.
400.0 × 52.3 × 28.4 feet.
T.3-cyl. (27″, 44″ & 73″ × 48″) engine manufactured by the Central Marine Engine Works, W. Hartlepool. 2,585 hp.
Ocean-going tanker.

11.1918: Completed as WAR SIKH by Wm. Gray & Company Ltd., Hartlepool (Yard No. 907), for the Shipping Controller (T. W. Tamplin & Company, managers). 4.10.1919: Purchased by the British Tanker Company Ltd., and renamed BRITISH SOLDIER. 1952: Sold to Vivalet Shipping & Trading Company S. A., Panama, and renamed MARINA. 1954: Sold to A. Romano, Greece, and renamed ROMANO. 1959: Sold to Menora Cia. Maritima, Panama, and renamed MENORA. 18.7.1959: Arrived at Savona for demolition, by A.R.D.E.M. 13.8.1959: Work commenced.

BT. 21. BRITISH MAPLE (1) (1919–1932)

O.N. 109498. 4,559g. 7,045n. 470.0 × 56.0 × 32.0 feet.
Post 1908: 5,926g. 7,998n. 3,040 hp.
Post 1915: 5,806g. 8,039n. 10,790d.
T.3-cyl. (28″, 46″ & 75 ″ × 54 ″) engine manufactured by the Central Marine Engine Works, W. Hartlepool. 2,525 hp.
Ocean-going tanker.

17.8.1898: Launched as MOUNT ROYAL by C. S. Swan & Hunter, Wallsend (Yard No. 230), for Elder Dempster & Company, Liverpool. 11.1898: Completed. 1900: Transferred to the Elder Line Ltd. 6.4.1903: Sold to the Canadian Pacific Railway Company. 1908: Reboilered. 10.1914: Requisitioned by the Admiralty and converted into a dummy battleship representing HMS MARLBOROUGH. 1915: Converted into a naval oiler by inserting circular tanks in the holds, and renamed RANGOL. 10.7.1916: Purchased outright by the Admiralty (Lane & MacAndrew Ltd., appointed as managers), and renamed MAPLELEAF. 1917: Transferred to the Shipping Controller (same managers). 4.10.1919: Purchased by the British Tanker Company Ltd., and renamed BRITISH MAPLE. 6.6.1922: Stationed at Southampton Water as a bunker depot ship. 12.1932: Sold for £4,000, to Metal Industries Ltd., for demolition. 25.1.1933: Work commenced at Rosyth.

BT. 22. VINELEAF/BRITISH VINE (1) (1919–1923)

O.N. 113459. 7,678g. 4,837n. 11,000d.
470.0 × 56.2 × 31.8 feet.
T.3-cyl. (27½″, 45½″ & 75″ × 60″) engine manufactured by the Wallsend Slipway & Engineering Company Ltd., Wallsend. 2,960 hp.
Ocean-going tanker.

22.2.1901: Launched as PATRICIAN by C. S. Swan & Hunter, Wallsend (Yard No. 261), for Thos. and Jas Harrison, Liverpool. 3.4.1901: Completed. 30.11.1914: Requisitioned by the Admiralty and converted into a dummy battleship representing HMS INVINCIBLE. 1915: Purchased outright by the Admiralty, and converted into a naval oiler by inserting circular tanks in the holds, and renamed TEAKOL. 1917: Transferred to the Shipping Controller (Lane & MacAndrew Ltd., appointed as managers), and renamed VINELEAF. 12.7.1919: Purchased by the British Tanker Company Ltd., London, 4.10.1919: Renamed BRITISH VINE. 1923: Sold to A/S Tonsberg Hvalfangerei (H. Borge, manager), Norway, and renamed BUSEN. 29.7.1935: Arrived at Genoa for demolition.

BT.23. HERALD (1919–1921)

O.N. 124072. 387g. 46n. 125.5 × 28.2 × 13.0 feet.
Post 1914: 387g. 153n.
Post 1919: 367g. 4n.
T.3-cyl. (17″ 28½″ & 46″ × 30″) engine manufactured by G. T. Grey, South Shields.
Tug/tender.

15.4.1907: Launched by J. T. Eltringham & Company, S. Shields (Yard No. 261), for the Alexandra Towing Company Ltd., Liverpool. 6.1907: Completed. 1919: Sold to G. T. Grey, S. Shields. 1919: Sold to the British Tanker Company Ltd. 1921: Transferred to the Petroleum Steam Ship Company Ltd. 1953: Demolished at Bombay.

BT. 24. BRITISH ROSE (1) (1920–1930)

O.N. 137518. 6,572g. 3,817n. 9,250d.
400.0 × 54.1 × 32.5 feet.
T.3-cyl. (27″, 45″ & 74″ × 48″) engine manufactured by the North Eastern Marine Engineering Company Ltd., Newcastle. 2,475 hp.
Ocean-going tanker.

2.5.1916: Launched as CALIFOL by Sir Raylton Dixon & Company Ltd., Middlesbrough (Yard No. 594), for the Admiralty, London. 8.1916: Completed. 1917: Transferred to the Shipping Controller (Lane & MacAndrew Ltd., appointed as managers), and renamed ROSELEAF. 5.1.1920: Purchased by the British Tanker Company Ltd., and renamed BRITISH ROSE. 1930: Sold to La Riviera Societa Anonima di Nav. (A. Lauro, manager), Italy, and renamed PORTOFINO. 11.1942: Sunk as a war loss.

BT. 25. BRITISH FERN (1) (1920–1931)

O.N. 139189. 5,838g. 3,389n. 8,400d.
408.8 × 54.1 × 28.8 feet.
T.3-cyl. (27″, 44″ & 75″ × 48″) engine manufactured by Dunsmuir & Jackson Ltd., Glasgow. 2,905 hp.
Ocean-going tanker.

1.1917: Completed as FERNLEAF by Napier & Miller Ltd., Glasgow (Yard No. 200), for the Admiralty (Lane & MacAndrew Ltd., appointed as managers). 1917: Transferred to the Shipping Controller (same managers). 9.2.1920: Purchased by the British Tanker Company Ltd., and renamed BRITISH FERN. 1931: Sold for demolition.

BT. 26. BRITISH EMPEROR (1920–1941)

see ship No. BT. 5 above.

BT. 27. BRITISH EMPRESS (1) (1920–1936)

see ship No. BT. 6 above.

Herald. (World Ship Society Photograph Library)

BT. 28. BRITISH PRINCESS (1) (1920–1946)

see ship No. BT. 7 above.

BT. 29. BRITISH ADMIRAL (1) (1920–1936)

see ship No. BT. 8 above.

BT. 30. BRITISH SOVEREIGN (1) (1920–1951)

see ship No. BT. 9 above.

BT. 31. BRITISH ENSIGN (1) (1920–1937)

see ship No. BT. 10 above.

BT. 32. PETROLEA (1920–1924)

O.N. 125755. 202g. 95n. 300d. 119.0 × 21.9 × 10.0 feet.
T.3-cyl. ($7\frac{3}{4}$″, $12\frac{3}{8}$″ & $19\frac{1}{2}$″ × $11\frac{13}{16}$″) engine manufactured by the shipbuilder. 20 rhp.
Powered tank barge.

1905: Completed by L Zobel, Bromberg, for Deutsche Petroleum Verkaufs G.m.b.H., Hamburg. 1908: Purchased by the British Petroleum Company Ltd. 1914: Company title and assets seized by the British Government. 1915: Assets allocated to the Anglo-Persian Oil Company Ltd., without name change. 10.12.1920: Transferred to the British Tanker Company Ltd. 1924: Sold to Det. Danske Petroleum A/S (C. Fromholm, manager), Denmark. 1950: Sold to C. Marquandt, Denmark, and renamed TANKBJERG. 1959: Lloyd's Register deleted entry due to lack of up-to-date information.

BT. 33. SCANDINAVIA (1920–1922)

As built: 461g. 279n. 164.0 × 27.3 × 11.9 feet.
O.N. 132664. 456g. 207n. 171.0 × 27.3 × 11.0 feet.
6-cyl. 2 S.C.S.A. (13″ × $13\frac{1}{2}$″) paraffin oil engine – manufacturers unspecified. 77 nhp.
Aux. schooner.

1905: Completed by N. V. Werf V. Rijkee & Company, Rotterdam (Yard No. 118), for Wm. H. Muller & Company's Algemeene Scheeps Maatscahppij (Wm. H. Muller & Company, managers), Rotterdam. 1912: Purchased by the British Petroleum Company Ltd. 1914: Company title and assets seized by the British Government. 1915: Assets allocated to the Anglo-Persian Oil Company Ltd., without name change. 1917: British Tanker Company Ltd., appointed as managers. 1917: Transferred to Petroleum Steam Ship Company Ltd. 10.12.1920: Transferred to the British Tanker Company Ltd. 5.8.1922: Beached following a collision. 6.8.1922: Refloated. 20.12.1922: Wrecked on Portland Breakwater whilst on a voyage from London to Manchester. Wreck sold for demolition.

BT. 34. KURA (1920–1924)

O.N. 96153. 2,372g. 1,558n. 294.0 × 37.7 × 20.2 feet.
T.3-cyl. ($22\frac{1}{2}$″, $36\frac{1}{2}$″ & 60″ × 39″) engine manufactured by the Wallsend Slipway & Engineering Company Ltd., Wallsend. 1,170 hp.
Ocean-going tanker.

3.8.1889: Launched by Sir W. G. Armstrong, Mitchell & Company Ltd., Walker (Yard No. 555), for Kura Steam Ship Company Ltd. (Bessler, Waechter & Company, London) (Stephens & Mawson, managers). 8.1889: Completed. 1901: Managers restyled as Stephens, Sutton & Stephens. 16.11.1917: British Tanker Company Ltd., appointed as managers. 25.10.1918: Sold to Petroleum Steamship Company Ltd. 1920: Transferred to The British Tanker Company Ltd. 1924: Sold to Societa Armatrice Italiana, Italy, and renamed PERSIANO. 1938: Sold to Ditta G. M. Barbagelata, Italy. 12.4.1941: Whilst on passage from Palermo to Tripoli with benzine, was torpedoed and sunk by the British submarine HMS TETRARCH, off Tripoli.

BT. 35. BRITISH SAILOR (1) (1920–1951)

O.N. 142723. 5,576g. 3,444n. 8,450d. 400.0 × 52.3 × 28.4 feet.
T.3-cyl. (27″, 44″ & 73″ × 48″) engine manufactured by the shipbuilder. 2,585 hp.
Ocean-going tanker.

5.11.1918: Launched as WAR RAJAH by Swan, Hunter & Wigham, Richardson Ltd., Newcastle (Yard No. 1077), for the Shipping Controller (The British Tanker Company Ltd., managers). 12.1918: Completed. 16.2.1920: Purchased by the British Tanker Company Ltd., and renamed BRITISH SAILOR. 1951: Sold to Vivalet Shipping and Trading Company S. A., Panama, and renamed VIVA. 1953: Sold to Soc. Anon. Hellenique Transpetrol, Panama, and renamed LEROS. 4.1.1954: Grounded near the Elbe lightvessel and sustained severe damage. 9.1.1954: Refloated and subsequently condemned. 23.3.1954: Sold to the British Iron & Steel Corporation for demolition and allocated to Hughes, Bolckow Shipbreaking Company Ltd., Blyth. 3.4.1954: Arrived in tow at Blyth and work commenced the same day.

British Sailor at Cape Town. (World Ship Society Photograph Library)

BT.36. MUMBLES (1921–1931)

O.N. 137265. 195g. 17n. 100.2 × 24.0 × 11.2 feet.
C.2-cyl. (20″ & 42″ × 27″) engine manufactured by the shipbuilder. 700ihp.
Tug.

9.1917: Completed as MARSDEN by J. P. Rennoldson & Sons, S. Shields (Yard No. 303), for Sunderland Towage Company Ltd., Sunderland. 1.10.1917 until 11.11.1919: Requisitioned by the Admiralty. 5.1918: Sold to France, Fenwick, Tyne & Wear Company Ltd., Newcastle. 4.1921: Sold to the British Tanker Company Ltd., and renamed MUMBLES, for employment at Swansea. 25.2.1931: Wrecked at Oxwich Point, Swansea Bay.

BT.37. TANKARD x 8 (1922–1950)

134g. 102n. c110 × 21 × 8 feet.
Fresh water tank barge based at Swansea.

1915: Built for Government purposes. 1922: Purchased by the British Tanker Company Ltd., and stationed at Swansea. 1950: Sold to the Prince of Wales Dry Dock Company (Swansea) Ltd. No further details located.

BT. 38. BRITISH TOMMY (1921–1946)

O.N. 143971. 1,411g. 805n. 1,874d. 229.9 × 36.2 × 19.0 feet.
T.3-cyl. ($17\frac{1}{2}$″, 28″ & 47″ × 33″) engine manufactured by Rankin & Blackmore Ltd., Greenock. 805 hp.
Coastal tanker.

24.6.1921: Launched by Lithgows Ltd., Port Glasgow (Yard No. 745), for the British Tanker Company Ltd. 8.1921: Completed. 1946: Sold to Van Heyghen Freres, Ghent, for demolition. 4.12.1946: Departed in tow from the R. Tyne. 8.12.1946: Delivered at Ghent.

BT. 39. BRITISH VISCOUNT (2) (1921–1941)

O.N. 145236. 6,895g. 4,091n. 10,924d. 440.0 × 57.0 × 33.7 feet.
Two, steam turbines manufactured by the shipbuilder, double reduction geared to a single screw. 3,220 shp.
Ocean-going tanker.

24.1.1921: Launched by Swan, Hunter & Wigham, Richardson Ltd., Newcastle (Yard No. 1112), for the British Tanker Company Ltd. 6.1921: Completed. 3.4. 1941: Whilst on a voyage from Curacao to Scapa Flow, via Halifax, in Convoy SC26, was sunk by a torpedo from the German submarine U-73, at position 58.15N., 27.30W., with the loss of 28 crew.

BT. 40. BRITISH COLONEL (1921–1953)

O.N. 145243. 6,999g. 4,136n. 10,995d. 440.8 × 57.1 × 34.0 feet.
Two, steam turbines manufactured by G. Clark & Company Ltd., Sunderland, double reduction geared to a single screw. 3,220 shp.
Ocean-going tanker.

1.2.1921: Launched by Sir James Laing & Sons Ltd., Sunderland (Yard No. 626), for the British Tanker Company Ltd. 7.1921: Completed. 1953: Sold to the British Iron & Steel Corporation and allocated to P. & W. MacLellan Ltd., for demolition. 4.5.1953: Handed over at Bo'ness. 15.6.1953: Work commenced.

BT. 41. BRITISH TRADER (1) (1921–1953)

O.N. 146163. 4,204g. 2,314n. 6,089d. 351.4 × 49.1 × 27.1 feet.
T.3-cyl. (23″, $36\frac{1}{8}$″ & 58″ × 42″) engine manufactured by the shipbuilder. 1,745 hp.
Ocean-going tanker.

British Viscount. (World Ship Society Photograph Library)

8.7.1921: Launched by Wm. Beardmore & Company Ltd., Glasgow (Yard No. 621), for the British Tanker Company Ltd. 11.1921: Completed. 1953: Sold to Cheam Steam Ship Company Ltd., London, and renamed FLISVOS. 1954: Sold to Naviera Peruana de Pacifico S. A., Peru, and renamed MANCO CAPAC. 1961: Entry deleted from Lloyd's Register.

BT.42. BRITISH CHANCELLOR (1) (1921–1952)

O.N. 146197. 7,085g. 4,215n. 10,925d.
440.3 × 57.1 × 34.0 feet.
Two, steam turbines manufactured by G. Clark & Company Ltd., Sunderland, double reduction geared to a single screw. 3,220 shp.
Ocean-going tanker.

4.8.1921: Launched by Sir James Laing & Sons Ltd., Sunderland (Yard No. 681), for the British Tanker Company Ltd. 7.1921: Completed. 1952: Sold to Cia. Maritime Wanmas S. A., Panama, and renamed WANMAS. 1954: Sold to Compania Linea Roja Limitida, Liberia, and renamed FILITRIC. 1954: Sold to Vivalet Shipping and Trading Company S. A., Panama, and renamed VIVA. 1955: Sold to Tankers and Freighters (Israel) Ltd., Haifa, and renamed GAATON. 11.2.1961: Arrived at Spezia for demolition by Cantiera Nav. Santa Maria S.p.A. 23.2.1963: Work commenced.

British Chancellor. (World Ship Society Photograph Library)

BT. 43. BRITISH JUDGE (1) (1921–1953)

O.N. 146208. 6,735g. 4,011n. 10,573d.
420.5 × 56.4 × 33.4 feet.
T.3-cyl. (28″, 46″ & 75″ × 51″) engine manufactured by G. Clark & Company Ltd., Sunderland. 2,800 hp.
Ocean-going tanker.

18.10.1921: Launched by Sir James Laing & Sons Ltd., Sunderland (Yard No. 679), for the British Tanker Company Ltd. 12.1921: Completed. 28.2.1942: Whilst at a position 10 miles S. of Princes Island, Dutch E. Indies, was damaged by a torpedo from a German submarine. 1953: Sold to the British Iron & Steel Corporation, and allocated to T. W. Ward Ltd., Sheffield, for demolition. 8.6.1953: Arrived at their Preston facility. 15.6.1953: Work commenced.

BT. 44. ST. PATRICE (1) (1922)

O.N. 143977. 1,920g. 1,077n. 2,645d.
264.7 × 42.2 × 17.7 feet.
T.3-cyl. (21″, 34″ & 56″ × 36″) engine manufactured by the North Eastern Marine Engineering Company Ltd., Newcastle. 188 nhp.
Coastal tanker.

1919: Completed by Antwerp Engineering Company, Hoboken, for Societe Navale de L'Ouest, France. 1921: Transferred to Association Petroliere, France. 6.4.1922: Purchased by the Anglo-Persian Oil Company Ltd. (British Tanker Company Ltd., managers). 3.5.1922: Transferred to British Tanker Company Ltd. 21.5.1922: Whilst on a voyage from Swansea to Jarrow, stranded on the Man O' War Rocks, Lizard. 8.6.1922: Refloated and beached to prevent sinking. 16.7.1922: Refloated and taken to Falmouth for inspection. Declared a total loss. Subsequently foundered whilst in tow to Wilhelmshavn, for demolition.

British Judge. (World Ship Society Photograph Library)

British Trader. (World Ship Society Photograph Library)

BT. 45. BRITISH ENTERPRISE (1) (1922–1936)

O.N. 146219. 4,204g. 2,312n. 6,089d.
351.4 × 49.1 × 27.1 feet.
T.3-cyl. (23″, 36″ & 58″ × 42″) engine manufactured by the shipbuilder. 1,745 hp.
Ocean-going tanker.

19.10.1921: Launched by Wm. Beardmore & Company Ltd., Glasgow (Yard No. 623), for the British Tanker Company Ltd. 1.1922: Completed. 1936: Sold to the West of Scotland Shipbreaking Company Ltd., for demolition at Troon.

British Enterprise. (World Ship Society Photograph Library)

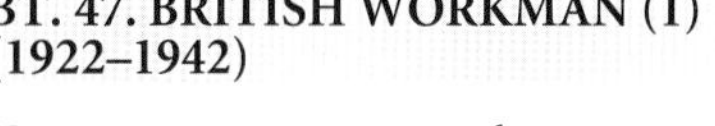

BT. 47. BRITISH WORKMAN (1) (1922–1942)

O.N. 146550. 6,994g. 4,066n. 10,898d.
440.4 × 57.0 × 33.9 feet.
Two, steam turbines manufactured by the shipbuilder, double reduction geared to a single screw. 3,220 shp.
Ocean-going tanker.

17.1.1922: Launched by Workman, Clark & Company Ltd., Belfast (Yard No. 465), for the British Tanker Company Ltd. 4.1922: Completed. 9.4.1941: Damaged by aircraft bombing at position 58.31N., 12.40W. 3.5.1942: Having suffered machinery problems and straggled whilst on a voyage in Convoy ON 89, from Greenock to Galveston, was sunk by a torpedo from the German submarine U-455, at position 44.7N., 51.53W., 300 miles south of Cape Race.

British Mariner. (World Ship Society Photograph Library)

BT. 48. BRITISH CORPORAL (1) (1922–1940)

O.N. 146561. 6,972g. 4,072n. 10,817d.
440.0 × 57.1 × 33.8 feet.
Two, steam turbines manufactured by the shipbuilder, double reduction geared to a single screw. 3,270 shp.
Ocean-going tanker.

29.11.1921: Launched by Palmer's Shipbuilding & Iron Company Ltd., Jarrow (Yard No. 923), for the British Tanker Company Ltd. 23.5.1922: Completed. 4.7.1940: Whilst at position 50.13N., 12.35W., 10 miles south from Portland Bill, was severely damaged by a German 'E' boat. Declared a total loss, the vessel was taken over by the Ministry of Shipping (subsequently restyled as the Ministry of War Transport), repaired and renamed EMPIRE CORPORAL (the British Tanker Company Ltd., appointed as managers). 10.8.1942: Departed from Curacao as part of Convoy TAW 12 J, bound to Key West. 14.8.1942: Sunk by a torpedo from the German submarine U-598, at position 21.45N., 76.10W., off the north coast of Cuba.

BT. 46. BRITISH MARINER (1) (1922–1941)

O.N. 146530. 6,996g. 4,083n. 10,772d.
440.2 × 57.1 × 33.8 feet.
Two, steam turbines manufactured by the shipbuilder, double reduction geared to a single screw. 3,270 shp.
Ocean-going tanker.

4.10.1921: Launched by Palmer's Shipbuilding & Iron Company Ltd., Jarrow (Yard No. 924), for the British Tanker Company Ltd. 7.3.1922: Completed. 20.10.1941: Sunk by a torpedo from the German submarine U-126, at position 7.43N., 14.20W., 100 miles west of Freetown.

British Corporal. (World Ship Society Photograph Library)

British Workman. (World Ship Society Photograph Library)

BT. 49. BRITISH COUNCILLOR (1) (1922–1940)

O.N. 146562. 7,045g. 4,190n. 10,925d.
440.3 × 57.1 × 33.9 feet.
Two, steam turbines manufactured by G. Clark & Company Ltd., Sunderland, double reduction geared to a single screw. 3,210 shp.
Ocean-going tanker.

12.2.1921: Launched by Sir J. Laing & Sons Ltd., Sunderland (Yard No.682), for the British Tanker Company Ltd. 5.1922: Completed. 2.2.1940: Whilst on a ballast voyage from R. Tyne to Abadan, in Convoy FS 84, exploded a mine off the Humber Estuary. 3.2.1940: Sank at position 53.44.52N.,

British Engineer. (World Ship Society Photograph Library)

0.24.05W., 20 miles N.E. of Spurn Head. (Other sources state torpedo from "E"boat, or submarine as cause of loss)

BT. 50. BRITISH ENGINEER (1) (1922–1952)

O.N. 146578. 7,016g. 4,059n. 10,898d. 440.4 × 57.0 × 33.9 feet.
Two, steam turbines manufactured by the shipbuilder, double reduction geared to a single screw. 3,025 shp.
Ocean-going tanker.

27.4.1922: Launched by Workman, Clark & Company Ltd., Belfast (Yard No. 466), for the British Tanker Company Ltd. 6.1922: Completed. 12.6.1944: Suffered mine damage at position 50.10N., 00.59W. 1952: Sold to Vivalet Shipping and Trading Company S.A., Panama, and renamed EMILY. 1954: Sold to Traders & Shippers (Tankers) Ltd., Israel, and renamed YARKON. 11.1958: Sold to Cantiera Nav.Santa Maria S.p.A., La Spezia, for demolition but was resold to Brodospas. 1.1959: Arrived at Split.

BT. 51. BRITISH GRENADIER (1) (1922–1941)

O.N. 146591. 6,888g. 4,078n. 10,750d. 440.0 × 57.0 × 33.7 feet.
Two, steam turbines manufactured by Metropolitan-Vickers Electric Company Ltd., Manchester, double reduction geared to a single screw. 3,025 shp.
Ocean-going tanker.

14.2.1922: Launched by Swan, Hunter & Wigham, Richardson Ltd., Newcastle (Yard No. 1126), for the British Tanker Company Ltd. 2.1922: Completed. 22.5.1941: Whilst on a ballast voyage from Freetown to Aruba and Curacao, was sunk by a torpedo from the German submarine U-103, at position 6.15N., 12.59W., 150 miles west of Monrovia.

BT. 52. BRITISH INDUSTRY (1) (1922)

4,121g. 2,261n. 351.4 × 49.1 × 27.1 feet.
T.3-cyl. (23″ 36″ & 58″ × 42″) engine manufactured by the shipbuilder. 349 nhp.
Ocean-going tanker.

1.1922: Launched as BRITISH INDUSTRY by Wm. Beardmore & Company Ltd., Glasgow (Yard No. 624), for British Tanker Company Ltd. 4.1922: Completed as ST. JEROME for Association Petroliere, France. 1928: Renamed SHAPUR. 1939: Sold to the French Navy for conversion into a pontoon.

BT. 53. BRITISH COMMERCE (1) (1922–1937)

O.N. 146615. 4,205g. 2,310n. 6,089d. 351.4 × 49.1 × 27.1 feet.
T.3-cyl. (23″ 36″ & 58″ × 42″) engine manufactured by the shipbuilder. 1,745 hp.
Ocean-going tanker.

26.5.1922: Launched by Wm. Beardmore & Company Ltd., Glasgow (Yard No. 625), for the British Tanker Company Ltd. 22.8.1922: Completed. 1937: Sold for demolition.

BT. 54. BRITISH GENERAL (2) (1922–1940)

O.N. 146610. 6,985g. 4,073n. 10,822d. 440.2 × 57.1 × 33.8 feet.
Two, steam turbines manufactured by the shipbuilder, double reduction geared to a single screw shaft. 3,270 hp.
Ocean-going tanker.

15.11.1921: Launched by Palmer's Shipbuilding & Iron Company Ltd., Jarrow (Yard No. 926), for the British Tanker Company Ltd. 6.1922: Completed. 6.10.1940: Whilst of a voyage from the R. Tyne to Abadan, in Convoy OA 222, was damaged by a torpedo from the German submarine U-37, at position 51.42N. 24.03W., 700 miles west of Ireland. 7.10.1940: Sank at position 51.42N. 24.50W.

BT. 55. BRITISH ADVOCATE (1) (1922–1941)

O.N. 146629. 6,993g. 4,151n. 10,925d. 440.3 × 57.1 × 33.9 feet.

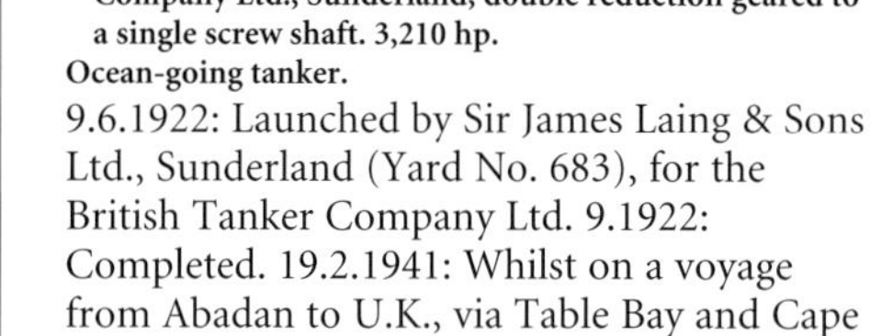
Two, steam turbines manufactured by G. Clark & Company Ltd., Sunderland, double reduction geared to a single screw shaft. 3,210 hp.
Ocean-going tanker.

9.6.1922: Launched by Sir James Laing & Sons Ltd., Sunderland (Yard No. 683), for the British Tanker Company Ltd. 9.1922: Completed. 19.2.1941: Whilst on a voyage from Abadan to U.K., via Table Bay and Cape Town was captured and taken as a prize by the German pocket battleship ADMIRAL SCHEER, at position 7.10N., 45.30E., west of the Seychelles. 29.4.1941: Arrived at Bordeaux, and subsequently renamed ADOLF. 1941: Renamed NORDSTERN. 25.9.1943: Sunk at Nantes. Subsequently raised. 23.7.1944: Sunk by aircraft bombing at Donges. 1947: Raised for demolition.

British Gunner (World Ship Society Photograph Library)

BT. 56. BRITISH GUNNER (1) (1922–1941)

O.N. 146639. 6,894g. 4,073n. 10,750d. 440.0 × 57.0 × 33.7 feet.
Two, steam turbines manufactured by the shipbuilder, double reduction geared to a single screw shaft. 3,210 hp.
Ocean-going tanker.

10.8.1922: Launched by Swan, Hunter & Wigham, Richardson, Newcastle (Yard No. 1130), for the British Tanker Company Ltd. 10.1922: Completed. 24.2.1941: Whilst on a voyage in Convoy OB 289 from Swansea to Aruba, was sunk by a torpedo from the German submarine U-97, at position 61.09N., 12.04W., near the Faroes.

BT. 57. BRITISH SCOUT (1922–1957)

O.N. 143979. 1,507g. 836n. 2,210d. 245.0 × 37.2 × 19.8 feet.
T.3-cyl. (17½″, 29″ & 48″ × 33″) engine manufactured by the shipbuilder. 910 hp.
Coastal tanker.

25.8.1922: Launched by Swan, Hunter &

British Commerce wearing the original funnel markings. (World Ship Society Photograph Library)

Wigham, Richardson Ltd., Newcastle (Yard No. 1136), for the British Tanker Company Ltd. 10.1922: Completed. 1.6.1956: Owners restyled as BP Tanker Company Ltd. 1957: Sold to the British Iron & Steel Corporation and allocated to Metal Industries Ltd., for demolition. 3.4.1957: Arrived at Rosyth and work commenced.

British Scout (World Ship Society Photograph Library)

BT. 58. BRITISH SERGEANT (1) (1922–1942)

O.N. 146647. 5,868g. 3,387n. 9,120d.
400.6 × 54.2 × 32.7 feet.
Two, steam turbines manufactured by the shipbuilder, double reduction geared to a single screw shaft. 2,965 hp.
Ocean-going tanker.

27.2.1922: Launched by Palmer's Shipbuilding & Iron Company Ltd., Newcastle (Yard No. 931), for the British Tanker Company Ltd. 10.1922: Completed. 9.4.1942: Whilst in the Bay of Bengal, on a voyage from Trincomalee, was sunk by Japanese aircraft, at position 08.10N., 81.38E.

British Sergeant wearing the original funnel markings. (World Ship Society Photograph Library)

BT. 59. BRITISH OFFICER (1) (1922–1940)

O.N. 146646. 6,990g. 4,083n. 10,822d.
440.2 × 57.1 × 33.8 feet.
Two, steam turbines manufactured by the shipbuilder, double reduction geared to a single screw shaft. 3,270 hp.
Ocean-going tanker.

22.8.1922: Launched by Palmer's Shipbuilding & Iron Company Ltd., Newcastle (Yard No. 934), for the British Tanker Company Ltd. 11.1922: Completed. 1.12.1940: Whilst on a voyage from Sheerness to R. Tyne, exploded a mine at a position 1/2 mile east of the north pier of the R. Tyne, and was beached to prevent sinking. 12.12.1940: Broke in two, stern sank and bow subsequently demolished.

BT. 60. BRITISH MERCHANT (1) (1922–1949)

O.N. 146655. 7,012g. 4,004n. 10,729d.
440.7 × 57.2 × 34.1 feet.
Two, steam turbines manufactured by the shipbuilder, double reduction geared to a single screw shaft. 3,365 hp.
Ocean-going tanker.

23.8.1922: Launched by Wm. Beardmore & Company Ltd., Glasgow (Yard No. 622), for the British Tanker Company Ltd. 11.1922: Completed. 1949: Sold to the British Iron & Steel Corporation and allocated to Hughes Bolckow Shipbreaking Company Ltd., Blyth, for demolition. 8.1949: Arrived in tow from Newport and work commenced.

British Merchant. (World Ship Society Photograph Library)

BT. 61. BRITISH LORD (1922–1953)

O.N. 146658. 6,098g. 3,520n. 9,517d.
412.0 × 54.8 × 32.9 feet.
Two, steam turbines manufactured by Metropolitan-Vickers Electric Company Ltd., Manchester, double reduction geared to a single screw shaft. 3,220 hp.
Ocean-going tanker.

24.7.1922: Launched by J. L. Thompson & Sons Ltd., Sunderland (Yard No. 547), for the British Tanker Company Ltd. 11.1922: Completed. 21.4.1941: Damaged by aircraft at position 34.35N., 23.32E. 1953: Sold to the British Iron & Steel Corporation and allocated to T. W. Ward Ltd., Sheffield, for demolition at their Milford Haven facility. 22.5.1953: Arrived at Milford Haven from Dunkirk. 8.6.1953: Work commenced.

British Officer. (World Ship Society Photograph Library)

British Lord wearing the original funnel markings. (World Ship Society Photograph Library)

BT. 62. BRITISH COMMANDER (1) (1922–1940)

O.N. 146652. 6,898g. 4,072n. 11,028d.
440.0 × 57.0 × 33.8 feet.
Two, steam turbines manufactured by Metropolitan-Vickers Electric Company Ltd., Manchester, double reduction geared to a single screw shaft. 3,215 hp.
Ocean-going tanker.

11.7.1922: Launched by the Caledon Shipbuilding & Engineering Company Ltd., Dundee (Yard No. 282), for the British Tanker Company Ltd. 12.1922: Completed. 27.8.1940: Whilst on an independent ballast voyage from Falmouth to Abadan, via Table Bay, was sunk with torpedo and gunfire by the German raider PINGUIN, at position 29.37N., 45.50E., 250 miles south of Pointe Barrow. (Another source states 39.30N., 46.06E., south of Madagascar.)

British Commander at Cape Town. (World Ship Society Photograph Library)

British Premier. (World Ship Society Photograph Library)

BT. 63. BRITISH ARCHITECT (1) (1922–1953)

O.N. 146680. 7,388g. 4,136n. 11,624d.
440.4 × 56.1 × 34.6 feet.
T.3-cyl. (25″, $42^{1}/_{2}$″ & 72″ × 54″) engine manufactured by Dunsmuir & Jackson Ltd., Glasgow. 3,080 hp.
Ocean-going tanker.

21.9.1922: Launched by the Blythswood Shipbuilding Company Ltd., Glasgow (Yard No.1), for the British Tanker Company Ltd. 12.1922: Completed. 2.4.1953: Departed from Aden bound to the U.K. 5.1953: Sold to the British Iron & Steel Corporation and allocated to Smith & Houston Ltd., for demolition. 5.5.1953: Delivered at Port Glasgow. 13.5.1953: Work commenced.

BT. 64. BRITISH PREMIER (1) (1922–1940)

O.N. 146684. 5,872g. 3,377n. 9,132d.
440.6 × 53.7 × 32.7 feet.
Two, steam turbines manufactured by the shipbuilder, double reduction geared to a single screw shaft. 2,615 hp.
Ocean-going tanker.

25.8.1922: Launched by Palmer's Shipbuilding & Iron Company Ltd., Newcastle (Yard No. 925), for the British Tanker Company Ltd. 12.1922: Completed. 24.12.1940: Whilst on a voyage from Abadan to Swansea via Table Bay and Freetown, was sunk by a torpedo from the German submarine U-65, at position 6.20N., 13.20W., 200 miles S. W, from Freetown.

BT. 65. BRITISH STATESMAN (1) (1923–1953)

O.N. 146686. 6,991g. 4,150n. 10,925d.
440.3 × 57.1 × 33.9 feet.
Two, steam turbines manufactured by G. Clark & Company Ltd., Sunderland, double reduction geared to a single screw shaft. 3,210 hp.
Ocean-going tanker.

5.10.1922: Launched by Sir James Laing & Sons Ltd., Sunderland (Yard No. 685), for the British Tanker Company Ltd. 1.1923: Completed. 9.4.1941: Damaged by aircraft whilst off Harwich. 9/10.5.1941: Damaged by aircraft whilst off Spurn Head. 7.1953: Sold to the British Iron & Steel Corporation and allocated to P. & W. MacLellan Ltd., for demolition. 10.7.1953: Arrived at Bo'ness.

BT. 66. BRITISH FUSILIER (1923–1953)

O.N. 146692. 6,943g. 4,083n. 10,873d.
440.0 × 57.0 × 33.7 feet.
Two, steam turbines manufactured by the shipbuilder, double reduction geared to a single screw shaft. 3,210 hp.
Ocean-going tanker.

5.12.1922: Launched by Swan, Hunter & Wigham, Richardson Ltd., Newcastle (Yard No. 1134), for the British Tanker Company Ltd. 1.1923: Completed. 1953: Sold to the British Iron & Steel Corporation and allocated to Metal Industries Ltd., for demolition. 10.1.1953: Arrived at Faslane. 15.1.1953: Work commenced.

British Statesman. (World Ship Society Photograph Library)

British Fusilier. (World Ship Society Photograph Library)

BT. 67. BRITISH CAPTAIN (1) (1923–1941)

O.N. 146691. 6,968g. 4,073n. 10,822d.
440.0 x 57.1 x 33.8 feet.
Two, steam turbines manufactured by the shipbuilder, double reduction geared to a single screw shaft. 3,270 hp.
Ocean-going tanker.

17.11.1922: Launched by Palmer's Shipbuilding & Iron Company Ltd., Newcastle (Yard No. 933), for the British Tanker Company Ltd. 2.1923: Completed. 2.12.1941: Whilst on a loaded voyage from Corpus Christi to Shell haven, via Halifax and Methil, in Convoy FS 661, exploded a mine and sank at position 52.11.48N., 1.53.17E., 15 miles east from Aldeburgh.

BT. 68. BRITISH LADY (1) (1923–1939)

O.N. 146698. 6,098g. 3,520n. 9,517d.
412.0 × 54.8 × 32.9 feet.
Two, steam turbines manufactured by Metropolitan-Vickers Electric Company Ltd., Manchester, double reduction geared to a single screw shaft. 3,200 hp.
Ocean-going tanker.

19.10.1922: Launched by J. L. Thompson & Sons Ltd., Sunderland (Yard No. 548), for the British Tanker Company Ltd. 2.1923: Completed. 1939: Sold to the Admiralty for employment as a Naval oiler in the Scapa Flow area. 1946: Sold for demolition, at Sunderland.

BT. 69. BRITISH COMMODORE (1) (1923–1953)

O.N. 146710. 6,865g. 4,036n. 11,028d.
440.0 × 56.3 × 30.0 feet.
Two, steam turbines manufactured by Metropolitan-Vickers Electric Company Ltd., Manchester, double reduction geared to a single screw shaft. 3,215 hp.
Ocean-going tanker.

5.10.1922: Launched by the Caledon Shipbuilding & Engineering Company Ltd., Dundee (Yard No.283), for the British Tanker Company Ltd. 3.1923: Completed. 1953: Sold to the British Iron & Steel Corporation and allocated to Metal Industries Ltd., for demolition. 30.4.1953: Arrived at Faslane in tow. 4.5.1953: Work commenced.

BT. 70. BRITISH YEOMAN (1) (1923–1942)

O.N. 147491. 6,990g. 4,084n. 10,822d.
440.0 × 57.1 × 33.8 feet.
Two, steam turbines manufactured by the shipbuilder, double reduction geared to a single screw shaft. 3,210 hp.
Ocean-going tanker.

17.4.1923: Launched by Palmer's Shipbuilding & Iron Company Ltd., Newcastle (Yard No. 936), for the British Tanker Company Ltd. 6.1923: Completed. 14.7.1942: Whilst on a voyage from Curacao to Gibraltar, was sunk by a torpedo from the German submarine U-201, at position 26.42N., 24.20W., S.W. of the Canary Islands.

British Yeoman wearing the original funnel markings. (World Ship Society Photograph Library)

British Hussar wearing the original funnel markings. (World Ship Society Photograph Library)

BT. 71. BRITISH HUSSAR (1) (1923–1953)

O.N. 147544. 6,944g. 4,098n. 10,929d.
440.2 × 57.0 × 33.7 feet.
Two, steam turbines manufactured by the shipbuilder, double reduction geared to a single screw shaft. 3,210 hp.
Ocean-going tanker.

14.8.1923: Launched by Swan, Hunter & Wigham, Richardson Ltd., Newcastle (Yard No. 1138), for the British Tanker Company Ltd. 10.1923: Completed. 30.6.1953: Sold, for £40,000, to the British Iron & Steel Corporation and allocated to Metal Industries Ltd., for demolition. 10.8.1953: Arrived at Rosyth from Grangemouth. 11.8.1953: Work commenced.

(n.b. Almost 30 years to the day from launch to start of demolition.)

BT. 72. BRITISH AMBASSADOR (1) (1924–1954)

O.N. 147595. 6,996g. 4,106n. 11,008d.
435.0 × 57.3 × 33.8 feet.
T.3-cyl. (28″, 46″ & 76″ × 51″) engine manufactured by Palmer's Shipbuilding & Iron Company Ltd., Newcastle. 2,905 hp.
Ocean-going tanker.

21.1.1924: Launched by Sir J. Laing & Sons Ltd., Sunderland (Yard No. 686), for the British Tanker Company Ltd. 2.1924: Completed. 1954: Sold to the British Iron & Steel Corporation and allocated to P. & W. MacLellan Ltd., for demolition. 30.7.1954: Arrived at Bo'ness from Pernis.

BT. 73. BRITISH DUCHESS (1) (1924–1952)

O.N. 147647. 5,981g. 3,443n. 9,405d.
405.0 × 54.8 × 32.9 feet.
T.3-cyl. (28″, 46″ & 76″ × 51″) engine manufactured by Palmer's Shipbuilding & Iron Company Ltd., Newcastle. 2,905 hp.
Ocean-going tanker.

6.3.1924: Launched by J. L. Thompson & Sons Ltd., Sunderland (Yard No. 549), for the British Tanker Company Ltd. 5.1924: Completed. 1952: Sold to Vivalet Shipping & Trading Company S.A., Panama, and renamed DUCHESS. 21.1.1959: Arrived at Eastham. 23.1.1959: Sold to the Indian Trading Company, Leichtenstein, for demolition, thence to Societa Cantiera di Portovenero, Italy. 9.2.1959: Arrived at Spezia for demolition. 10.3.1959: Work commenced.

BT. 74. BRITISH AVIATOR (1) (1924–1953)

O.N. 147700. 6,998g. 4,136n. 10,762d.
439.8 × 57.1 × 33.8 feet.
6-cyl. 2 S.C.S.A. (23″ × 72″) oil engine manufactured by the shipbuilder. 4,925 bhp.
Post 1930: 4-cyl. 2 S.C.S.A. (23⅝″ × 91$^{5}/_{16}$″) oil engine manufactured by Wm. Doxford & Sons Ltd., Sunderland. 3,435 bhp.
Ocean-going tanker.

20.5.1924: Launched by Palmer's Shipbuilding & Iron Company Ltd., Newcastle (Yard No. 935), for the British Tanker Company Ltd. 8.1924: Completed. 2.1930: Re-engined. 8.1953: Sold to the British Iron & Steel Corporation and allocated to J. Cashmore &

British Aviator. (World Ship Society Photograph Library)

Company Ltd., for demolition. 7.9.1953: Arrived at Newport. 12.1953: Work commenced.

BT. 75. BRITISH MOTORIST (1924–1942)

O.N. 148491. 6,891g. 4,103n. 10,772d.
440.2 × 57.0 × 33.8 feet.
8-cyl. 2 S.C.S.A. (24″ × 50″) oil engine manufactured by the shipbuilder. 3,980 bhp.
Ocean-going tanker.

14.8.1924: Launched by Swan, Hunter & Wigham, Richardson Ltd., Newcastle (Yard No. 1162), for the British Tanker Company Ltd. 10.1924: Completed. 19.2.1942: Sunk by Japanese aircraft at Darwin, Australia. 18.9.1959: Refloated by Japanese salvage operators and towed to Japan for demolition.

BT. 76. BRITISH CONSUL (1) (1924–1942)

O.N. 148511. 6,940g. 4,114n. 11,008d.
435.0 × 57.3 × 33.8 feet.
T.3-cyl. (28″, 46″ & 76″ × 51″) engine manufactured by Palmer's Shipbuilding and Iron Company Ltd., Newcastle.
Ocean-going tanker.

30.9.1924: Launched by Sir James Laing & Sons Ltd., Sunderland (Yard No. 691), for the British Tanker Company Ltd. 12.1924: Completed. 18.2.1942: Sustained torpedo damage at position 10.37N., 61.34W. 19.8.1942: Whilst on a voyage from Trinidad to Key West, was sunk by a torpedo from the German submarine U-564 (another source gives U-161), at position 11.58N., 62.38W., west of Grenada, W. Indies.

BT. 77. BRITISH CHEMIST (1925–1953)

O.N. 148643. 6,997g. 4,129n. 10,762d.
439.7 × 57.1 × 33.8 feet.
6-cyl. 2 S.C.S.A. (23″ × 72″) oil engine manufactured by the shipbuilder. 4,925 bhp.
Post 1930: 4-cyl. 2 S.C.S.A. (23⅝″ × 91¼″) oil engine manufactured by Wm. Doxford & Sons Ltd., Sunderland. 3,435 bhp.
Ocean-going tanker.

7.5.1925: Launched by Palmer's Shipbuilding & Iron Company Ltd., Newcastle (Yard No. 937), for the British Tanker Company Ltd. 7.1925: Completed. 4.1930: Re-engined. 8.1953: Sold to the British Iron & Steel Corporation and allocated to T. W. Ward Ltd., for demolition at their Inverkeithing facility. 8.9.1953: Arrived at Inverkeithing from Swansea. 9.9.1953: Handed over and work commenced.

BT. 78. BRITISH PETROL (1925–1940)

O.N. 148676. 6906g. 4,113n. 10,774d.
440.2 × 57.0 × 33.8 feet.
8-cyl. 2 S.C.S.A. (24″ × 50″) oil engine manufactured by the shipbuilder. 3,980 bhp.
Ocean-going tanker.

8.6.1925: Launched by Swan, Hunter & Wigham, Richardson Ltd., Newcastle (Yard No. 1196), for the British Tanker Company Ltd. 9.1925: Completed. 9.1939: Requisitioned by the Admiralty as a Naval oiler. 13.6.1940: Shelled and sunk by the German raider WIDDER, at position approximately 20.00N., 50.00W., mid Atlantic.

British Petrol at Cape Town. (World Ship Society Photograph Library)

BT. 79. BRITISH DIPLOMAT (1) (1926–1940)

O.N. 148786. 6,484g. 4,555n. 9,151d.
420.2 × 54.4 × 32.7 feet.
Two, 8-cyl. 2 S.C.S.A. (23⅝″ × 41¾″) oil engines manufactured by the shipbuilder. 7,760 bhp.
Ocean-going tanker.

2.4.1926: Launched by J. Brown Ltd., Clydebank (Yard No. 507), for the British Tanker Company Ltd. 7.1926: Completed. 17.5.1940: Sold to the Ministry of Shipping (subsequently restyled as the Ministry of War Transport), and renamed EMPIRE DIPLOMAT (British Tanker Company Ltd., managers). 6.5.1944: Sustained grounding damage and was laid up at Newcastle. 1.1946: Demolition completed by Clayton & Davie Ltd., Newcastle.

British Diplomat with a leaning foremast. (World Ship Society Photograph Library)

BT. 80. BRITISH INVENTOR (1) (1926–1940)

O.N. 148785. 7,101g. 4,226n. 11,693d.
430.0 × 58.1 × 34.0 feet.
T.3-cyl. (28″, 46″ & 76″ × 51″) engine manufactured by the shipbuilder. 2,835 hp.
Ocean-going tanker.

1925: Laid down as BRITISH ASH by Palmer's Shipbuilding & Iron Company Ltd., Newcastle (Yard No. 959), for the British Tanker Company Ltd. 11.5.1926: Launched as BRITISH INVENTOR. 7.1926: Completed. 5.5.1940: Departed from Abadan en route to Hamble. 5.6.1940: Sailed from Gibraltar. 12.6.1940: Exploded a mine off St. Albans Head, and beached to prevent sinking. 30.6. 1940: Deliberately broken into two by salvors, the stern section then towed by two tugs to Ringstead Bay. Forward section broken up in-situ. 2.7.1940: Afterpart beached near White Nothe to be prepared for sea tow. 4.7.1940: Afterpart moored at Portland for discharge. 31.7.1940: Towed to Southampton for demolition. 2.11.1940: Demolition reported as being in hand, the machinery having been removed weeks earlier, for refitting into the new EMPIRE GRANITE, then under construction. Details of the shipbreaker not located.

BT. 81. BRITISH GOVERNOR (1926–1953)

O.N. 149735. 6,840g. 4,037n. 10,904d.
440.2 × 57.0 × 33.7 feet.
T.3-cyl. (26½″, 44″ & 74″ × 51″) engine manufactured by the shipbuilder. 2,920 hp.
Ocean-going tanker.

10.9.1926: Launched by Swan, Hunter & Wigham, Richardson Ltd., Newcastle (Yard No. 1218), for the British Tanker Company

British Governor. (World Ship Society Photograph Library)

Ltd. 10.1926: Completed. 4.4. 1943: Whilst at Mishukov Anchorage, Kola Inlet, was damaged by aircraft. 5.12.1953: Arrived at Osaka from Pulo Bukom. 7.12.1953: Sold to Yamato & Company Ltd., Osaka, for demolition. 25.12.1953: Work commenced. 6.1954: Completed.

BT. 82. BRITISH COLONY (1927–1942)

O.N. 149828. 6,917g. 4,143n. 10,840d.
440.2 × 57.0 × 33.7 feet.
T.3-cyl. (26½″, 44″ & 74″ × 51″) engine manufactured by the shipbuilder. 2,920 hp.
Ocean-going tanker.

4.4.1927: Launched by Swan, Hunter & Wigham, Richardson Ltd., Newcastle (Yard No. 1224), for the British Tanker Company Ltd. 5.1927: Completed. 13.5.1942: Whilst on a voyage from Trinidad to Gibraltar, sunk by a torpedo from the German submarine U-162, at a position east of Barbados.

BT. 83. BRITISH INDUSTRY (2) (1927–1953)

O.N. 149836. 4,297g. 2,425n. 6,631d.
366.2 × 49.2 × 27.2 feet.
T.3-cyl. (23″, 39″ & 66″ × 45″) engine manufactured by the shipbuilder. 2,035 hp.
Ocean-going tanker.

3.5.1927: Launched by Palmer's Shipbuilding & Iron Company Ltd., Newcastle (Yard No. 963), for the British Tanker Company Ltd. 5.1927: Completed. 1953: Sold to the British Iron & Steel Corporation and allocated to T. W. Ward Ltd., Sheffield for demolition at their Grays, Essex Facility. 7.7.1953: Arrived at Columbia Wharf, Grays, Essex.

BT. 84. BRITISH ENDEAVOUR (1) (1927–1940)

O.N. 149914. 4,580g. 2,641n. 6,906d.
381.2 × 50.4 × 27.6 feet.
T.3-cyl. (25″, 42″ & 70″ × 48″) engine manufactured by the Wallsend Slipway Company Ltd., Wallsend. 2,110 hp.
Ocean-going tanker.

12.8.1927: Launched by Sir W. G. Armstrong, Whitworth & Company Ltd., Newcastle (Yard No. 1025), for the British Tanker Company Ltd. 10.1927: Completed. 21.2.1940: Whilst sailing in Convoy OGF 19, sunk by a torpedo from the German submarine U-50, at a position 120 miles west of Vigo.

BT. 85. BRITISH PROGRESS (1) (1927–1943)

O.N. 149926. 4,581g. 2,639n. 6,906d.
381.2 × 50.4 × 27.6 feet.
T.3-cyl. (25″, 42″ & 70″ × 48″) engine manufactured by the Wallsend Slipway Company Ltd., Wallsend. 2,110 hp.
Ocean-going tanker.

9.9.1927: Launched by Sir W. G. Armstrong, Whitworth & Company Ltd., Newcastle (Yard No. 1026), for the British Tanker Company Ltd. 11.1927: Completed. 1.11.1943: Departed Thames Haven bound to Grangemouth. 4.11.1943: Damaged by a torpedo from a German 'E' boat, at position 52.55N., 02.00E., Norfolk coast. Subsequently towed into Gt. Yarmouth Roads. 9.11.1943: Departed in tow bound to R. Tyne. 11.11.1943: Arrived. 27.11.1943: Laid-up pending a decision on her future, and subsequently condemned. 25.4.1944: Departed from North Shields for demolition by unspecified shipbreakers. 12.5.1944: Signal letters cancelled.

British Endeavour. (World Ship Society Photograph Library)

British Progress. (World Ship Society Photograph Library)

British Industry. (World Ship Society Photograph Library)

BT. 86. BRITISH UNION (1) (1927–1941)

O.N. 149943. 6,987g. 4,163n. 10,912d.
440.1 × 57.0 × 33.9 feet.
6-cyl. 2 S.C.S.A. (26¾″ × 47¼″) oil engine manufactured by the Wallsend Slipway Company Ltd., Wallsend. 3,745 bhp.
Ocean-going tanker.

British Valour. (World Ship Society Photograph Library)

26.9.1927: Launched by Swan, Hunter & Wigham, Richardson Ltd., Newcastle (Yard No. 1226), for the British Tanker Company Ltd. 11.1927: Completed. 18.1.1941: Whilst requisitioned by the Admiralty, on a voyage from Gibraltar to Curacao, was sunk by the German raider KORMORAN, at position 26.34N., 30.58W., north-west of the Cape Verde Islands.

BT. 87. BRITISH VALOUR (1) (1927–1953)

O.N. 149945. 7,118g. 4,225n. 10,959d.
440.5 × 57.0 × 33.8 feet.
8-cyl. 4 S.C.S.A. (29 1/8″ × 59 1/16″) B&W type oil engine manufactured by J. G. Kincaid & Company Ltd., Greenock. 3,265 bhp.
Ocean-going tanker.
31.8.1927: Launched by Lithgows Ltd., Greenock (Yard No. 796), for the British Tanker Company Ltd. 11.1927: Completed. 25.9.1953: Sold to the British Iron & Steel Corporation and allocated to Shipbreaking Industries Ltd., for demolition. 21.5.1954: Departed in tow from Newport. 24.5.1954: Arrived at Faslane.

BT. 88. BRITISH FAITH (1) (1928–1956)

O.N. 149974. 6,959g. 4,133n. 10,887d.
441.8 × 56.9 × 33.7 feet.
8-cyl. 4 S.C.S.A. (29 1/8″ × 59 1/16″) oil engine manufactured by Akt. Burmeister & Wains Maskin-og-Skipsbyggeri, Copenhagen. 3,265 bhp.
Ocean-going tanker.
12.10.1927: Launched by the Caledon Shipbuilding & Engineering Company Ltd., Dundee (Yard No. 313), for the British Tanker Company Ltd. 1.1928: Completed. 6.4.1956: Arrived at Swansea. 9.4.1956: Sold to the British Iron & Steel Corporation for and allocated to T. W. Ward Ltd., Sheffield, for demolition at their Milford Haven facility. 16.4.1956: Arrived at Milford Haven.

BT. 89. BRITISH LOYALTY (1) (1928–1946)

O.N. 149977. 6,993g. 4,167n. 10,440d.
440.7 × 57.1 × 33.9 feet.
6-cyl. 2 S.C.S.A. (26 3/4″ × 47 1/4″) oil engine manufactured by Sulzer Bros., Winterthur. 3,740 bhp.
Ocean-going tanker.
27.9.1927: Launched by Palmer's Shipbuilding & Iron Company Ltd., Newcastle (Yard No. 969), for the British Tanker Company Ltd. 1.1928: Completed. 30.5.1942: Sustained torpedo damage whilst at a position 5 cables from the Antsivana Lighthouse, Diego Suarez, Madagascar. 9.3.1944: Sustained torpedo damage whilst in Addu Atoll Harbour. 5.1.1946: Scuttled in the Indian Ocean.

BT. 90. BRITISH GLORY (1) (1928–1954)

O.N. 160364. 6,993g. 4,159n. 10,876d.
435.0 × 57.3 × 33.8 feet.
6-cyl. 4 S.C.S.A. (29 1/8″ × 59 1/16″) B&W type oil engine manufactured by Harland & Wolff Ltd., Glasgow. 3,210 bhp.
Ocean-going tanker.
9.12.1927: Launched by Sir James Laing & Sons Ltd., Sunderland (Yard No. 701), for the British Tanker Company Ltd. 2.1928: Completed. 15.10.1940: Sustained torpedo damage at position 57.10N., 08.36W. 28.1.1954: Arrived on the R. Tyne from Hamburg and subsequently sold to the British Iron & Steel Corporation and allocated to Hughes Bolckow Shipbreaking Company Ltd., for demolition. 2.2.1954: Arrived at Blyth.

BT. 91. BRITISH RELIANCE (1) (1928–1941)

O.N. 160357. 7,000g. 4,132n. 11,066d.
440.3 × 57.0 × 33.8 feet.
8-cyl. 4 S.C.S.A. (29 1/8″ × 59 1/16″) B&W type oil engine manufactured by J. G. Kincaid & Company Ltd., Greenock. 3,265 bhp.
Ocean-going tanker.
8.12.1927: Launched by the Greenock Dockyard Company Ltd., Greenock (Yard No. 413), for the British Tanker Company Ltd. 2.1928: Completed. 2.4.1941: Whilst on a voyage in Convoy SC 26, Sydney, Cape Breton, to the U.K., sunk by a torpedo from the German submarine U-46, at position 58.21N., 28.30W, in the Atlantic.

BT. 92. BRITISH HOPE (1928–1957)

O.N. 160382. 7,083g. 4,187n. 10,830d.
441.8 × 56.9 × 33.7 feet.
8-cyl. 4 S.C.S.A. (29 1/8″ × 59 1/16″) 3,265 bhp oil engine manufactured by Akt. Burmeister & Wains Maskin-og-Skipsbyggeri, Copenhagen.
Ocean-going tanker.
7.12.1927: Launched by the Caledon Shipbuilding & Engineering Company Ltd., Dundee (Yard No. 314), for the British Tanker Company Ltd. 3.1928: Completed. 1.6.1956: Owners restyled as BP Tanker Company Ltd. 10.9.1957: Departed from Port Said. 10.1957: Sold to the British Iron & Steel Corporation and allocated to T. W. Ward Ltd., Sheffield, for demolition at their Milford Haven facility. 11.10.1957: Arrived at Milford Haven.

BT. 93. BRITISH COURAGE (1) (1928–1953)

O.N. 160390. 6,952g. 4,132n. 10,927d.
440.5 × 57.0 × 33.8 feet.
6-cyl. 4 S.C.S.A. (29 1/8″ × 59 1/16″) B&W type oil engine manufactured by Harland & Wolff Ltd., Glasgow. 3,265 bhp.
Ocean-going tanker.
23.12.1927: Launched by Lithgows Ltd., Port Glasgow (Yard No. 802), for the British Tanker Company Ltd. 3.1928: Completed. 12.1953: Sold to the British Iron & Steel Corporation and allocated to T. W. Ward Ltd., Sheffield, for demolition at their Inverkeithing facility. 24.12.1953: Arrived at Inverkeithing from Rosyth.

BT. 94. BRITISH DOMINION (1928–1943)

O.N. 160400. 6,983g. 4,141n. 10,912d.
440.0 × 57.0 × 33.9 feet.
4-cyl. 2 S.C.S.A. (22 13/16″ × 91 1/4″) oil engine manufactured by Wm. Doxford & Sons Ltd., Sunderland. 3,210 bhp.
Ocean-going tanker.
7.2.1928: Launched by Swan, Hunter & Wigham, Richardson Ltd., Newcastle (Yard No. 1240), for the British Tanker Company Ltd. 4.1928: Completed. 11.1.1943: Whilst on a voyage from Trinidad to West Africa, sunk by a torpedo from the German submarine U-522, at position 30.30N., 19.55W., off the Canary Islands.

British Hope. (World Ship Society Photograph Library)

British Loyalty. (World Ship Society Photograph Library)

British Courage at Cape Town. (World Ship Society Photograph Library)

British Dominion. (World Ship Society Photograph Library)

BT. 95. BRITISH RENOWN (1) (1928–1954)

O.N. 160397. 7,066g. 4,150n. 10,950d.
435.0 × 57.3 × 33.8 feet.
4-cyl. 2 S.C.S.A. ($22^{13}/_{16}'' \times 91^{1}/_{4}''$) Doxford type oil engine manufactured by Richardsons, Westgarth & Company Ltd., Hartlepool. 3,210 bhp.
Ocean-going tanker.

9.11.1927: Launched by Sir James Laing & Sons Ltd., Sunderland (Yard No. 700), for the British Tanker Company Ltd. 4.1928: Completed. 21.4.1941: Damaged by aircraft whilst 3 miles S.E. of Dartmouth. 21.11.1942: Damaged by a torpedo at position 43.53N., 55.02W. 1954: Sold to the British Iron & Steel Corporation and allocated to Smith & Houston Ltd., for demolition. 24.7.1954: Arrived at Port Glasgow.

BT. 96. BRITISH FREEDOM (1) (1928–1945)

O.N. 160493. 6,985g. 4,171n. 10,440d.
440.1 × 57.1 × 33.9 feet.
4-cyl. 2 S.C.S.A. ($22^{13}/_{16}'' \times 91^{1}/_{4}''$) Doxford type oil engine manufactured by Richardsons, Westgarth & Company Ltd., Hartlepool. 3,210 bhp.
Ocean-going tanker.

9.12.1928: Launched by Palmer's Shipbuilding & Iron Company Ltd., Newcastle (Yard No. 968), for the British Tanker Company Ltd. 6.1928: Completed. 14.1.1945: Whilst requisitioned by the Admiralty, on a voyage from Halifax to the U.K., was sunk by a torpedo from the German submarine U-1232, at a position near Halifax.

BT. 97. BRITISH ARDOUR (1) (1928–1943)

O.N. 160525. 7,124g. 4,261n. 11,196d.
440.6 × 57.1 × 33.9 feet.
Q.4-cyl. (24″, 35″, $50^{1}/_{2}''$ & 73″ × 51″) engine manufactured by the shipbuilder. 2,765 hp.
Ocean-going tanker.

4.5.1928: Launched by Palmer's Shipbuilding & Iron Company Ltd., Newcastle (Yard No. 978), for the British Tanker Company Ltd. 7.1928: Completed. 5.4.1943: Whilst requisitioned by the Admiralty, on a voyage in Convoy HX231, from New York to Londonderry, was sunk by a torpedo from the German submarine U-706, at position 58.08N., 33.04W.

BT. 98. BRITISH HONOUR (1) (1928–1953)

O.N. 160530. 6,991g. 4,174n. 11,135d.
440.5 × 57.1 × 33.9 feet.
6-cyl. 2 S.C.S.A. ($26^{3}/_{4}'' \times 47^{1}/_{4}''$) oil engine manufactured by Sulzer Bros., Winterthur. 3,740 bhp.
Ocean-going tanker.

7.3.1928: Launched by Palmer's Shipbuilding & Iron Company Ltd., Newcastle (Yard No. 970), for the British Tanker Company Ltd. 7.1928: Completed. 1953: Sold to Spedizioni Italiana Maritima Terrestri (SPIMAR), Italy, and renamed MARISIN M. 1957: Renamed MARIO MARTINI. 21.3.1961: Laid up at Genoa. 13.1.1962: Arrived at Spezia, in tow, for demolition by Cantieri Lotti S.p.A. 25.2.1962: Work commenced.

BT. 99. BRITISH PLUCK (1) (1928–1936)

O.N. 143990. 1,025g. 514n. 1,087d.
230.0 × 32.7 × 13.8 feet.
6-cyl. 2 S.C.S.A. ($16^{9}/_{16}'' \times 28^{3}/_{4}''$) oil engine manufactured by the shipbuilder. 1,430 bhp.
Coastal tanker.

4.4.1928: Launched by Swan, Hunter & Wigham, Richardson Ltd., Newcastle (Yard No. 1254), for the British Tanker Company Ltd. 8.1928: Completed. 1936: Renamed SHELLBRIT 1 (Shell-Mex & BP Ltd., operators). 17.9.1940: Whilst on a voyage from Grangemouth to Inverness, exploded a mine and sank at a position 3 miles from the entrance to the Cromarty Firth.

British Renown. (World Ship Society Photograph Library)

British Freedom. (World Ship Society Photograph Library)

British Ardour. (World Ship Society Photograph Library)

British Pluck. (World Ship Society Photograph Library)

BT.100. BRITISH JUSTICE (1) (1928–1954)

O.N. 160548. 6,982g. 4,122n. 11,174d.
440.7 × 57.1 × 33.9 feet.
4-cyl. 2 S.C.S.A. ($22\frac{13}{16}$″ × $45\frac{5}{8}$″) Doxford type oil engine manufactured by Richardsons, Westgarth & Company Ltd., Hartlepool. 3,270 bhp.
Ocean-going tanker.

6.3.1928: Launched by Palmer's Shipbuilding & Iron Company Ltd., Newcastle (Yard No. 977), for the British Tanker Company Ltd. 8.1928: Completed. 5.1.1954: Sold, for £40,000 to the British Iron & Steel Corporation and allocated to Shipbreaking Industries Ltd., for demolition. 26.1.1954: Arrived at Rosyth from Grangemouth and work commenced.

BT. 101. BRITISH THRIFT (1928–1935)

O.N. 143992. 695g. 247n. 690d. 185.3 × 31.6 × 11.2 feet.
Post 1953: 707g. 254n. 690d. 194′0″ × 31′7″ × 10′9″ .
4-cyl. 2 S.C.S.A. ($16\frac{1}{2}$″ × $28\frac{3}{8}$″) oil engine manufactured by the shipbuilder. 955 bhp.
Post 1953: 6-cyl. 2 S.C.S.A. (265 × 245mm) oil engine manufactured by Crossley Bros. Ltd., Manchester. 570 bhp.
Coastal tanker.

14.6.1928: Launched by Swan, Hunter & Wigham, Richardson Ltd., Newcastle (Yard No. 1256), for the British Tanker Company Ltd. 9.1928: Completed. 1935: Refitted with a new double bottom, and renamed THRIFTIE (Medway Oil & Storage Company Ltd., operators). 1936: Renamed SHELLBRIT 2 (Shell-Mex & BP Ltd., operators). 9.11.1940: Damaged by aircraft at Shoreham. 1943: Sold to Shell-Mex & BP Ltd., and renamed SHELL LOADER. 12.1953: Re-engined. 1961: Sold to Express Argosarinikos, Greece, and renamed AMPHITRITE. 1977: Sold to Hellenic Shipyards Company Ltd., Greece. 1985: Sold for demolition at Salamina.

BT.102. BRITISH CHIVALRY (1) (1929–1944)

O.N. 161198. 7,118g. 4,238n. 11,220d.
440.8 × 57.1 × 34.0 feet.
Q.4-cyl. (24″, 35″, $50\frac{1}{2}$″ & 73″ × 51″) engine manufactured by the shipbuilder. 2,765 hp.
Ocean-going tanker.

24.1.1929: Launched by Palmer's Shipbuilding & Iron Company Ltd., Newcastle (Yard No. 979), for the British Tanker Company Ltd. 2.1929: Completed. 22.2.1944: Sunk by a torpedo from the Japanese submarine I-37, at position 0.50S., 68.00E., off the Maldive Islands.

BT.103. BRITISH FORTUNE (1) (1930–1941)

O.N. 162486. 4,696g. 2,619n. 6,913d.
384.6 × 50.2 × 27.7 feet.
T.3-cyl. (25″, 42″ & 70″ × 48″) engine manufactured by Rankine & Blackmore Ltd. 2,150 hp.
Ocean-going tanker.

7.8.1930: Launched by Lithgows Ltd., Port Glasgow (Yard No. 846), for the British Tanker Company Ltd. 9.1930: Completed. 31.10.1941: Sunk by aircraft bombing 1 mile from the Aldeburgh light buoy.

BT.104. PAHRA (1930–1931)

O.N. 162476. 85g. 78n. ? × ? × ? feet.
Dumb tank barge.

9.1930: Completed by W. & E. Hill Ltd., South Shields, for the British Tanker Company Ltd. 1931: Transferred to Petroleum Steamship Company Ltd. *Due to small size and type of this vessel no further details have been recorded by the authors.*

BT.105. PESHIN (1930–1931)

O.N. 162477. 85g. 78n. ? × ? × ? feet.
Dumb tank barge.

9.1930: Completed by W. & E. Hill Ltd., South Shields, for the British Tanker Company Ltd. 1931: Transferred to Petroleum Steamship Company Ltd. *Due to small size and type of this vessel no further details have been recorded by the authors.*

British Justice. (World Ship Society Photograph Library)

British Chivalry. (World Ship Society Photograph Library)

British Fortune. (World Ship Society Photograph Library)

British Venture. (World Ship Society Photograph Library)

BT.106. BRITISH VENTURE (1) (1930–1943)

O.N. 162502. 4,696g. 2,619n. 6,922d.
384.6 × 50.2 × 27.7 feet.
T.3-cyl. (25″, 42″ & 70″ × 48″) engine manufactured by Rankine & Blackmore Ltd. 2,150 hp.
Ocean-going tanker.

25.9.1930: Launched by Lithgows Ltd., Port Glasgow (Yard No. 847), for the British Tanker Company Ltd. 11.1930: Completed. 24.6.1943: Sunk by a torpedo from the Japanese submarine I-27, at position 25.13N., 58.02E, in the Gulf of Oman.

BT. 107. BRITISH SCIENCE (1931–1941)

O.N. 162532. 7,138g. 4,172n. 11,082d.
441.2 × 59.7 × 33.0 feet.
4-cyl. 2 S.C.S.A. (23⁵/₈″ × 91⁵/₁₆″) oil engine manufactured by Wm. Doxford & Sons Ltd., Sunderland. 2,250 bhp.
Ocean-going tanker.

21.10.1930: Launched by Palmer's Shipbuilding & Iron Company Ltd., Newcastle (Yard No. 1003), for the British Tanker Company Ltd. 1.1931: Completed. 18.4.1941: Whilst on a voyage from Haifa to Piraeus, sunk by a torpedo from a German aircraft, at a position 50 miles N.W. from Cape Spanda, Crete.

BT. 108. BRITISH PRIDE (1) (1931–1955)

O.N. 162533. 7,106g. 4,180n. 11,040d.
440.6 × 59.5 × 33.0 feet.
8-cyl. 4 S.C.S.A. (29¹/₈″ × 59¹/₁₆″) B&W type oil engine manufactured by J. G. Kincaid & Company Ltd., Greenock. 3,265 bhp.
Ocean-going tanker.

25.11.1930: Launched by Lithgows Ltd., Port Glasgow (Yard No. 849), for the British Tanker Company Ltd. 1.1931: Completed. 1955: Sold to the British Iron & Steel Corporation, and allocated to T. W. Ward Ltd., Sheffield, for demolition at their Grays, Essex facility. 21.6.1955: Arrived at Columbia Wharf, Grays, Essex.

BT. 109. BRITISH SPLENDOUR (1) (1931–1942)

O.N. 162546. 7,138g. 4,172n. 11,095d.
441.2 × 59.7 × 33.0 feet.
4-cyl. 2 S.C.S.A. (23⁵/₈″ × 91⁵/₁₆″) oil engine manufactured by Wm. Doxford and Sons Ltd., Sunderland. 2,250 bhp.
Ocean-going tanker.

20.11.1930: Launched by Palmer's Shipbuilding & Iron Company Ltd., Newcastle (Yard No. 1004), for the British Tanker Company Ltd. 2.1931: Completed. 20.2.1941: Damaged by aircraft whilst ½ mile south of Black Head, near Lizard. 7.4.1942: Whilst on a voyage from Houston to Halifax, sunk by a torpedo from the German submarine U-552, at a position close to Cape Hatteras.

BT. 110. BRITISH RESOURCE (1) (1931–1942)

O.N. 162547. 7,209g. 4,197n. 11,186d.
440.6 × 59.4 × 32.9 feet.
8-cyl. 4 S.C.S.A. (29¹/₈″ × 59¹/₁₆″) B&W type oil engine manufactured by J. G. Kincaid & Company Ltd., Greenock. 3,265 bhp.
Ocean-going tanker.

23.12.1930: Launched by the Greenock Dockyard Company Ltd., Greenock (Yard No. 421), for the British Tanker Company Ltd. 3.1931: Completed. 14.3.1942: Whilst on a voyage from Curacao to Halifax, sunk by a torpedo from the German submarine U-124, at position 36.04N., 65.38W.

BT. 111. BRITISH PRESTIGE (1) (1931–1956)

O.N. 162553. 7,106g. 4,180n. 11,040d.
440.6 × 59.5 × 33.0 feet.
8-cyl. 4 S.C.S.A. (29¹/₈″ × 59¹/₁₆″) B&W type oil engine manufactured by J. G. Kincaid & Company Ltd., Greenock. 3,265 bhp.
Ocean-going tanker.

23.12.1930: Launched by Lithgows Ltd., Port Glasgow (Yard No. 850), for the British Tanker Company Ltd. 3.1931: Completed. 13.11.1940: Sustained mine damage off Humber Boom. 9.2.1956: Arrived at Swansea. 24.2.1956: Sold to the British Iron & Steel Corporation, and allocated to T. W. Ward Ltd., Sheffield for demolition at their Barrow in Furness facility. 29.2.1956: Arrived at their Briton Ferry facility, having been re-allocated.

BT. 112. BRITISH STRENGTH (1) (1931–1941)

O.N. 162575. 7,139g. 4,169n. 11,095d.
441.2 × 59.7 × 33.0 feet.

British Science. (World Ship Society Photograph Library)

British Pride. (World Ship Society Photograph Library)

British Prestige. (World Ship Society Photograph Library)

British Strength. (World Ship Society Photograph Library)

4-cyl. 2 S.C.S.A. (23$^{5}/_{8}$″ × 91$^{5}/_{16}$″) Doxford type oil engine manufactured by Richardsons, Westgarth & Company Ltd., Hartlepool. 2,250 bhp.
Ocean-going tanker.
17.5.1931: Launched by Palmer's Shipbuilding and Iron Company Ltd., Newcastle (Yard No. 1005), for the British Tanker Company Ltd. 4.1931: Completed. 13.3.1941: Sunk by either or both of the German battlecruisers SCHARNHORST and GNEISENAU, at a position approximately 42.00N., 43.00W.

BT. 113. BRITISH ENERGY (1) (1931–1955)

O.N. 162588. 7,209g. 4,197n. 11,186d.
440.6 × 59.4 × 32.9 feet.
8-cyl. 4 S.C.S.A. (29$^{1}/_{8}$″ × 59$^{1}/_{16}$″) B&W type oil engine manufactured by J. G. Kincaid & Company Ltd., Greenock. 3,265 bhp.
Ocean-going tanker.
2.4.1931: Launched by the Greenock Dockyard Company Ltd., Greenock (Yard No. 422), for the British Tanker Company Ltd. 5.1931: Completed. 31.8.1940: Damaged by aircraft at Birkenhead. 16.9.1955: Arrived at Grangemouth. 18.9.1955: Sold to the British Iron & Steel Corporation, and allocated to P. & W. MacLellan Ltd., for demolition. 27.9.1955: Arrived at Bo'ness.

BT. 114. THRIFTIE (1935–1936)

see ship No. BT. 101 above.

BT. 115. SHELLBRIT 1 (1936–1940)

see ship No. BT. 99 above.

BT. 116. SHELLBRIT 2 (1936–1943)

see ship No. BT. 101 above.

BT. 117. BRITISH FAME (1) (1936–1940)

O.N. 164701. 8,303g. 4,939n. 12,250d.
466.3 × 61.3 × 33.9 feet.
4-cyl. 2 S.C.S.A. (23$^{5}/_{8}$″ × 91$^{5}/_{16}$″) oil engine manufactured by Wm. Doxford & Sons Ltd., Sunderland. 2,250 bhp.
Ocean-going tanker.
19.6.1936: Launched by Swan, Hunter & Wigham, Richardson Ltd., Wallsend (Yard No. 1498), for the British Tanker Company Ltd. 8.1936: Completed. 12.8. 1940: Whilst on a voyage in Convoy OB 193, sunk by a torpedo from the Italian submarine MALASPINA, at position 37.44N., 22.56W., in the Atlantic.

BT. 118. BRITISH ENDURANCE (1) (1936–1959)

O.N. 164726. 8,406g. 4,918n. 12,250d.
466.3 × 61.3 × 33.9 feet.
4-cyl. 2 S.C.S.A. (23$^{5}/_{8}$″ × 91$^{5}/_{16}$″) oil engine manufactured by Wm. Doxford & Sons Ltd., Sunderland. 3,435 bhp.
Ocean-going tanker.
19.8.1936: Launched by Swan, Hunter & Wigham, Richardson Ltd., Newcastle (Yard No. 1500), for the British Tanker Company Ltd. 10.1936: Completed. 1.6.1956: Owners restyled as BP Tanker Company Ltd. 24.1.1959: Arrived at Plymouth. 28.1.1959: Sold via Rederi Wijsmuller, Holland, for demolition. 3.2.1959: Arrived at Rotterdam, for conversion into a dry cargo vessel, and renamed REDWIJS II. 21.6.1959: Departed from Rotterdam loaded with scrap metal. 11.8.1959: Arrived at Yawata, for demolition by Matsukura Shoten K.K., at their Hirao Works.

BT. 119. BRITISH CONFIDENCE (1) (1936–1957)

O.N. 164737. 8,494g. 4,993n. 12,262d.
466.9 × 62.0 × 34.0 feet.
4-cyl. 2 S.C.S.A. (23$^{5}/_{8}$″ × 91$^{5}/_{16}$″) oil engine manufactured by Wm. Doxford & Sons Ltd., Sunderland. 3,435 bhp.
Ocean-going tanker.
18.8.1936: Launched by Cammell, Laird & Company Ltd., Birkenhead (Yard No. 1013), for the British Tanker Company Ltd. 10.1936: Completed. 1.6.1956: Owners restyled as BP Tanker Company Ltd. 1957: Renamed ANGLIAN CONFIDENCE (Common Bros. Ltd, Newcastle, appointed as managers). 12.5.1958: Arrived at Inverkeithing for demolition by T. W. Ward Ltd., Sheffield.

British Energy. (World Ship Society Photograph Library)

British Fame. (World Ship Society Photograph Library)

British Endurance. (World Ship Society Photograph Library)

British Confidence at Cape Town. Note the wartime Carley Floats on the foredeck. (World Ship Society Photograph Library)

British Power at Cape Town. (World Ship Society Photograph Library)

British Destiny at Cape Town. (World Ship Society Photograph Library)

BT. 120. BRITISH TRIUMPH (1) (1936–1940)

O.N. 165358. 8,402g. 5,008n. 12,200d.
467.6 × 61.7 × 33.9 feet.
6-cyl. 4 S.C.S.A. (29¹/₈″ × 59¹/₁₆″) B&W type oil engine manufactured by J. G. Kincaid & Company Ltd., Greenock. 3,200 bhp.
Ocean-going tanker.

14.10.1936: Launched by Lithgows Ltd., Port Glasgow (Yard No. 886), for the British Tanker Company Ltd. 12.1936: Completed. 12.2.1940: Whilst on a voyage from Hull to Aruba, exploded a mine and sank at position 53.06N., 01.25E., off the Norfolk coast.

BT. 121. BRITISH POWER (1) (1936–1958)

O.N. 165354. 8,451g. 4,967n. 12,172d.
467.8 × 61.7 × 33.8 feet.
6-cyl. 4 S.C.S.A. (29¹/₈″ × 59¹/₁₆″) B&W type oil engine manufactured by the shipbuilder. 3,200 bhp.
Ocean-going tanker.

16.9.1936: Launched by Harland & Wolff Ltd., Glasgow (Yard No. 968 G), for the British Tanker Company Ltd. 16.12.1936: Completed. 1.6.1956: Owners restyled as BP Tanker Company Ltd. 18.7.1958: Arrived at Rotterdam for demolition by Frank Rijsdiyks Industries Ltd., at Henrik Ido Ambacht.

BT. 122. BRITISH DESTINY (1) (1937–1957)

O.N. 165385. 8,470g. 4,971n. 12,176d.
467.8 × 61.7 × 33.8 feet.
6-cyl. 4 S.C.S.A. (29¹/₈″ × 59¹/₁₆″) B&W type oil engine manufactured by the shipbuilder. 3,200 bhp.
Ocean-going tanker.

3.11.1936: Launched by Harland & Wolff Ltd., Glasgow (Yard No. 969 G), for the British Tanker Company Ltd. 21.1.1937: Completed. 1.6.1956: Owners restyled as BP Tanker Company Ltd. 1957: Renamed GAELIC DESTINY (J. and J. Denholm Ltd., Glasgow, appointed as managers). 20.12.1958: Arrived at Rotterdam for demolition by Frank Rijsdiyks Industries Ltd., at Henrik Ido Ambacht. 8. 1959: Work commenced.

BT. 123. BRITISH FORTITUDE (1937–1957)

O.N. 165448. 8,482g. 4,993n. 12,265d.
466.9 × 62.0 × 34.0 feet.
4-cyl. 2 S.C.S.A. (23⁵/₈″ × 91⁵/₁₆″) oil engine manufactured by Wm. Doxford & Sons Ltd., Sunderland. 3,435 bhp.
Ocean-going tanker.

11.2.1937: Launched by Cammell, Laird & Company Ltd., Birkenhead (Yard No. 1020), for the British Tanker Company Ltd. 4.1937: Completed. 23.2.1943: Whilst on a ballast voyage from the Bristol Channel to Curacao, was damaged by a torpedo from the German submarine U-202, at position 31.10.N., 27.30.W. 8.3.1943: Arrived at Guantanamo Bay, Cuba. 14.3.1943: Arrived at Tampa, Florida for repair. 1.6.1956: Owners restyled as BP Tanker Company Ltd. 1957: Renamed ANGLIAN FORTITUDE (Common Bros. Ltd., Newcastle, appointed as managers). 26.8.1958: Arrived at Rotterdam for demolition by Frank Rijsdiyks Industries Ltd., at Henrik Ido Ambacht. Resold and 27.8.1958: Arrived at Antwerp for demolition by Jos De Smedt, at Burcht. 9.1958: Work commenced.

British Diligence at Cape Town. (World Ship Society Photograph Library)

BT. 124. BRITISH DILIGENCE (1937–1957)

O.N. 165466. 8,408g. 4,930n. 12,235d.
466.3 × 61.9 × 33.9 feet.
4-cyl. 2 S.C.S.A. ($23\frac{5}{8}'' \times 91\frac{5}{16}''$) oil engine manufactured by Wm. Doxford & Sons Ltd., Sunderland. 3,435 bhp.
Ocean-going tanker.

23.12.1936: Launched by Swan, Hunter & Wigham, Richardson Ltd., Newcastle (Yard No. 508), for the British Tanker Company Ltd. 6.1937: Completed. 1.6.1956: Owners restyled as BP Tanker Company Ltd. 1957: Renamed ANGLIAN DILIGENCE (Common Bros. Ltd., Newcastle, appointed as managers). 12.10.1958: Arrived at Killingholme. 18.10.1958: Arrived at Rotterdam for demolition by Frank Rijsdiyks Industries Ltd., at Henrik Ido Ambacht. Resold and 19.11.1958: Arrived at Genoa for demolition by A.R.D.E.M., who commenced work the same day.

BT. 125. BRITISH RESOLUTION (1) (1937–1959)

O.N. 165539. 8,408g. 4,927n. 12,235d.
466.3 × 61.9 × 33.9 feet.
4-cyl. 2 S.C.S.A. ($23\frac{5}{8}'' \times 91\frac{5}{16}''$) oil engine manufactured by Wm. Doxford & Sons Ltd., Sunderland. 3,435 bhp.
Ocean-going tanker.

23.2.1937: Launched by Swan, Hunter & Wigham, Richardson Ltd., Newcastle (Yard No. 1514), for the British Tanker Company Ltd. 8.1937: Completed. 1.6.1956: Owners restyled as BP Tanker Company Ltd. 1959: Sold for conservation and for machinery removal but transaction not concluded. 24.4.1959: Arrived at Rotterdam for demolition by Boele Oosterwijk B. V. 15.12.1959: Resold for demolition by Frank Rijsdiyks Industries Ltd., at Henrik Ido Ambacht. 3.1960: Work commenced.

British Zeal at Cape Town. (World Ship Society Photograph Library)

BT. 126. BRITISH INTEGRITY (1) (1937–1957)

O.N. 165562. 8,412g. 4,940n. 12,145d.
467.8 × 61.7 × 33.8 feet.
6-cyl. 4 S.C.S.A. ($29\frac{1}{8}'' \times 59\frac{1}{16}''$) B&W type oil engine manufactured by the shipbuilder. 3,200 bhp.
Ocean-going tanker.

22.6.1937: Launched by Harland & Wolff Ltd., Glasgow (Yard No. 972 G), for the British Tanker Company Ltd. 8.9.1937: Completed. 1.6.1956: Owners restyled as BP Tanker Company Ltd. 1957: Renamed GAELIC INTEGRITY (J. & J. Denholm Ltd., Glasgow, appointed as managers). 24.5.1958: Arrived at Rotterdam for demolition by Frank Rijsdiyks Industries Ltd., at Henrik Ido Ambacht. 9.1958: Work commenced.

BT. 127. BRITISH ZEAL (1937–1959)

O.N. 165624. 8,532g. 5,005n. 12,180d.
467.6 × 61.7 × 33.9 feet.
6-cyl. 4 S.C.S.A. ($29\frac{1}{8}'' \times 59\frac{1}{16}''$) B&W type oil engine manufactured by J. G. Kincaid & Company Ltd., Greenock. 3,200 bhp.
Ocean-going tanker.

3.11.1937: Launched by Lithgows Ltd., Port Glasgow (Yard No. 888), for the British Tanker Company Ltd. 12.1937: Completed. 31.10.1940: Damaged by submarine at position 15.40N., 20.43W. 1.6.1956: Owners restyled as BP Tanker Company Ltd. 3.2.1959: Arrived at the Isle of Grain. 8.2.1959: Sold via Rederi Wijsmuller, Holland, for demolition. 12.2.1959: Arrived at Rotterdam, for conversion into a dry cargo vessel, and renamed REDWIJS I. 3.4.1959: Departed from Rotterdam, loaded with scrap metal. 8.6.1959: Arrived at Yawata, for demolition by Matsukura Shoten K.K., at their Hirao Works. 24.6.1959: Work commenced at Hirao.

BT. 128. BRITISH FIDELITY (1) (1938–1957)

O.N. 166592. 8,465g. 4,906n. 12,201d.
467.8 × 61.7 × 33.8 feet.
6-cyl. 4 S.C.S.A. ($29\frac{1}{8}'' \times 59\frac{1}{16}''$) B&W type oil engine manufactured by the shipbuilder. 3,200 bhp.
Ocean-going tanker.

25.8.1938: Launched by Harland & Wolff Ltd., Glasgow (Yard No. 1010 G), for the British Tanker Company Ltd. 26.10.1938: Completed. 11.1.1941: Exploded a mine and sustained damage at position 51.22N., 03.05W. 1.6.1956: Owners restyled BP Tanker Company Ltd. 1957: Renamed GAELIC FIDELITY (J. & J. Denholm Ltd., Glasgow, appointed as managers). 19.5.1958: Arrived at Antwerp for demolition by Jos de Smedt, at Burght. 25.5.1958: Work commenced.

BT. 129. BRITISH SECURITY (1) (1937–1941)

O.N. 166328. 8,334g. 4,967n. 12,121d.
467.8 × 61.7 × 33.8 feet.
6-cyl. 4 S.C.S.A. ($29\frac{1}{8}'' \times 59\frac{1}{16}''$) B&W type oil engine manufactured by the shipbuilder. 3,200 bhp.
Ocean-going tanker.

4.11.1937: Launched by Harland & Wolff Ltd., Glasgow (Yard No. 974 G), for the British Tanker Company Ltd. 29.12.1937: Completed. 20.5.1941: Whilst on a voyage in Convoy HX 126, Halifax to R. Clyde, sunk by a torpedo from the German submarine U-556, at position 57.28N., 41.07W.

BT. 130. BRITISH GENIUS (1939–1961)

O.N. 167160. 8,553g. 4,961n. 12,416d.
466.9 × 62.0 × 33.7 feet.
4-cyl. 2 S.C.S.A. ($23\frac{5}{8}'' \times 91\frac{5}{16}''$) oil engine manufactured by the shipbuilder. 3,435 bhp.
Ocean-going tanker.

8.11.1938: Launched by Wm. Doxford & Sons Ltd., Sunderland (Yard No. 644), for the British Tanker Company Ltd. 1.1939:

British Integrity. (World Ship Society Photograph Library)

British Fidelity. (World Ship Society Photograph Library)

Completed. 1.6.1956: Owners restyled as BP Tanker Company Ltd. 12.5.1961: Arrived at Briton Ferry for demolition by T. W. Ward Ltd., Sheffield.

BT. 131. BRITISH TRUST (1) (1939–1943)

O.N. 167167. 8,446g. 4,967n. 12,416d.
467.8 × 61.7 × 33.8 feet.
6-cyl. 4 S.C.S.A. ($29^{1}/_{8}$″ × $59^{1}/_{16}$″) B&W type oil engine manufactured by the shipbuilder. 3,200 bhp.
Ocean-going tanker.

27.10.1938: Launched by Harland & Wolff Ltd., Glasgow (Yard No. 1011 G), for the British Tanker Company Ltd. 19.1.1939: Completed. 1.5.1943: Whist on a voyage from Alexandria to Benghazi, sunk by a torpedo from German aircraft, at a position 25 miles north from Benghazi.

BT. 132. BRITISH SINCERITY (1939–1958)

O.N. 167168. 8,533g. 4,898n. 12,207d.
466.9 × 62.0 × 34.0 feet.
4-cyl. 2 S.C.S.A. ($23^{5}/_{8}$″ × $91^{5}/_{16}$″) oil engine manufactured by Wm. Doxford & Sons Ltd., Sunderland. 3,435 bhp.
Ocean-going tanker.

22.11.1938: Launched by Cammell, Laird & Company Ltd., Birkenhead (Yard No. 1035), for the British Tanker Company Ltd. 2.1939: Completed. 1.6.1956: Owners restyled as BP Tanker Company Ltd. 29.6.1958: Arrived at Antwerp for demolition. 9.1958: O. Bulens commenced work at Hoboken.

BT. 133. BRITISH TENACITY (1) (1939–1959)

O.N. 167170. 8,439g. 4,855n. 12,254d.
466.3 × 61.9 × 33.9 feet.
4-cyl. 2 S.C.S.A. ($23^{5}/_{8}$″ × $91^{5}/_{16}$″) oil engine manufactured by Wm. Doxford & Sons Ltd., Sunderland. 3,435 bhp.
Ocean-going tanker.

8.12.1938: Launched by Swan, Hunter & Wigham, Richardson Ltd., Newcastle (Yard No. 1592), for the British Tanker Company Ltd. 2.1939: Completed. 1.6.1956: Owners restyled as the BP Tanker Company Ltd. 12.1.1959: Arrived at Blyth for demolition by Hughes, Bolckow Shipbreaking Company Ltd.

British Tenacity at Cape Town. (World Ship Society Photograph Library)

BT. 134. BRITISH LIBERTY (1) (1939–1940)

O.N. 167191. 8,485g. 4,871n. 12,490d.
466.8 × 62.0 × 33.9 feet.
4-cyl. 2 S.C.S.A. ($23^{5}/_{8}$″ × $91^{5}/_{16}$″) oil engine manufactured by Wm. Doxford & Sons Ltd., Sunderland. 3,435 bhp. 687nhp.
Ocean-going tanker.

30.10.1937: Keel laid by the Furness Shipbuilding Company Ltd., Haverton Hill on Tees (Yard No. 287), for the British Tanker Company Ltd. 17.1.1939: Launched. 2.1939: Completed. 6.1.1940: Whilst on a voyage from Haifa to Dunkirk, under command of Capt. Templeton, fouled and exploded a mine and sank at a position 4 miles N.E. of the Dyck light vessel, in an Allied minefield.

BT. 135. BRITISH PRUDENCE (1) (1939–1942)

O.N. 167217. 8,620g. 4,903n. 12,451d.
474.6 × 62.0 × 33.9 feet.
4-cyl. 2 S.C.S.A. ($23^{5}/_{8}$″ × $91^{5}/_{16}$″) oil engine manufactured by Wm. Doxford & Sons Ltd., Sunderland. 3,435 bhp.
Ocean-going tanker.

6.2.1939: Launched by Sir J. Laing & Sons Ltd., Sunderland (Yard No. 723), for the British Tanker Company Ltd. 4.1939: Completed. 23.3.1942: Whilst on an Admiralty voyage from Halifax to the R. Clyde, sunk by a torpedo from a German submarine, at position 45.28N., 56.13W., 300 miles east of Sydney, Cape Breton.

BT. 136. BRITISH UNITY (1) (1939–1961)

O.N. 167215. 8,407g. 4,881n. 12,300d.
467.9 × 61.7 × 33.9 feet.

British Genius. (World Ship Society Photograph Library)

British Sincerity. (World Ship Society Photograph Library)

British Unity. (World Ship Society Photograph Library)

British Harmony. (World Ship Society Photograph Library)

8-cyl. 4 S.C.S.A. (29 1/8″ × 59 1/16″) B&W type oil engine manufactured by J. G. Kincaid & Company Ltd., Greenock. 3,200 bhp.
Ocean-going tanker.

28.12.1938: Launched by Lithgows Ltd., Port Glasgow (Yard No. 914), for the British Tanker Company Ltd. 4.1939: Completed. 1.6.1956: Owners restyled as BP Tanker Company Ltd. 2.6.1961: Arrived at Briton Ferry for demolition, by T. W. Ward Ltd., Sheffield.

BT. 137. BRITISH INFLUENCE (1939)

O.N. 167227. 8,431g. 4,930n. 12,443d.
466.3 × 61.9 × 33.9 feet.
4-cyl. 2 S.C.S.A. (23 5/8″ × 91 5/16″) oil engine manufactured by Wm. Doxford & Sons Ltd., Sunderland. 3,435 bhp.
Ocean-going tanker.

8.3.1939: Launched by Swan, Hunter & Wigham, Richardson Ltd., Newcastle (Yard No.1 593), for the British Tanker Company Ltd. 5.1939: Completed. 14.9.1939: Whilst on a voyage from Abadan to Hull, damaged by a torpedo and sunk by gunfire from the German submarine U-29, at position 49.43N., 12.49W., in the Western Approaches.

BT. 138. BRITISH HARMONY (1) (1941–1960)

O.N. 168214. 8,453g. 4,897n. 12,458d.
466.3 × 61.9 × 33.9 feet.
4-cyl. 2 S.C.S.A. (23 5/6″ × 91 5/16″) Doxford type oil engine manufactured by the shipbuilder. 3,435 bhp.
Ocean-going tanker.

9.6.1941: Launched by Swan, Hunter & Wigham, Richardson Ltd., Newcastle (Yard No. 1696), for the British Tanker Company Ltd. 9.1941: Completed. 1.6.1956: Owners restyled as BP Tanker Company Ltd. 23.9.1957: Laid up at Falmouth. 29.9.1960: Towed to Cardiff thence to Glasgow to be prepared for scrapping. 16.10.1960: Arrived at Troon for demolition by West of Scotland Shipbreaking Company Ltd. 3.11.1960: Work commenced.

BT. 139. BRITISH CHARACTER (1941–1959)

O.N. 168246. 8,453g. 4,897n. 12,458d.
466.3 × 61.9 × 33.9 feet.
4-cyl. 2 S.C.S.A. (23 5/8″ × 91 5/16″) Doxford type oil engine manufactured by the shipbuilder. 3,435 bhp.
Ocean-going tanker.

25.8.1941: Launched by Swan, Hunter & Wigham, Richardson Ltd., Newcastle (Yard No. 1698), for the British Tanker Company Ltd. 12.1941: Completed. 1.6.1956: Owners restyled as BP Tanker Company Ltd. 19.3.1959: Arrived at Bo'ness for demolition by P. & W. MacLellan Ltd. 6.1959: Work commenced.

BT. 140. BRITISH VIGILANCE (1) (1942–1943)

O.N. 168286. 8,093g. 4,755n. 12,028d.
463.2 × 61.2 × 33.1 feet.
6-cyl. 4 S.C.S.A. (29 1/8″ × 59 1/16″) B&W type oil engine manufactured by the shipbuilder. 3,200 bhp.
Ocean-going tanker.

18.2.1942: Launched as EMPIRE VIGILANCE by Harland & Wolff Ltd., Glasgow (Yard No. 1116 G), for the Ministry of War Transport. 23.5.1942: Completed as BRITISH VIGILANCE for the British Tanker Company Ltd. 3.1.1943: Whilst on a voyage from Curacao to Gibraltar was damaged by a torpedo fired by the German submarine U-514, at position 20.58N., 44.40W., in the north Atlantic, was abandoned in a drifting condition. 24.1.1943: Torpedoed and sunk by the German submarine U-105.

BT. 141. BRITISH MERIT (1942–1961)

O.N. 168295. 8,093g. 4,755n. 11,961d.
463.2 × 61.2 × 33.1 feet.
6-cyl. 4 S.C.S.A. (29 1/8″ × 59 1/16″) B&W type oil engine manufactured by the shipbuilder. 2,450 bhp.
Ocean-going tanker.

British Character. (World Ship Society Photograph Library)

British Merit. (World Ship Society Photograph Library)

British Tradition. (World Ship Society Photograph Library)

16.4.1942: Launched by Harland & Wolff Ltd., Glasgow (Yard No. 1117 G), for the British Tanker Company Ltd. 9.7.1942: Completed. 25.7.1942: Whilst sailing in Convoy ON 113 to Newfoundland, was damaged by a torpedo fired by the German submarine U-552, at position 49.03N., 40.36W., 600 miles east from Newfoundland. Subsequently taken in tow. 2.8.1942: Arrived at Newfoundland. 24.8.1942: Departed for New York, in tow for repairs. 1.6.1956: Owners restyled as BP Tanker Company Ltd. 9.12.1960: Arrived in tow at Cardiff, from lay-up at Portland, to be prepared for demolition. 17.3.1961: Arrived in tow at Briton Ferry for demolition by T. W. Ward Ltd., Sheffield. 1.4.1961: Work commenced.

BT. 142. BRITISH TRADITION (1942–1961)

O.N. 168301. 8,443g. 4,825n. 12,322d.
466.3 × 61.9 × 33.9 feet.
6-cyl. 4 S.C.S.A. (29$^{1}/_{8}$″ × 59$^{1}/_{16}$″) B&W type oil engine manufactured by Harland & Wolff Ltd., Belfast. 2,450 bhp.
Ocean-going tanker.

5.3.1942: Launched by Cammell, Laird & Company Ltd., Birkenhead (Yard No. 1067), for the British Tanker Company Ltd. 8.1942: Completed. 1.6.1956: Owners restyled as BP Tanker Company Ltd. 2.9.1958: Laid up at Portland. 29.10.1960: Arrived in tow at Cardiff to be prepared for demolition. 20.1.1961: Arrived in tow at Briton Ferry for demolition by T. W. Ward Ltd., Sheffield. 15.2. 1961: Work commenced.

BT. 143. BRITISH PROMISE (1) (1942–1959)

O.N. 168331. 8,443g. 4,825n. 12,415d.
466.3 × 61.9 × 33.9 feet.
6-cyl. 4 S.C.S.A. (29$^{1}/_{8}$″ × 59$^{1}/_{16}$″) B&W type oil engine manufactured by Harland & Wolff Ltd., Belfast. 2,450 bhp.
Ocean-going tanker.

30.7.1942: Launched by Cammell, Laird & Company Ltd., Birkenhead (Yard No. 1068), for the British Tanker Company Ltd. 11.1942: Completed. 20.11.1942: Damaged by a torpedo fired by the German submarine U-518, at position 43.53N., 55.02W., 200 miles south of Newfoundland. 22.11.1942: Arrived at Newfoundland, and subsequently repaired. 1.6.1956: Owners restyled as BP Tanker Company Ltd. 3.1.1958: Laid up at Methil. 24.2.1959: Arrived at Rosyth for demolition by Shipbreaking Industries Ltd.

British Gratitude. (World Ship Society Photograph Library)

BT. 144. BRITISH GRATITUDE (1942–1959)

O.N. 168355. 8,463g. 4,914n. 12.355d.
470.1 × 61.9 × 33.9 feet.
6-cyl. 4 S.C.S.A. (29$^{1}/_{8}$″ × 59$^{1}/_{16}$″) B&W type oil engine manufactured by Harland & Wolff Ltd., Glasgow. 2,450 bhp.
Ocean-going tanker.

26.9.1942: Launched by Swan, Hunter & Wigham, Richardson Ltd., Wallsend (Yard No. 1673), for the British Tanker Company Ltd. 12.1942: Completed. 1.6.1956: Owners restyled as BP Tanker Company Ltd. 12.5.1959: Arrived at Tamise in tow from lay-up at Falmouth. 7.7.1959: Jos Boel and Fils S. A., commenced demolition.

British Vigour. (World Ship Society Photograph Library)

British Promise at Cape Town. (World Ship Society Photograph Library)

BT. 145. BRITISH VIGOUR (1943–1959)

O.N. 168398. 5,844g. 3,163n. 8,485d.
406.2 × 56.3 × 29.9 feet.
3-cyl. 2 S.C.S.A. (23$^{5}/_{8}$″ × 91$^{5}/_{16}$″) oil engine manufactured by Wm. Doxford & Sons Ltd., Sunderland. 2,580 bhp. 516nhp.
Ocean-going tanker.

19.2.1942: Keel laid by the Furness Ship Building Company, Haverton Hill on Tees (Yard No. 347), for the British Tanker Company Ltd. 21.12.1942: Launched. 2.1943: Completed. 1.6.1956: Owners restyled as BP Tanker Company Ltd. 1959: Sold to Compagnie d'Armement Maritime, France, and renamed THORONET. 25.6.1964: Arrived at Aviles for demolition by Disguaces y Salvamentos S.A. 30.6.1964: Work commenced.

BT. 146. BRITISH RESPECT (1) (1943–1959)

O.N. 168416. 8,479g. 4,967n. 12,319d.
469.8 × 61.9 × 33.9 feet.
4-cyl. 2 S.C.S.A. ($23\frac{5}{8}''$ × $91\frac{5}{16}''$) Doxford type oil engine manufactured by the shipbuilder. 3,435 bhp.
Ocean-going tanker.

4.2.1943: Launched by Swan, Hunter & Wigham, Richardson Ltd., Newcastle (Yard No. 1724), for the British Tanker Company Ltd. 4.1943: Completed. 1.6.1956: Owners restyled as BP Tanker Company Ltd. 13.6.1959: Arrived, in tow of CRUISER (304g./53), at Barrow in Furness for demolition by T. W. Ward Ltd., Sheffield. 9.1959: Work commenced.

British Patience. (World Ship Society Photograph Library)

BT. 147. BRITISH PURPOSE (1) (1943–1959)

O.N. 168424. 5,845g. 3,164n. 8,485d.
406.2 × 56.3 × 29.9 feet.
3-cyl. 2 S.C.S.A. ($23\frac{5}{8}''$ × $91\frac{5}{16}''$) oil engine manufactured by Wm. Doxford & Sons Ltd., Sunderland. 2,580 bhp. 516nhp.
Ocean-going tanker.

23.4.1942: Keel laid by the Furness Ship Building Company, Haverton Hill on Tees (Yard No. 348), for the British Tanker Company Ltd. 22.2.1943: Launched. 4.1943: Completed. 20.10.1943: Whilst at position 11.49N., 74.54E., was damaged by a torpedo from a German submarine. 1.6.1956: Owners restyled as BP Tanker Company Ltd. 1959: Sold to Sameiet Anella (A. Blystad, manager), Norway, and renamed ANELLA. 22.12.1961: Arrived at Bremerhaven for demolition. 4.1.1962: Eisen Und Metall A.G., commenced work.

British Restraint. (World Ship Society Photograph Library)

British Purpose. (World Ship Society Photograph Library)

BT. 148. BRITISH PATIENCE (1) (1943–1961)

O.N. 168451. 8,097g. 4,757n. 11,961d.
463.2 × 61.2 × 33.1 feet.
6-cyl. 4 S.C.S.A. ($29\frac{1}{8}''$ × $59\frac{1}{16}''$) B&W type oil engine manufactured by the shipbuilder. 3,200 bhp.
Ocean-going tanker.

23.3.1943: Launched by Harland & Wolff Ltd., Glasgow (Yard No. 1166 G), for the British Tanker Company Ltd. 15.6.1943: Completed. 1.6.1956: Owners restyled as BP Tanker Company Ltd. 8.9.1961: Arrived at Troon for demolition by the West of Scotland Shipbreaking Company Ltd.

BT. 149. BRITISH RESTRAINT (1943–1959)

O.N. 168473. 8,448g. 4,831n. 12,273d.
466.3 × 61.9 × 33.9 feet.
6-cyl. 2 S.C.S.A. ($29\frac{1}{8}''$ × $59\frac{1}{16}''$) B&W type oil engine manufactured by Harland & Wolff Ltd., Belfast. 3,300 bhp.
Ocean-going tanker.

8.4.1943: Launched by Cammell, Laird & Company Ltd., Birkenhead (Yard No. 1105), for the British Tanker Company Ltd. 7.1943: Completed. 1.6.1956: Owners restyled as BP Tanker Company Ltd. 31.12.1957: Laid up at Falmouth. 4.1959: Sold to the Indian Trading and Transport Establishment, Vaduz, Leichtenstein. 26.5.1959: Resold to Terreste Marittima S.p.A., Spezia, for demolition. 29.5.1959: Arrived at Spezia, in tow of TURMOIL (1,136g./45).

BT. 150. BRITISH MIGHT (1945–1961)

O.N. 180565. 8,269g. 4,806n. 12,202d.
466.0 × 59.5 × 34.8 feet.
6-cyl. 4 S.C.S.A. ($29\frac{1}{8}''$ × $59\frac{1}{16}''$) B&W type oil engine manufactured by the shipbuilder. 3,200 bhp.
Ocean-going tanker.

29.3.1945: Launched by Harland & Wolff Ltd., Glasgow (Yard No. 1196 G), for the British Tanker Company Ltd. 7.6.1945: Completed. 1.6.1956: Owners restyled as BP Tanker Company Ltd. 9.5.1961: Arrived at Troon for demolition by West of Scotland Shipbreaking Company Ltd. 17.5.1961: Work commenced.

BT. 151. BRITISH VIRTUE (1945–1962)

O.N. 180567. 8,553g. 4,953n. 12,390d.
469.1 × 61.9 × 33.9 feet.
4-cyl. 2 S.C.S.A. ($23\frac{5}{8}''$ × $91\frac{5}{16}''$) Doxford type oil engine manufactured by the shipbuilder. 3,435 bhp.
Ocean-going tanker.

17.3.1945: Launched by Swan, Hunter & Wigham, Richardson Ltd., Newcastle (Yard No. 1762), for the British Tanker Company Ltd. 6.1945: Completed. 1.6.1956: Owners restyled as BP Tanker Company Ltd. 18.6.1958: Arrived at Barry and laid up. 16.7.1961: Arrived in tow at Cardiff to be prepared for demolition. 1.5.1962: Departed under to from CardifF. 4.5.1962: Arrived at Troon for demolition by West of Scotland Shipbreaking Company Ltd. 10.5.1962: Work commenced.

BT. 152. BRITISH WISDOM (1945–1960)

O.N. 180577. 8,295g. 4,800n. 12,282d.
466.6 × 61.2 × 33.2 feet.
4-cyl. 2 S.C.S.A. ($23\frac{5}{8}''$ × $91\frac{5}{16}''$) Doxford type oil engine manufactured by Barclay, Curle & Company Ltd., Glasgow. 3,315 bhp.
Ocean-going tanker.

12.4.1945: Launched by the Blythswood Shipbuilding Company Ltd., Glasgow (Yard No.78), for the British Tanker Company Ltd. 7.1945: Completed. 1.6.1956: Owners restyled as BP Tanker Company Ltd. 10.2.1958: Laid up at Falmouth. 9.9.1960: Arrived in tow at

British Might, 12 April 1955. (World Ship Society Photograph Library)

British Virtue alongside *British Major*. (World Ship Society Photograph Library)

British Wisdom in the course of demolition. (World Ship Society Photograph Library)

British Cavalier in the course of demolition. (World Ship Society Photograph Library)

Cardiff to be prepared for demolition. 6.10.1960: Sold to T. W. Ward Ltd., Sheffield., for demolition, but remained at Cardiff. 8.5.1962: Arrived in tow at Briton Ferry. 12.5.1962: Work commenced.

BT. 153. BRITISH CAVALIER (1) (1945–1959)

O.N. 169033. 9,891g. 5,912n. 482.7 × 68.3 × 36.1 feet.
8-cyl. 4 S.C.S.A. (25 9/16″ × 55 1/8″) B&W type oil engine manufactured by R. & W. Hawthorn, Leslie & Company Ltd., Newcastle. 2,510 bhp.
Ocean-going tanker.

27.8.1942: Launched as EMPIRE CAVALIER by Sir James Laing & Sons Ltd., Sunderland (Yard No. 743), for the Ministry of War Transport (Mungo, Campbell & Company Ltd., Newcastle, managers). 11.1942: Completed. 1944: British Tanker Company Ltd., appointed as managers. 1945: Purchased by the British Tanker Company Ltd., and renamed BRITISH CAVALIER. 1.6.1956: Owners restyled as BP Tanker Company Ltd. 13.11.1957: Laid up at Swansea. 20.5.1959: Handed over to T. W. Ward Ltd., Sheffield, at Swansea. 23.5.1959: Arrived in tow at Briton Ferry for demolition. 6.1959: Work commenced.

BT. 154. BRITISH LANCER (1) (1945–1960)

O.N. 169027. 9,891g. 5,912n. 482.7 × 68.3 × 36.1 feet.
8-cyl. 4 S.C.S.A. (25 9/16″ × 55 1/8″) B&W type oil engine manufactured by R. & W. Hawthorn, Leslie & Company Ltd., Newcastle. 2,510 bhp.
Ocean-going tanker.

29.5.1942: Launched as EMPIRE WORDSWORTH by Sir James Laing & Sons Ltd., Sunderland (Yard No. 742), for the Ministry of War Transport (Hunting & Sons Ltd., Newcastle, managers). 9.1942: Completed. 1944: British Tanker Company Ltd., appointed as managers. 1945: Purchased by the British Tanker Company Ltd., and renamed BRITISH LANCER. 1.6.1956: Owners restyled as BP Tanker Company Ltd. 10.9.1960: Arrived at Briton Ferry for demolition by T. W. Ward Ltd., Sheffield. 15.12.1960: Work commenced.

BT. 155. BRITISH DRAGOON (1) (1945–1962)

O.N. 169117. 9,909g. 5,924n. 482.7 × 68.3 × 36.1 feet.
6-cyl. 4 S.C.S.A. (29 1/8″ × 59 1/16″) B&W type oil engine manufactured by Harland & Wolff Ltd., Glasgow. 2,450 bhp.
Ocean-going tanker.

8.3.1943: Launched as EMPIRE ALLIANCE by Sir James Laing & Sons Ltd., Sunderland (Yard No. 747), for the Ministry of War Transport (the Anglo-Saxon Petroleum Company Ltd., managers). 6.1943: Completed. 1944: The British Tanker Company Ltd., appointed as managers. 1945: Purchased by the British Tanker Company Ltd., and renamed BRITISH DRAGOON. 1.6.1956: Owners restyled as BP Tanker Company Ltd. 12.12.1962: Arrived at Blyth for demolition by Hughes Bolckow Shipbreaking Company Ltd.

BT. 156. BRITISH GUARDSMAN (1) (1945–1951)

O.N. 165832. 8,128g. 4,626n. 465.9 × 59.4 × 33.8 feet.
T.3-cyl. (26 1/2″, 44″ & 73″ × 48″) engine manufactured by the shipbuilder. 3,145 hp.
Ocean-going tanker.

British Lancer arriving at Swansea. (World Ship Society Photograph Library)

British Dragoon arriving at Cape Town. (World Ship Society Photograph Library)

14.5.1942: Launched as EMPIRE GARRICK by Swan, Hunter & Wigham, Richardson Ltd., Newcastle (Yard No. 1710), for the Ministry of War Transport (James German & Company Ltd., managers). 7.1942: Completed. 1944: British Tanker Company Ltd., appointed as managers. 1945: Purchased by the British Tanker Company Ltd., and renamed BRITISH GUARDSMAN. 1951: Sold to the British Oil Shipping Company (Stevenson, Hardy & Company Ltd., managers), and renamed ALAN EVELYN. 1955: Sold to Duff, Herbert & Mitchell Ltd., and renamed WESTBROOK. 28.7.1959: Whilst laid up at Barry, sustained considerable fire damage to her superstructure and was declared a total loss. 15.3.1960: Whilst under tow to J. Cashmore & Company, Newport, grounded at the entrance to the R. Usk, but was refloated later in the day. 16.3.1960: Berthed at breaker's yard.

BT. 157. BRITISH SUPREMACY (1945–1961)

O.N. 180785. 8,242g. 4,816n. 12,330d.
466.0 × 59.5 × 34.8 feet.
6-cyl. 4 S.C.S.A. ($29^{1}/_{8}''$ × $59^{1}/_{16}''$) B&W type oil engine manufactured by the shipbuilder's Glasgow works. 3,200 bhp.
Ocean-going tanker.

26.7.1945: Launched by Harland & Wolff Ltd., Belfast (Yard No. 1284), for the British Tanker Company Ltd. 12.1945: Completed. 1.6.1956: Owners restyled as BP Tanker Company Ltd. 11.7.1957: Laid up at Falmouth. 21.9.1961: Departed in tow from Falmouth. 26.9.1961: Arrived at Troon for demolition by West of Scotland Shipbreaking Company Ltd. 7.8.1962: Work commenced.

BT. 158. BRITISH SUCCESS (1) (1946–1961)

O.N. 180817. 8,215g. 4,769n. 12,382d.
466.0 × 59.2 × 34.8 feet.
6-cyl. 4 S.C.S.A. ($29^{1}/_{8}''$ × $59^{1}/_{16}''$) B&W type oil engine manufactured by J. G. Kincaid & Company Ltd., Greenock. 3,375 bhp.
Ocean-going tanker.

7.11.1945: Launched by the Blythswood Shipbuilding Company Ltd., Glasgow (Yard No. 81), for the British Tanker Company Ltd. 2.1946: Completed. 1.6.1956: Owners restyled as BP Tanker Company Ltd. 22.9.1957: Laid up at Falmouth. 29.8.1961: Arrived in tow at Troon for demolition by West of Scotland Shipbreaking Company Ltd. 20.10.1961: Work commenced.

BT. 159. BRITISH CAUTION (1946–1961)

O.N. 180823. 8,552g. 4,923n. 12,490d.
469.1 × 61.9 × 33.9 feet.
4-cyl. 2 S.C.S.A. ($23^{5}/_{8}''$ × $91^{5}/_{16}''$) Doxford type oil engine manufactured by the shipbuilder. 3,435 bhp.
Ocean-going tanker.

21.9.1945: Launched by Swan, Hunter & Wigham, Richardson Ltd., Newcastle (Yard No. 1764), for the British Tanker Company Ltd. 2.1946: Completed. 1.6.1956: Owners restyled as BP Tanker Company Ltd. 16.8.1959: Laid up at Barry. 10.12.1961: Arrived in tow at Newport, for demolition by J. Cashmore Ltd.

British Supremacy. (World Ship Society Photograph Library)

British Success. (World Ship Society Photograph Library)

British Caution. (World Ship Society Photograph Library)

British Major, 20 September 1948. (World Ship Society Photograph Library)

British Bombardier. (World Ship Society Photograph Library)

BT. 161. BRITISH MARQUIS (2) (1946–1961)

O.N. 180869. 8,563g. 4,906n. 12,310d.
469.6 × 62.0 × 33.9 feet.
4-cyl. 2 S.C.S.A. ($23\frac{5}{8}'' \times 91\frac{5}{16}''$) oil engine manufactured by the shipbuilder. 3,435 bhp.
Ocean-going tanker.

3.4.1946: Launched by Wm. Doxford & Sons Ltd., Sunderland (Yard No. 735), for the British Tanker Company Ltd. 5.1946: Completed. 1.6.1956: Owners restyled as BP Tanker Company Ltd. 22.9.1957: Laid up at Falmouth. 21.9.1961: Departed in tow from Falmouth. 25.9.1961: Arrived at Bo'ness for demolition by P. & W. MacLellan Ltd. 28.2.1962: Work commenced.

BT. 162. BRITISH BOMBARDIER (1) (1946–1959)

O.N. 168521. 8,202g. 4,781n. 11,742d.
465.6 × 59.5 × 33.8 feet.
8-cyl. 4 S.C.S.A. ($25\frac{9}{16}'' \times 55\frac{1}{8}''$) B&W type oil engine manufactured by the shipbuilder. 2,510 bhp.
Ocean-going tanker.

8.8.1942: Launched as EMPIRE FUSILIER by Harland & Wolff Ltd., Belfast (Yard No. 1158), for the Ministry of War Transport (Dodd, Thompson & Company Ltd., managers). 2.1943: Completed, as EMPIRE BOMBARDIER. 1944: British Tanker Company Ltd., appointed as managers. 1946: Purchased by the British Tanker Company Ltd., and renamed BRITISH BOMBARDIER. 1.6.1956: Owners restyled as BP Tanker Company Ltd. 28.5.1958: Laid up at Devonport. 1.1959: Sold to Van Heyghen Freres, Ghent, thence to Chantiers Navals Jos Boels et Fils S. A. 13.3.1959: Arrived in tow at Tamise. 23.3.1959: Demolition commenced.

BT. 163. BRITISH BUGLER (1946–1957)

O.N. 180161. 3,766g. 1,974n. 343.5 × 48.3 × 26.5 feet.
3-cyl. 2 S.C.S.A. ($23\frac{5}{8}'' \times 91\frac{5}{16}''$) oil engine manufactured by Wm. Doxford & Sons Ltd., Sunderland. 3,435 bhp.
Ocean-going tanker.

27.4.1945: Launched as EMPIRE ARROW by J. L. Thompson & Sons Ltd., Sunderland (Yard No. 641), for the Ministry of War Transport (British Tanker Company Ltd., managers). 8. 1945: Completed. 1946: Purchased by the British Tanker Company Ltd., and renamed BRITISH BUGLER. 1.6.1956: Owners restyled as BP Tanker Company Ltd. 1957: Sold to Cie. d'Armement Maritime, Djibouti, and renamed MONTMAJOUR. 1963: Sold to Greek Tanker Shipping Company, Greece, and renamed

BT. 160. BRITISH MAJOR (2) (1946–1961)

O.N. 180838. 8,564g. 4,908n. 12,310d.
469.6 × 62.0 × 33.9 feet.
4-cyl. 2 S.C.S.A. ($23\frac{5}{8}'' \times 91\frac{5}{16}''$) oil engine manufactured by the shipbuilder. 3,435 bhp.
Ocean-going tanker.

15.1.1946: Launched by Wm. Doxford & Sons Ltd., Sunderland (Yard No. 734), for the British Tanker Company Ltd. 26.3.1946: Completed. 1.6.1956: Owners restyled as BP Tanker Company Ltd. 5.5.1959: Laid up at Falmouth. 29.9.1961: Arrived in tow at Cardiff to be prepared for demolition. 8.4.1962: Departed in tow from Cardiff and arrived at Newport for demolition by J. Cashmore Ltd. 9.4.1962: Work commenced.

British Bugler. (World Ship Society Photograph Library)

British Commando. (World Ship Society Photograph Library)

British Drummer arriving at Swansea. (World Ship Society Photograph Library)

MANTINIA. 1.1.1978: Laid up at Piraeus. 6.1981: Demolished at Kynosoura.

BT. 164. BRITISH COMMANDO (1946–1958)

O.N. 168512. 8,194g. 4,777n. 465.6 × 59.5 × 33.8 feet.
8-cyl. 4 S.C.S.A. ($25\frac{9}{16}'' \times 55\frac{1}{8}''$) B&W type oil engine manufactured by the shipbuilder. 2,510 bhp.
Ocean-going tanker.

17.1.1942: Launched as EMPIRE CHAPMAN by Harland & Wolff Ltd., Belfast (Yard No. 1080), for the Ministry of War Transport (British Tanker Company Ltd., managers). 25.6. 1942: Completed. 1946: Purchased by the British Tanker Company Ltd., and renamed BRITISH COMMANDO. 1.6.1956: Owners restyled as BP Tanker Company Ltd. 3.3.1958: Arrived in tow at Bruges for demolition. 21.1. 1959: Van Heyghen Freres commenced work at Ghent.

BT. 165. BRITISH DRUMMER (1946–1957)

O.N. 180152. 3,758g. 1,978n. 343.5 × 48.3 × 26.5 feet.
3-cyl. 2 S.C.S.A. ($23\frac{5}{8}'' \times 91\frac{5}{16}''$) oil engine manufactured by Wm. Doxford & Sons Ltd., Sunderland. 2,250 bhp.
Ocean-going tanker.

16.12.1944: Launched as EMPIRE ENSIGN by J. L. Thompson & Sons Ltd., Sunderland (Yard No. 637), for the Ministry of War Transport (British Tanker Company Ltd., managers). 3.1945: Completed. 1946: Purchased by the British Tanker Company Ltd., and renamed BRITISH DRUMMER. 1.6.1956: Owners restyled as BP Tanker Company Ltd. 1957: Sold to Pedersen & Blystad, Norway, and renamed ANELLA. 1958: Sold to Bucha Godager & Company, Norway, and renamed NORSE COMMANDER. 6.9.1966: Arrived in tow with boiler damage at Singapore. Subsequently declared a constructive total loss. 12.11.1966: Delivered to Hong Huat Hardware Company Ltd., Singapore, for demolition. 4.4.1967: Work commenced.

BT. 166. BRITISH ESCORT (1946–1959)

O.N. 169174. 8,477g. 4,949n. 469.8 × 61.9 × 33.9 feet.
4-cyl. 2 S.C.S.A. ($23\frac{5}{8}'' \times 91\frac{5}{16}''$) Doxford type oil engine manufactured by the shipbuilder. 3,435 bhp.
Ocean-going tanker.

1942: Laid down as BRITISH VIRTUE by Swan, Hunter & Wigham, Richardson Ltd., Newcastle (Yard No. 1726), by the British Tanker Company Ltd. 18.5.1943: Launched as EMPIRE MACCABE, for the Ministry of War Transport (British Tanker Company Ltd., managers). 11.1943: Completed. 1946: Purchased by the British Tanker Company Ltd., and renamed BRITISH ESCORT. 1.6.1956: Owners restyled as BP Tanker Company Ltd. 1959: Sold to Easthill Shipping Company Ltd., London, and renamed EASTHILL ESCORT. 1960: Sold to River Line Ltd. (Mollers Ltd., Hong Kong, managers), Bermuda. 31.12.1961: Laid up at Hong Kong. 13.3.1962: Handed over to Hong Kong Chiap Hua Manufacturing Company (1947) Ltd., for demolition at Hong Kong. 20.3.1962: Work commenced.

BT.167. BRITISH PILOT (1946–1962)

O.N. 168869. 8,452g. 4,865n. 466.3 × 61.9 × 33.9 feet.
6-cyl. 4 S.C.S.A. ($29\frac{1}{8}'' \times 59\frac{1}{16}''$) B&W type oil engine manufactured by Harland & Wolff Ltd., Glasgow. 2,450 bhp.
Ocean-going tanker.

1943: Laid down as BRITISH CAUTION by Cammell, Laird & Company Ltd., Birkenhead (Yard No. 1106), for the British Tanker Company Ltd. 21.7.1943: Launched as EMPIRE MACCOLL, for the Ministry of War Transport (British Tanker Company Ltd., managers). 11.1943: Completed. 1946: Purchased by the British Tanker Company Ltd., and renamed BRITISH PILOT. 1.6.1956: Owners restyled as BP Tanker Company Ltd. 21.8.1962: Arrived at Faslane for demolition

British Escort on the Mersey. (World Ship Society Photograph Library)

British Pilot. (World Ship Society Photograph Library)

by Shipbreaking Industries Ltd. 27.8.1962: Work commenced.

BT.168. BRITISH PIPER (1946–1961)

O.N. 169467. 8,238g. 4,796n. 466.0 × 59.5 × 34.8 feet.
6-cyl. 4 S.C.S.A. ($29^{1}/_{8}''$ × $59^{1}/_{16}''$) B&W type oil engine manufactured by the shipbuilder. 3,200 bhp.
Ocean-going tanker.

20.12.1945: Launched as EMPIRE GRENADA by Harland & Wolff Ltd., Glasgow (Yard No. 1197), for the Ministry of War Transport (British Tanker Company Ltd., managers). 11.4. 1946: Completed as BRITISH PIPER for the British Tanker Company Ltd. 1.6. 1956: Owners restyled as BP Tanker Company Ltd. 1.10.1960: Laid up at Falmouth. 25.9.1961: Arrived in tow at Cardiff to be prepared for demolition. 10.10.1961: Towed from Cardiff to Newport for demolition by J. Cashmore Ltd. 11.10.1961: Work commenced.

BT. 169. BRITISH SWORDFISH (1946–1959)

O.N. 168770. 8,106g. 4,735n. 463.2 × 61.2 × 33.1 feet.
6-cyl. 4 S.C.S.A. ($29^{1}/_{8}''$ × $59^{1}/_{16}''$) B&W type oil engine manufactured by the shipbuilder. 2,450 bhp.
Ocean-going tanker.

1943: Laid down as BRITISH WISDOM by Harland & Wolff Ltd., Glasgow (Yard No. 1167 G), for the British Tanker Company Ltd. 17.6.1943: Launched as EMPIRE MACKAY, for the Ministry of War Transport (British Tanker Company Ltd., managers). 10.1943: Completed. 1946: Purchased by the British Tanker Company Ltd., and renamed BRITISH SWORDFISH. 21.5.1959: Arrived at Rotterdam for demolition by Frank Rijdiyk Industrielle. 11.1959: Work commenced at Hendrik Ido Ambacht.

BT. 170. BRITISH COMMERCE (2) (1946–1961)

O.N. 180903. 6,092g. 3,335n. 8,380d. 406.0 × 56.3 × 30.0 feet.
3-cyl. 2 S.C.S.A. ($23^{5}/_{8}''$ × $91^{5}/_{16}''$) oil engine manufactured by the shipbuilder. 2,670 bhp.
Ocean-going tanker.

15.5.1946: Launched by Wm. Doxford & Sons Ltd., Sunderland (Yard No. 736), for the British Tanker Company Ltd. 7.1946: Completed. 1.6.1956: Owners restyled as BP Tanker Company Ltd. 1.10.1960: Arrived in tow at Falmouth and laid up. 12.6.1961: Arrived in tow at Antwerp for demolition by Scrappingco S.p.r.l. 20.6.1961: Work commenced.

BT. 171. BRITISH PRINCESS (2) (1946–1962)

O.N. 180928. 8,582g. 4,918n. 12,354d. 469.6 × 62.0 × 33.9 feet.
3-cyl. 2 S.C.S.A. ($23^{5}/_{8}''$ × $91^{5}/_{16}''$) oil engine manufactured by Wm. Doxford & Sons Ltd., Sunderland. 3,435 bhp.
Ocean-going tanker.

30.4.1946: Launched by Sir James Laing & Sons Ltd., Sunderland (Yard No. 768), for the British Tanker Company Ltd. 8.1946: Completed. 1.6.1956: Owners restyled as BP Tanker Company Ltd. 22.4.1959: Laid up at Swansea. 8.2.1962: Arrived in tow at Briton Ferry for demolition by T. W. Ward Ltd., Sheffield. 26.2.1962: Work commenced.

BT. 172. BRITISH MARSHAL (2) (1946–1961)

O.N. 180959. 8,582g. 4,918n. 12,310d. 469.6 × 62.0 × 33.9 feet.
4-cyl. 2 S.C.S.A. ($23^{5}/_{8}''$ × $91^{5}/_{16}''$) oil engine manufactured by the shipbuilder. 3,435 bhp.
Ocean-going tanker.

6.6.1946: Launched by Wm. Doxford & Sons Ltd., Sunderland (Yard No. 737), for the British Tanker Company Ltd. 7.1946: Completed. 1.6.1956: Owners restyled as BP Tanker Company Ltd. 9.7.1957: Laid up at Falmouth. 6.11.1961: Arrived in tow at Blyth for demolition by Hughes Bolckow Shipbreaking Company Ltd.

British Piper. (World Ship Society Photograph Library)

British Swordfish at Cape Town. (World Ship Society Photograph Library)

British Commerce. (World Ship Society Photograph Library)

British Princess. (World Ship Society Photograph Library)

BT. 173. BRITISH KNIGHT (2) (1946–1961)

O.N. 180961. 8,629g. 4,999n. 12,300d. 471.6 × 61.8 × 33.6 feet.
6-cyl. 4 S.C.S.A. ($29^{1}/_{8}''$ × $59^{1}/_{16}''$) B&W type oil engine manufactured by the shipbuilder. 3,485 bhp.
Ocean-going tanker.

12.6.1946: Launched by Harland & Wolff Ltd., Glasgow (Yard No. 1307 G), for the British Tanker Company Ltd. 25.9.1946: Completed.

British Marshal. (World Ship Society Photograph Library)

British Rose. (World Ship Society Photograph Library)

1.6.1956: Owners restyled as BP Tanker Company Ltd. 3.3.1959: Laid up at Falmouth. 7.10.1961: Arrived at Bo'ness for demolition by P. & W. MacLellan Ltd. 26.9.1962: Work commenced.

BT. 174. BRITISH ROSE (2) (1946–1961)

O.N. 180973. 6,101g. 3,332n. 8,396d.
406.0 × 56.3 × 30.0 feet.
3-cyl. 2 S.C.S.A. ($23\frac{5}{8}'' \times 91\frac{5}{16}''$) Doxford type oil engine manufactured by the North Eastern Marine Engineering Works (1938) Ltd., Wallsend. 2,670 bhp.
Ocean-going tanker.

29.5.1946: Launched by J. L. Thompson & Sons Ltd., Sunderland (Yard No. 646), for the British Tanker Company Ltd. 10.1946: Completed. 1.6.1956: Owners restyled as BP Tanker Company Ltd. 25.4.1959: Laid up at Falmouth. 16.6.1961: Arrived in tow at Bruges for demolition by Van Heyghen Freres. 17.7.1961: Work commenced.

BT. 175. BRITISH EARL (2) (1946–1961)

O.N. 181583. 8,745g. 4,988n. 12,250d.
472.6 × 62.0 × 33.6 feet.
4-cyl. 2 S.C.S.A. ($23\frac{5}{8}'' \times 91\frac{5}{16}''$) Doxford type oil engine manufactured by the shipbuilder. 3,435 bhp.
Ocean-going tanker.

28.6.1946: Launched by Swan, Hunter & Wigham, Richardson Ltd., Newcastle (Yard No. 1772), for the British Tanker Company Ltd. 10.1946: Completed. 18.1.1947: Whilst on a voyage from Abadan to Stockholm, exploded a mine in the Great Belt, Denmark, and beached off Langeland Island to prevent sinking. 25.1.1947: Refloated and towed to Nyborg for repairs. Whilst en route temporarily grounded south of Sprogo. Subsequently towed to the U.K. for permanent repairs which included the cutting of her hull into sections to enable it to be realigned. 1.6.1956: Owners restyled as BP Tanker Company Ltd. 15.7.1957: Laid up at Falmouth. 18.7.1961: Departed from Falmouth in tow of ENGLISHMAN (716g./45). 25.7.1961: Arrived at Inverkeithing for demolition by T. W. Ward Ltd., Sheffield. 10.1961: Work commenced.

BT. 176. BRITISH ENTERPRISE (2) (1946–1961)

O.N. 181519. 6,095g. 3,329n. 8,370d.
406.0 × 56.3 × 30.0 feet.
3-cyl. 2 S.C.S.A. ($23\frac{5}{8}'' \times 91\frac{5}{16}''$) oil engine manufactured by the shipbuilder. 2,670 bhp.
Ocean-going tanker.

10.9.1946: Launched by Wm. Doxford & Sons Ltd., Sunderland (Yard No. 738), for the British Tanker Company Ltd. 11.1946: Completed. 1.6.1956: Owners restyled as BP Tanker Company Ltd. 15.7.1959: Laid up at Falmouth. 20.6.1961: Arrived in tow at Gateshead for demolition by Clayton & Davie Ltd. 23.7.1961: Work commenced.

BT. 177. BRITISH HOLLY (2) (1946–1964)

O.N. 183530. 8,582g. 4,919n. 12,354d.
469.6 × 62.0 × 33.9 feet.
4-cyl. 2 S.C.S.A. ($23\frac{5}{8}'' \times 91\frac{5}{16}''$) oil engine manufactured by Wm. Doxford & Sons Ltd., Sunderland. 3,435 bhp.
Ocean-going tanker.

26.8.1946: Launched by Sir James Laing & Sons Ltd., Sunderland (Yard No. 770), for the British Tanker Company Ltd. 12.1946: Completed. 1.6.1956: Owners restyled as BP Tanker Company Ltd. 23.3.1964: Arrived at Faslane for demolition by Shipbreaking Industries Ltd. 26.3.1964: Work commenced.

BT. 178. BRITISH VETERAN (1946–1948)

see ship No. BT. 7 above.

BT. 179. BRITISH ADMIRAL (2) (1947–1961)

O.N. 181504. 8,378g. 4,948n. 12,283d.
472.6 × 62.0 × 33.6 feet.

British Holly. (World Ship Society Photograph Library)

British Admiral. (World Ship Society Photograph Library)

4-cyl. 2 S.C.S.A. (23⁵/₈″ × 91⁵/₁₆″) oil engine manufactured by Wm. Doxford & Sons Ltd., Sunderland. 3,435 bhp.
Ocean-going tanker.

3.4.1945: Keel laid by the Furness Shipbuilding Company, Haverton Hill on Tees (Yard No. 390), for the British Tanker Company Ltd. 16.7.1946: Launched. 1.1947: Completed. 1.6.1956: Owners restyled as BP Tanker Company Ltd. 6.5.1959: Laid up at Falmouth. 29.9.1961: Arrived in tow at Blyth for demolition by Hughes Bolckow Shipbreaking Company Ltd. 20.3.1962: Work commenced.

BT. 180. BRITISH BARON (2) (1947–1962)

O.N. 181568. 8,556g. 4,948n. 12,412d.
471.0 × 61.9 × 33.9 feet.
4-cyl. 2 S.C.S.A. (23⁵/₈″ × 91⁵/₁₆″) Doxford type oil engine manufactured by Richardsons, Westgarth & Company Ltd., Hartlepool. 3,435 bhp.
Ocean-going tanker.

29.10.1946: Launched by Cammell, Laird & Company Ltd., Birkenhead (Yard No. 1177), for the British Tanker Company Ltd. 2.1947: Completed. 1.6.1956: Owners restyled as BP Tanker Company Ltd. 7.10.1960: Laid up at Falmouth. 9.1.1962: Arrived in tow at Inverkeithing for demolition by T. W. Ward Ltd., Sheffield. 15.1.1962: Work commenced.

BT. 181. BRITISH EMPRESS (2) (1947–1961)

O.N. 181588. 8,745g. 4,988n. 12,245d.
472.6 × 62.0 × 33.6 feet.
4-cyl. 2 S.C.S.A. (23⁵/₈″ × 91⁵/₁₆″) oil engine manufactured by Wm. Doxford & Sons Ltd., Sunderland. 3,435 bhp.
Ocean-going tanker.

29.4.1945: Keel laid by the Furness Shipbuilding Company, Haverton Hill on Tees (Yard No. 391), for the British Tanker Company Ltd. 24.10.1946: Launched. 3.1947: Completed. 1.6.1956: Owners restyled as BP Tanker Company Ltd. 29.3.1959: Laid up at Methil. 28.7.1961: Arrived in tow at Charlestown Roads. 31.7.1961: Arrived in tow at Rosyth for demolition by Shipbreaking Industries Ltd. 4.9.1961: Work commenced.

BT. 182. BRITISH ENSIGN (2) (1947–1961)

O.N. 181615. 8,738g. 4,984n. 12,257d.
472.6 × 62.0 × 33.6 feet.
4-cyl. 2 S.C.S.A. (23⁵/₈″ × 91⁵/₁₆″) oil engine manufactured by Wm. Doxford & Sons Ltd., Sunderland. 3,435 bhp.
Ocean-going tanker.

23.11.1945: Keel laid by the Furness Shipbuilding Company, Haverton Hill on Tees (Yard No. 393), for the British Tanker Company Ltd. 10.12.1946: Launched. 5.1947: Completed. 1.6.1956: Owners restyled as BP Tanker Company Ltd. 24.2.1959: Laid up at Methil. 29.8.1961: Arrived in tow at Rosyth for demolition by Shipbreaking Industries Ltd.

BT. 183. ROGUE RIVER (1947–1959)

O.N. 181727. 10,647g. 6,310n. 16,494d.
506.5 × 68.2 × 39.2 feet.
Post 1961: 15,781g. 9,611n. 24,015d.
574′ 6″ × 78′ 7″ × 46′ 9″ .
Two, steam turbines (6,600 shp) manufactured by the General Electric Company, Shenectady, U.S.A., powering 1 electric generator connected to an electric motor in turn connected to screw shaft. 6,000 shp.
Ocean-going tanker.

19.11.1944: Launched by the Alabama Drydock & Shipbuilding Company, Mobile (Yard No. 316), for United States War Shipping Administration (subsequently the United States Maritime Commission). 12.1944: Completed. 1947: Purchased by the British Tanker Company Ltd. 1.6.1956: Owners restyled as BP Tanker Company Ltd. 1959: Sold to A/S Gerrards Rederi, Norway, renamed HUNSFORS, and used as an electricity generating plant. 1960: Renamed APACHE. 1961: Lengthened and converted into a bulk carrier by Blohm & Voss A. G., Hamburg. 1968: Sold to Philippine Pacific Shipping Company, Panama, and renamed

British Baron. (World Ship Society Photograph Library)

British Empress. (World Ship Society Photograph Library)

British Ensign. (World Ship Society Photograph Library)

Rogue River at Cape Town. (World Ship Society Photograph Library)

Cottonwood Creek at Cape Town. (World Ship Society Photograph Library)

British Fern. (World Ship Society Photograph Library)

PACMERCHANT. 26.2.1977: Arrived at Kaohsiung for demolition.

BT. 184. COTTONWOOD CREEK (1947–1955)

O.N. 181691. 10,647g. 6,310n. 16,505d.
506.5 × 68.2 × 39.2 feet.
Post 1959: 10,232g. 5,995n. 15,200d.
Two, steam turbines (7,425 shp) manufactured by the General Electric Company, Lynn, U.S.A., powering 1 electric generator connected to an electric motor in turn connected to screw shaft. 6,000 shp.
Ocean-going tanker.

2.11.1944: Launched by the Alabama Drydock & Shipbuilding Company, Mobile (Yard No. 313), for United States War Shipping Administration (subsequently United Stated Maritime Commission). 11.1944: Completed. 1947: Purchased by the British Tanker Company Ltd. 1955: Transferred to Soc. Maritime de Petroles BP., France, and renamed BRISSAC. 12.1959: Sold to Zeeland Transportation Ltd., Liberia, converted into a bulk carrier by A/S Stord Verft, Norway, and renamed BULK MARINER. 1960: Reverted to COTTONWOOD CREEK. 1965: Sold to Ogden Bulk Transport Inc., U.S.A. 5.1.1970: Whilst on a voyage from New Orleans to Saigon, with a cargo of wheat, grounded on coral at position 15.51N., 82.18W, off Honduras. Salvors in attendance but beaten by heavy weather which began to break vessel up. 2.1970: Abandoned as a total loss.

BT. 185. FORT STEVENS (1947–1959)

O.N. 181690. 10,639g. 6,274n. 16,512d.
506.5 × 68.2 × 39.2 feet.
Two, steam turbines (7,240 shp) manufactured by the General Electric Company, Lynn, U.S.A., powering 1 electric generator connected to an electric motor in turn connected to screw shaft. 6,000 shp.
Ocean-going tanker.

16.9.1944: Launched by the Alabama Drydock & Shipbuilding Company, Mobile (Yard No. 307), for United States War Shipping Administration (subsequently the United States Maritime Commission). 10.1944: Completed. 1947: Purchased by the British Tanker Company Ltd. 1.6.1956: Owners restyled as BP Tanker Company Ltd. 5.10.1959: Arrived at Blyth for demolition by Hughes, Bolckow Shipbreaking Company Ltd.

BT. 186. BRITISH FERN (2) (1947–1961)

O.N. 181663. 8,582g. 4,919n. 12,310d.
469.6 × 62.0 × 33.9 feet.
4-cyl. 2 S.C.S.A. (23⅝″ × 91$^{5}/_{16}$″) oil engine manufactured by Wm. Doxford & Sons Ltd., Sunderland. 3,435 bhp.
Ocean-going tanker.

6.2.1947: Launched by Sir James Laing & Sons Ltd., Sunderland (Yard No. 771), for the British Tanker Company Ltd. 7.1947: Completed. 1.6.1956: Owners restyled as BP Tanker Company Ltd. 7.2.1959: Laid up at Falmouth. 1.9.1961: Arrived at Blyth for demolition by Hughes, Bolckow Shipbreaking Company Ltd.

BT. 187. RED BANK (1947–1959)

O.N. 181711. 10,639g. 6,274n. 16,546d.
506.5 × 68.2 × 39.2 feet.
Two, steam turbines (7,240 shp) manufactured by the General Electric Company, Lynn, U.S.A., powering 1 electric generator connected to an electric motor in turn connected to screw shaft. 6,000 shp.
Ocean-going tanker.

19.10.1944: Launched by the Alabama Drydock & Shipbuilding Company, Mobile (Yard No. 311), for United States War Shipping Administration (subsequently the United States Maritime Commission). 11.1944: Completed. 1947: Purchased by the British Tanker Company Ltd. 1.6.1956: Owners restyled as BP Tanker Company Ltd. 1959: Sold to Christiania Portland Cementfabrik, Norway, renamed BANK, for use as an electricity generating station. 20.1.1960 Arrived in tow at Spezia for demolition by Terreste Marittima S.p.A. 4.1960: Work commenced.

BT. 188. BRITISH ISLES (2) (1947–1962)

O.N. 181703. 8,738g. 4,984n. 12,275d.
472.6 × 62.0 × 33.6 feet.
4-cyl. 2 S.C.S.A. (23⅝″ × 91$^{5}/_{16}$″) oil engine manufactured by Wm. Doxford & Sons Ltd., Sunderland. 3,100 bhp.
Ocean-going tanker.

29.2.1946: Keel laid by the Furness Shipbuilding Company, Haverton Hill on Tees (Yard No. 394), for the British Tanker Company Ltd. 24.3.1947: Launched. 8.1947: Completed. 1.6.1956: Owners restyled as BP Tanker Company Ltd. 8.3.1962: Arrived at Antwerp for demolition by Jos de Smedt. 20.3.1962: Work commenced.

BT. 189. CHISHOLM TRAIL (1947–1955)

O.N. 181763. 10,660g. 6,322n. 16,501d.
506.5 × 68.2 × 39.2 feet.
Two, steam turbines (7,240 shp) manufactured by the General Electric Company, Lynn, U.S.A., powering 1

Red Bank at Cape Town. (World Ship Society Photograph Library)

electric generator connected to an electric motor in turn connected to screw shaft. 6,000 shp.
Ocean-going tanker.
2.1945: Completed by the Kaiser Company Inc., Portland, Oregon (Yard No. 120), for United States War Shipping Administration (subsequently the United States Maritime Commission). 1947: Purchased by the British Tanker Company Ltd. 1955: Transferred to Societe Maritime de Petroles BP, France, and renamed MONTSOREAU. 6.12.1961: Whilst on a voyage from La Skhirra to Dunkirk, collided with the French tanker ISIDORA (20,704g./55) in fog, sustaining considerable damage, at a position 12 miles north of Cape Spartel. Towed to Gibraltar by ISIDORA and beached to prevent sinking. 19.12.1961: Having received temporary repairs, was refloated and towed by the French tug LAURENT CHAMBON (263g./60), to Port de Bouc, where she was declared a total loss. 10.2.1962: Societe de Material Navaldu Midi, Marseilles, commenced demolition at La Seyne.

BT. 190. FORT FREDERICA (1947–1959)

O.N. 181768. 10,672g. 6,322n. 16,385d.
506.5 × 68.2 × 39.2 feet.
Two, steam turbines (7,240 shp) manufactured by the General Electric Company, Lynn, U.S.A., powering 1 electric generator connected to an electric motor in turn connected to screw shaft. 6,000 shp.
Ocean-going tanker.
2.1945: Completed by the Kaiser Company Inc., Portland, Oregon (Yard No. 118), for United States War Shipping Administration (subsequently the United States Maritime Commission). 1947: Purchased by the British Tanker Company Ltd. 1.6.1956: Owners restyled as BP Tanker Company Ltd. 11.12.1959: Hong Kong Salvage and Towage Company Ltd., commenced demolition at Hong Kong.

BT. 191. MESA VERDE (1947–1955)

O.N. 181779. 10,660g. 6,322n. 16,377d.
506.5 × 68.2 × 39.2 feet.
Two, steam turbines (7,240 shp) manufactured by the General Electric Company, Lynn, U.S.A., powering 1 electric generator connected to an electric motor in turn connected to screw shaft. 6,000 shp.
Ocean-going tanker.
11.1944: Completed by the Kaiser Company Inc., Portland, Oregon (Yard No. 99), for United States War Shipping Administration (subsequently the United States Maritime Commission). 1947: Purchased by the British Tanker Company Ltd. 1955: Transferred to Societe Maritime de Petroles BP, France, and renamed VILLANDRY. 6.1961: Compagnie de Remorquage et de Sauvetage Les Abielles commenced demolition at Toulon.

BT. 192. EL MORRO (1947–1959)

O.N. 181790. 10,673g. 6,320n. 16,401d.
506.5 × 68.2 × 39.2 feet.
Two, steam turbines (7,240 shp) manufactured by the General Electric Company, Lynn, U.S.A., powering 1 electric generator connected to an electric motor in turn connected to screw shaft. 6,000 shp.
Ocean-going tanker.
12.1944: Completed by the Kaiser Company Inc., Portland, Oregon (Yard No. 101), for United States War Shipping Administration (subsequently the United States Maritime Commission). 1947: Purchased by the British Tanker Company Ltd. 1.6.1956: Owners

British Isles. (World Ship Society Photograph Library)

Chisholm Trail. (World Ship Society Photograph Library)

Fort Frederica at Cape Town. (World Ship Society Photograph Library)

El Morro. (World Ship Society Photograph Library)

Smoky Hill at Cape Town. (World Ship Society Photograph Library)

restyled as BP Tanker Company Ltd. 4.11.1959: Arrived at Blyth for demolition by Hughes Bolckow Shipbreaking Company Ltd. 2.12.1959: Work commenced.

BT. 193. BEECHER ISLAND (1947–1959)

O.N. 181808. 10,668g. 6,317n. 16,495d. 506.5 × 68.2 × 39.2 feet.
Two, steam turbines (7,240 shp) manufactured by the General Electric Company, Lynn, U.S.A., powering 1 electric generator connected to an electric motor in turn connected to screw shaft. 6,000 shp.
Ocean-going tanker.

30.11.1944: Launched by the Alabama Drydock & Shipbuilding Company, Mobile (Yard No. 318), for United States War Shipping Administration (subsequently the United States Maritime Commission). 12.1944: Completed. 1947: Purchased by the British Tanker Company Ltd. 1.6.1956: Owners restyled as BP Tanker Company Ltd. 5.10.1959: Sold to Hughes, Bolckow Shipbreaking Company Ltd., Blyth, thence T. W. Ward Ltd, Sheffield., for demolition at their Barrow in Furness facility. 8.10.1959: Arrived at Barrow in Furness. 9.10.1959: Work commenced.

BT. 194. SMOKY HILL (1947–1957)

O.N. 181817. 10,660g. 6,322n. 16,387d. 506.5 × 68.2 × 39.2 feet.
Two, steam turbines (7,240 shp) manufactured by the General Electric Company, Lynn, U.S.A., powering 1 electric generator connected to an electric motor in turn connected to screw shaft. 6,000 shp.
Ocean-going tanker.

9.1944: Completed by the Kaiser Company Inc., Portland, Oregon (Yard No. 88), for United States War Shipping Administration (subsequently the United States Maritime Commission). 1947: Purchased by the British Tanker Company Ltd. 1.6.1956: Owners restyled as BP Tanker Company Ltd. 1957: Sold to Mariblanca Nav. S. A., Greece, and renamed MARIPOSA. 9.7.1964: Laid up at Perama. 17.1.1965: Whilst en route from Piraeus to Castellon for demolition, grounded at Augusta but was refloated. 30.1.1965: Arrived at Castellon as MARIPOSA II, for demolition by L. E. Varela Davillo. 7.1966: Work commenced.

BT. 195. IRAN (1947–1958)

O.N. 169103. 798g. 373n. 840d. 193.0 × 30.0 × 14.1 feet.
T.3-cyl. (15″, 25$^{1}/_{2}$″ & 41″ × 30″) engine manufactured by Aitchison, Blair Ltd., Clydebank.
Coastal tanker.

11.10.1943: Launched as EMPIRE SETTLER by the Grangemouth Dockyard Company Ltd., Grangemouth (Yard No. 453), for the Ministry of War Transport (Anglo -Saxon Petroleum Company Ltd., managers). 11.1943: Completed. 3.10.1947: Sold to the British Tanker Company Ltd., and renamed IRAN. 1.6.1956: Owners restyled BP Tanker Company Ltd. 1958: Renamed WIDAD. 1962: Sold to N. E. Vernicos Shipping Company Ltd. (D. C. & A. Vernicos, managers), Greece, and renamed MOTOL VII. 4.1968: Demolition commenced at Piraeus.

BT. 196. BLACKBIRD (1947–1948)

O.N. 177007. 13g 10n 38.0 × 10.0 × 3.5 feet.
286bhp, oil engine
Wooden hulled unspecified vessel.

1940: Completed by unspecified builders at Bay Head, New Jersey, USA, for the U. S. Navy. 12.1947: Acquired by the British Tanker Company Ltd. (Anglo-Bahamian Oil Company Ltd., managers), Bahamas. 8.1948: Sold to unspecified buyers. *Due to small size and type of this vessel no further details have been recorded by the authors.*

BT. 197. SUILVEN (1947)

O.N. 147904. 882g. 390n. 197.0 × 7.5 × 13.3 feet.
Two, T.4-cyl. (12″, 19$^{1}/_{2}$″, 22″ & 22″ × 20″) engines manufactured by the shipbuilder. 395 shp.
Steel steam yacht converted into a pilot vessel.

6.1924: Completed as THALASSA by J. Brown & Company Ltd., Clydebank, for Eugene Higgins, New York. 1944: Acquired by the British Government. 1945: Sold to W. G. Hetherington, Glasgow, and renamed SUILVEN. 1946: Taken over by the Executors of the Late W. G. Hetherington. 1947: Purchased by the British Tanker Company Ltd., and converted into a pilot vessel. 27.4.1947: Upon completion was sold to Government of Iran. No further details located.

BT. 198. BRITISH DUKE (2) (1948–1962)

O.N. 181834. 8,562g. 4,950n. 12,420d. 471.0 × 61.9 × 33.9 feet.
4-cyl. 2 S.C.S.A. (23$^{5}/_{8}$″ × 91$^{5}/_{16}$″) Doxford type oil engine manufactured by Richardsons, Westgarth & Company Ltd., Hartlepool. 3,435 bhp.
Ocean-going tanker.

19.6.1947: Launched by Cammell, Laird & Company Ltd., Birkenhead (Yard No. 1178), for the British Tanker Company Ltd. 2.1948: Completed. 1.6.1956: Owners restyled as BP Tanker Company Ltd. 17.7.1962: Arrived at Dalmuir for demolition by W. H. Arnott, Young & Company Ltd. 3.8.1962: Work commenced.

BT. 199. BRITISH RANGER (1) (1948–1957)

O.N. 181916. 8,575g. 4,949n. 12,344d. 470.4 × 61.8 × 33.8 feet.
6-cyl. 4 S.C.S.A. (29$^{1}/_{8}$″ × 59$^{1}/_{16}$″) B&W type oil engine manufactured by the shipbuilder. 3,200 bhp.
Ocean-going tanker.

11.12.1947: Launched by Harland & Wolff

Iran. (World Ship Society Photograph Library)

British Duke leaving Swansea. (World Ship Society Photograph Library)

British Ranger. (World Ship Society Photograph Library)

British Security at Swansea, alongside a laid-up member of the fleet. (World Ship Society Photograph Library)

Ltd., Glasgow (Yard No. 1362 G), for the British Tanker Company Ltd. 3.6.1948: Completed. 1.6.1956: Owners restyled as BP Tanker Company Ltd. 1957: Transferred to BP Clyde Tanker Company Ltd., and renamed CLYDE RANGER. 1.3.1963: Arrived at Faslane for demolition by Shipbreaking Industries Ltd. 23.3.1963: Work commenced.

BT. 200. BRITISH SECURITY (2) (1948–1966)

O.N. 181947. 8,583g. 4,941n. 12,306d.
470.6 × 61.8 × 33.8 feet.
6-cyl. 4 S.C.S.A. ($29^{1}/_{8}$″ × $59^{1}/_{16}$″) B&W type oil engine manufactured by the shipbuilder. 3,475 bhp.
Ocean-going tanker.

27.2.1948: Launched by Harland & Wolff Ltd., Belfast (Yard No. 1364), for the British Tanker Company Ltd. 7.7.1948: Completed. 1.6.1956: Owners restyled as BP Tanker Company Ltd. 1966: Sold to A. Halcoussis, Greece, and renamed MANA. 1967: Sold to Ypatia Eidiki, Greece, and renamed YPATIA. 3.9.1968: Departed from Ras Tanura bound to Constantza. 14.9.1968: Arrived at Lourenco Marques (Maputo) having sustained grounding damage on Danae Reef, off Cape Inhaca, Mozambique. Declared as beyond economical repair and sold for demolition. Subsequently towed to Kaohsiung. 5.1969: Demolition was commenced by unspecified shipbreakers.

BT. 201. BRITISH ADVOCATE (2) (1948–1962)

O.N. 181956. 8,573g. 4,937n. 12,306d.
470.4 × 61.8 × 33.8 feet.
6-cyl. 4 S.C.S.A. ($29^{1}/_{8}$″ × $59^{1}/_{16}$″) B&W type oil engine manufactured by J. G. Kincaid & Company Ltd., Greenock. 3,125 bhp.
Ocean-going tanker.

27.4.1948: Launched by Lithgows Ltd., Port Glasgow (Yard No. 1033), for the British Tanker Company Ltd. 7.1948: Completed. 1.6.1956: Owners restyled as BP Tanker Company Ltd. 11.7.1962: Departed in tow from R. Tyne for demolition by Netransmar Schoenmarkt S. A., Antwerp. Resold and 22.7.1962: Arrived in tow at Bilbao for demolition by Bugues y Materiales. 15.9.1962: Work commenced.

BT. 202. BRITISH SCIENTIST (1) (1948–1957)

O.N. 182846. 8,545g. 4,873n. 12,362d.
471.6 × 61.9 × 33.9 feet.

British Advocate. (World Ship Society Photograph Library)

British Councillor. (World Ship Society Photograph Library)

6-cyl. 4 S.C.S.A. ($29^{1}/_{8}$″ × $59^{1}/_{16}$″) B&W type oil engine manufactured by J. G. Kincaid & Company Ltd., Greenock. 3,125 bhp.
Ocean-going tanker.

9.6.1948: Launched by Cammell, Laird & Company Ltd., Birkenhead (Yard No. 1190), for the British Tanker Company Ltd. 9.1948: Completed. 1.6.1956: Owners restyled as BP Tanker Company Ltd. 1957: Transferred to BP Clyde Tanker Company Ltd., and renamed CLYDE SCIENTIST. 27.2.1963: Arrived at Milford Haven for demolition by T. W. Ward Ltd., Sheffield, but was transferred to their Briton Ferry facility. 12.3.1963: Arrived in tow. 15.3.1963: Work commenced.

BT. 203. BRITISH COUNCILLOR (2) (1948–1967)

O.N. 182876. 8,573g. 4,937n. 12,275d.
470.4 × 61.8 × 33.8 feet.
6-cyl. 4 S.C.S.A. ($29^{1}/_{8}$″ × $59^{1}/_{16}$″) B&W type oil engine manufactured by J. G. Kincaid & Company Ltd., Greenock. 3,200 bhp.
Ocean-going tanker.

9.8.1948: Launched by Lithgows Ltd., Port Glasgow (Yard No. 1034), for the British Tanker Company Ltd. 10.1948: Completed. 1.6.1956: Owners restyled as BP Tanker Company Ltd. 10.4.1967: Arrived at Faslane for demolition by Shipbreaking Industries Ltd.

BT. 204. BRITISH STRENGTH (2) (1948–1966)

O.N. 182859. 8,580g. 4,936n. 12,278d.
470.6 × 61.8 × 33.8 feet.
6-cyl. 4 S.C.S.A. ($29^{1}/_{8}$″ × $59^{1}/_{16}$″) B&W type oil engine manufactured by the shipbuilder. 3,475 bhp.
Ocean-going tanker.

8.6.1948: Launched by Harland & Wolff Ltd., Belfast (Yard No. 1365), for the British Tanker Company Ltd. 12.11.1948: Completed.

British Strength. (World Ship Society Photograph Library)

British Venture with funnel covered during a period of lay-up. (World Ship Society Photograph Library)

British Progress. (World Ship Society Photograph Library)

British Chivalry. (J K Byass)

1.6.1956: Owners restyled as BP Tanker Company Ltd. 29.3.1966: Arrived at London. 5.4.1976: Sold to Eckhardt & Company G.m.b.H., Bremen, for demolition. 7.4.1966: Departed in tow, bound to Hamburg. En route was resold to Repcuperaciones Submarinos S. A., Spain. 11.4.1966: Arrived in tow at Santander for demolition.

BT. 205. BRITISH VENTURE (2) (1948–1961)

O.N. 182921. 6,119g. 3,348n. 8,396d.
406.0 × 56.3 × 30.0 feet.
3-cyl. 2 S.C.S.A. $(23^{5}/_{8}'' \times 91^{5}/_{16}'')$ Doxford type oil engine manufactured by Richardsons, Westgarth & Company Ltd., Hartlepool. 2,670 bhp.
Ocean-going tanker.

21.5.1948: Launched by J. L. Thompson & Sons Ltd., Sunderland (Yard No. 656), for the British Tanker Company Ltd. 12.1948: Completed. 1.6.1956: Owners restyled as BP Tanker Company Ltd. 2.7.1961: Arrived at Newport for demolition by J. Cashmore Ltd.

BT. 206. BRITISH PROGRESS (2) (1948–1963)

O.N. 182916. 8,577g. 4,937n. 12,560d.
470.4 × 61.8 × 33.8 feet.
6-cyl. 4 S.C.S.A. $(29^{1}/_{8}'' \times 59^{1}/_{16}'')$ B&W type oil engine manufactured by J. G. Kincaid & Company Ltd., Greenock. 3,125 bhp.
Ocean-going tanker.

23.8.1948: Launched by the Blythswood Shipbuilding Company, Glasgow (Yard No. 89), for the British Tanker Company Ltd. 12.1948: Completed. 1.6.1956: Owners restyled as BP Tanker Company Ltd. 13.3.1963: Arrived at Hamburg en route for demolition. 3.4.1963: Eckhardt & Company G.m.b.H., commenced work at Bremen.

BT. 207. BRITISH MARINER (2) (1948–1962)

O.N. 182898. 8,576g. 4,949n. 12,303d.
470.4 × 61.8 × 33.8 feet.
6-cyl. 4 S.C.S.A. $(29^{1}/_{8}'' \times 59^{1}/_{16}'')$ B&W type oil engine manufactured by the shipbuilder. 3,200 bhp.
Ocean-going tanker.

16.9.1948: Launched by Harland & Wolff Ltd., Glasgow (Yard No.1 378 G), for the British Tanker Company Ltd. 29.12.1948: Completed. 1.6.1956: Owners restyled as BP Tanker Company Ltd. 27.3.1962: Collided with and sank the W. German PALMYRA (1,944g./44) at position 18 miles off Ushant. Subsequently berthed on the Tyne for inspection but declared as beyond economical repair. 1.5.1962: Departed in tow from the R. Tyne. 4.5.1962: Arrived at Bruges for demolition. 5.5.1962: Brugse Scheepssloperij S. A., commenced work.

BT. 208. BRITISH CHIVALRY (2) (1949–1958)

O.N. 182927. 11,217g. 6,467n. 16,847d.
525.5 × 69.8 × 37.5 feet.
6-cyl. 2 S.C.S.A. $(26^{3}/_{8}'' \times 91^{5}/_{16}'')$ Doxford type oil engine manufactured by Barclay, Curle & Company Ltd., Glasgow. 6,450 bhp.
Ocean-going tanker.

27.4.1948: Launched by the Blythswood Shipbuilding Company, Glasgow (Yard No. 88), for the British Tanker Company Ltd. 1.1949: Completed. 1.6.1956: Owners restyled as BP Tanker Company Ltd. 1958: Transferred to BP Clyde Tanker Company Ltd., and renamed CLYDE CHIVALRY. 1963: Reverted to the BP Tanker Company Ltd., and BRITISH CHIVALRY. 15:30 hours, 3.3.1972: Sold to Eckhardt & Company G.m.b.H., Bremen, for demolition but was subsequently resold to Recuperaciones Submarinos S. A., Santander. 16.3.1972: Arrived from Swansea in tow, at Santander for demolition. 28.4.1972: Work commenced.

BT. 209. BRITISH ENDEAVOUR (2) (1949–1962)

O.N. 182929. 8,589g. 4,954n. 12,250d.
469.6 × 61.9 × 33.9 feet.
4-cyl. 2 S.C.S.A. $(23^{5}/_{8}'' \times 91^{5}/_{16}'')$ Doxford type oil engine manufactured by the shipbuilder. 3,560 bhp.
Ocean-going tanker.

3.9.1948: Launched by R. & W. Hawthorn, Leslie & Company Ltd., Hebburn (Yard No. 695), for the British Tanker Company Ltd.

1.1949: Completed. 1.6.1956: Owners restyled as BP Tanker Company Ltd. 29.3.1962: Arrived at Inverkeithing for demolition by T. W. Ward Ltd., Sheffield.

BT. 210. BRITISH FORTUNE (2) (1949–1961)

O.N. 182931. 6,108g. 3,334n. 8,380d.
406.0 × 56.3 × 30.0 feet.
3-cyl. 2 S.C.S.A. (23 3/8″ × 91 5/16″) oil engine manufactured by the shipbuilder. 2,500 bhp.
Ocean-going tanker.

9.6.1948: Launched by Wm. Doxford & Sons Ltd., Sunderland (Yard No. 763), for the British Tanker Company Ltd. 1.1949: Completed. 1.6.1956: Owners restyled as BP Tanker Company Ltd. 12.9.1961: Arrived at Briton Ferry for demolition by T. W. Ward Ltd., Sheffield.

BT. 211. BRITISH FAME (2) (1949–1972)

O.N. 182948. 11,203g. 6,458n. 16,849d.
525.5 × 69.8 × 37.5 feet.
6-cyl. 2 S.C.S.A. (26 3/8″ × 91 5/16″) Doxford type oil engine manufactured by the shipbuilder. 6,455 bhp.
Ocean-going tanker.

25.2.1948: Launched by Swan, Hunter & Wigham, Richardson Ltd., Wallsend (Yard No. 1761), for the British Tanker Company Ltd. 2.1949: Completed. 1.6.1956: Owners restyled as BP Tanker Company Ltd. 13.9.1971: Laid up at Swansea. 17.2.1972: Arrived at Briton Ferry for demolition by T. W. Ward Ltd., Sheffield.

BT. 212. BRITISH YEOMAN (2) (1949–1963)

O.N. 182969. 8,741g. 5,038n. 12,243d.
472.6 × 62.0 × 33.6 feet.
4-cyl. 2 S.C.S.A. (23 3/8″ × 91 5/16″) Doxford type oil engine manufactured by the North Eastern Marine Engineering Works (1938) Ltd., Wallsend. 3,435 bhp.
Ocean-going tanker.

25.8.1947: Keel laid by the Furness Shipbuilding Company, Haverton Hill on Tees (Yard No. 412), for the British Tanker Company Ltd. 20.10.1948: Launched. 3.1949: Completed. 1.6.1956: Owners restyled as BP Tanker Company Ltd. 25.5.1963: Arrived at Castellon for demolition by Amceto Fernandez Ordas. 2.7.1963: Work commenced.

BT. 213. BRITISH WORKMAN (2) (1949–1967)

O.N. 182972. 8,575g. 4,949n. 12,328d.
470.4 × 61.8 × 33.8 feet.
6-cyl. 4 S.C.S.A. (29 1/8″ × 59 1/16″) B&W type oil engine manufactured by the shipbuilder. 3,480 bhp
Ocean-going tanker.

16.11.1948: Launched by Harland & Wolff Ltd., Glasgow (Yard No. 1379 G), for the British Tanker Company Ltd. 24.3.1949: Completed. 1.6.1956: Owners restyled as BP Tanker Company Ltd. 5.1967: Sold to Isaac Varela, for demolition at Bilbao, thence to L. E. Varela Davillo, Castellon. 18.5.1967: Arrived at Castellon for demolition.

BT. 214. BRITISH PRUDENCE (2) (1949–1966)

O.N. 182976. 8,577g. 4,937n. 12,545d.
470.4 × 61.8 × 33.8 feet.
6-cyl. 4 S.C.S.A. (29 1/8″ × 59 1/16″) B&W type oil engine manufactured by J. G. Kincaid & Company Ltd., Greenock. 3,200 bhp.
Ocean-going tanker.

British Endeavour at Cape Town. (World Ship Society Photograph Library)

British Fortune. (World Ship Society Photograph Library)

British Fame. (World Ship Society Photograph Library)

British Yeoman. (World Ship Society Photograph Library)

British Workman. (World Ship Society Photograph Library)

British Prudence. (World Ship Society Photograph Library)

20.12.1948: Launched by the Blythswood Shipbuilding Company, Glasgow (Yard No. 90), for the British Tanker Company Ltd. 3.1949: Completed. 1.6.1956: Owners restyled as BP Tanker Company Ltd. 28.8.1966: Arrived at Hamburg for demolition by Eisen und Metall A. G. 12.9.1966: Work commenced.

BT. 215. TAFT (1949–1960)

O.N. 182985. 209g. 11n. 104.4 × 23.2 × 8.4 feet.
Two, C.2-cyl. (11″ & 22″ × 16″) engines manufactured by Plenty & Son Ltd., Newbury.
Twin screw tug.

16.2.1949: Launched by Scott & Sons, Bowling (Yard No. 387), for the Petroleum Steam Ship Company Ltd. 4.1949: Completed. 5.1949: Transferred to the British Tanker Company Ltd. 1960: Sold to the Government of Iraq (Directorate General of Ports & Navigation), Iraq, and renamed THAIR. 1966: Renamed HEET. 1963: Owners restyled Government of Iraq (Directorate General of Ports and Navigation). 1975: Owners restyled as Government of Iraq (Iraqi Ports Administration). 2.1975: Laid up – surveys overdue. 1976: Owners restyled as State Organisation of Iraqi Ports. 1978: Owners restyled as Government of Iraq (State Organisation of Iraqi Ports). 1979: Owners restyled as Government of the Republic of Iraq (State Organisation of Iraqi Ports). Still listed in Lloyd's Register 2003/04

BT. 216. TANB (1949–1951)

O.N. 182986. 209g. 11n. 104.4 × 23.2 × 8.4 feet.
Two, C.2-cyl. (11″ & 22″ × 16″) engines manufactured by Plenty & Son Ltd., Newbury
Twin screw tug.

3.1.1949: Launched by Scott & Sons, Bowling (Yard No.388), for the Petroleum Steam Ship Company Ltd. 4.1949: Completed. 5.1949: Transferred to the British Tanker Company Ltd. 1951: Seized by the Persian Authorities. 1955: Transferred to the National Iranian Oil Company Ltd., Iran, and renamed TAFRASH.1963: Sold to Nain Kawaiti, Iran. 3.1963: Lloyd's Register class suspended – dry-docking overdue. 1998: Lloyd's Register entry deleted – 'Continued existence in doubt'.

BT. 217. BRITISH LIBERTY (2) (1949–1964)

O.N. 183009. 8,589g. 4,952n. 12,250d. 469.6 × 62.0 × 33.9 feet.
4-cyl. 2 S.C.S.A. ($23^{5}/_{8}''$ × $91^{5}/_{16}''$) oil engine manufactured by the shipbuilder. 3,435 bhp.
Ocean-going tanker.

2.9.1948: Launched by Wm. Doxford & Sons Ltd., Sunderland (Yard No. 765), for the British Tanker Company Ltd. 5.1949: Completed. 1.6.1956: Owners restyled as BP Tanker Company Ltd. 27.6.1964: Having suffered machinery failure, arrived at Hong Kong in tow of BRITISH OFFICER, and was subsequently sold for demolition by Mollers Ltd., at Hong Kong. 23.7.1964: Work commenced.

BT. 218. BRITISH LOYALTY (2) (1949–1967)

O.N. 183050. 8,592g. 4,951n. 12,250d. 469.6 × 62.0 × 33.9 feet.
4-cyl. 2 S.C.S.A. ($23^{5}/_{8}''$ × $91^{5}/_{16}''$) oil engine manufactured by the shipbuilder. 3,435 bhp.
Ocean-going tanker.

18.11.1948: Launched by Wm. Doxford &

British Liberty. (World Ship Society Photograph Library)

British Loyalty. (World Ship Society Photograph Library)

Sons Ltd., Sunderland (Yard No. 766), for the British Tanker Company Ltd. 7.1949: Completed. 1.6.1956: Owners restyled as BP Tanker Company Ltd. 1967: Sold via unspecified Dutch intermediaries to Spanish shipbreakers. 22.6.1967: Arrived in tow at Bilbao for demolition by Hierros Arbulu. 7.8.1967: Work commenced.

BT. 219. BRITISH RESOURCE (2) (1949–1972)

O.N. 183096. 11,200g. 6,490n. 16,880d. 525.5 × 69.8 × 37.5 feet.
6-cyl. 2 S.C.S.A. (26 3/8″ × 91 5/16″) Doxford type oil engine manufactured by the shipbuilder. 6,460 bhp.
Ocean-going tanker.

16.3.1949: Launched by R. & W. Hawthorn, Leslie & Company Ltd., Hebburn (Yard No. 694), for the British Tanker Company Ltd. 9.1949: Completed. 1.6.1956: Owners restyled as BP Tanker Company Ltd. 24.4.1972: Arrived at Castellon for demolition by M. Varela Davillo. 5.1972: Work commenced.

British Resource. (World Ship Society Photograph Library)

BT. 220. BRITISH ARDOUR (2) (1949–1962)

O.N. 183137. 8,616g. 4,982n. 12,198d. 469.6 × 61.9 × 33.9 feet.
4-cyl. 2 S.C.S.A. (23 5/8″ × 91 5/16″) Doxford type oil engine manufactured by the shipbuilder. 3,435 bhp.
Ocean-going tanker.

12.4.1949: Launched by Swan, Hunter & Wigham, Richardson Ltd., Newcastle (Yard No. 1866), for the British Tanker Company Ltd. 11.1949: Completed. 1.6.1956: Owners restyled as BP Tanker Company Ltd. 30.10.1962: Scrappingco S. A., commenced demolition at Antwerp.

British Ardour. (World Ship Society Photograph Library)

BT. 221. BRITISH CAPTAIN (2) (1949–1962)

O.N. 183119. 8,700g. 5,024n. 12,303d. 471.6 × 61.8 × 33.6 feet.
6-cyl. 4 S.C.S.A. (29 1/8″ × 59 1/16″) B&W type oil engine manufactured by the shipbuilder. 3,480 bhp.
Ocean-going tanker.

11.8.1949: Launched by Harland & Wolff Ltd., Glasgow (Yard No. 1397 G), for the British Tanker Company Ltd. 25.11.1949: Completed. 1.6.1956: Owners restyled as BP Tanker Company Ltd. 4.12.1962: Arrived at Faslane for demolition by Shipbreaking Industries Ltd.

BT. 222. HAFFAR (1949–1960)

O.N. 183139. 1,180g. 453n. 192.9 × 40.1 × 17.8 feet.
Two, T.3-cyl. (11 3/8″, 18 1/2″ & 30″ × 21″) engines manufactured by the shipbuilder. 1,000ihp. 10kts.
Twin screw suction hopper dredger.

11.8.1949: Launched by Lobnitz & Company Ltd., Renfrew (Yard No. 1111), for the British Tanker Company Ltd. 11.1949: Completed. 1960: Sold to The J. P. Porter Company Company Ltd., Halifax N.S., and renamed LOCKEPORT, retaining London registry. 1965: Transferred to Halifax Registry. 1979: Sold to Sceptre Dredging Ltd. 1989: Sold to Fraser River Pile & Dredge Ltd., Sorel. 1992: Sold to Verreault Maritime Inc., and renamed PORT MECHINS. Still listed in Lloyd's Register 2003/04.

BT. 223. BRITISH TRIUMPH (2) (1949–1963)

O.N. 183162. 8,640g. 4,934n. 12,245d. 471.0 × 61.9 × 33.9 feet.
6-cyl. 4 S.C.S.A. (29 1/8″ × 59 1/16″) B&W type oil engine manufactured by Harland & Wolff Ltd., Glasgow. 3,200 bhp.

British Triumph. (World Ship Society Photograph Library)

Ocean-going tanker.

23.9.1949: Launched by Cammell, Laird & Company Ltd., Birkenhead (Yard No. 1199), for the British Tanker Company Ltd. 12.1949: Completed. 1.6.1956: Owners restyled as BP Tanker Company Ltd. 6.1.1963: Arrived at Faslane for demolition by Shipbreaking Industries Ltd.

BT. 224. PAZAN (1949–1956)

O.N. 182839. 483g. 171n. 189.7 × 26.3 × 7.5 feet.
Two, 6-cyl. 4 S.C.S.A.(19 7/16″ × 14 3/16″) oil engines manufactured by Kloeckner Humboldt Deutz A.G., Koeln-Deutz.
Coastal tanker.

1942: Completed as AUGUST by Greifenwerft G.m.b.H., Stettin (Yard No. ?), for unspecified German owners. 1948: Sold to the Anglo-Iranian Oil Company Ltd., and renamed ANGLIRAN 20. 1948: Transferred to The Petroleum Steamship Company Ltd., and renamed ANGLIRAN 16. 1949: Transferred to the British Tanker Company Ltd., and renamed PAZAN, 1956: Sold to A. W. Bentley-Buckle, Mombassa, and renamed

British Reliance. (World Ship Society Photograph Library)

British Freedom. (World Ship Society Photograph Library)

SOUTHERN PIONEER. 1957: Sold to Southern Line Ltd., Mombasa. 11.1964: Gutted by fire.

BT. 225. BRITISH RELIANCE (2) (1950–1973)

O.N. 183186. 11,201g. 6,490n. 16,687d.
525.5 × 69.8 × 37.5 feet.
6-cyl. 2 S.C.S.A. ($26^{3}/_{8}''$ × $91^{5}/_{16}''$) oil engine manufactured by Wm. Doxford & Sons Ltd., Sunderland. 6,400 bhp.
Ocean-going tanker.

23.9.1949: Launched by Sir James Laing & Sons Ltd., Sunderland (Yard No. 784), for the British Tanker Company Ltd. 2.1950: Completed. 1.6.1956: Owners restyled as BP Tanker Company Ltd. 1973: Sold to Atlantic Research Ltd., Bermuda, and renamed BANGOR BAY. 1974: Sold to Suffolk Navigation Company Ltd., Greece, and renamed OCEAN PRINCESS. 24.3.1975: Arrived at Castellon for demolition. 26.3.1975: Handed over to INCOLESA. 4.1975: Work commenced.

BT. 226. BRITISH FREEDOM (2) (1950–1972)

O.N. 183097. 11,207g. 6,494n. 16,849d.
525.5 × 69.8 × 37.5 feet.
6-cyl. 2 S.C.S.A. ($26^{3}/_{8}''$ × $91^{5}/_{16}''$) Doxford type oil engine manufactured by Wallsend Slipway Company Ltd., Wallsend. 6,400 bhp.
Ocean-going tanker.

30.3.1949: Launched by Swan, Hunter & Wigham, Richardson Ltd., Wallsend (Yard No. 1765), for the British Tanker Company Ltd. 2.1950: Completed. 1.6.1956: Owners restyled as BP Tanker Company Ltd. 15.3.1972: Sold to Nissho-Iwai Company Ltd., Japan, for demolition at Nagasaki. Resold and 7.4.1972: Arrived at Kaohsiung for demolition by I. Chong Steel & Iron Works. 20.4.1972: Work commenced.

BT. 227. BRITISH COMMANDER (2) (1950–1962)

O.N. 183184. 8,655g. 4,995n. 12,244d.
471.6 × 61.5 × 33.6 feet.
6-cyl. 4 S.C.S.A. ($29^{1}/_{8}''$ × $59^{1}/_{16}''$) B&W type oil engine manufactured by the shipbuilder. 3,200 bhp.
Ocean-going tanker.

21.11.1949: Launched by Harland & Wolff Ltd., Glasgow (Yard No. 1398 G), for the British Tanker Company Ltd. 23.2.1950: Completed. 1.6.1956: Owners restyled as BP Tanker Company Ltd. 24.7.1962: Arrived at Antwerp for demolition by Scrappingco S. A. 26.7.1962: Work commenced.

BT. 228. BRITISH PATRIOT (1950–1963)

O.N. 183195. 8,661g. 4,975n. 12,120d.
471.1 × 61.8 × 33.8 feet.
6-cyl. 4 S.C.S.A. ($29^{1}/_{8}''$ × $59^{1}/_{16}''$) B&W type oil engine manufactured by J. G. Kincaid & Company Ltd., Greenock. 3,200 bhp.
Ocean-going tanker.

27.10.1949: Launched by Lithgows Ltd., Port Glasgow (Yard No. 1042), for the British Tanker Company Ltd. 2.1950: Completed. 1.6.1956: Owners restyled BP Tanker Company Ltd. 4.6.1963: Arrived at Antwerp for demolition by Scrappingco S. A. 6.6.1963: Work commenced.

British Commander. (World Ship Society Photograph Library)

British Patriot. (World Ship Society Photograph Library)

BT. 229. BRITISH GENERAL (3) (1950–1964)

**O.N. 183232. 8,775g. 5,039n. 12,150d.
472.6 × 62.0 × 33.6 feet.
4-cyl. 2 S.C.S.A. (23⅝″ × 91$^5/_{16}$″) Doxford type oil engine manufactured by Vickers-Armstrongs Ltd., Barrow. 3,300 bhp.
Ocean-going tanker.**

20.1.1949: Keel laid by the Furness Shipbuilding Company, Haverton Hill on Tees (Yard No. 434), for the British Tanker Company Ltd. 20.12.1949: Launched. 5.1950: Completed. 1.6.1956: Owners restyled as BP Tanker Company Ltd. 1.6.1964: Arrived at Inverkeithing for demolition by T. W. Ward Ltd., Sheffield.

British General. (World Ship Society Photograph Library)

BT. 230. BRITISH UNION (2) (1950–1962)

**O.N. 183237. 8,663g. 4,985n. 12,167d.
469.6 × 61.9 × 33.9 feet.
4-cyl. 2 S.C.S.A. (23⅝″ × 91$^5/_{16}$″) Doxford type oil engine manufactured by the shipbuilder. 3,100 bhp.
Ocean-going tanker.**

20.12.1949: Launched by Swan, Hunter & Wigham, Richardson Ltd., Newcastle (Yard No. 1876), for the British Tanker Company Ltd. 5.1950: Completed. 1.6.1956: Owners restyled as BP Tanker Company Ltd. 19.12.1962: Arrived at Inverkeithing for demolition by T. W. Ward Ltd., Sheffield.

British Union. (World Ship Society Photograph Library)

BT. 231. BRITISH CONSUL (2) (1950–1963)

**O.N. 183236. 8,655g. 4,995n. 12,275d.
471.6 × 61.8 × 33.6 feet.
6-cyl. 4 S.C.S.A. (29⅛″ × 59$^1/_{16}$″) B&W type oil engine manufactured by the shipbuilder. 3,500 bhp.
Ocean-going tanker.**

2.3.1950: Launched by Harland & Wolff Ltd., Glasgow (Yard No. 1399 G), for the British Tanker Company Ltd. 9.6.1950: Completed. 1.6.1956: Owners restyled as BP Tanker Company Ltd. 30.4.1963: Arrived at Blyth for demolition by Hughes, Bolckow Shipbreaking Company Ltd.

British Consul. (World Ship Society Photograph Library)

BT. 232. BRITISH TRUST (2) (1950–1957)

**O.N. 183265. 8,640g. 4,934n. 12,248d.
471.0 × 61.9 × 33.9 feet.
6-cyl. 4 S.C.S.A. (29⅛″ × 59$^1/_{16}$″) B&W type oil engine manufactured by J. G. Kincaid & Company Ltd., Greenock. 3,520 bhp.
Ocean-going tanker.**

5.4.1950: Launched by Cammell, Laird & Company Ltd., Birkenhead (Yard No. 1200), for the British Tanker Company Ltd. 6.1950: Completed. 1.6.1956: Owners restyled as BP Tanker Company Ltd. 1957: Transferred to BP Clyde Tanker Company Ltd., and renamed CLYDE INVENTOR. 17.10.1963: Arrived at Hamburg for demolition by Eisen Und Metall A. G. 2.12.1963: Work commenced.

BT. 233. KANGAVAR (1950–1955)

**O.N. 183283. 328g. 160.0 × 25.1 × 8.0 feet.
Dumb tank barge.**

6.1950: Completed by Clelands (Successors) Ltd., Willington Quay on Tyne (Yard No. 162), for the British Tanker Company Ltd. 1955: Sold to the National Iranian Oil Company Ltd. *Due to the small size and type of this vessel the Authors. have not recorded any further details.*

BT. 234. BRITISH EXPLORER (1) (1950–1958)

**O.N. 183275. 8,644g. 4,970n. 12,243d.
470.6 × 61.8 × 33.8 feet.
6-cyl. 4 S.C.S.A. (29⅛″ × 59$^1/_{16}$″) B&W type oil engine manufactured by the shipbuilder. 3,500 bhp.
Ocean-going tanker.**

21.3.1950: Launched by Harland & Wolff Ltd., Belfast (Yard No. 1400), for the British Tanker Company Ltd. 8.7.1950: Completed. 1.6.1956: Owners restyled as BP Tanker Company Ltd. 1958: Transferred to BP Clyde Tanker Company Ltd., and renamed CLYDE EXPLORER. 12.1.1964: Arrived at Santander for demolition by Recuperaciones Submarinos S. A. 15.1.1964: Work commenced.

BT. 235. BRITISH DEFENDER (1950–1965)

**O.N. 183298. 6,138g. 3,335n. 8,420d.
406.0 × 56.2 × 30.0 feet.
Post 1969; 4,421g. 2,454n. 7,229d. 400′ 0″ × 56′ 0″ × 30′ 1″ BP
3-cyl. 2 S.C.S.A. (23⅝″ × 91$^5/_{16}$″) oil engine manufactured by the shipbuilder. 2,450 bhp. Post 1969; Engine rated at 2,500 bhp.
Ocean-going tanker.**

Farahmand. (World Ship Society Photograph Library)

British Peer. (World Ship Society Photograph Library)

2.2.1950: Launched by Wm. Doxford & Sons Ltd., Sunderland (Yard No. 779), for the British Tanker Company Ltd. 7.1950: Completed. 1.6.1956: Owners restyled as BP Tanker Company Ltd. 1965: Sold to the Trustees Secretaries Ltd. (F. C. Strick & Company (Newcastle) Ltd., managers), and renamed EL FLAMINGO. 1969: Converted into a self-unloading suction/hopper dredger with bottom doors. 1970: Sold to J. Murphy & Sons Ltd., London. 1970: Sold to Transworld Marine Trailers Ltd., Liberia, 1972: Sold to Marcon (RMC) Ltd. (J. Murphy & Sons Ltd., managers), London. 2.2.1982: Sold to Belcon Shipping & Trading Company Ltd., London, thence to Bruges Scheepsloperij, for demolition. 10.2.1982: Arrived at Bruges, in tow from London.

BT. 236. KARKUNAN (1950–1955)

O.N. 183282. 328g. 160.0 × 25.1 × 8.0 feet.
Dumb tank barge.

7.1950: Completed by Clelands (Successors) Ltd., Willington Quay on Tyne (Yard No.163), for the British Tanker Company Ltd. 1955: Sold to the National Iranian Oil Company Ltd. *Due to the small size and type of this vessel the Authors. have not recorded any further details.*

BT. 237. KUSA (1950–1952)

O.N. 184263. 92g. 26n 76.9 × 18.3 × 9.0 feet.
Two, 8-cyl. 4 S.C.S.A. (5$^{1}/_{2}$″ × 7$^{3}/_{4}$″) oil engines manufactured by L. Gardner & Sons Ltd., Manchester.
Wooden hulled, twin screw refrigerated fish carrier for operation between Abadan and Muscat.

8.1950: Completed by J. A. Silver Ltd., Roseneath, Dumbarton, for the British Tanker Company Ltd. 2.9.1950: Departed Clyde bound in tow to Abadan. 1952: Seized by the Persian Authorities. No further details located.

BT. 238. FARAHMAND (1) (1950–1955)

O.N. 184262. 450g. 20n. 127.7 × 32.6 × 13.4 feet.
T.3-cyl. (17$^{1}/_{8}$″, 28$^{1}/_{2}$″ & 48$^{1}/_{4}$″ × 30″) engine manufactured by the shipbuilder.
Tug.

17.5.1950: Launched by Ferguson Bros. (Port Glasgow) Ltd. (Yard No. 394), for the Petroleum Steam Ship Company Ltd. 8.1950: Completed for the British Tanker Company Ltd. 1955: Renamed BP GUARD. 1972: Transferred to the BP Clyde Tanker Company Ltd. 1975: Sold to Gulf Shipping Company S.A., Iran, and renamed FARROKH. 1998: Lloyd' Register entry removed – 'Continued existence in doubt'.

BT. 239. BRITISH PEER (2) (1950–1963)

O.N. 183308. 8,661g. 4,977n. 12,120d. 471.1 × 61.8 × 33.8 feet.
6-cyl. 4 S.C.S.A. (29$^{1}/_{8}$″ × 59$^{1}/_{16}$″) B&W type oil engine manufactured by J. G. Kincaid & Company Ltd., Greenock. 3,520 bhp.
Ocean-going tanker.

6.4.1950: Launched by Lithgows Ltd., Port Glasgow (Yard No. 1043), for the British Tanker Company Ltd. 8.1950: Completed. 1.6.1956: Owners restyled as BP Tanker Company Ltd. 1963: Sold to Aniceto Fernandez Ordas, Madrid, for demolition at Valencia. 5.8.1963: Work commenced.

BT. 240. BRITISH PROSPECTOR (1) (1950–1958)

O.N. 184267. 8,655g. 4,977n. 12,243d. 470.6 × 61.8 × 33.8 feet.
6-cyl. 4 S.C.S.A. (29$^{1}/_{8}$″ × 59$^{1}/_{16}$″) B&W type oil engine manufactured by the shipbuilder. 3,500 bhp.
Ocean-going tanker.

1.6.1950: Launched by Harland & Wolff Ltd., Belfast (Yard No. 1401), for the British Tanker Company Ltd. 28.9.1950: Completed. 1.6.1956: Owners restyled as BP Tanker Company Ltd. 1958: Transferred to BP Clyde Tanker Company Ltd., and renamed CLYDE PROSPECTOR. 3.1964: Sold for demolition by Scrappingco S. A., at Willebroek. 2.4.1964: Work commenced.

BT. 241. KARAJ (1950–1955)

O.N. 183309. 328g. 160.0 × 25.1 × 8.0 feet.
Dumb tank barge.

9.1950: Completed by Clelands (Successors) Ltd., Willington Quay on Tyne (Yard No.164), for the British Tanker Company Ltd. 1955: Sold to the National Iranian Oil Company Ltd., Iran. *Due to the small size and type of this vessel the Authors. have not recorded any further details*

BT. 242. BRITISH DIPLOMAT (2) (1950–1961)

O.N. 184275. 6,155g. 3,346n. 8,420d. 406.0 × 56.2 × 30.0 feet.
3-cyl. 2 S.C.S.A. (23$^{5}/_{8}$″ × 91$^{5}/_{16}$″) oil engine manufactured by the shipbuilder. 2,250 bhp.
Ocean-going tanker.

British Prospector. (World Ship Society Photograph Library)

British Diplomat. (World Ship Society Photograph Library)

British Splendour laying to anchor. (World Ship Society Photograph Library)

18.4.1950: Launched by Wm. Doxford & Sons Ltd., Sunderland (Yard No.781), for the British Tanker Company Ltd. 10.1950: Completed. 1.6.1956: Owners restyled as BP Tanker Company Ltd. 22.12.1961: Arrived at Grays, Essex for demolition by T. W. Ward Ltd., Sheffield.

BT. 243. KALMAS (1950–1955)

O.N. 184298. 328g. 160.0 × 25.1 × 8.0 feet.
Dumb tank barge.

11.1950: Completed by Clelands (Successors) Ltd., Willington Quay on Tyne (Yard No.165), for the British Tanker Company Ltd. 1955: Sold to the National Iranian Oil Company Ltd. *Due to the small size and type of this vessel the Authors. have not recorded any further details*

BT. 244. BRITISH SURVEYOR (1) (1950–1961)

O.N. 184318. 8,655g. 4,977n. 12,250d.
470.6 × 61.8 × 33.8 feet.
6-cyl. 4 S.C.S.A. (29$^{1}/_{8}$″ × 59$^{1}/_{16}$″) B&W type oil engine manufactured by the shipbuilder. 3,500 bhp.
Ocean-going tanker.

15.8.1950: Launched by Harland & Wolff Ltd., Belfast (Yard No. 1402), for the British Tanker Company Ltd. 8.12.1950: Completed. 1.6.1956: Owners restyled as BP Tanker Company Ltd. 1961: Transferred to BP Clyde Tanker Company Ltd., and renamed CLYDE SURVEYOR. 15.4.1964: Arrived at Ystad for demolition by Carl Persohn & Soner AB. 5.6.1964: Work commenced.

BT. 245. BRITISH SPLENDOUR (2) (1950–1972)

O.N. 184335. 11,233g. 6,500n. 16,823d.
525.5 × 69.8 × 37.5 feet.
6-cyl. 2 S.C.S.A. (26$^{3}/_{8}$″ × 91$^{5}/_{16}$″) Doxford type oil engine manufactured by the Wallsend Slipway Company Ltd., Wallsend. 6,400 bhp.
Ocean-going tanker.

16.8.1950: Launched by Swan, Hunter & Wigham, Richardson Ltd., Wallsend (Yard No. 1789), for the British Tanker Company Ltd. 12.1950: Completed. 1.6.1956: Owners restyled as BP Tanker Company Ltd. At 15:30hrs. 3.3.1972: Sold, at Swansea, to Recuperaciones Submarinos S. A., Santander, for demolition. 26.3.1972: Arrived in tow at Santander. 9.6.1972: Work commenced.

BT. 246. BRITISH NAVIGATOR (1) (1951 – 1964)

O.N. 184357. 6,135g. 3,340n. 8,520d.
406.0 × 56.3 × 30.0 feet.
3-cyl. 2 S.C.S.A. (23$^{5}/_{8}$″ × 91$^{5}/_{16}$″) oil engine manufactured by Wm. Doxford & Sons Ltd., Sunderland. 2,250 bhp.
Ocean-going tanker.

26.9.1950: Launched by J. L. Thompson & Sons Ltd., Sunderland (Yard No. 664), for the British Tanker Company Ltd. 2.1951: Completed. 1.6.1956: Owners restyled as BP Tanker Company Ltd. 29.4.1964: Arrived at the Isle of Grain. 22. 6.1964: Departed, in tow, from the Thames and arrived at Bruges later in the day for demolition by Brugse Scheepsslopperij. 10.7.1964: Work commenced.

BT. 247. BRITISH SPORTSMAN (1951–1972)

O.N. 184364. 11,231g. 6,506n. 16,798d.
525.5 × 69.8 × 37.5 feet.
6-cyl. 2 S.C.S.A. (26$^{3}/_{8}$″ × 91$^{5}/_{16}$″) Doxford type oil engine manufactured by the Wallsend Slipway Company Ltd., Wallsend. 7,040 bhp.
Ocean-going tanker.

12.10.1950: Launched by Swan, Hunter & Wigham, Richardson Ltd., Wallsend (Yard No. 1791), for the British Tanker Company Ltd. 2.1951: Completed. 1.6.1956: Owners restyled as BP Tanker Company Ltd. 24.1.1972: Arrived at Inverkeithing for demolition by T. W. Ward Ltd., Sheffield.

BT. 248. FIRUZMAND (1951–1955)

O.N. 184362. 462g. 14n. 127.7 × 32.6 × 13.4 feet.
T.3-cyl. (17″ 28″ & 46″ × 33″) engine manufactured by Plenty & Sons Ltd., Newbury. 1,250 ihp.
Tug.

9.11.1950: Launched by Scott & Sons, Bowling (Yard No. 392), for the Petroleum Steam Ship Company Ltd. 2.1951: Completed for the British Tanker Company Ltd. 1955: Renamed BP WARDEN. 1972: Transferred to the BP Clyde Tanker Company Ltd. 1976: Sold to Gulf Shipping Company S.A., Iran, and renamed FIROUZMAND.1998: Lloyd's Register entry removed – 'Continued existence in doubt'.

BT. 249. BRITISH PREMIER (2) (1951–1964)

O.N. 184387. 8,661g. 4,977n. 12,250d.
471.1 × 61.8 × 33.8 feet.
6-cyl. 4 S.C.S.A. (29$^{1}/_{8}$″ × 59$^{1}/_{16}$″) B&W type oil engine manufactured by J. G. Kincaid & Company Ltd., Greenock. 3,200 bhp.
Ocean-going tanker.

29.11.1950: Launched by Lithgows Ltd., Port Glasgow (Yard No. 1052), for the British Tanker Company Ltd. 13.3.1951: Completed. 1.6.1956: Owners restyled as BP Tanker Company Ltd. 22.5.1964: Arrived at Antwerp for demolition by Scrappingco S. A. 11.6.1964: Work commenced.

British Navigator. (World Ship Society Photograph Library)

British Sportsman. (World Ship Society Photograph Library)

British Premier. (World Ship Society Photograph Library)

BT. 250. BRITISH BUILDER (1951–1963)

O.N. 184397. 8,699g. 5,008n. 12,270d.
469.6 × 62.0 × 33.9 feet.
4-cyl. 2 S.C.S.A. (23⅝″ × 91$^{5}/_{16}$″) oil engine manufactured by the shipbuilder. 3,100 bhp.
Ocean-going tanker.

22.3.1951: Launched by Wm. Doxford & Sons Ltd., Sunderland (Yard No. 782), for the British Tanker Company Ltd. 3.1951: Completed. 1.6.1956: Owners restyled as BP Tanker Company Ltd. 1.9.1963: Arrived at Bruges for demolition by Bruges Scheepsslopperij. 14.10.1963: Work commenced.

BT. 251. BRITISH ROVER (1951–1961)

O.N. 184404. 6,137g. 3,334n. 8,420d.
406.0 × 56.3 × 30.0 feet.
3-cyl. 2 S.C.S.A. (23⅝″ × 91$^{5}/_{16}$″) oil engine manufactured by Wm. Doxford & Sons Ltd., Sunderland. 2,250 bhp.
Ocean-going tanker.

24.11.1950: Launched by J. L. Thompson & Sons Ltd., Sunderland (Yard No. 665), for the British Tanker Company Ltd. 4.1951: Completed. 1.6.1956: Owners restyled as BP Tanker Company Ltd. 1961: Sold to the Palm Line Ltd., London, and renamed MAKENI PALM. 1967: Sold to Sulina Cia. Nav., Italy, and renamed KERKENNAH. 1971: Renamed PALAU. 1976: Sold to Sarda Armatoriale Punta Scorno, Italy. 11.6.1978: Arrived at Brindisi for demolition.

BT. 252. BRITISH SEAFARER (1951–1973)

O.N. 184410. 11,220g. 6,509n. 16,800d.
525.5 × 69.8 × 37.5 feet.
6-cyl. 2 S.C.S.A. (26⅜″ × 91$^{5}/_{16}$″) Doxford type oil engine manufactured by the shipbuilder. 6,400 bhp.
Ocean-going tanker.

8.1.1951: Launched by R. & W. Hawthorn, Leslie & Company Ltd., Hebburn (Yard No. 703), for the British Tanker Company Ltd. 4.1951: Completed. 1.6.1956: Owners restyled as BP Tanker Company Ltd. 26.3.1973: Arrived at Villaneuve y Geltrue for demolition by Hierros Ardes.

BT. 253. BRITISH CRAFTSMAN (1951–1964)

O.N. 184438. 8,697g. 5,008n. 12,270d.
469.6 × 62.0 × 33.9 feet.
4-cyl. 2 S.C.S.A. (23⅝″ × 91$^{5}/_{16}$″) oil engine manufactured by the shipbuilder. 3,100 bhp.
Ocean-going tanker.

29.8.1950: Launched by Wm. Doxford & Sons Ltd., Sunderland (Yard No. 783), for the British Tanker Company Ltd. 6.1951: Completed. 1.6.1956: Owners restyled as BP Tanker Company Ltd. 24.8.1964: Arrived at Hamburg for demolition. 2.9.1964: Handed over to Eisen Und Metall A. G. 3.10.1964: Work commenced.

BT. 254. BRITISH BIRCH (2) (1951–1964)

O.N. 184429. 8,688g. 4,992n. 12,270d.
469.6 × 61.9 × 33.9 feet.
4-cyl. 2 S.C.S.A. (23⅝″ × 91$^{5}/_{16}$″) Doxford type oil engine manufactured by Richardsons, Westgarth & Company Ltd., Hartlepool. 3,100 bhp.
Ocean-going tanker.

11.12.1950: Launched by Sir James Laing & Sons Ltd., Sunderland (Yard No. 791), for the British Tanker Company Ltd. 6.1951: Completed. 1.6.1956: Owners restyled as BP Tanker Company Ltd. 12.6.1964: Departed R. Tyne en route for demolition by Christiania Spigerwerk, Oslo, Norway. 14.6.1964: Arrived at Grimstad for demolition by Norsk Skipsopphugnings Company, having been resold.

BT. 255. BRITISH VISCOUNT (3) (1951–1965)

O.N. 184451. 8,664g. 4,986n. 12,167d.
469.6 × 62.0 × 33.9 feet.
4-cyl. 2 S.C.S.A. (23⅝″ × 91$^{5}/_{16}$″) Doxford type oil engine manufactured by the shipbuilder. 3,100 bhp.
Ocean-going tanker.

8.1.1951: Launched by Swan, Hunter & Wigham, Richardson Ltd., Wallsend (Yard No. 1873), for the British Tanker Company Ltd. 6.1951: Completed. 1.6.1956: Owners restyled as BP Tanker Company Ltd. 27.1.1965: Arrived at Santander for demolition by Recuperaciones Submarinos S. A. 28.1.1965: Work commenced.

BT. 256. BRITISH LADY (2) (1951–1963)

O.N. 184466. 6,140g. 3,320n. 8,463d.
406.7 × 56.2 × 30.0 feet.

British Builder. (World Ship Society Photograph Library)

British Seafarer. (World Ship Society Photograph Library)

British Craftsman. (World Ship Society Photograph Library)

3-cyl. 2 S.C.S.A. (23$^{5}/_{8}$" × 91$^{5}/_{16}$") Doxford type oil engine manufactured by R. & W. Hawthorn, Leslie & Company Ltd., Newcastle. 2,250 bhp.
Ocean-going tanker.
24.1.1951: Launched by Smiths Dock Company Ltd., Middlesbrough (Yard No. 1211), for the British Tanker Company Ltd. 6.1951: Completed. 1.6.1956: Owners restyled as BP Tanker Company Ltd. 8.8.1963: Arrived at Bo'ness for demolition by P. &W. MacLellan Ltd.

BT. 257. BRITISH PLUCK (2) (1951–1954)

O.N. 169461. 930g. 341n. 193.5 × 34.2 × 14.7 feet.
T.3-cyl. (13$^{1}/_{2}$", 22$^{3}/_{4}$" and 38" × 27") engine manufactured by the shipbuilder's Belfast works. 725 bhp.
Coastal tanker.
31.10.1945: Launched as EMPIRE TESELLA by Harland & Wolff Ltd., Glasgow (Yard No. 1318 G), for the Ministry of War Transport (the British Tanker Company Ltd., managers). 7.2.1946: Completed. 1951: Purchased by the British Tanker Company Ltd., and renamed BRITISH PLUCK. 4.1954: Demolished by Akbaruli Noorbhai & Company, Bombay.

BT. 258. BRITISH GUIDE (1951–1963)

O.N. 184472. 8,778g. 5,036n. 12,125d. 472.6 × 62.0 × 33.6 feet.
4-cyl. 2 S.C.S.A. (23$^{5}/_{8}$" × 91$^{5}/_{16}$") Doxford type oil engine manufactured by R. & W. Hawthorn, Leslie & Company Ltd., Newcastle. 3,300 bhp.
Ocean-going tanker.
22.12.1949: Keel laid by the Furness Shipbuilding Company, Haverton Hill on Tees (Yard No. 435), for the British Tanker Company Ltd. 7.2.1951: Launched. 7.1951: Completed. 1.6.1956: Owners restyled as BP Tanker Company Ltd. 6.11.1963: Collided with OCEAN ENTERPRISE (5,809g./49), off Spurn Head and returned to Saltend Terminal to discharge. 10.11.1963: Departed from Saltend bound to Sunderland for dry-docking and inspection. 23.11.1963: Declared as beyond economical repair. 10.12.1963: Arrived at Antwerp for demolition by Scrappingco S. A. 23.12.1963: Work commenced.

British Birch. (World Ship Society Photograph Library)

BT. 259. BRITISH WARRIOR (1951–1961)

O.N. 184470. 6,143g. 3,337n. 8,490d. 406.0 × 56.3 × 30.0 feet.
3-cyl. 2 S.C.S.A. (23$^{5}/_{8}$" × 91$^{5}/_{16}$") oil engine manufactured by Wm. Doxford & Sons Ltd., Sunderland. 3,200 bhp.
Ocean-going tanker.
22.2.1951: Launched by J. L. Thompson & Sons Ltd., Sunderland (Yard No. 669), for the British Tanker Company Ltd. 7.1951: Completed. 1.6.1956: Owners restyled as BP Tanker Company Ltd. 1961: Sold to A. Blystaad, Norway, and renamed ANNE. 1964: Sold to Luzon Stevedoring Corporation, Philippines, and renamed LSCO PANDACAN. 4.1977: Arrived at Kaohsiung for demolition.

British Viscount. (World Ship Society Photograph Library)

BT. 260. BRITISH ADVENTURE (1) (1951–1973)

O.N. 184497. 18,573g. 11,281n. 30,218d. 619.5 × 81.3 × 44.7 feet.
Two, steam turbines manufactured by the shipbuilder, double reduction geared to a single screw shaft. 13,750 shp.
Ocean-going tanker.
12.12.1950: Launched by Vickers-Armstrongs Ltd., Barrow in Furness (Yard No. 994), for the British Tanker Company Ltd. 9.1951: Completed. 1.6.1956: Owners restyled as BP Tanker Company Ltd. 1973: Sold to Philoship Company S. A., Greece, and renamed VRAHOS. 5.3.1975: Departed from Singapore Roads. 12.3.1975: Arrived at Kaohsiung for demolition by Tai Kien Industry Company Ltd. 29.4.1975: Work commenced.

British Guide. (World Ship Society Photograph Library)

British Warrior. (World Ship Society Photograph Library)

British Adventurer. (World Ship Society Photograph Library)

BT. 261. BRITISH PIONEER (1) (1951–1958)

O.N. 184455. 8,651g. 4,960n. 12,390d.
470.5 × 61.8 × 33.8 feet.
6-cyl. 4 S.C.S.A. ($29\frac{1}{8}'' \times 59\frac{1}{16}''$) B&W type oil engine manufactured by J. G. Kincaid & Company Ltd., Greenock. 3,520 bhp.
Ocean-going tanker.

24.4.1951: Launched by the Blythswood Shipbuilding Company, Glasgow (Yard No. 97), for the British Tanker Company Ltd. 9.1951: Completed. 1.6.1956: Owners restyled as BP Tanker Company Ltd. 1958: Transferred to the BP Clyde Tanker Company Ltd., and renamed CLYDE PIONEER. 17.4.1965: Arrived at Antwerp for demolition by Scrappingco S. A. 3.5.1965: Work commenced.

BT. 262. BRITISH BULLDOG (1951–1972)

O.N. 184521. 18,593g. 11,289n. 30,099d.
619.5 × 81.2 × 44.7 feet.
Two, steam turbines manufactured by the Wallsend Slipway Company Ltd., Wallsend, double reduction geared to a single screw shaft. 13,750 shp.
Ocean-going tanker.

22.5.1951: Launched by Swan, Hunter & Wigham, Richardson Ltd., Wallsend (Yard No. 1803), for the British Tanker Company Ltd. 11.1951: Completed. 1.6.1956: Owners restyled as BP Tanker Company Ltd. 12.7.1972: Arrived at Castellon for demolition by Desguaces Maritimos S. A.

BT. 263. BRITISH MAPLE (2) (1951–1965)

O.N. 184546. 8,686g. 4,995n. 12,160d.
469.6 × 61.8 × 33.9 feet.
4-cyl. 2 S.C.S.A. ($23\frac{5}{8}'' \times 91\frac{5}{16}''$) oil engine manufactured by Wm. Doxford & Sons Ltd., Sunderland. 3,440 bhp.
Ocean-going tanker.

19.6.1951: Launched by Sir James Laing & Sons Ltd., Sunderland (Yard No. 792), for the British Tanker Company Ltd. 12.1951: Completed. 1.6.1956: Owners restyled as BP Tanker Company Ltd. 13.4.1965: Arrived in tow at Hamburg for demolition by Eisen Und Metall A. G. 1.6.1965: Work commenced.

BT. 264. BRITISH TALENT (1952–1972)

O.N. 184569. 18,593g. 11,278n. 30,132d.
619.5 × 81.3 × 44.7 feet.
Two, steam turbines manufactured by the shipbuilder, double reduction geared to a single screw shaft. 13,750 shp.
Ocean-going tanker.

17.8.1951: Launched by R. & W. Hawthorn, Leslie & Company Ltd., Hebburn (Yard No. 709), for the British Tanker Company Ltd. 3.1952: Completed. 1.6.1956: Owners restyled as BP Tanker Company Ltd. 23.3.1972: Arrived at Bilbao for demolition by Hierros Ardes.

BT. 265. BRITISH REALM (1952–1970)

O.N. 184601. 18,571g. 11,268n. 30,108d.
619.5 × 81.3 × 44.7 feet.
Two, steam turbines manufactured by the shipbuilder, double reduction geared to a single screw shaft. 13,750 shp.
Ocean-going tanker.

7.6.1951: Launched by Fairfield Company Ltd., Glasgow (Yard No. 749), for the British Tanker Company Ltd. 4.1952: Completed. 1.6.1956: Owners restyled as BP Tanker Company Ltd. 9.6.1970: Arrived at Kaohsiung for demolition by Li Chong Steel & Iron Works. 20.6.1970: Work commenced.

BT. 266. BRITISH SKILL (1) (1952–1972)

O.N. 184651. 18,550g. 11,240n. 29,891d.
619.5 × 81.3 × 44.7 feet.
Two, steam turbines manufactured by the shipbuilder, double reduction geared to a single screw shaft. 13,750 shp.
Ocean-going tanker.

16.1.1952: Launched by Harland & Wolff Ltd., Belfast (Yard No. 1425), for the British Tanker Company Ltd. 12.6.1952: Completed.

British Bulldog. (World Ship Society Photograph Library)

British Maple. (World Ship Society Photograph Library)

British Realm. (World Ship Society Photograph Library)

British Skill. (World Ship Society Photograph Library)

1.6.1956: Owners restyled as BP Tanker Company Ltd. 1.12.1972: Sold to Willtops (Asia) Ltd., Singapore. 27.12.1972: Arrived in tow at Kaohsiung for demolition by Yung Tai Steel & Iron Works Company Ltd. 23.1.1973: Work commenced.

BT. 267. BRITISH CROWN (1952–1966)

O.N. 184648. 18,570g. 11,252n. 28,598d.
619.5 × 81.3 × 44.7 feet.
Two, steam turbines manufactured by the shipbuilder, double reduction geared to a single screw shaft. 13,750 shp.
Ocean-going tanker.

14.6.1952: Launched by Cammell, Laird & Company Ltd., Birkenhead (Yard No. 1208), for the British Tanker Company Ltd. 7.1952: Completed. 1.6.1956: Owners restyled as BP Tanker Company Ltd. 20.8.1966: Sustained explosion and fire damage at Umm Said and was on 3.11.1966: Declared a CTL., the forepart having sunk.

BT. 268. BURGAN (1952–1956)

O.N. 166966. 134g. 41n. 112.1 × 18.5 × ? feet.
Two, 6-cyl. 4 S.C.S.A. ($5^{3}/_{4}'' \times 7''$) petrol engines manufactured in 1942 by Hall, Scott Ltd.
Wooden hulled yacht converted into a survey vessel.

1945: Completed as ABINGDON by Johnson & Jago, Southend, for Major Douglas F. Bostock, Ipswich. 1948: Reconstructed at Chertsey. 1952: Purchased by the British Tanker Company Ltd., converted into a survey vessel, and renamed BURGAN. 1956: Transferred to Abu Dhabi Marine Areas Ltd. 1957: Owners restyled as BP Exploration Company Ltd., and vessel sold to Iranian buyers. *Due to the small size and type of this vessel the Authors. have not recorded any further details.*

BT. 269. BRITISH SAILOR (2) (1953–1972)

O.N. 185865. 20,961g. 12,592n. 33,682d.
640.6 × 85.7 × 47.0 feet.
Two, steam turbines manufactured by the shipbuilder, double reduction geared to a single screw shaft. 13,750 shp.
Ocean-going tanker.

18.12.1952: Launched by J. Brown & Company (Clydebank) Ltd., Clydebank (Yard No. 677), for the British Tanker Company Ltd. 4.1953: Completed. 1.6.1956: Owners restyled as BP Tanker Company Ltd. 1972: Sold to Marisira Nav. Company Ltd., Cyprus, and renamed MARISIRA. 1974: Sold to the Egyptian General Petroleum Organization, Egypt, and renamed FAGR. 1980: Arrived at Kaohsiung for demolition.

BT. 270. BRITISH FLAG (1953–1971)

O.N. 185934. 11,327g. 6,545n. 16,750d.
525.5 × 69.8 × 37.5 feet.
6-cyl. 2 S.C.S.A. ($26^{3}/_{8}'' \times 91^{5}/_{16}''$) Doxford type oil engine manufactured by the shipbuilder. 6,400 bhp.
Ocean-going tanker.

12.12.1952: Launched by R. & W. Hawthorn, Leslie & Company Ltd., Hebburn (Yard No. 716), for the British Tanker Company Ltd. 7.1953: Completed. 1.6.1956: Owners restyled as BP Tanker Company Ltd. 19.7.1971: Arrived at Burriani for demolition by Ciqualar y Peris. 22.7.1971: Handed over. 2.8.1971: Work commenced.

BT. 271. BRITISH OAK (1) (1953–1972)

O.N. 185963. 11,307g. 6,525n. 16,562d.
525.5 × 69.8 × 37.5 feet.
6-cyl. 2 S.C.S.A. ($29^{1}/_{2}'' \times 59^{1}/_{16}''$) B&W type oil engine manufactured by Harland & Wolff Ltd., Glasgow. 7,050 bhp.
Ocean-going tanker.

28.5.1953: Launched by Smiths Dock Company Ltd., Middlesbrough (Yard No. 1227), for British Tanker Company Ltd.

British Crown. (World Ship Society Photograph Library)

British Sailor. (World Ship Society Photograph Library)

British Flag. (World Ship Society Photograph Library)

British Oak. (World Ship Society Photograph Library)

10.1953: Completed. 1.6.1956: Owners restyled as BP Tanker Company Ltd. 12.1.1972: Arrived at Vinaroz for demolition. 14.1.1972: Handed over to Desguaces Maritimos S. A.

BT. 272. BRITISH GUARDIAN (1953–1958)

O.N. 185976. 11,359g. 6,537n. 16,481d.
525.5 × 69.8 × 37.5 feet.
6-cyl. 2 S.C.S.A. (29½″ × 59¹/₁₆″) B&W type oil engine manufactured by J. G. Kincaid and Company Ltd., Greenock. 6,400 bhp.
Ocean-going tanker.

29.4.1953: Launched by Lithgows Ltd., Port Glasgow (Yard No. 1078), for the British Tanker Company Ltd. 11.1953: Completed. 1.6.1956: Owners restyled as BP Tanker Company Ltd. 1958: Transferred to the BP Clyde Tanker Company Ltd., and renamed CLYDE GUARDIAN. 1963: Reverted to the BP Tanker Company Ltd., and BRITISH GUARDIAN. 26.1.1972: Arrived at Gandia, Spain for demolition. 28.1.1972: Handed over to Aureliano Perez Ibarra.

BT. 273. BRITISH ENVOY (1953–1958)

O.N. 185985. 11,349g. 6,561n. 16,768d.
525.5 × 69.8 × 37.5 feet.
6-cyl. 2 S.C.S.A. (26⅜″ × 91⁵/₁₆″) Doxford type oil engine manufactured by the shipbuilder. 6,400 bhp.
Ocean-going tanker.

29.6.1953: Launched by Wm. Doxford & Sons Ltd., Sunderland (Yard No. 798), for British Tanker Company Ltd. 12.1953: Completed. 1.6.1956: Owners restyled as BP Tanker Company Ltd. 1958: Transferred to the BP Clyde Tanker Company Ltd., and renamed CLYDE ENVOY. 1963: Reverted to the BP Tanker Company Ltd., and BRITISH ENVOY. 4.4.1970: Arrived at Inverkeithing for demolition by T. W. Ward Ltd., Sheffield.

BT. 274. BRITISH MERCHANT (2) (1954–1973)

O.N. 186002. 21,064g. 12,701n. 31,750d.
640.6 × 85.7 × 47.0 feet.
Two, steam turbines manufactured by the Wallsend Slipway Company Ltd., Wallsend, double reduction geared to a single screw shaft. 13,750 shp.
Ocean-going tanker.

24.7.1953: Launched by Swan, Hunter & Wigham, Richardson Ltd., Wallsend (Yard No. 1825), for the British Tanker Company Ltd. 1.1954: Completed. 1.6.1956: Owners restyled as BP Tanker Company Ltd. 1973: Sold to Possidon Shipping & Trading Corp. (John S. Latsis, manager), Greece, and renamed PETROLA VII. 1976: Sold to Aroania Shipping & Trading Corp. (same managers), Greece, and renamed PETROLA 7. 6.10.1978: Arrived at Castellon for demolition by M. Varela Davillo.

BT. 275. BRITISH CRUSADER (1954–1957)

O.N. 186000. 11,346g. 6,538n. 16,529d.
547′ 0″ × 69′ 10″ × 30′ 0¼″ .
6-cyl. 2 S.C.S.A. (29½″ × 59¹/₁₆″) B&W type oil engine manufactured by Harland & Wolff Ltd., Glasgow. 7,050 bhp.
Ocean-going tanker.

23.9.1953: Launched by Cammell, Laird & Company (Shipbuilders & Engineers) Ltd., Birkenhead (Yard No. 1228), for British Tanker Company Ltd. 2.1954: Completed. 1.6.1956: Owners restyled as BP Tanker Company Ltd. 1957: Transferred to the BP Clyde Tanker Company Ltd., and renamed CLYDE CRUSADER. 1964: Reverted to the BP Tanker Company Ltd., and BRITISH CRUSADER. 27.6.1972: Sold to Nissho-Iwai Company Ltd., Japan, for demolition. Resold and 11.7.1972: Departed from Singapore Roads. 26.7.1972: Arrived at Kaohsiung for

British Guardian at Cape Town. (World Ship Society Photograph Library)

British Envoy. (World Ship Society Photograph Library)

British Merchant. (World Ship Society Photograph Library)

British Crusader. (World Ship Society Photograph Library)

demolition by Tung Ho Steel Corp. 15.8.1972: Work commenced.

BT. 276. BRITISH ENGINEER (2) (1954–1972)

O.N. 186053. 21,077g. 12,716n. 31,785d.
664′ 10″ × 86′ 8″ × 34′ $11^{3}/_{4}$″ .
Two, steam turbines manufactured by the shipbuilder, double reduction geared to a single screw shaft. 13,750 shp.
Ocean-going tanker.

24.11.1953: Launched by Harland & Wolff Ltd., Belfast (Yard No. 1464), for the British Tanker Company Ltd. 30.5.1954: Completed. 1.6.1956: Owners restyled as BP Tanker Company Ltd. 1972: Sold to Lykavittos Shipping & Trading Corp. (John S. Latsis, manager), Greece, and renamed PETROLA V. 21.6.1976: Arrived at Castellon, for demolition by M. Varela Davillo.

British Engineer. (World Ship Society Photograph Library)

BT. 277. BRITISH GUNNER (2) (1954–1961)

O.N. 186055. 10,076g. 5,792n. 14,571d.
516' 6" x 65' 4" x 28' 3".
6-cyl. 2 S.C.S.A. (620 x 1400mm) B&W type oil engine manufactured by the shipbuilder. 4,950 bhp.
Ocean-going tanker.

22.12.1953: Launched by Harland & Wolff Ltd., Glasgow (Yard No. 1466 G), for the British Tanker Company Ltd. 6.5.1954: Completed. 1.6.1956: Owners restyled as BP Tanker Company Ltd. 1961: Transferred to the BP Clyde Tanker Company Ltd., and renamed CLYDE GUNNER. 1964: Reverted to the BP Tanker Company Ltd., and BRITISH GUNNER. 17.5.1972: Arrived at Vinaroz, Spain for demolition by Desguaces Maritimos S. A.

BT. 278. BRITISH HERO (1954–1972)

O.N. 186086. 11,358g. 6,545n. 15,800d.
547′ 0″ × 69′ 10″ × 30′ $0^{1}/_{2}$″ .
6-cyl. 2 S.C.S.A. (750 × 1500mm) B&W type oil engine manufactured by J. G. Kincaid & Company Ltd., Greenock. 6,400 bhp
Ocean-going tanker.

9.3.1954: Launched by Lithgows Ltd., Port Glasgow (Yard No. 1080), for the British Tanker Company Ltd. 6.1954: Completed. 1.6.1956: Owners restyled as BP Tanker Company Ltd. 5.6.1972: Arrived at Santander for demolition by Recuperaciones Submarinas S. A.

BT. 279. BRITISH CORPORAL (2) (1954–1960)

O.N. 186092. 10,071g. 5,767n. 14,577d.
516′ 6″ × 65′ 4″ × 28′ $3^{1}/_{4}$″ .
6-cyl. 2 S.C.S.A. (620 × 1400mm) B&W type oil engine manufactured by the shipbuilder. 4,950 bhp.
Ocean-going tanker.

9.12.1953: Launched by Harland & Wolff Ltd., Belfast (Yard No. 1465), for the British Tanker Company Ltd. 1.7.1954: Completed. 1.6.1956: Owners restyled as BP Tanker Company Ltd. 1960: Transferred to the BP Clyde Tanker Company Ltd., and renamed CLYDE CORPORAL. 1964: Reverted to the BP Tanker Company Ltd., and BRITISH CORPORAL. 1.5.1972: Sold to Nissho-Iwai Company Ltd., for demolition. 2.5.1972: Resold to Lung Yung Steel Company Ltd., Taiwan. 10.5.1972: Departed, in tow of the Japanese tug TOKO MARU (482g./67), from Singapore Roads. 20.5.1972: Arrived at Kaohsiung. 20.6.1972: Work commenced. 30.7.1972: Work completed.

British Gunner. (World Ship Society Photograph Library)

British Hero. (World Ship Society Photograph Library)

British Corporal. (World Ship Society Photograph Library)

BT. 281. BRITISH CHANCELLOR (2) (1954–1961)

O.N. 186111. 11,356g. 6,511n. 16,808d.
547′ 0″ × 69′ 10″ × 30′ 0½″ .
6-cyl. 2 S.C.S.A. (670 × 2320mm) Doxford type oil engine manufactured by Barclay, Curle & Company Ltd., Glasgow. 6,400 bhp.
Ocean-going tanker.

21.4.1954: Launched by the Blythswood Shipbuilding Company, Glasgow (Yard No. 107), for the British Tanker Company Ltd. 8.1954: Completed. 1.6.1956: Owners restyled as BP Tanker Company Ltd. 1961: Transferred to the BP Clyde Tanker Company Ltd., and renamed CLYDE CHANCELLOR. 1964: Reverted to the BP Tanker Company Ltd., and BRITISH CHANCELLOR. 30.2.1972: Laid up at Hong Kong. 20.4.1972: Sold to Great Eastern Ltd., Hong Kong. 24.4.1972: Departed from Hong Kong, in tow of TAKUSEI MARU No. 25 (455g./71), for demolition. 14.5.1972: Arrived at Kaohsiung for demolition by Keun Hwa Steel Enterprise. 20.5.1972: Work commenced. 25.6.1972: Work completed.

BT. 282. BRITISH SERGEANT (2) (1954–1960)

O.N. 186113. 10,073g. 5,792n. 13,712d.
516′ 6″ × 65′ 4″ × 28′ 3″ .
6-cyl. 2 S.C.S.A. (620 × 1400mm) B&W type oil engine manufactured by the shipbuilder. 4,950 bhp.
Ocean-going tanker.

14.4.1954: Launched by Harland & Wolff Ltd., Glasgow (Yard No. 1467 G), for the British Tanker Company Ltd. 20.8.1954: Completed. 1.6.1956: Owners restyled as BP Tanker Company Ltd. 1960: Transferred to the BP Clyde Tanker Company Ltd., and renamed CLYDE SERGEANT. 1963: Reverted to the BP Tanker Company Ltd., and BRITISH SERGEANT. 22.10.1972: Sold at Singapore to Nissho-Iwai Company Ltd., Japan, for demolition. Resold and 27.10.1972: Departed in tow from Shimonoseki. 2.11.1972: Arrived at Hua Lien for demolition by Kuang Yih Steel & Iron Works Company Ltd.

BT. 283. BRITISH SOLDIER (2) (1954–1972)

O.N. 186142. 21,082g. 12,709n. 33,601d.
664′ 10″ × 85′ 8″ × 35′ 0″ .
Two, steam turbines manufactured by the shipbuilder, double reduction geared to screw shaft. 13,750 shp.
Ocean-going tanker.

30.6.1954: Launched by J. Brown & Company (Clydebank) Ltd., Clydebank (Yard No. 678), for the British Tanker Company Ltd. 10.1954: Completed. 1.6.1956: Owners restyled as BP Tanker Company Ltd. 1972: Sold to Armadoras Marisurf S. A. (D. J. Chandris,

BT. 280. BRITISH VISION (1954–1972)

O.N. 186096. 11,349g. 6,532n. 16,870d.
547′ 0″ × 69′ 10″ × 30′ 0¼″ .
6-cyl. 2 S.C.S.A. (670 × 2320mm) Doxford type oil engine manufactured by North Eastern Marine Engineering Company (1938) Ltd., Wallsend. 6,800 bhp.
Ocean-going tanker.

5.3.1954: Launched by J. L. Thompson & Sons Ltd., Sunderland (Yard No. 679), for the British Tanker Company Ltd. 7.1954: Completed. 1.6.1956: Owners restyled as BP Tanker Company Ltd. 4.10.1972: Arrived at Castellon for demolition by M. Varela Davillo.

British Vision. (World Ship Society Photograph Library)

British Chancellor. (World Ship Society Photograph Library)

British Sergeant. (World Ship Society Photograph Library)

manager), Cyprus, and renamed MARIBRUNA. 20.5.1976: Arrived at Kaohsiung for demolition.

BT. 284. BRITISH PATROL (1954–1973)

O.N. 186162. 11,380g. 6,580n. 16,518d. 547′ 0″ × 69′ 10″ × 30′ $0^{1}/_{4}$″.
6-cyl. 2 S.C.S.A. (670 × 2320mm) Doxford type oil engine manufactured by the shipbuilder. 6,900 bhp.
Ocean-going tanker.

30.8.1954: Launched by Swan, Hunter & Wigham, Richardson Ltd., Newcastle (Yard No. 1900), for the British Tanker Company Ltd. 11.1954: Completed. 1.6.1956: Owners restyled as BP Tanker Company Ltd. 1973: Sold Marifoam Shipping Company Ltd. (D. J. Chandris, manager), Cyprus, and renamed MARIPATROL. 1980: Sold to Fiorita Maritime Company, Greece, and renamed NONA MARO. 14.6.1980: Damaged by explosion and fire at Flushing. 18.3.1981: Arrived at Cartagena for demolition.

BT. 285. BRITISH SOVEREIGN (2) (1954–1972)

O.N. 186164. 21,138g. 12,748n. 32,154d. 664′ 10″ × 85′ 8″ × 35′ 0″.
Two, steam turbines manufactured by the shipbuilder, double reduction geared to screw shaft. 13,750 shp.
Ocean-going tanker.

31.8.1954: Launched by Vickers-Armstrongs Ltd., Barrow in Furness (Yard No. 1019), for the British Tanker Company Ltd. 12.1954: Completed. 1.6.1956: Owners restyled as BP Tanker Company Ltd. 1972: Sold to Possidon Shipping & Trading Corp. (John S. Latsis, manager), Greece, and renamed PETROLA VI. 1976: Renamed PETROLA 6. 16.2.1977: Arrived at Barcelona for demolition.

BT. 286. BRITISH OFFICER (2) (1955–1973)

O.N. 186176. 11,362g. 6,546n. 15,839d. 547′ 0″ × 69′ 10″ × 30′ $0^{1}/_{4}$″.
6-cyl. 2 S.C.S.A. (750 × 1500mm) B&W type oil engine manufactured by J. G. Kincaid & Company Ltd., Greenock. 6,400 bhp.
Ocean-going tanker.

26.10.1954: Launched by W. Hamilton & Company Ltd., Port Glasgow (Yard No. 500), for the British Tanker Company Ltd. 1.1955: Completed. 1.6.1956: Owners restyled as BP Tanker Company Ltd. 29.3.1973: Arrived at Villanueva y Geltru, Spain, for demolition. Resold and 13.5.1973: Arrived at Castellon for demolition by Hierros Ardes.

BT. 287. BRITISH VICTORY (1955–1973)

O.N. 186229. 21,153g. 12,739n. 34,118d. 664′ 10″ × 85′ 8″ × 35′ 0″.
Two, steam turbines manufactured by the shipbuilder, double reduction geared to screw shaft. 13,750 shp.
Ocean-going tanker.

13.12.1954: Launched by Vickers-Armstrongs Ltd., Barrow in Furness (Yard No. 1020), for the British Tanker Company Ltd. 4.1955: Completed. 1.6.1956: Owners restyled as BP Tanker Company Ltd. 1973: Sold to Aquarella Navigation Company Ltd. (D. J. Chandris, manager), Cyprus, and renamed MARIVIC. 1.5.1977: Arrived at Kaohsiung for demolition.

BT. 288. BP PROTECTOR (1955–1961)

O.N. 166354. 361g. 3n. 120.5 × 31.1 × 13.0 feet.
T.3-cyl. ($16^{1}/_{2}$″, 27″ & 46″ × 30″) engine manufactured by Plenty & Son Ltd., Newbury. 870 hp.
Tug.

21.12.1937: Launched as ZURMAND by Scott & Sons, Bowling (Yard No. 344), for the Petroleum Steam Ship Company Ltd. 2.1938: Completed. 7.3.1938: Sailed from Glasgow. 22.4.1938: Arrived at Abadan, but was subsequently returned to U.K. for port operations. 1955: Transferred to the BP Tanker Company Ltd., and renamed BP PROTECTOR. 1961: Sold to the Alexandra

British Soldier. (World Ship Society Photograph Library)

British Patrol. (J K Byass)

British Sovereign. (World Ship Society Photograph Library)

British Officer. (World Ship Society Photograph Library)

British Victory. (World Ship Society Photograph Library)

BP Protector. (The late Des Harris (Fotoship), courtesy of Paul Andow)

Towing Company Ltd., Liverpool, and renamed FLYING BREEZE. 1968: Sold to Tsavliris (Shipping & Towage) Company Ltd., Greece, and renamed NISOS THIRA. 1974: Entry deleted from Lloyd's Register – believed demolished.

BT. 289. BP GUARD (1955–1972)

see ship No. BT. 238 above.

BT. 290. BP WARDEN (1955–1972)

see ship No. BT. 248 above.

BT. 291. BP DEFENDER (1955–1956)

O.N. 180919. 307g. 105.9 × 30.1 × 12.4 feet.
T.3-cyl. (16½″, 27″ & 46″ × 30″) 1,100 ihp engine manufactured by Plenty & Son Ltd., Newbury.
Tug.

1945: Laid down as EMPIRE DOREEN by Scott & Sons, Bowling (Yard No. 377), for the Ministry of War Transport. 1.5.1946: Launched as NIRUMAND for the Petroleum Steam Ship Company Ltd. 14.8.1946: Completed. 1955: Transferred to the British Tanker Company Ltd., and renamed BP DEFENDER (BP FRISKY proposed). 1956: Owners restyled as BP Tanker Company Ltd., and renamed NIRUMAND. 1971: Sold to Gulf Shipping Company S. A., Iran, and renamed NIRU. Last reported as lying sunk 2 km north of Abadan.

BT. 292. NIRUMAND (1956–1971)

see ship No. BT. 291 above.

BT. 293. BRITISH RENOWN (2) (1957)

O.N. 187575. 11,359g. 6,528n. 16,672d.
547′ 4″ × 69′ 10″ × 30′ 0½″ .
6-cyl. 2 S.C.S.A. (670 × 2320mm) Doxford type oil engine manufactured by R. & W. Hawthorn, Leslie (Engineering) Ltd., Newcastle. 6,600 bhp.
Ocean-going tanker.

31.1.1957: Launched by J. L. Thompson & Sons Ltd., Sunderland (Yard No. 680), for the BP Tanker Company Ltd. 5.1957: Completed. 7.1957: Transferred to the Tanker Charter Company Ltd. 13.2.1970: Whilst on a voyage from Bandar Mashar to Yokohama, suffered severe engine damage and taken to Singapore. 17.3.1970: Following discharge, sold to Harbour Line Ltd., Hong Kong, for demolition. 25.3.1970: Departed in tow from Singapore bound to Taiwan. 11.4.1970: Resold to Yi Ho Steel Enterprise Corp., Taiwan. 15.4.1970: Handed over at Kaohsiung for demolition. 25.4.1970: Work commenced.

BT. 294. BRITISH VIGILANCE (2) (1957)

O.N. 187576. 11,349g. 6,498n. 16,672d.
547′ 4″ × 69′ 10″ × 30′ 0½″ .
6-cyl. 2 S.C.S.A. (670 × 2320mm) Doxford type oil engine manufactured by North Eastern Marine Engineering Company Ltd., Newcastle. 6,800 bhp.
Ocean-going tanker.

20.12.1956: Launched by Sir James Laing & Sons Ltd., Sunderland (Yard No. 802), for the BP Tanker Company Ltd. 5.1957: Completed. 7.1957: Transferred to the Tanker Charter Company Ltd. 14.1.1972: Laid up at Rosyth. 15.2.1973: Arrived in tow at Vinaroz for demolition by Desguaces Maritimos S. A.

BT. 295. BRITISH GLORY (2) (1957)

O.N. 187582. 21,001g. 12,462n. 33,702d.
664′ 9″ × 85′ 10″ × 35′ 0″ .
Two, steam turbines manufactured by Vickers-Armstrongs (Engineering) Ltd., Barrow in Furness, double reduction geared to screw shaft. (15,500 shp).
Ocean-going tanker.

1.2.1957: Launched by Vickers-Armstrongs (Shipbuilders) Ltd., Barrow in Furness (Yard No. 1044), for the BP Tanker Company Ltd. 6.1957: Completed. 9.1957: Transferred to the Tanker Charter Company Ltd. 1973: Sold to Ostria Armadora S. A., Greece, and renamed EVROS. 13.1.1975: Whilst undergoing repairs at Rio Grande, sank in port due to ingress of seawater through sea cocks which had not been closed before removal of a condenser.

BP Warden. (World Ship Society Photograph Library)

British Renown. (World Ship Society Photograph Library)

Subsequently raised and laid up. 1.1977: Towed to Vitoria for demolition.

BT. 296. BRITISH VALOUR (2) (1957)

O.N. 187598. 22,001g. 12,987n. 35,246d. 680′ 0″ × 86′ 5″ × 35′ 1¾″.
Two, steam turbines manufactured by the Wallsend Slipway & Engineering Company, Wallsend, double reduction geared to screw shaft. (25,000 shp.)
Ocean-going tanker.

19.12.1956: Launched by Swan, Hunter & Wigham, Richardson Ltd., Newcastle (Yard No. 1853), for the BP Tanker Company Ltd. 7.1957: Completed. 10.1957: Transferred to the Tanker Charter Company Ltd. 1973: Sold to Transportes Intermar Armadora S. A., Liberia, and renamed MESIS. 25.10.1975: Arrived at Castellon for demolition.

BT. 297. BRITISH TRADER (2) (1957)

O.N. 187660. 21,019g. 12,492n. 33,363d. 664′ 9″ × 85′ 10″ × 35′ 0¼″.
Two, steam turbines manufactured by the shipbuilder, double reduction geared to screw shaft. (15,500 shp).
Ocean-going tanker.

26.6.1957: Launched by J. Brown & Company (Clydebank) Ltd., Clydebank (Yard No. 698), for the BP Tanker Company Ltd. 10.1957: Completed. 12.1957: Transferred to the Tanker Charter Company Ltd. 1973: Sold to Parorys Cia. Nav. S. A., Panama, and renamed PELOPIDAS. 28.8.1976: Arrived at Kaohsiung for demolition.

BT. 298. BRITISH COURAGE (2) (1957)

O.N. 187666. 22,001g. 12,987n. 35,572d. 680 ′0″ × 86′ 5″ × 35′ 1¾″.
Two, steam turbines manufactured by R. & W. Hawthorn, Leslie (Engineering) Ltd., Hebburn, double reduction geared to screw shaft. (25,000 shp).
Ocean-going tanker.

13.5.1957: Launched by R. & W. Hawthorn, Leslie (Shipbuilders) Ltd., Hebburn (Yard No. 733), for the BP Tanker Company Ltd. 11.1957: Completed. 12.1957: Transferred to the Tanker Charter Company Ltd. 1973: Sold to Sociadad de Transportes Maritimas S. A., Panama, and renamed POUNENTES. 16.9.1976: Arrived in tow at Curacao with boiler damage. 10.12.1977: Arrived at Kaohsiung for demolition.

BT. 299. ANGLIAN CONFIDENCE (1957–1958)

see ship No. BT.119 above.

BT. 300. ANGLIAN FORTITUDE (1957–1958)

see ship No. BT.123 above.

BT. 301. ANGLIAN DILIGENCE (1957–1958)

see ship No. BT.124 above.

BT. 302. GAELIC INTEGRITY (1957–1958)

see ship No. BT.126 above.

BT. 303. GAELIC FIDELITY (1957–1958)

see ship No. BT.129 above.

BT. 304. GAELIC DESTINY (1957–1958)

see ship No. BT.122 above.

BT. 305. ZURMAND (2) (1957–1966)

O.N. 167032. 600g. 45n. 156′ 8″ × 33′ 2″ × 14′ 9½″.
T.3-cyl. (17″, 28″ & 46″ × 33″) engine manufactured by C. D. Holmes & Company Ltd., Hull. 1,350 ihp.
Salvage tug.

17.4.1942: Launched as DEXTEROUS by Cochrane & Sons Ltd., Selby (Yard No. 1247), for the Admiralty. 9.1942: Completed. 1946: Transferred to the Ministry of War Transport (J. D. McLaren & Company Ltd., managers). 1946: Owners restyled as Ministry of Transport. 1957: Purchased by the BP Tanker Company Ltd., and renamed ZURMAND. 1966: Sold to Waterloo Shipping Company Ltd. (Tsavliris (Shg) Ltd., managers). 1967: Sold to Tsavliris (Salvage & Towage) Ltd. 1968: Renamed NISOS IKARIA. 1971: Sold for demolition.

BT. 306. BAHRAMAND (1958–1968)

O.N. 169410. 302g. 105.9 × 30.1 × 12.4 feet.
T.3-cyl. (16½″, 27″ & 46″ × 30″) engine manufactured by Plenty & Son Ltd., Newbury. 1,100 ihp.
Tug.

14.3.1944: Launched as EMPIRE DORIS by Scott & Sons, Bowling (Yard No. 371), for the Ministry of War Transport. 25.4.1944:

British Vigilance. (World Ship Society Photograph Library)

British Glory. (World Ship Society Photograph Library)

British Trader. (World Ship Society Photograph Library)

British Courage (World Ship Society Photograph Library)

Completed and handed over to Overseas Towage & Salvage Company Ltd., the appointed managers. 12.1945: Taken on charter by Anglo-Iranian Oil Company Ltd. (British Tanker Company Ltd., managers). 1947: Sold to the Petroleum Steam Ship Company Ltd. 5.1948: Renamed BAHRAMAND. 1958: Transferred to the BP Tanker Company Ltd. 1968: Sold to A. Shafei and Partners, Iran, and renamed TAHAMTAN. 1998: Entry removed from Lloyd's Register – continued existence in doubt.

BT. 307. DANESHMAND (1958–1972)

O.N. 181120. 302g. 105.9 × 30.1 × 12.4 feet.
T.3-cyl. (16½″, 27″ & 46″ × 30″) engine manufactured by the North Eastern Marine Engineering Company (1938) Ltd., Sunderland. 1,100 ihp.
Tug.

18.9.1945: Launched as EMPIRE SALLY by J. Crown & Sons Ltd., Sunderland (Yard No. 219), for the Ministry of War Transport. 22.12.1945: Completed and handed over to Townsend Brothers Ferries Ltd., London, for onward delivery to the East Indies but this being cancelled was laid up as surplus to requirements. 4.1946: Sold, for £37,500, to the Petroleum Steam Ship Company Ltd., London. 4.1947: Renamed DANESHMAND. 1958: Transferred to the BP Tanker Company Ltd. 1972: Sold to Gulf Shipping Company S. A., Iran, and renamed DANESH. 1.1975: Reported as sunk in a collision.

BT. 308. TANUMAND (1958–1971)

O.N. 181509. 307g. 105.9 × 30.1 × 12.4 feet.
T.3-cyl. (16½″, 27″ & 45″ × 30″) engine manufactured by Aitchison, Blair Ltd., Clydebank. 1,100 ihp.
Tug.

1945: Laid down as EMPIRE TERENCE by Scott & Sons, Bowling (Yard No. 378), for the Ministry of War Transport. 16.9.1946: Launched as TANUMAND for the Petroleum Steam Ship Company Ltd. 14.8.1946: Completed. 1958: Transferred to the BP Tanker Company Ltd. 1971: Sold to Mohammed Reza Samadpour, Iran. 1973: Sold to Famshek Marine Service Company, Iran. 1998: Entry removed from Lloyd's Register – continued existence in doubt.

BT. 309. TAVANA (1958–1967)

O.N. 167183. 361g. 4n. 120.5 × 31.1 × 13.0 feet.
T.3-cyl. (16½″ 27″ & 46″ × 30″) engine manufactured by Plenty & Son Ltd., Newbury. 870 hp.
Tug.

24.1.1939: Launched by Scott & Sons, Bowling (Yard No. 351), for the Petroleum Steam Ship Company Ltd. 2.1939: Completed. 4.3.1939: Sailed from Leith with barges in tow. 29.4.1939: Arrived at Abadan. 1958: Transferred to the British Tanker Company Ltd. 1967: Sold to A. Rasoolzadeh and Y. Assadpourfad, Iran. 1973: Sold to Hamad Adibzadeh, Iran. 1998: Entry removed from Lloyd's Register – continued existence in doubt.

BT. 310. WIDAD (1958–1962)

see ship No. BT. 195 above.

BT. 311. BRITISH JUSTICE (2) (1958)

O.N. 187696. 21,079g. 12,534n. 33,769d.
665′ 1″ × 85′ 10″ × 35′ 0″ .
Two, steam turbines manufactured by the shipbuilder, double reduction geared to screw shaft. (15,500 shp).
Ocean-going tanker.

26.7.1957: Launched by Cammell, Laird & Company (Shipbuilders & Engineers) Ltd., Birkenhead (Yard No. 1270), for the BP

Gaelic Destiny. (World Ship Society Photograph Library)

British Justice. (World Ship Society Photograph Library)

Tanker Company Ltd. 1.1958: Completed. 3.1958: Transferred to the Tanker Charter Company Ltd. 1972: Transferred to the BP Tanker Company Ltd. 1973: Sold to Tex-Darien Shipping Company S. A., Panama, and renamed SALAMIS. 22.12.1975: Arrived at Kaohsiung for demolition.

BT. 312. BRITISH HONOUR (2) (1958)

O.N. 187721. 21,031g. 12,432n. 33,454d.
664′ 8″ × 85′ 10″ × 35′ 0¼″.
Two, steam turbines manufactured by the shipbuilder, double reduction geared to screw shaft. (15,500 shp).
Ocean-going tanker.

25.9.1957: Launched by Harland & Wolff Ltd., Belfast (Yard No. 1531), for the BP Tanker Company Ltd. 31.1.1958: Completed. 3.1958: Transferred to the Tanker Charter Company Ltd. 1973: Sold to Gantline Cia. Nav. S. A., Greece, and renamed NEDI. 18.10.1976: Arrived at Kaohsiung for demolition.

British Honour. (World Ship Society Photograph Library)

BT. 313. BRITISH ARCHITECT (2) (1958)

O.N. 187785. 23,124g. 12,343n. 36,046d.
683′ 3″ × 86′ 5″ × 37′ 7¼″.
Two, steam turbines manufactured by the Wallsend Slipway & Engineering Company, Wallsend, double reduction geared to screw shaft. (15,500 shp).
Ocean-going tanker.

7.11.1957: Launched by Swan, Hunter & Wigham, Richardson Ltd., Wallsend (Yard No. 1869), for the BP Tanker Company Ltd. 6.1958: Completed. 7.1958: Transferred to the Tanker Charter Company Ltd. 16.6.1970: Whilst on a ballast voyage from Chiba to Persian Gulf was struck by lightning forward of the quarterdeck causing an explosion and damage to main deck. 23.6.1970: Arrived at Hong Kong under own power for repairs. 1972: Transferred to the BP Tanker Company Ltd. 31.1.1975: Laid up at London. 29.11.1975: Arrived in tow at Dalmuir for demolition by W. H. Arnott, Young & Company Ltd.

British Architect. (World Ship Society Photograph Library)

British Architect arriving at Hong Kong 23.6.1970 with explosion damage – seen in the area immediately behind the tug. (World Ship Society Photograph Library)

BT. 314. BRITISH ENERGY (2) (1958)

O.N. 300760. 23,124g. 12,343n. 37,244d.
683′ 0″ × 86′ 5″ × 37′ 7½″.
Two, steam turbines manufactured by the shipbuilder, double reduction geared to screw shaft. (15,500 shp).
Ocean-going tanker.

11.12.1957: Launched by Fairfield Shipbuilding and Engineering Company Ltd., Glasgow (Yard No. 782), for the BP Tanker Company Ltd. 10.1958: Completed. 12.1958: Transferred to the Tanker Charter Company Ltd. 1972: Transferred to the BP Tanker Company Ltd. 13.5.1975: Arrived at Kaohsiung for demolition by Swie Heng Steel Enterprise Company Ltd.

BT. 315. BRITISH AVIATOR (2) (1958)

O.N. 300770. 23,124g. 12,343n. 37,232d.
683′ 3″ × 86′ 5″ × 37′ 7¼″.
Two, steam turbines manufactured by the Wallsend Slipway & Engineering Company, Wallsend, double reduction geared to screw shaft. (15,500 shp).
Ocean-going tanker.

23.12.1957: Launched by Swan, Hunter & Wigham, Richardson Ltd., Wallsend (Yard No. 1871), for the BP Tanker Company Ltd. 10.1958: Completed. 12.1958: Transferred to the Tanker Charter Company Ltd. 1972: Transferred to the BP Tanker Company Ltd. 26.4.1976: Arrived at Kaohsiung. 7.5.1976: Sold to Kanematsu-Goshi (Belgium) S. A. for demolition. Resold and 12.6.1976: Yi Ho Steel Enterprise Corp., commenced demolition.

British Energy. (World Ship Society Photograph Library)

BT. 316. BRITISH DUCHESS (2) (1958)

O.N. 300772. 27,585g. 14,849n. 44,824d.
710′ 1″ × 95′ 3″ × 38′ 8″.
Two, steam turbines manufactured by the shipbuilder, double reduction geared to screw shaft. (17,600 shp).
Ocean-going tanker.

2.6.1958: Launched by J. Brown & Company (Clydebank) Ltd., Clydebank (Yard No. 703), for the BP Tanker Company Ltd. 10.1958: Completed. 10.1958: Transferred to the Tanker Charter Company Ltd. 1972: Transferred to the BP Tanker Company Ltd. 1975: Sold to Hermas Shipping & Trading Corp. S.A. (J. S. Latsis, manager), Greece, and renamed PETROLA XXV. 1976: Renamed PETROLA 25. 31.8.1978: Arrived in tow at Barcelona for demolition.

BT. 317. DELAVAR (2) (1958–1972)

O.N. 300774. 357g. 45n. 130′ 10″ × 33′ 2″ × 13′ 5″.
8-cyl. 2 S.C.S.A. (14½″ × 19″) oil engine manufactured by Crossley Bros.Ltd., Manchester, double reduction, reverse geared with flexible couplings to screw shaft. 1,500 bhp. 12 kts.
Salvage tug.

17.6.1957: Launched by Scott & Sons, Bowling (Yard No.418), for the BP Tanker Company Ltd. 21.10.1958: Completed. 1972: Transferred

British Aviator. (World Ship Society Photograph Library)

British Duchess. (World Ship Society Photograph Library)

to the BP Clyde Tanker Company Ltd. 1975: Sold to the National Iranian Oil Company Ltd. (Oil Service Company Of Iran (Private Company), managers), Iran. Still listed in Lloyd's Register 2003/04.

BT. 318. BRITISH AMBASSADOR (2) (1958–1975)

O.N. 300812. 27,499g. 14,801n. 44,929d.
710′ 1″ × 95′ 5″ × 38′ 8″ .
Two, steam turbines manufactured by Vickers-Armstrongs (Engineering) Ltd., Barrow in Furness, double reduction geared to screw shaft. (17,600 shp).
Ocean-going tanker.

16.8.1958: Launched by Vickers-Armstrongs (Shipbuilders) Ltd., Barrow in Furness (Yard No. 1057), for the BP Tanker Company Ltd. 12.1958: Completed. 14.1.1975: Whilst on a voyage from Ras Tanura to Los Angeles, suffered engine room flooding and sank at position 25.42N., 137.19E., 180 miles west of Iwo Jima.

BT. 319. ZERANG (2) (1959–1972)

O.N. 300848. 357g. 45n. 130′ 10″ × 33′ 2″ × 13′ 5″.
8-cyl. 2 S.C.S.A. (14$^1/_2$″ × 19″) oil engine manufactured by Crossley Bros. Ltd., Manchester, double reduction, reverse geared with flexible couplings to screw shaft. 1,500 bhp. 12 kts.
Salvage tug.

27.11.1958: Launched by Scott & Sons, Bowling (Yard No. 419), for the BP Tanker Company Ltd. 3.1959: Completed. 1972: Transferred to the BP Clyde Tanker Company Ltd. 1975: Sold to the National Iranian Oil Company Ltd. (Oil Service Company Of Iran (Private Company), managers), Iran. Still listed in Lloyd's Register 2003/04

BT. 320. BRITISH LIGHT (2) (1959–1975)

O.N. 300867. 23,015g. 12,701n. 36,754d.
683′ 0″ × 86′ 4″ × 37′ 7$^1/_2$″ .
Two, De Laval type steam turbines manufactured by Ansaldo Stabilo Meccanista, Genoa, double reduction geared to screw shaft. (15,500 shp).
Ocean-going tanker.

12.10.1958: Launched by Ansaldo Societa Per Azioni, Genoa (Yard No. 1530), for the BP Tanker Company Ltd. 4.1959: Completed. 24.1.1975: Laid up at London. 27.5.1975: Arrived in tow at Bilbao for demolition.

BT. 321. BRITISH STATESMAN (2) (1959)

O.N. 300871. 27,586g. 15,036n. 44,701d.
710′ 1″ × 95′ 5″ × 38′ 8$^1/_4$″ .
Two, steam turbines manufactured by the shipbuilder, double reduction geared to screw shaft. (17,600 shp).
Ocean-going tanker.

27.11.1958: Launched by Harland & Wolff Ltd., Belfast (Yard No. 1572), for the BP Tanker Company Ltd. 18.4.1959: Completed. 22.4.1959: Transferred to the Tanker Charter Company Ltd. 1972: Transferred to the BP Tanker Company Ltd. 4.4.1975: Arrived at Kaohsiung for demolition. 5.4.1975: Sold to the Nissho-Iwai American Corp., New York, for $103 per light ton. 7.4.1975: Resold to Tung Ho Steel Enterprise Company Ltd., Taiwan. 6.5.1975: Demolition commenced.

BT. 322. BRITISH JUDGE (2) (1959)

O.N. 300879. 27,585g. 14,852n. 44,804d.
710′ 1″ × 95′ 3″ × 38′ 8″ .
Two, steam turbines manufactured by the shipbuilder, double reduction geared to screw shaft. (17,600 shp).
Ocean-going tanker.

11.12.1958: Launched by J. Brown & Company (Clydebank) Ltd., Clydebank (Yard No. 705), for the BP Tanker Company Ltd. 4.1959: Completed. 6.1959: Transferred to the Tanker Charter Company Ltd. 1972: Transferred to the BP Tanker Company Ltd. 17.1.1975: Laid up at London. 15.5.1975: Departed from London, in tow for Falmouth. 12.6.1975: Sold to Aquilary Peris, Valencia, for demolition. 14.6.1975: Departed in tow from Falmouth bound to Valencia, but for unknown reasons the sale was cancelled whilst vessel was en route. 24.6.1975: Arrived at Valencia for sale. 29.7.1975: Resold, at Valencia, to Intershitra (Holland) B. V., for demolition. 3.9.1975: Work reported as having commenced at an unspecified location.

British Ambassador. (World Ship Society Photograph Library)

British Statesman. (World Ship Society Photograph Library)

British Judge. (World Ship Society Photograph Library)

British Beacon. (World Ship Society Photograph Library)

BT. 323. BRITISH BEACON (2) (1959–1960)

**O.N. 300998. 23,015g. 12,418n. 35,031d.
683′ 0″ × 86′ 4″ × 37′ 7½″.
Two, De Laval type steam turbines manufactured by Ansaldo Stabilo Meccanista, Genoa, double reduction geared to screw shaft. (15,500 shp).
Ocean-going tanker.**

19.4.1959: Launched by Ansaldo Societa Per Azioni, Genoa (Yard No. 1531), for the BP Tanker Company Ltd. 10.1959: Completed. 1.1960: Transferred to the Clyde Charter Company Ltd. 1972: Transferred to the BP Tanker Company Ltd. 1973: Sold Cecil Shipping Corp., Liberia, and renamed BEACON. 18.3.1976: Departed from Chiba bound to Busan for demolition. 23.3.1976: Work commenced at Masan, Korea.

BT. 324. BRITISH STAR (2) (1959–1973)

**O.N. 300907. 23,015g. 12,418n. 36,954d.
683′ 0″ × 86′ 4″ × 37′ 7¾″.
Two, De Laval type steam turbines manufactured by the shipbuilder, double reduction geared to screw shaft. (15,500 shp).
Ocean-going tanker.**

21.6.1958: Launched by Cantieri Riuniti Dell' Adriatico, Trieste (Yard No. 1842), for the BP Tanker Company Ltd. 11.1959: Completed. 1973: Sold to Cosmopolitan Shipping Compania S. A., Liberia, and renamed LESLIE CONWAY. Prior to 14.3.1975: Arrived at Kaohsiung for demolition.

BT. 325. BRITISH TRUST (3) (1959)

**O.N. 301003. 11,169g. 5,952n. 15,600d.
524′ 8″ × 69′ 4″ × 29′ 4½″.
6-cyl. 2 S.C.S.A. (750 × 1500mm) B&W 6-75VTBF-150/50 type oil engine manufactured by J. G. Kincaid & Company Ltd., Glasgow. 8,600 bhp.
Ocean-going tanker.**

1958: Laid down as BRITISH THRUSH by Lithgows Ltd., Port Glasgow (Yard No. 1125), for the BP Tanker Company Ltd. 26.6.1959: Launched as BRITISH TRUST. 30.9.1959: Completed. 10.1959: Transferred to the Clyde Charter Company Ltd. 1972: Transferred to the BP Tanker Company Ltd. 1973: Transferred to Scalesdrene Ltd. 1976: Sold to United Freighter Corp., Panama, and renamed JINJIANG. 1979: Sold to the Peoples Republic of China, and renamed TA CHING 235. 1980: Renamed DA QING 235. 1995: Reported as having been demolished.

BT. 326. BRITISH SWIFT (1) (1959)

**O.N. 301009. 11,174g. 5,929n. 16,041d.
525′ 5″ × 69′ 3″ × 29′ 4½″.
6-cyl. 2 S.C.S.A. (670 × 2320mm) Doxford type oil engine manufactured by the shipbuilder. 8,000 bhp.
Ocean-going tanker.**

24.6.1959: Launched by Scott's Shipbuilding & Engineering Company Ltd., Greenock (Yard No. 681), for the BP Tanker Company Ltd. 22.10.1959: Completed. 27.10.1959: Transferred to the Clyde Charter Company Ltd. 1972: Transferred to the BP Tanker Company Ltd. 1973: Transferred to Erynflex Ltd. 1977: Sold to Noah Shipping Company, Honduras, and renamed NOAH VI. 19.5.1982: Collided with CAST GULL (79,279g./72), and proceeded into Bahrain. 1998: Owners, flag and port of registry deleted from Lloyd's Register. 2000: Lloyd's Register entry deleted – 'continued existence in doubt'.

British Star. (World Ship Society Photograph Library)

British Trust. (World Ship Society Photograph Library)

British Swift. (World Ship Society Photograph Library)

BT. 327. BRITISH POWER (2) (1959)

O.N. 301015. 27,586g. 14,686n. 44,799d.
710′ 0″ × 95′ 4″ × 38′ 8″.
Two, steam turbines manufactured by the shipbuilder, double reduction geared to screw shaft. (17,600 shp).
Ocean-going tanker.

22.5.1959: Launched by Harland & Wolff Ltd., Belfast (Yard No. 1573), for the BP Tanker Company Ltd. 15.11.1959: Completed. 12.1959: Transferred to the Clyde Charter Company Ltd. 1972: Transferred to the BP Tanker Company Ltd. 5.5.1975: Arrived at Kaohsiung for demolition by Chi Yuang Steel Enterprise Company Ltd. 20.11.1975: Work commenced.

British Power. (World Ship Society Photograph Library)

BT. 328. BRITISH GANNET (1) (1959)

O.N. 301021. 11,238g. 5,960n. 15,262d.
525′ 4″ × 69′ 3″ × 29′ 4¼″.
6-cyl. 2 S.C.S.A. (750 × 1500mm) B&W 6-75VTBF-150/50 type oil engine manufactured by J. G. Kincaid & Company Ltd., Glasgow. 8,600 bhp.
Ocean-going tanker.

5.6.1959: Launched by the Blythswood Shipbuilding Company, Glasgow (Yard No. 127), for the BP Tanker Company Ltd. 5.11.1959: Completed. 12.1959: Transferred to the Clyde Charter Company Ltd. 1972: Transferred to the BP Tanker Company Ltd. 1973: Transferred to Crestaford Ltd. 1976: Sold to United Freighter Corp. S. A., Panama, and renamed HANJIANG. 1980: Sold to Newstead Shipping Corp. (Ocean Tramping Company Ltd., managers), Panama, and renamed NEWHAVEN. 26.5.1983: Departed from Bahrain for demolition at Gadani Beach.

British Gannet. (World Ship Society Photograph Library)

BT. 329. BRITISH DESTINY (2) (1959)

O.N. 301028. 27,585g. 14,690n. 44,902d.
710′ 3″ × 95′ 4″ × 38′ 8″.
Two, steam turbines manufactured by the Wallsend Slipway & Engineering Company Ltd., Wallsend, double reduction geared to screw shaft. (17,600 shp).
Ocean-going tanker.

11.3.1959: Launched by Swan, Hunter & Wigham, Richardson Ltd., Wallsend (Yard No. 1873), for the BP Tanker Company Ltd. 12.12.1959: Completed. 16.12.1959: Transferred to the Clyde Charter Company Ltd. 1972: Transferred to the BP Tanker Company Ltd. 1975: Sold Marine Transporters and Suppliers Corp., Liberia, and renamed AGIA TRIAS. 1979: Sold to Nai Tio Ocean Transport Pte. Ltd., Singapore, and renamed RALLYTIME I. 27.12.1982: Arrived at Gadani Beach for demolition.

BT. 330. BRITISH QUEEN (1959)

O.N. 301036. 32,431g. 19,040n. 49,967d.
760′ 0″ × 97′ 5″ × 40′ 6¼″.
Two, steam turbines manufactured by the shipbuilder, double reduction geared to screw shaft. (17,600 shp).
Ocean-going tanker.

16.9.1959: Launched by J. Brown & Company (Clydebank) Ltd., Clydebank (Yard No. 704), for the BP Tanker Company Ltd. 12.1959: Completed and transferred to the Tanker Charter Company Ltd., London. 1972: Transferred to the BP Tanker Company Ltd. 8.4.1975: Arrived at Kaohsiung for demolition by Li Chong Steel & Iron Works Company Ltd. 16.6.1975: Work commenced.

British Queen. (World Ship Society Photograph Library)

BT. 331. BRITISH KIWI (1960)

O.N. 301042. 11,178g. 5,941n. 16,183d.
525′ 2″ × 69′ 3″ × 29′ 4½″.
6-cyl. 2 S.C.S.A. (670 × 2320mm) Doxford type oil engine manufactured by R. & W. Hawthorn, Leslie (Engineering) Ltd., Newcastle. 8,000 bhp.
Ocean-going tanker.

21.7.1959: Launched by Smiths Dock Company Ltd., Middlesbrough (Yard No. 1256), for the BP Tanker Company Ltd. 14.1.1960: Completed. 3.1960: Transferred to the Clyde Charter Company Ltd. 1972: Transferred to the BP Tanker Company Ltd. 1976: Transferred to BP Oil Development Company Ltd., converted into an offshore support vessel, and renamed FORTIES KIWI. 1982: Renamed COLTAIR. 1986: Sold to Waterloo Shipping Company Ltd., Malta, and renamed KITTY. 10.2.1986: Laid up on the R. Blackwater. 30.4.1989: Passed Suez, en route to India for demolition.

British Kiwi. (J K Byass)

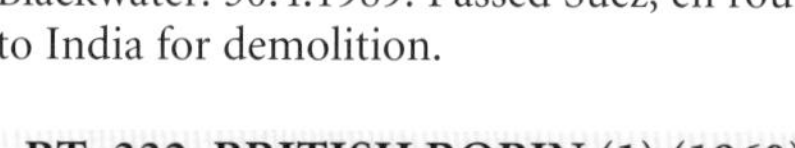

BT. 332. BRITISH ROBIN (1) (1960)

O.N. 301093. 11,211g. 5,954n. 15,450d.
525′ 6″ × 69′ 3″ × 29′ 4¾″.
6-cyl. 2 S.C.S.A. (750 × 1500mm) B&W 6-75VTBF-150/50 type oil engine manufactured by J. G. Kincaid & Company Ltd., Greenock. 8,600 bhp.
Ocean-going tanker.

19.11.1959: Launched by Lithgows Ltd., Port Glasgow (Yard No. 1126), for the BP Tanker Company Ltd. 9.3.1960: Completed. 3.1960 Transferred to the Clyde Charter Company Ltd. 1972: Transferred to the BP Tanker Company Ltd. 1977: Sold to Locofrance Service S. A., France, and renamed LOT. 1983: Sold to Fal Bunkering Company Ltd., Dubai, and renamed FAL XI. 8.7.1986: Whilst awaiting demolition, drove ashore at Clifton Beach, Pakistan, and declared a total loss.

British Lantern. (World Ship Society Photograph Library)

BT. 333. BRITISH LANTERN (2) (1960–1973)

O.N. 301111. 23,015g. 12,701n. 36,194d.
683′ 0″ × 86′ 4″ × 37′ 8″ .
Two, De Laval type steam turbines manufactured by the shipbuilder, double reduction geared to screw shaft. ((15,500 shp).
Ocean-going tanker.

28.4.1959: Launched by Cantieri Riuniti Del' Adriatico, Trieste (Yard No. 1843), for the BP Tanker Company Ltd. 4.1960: Completed. 1973: Sold to Emblema Hidalgo Naviera S. A., of Panama, Greece, and renamed KAVO VRETTANOS. 1974: Sold to Triton Corp., Greece. 8.7.1975: Laid up at Itea. 1.1979: Demolition commenced at Castellon.

British Gull in the Straits of Malacca. (World Ship Society Photograph Library)

BT. 334. BRITISH GULL (1960)

O.N. 301136. 11,156g. 5,922n. 15,939d.
525′ 2″ × 69′ 2″ × 29′ 4³/4″ .
6-cyl. 2 S.C.S.A. (750 × 1500mm) B&W 6-75VTBF-150/50 type oil engine manufactured by the shipbuilder. 8,600 bhp.
Ocean-going tanker.

1959: Laid down as BRITISH SEAGULL by Harland & Wolff Ltd., Glasgow (Yard No. 1589 G), for the BP Tanker Company Ltd. 29.12.1959: Launched as BRITISH GULL. 29.4.1960: Completed. 6.1960 Transferred to the Clyde Charter Company Ltd. 1972: Transferred to the BP Tanker Company Ltd. 1976: Converted into a depot ship for laid-up BP tankers at Brunei Bay. 4.1982: Arrived at Kaohsiung for demolition.

British Mallard. (World Ship Society Photograph Library)

BT. 335. BRITISH MALLARD (1) (1960)

O.N. 301137. 11,174g. 5,924n. 15,866d.
525′ 2″ × 69′ 2″ × 29′ 4¹/4″ .
6-cyl. 2 S.C.S.A. (750 × 1500mm) B&W 6-75VTBF-150/50 type oil engine manufactured by the shipbuilder. 8,600 bhp.
Ocean-going tanker.

3.11.1959: Launched by Harland & Wolff Ltd., Belfast (Yard No. 1588), for the BP Tanker Company Ltd. 6.5.1960: Completed. 3.6.1960: Transferred to the Clyde Charter Company Ltd. 1972: Transferred to the BP Tanker Company Ltd. 1977: Sold to SOCOTRA, France, and renamed PENHORS. 1984: Sold to Fal Bunkering Company Ltd., Dubai, and renamed FAL XII. 9.1987: Arrived at Gadani Beach for demolition.

BT. 336. BRITISH CURLEW (1) (1960)

O.N. 301161. 11,157g. 5,922n. 15,389d.
524′ 8″ × 69′ 3″ × 29′ 4³/4″ .
7-cyl. 2 S.C.S.A. (760 × 1550mm) Sulzer 6RND76 type oil engine manufactured by the shipbuilder. 7,500 bhp.
Ocean-going tanker.

12.1.1960: Launched by A. Stephen & Sons Ltd., Glasgow (Yard No. 670), for the BP Tanker Company Ltd. 12.6.1960: Completed. 6.1960 Transferred to the Clyde Charter Company Ltd. 1972: Transferred to the BP Tanker Company Ltd. 1976: Sold to Hemisphere Shipping Company Ltd. (Ocean Tramping Company Ltd., managers), Hong Kong, and renamed WENJIANG. 9.1980: Detained at Basrah at the outbreak of hostilities. 3.10.1980: Damaged by shellfire in the area of the steering flat sustaining a 3ft.hole. 18.5.1981: Anchored in the Shatt Al Arab Waterway. 1990: Owners and managers deleted from Lloyd's Register. 22.1.1992: Lloyd's Register Class withdrawn and entry amended to 10.1981: Lost during hostilities.

British Robin. (World Ship Society Photograph Library)

BT. 337. FARAHMAND (2) (1960–1975)

O.N. 301181. 362g. 133′ 6″ × 33′ 0″ × 12′ 6³/4″.
8-cyl. 2 S.C.S.A. (14¹/2″ × 19″) oil engine manufactured by Crossley Bros. Ltd., Manchester, single reduction, reverse geared to screw shaft.
Salvage tug.

12.4.1960: Launched by Ferguson Bros. (Port Glasgow) Ltd., Port Glasgow (Yard No. 429), for the BP Tanker Company Ltd. 7.1960: Completed. Subsequently transferred to the BP Clyde Tanker Company Ltd. 1975: Sold to the National Iranian Oil Company Ltd. (Oil Service Company Of Iran (Private Company), managers), Iran. 21.5.1986: Lloyd's Register Class withdrawn. 1986 – 1996: Two unrecorded transactions were undertaken wherein vessel was renamed GULF SPAN 10 then ARASHI. 1996: Lloyd's Register recorded a sale to unspecified Honduras owners quoting the two unrecorded names and the further renaming to HOMELAND under Belize flag. 2000: Entry deleted from Lloyd's Register.

BT. 338. BRITISH COMET (1960–1974)

O.N. 301191. 23,015g. 12,701n. 36,903d.
683′ 0″ × 86′ 4″ × 37′ 7³/4″ .
Two, De Laval type steam turbines manufactured by the

British Curlew. (J K Byass)

British Comet. (World Ship Society Photograph Library)

shipbuilder, double reduction geared to screw shaft. (15,500 shp).
Ocean-going tanker.
24.1.1960: Launched by Cantieri Riuniti Del' Adriatico, Trieste (Yard No. 1844), for the BP Tanker Company Ltd. 9.1960: Completed. 22.6.1974: Arrived at Kaohsiung for demolition by Swie Hung Steel Enterprise Company Ltd. Resold and 16.9.1975: Zui Feng Steel Corp., commenced work at Kaohsiung.

BT. 339. BRITISH SIGNAL (1961–1971)

O.N. 302560. 23,015g. 12,701n. 35,275d.
683′ 0″ × 86′ 4″ × 37′ 7½″ .
Two, De Laval type steam turbines manufactured by the shipbuilder, double reduction geared to screw shaft. (15,500 shp).
Ocean-going tanker.
20.9.1959: Launched by Ansaldo Societa Per Azioni, Genoa (Yard No.1532), for the BP Tanker Company Ltd. 2.1961: Completed. 1971: Sold to Enterprise Cia.Nav.S.A., Greece, and renamed LESTE. 1978: Converted into an oil storage vessel. 1984: Sold for demolition following a long period of lay-up at Salamis.

BT. 340. BRITISH CORMORANT (1) (1961–1977)

O.N. 302680. 11,132g. 5,880n. 16,039d.
525′ 2″ × 69′ 4″ × 29′ 5″ .
6-cyl. 2 S.C.S.A. (750 × 1500mm) B&W 6-75VTBF-150/50 type oil engine manufactured by the shipbuilder. 8,600 bhp.
Ocean-going tanker.
19.1.1961: Launched by Harland & Wolff Ltd., Belfast (Yard No. 1604), for the BP Tanker Company Ltd. 6.7.1961: Completed. 1977: Sold to Trans-Ocean Maritime Transport Inc., Liberia, and renamed ORIENTAL ENDEAVOUR thence, without trading, renamed ORIENTAL BANKER. 15.9.1983: Arrived in tow from Singapore, at Ko-Sichang, Thailand, for demolition.

BT. 341. BRITISH OSPREY (1) (1962–1977)

O.N. 302847. 11,132g. 5,880n. 16,055d.
525′ 9″ × 69′ 5″ × 29′ 5″ .
6-cyl. 2 S.C.S.A. (750 × 1500mm) B&W 6-75VTBF-150/50 type oil engine manufactured by the shipbuilder. 8,600 bhp.
Ocean-going tanker.
24.8.1961: Launched by Harland & Wolff Ltd., Glasgow (Yard No. 1605 G), for the BP Tanker Company Ltd. 12.1.1962: Completed. 1977: Sold to Pacific Tanker Transport Inc., Liberia, and renamed ORIENTAL PEACE. 24.7.1982: Laid-up at Singapore. 1983: Renamed ALLOCEAN No.2. 11.1983: Arrived at Kaohsiung for demolition.

BT. 342. BRITISH PRESTIGE (2) (1962–1975)

O.N. 302872. 27,480g. 14,638n. 44,924d.
710′ 1″ × 95′ 5″ × 40′ 5″ .
Two, steam turbines manufactured by Vickers-Armstrongs (Engineering) Ltd., Barrow in Furness, double reduction geared to screw shaft. (17,600 shp).
Ocean-going tanker.
28.7.1961: Launched by Vickers-Armstrongs (Shipbuilders) Ltd., Barrow in Furness (Yard No. 1058), for the BP Tanker Company Ltd. 2.1962: Completed. 30.4.1975: Arrived at Kaohsiung for demolition. 10.11.1975: Kuo Tah Enterprise Company Ltd., commenced work.

BT. 343. BRITISH KESTREL (1) (1962–1976)

O.N. 302906. 11,171g. 5,913n. 15,922d.
525′ 3″ × 69′ 4″ × 29′ 4¼″ .
6-cyl. 2 S.C.S.A. (750 × 1500mm) B&W 6-75VTBF-150/50 type oil engine manufactured by J. G. Kincaid & Company Ltd., Greenock. 8,600 bhp.
Ocean-going tanker.
27.10.1961: Launched by Wm. Hamilton & Sons Ltd., Port Glasgow (Yard No. 524), for BP Tanker Company Ltd. 3.1962: Completed. 1976: Sold to Peninsular Shipping Company Ltd. (Ocean Tramping Company Ltd., managers), Hong Kong, and renamed SUNJIANG. 24.5.1983: Departed from Hong Kong for demolition at Shanghai.

BT. 344. BRITISH MERLIN (1) (1962–1965)

O.N. 302934. 11,134g. 5,875n. 16,116d.
525′ 9″ × 69′ 5″ × 29′ 5¼″ .
6-cyl. 2 S.C.S.A. (750 × 1500mm) B&W 6-75VTBF-150/50 type oil engine manufactured by the shipbuilder. 8,600 bhp.

British Signal. (World Ship Society Photograph Library)

British Cormorant in the Straits of Malacca. (World Ship Society Photograph Library)

British Osprey in the Straits of Malacca. (World Ship Society Photograph Library)

British Prestige in the Straits of Malacca. (World Ship Society Photograph Library)

British Kestrel. (J K Byass)

British Merlin. (World Ship Society Photograph Library)

Ocean-going tanker.

23.11.1961: Launched by Harland & Wolff Ltd., Glasgow (Yard No. 1606 G), for BP Tanker Company Ltd. 19.5.1962: Completed. 1965: Renamed BP ENTERPRISE. 1968: Reverted to BRITISH MERLIN. 1977: Sold to Luzon Stevedoring Corp., Philippines, and renamed LSCO BASILAN. 1980: Sold to PNOC-Shipping and Transport Corp., Philippines, and renamed PNOC BASILAN. 26.11.1983: Suffered an explosion followed by fire and sank at position 16.21N., 120.19E., off the west coast of Luzon.

BT. 345. BRITISH HUSSAR (2) (1962–1975)

O.N. 302958. 32,341g. 18,391n. 52,546d.
759′ 0″ × 97′ 3″ × 42′ 9¾″.
Two, steam turbines manufactured by the shipbuilder, double reduction geared to screw shaft. (16,000 shp).
Ocean-going tanker.

23.1.1962: Launched by J. Brown & Company (Clydebank) Ltd., Clydebank (Yard No. 714), for the BP Tanker Company Ltd. 5.1962: Completed. 12.1975: Sold Hua Engineering Copper and Iron Industry Company, for demolition at Kaohsiung. 26.12.1975: Arrived at Kaohsiung. 26.2.1976: Sub-contractors, Taiwan Scrap Company, commenced work.

BT. 346. BRITISH CYGNET (1) (1962–1964)

O.N. 303009. 11,137g. 5,907n. 15,441d.
525′ 2″ × 69′ 4″ × 29′ 5″.
6-cyl. 2 S.C.S.A. (750 × 1500mm) B&W 6-75VTBF-150/50 type oil engine manufactured by the shipbuilder. 8,600 bhp.
Ocean-going tanker.

9.1.1962: Launched by Harland & Wolff Ltd., Belfast (Yard No. 1607), for the BP Tanker Company Ltd. 7.6.1962: Completed. 1964: Renamed BP ENDEAVOUR. 1967: Renamed BP EXPLORER. 1969: Reverted to BRITISH CYGNET. 1977: Sold to Atlantic Tanker Transport Inc., Liberia, and renamed ORIENTAL UNITY. 13.9.1982: Arrived at Djakarta, for demolition.

BT. 346. BRITISH BOMBARDIER (2) (1962–1976)

O.N. 304314. 32,351g. 18,404n. 54,116d.
759′ 8″ × 97′ 5″ × 42′ 10″.
Two, steam turbines manufactured by the shipbuilder, double reduction geared to screw shaft. (16,000 shp).
Ocean-going tanker.

18.5.1962: Launched by A. Stephen & Sons Ltd., Glasgow (Yard No. 672), for the BP Tanker Company Ltd. 9.1962: Completed. 9.4.1976: Arrived at Kaohsiung for demolition. 29.5.1976: Jui Fu Steel and Iron Company Ltd., commenced work.

BT. 348. BRITISH CAVALIER (2) (1962–1975)

O.N. 304338. 32,417g. 18,342n. 54,577d.
759′ 8″ × 97′ 4″ × 41′ 5″.
Two, steam turbines manufactured by the Parsons Marine Turbine Company, Wallsend, double reduction geared to screw shaft. (16,000 shp).
Ocean-going tanker.

19.6.1962: Launched by J. L. Thompson & Sons Ltd., Sunderland (Yard No. 700), for the BP Tanker Company Ltd. 11.1962: Completed. 10.12.1975: Arrived at Kaohsiung for demolition. 8.1.1976: Yung Tai Steel & Iron Works Company Ltd., commenced work.

British Cygnet in the Straits of Malacca. (World Ship Society Photograph Library)

British Cavalier. (World Ship Society Photograph Library)

BT. 349. BRITISH GRENADIER (2) (1963–1976)

O.N. 304387. 32,302g. 18,427n. 54,788d.
759′ 8″ × 97′ 5″ × 42′ 9¼″.
Two, steam turbines manufactured by Vickers-Armstrongs (Engineering) Ltd., Barrow in Furness, double reduction geared to screw shaft. (16,000 shp).
Ocean-going tanker.

16.8.1962: Launched by Vickers-Armstrongs (Shipbuilders) Ltd., Barrow in Furness (Yard No. 1067), for the BP Tanker Company Ltd. 1.1963: Completed. 17.11.1975: Laid up at Singapore Roads. 24.2.1976: Sold to Kanematsu-Goshi (Belgium) S. A., for demolition. 28.2.1976: Departed from Singapore. 5.3.1976: Arrived at Kaohsiung. Resold and 11.3.1976: Handed over to Yi Ho Steel Enterprise Corp., at Kaohsiung. 3.4.1976: Demolition commenced.

BT. 350. BRITISH VENTURE (3) (1963–1978)

O.N. 304488. 23,397g. 12,566n. 38,112d.
677′ 11″ × 86′ 4″ × 38′ 11½″.
8-cyl. 2 S.C.S.A. (900 × 1550mm) Sulzer type oil engine manufactured by R. & W. Hawthorn, Leslie & Company (Engineering) Ltd., Hebburn. 16,000 bhp.
Ocean-going tanker.

8.12.1961: Launched by R. & W. Hawthorn, Leslie & Company (Shipbuilders) Ltd., Hebburn (Yard No. 742), for the BP Tanker Company Ltd. 4.1963: Completed. 13.4.1978: Arrived at Kaohsiung for demolition. 7.5.1978: Kuo Dar Steel and Iron Enterprise Company Ltd., commenced work.

BT. 351. BRITISH GUARDSMAN (2) (1963–1975)

O.N. 304601. 32,557g. 18,508n. 54,611d.
760′ 0″ × 97′ 4″ × 42′ 8¾″.
Two, steam turbines manufactured by Fairfield-Rowan Ltd., Glasgow, double reduction geared to screw shaft. (16,000 shp).
Ocean-going tanker.

12.12.1962: Launched by Fairfield Shipbuilding and Engineering Company Ltd., Glasgow (Yard No. 796), for the BP Tanker Company Ltd. 6.1963: Completed. 14.11.1975: Arrived at Kaohsiung for demolition. 8.1.1976: Pai Chow Steel and Iron Works, commenced work.

BT. 352. BRITISH DIPLOMAT (3) (1963–1975)

O.N. 304591. 31,259g. 16,981n. 49,320d.
747′ 11″ × 99′ 10″ × 39′ 4¾″.
Two, steam turbines manufactured by Ateliers et Chantiers de Bretagne, Nantes, double reduction geared to screw shaft. (17,800 shp).
Ocean-going tanker.

12.3.1963: Launched by Ateliers et Chantiers de Dunkerque et Bordeaux (France Gironde), Dunkirk (Yard No. 234), for the BP Tanker Company Ltd. 6.1963: Completed. 13.11.1975: Arrived at Kaohsiung for demolition. 10.12.1975: Sing Chen Yung Iron and Steel Corp., commenced work.

BT. 353. BRITISH LANCER (2) (1963–1976)

O.N. 304614. 32,547g. 18,262n. 54,694d.
759′ 6″ × 97′ 4″ × 42′ 9″.
Two, steam turbines manufactured by the shipbuilder, double reduction geared to screw shaft. (16,000 shp).
Ocean-going tanker.

28.9.1962: Launched by Harland & Wolff Ltd., Belfast (Yard No. 1600), for the BP Tanker Company Ltd. 28.6.1963: Completed. 1976: Sold to Pro Li-Ja Shipping Company S. A., Panama, and renamed LANCER I. 31.8.1976: Arrived at Kaohsiung for demolition.

BT. 354. BRITISH MARINER (3) (1963–1975)

O.N. 304700. 43,605g. 25,870n. 74,635d.
815′ 0″ × 112′ 11″ × 45′ 7¾″.
Two, steam turbines manufactured by the shipbuilder, double reduction geared to screw shaft. (20,000 shp).
Ocean-going tanker.

23.4.1963: Launched by J. Brown & Company (Clydebank) Ltd., Clydebank (Yard No. 715), for the BP Tanker Company Ltd. 10.1963: Completed. 9.11.1975: Arrived at Kaohsiung for demolition by Gi Yuen Steel Works Ltd.

BT. 355. BRITISH DRAGOON (2) (1963–1982)

O.N. 304714. 31,544g. 17,851n. 52,928d.
726′ 4″ × 102′ 4″ × 41′ 2¼″.
Two, steam turbines manufactured by R. & W. Hawthorn, Leslie & Company (Engineering) Ltd., Hebburn, double reduction geared to screw shaft. (16,000 shp).
Ocean-going tanker.

25.4.1963: Launched by R. & W. Hawthorn, Leslie & Company (Shipbuilders) Ltd., Hebburn (Yard No. 748), for the BP Tanker Company Ltd. 11.1963: Completed. 6.12.1982: Arrived at Kaohsiung for demolition.

British Grenadier at Gibraltar. (World Ship Society Photograph Library)

British Venture. (World Ship Society Photograph Library)

British Guardsman at Falmouth. (World Ship Society Photograph Library)

British Diplomat. (World Ship Society Photograph Library)

British Lancer. (World Ship Society Photograph Library)

British Mariner. (World Ship Society Photograph Library)

BT. 356. BRITISH ENSIGN (3) (1964–1976)

O.N. 305930. 43,335g. 27,128n. 75,578d. 815′ 2″ × 112′ 11″ × 44′ 1¼″.

Two, steam turbines manufactured by the shipbuilder, double reduction geared to screw shaft. (20,000 shp). Ocean-going tanker.

4.10.1963: Launched by Cammell, Laird & Company (Shipbuilders & Engineers) Ltd., Birkenhead (Yard No. 1293), for the BP Tanker Company Ltd. 4.1964: Completed. 15.1.1976: Arrived at Kaohsiung for demolition. 26.2.1976: Nan Yung Steel and Iron Company Ltd., commenced work.

BT. 357. BRITISH HAZEL (1) (1964–1982)

O.N. 305982. 13,100g. 7,611n. 20,462d. 561′ 1″ × 73′ 9″ × 30′ 2¼″.
6-cyl. 2 S.C.S.A. (760 × 1550mm) Sulzer 6RND76 type oil engine manufactured by the Wallsend Slipway & Engineering Company, Wallsend. 7,500 bhp. Ocean-going tanker.

31.10.1963: Launched by Swan, Hunter & Wigham, Richardson Ltd., Wallsend (Yard No. 1895), for the BP Tanker Company Ltd. 5.1964: Completed. 1982: Sold to Petrostar Company Ltd., Saudi Arabia, and renamed PETROSTAR XVII. 1983: Renamed NEJMAT EL PETROL XVII. 1988: Sold to Fal Bunkering Company Ltd., United Arab Emirates, and renamed FAL XXII. 1989: Sold to National Marine Services (NMS), United Arab Emirates, and renamed AL HAMRIA. 1990: Sold to Fal Shipping Company Ltd., United Arab Emirates, and renamed FAL XVIII. 8.1.2003: Demolition commenced at an unrecorded location

BT. 358. BRITISH CHIVALRY (2) (1963–1972)

see ship No. BT. 208 above.

BT. 359. BRITISH GUARDIAN (1963–1972)

see ship No. BT. 272 above.

BT. 360. BRITISH ENVOY (1963–1970)

see ship No. BT. 273 above.

BT. 361. BRITISH SERGEANT (2) (1963–1972)

see ship No. BT. 282 above.

BT. 362. BRITISH CHANCELLOR (2) (1964–1972)

see ship No. BT. 281 above.

BT. 363. BRITISH CORPORAL (2) (1964–1972)

see ship No. BT. 279 above.

BT. 364. BRITISH GUNNER (2) (1964–1972)

see ship No. BT. 278 above.

BT. 365. BRITISH CRUSADER (1964–1972)

see ship No. BT. 275 above.

BT. 366. BP ENDEAVOUR (1) (1964–1967)

see ship No. BT. 346 above.

BT. 367. BRITISH HAWTHORN (1) (1964–1983)

O.N. 306128. 13,119g. 7,627n. 20,551d. 561′ 1″ × 73′ 9″ × 30′ 2½″.
6-cyl. 2 S.C.S.A. (760 × 1550mm) Sulzer 6RND76 type oil engine manufactured by R. & W. Hawthorn, Leslie & Company (Engineering) Ltd., Hebburn. 7,500 bhp. Ocean-going tanker.

16.3.1964: Launched by R. & W. Hawthorn, Leslie & Company (Shipbuilders) Ltd., Hebburn (Yard No. 749), for the BP Tanker Company Ltd. 10.1964: Completed. 1983: Sold

British Ensign. (World Ship Society Photograph Library)

British Hazel on 20 October 1979. (World Ship Society Photograph Library)

British Hawthorn. (World Ship Society Photograph Library)

to Vergina Shipping Company S. A., Panama, and renamed NEW FORTUNE. 1984: Renamed KYRA POPI. 1985: Sold to Misano di Navigazione S.p.A., Italy, and renamed MARE EQUATORIALE. 1986: Sold to Societe Marittima Internazionale SpA. (Misano di Navigazione S.p.A., managers), Palermo. 1992: Sold to Prismar Srl, (same managers). 1995: Sold to Five Star General Trading Ltd., St.Vincent and The Grenadines. 29.9.1996: Arrived at Alang for demolition.

BT. 368. BRITISH FERN (3) (1964–1983)

O.N. 306201. 13,252g. 7,621n. 20,638d.
561′ 0″ × 73′ 9″ × 30′ 2¼″.
6-cyl. 2 S.C.S.A. (740 × 1600mm) B&W 6-74VT2BF-160 type oil engine manufactured by J. G. Kincaid & Company Ltd., Greenock. 7,500 bhp.
Ocean-going tanker.

14.5.1964: Launched by Lithgows Ltd., Port Glasgow (Yard No. 1131), for the BP Tanker Company Ltd. 12.1964: Completed. 1983: Sold to Armatoriale Orseolo S.p.A., Italy, and renamed CHERSO. 19 26.12.1991: Sustained heavy weather damage whilst outward from Augusta and put back. 29.1.1992: Arrived at Izola for repairs. 5.1992: Arrested at Izola in respect of alleged unpaid bills. 1992: Sold to Armatoriale Orio S.p.A., Italy. 1994: Sold for demolition.

BT. 369. BRITISH HOLLY (3) (1965)

O.N. 306308. 13,271g. 7,634n. 20,638d.
561′ 0″ × 73′9″ × 30′ 2¼″.
6-cyl. 2 S.C.S.A. (740 × 1600mm) B&W 6-74VT2BF-160 type oil engine manufactured by J. G. Kincaid & Company Ltd., Greenock. 7,500 bhp.
Ocean-going tanker.

9.9.1964: Launched by Lithgows Ltd., Port Glasgow (Yard No. 1155), for the BP Tanker Company Ltd. 20.3.1965: Completed. 26.3.1965: Transferred to BP Thames Tanker Company Ltd. 1983: Sold to Nova Industria Armamento S.p.A., Italy, and renamed HUMANITAS. 1984: Sold to Marisud S.p.A., Italy, and renamed MARISUD PRIMA. 1988: Sold to Misano di Navigazione S.p.A., Italy, and renamed LABRADOR. 1990: Sold to Anadolu Petrolleri-Ali Sukru Iskefyeli, Turkey, and renamed EMIRE. 1990: Sold to Seydi Reis Denizcilik Isletmesi A. S. (Genel Denizcilik Nakliyati A.S. (GEDEN LINE), managers, Turkey, and renamed PARA. Still listed in Lloyd's Register 2004/05.

BT. 370. BRITISH VINE (2) (1965–1983)

O.N. 306241. 13,408g. 7,726n. 20,835d.
559′ 0″ × 73′ 9″ × 30′ 1″.
6-cyl. 2 S.C.S.A. (740 × 1600mm) B&W 6-74VT2BF-160 type oil engine manufactured by the shipbuilder. 7,500 bhp.
Ocean-going tanker.

23.9.1964: Launched by Harland & Wolff Ltd., Belfast (Yard No. 1601), for the BP Tanker Company Ltd. 26.3.1965: Completed. 1983: Sold to Lefkaritas Bros., Greece, and renamed PETROLINA VI. 1988: Sold to Tenca Cia. Nav. S. A., Panama, and renamed VINE. 1993: Sold to Lefkaritis Bros. Shipping Ltd., Cyprus. 1996: Sold to Bozeman Holdings S. A. (Iran Marine Services Ltd., Tehran, managers), and to be renamed SAVEH, under Panamanian registry. 12.4.1997: Arrived at Alang, under the St. Vincent & Grenadines registry for demolition.

BT. 371. BRITISH WILLOW (1) (1965)

O.N. 307771. 13,136g. 7,553n. 20,750d.
561′ 2″ × 73′ 8″ × 30′ 0¼″.
6-cyl. 2 S.C.S.A. (740 × 1600mm) B&W 6-74VT2BF-160 type oil engine manufactured by Harland & Wolff Ltd., Belfast. 7,500 bhp.
Ocean-going tanker.

7.10.1964: Launched by Sir James Laing &

British Fern. (World Ship Society Photograph Library)

British Vine in New Zealand waters. (World Ship Society Photograph Library)

British Willow in New Zealand waters. (J K Byass)

Sons Ltd., Sunderland (Yard No. 835), for the BP Tanker Company Ltd. 11.5.1965: Completed. 21.5.1965: Transferred to BP Thames Tanker Company Ltd. 1983: Sold to Castle Shipping Company (Dilmun Marine Services, manager), Gibraltar, and renamed NEWCASTLE. 1988: Sold to Flamingo Shipping Company Ltd. (Mayamar Marine Enterprises S.A., managers), Malta, and renamed FLAMINGO I. 1994: Reported as demolished.

BT. 372. BRITISH COMMERCE (3) (1965)

O.N. 306271. 37,814g. 24,707n. 69,579d.
815′ 9″ × 108′ 3″ × 42′ 3¾″.
9-cyl. 2 S.C.S.A. (900 × 1550mm) Sulzer type oil engine manufactured by G. Clark and North Eastern Marine Ltd., Sunderland. 18,000 bhp.
Ocean-going tanker.

10.7.1964: Launched by J. L. Thompson & Sons Ltd., Sunderland (Yard No. 702), for the BP Tanker Company Ltd. 5.1965: Completed. 9.1965: Transferred to BP Tyne Tanker Company Ltd. 31.1.1983: Arrived at Kaohsiung for demolition.

BT. 373. BRITISH LAUREL (1) (1965–1981)

O.N. 307781. 13,512g. 7,760n. 20,826d.
561′ 0″ × 73′ 8″ × 30′ 0¾″.
6-cyl. 2 S.C.S.A. (740 × 1600mm) B&W 6-74VT2BF-160 type oil engine manufactured by the shipbuilder. 7,500 bhp.
Ocean-going tanker.

19.2.1965: Launched by Eriksberg M/V Ab, Gothenburg (Yard No. 589), for the BP Tanker Company Ltd. 6.1965: Completed. 1981: Sold to Armadores Mariella S. A., Panama, and renamed MARIBRUNA IV. 1983: Sold to Globemaster Shipping Inc., Panama, and renamed MARIANTHI M. 12.10.1987: Struck by an Iraqi aircraft-launched missile and bombs at position 28.02N., 51.07E., 60 miles south of Kharg Island. 1 missile lodged in her boiler and failed to explode. One crewman killed. 1990: Sold to Sea King Maritime Inc., Panama, and renamed SEA MOON. 1992: Sold to Bakri Navigation Company Ltd., Saudi Arabia, and renamed MOUG AL BAHR. 1994: Red Sea Marine Services appointed as managers. 7.11.1995: Nicksons Exports (Pvt) Ltd., commenced demolition at Alang.

BT. 374. BRITISH ADMIRAL (3) (1965)

O.N. 306310. 61,768g. 39,858n. 111,274d.
917′ 6″ × 128′ 6″ × 51′ 8¾″.
Two, steam turbines manufactured by the shipbuilder, double reduction geared to screw shaft. (25,000 shp).
Ocean-going tanker.

17.3.1965: Launched by Vickers Ltd., Barrow in Furness (Yard No. 1069), for the BP Tanker Company Ltd. 8.1965: Completed. 9.1965: Transferred to BP Tyne Tanker Company Ltd. 15.7.1976: Arrived at Kaohsiung for demolition. 30.8.1976: Tung Ho Steel Enterprise Company Ltd., commenced work.

BT. 375. BP ENTERPRISE (1) (1965 -1968)

see ship No. BT. 344 above.

BT. 376. BRITISH POPLAR (1965–1982)

O.N. 307928. 13,530g. 7,773n. 20,774d.
561′ 0″ × 73′ 8″ × 30′ 0¾″.
6-cyl. 2 S.C.S.A. (740 × 1600mm) B&W 6-74VT2BF-160 type oil engine manufactured by the shipbuilder. 7,500 bhp.
Ocean-going tanker.

1.4.1965: Launched by Eriksberg M/V Ab, Gothenburg (Yard No. 590), for the BP Tanker Company Ltd. 10.1965: Completed. 1982: Sold to Nova Industria Armamento S.p.A., Italy, and renamed UTILITAS. 1991: Sold to SPEI Leasing S.p.A. (Misano di Navigazione S.p.A., managers), Italy, and renamed ALCANTARA. 1995: Sold to Indian shipbreakers. 6.9.1995: Anchored off Alang. 26.9.1995: Beached. 30.10.1995: Seth Shipbreaking Corporation, commenced work.

BT. 377. BRITISH IVY (1965–1982)

O.N. 307976. 13,271g. 7,634n. 20,638d.
561′ 0″ × 73′ 9″ × 30′ 0″.
Post 1993: 12,979g. 7,784n. 20,977d.
6-cyl. 2 S.C.S.A. (740 × 1600mm) B&W 6-74VT2BF-160 type oil engine manufactured by J. G Kincaid & Company Ltd., Greenock. 7,500 bhp.
Ocean-going tanker.

1.7.1965: Launched by Lithgows Ltd., Port Glasgow (Yard No. 1135), for the BP Tanker Company Ltd. 11.1965: Completed. 1982: Sold to Nova Industria Armamento S.p.A., Italy, and renamed CHARITAS. 1987: Sold to Franconia S.r.l., Italy. 1993: Sold to Fione Shipping Company Ltd., Antigua and Barbuda, and renamed CHAR. 1993: Sold to IMS Marine Services G.m.b.H., St.Vincent and The Grenadines, and renamed OHARA. 1996: Lloyd's Register deleted flag and port of registry. 1997: Reported as having been demolished.

British Commerce. (World Ship Society Photograph Library)

British Laurel. (J K Byass)

British Admiral. (World Ship Society Photograph Library)

British Enterprise. (World Ship Society Photograph Library)

British Poplar. (World Ship Society Photograph Library)

British Ivy. (World Ship Society Photograph Library)

BT. 378. BRITISH MAPLE (3) (1965–1982)

O.N. 307979. 13,530g. 7,773n. 20,774d. 561′ 0″ × 73′ 8″ × 30′ 1″.
6-cyl. 2 S.C.S.A. (740 × 1600mm) B&W 6-74VT2BF-160 type oil engine manufactured by the shipbuilder. 7,500 bhp.
Ocean-going tanker.

30.9.1965: Launched by Eriksberg M/V Ab, Gothenburg (Yard No. 591), for the BP Tanker Company Ltd. 12.1965: Completed. 1982: Sold to Loutra Shipping Company Ltd., Greece, and renamed MANAMARIA. 8.6.1982: Whilst on a voyage from Zawia Terminal, sustained extensive fire damage to her engine room, at a position 35 miles west of Lampedusa Island, near Malta. Sold for demolition.

BT. 379. BRITISH ARGOSY (1) (1966–1976)

O.N. 308175. 62,427g. 40,158n. 112,786d. 920′ 9″ × 128′ 5″ × 51′ 9″.
Two, steam turbines manufactured by the Wallsend Slipway & Engineering Company, Wallsend, double reduction geared to screw shaft. (25,000 shp).
Ocean-going tanker.

2.7.1966: Launched by Swan, Hunter & Wigham, Richardson Ltd., Wallsend (Yard No. 1897), for the BP Tanker Company Ltd. 7.1966: Completed. 1.7.1976: Arrived at Kaohsiung for demolition. 10.9.1976: Nan Feng Steel Enterprise Company Ltd., commenced work.

BT. 380. BRITISH COMMODORE (2) (1967–1975)

O.N. 309840. 38,288g. 24,994n. 67,862d. 819′ 6″ × 108′ 3″ × 42′ 3½″.
9-cyl. 2 S.C.S.A. (840 × 1800mm) B&W type oil engine manufactured by Harland & Wolff Ltd., Belfast. 18,000 bhp.
Ocean-going tanker.

18.8.1966: Launched by Fairfields (Glasgow) Ltd., Glasgow (Yard No. 795), for the BP Tanker Company Ltd. 2.1967: Completed. 1975: Transferred to the Tanker Charter Company Ltd. 28.11.1982: Arrived at Siracha, Thailand for demolition.

BT. 381. BRITISH CENTAUR (1967–1972)

O.N. 307991. 37,985g. 23,631n. 67,697d. 815′ 9″ × 108′ 4″ × 42′ 3¾″.
9-cyl. 2 S.C.S.A. (840 × 1800mm) B&W type oil engine manufactured by the shipbuilder. 18,000 bhp.
Ocean-going tanker.

15.6.1965: Launched by Harland & Wolff Ltd., Belfast (Yard No. 1602), for the BP Tanker Company Ltd. 11.1.1966: Completed for the Tanker Charter Company Ltd. 1967: Transferred to the BP Tanker Company Ltd. 1972: Transferred to the Tanker Charter Company Ltd. 1983: Sold to Harrisons (Clyde) Ltd., Glasgow, and renamed EARL OF SKYE. 28.6.1984: Arrived at Ulsan for demolition.

BT. 382. BRITISH CAPTAIN (3) (1967–1972)

O.N. 307961. 38,053g. 24,070n. 67,944d. 815′ 8″ × 108′ 3″ × 42′ 4½″.
Two, steam turbines manufactured by the shipbuilder, double reduction geared to screw shaft. 20,000 shp.
Ocean-going tanker.

30.4.1965: Launched by Cammell, Laird & Company (Shipbuilders & Engineers) Ltd., Birkenhead (Yard No. 1294), for the BP Tanker Company Ltd. 1.1966: Completed for the Tanker Charter Company Ltd. 1967:

British Maple. (World Ship Society Photograph Library)

British Commodore. (World Ship Society Photograph Library)

British Centaur. (World Ship Society Photograph Library)

British Captain. (World Ship Society Photograph Library)

Transferred to the BP Tanker Company Ltd. 1972: Transferred to the Tanker Charter Company Ltd. 1976: Sold to United Maritime Enterprises S. A., Greece, and renamed HALCYON MED. 1979: Sold to North Star Oceanic Ltd., Greece. 29.3.1982: Laid-up at Aliveri. 19.2.1985: Arrived at Kaohsiung for demolition.

BT. 383. BP EXPLORER (2) (1967–1969)

see ship No. BT. 346 above.

BT. 384. BP ENDEAVOUR (2) (1967–1987)

O.N. 191879. 13,187g. 8,217n. 19,500d.
560′ 6″ × 73′ 8″ × 30′ 10¼″.
6-cyl. 2 S.C.S.A. (760 × 1550mm) Sulzer 6RND76 type oil engine manufactured by the Commonwealth Government Engineering Works, Melbourne. 7,500 bhp.
Ocean-going tanker.

21.8.1967: Launched by the New South Wales Government Engineering and Shipbuilding Undertaking, State Dockyard, Newcastle N. S. W. (Yard No. 76), for the BP Tankers Australia Pty. Ltd., Australian registry. 9.1967: Completed and transferred to the BP Tanker Company Ltd. 1976: Adelaide Steamship Company Ltd., appointed as managers. 1978: Removed from management. 1987: Sold to Ark Shipping Company (Dilmun Marine Services, managers), Gibraltar, and renamed NEWARK. 17.12.1993: Lloyd's Register Class deleted, sold for demolition.

BT. 385. BRITISH LIBERTY (3) (1968–1981)

O.N. 335715. 15,115g. 8,777n. 24,000d.
556′ 6″ (BB) × 81′ 5″ × 31′ 4″.
6-cyl. 2 S.C.S.A. (740 × 1600mm) B&W 6-74VT2BF-160 type oil engine manufactured by the shipbuilder. 7,500 bhp.
Ocean-going tanker.

15.2.1968: Launched by Eriksberg M/V Ab, Gothenburg (Yard No. 619), for the BP Tanker Company Ltd. 5.1968: Completed. 1981: Sold to Societe d'Armement et de Transport (SOCATRA) and Compagnie Marseillaise de Reparations, France, and renamed FOLGOET. 15.9.1992 until 1.1996: In lay-up at Marseilles. 1.1996: Transferred to St. Vincent & The Grenadines registry. 12.3.1996: Anchored off Alang for demolition. 18.3.1996: Beached.

BT. 386. BP ENTERPRISE (2) (1968–1989)

O.N. 191880. 13,185g. 8,218n. 19,480d.
560′ 6″ × 73′ 8″ × 30′ 10¼″.
Post 1993: 12,319g. 8,344n. 20,640d.
6-cyl. 2 S.C.S.A. (760 × 1550mm) Sulzer 6RND76 type oil engine manufactured by the Commonwealth Government Engineering Works, Melbourne. 7,500 bhp.
Ocean-going tanker.

10.5.1968: Launched by the New South Wales Government Engineering and Shipbuilding Undertaking State Dockyard, Newcastle N. S. W. (Yard No. 77), for the BP Tankers Australia Pty. Ltd., Australian registry. 7.1968: Completed and transferred to the BP Tanker Company Ltd. 1976: Adelaide Steamship Company Ltd., appointed as managers. 1989: Sold to Redford Investment Inc. (Harry Borthen & Company, A/S managers), Liberia, and renamed LIV COB. 1993: Sold to Piebald International Ltd. (Borthen Ship Management A/S, managers), Liberia. Prior to 31.12.1995: Arrived at Alang for demolition.

BT. 387. BRITISH LOYALTY (3) (1968–1981)

O.N. 335919. 15,118g. 8,800n. 23,900d.
556′ 6″ (BB) × 81′ 5″ × 31′ 4″.
Post 1994: 14,785g. 8,921n. 24,290d.
6-cyl. 2 S.C.S.A. (740 × 1600mm) B&W 6-74VT2BF-160 type oil engine manufactured by the shipbuilder. 7,500 bhp.
Ocean-going tanker.

6.6.1968: Launched by Eriksberg M/V Ab, Gothenburg (Yard No. 620), for the BP Tanker Company Ltd. 9.1968: Completed. 1981: Sold to Kaymart Company Ltd., Saudi

BP Enterprise. (J K Byass)

British Loyalty. (J K Byass)

Arabia, and renamed HALA. 1981: Sold to Unifedo S. A., Switzerland, and renamed PETER KIRK. 1986: Sold to Korella Shipping Company S. A., Panama, and renamed KORTANK. 1992: Sold to Fal Shipping Company Ltd., United Arab Emirates, and renamed FAL XXVI. 1992: Sold to Gulf Horizon Inc., Panama (Fal Shipping Company Ltd., managers), and renamed GULF HORIZON 1. 1993: Removed from management. 1993: Owners deleted from Lloyd's Register, and tonnages amended. 13.12.1993: Anchored off Alang for demolition. 14.12.1993: Beached.

BT. 388. BRITISH MERLIN (1) (1968–1977)

see ship No. BT. 344 above.

BT. 389. BRITISH CYGNET(1) (1969–1977)

see ship No. BT. 346 above.

BT. 390. BRITISH SECURITY (3) (1969–1976)

O.N. 337045. 15,095g. 8,783n. 23,900d.
556′ 6″ (BB) × 81′ 5″ × 31′ 4″ .
6-cyl. 2 S.C.S.A. (740 × 1600mm) B&W 6-74VT2BF-160 type oil engine manufactured by the shipbuilder. 7,500 bhp.
Ocean-going tanker.

14.1.1969: Launched by Eriksberg M/V Ab, Gothenburg (Yard No. 621), for the BP Tanker Company Ltd. 3.1969: Completed. 1976: Transferred to BP Tyne Tanker Company Ltd. 1989: Sold to Societa Italiana Maritima S.r.L., Italy, and renamed TAURUS ERRE. 1992: Sold to Orizon Tanker Company Ltd. (Intermed S. A., managers), Malta, and renamed SEA HORSE. 1999: Sold to Petroma Shipping Ltd., Malta, and renamed POTI STAR. 2002: Sold to Petromar Shipping Ltd. (Dela Petrol, managers), under Cambodia registry. Still listed in Lloyd's Register 2004/05.

BT. 391. BRITISH TENACITY (2) (1969–1976)

O.N. 337753. 15,095g. 8,783n. 24,000d.
556′ 6″ (BB) × 81′ 5″ × 31′ 4″ .
6-cyl. 2 S.C.S.A. (740 × 1600mm) B&W 6-74VT2BF-160 type oil engine manufactured by the shipbuilder. 7,500 bhp.
Ocean-going tanker.

17.4.1969: Launched by Eriksberg M/V Ab, Gothenburg (Yard No. 622), for the BP Tanker Company Ltd. 6.1969: Completed. 1976: Transferred to BP Tyne Tanker Company Ltd. 1985: Transferred to BP Thames Tanker Company Ltd. 1989: Sold to Societa Italiana Maritima S.r.L., Italy, and renamed AQUARIUS ERRE. 1991: Sold to Orizon Tanker Company Ltd. (Intermed S. A., managers), Malta, and renamed BLUE SEA.1997: Sold to Egyptian Arabian Shipping Company, Panama, and renamed BLUE SEA II. 1999: Elhawi Shipping Company Ltd., appointed as managers. 26.4.2000: Lloyd's Register withdrew class. 2000: Sold to Elhawi Marine Technical Services & Salvage, Panama. 8.1.2001: Arrived at Gadani Beach, Pakistan, for demolition.

BT. 392. BRITISH UNITY (2) (1969–1981)

O.N. 337828. 15,260g. 9,070n. 24,386d.
558′ 10″ (BB) × 81′ 6″ × 31′ 1″ .
6-cyl. 2 S.C.S.A. (740 × 1600mm) B&W 6-74VT2BF-160 type oil engine manufactured by Brodogradaliste I Tvornica Dizel Motora 'Uljanik', Pula. 7,500 bhp.
Ocean-going tanker.

18.12.1968: Launched by Brodogradaliste I Tvornica Dizel Motora 'Split', Split (Yard No. 239), for the BP Tanker Company Ltd. 7.1969: Completed. 1981: Sold to Loira S. A., Panama, and renamed SEBASTIANI. 1985: Sold to Goldfin Corp. S. A., Bahamas, and renamed

British Security at Tacoma 12 May 1982. (World Ship Society Photograph Library)

British Tenacity. (World Ship Society Photograph Library)

SILVER CLOUD. 1987: Sold to Rubimar S. A., Panama, and renamed NOEL BAY. 1989: Sold to Zaza Navigation Ltd. (Acomarit Services Maritimes S. A., managers), Malta, and renamed BAYONNE. 15.1.1994: Anchored off Alang, for demolition.

BT. 393. BRITISH FIDELITY (2) (1969–1985)

O.N. 337993. 15,260g. 9,070n. 24,414d.
558′ 10″ (BB) × 81′ 7″ × 31′ 7″.
Post 1993: 14,721g. 8,540n. 24,775d.
6-cyl. 2 S.C.S.A. (740 × 1600mm) B&W 6-74VT2BF-160 type oil engine manufactured by Brodogradaliste I Tvornica Dizel Motora" Uljanik", Pula. 7,500 bhp.
Ocean-going tanker.

14.5.1969: Launched by Brodogradaliste I Tvornica Dizel Motora 'Split', Split (Yard No. 240), for the BP Tanker Company Ltd. 12.1969: Completed. 1985: Sold to Nova Industria Armamento S.p.A., Italy, and renamed FIDELITY. 1990: Sold to Tankersud S.p.A. (Morfini S.r.l., managers), Italy, and renamed PORTORIA. 1995: Removed from management. 7.6.1996: Anchored off Alang for demolition. 14.6.1996: Beached.

BT. 394. BRITISH BEACON (2) (1972–1973)

see ship No. BT. 323 above.

BT. 395. BRITISH POWER (2) (1972–1975)

see ship No. BT. 327 above.

BT. 396. BRITISH GANNET (1) (1972–1973)

see ship No. BT. 328 above.

BT. 397. BRITISH DESTINY (2) (1972–1975)

see ship No. BT. 329 above.

BT. 398. BRITISH QUEEN (1972–1975)

see ship No. BT. 330 above.

BT. 399. BRITISH INDUSTRY (3) (1972–1973)

O.N. 187530. 21,083g. 12,534n. 33,475d.
664′ 9″ × 85′ 10″ × 35′ 0¼″.
Two, steam turbines manufactured by the shipbuilder, double reduction geared to screw shaft.
Ocean-going tanker.

10.10.1956: Launched by J. Brown & Company (Clydebank) Ltd., Clydebank (Yard No. 697), for the BP Tanker Company Ltd. 2.1957: Completed for the Tanker Charter Company Ltd. 2.1972: Laid-up at Falmouth. 1972: Transferred to the BP Tanker Company Ltd. 1973: Sold to Cosmopolitan Shipping Company S. A., Liberia, and renamed STEPHANIE CONWAY. 21.2.1975: Arrived at Castellon for demolition.

BT. 400. BRITISH KIWI (1972–1976)

see ship No. BT. 331 above.

BT. 401. BRITISH ROBIN (1) (1972–1977)

see ship No. BT. 332 above.

BT. 402. BRITISH GULL (1972–1982)

see ship No. BT. 334 above.

BT. 403. BRITISH MALLARD (1) (1972–1977)

see ship No. BT. 335 above.

British Unity. (World Ship Society Photograph Library)

British Fidelity. (World Ship Society Photograph Library)

BT. 404. BRITISH CURLEW (1) (1972–1976)

see ship No. BT. 336 above.

BT. 405. BRITISH JUSTICE (2) (1972–1973)

see ship No. BT. 311 above.

BT. 406. BRITISH FAITH (2) (1972–1973)

O.N. 187742. 21,001g. 12,464n. 33,766d.
664′ 9″ × 85′ 10″ × 35′ 0″.
Two, steam turbines manufactured by Vickers-Armstrongs (Engineering) Ltd., Barrow in Furness, double reduction geared to screw shaft.
Ocean-going tanker.

10.12.1957: Launched by Vickers-Armstrongs (Shipbuilders) Ltd., Barrow in Furness (Yard No.1047), for the BP Tanker Company Ltd. 3.1958: Completed, for the Tanker Charter Company Ltd. 1972: Transferred to the BP Tanker Company Ltd. 1973: Sold to Wonco Cia. Nav. S. A., Greece, and renamed STELIOS. 1976: Sold to Evifar Cia. Nav. S. A., Greece, and renamed MONTAZA. 30.10.1976: Arrived at Kaohsiung for demolition.

BT. 407. BRITISH ARCHITECT (2) (1972–1975)

see ship No. BT. 313 above.

BT. 408. BRITISH ENERGY (2) (1972–1975)

see ship No. BT. 314 above.

BT. 409. BRITISH AVIATOR (2) (1972–1976)

see ship No. BT. 315 above.

British Faith. (World Ship Society Photograph Library)

BT. 410. BRITISH DUCHESS (2) (1972–1975)

see ship No. BT. 316 above.

BT. 411. BRITISH SWIFT (1) (1972–1973)

see ship No. BT. 317 above.

BT. 412. BRITISH FULMAR (1972–1973)

O.N. 300829. 11,169g. 5,952n. 15,983d.
524′ 8″ × 69′ 4″ × 29′ $4\frac{1}{2}$″ .
7-cyl. 2 S.C.S.A. (760 × 1550mm) Sulzer 6RND76 type oil engine manufactured by the shipbuilder. 7,500 bhp.
Ocean-going tanker.

30.9.1958: Launched by A. Stephen & Sons Ltd., Glasgow (Yard No. 664), for the BP Tanker Company Ltd. 2.1959: Completed for the Clyde Charter Company Ltd. 1972: Transferred to the BP Tanker Company Ltd. 1973: Transferred to Solamole Ltd. 1976: Sold to United Freighters Corp. (Ocean Tramping Company Ltd., managers), Panama, and renamed ZHUJIANG. 1977: Transferred to Ocean Freighters Corp. 1979: Sold to the Peoples Republic of China, and renamed TA CHING 236. 1980: Renamed DA QING 236. 1982: Transferred to Government of the Peoples Republic of China (Bureau of Maritime Transportation Administration). 10.1983: Sank following a collision.

BT. 413. BRITISH STATESMAN (2) (1972–1975)

see ship No. BT. 321 above.

BT. 414. BRITISH JUDGE (2) (1972–1975)

see ship No. BT. 322 above.

British Humber carried a 'River' name but was not a member of the class (J K Byass)

BT. 415. BRITISH TRUST (3) (1972–1973)

see ship No. BT. 325 above.

BT. 416. BRITISH DART (1972–1986)

O.N. 358605. 15,650g. 9,661n. 25,245d.
562′ 6″ (BB) × 82′ 2″ × 31′ $5\frac{1}{4}$″.
6-cyl. 2 S.C.S.A. (740 × 1600mm) B&W 6K74EF type oil engine manufactured by Uddevallavarvet AB, Uddevalla. 9,000 bhp.
Ocean-going tanker.

22.3.1972: Launched by M/V Eriksbergs Ab. (Lindholmen Div), Gothenburg (Yard No. 658), for BP Tanker Company Ltd. 9.1972: Completed. 1976: Irano-British Ship Service Company Ltd., appointed as managers. 1979: Removed from management. 1986: Sold to the National Iranian Tanker Company (NITC) and renamed MINAB 3. 3.2002: Sold for demolition. 5.2002: Work commenced at an unrecorded location.

BT. 417. BRITISH TEST (1973–1986)

O.N. 358731. 15,653g. 9,675n. 25,245d.
562′ 6″ (BB) × 82′ 1″ × 31′ 5″.
6-cyl. 2 S.C.S.A. (740 × 1600mm) B&W 6K74EF type oil engine manufactured by the shipbuilder. 9,000 bhp.
Ocean-going tanker.

15.8.1972: Launched by M/V Eriksbergs Ab (Lindholmen Div), Gothenburg (Yard No.659), for BP Tanker Company Ltd. 1.1973: Completed. 1976: Irano-British Ship Service Company Ltd., appointed as managers. 1979: Removed from management. 1986: Sold to the National Iranian Tanker Company (NITC), and renamed MINAB 4. 16.4.2004: Beached at Gadani Beach for demolition.

BT. 418. BRITISH HUMBER (1973–1985)

O.N. 358816. 15,204g. 8,999n. 24,448d.
558′ 6″ (BB) × 81′ 7″ × 31′ $7\frac{1}{4}$″.
6-cyl. 2 S.C.S.A. (740 × 1600mm) B&W 6K74EF type oil engine manufactured by Brodogradaliste " Uljanik", Pula. 9,000 bhp.
Ocean-going tanker.

15.6.1972: Launched by Brodogradiliste 'Split', Split (Yard No.259), for BP Tanker Company Ltd. 2.1973: Completed. 1985: Transferred to BP International Ltd., Bahamas (BP Shipping Ltd., managers), and renamed BP HUMBER. 1991: Sold to Roma Leasing S.p.A. (SBT Tankers S.p.A., managers), Italy, and renamed AKRADINA. 1996: Sold to Navigazione Alta Italia S.p.A. (Beam Gestioni S.r.l., managers), Naples. 1998: Sold to Navigazione Montanari S.p.A. (same managers), Italy. 18.5.2000: Anchored off Alang for demolition.

BT. 419. BRITISH TAY (1973–1992)

O.N. 360552. 15,650g. 9,660n. 25,650d.
562′ 6″ (BB) × 82′ 2″ × 31′ 4″.
Post 1992: 14,894g. 10,498n. 25,650d.
6-cyl. 2 S.C.S.A. (740 × 1600mm) B&W 6K74EF type oil engine manufactured by the shipbuilder. Ocean-going tanker.

23.1.1973: Launched by M/V Eriksbergs Ab (Lindholmen Div), Gothenburg (Yard No. 660), for BP Tanker Company Ltd. 6.1973: Completed. 1992: Sold to T. C. P. Marine Shipping Company Ltd., Panama, and renamed SOUTH WIND I. 1994: Sold to International Oil Tanking Company Ltd. (Eurasia Shipping & Management Company Ltd., managers), Panama. 1997: Removed from management. 23.7.1997: Anchored off Alang to await demolition.

BT. 420. BRITISH TRENT (1973–1993)

O.N. 360855. 15,649g. 9,675n. 25,550d.
562′ 6″ (BB) × 82′ 2″ × 31′ 5″.
6-cyl. 2 S.C.S.A. (740 × 1600mm) B&W 6K74EF type oil engine manufactured by the shipbuilder. 9,000 bhp.
Ocean-going tanker.

24.5.1973: Launched by M/V Eriksbergs Ab (Lindholmen Div), Gothenburg (Yard No.

British Fulmar.(J K Byass)

British Dart. (World Ship Society Photograph Library)

661), for BP Tanker Company Ltd. 11.1973: Completed. 3.6.1993: Whilst outward bound in thick fog from Antwerp to Fiumicino and having just landed her Pilot in Flushing Roads, collided with the Panamanian bulk carrier WESTERN WINNER (15,954g/82), inward bound to pick up a Pilot in Flushing Roads. BRITISH TRENT burst into flames and was abandoned with the loss of seven lives and a further two missing. The WESTERN WINNER proceeded into port for examination. Following the dowsing of the flames by six fire-fighting tugs, the gutted BRITISH TRENT was towed stern-first toward an anchorage outside Rotterdam for safety inspection before entering that port for the remaining cargo to be discharged. 10.6.1993: Berthed at Botlek, Rotterdam and subsequently sold to the salvors, Smit Internationale Sleepbootmaatschappij "Smit New York" B. V., St. Vincent and the Grenadines, and renamed RITIS. 28.6.1993: Departed in tow from Rotterdam en route to Aliaga for demolition. 21.7.1993: Arrived. 9.1993: Demolition commenced by Kalkavan Gemi Sokum Ticaret A. S.

British Wye. (J K Byass)

BT. 421. BRITISH WYE (1974–1992)

O.N. 360982. 15,649g. 9,658n. 25,600d.
562′ 6″ (BB) × 82′ 2″ × 31′ 5″.
Post 1992: 14,943g. 10,429n. 25,196d.
6-cyl. 2 S.C.S.A. (740 × 1600mm) B&W 6K74EF type oil engine manufactured by the shipbuilder. 9,000 bhp.
Ocean-going tanker.

4.7.1973: Launched by M/V Eriksbergs Ab (Lindholmen Div), Gothenburg (Yard No. 675), for BP Tanker Company Ltd. 1.1974: Completed. 1976: Transferred to the BP Tanker Company Ltd. 1976: Irano-British Ship Service Company Ltd., appointed as managers. 1979: Removed from management. 1992: Sold to Xanthe Shipping Ltd. (Compagnie Monegasque Maritime S. A. metres. (COMOMAR), managers), Malta, and renamed SEA CASTLE. 1997: Sold to Lorsil Shipping Ltd., Malta, and renamed TOREPO. 2002: Sold to Landsvale Investments Inc., Panama (Sea World Management, Monte Carlo), and renamed SEA STREAM. 28.5.2002: Beached at Alang for demolition.

BT. 422. BRITISH NEATH (1974–1976)

O.N. 360939. 15,641g. 9,664n. 25,246d.
562′ 6″ (BB) × 82′ 2″ × 31′ 6″.
Post 1987: 16,015g. 9,876n. 25,651d.
6-cyl. 2 S.C.S.A. (740 × 1600mm) B&W 6K74EF type oil engine manufactured by S. A. Cockerill-Ougree-Providence, Seraing. 9,000 bhp.
Ocean-going tanker.

29.6.1973: Launched by Cockerill Yards Hoboken, Hoboken (Yard No. 869), for BP Tanker Company Ltd. 1.1974: Completed. 1976: Sold to National Iranian Tanker Company (NITC), Iran, and renamed MOKRAN. 15.2.1982: Attacked by Iraqi aircraft at Kharg Island. Damage not reported. 5.9.1986: Attacked by Iraqi aircraft whilst loading at Lavan Island. Extensively damaged in the cargo tanks area. 3.5.1987: Afterpart arrived, in tow, at Singapore for repair and to be joined to the forepart of MINAB (ex BRITISH FAL q.v.). by Jurong Shipyards Ltd., who estimated that the work would take six months and would include reconstruction and refurbishment of the accommodation and the complete overhauling and repairing of machinery in the engine room which had flooded during salvage operations. The resultant 'New vessel' to remain as MOKRAN. 24.10.1987: New vessel departed for Sitra Island. 3.2.1988: 21:00hrs., local time, struck by an Iraqi Exocet missile at position 27.14N., 52.28E., en route to Kharg Island. Sustained fire damage aft. Taken initially to Bandar Abbas. 13.4.1988: Arrived back at Singapore for further repairs. 6.4.2004: Beached at Chittagong for demolition.

British Tay. (J K Byass)

British Trent. (World Ship Society Photograph Library)

BT. 423. BRITISH SEVERN (1974–1976)

O.N. 363283. 15,641g. 9,664n. 25,245d.
562′ 6″ (BB) × 82′ 2″ × 31′ 6″.
Post 19 : 14,947g. 10,429n. 25,651d.
6-cyl. 2 S.C.S.A. (740 × 1600mm) B&W 6K74EF type oil engine manufactured by S. A. Cockerill-Ougree-Providence, Seraing. 9,000 bhp.
Ocean-going tanker.

8.1.1974: Launched by Cockerill Yards Hoboken, Hoboken (Yard No. 870), for BP Tanker Company Ltd. 5.1974: Completed. 1976: Sold to the National Iranian Tanker Company (NITC), Iran, and renamed MARUN. 12.9.1986: Struck by an Iraqi missile at position 28.30N., 50.47E. Towed to Sirri Island by the Singapore tug SALVERITAS for inspection and temporary repairs. 1.5.1987: Arrived at Singapore Roads en route to Jurong Shipyards Ltd. for repairs Still listed in Lloyd's Register 2004/05.

BT. 424. BRITISH FAL (1974–1976)

O.N. 363415. 16,495g. 9,675n. 25,244d.
562′ 6″ (BB) × 82′ 2″ × 31′ 6″.
6-cyl. 2 S.C.S.A. (740 × 1600mm) B&W 6K74EF type oil engine manufactured by the shipbuilder. 9,000 bhp.
Ocean-going tanker.

14.2.1974: Launched by M/V Eriksbergs Ab (Lindholmen Div), Gothenburg (Yard No. 676), for BP Tanker Company Ltd. 9.1974: Completed. 1976: Sold to the National Iranian Tanker Company, Iran, and renamed MINAB. 27.4.1986: Struck in the starboard bunker tank

British Severn. (World Ship Society Photograph Library)

British Fal. (World Ship Society Photograph Library)

by an Iraqi missile at position 28.23N., 51. 05E., 50 miles south of Kharg Island. Extensively damaged by fire aft and subsequently towed to Bandar Abbas. Damage reported as accommodation, emergency generator and control room, pump room and engine room destroyed by fire and auxiliary machinery extensively damaged. Subsequently declared as a partial war constructive total loss. 2.5.1987: Forepart arrived at Singapore in tow for repair. To be joined to the afterpart of MOKRAN (ex BRITISH NEATH q.v.) by Jurong Shipyards Ltd., who estimated that the work would take six months. It would include reconstruction and refurbishment of the accommodation and the complete overhauling and repairing of machinery in the engine room which had flooded during salvage operations. The resultant 'New vessel' to remain as MOKRAN. From this point the ship history becomes that of BRITISH NEATH above.

BT. 425. BRITISH BEECH (1) (1975–1976)

O.N. 306205. 13,138g. 7,555n. 20,750d.
561′ 2″ × 73′ 8″ × 30′ 0″ .
6-cyl. 2 S.C.S.A. (740 × 1600mm) B&W 6-74VT2BF-160 type oil engine manufactured by Harland & Wolff Ltd., Belfast. 7,500 bhp.
Ocean-going tanker.

26.5.1964: Launched by Sir James Laing & Sons Ltd., Sunderland (Yard No. 834), for the BP Tanker Company Ltd. 12.1964: Completed for BP Thames Tanker Company Ltd. 1975: Transferred to the BP Tanker Company Ltd. 1976: Transferred to Solamole Ltd. 1992: Sold to Schiff Holdings Inc. (Bakri Navigation Company Ltd., managers), Panama, and renamed SEAWIND. 24.8.2002: Demolition commenced at an unspecified location.

BT. 426. BRITISH RESOURCE (3) (1976–2000)

O.N. 365861. 133,035g. 108,525n. 265,450d.
338.64(BB) × 53.68 × 20.708 metres.
Two, steam turbines manufactured by the shipbuilder, double reduction geared to screw shaft. 34,000 shp.
Post 1982: 6-cyl. 2 S.C.S.A. (900 × 2180mm) B&W 6L90GF type oil engine manufactured by the shipbuilder. 21,350 bhp.
Very large crude carrier (VLCC)

5.3.1975: Launched by Mitsubishi Heavy Industries Ltd., Nagasaki (Yard No. 1738), for Erynflex Ltd., London. 25.7.1975: Completed, BP Tanker Company Ltd., appointed as managers. 1976: Transferred to the BP Tanker Company Ltd. 4.1982: Converted into a motorship. 1988: Transferred to Bermuda registry. 1990: Transferred to BP Shipping Ltd. 1999: Owners restyled as BP Amoco Shipping Ltd. 25.3.2000: Arrived at Xinhui, China, for demolition by Xinhui Ship Breaking Iron & Steel Company.

BT. 427. BORDER CASTLE (1979–1981)

O.N. 186915. 13,235g. 7,519n. 19,925d.
569′ 2″ × 72′ 8″ × 31′ 7″ .
6-cyl. 2 S.C.S.A. (700 × 2320mm) Doxford type oil engine manufactured by the shipbuilder. 7,200bhp.
Ocean-going tanker.

19.10.1960: Launched by Swan, Hunter & Wigham, Richardson Ltd., Newcastle (Yard No. 1956), for the Lowland Tanker Company Ltd. (Common Bros. Ltd., managers), Newcastle. 9.3.1961: Completed. 1970: Common Bros. (Management) Ltd., appointed as managers. 1976: BP Tanker Company Ltd., assumed management. 1979: Sold to the BP Tanker Company Ltd. 1980: Owners restyled as BP Shipping Ltd. 1981: Sold to Relay Maritime Inc. (Gulf Shipping Lines Ltd., London, managers), Panama, and renamed FIVE BROOKS. 17.10.1986: Whilst on a loaded voyage from Kuwait to Khor Fakkan was attacked by Iranian gunboats and accommodation set on fire at position 26.15N., 56.08E., Straits of Hormuz. Engine room flooded and 10 crewmen killed. Towed to Khor Fakkan for inspection and declared a war constructive total loss. 4.1.1987: Arrived at Gadani Beach for demolition by World Marine Shipping. 5.1.1987: Work commenced.

British Beach. (World Ship Society Photograph Library)

British Resource. (World Ship Society Photograph Library)

BT. 428. BORDER FALCON (1979–1982)

O.N. 186921. 13,230g. 7,528n. 19,949d.
569′ 1″ × 72′ 8″ × 31′ 7″ .
6-cyl. 2 S.C.S.A. (700 × 2320mm) Doxford type oil engine manufactured by Hawthorn, Leslie (Engineers) Ltd., Newcastle. 8,000bhp.
Ocean-going tanker.

3.3.1961: Launched by Smiths Dock Company Ltd., Middlesbrough (Yard No. 1262), for the Lowland Tanker Company Ltd. (Common Bros. Ltd., managers), Newcastle. 20.10.1961: Completed. 1970: Common Bros. (Management) Ltd., appointed as managers. 1976: BP Tanker Company Ltd., assumed management. 1979: Sold to the BP Tanker Company Ltd. 1980: Owners restyled as BP Shipping Ltd. 1982: Sold to Ajax Alpha Ltd. (Ajax Marine Ltd., Grimsby, managers), Bermuda, and renamed GARDENIA B. 1984: Transferred to Gardenia B Inc., Panama. 30.1.1985: Arrived at Kaohsiung for demolition by Sing Cheng Yung Iron & Steel. 6.2.1985: Work commenced.

BT. 429. BORDER PELE (1979–1981)

O.N. 186913. 13,228g. 7,523n. 19,925d.
569′ 2″ × 72′ 8″ × 31′ 7″ .
6-cyl. 2 S.C.S.A. (700 × 2320mm) Doxford type oil engine manufactured by the Wallsend Slipway & Engineering Company Ltd., Wallsend. 7,200bhp.
Ocean-going tanker.

8.6.1960: Launched by Swan, Hunter & Wigham, Richardson Ltd., Wallsend (Yard No. 1893), for the Lowland Tanker Company Ltd. (Common Bros. Ltd., managers), Newcastle. 21.1.1961: Completed. 1970: Common Bros. (Management) Ltd., appointed as managers. 1976: BP Tanker Company Ltd., assumed management. 1979: Sold to the BP Tanker Company Ltd. 1980: Owners restyled as BP Shipping Ltd. 1981: Sold to Elan Maritime Inc. (Gulf Shipping Lines Ltd., London, managers), Panama, and renamed FIVE STREAMS. 14.5.1984: Arrived at Chittagong Roads, for demolition by Khalil & Sons.

BT. 430. BORDER SHEPHERD (1979–1981)

O.N. 186906. 13,600g. 7,679n. 20,914d.
572′ 0″ × 73′ 0″ × 31′ 7½″ .
6-cyl. 2 S.C.S.A. (750 × 1500mm) B&W type oil engine manufactured by J. G. Kincaid & Company Ltd., Greenock. 8,800bhp.
Ocean-going tanker.

31.3.1960: Launched by Lithgows Ltd., Port Glasgow (Yard No. 1130), for the Lowland Tanker Company Ltd. (Common Bros. Ltd., managers), Newcastle. 28.7.1960: Completed. 1970: Common Bros. (Management) Ltd., appointed as managers. 1976: BP Tanker Company Ltd., assumed management. 1979: Sold to the BP Tanker Company Ltd. 1980: Owners restyled as BP Shipping Ltd. 1981: Sold to Almizar Shipping Company S. A. (D. J. Chandris, Greece, manager), Panama, and renamed MARIVERDA IV. 1983: Sold to Pyramid Navigation Company E. S. A., Egypt, and renamed AL NABILA II. 26.5.1993: Arrived at Alang for demolition.

British Skill. (World Ship Society Photograph Library)

British Spirit. (J K Byass)

BT. 431. BORDER CHIEFTAIN (1979)

O.N. 186924. 13,238g. 7,528n. 19,939d.
569′ 2″ × 72′ 8″ × 31′ 7″ .
6-cyl. 2 S.C.S.A. (700 × 2320mm) Doxford type oil engine manufactured by Hawthorn, Leslie (Engineers) Ltd., Newcastle. 8,000bhp.
Ocean-going tanker.

30.6.1961: Launched by Smiths Dock Company Ltd., Middlesbrough (Yard No. 1264), for the Lowland Tanker Company Ltd. (Common Bros. Ltd., managers), Newcastle. 18.1.1962: Completed. 1970: Common Bros. (Management) Ltd., appointed as managers. 1976: BP Tanker Company Ltd., assumed management. 1979: Sold via the BP Tanker Company Ltd. to Cosentino Shipping Company S. A. (A. Halcoussis & Company, managers), Greece, and renamed ACHILLET. 1987: Sold to Spiro Shipping Company Ltd. (Grecale Inc., Greece, managers), Malta, and renamed SPIRO. 27.9.1988: Arrived at Chittagong for demolition by Khalil & Sons Ltd. 29.9.1988: Work commenced.

Border Shepherd. (World Ship Society Photograph Library)

BT. 432. BRITISH SKILL (2) (1983–1999)

O.N. 703384. 66,034g. 36,211n. 127,778d.
260.99(BB) × 39.65 × 17.328 metres.
5-cyl. 2 S.C.S.A. (900 × 2180mm) B&W 5L90GFCA type oil engine manufactured by the shipbuilder. 16,250 bhp.
Ocean-going tanker.

31.3.1981: Keel laid by Harland & Wolff Ltd., Belfast (Yard No. 1718), for BP Thames Tanker Company Ltd. 3.7.1982: Launched. 26.4.1983: Completed for BP Shipping Ltd. 1999: Sold to Sogelease B.V. (same managers restyled as BP Amoco Shipping Ltd.), under Bermuda registry. 11.2002: Sold to Xin Dun Shipping Pte. Ltd. (Ocean Tankers (Pte.) Ltd., managers), Singapore, and renamed OCEAN SKILL. Still listed in Lloyd's Register 2004/05.

BT. 433. BRITISH SPIRIT (1983–1999)

O.N. 703252. 66,024g. 36,229n. 127,778d.
260.99(BB) × 39.65 × 16.222 metres.
5-cyl. 2 S.C.S.A. (900 × 2180mm) B&W 5L90GFCA type oil engine manufactured by J. G. Kincaid & Company Ltd., Greenock. 16,250 bhp.
Ocean-going tanker.

23.6.1980: Keel laid by Scott Lithgow Ltd., Port Glasgow (Yard No. 1201), for BP Thames Tanker Company Ltd. 30.3.1982: Launched. 15.3.1983: Completed for BP Shipping Ltd. 1999: Sold to Sogelease B.V. (same managers restyled as BP Amoco Shipping Ltd.,), under Bermuda registry. 11.2002: Sold to Da An Shipping Pte. Ltd. (Ocean Tankers (Pte.) Ltd., managers), Singapore, and renamed OCEAN POWER. Still listed in Lloyd's Register 2004/05.

British Success. (World Ship Society Photograph Library)

British Reliance. (World Ship Society Photograph Library)

BT. 434. BRITISH SUCCESS (2) (1984–1999)

O.N. 705470. 66,034g. 36,121n. 127,965d.
261.32(BB) × 39.65 × 14.877 metres.
5-cyl. 2 S.C.S.A. (900 × 2180mm) B&W 5L90GFCA type oil engine manufactured by the shipbuilder. 16,250 bhp.
Ocean-going tanker.

8.7.1981: Keel laid by Harland & Wolff Ltd., Belfast (Yard No. 1719), for BP Thames Tanker Company Ltd. 20.3.1983: Launched. 3.2.1984: Completed for BP Shipping Ltd. 1999: Sold to Sogelease B.V. (same managers restyled as BP Amoco Shipping Ltd.), under Bermuda registry. 9.2002: Sold to St. Andrews Shipping Company Ltd. (International Andromeda Shipping S.A.M., managers), and renamed ST ANDREWS under Norway (NIS) flag. Still listed in Lloyd's Register 2004/05.

BT. 435. BRITISH RELIANCE (3) (1985–2000)

O.N. 365920. 133,035g. 108,525n. 255,510d.
338.64(BB) × 53.68 × 20.708 metres.
Two, steam turbines manufactured by the shipbuilder, double reduction geared to screw shaft. 34,000 shp.
Very large crude carrier (VLCC).

23.5.1975: Launched by Mitsubishi Heavy Industries Ltd., Nagasaki (Yard No. 1739), for the BP Tanker Company Ltd., London. 9.1975: Completed for Crestaford Ltd. (BP Tanker Company Ltd., managers), and placed into lay-up. 9.1976: Commissioned. 1981: Managers restyled as BP Shipping Ltd. 1985: Sold to BP Shipping Ltd., under Bahamian registry. 1999: Owners restyled as BP Amoco Shipping Ltd. 1.2.2000: Reported as anchored off Zhuhai waiting demolition.

BT. 436. AUSTRALIAN SPIRIT (1987–1995)

O.N. 852251. 23,547g. 8,458n. 32,605d.
182.40(BB) × 26.83 × 10.526 metres.
6-cyl. 2 S.C.S.A. (520 × 1800mm) Mitsubishi 6RTA52 type oil engine manufactured by the shipbuilder. 8,750 bhp. Thwartship thrust controllable-pitch propeller forward.
Ocean-going tanker.

6.3.1986: Keel laid by Mitsubishi Heavy Industries Ltd., Nagasaki (Yard No. 1985), for BP Australia Ltd. 4.9.1986: Launched. 31.3.1987: Completed (Associated Steamships Pty Ltd., managers). 199 : Managers restyled as ASP Ship Management. 1995: Sold to Seabird Ltd., Coastal Tankers Ltd., managers), Wellington, New Zealand, and renamed TOANUI. 12.1999: Sold to Full Navi Logistica S.p.A. (V. Ships Management Inc., managers), Naples, and renamed LORENZA. 2.2000: Sold to Andoas Shipping Inc. (Petrolera Transoceanica S. A., managers), Panama, and renamed ANDOAS. 6.2000: Sold to Anake Navigation Corp. (same managers). Still listed in Lloyd's Register 2004/05.

BT. 437. BP ENERGY (1985–1987)

O.N. 399833. 18,343g. 12,122n. 32,265d.
170.97(BB) × 25.94 × 11.367 metres.
7-cyl. 2 S.C.S.A. (670 × 1400mm) B&W 7K67GF type oil engine manufactured by A/S Burmeister and Wain's Motor-og-Maschinfabrik af 1971, Copenhagen. 13,100 bhp.
Ocean-going tanker.

1.6.1975: Launched as LIBRA by Ab Finnboda Varv, Stockholm (Yard No. 395), for the Cherokee Shipping Corp. (Rethymnis & Kalukundis), Greece. 6.1976: Completed under Liberian registry. 1985: Purchased by BP Shipping Ltd., and renamed BP ENERGY. 1987: Transferred to Ash Marine (Bahamas) Ltd. (BP Shipping Ltd., managers), Bahamas. 1990: Sold to Olympius Posidon Maritime Company, Greece, and renamed ASPHALT LEADER. 2003: Demolished.

BT. 438. BP ADMIRAL (1990–1993)

O.N. 715345. 23,967g. 11,595n. 41,100d.
176.20(BB) × 30.82 × 11.525 metres.
6-cyl. 2 S.C.S.A. (520 × 1850mm) Mitsubishi 6UEC52LS type oil engine manufactured by the shipbuilder. 6,300 bhp.
Ocean-going tanker.

13.11.1989: Keel laid by Mitsubishi Heavy Industries Ltd., Nagasaki (Yard No. 2031), for BP Shipping Ltd., Bermuda registry. 9.2.1990: Launched. 26.9.1990: Completed. 1993: Renamed BRITISH ADMIRAL. 1999: Owners restyled as BP Amoco Shipping Ltd. 1.2004: Sold to unspecified buyers (Seaworld Management & Trading Inc., managers), and renamed ADMIRAL L. Still listed in Lloyd's Register 2004/05.

BT. 439. BP ADVENTURE (1990–1994)

O.N. 715349. 23,967g. 11,595n. 41,035d.
176.20(BB) × 30.82 × 11.525 metres.
6-cyl. 2 S.C.S.A. (520 × 1850mm) Mitsubishi 6UEC52LS type oil engine manufactured by the shipbuilder. 6,300 bhp.
Ocean-going tanker.

13.2.1990: Keel laid by Mitsubishi Heavy Industries Ltd., Nagasaki (Yard No. 2032), for BP Shipping Ltd., Bermuda registry. 27.4.1990: Launched. 21.12.1990: Completed. 1994: Renamed BRITISH ADVENTURE. 1999: Owners restyled as BP Amoco Shipping Ltd. 4.2004: Sold to unspecified buyers (Seaworld Management & Trading Inc., managers), and renamed ADVENTURE. Still listed in Lloyd's Register 2004/05.

BT. 440. BRITISH RESPECT (2) (1990–1992)

O.N. 363417. 136,601g. 112,534n. 277,746d.
336.03(BB) × 55.28 × 21.210 metres.
Two, steam turbines manufactured by the shipbuilder, double reduction geared to screw shaft. 36,000 shp.
Very large crude carrier (VLCC).

British Respect fresh from dry-docking, seen leaving the New Waterway in the summer of 1977 en route to Southampton Water to participate in the Queen's Silver Jubilee Fleet Review. (World Ship Society Photograph Library/W. J. Harvey)

29.4.1974: Launched by Kawasaki Heavy Industries, Sakaide (Yard No. 1204), for Scalesdrene Ltd., London. 9.1974: Completed, BP Tanker Company Ltd., appointed as managers. 1981: Managers restyled as BP Shipping Ltd. GMT 22.12.1987: At 10:30hrs, whilst lying at Larak Island, was bombed and set ablaze by Iraqi aircraft. Fire extinguished and vessel proceeded to Dubai for repairs. 4.2.1988: Returned to service. 1986: Transferred to Gibraltar registry. 1990: Transferred to BP Shipping Ltd., Bahamian registry. 1992: Sold to Delos Maritime Corp, Greece, and renamed DELOS. 1998: Owners restyled as E. N. E. Delos Ltd. (Aeolos Management S. A., managers), Greece. 10.10.1999: Arrived at Chittagong, for demolition.

British Resolution. (J K Byass)

BT. 441. BP ACHIEVER (1990–1991)

O.N. 850148. 66,031g. 41,323n. 127,575d. 261.35(BB) × 39.65 × 17.328 metres.
5-cyl. 2 S.C.S.A. (900 × 2180mm) B&W 5L90GB type oil engine manufactured by the shipbuilder. 16,250 bhp.

5.8.1980: Keel laid by Swan, Hunter Shipbuilders Ltd., Hebburn (Yard No. 112), for BP Thames Tanker Company Ltd. (Associated Steamships Pty Ltd., Australia, managers). 18.3.1983: Launched. 15.7.1983: Completed. 1990: Transferred to BP Shipping Ltd. 1991: Renamed AUSTRALIAN ACHIEVER (ASP Ship Management, managers). 1998: Renamed BRITISH STRENGTH. 1999: Sold to Sogelease B.V. (BP Amoco Shipping Ltd., managers), under Bermuda registry. 4.2003: Sold to Ocean Spirit Maritime Company (Liquimar Tankers Management Ltd., managers), and renamed AFRODITI. Still listed in Lloyd's Register 2004/05.

BT. 442. BRITISH RANGER (2) (1990–2000)

O.N. 366000. 133,035g. 108,525n. 265,617d. 338.64(BB) × 53.68 × 20.727 metres.
Two, steam turbines manufactured by the shipbuilder, double reduction geared to screw shaft. 34,000 shp.
Very large crude carrier (VLCC).

23.8.1975: Launched by Mitsubishi Heavy Industries Ltd., Nagasaki (Yard No. 1740), for the BP Tanker Company Ltd., London. 20.1.1976: Completed for Solamole Ltd. (BP Tanker Company Ltd., managers). 1981: Managers restyled as BP Shipping Ltd. 1990: Sold to BP Shipping Ltd. 1999: Owners restyled as BP Amoco Shipping Ltd. 2000: Sold for demolition.

BT. 443. BRITISH RENOWN (3) (1990–1994)

O.N. 363187. 133,035g. 108,854n. 270,025d. 338.64(BB) × 53.68 × 20.657 metres.
Two, steam turbines manufactured by the Nagasaki Shipbuilding & Engineering Works, Nagasaki, double reduction geared to screw shaft. 30,000 shp.
Very large crude carrier (VLCC)

10.11.1973: Launched by Mitsubishi Heavy Industries Ltd., Nagasaki (Yard No. 1703), for the BP Medway Tanker Company Ltd., London. 4.1974: Completed. 1978: Converted into a storage tanker. 1979: Re-converted into a tanker. 10.7.1984: At 12:02hrs local time, whilst en route to discharge TIBURON off Dubai was attacked by two Iranian aircraft at position 26.32N., 51.56.30E. Slight damage from a fire which was extinguished by crew. 11.7.1984: Arrived at Dubai Anchorage for repair to 1 metre diameter hole in Number Two starboard tank. 17.9.1984: Sailed for Gibraltar. 1985: Transferred to BP Thames Tanker Company Ltd. 1990: Transferred to BP Shipping Ltd., Bahamian registry. 1994: Demolished.

BT. 444. BRITISH RESOLUTION (2) (1990–1999)

O.N. 363468. 133,035g. 108,854n. 270,665d. 338.34(BB) × 53.62 × 20.708 metres.
Two, steam turbines manufactured by the shipbuilder, double reduction geared to screw shaft. 30,000 shp.
Very large crude carrier (VLCC)

5.7.1974: Launched by Mitsubishi Heavy Industries Ltd., Nagasaki (Yard No. 1704), for the BP Medway Tanker Company Ltd., London. 11.1974: Completed. 1978: Converted into a storage tanker. 1985: Transferred to BP Thames Tanker Company Ltd. 1986: Re-converted into a tanker. 1990: Transferred to BP Shipping Ltd. 1999: Owners restyled as BP Amoco Shipping Ltd. Previous to 25.12.1999: Arrived off Alang for demolition.

BT. 445. BRITISH TAMAR (1990–2000)

see ship No. Th. 5. in BP Thames Tanker section.

BT. 446. BRITISH ESK (1990–2001)

see ship No. Th. 7 in BP Thames Tanker section.

BT. 447. BRITISH FORTH (1990–1993)

see ship No. Th. 11 in BP Thames Tanker section.

BT. 448. BP ARGOSY (1991–1994)

O.N. 715350. 23,967g. 11,581n. 41,027d. 176.20(BB) × 30.82 × 11.525 metres.
6-cyl. 2 S.C.S.A. (520 × 1850mm) Mitsubishi 6UEC52LS type oil engine manufactured by the shipbuilder. 6,300 bhp.
Ocean-going refined products tanker.

4.6.1990: Keel laid by Mitsubishi Heavy Industries Ltd., Nagasaki (Yard No. 2033), for BP Shipping Ltd. 22.10.1990: Launched. 28.3.1991: Completed. 1994: Renamed BRITISH ARGOSY. 1999: Owners restyled as BP Amoco Shipping Ltd. 2.2004: Sold to Arctos Shipping Company Ltd., Marshall Islands, and renamed ARGOSY. Still listed in Lloyd's Register 2004/05.

BT. 449. AUSTRALIAN ACHIEVER (1991–1998)

see ship No. BT. 441 above.

BT. 450. BRITISH ADMIRAL (4) (1993–2004)

see ship No. BT. 438 above.

BT. 451. BRITISH ADVENTURE (2) (1994–2004)

see ship No. BT. 439 above.

BT. 452. BRITISH ARGOSY (2) (1994–2004)

see ship No. BT. 445 above.

British Argosy. (World Ship Society Photograph Library)

Cramond. (Tom Woolley – Targe Towing Ltd)

Dalmeny. (Tom Woolley – Targe Towing Ltd)

BT. 453. CRAMOND (1994–)

O.N. 722462. 449g. 134n. 34.85 × 11.13 × 4.650 metres.
Two, 8-cyl. 4 S.C.S.A. (256 × 310mm) 8 MDZC type oil engines manufactured by Anglo-Belgian Corp., B.V., Gent, geared to twin stern-mounted directional propellers. 4,800 bhp. Thwartship thrust propellers forward.
Fire-fighting pollution control tug.

23.4.1993: Keel laid by S.A. Balenciaga, Zumaya (Yard No.358), for BP Exploration Ltd. (Targe Towing Ltd., managers). 15.9.1993: Launched. 10.3.1994: Completed for BP Shipping Ltd., thence to Robert Fleming Leasing Ltd. (same managers).

BT. 454. DALMENY (1994–)

O.N. 722463. 449g. 134n. 34.85 × 11.13 × 4.650 metres.
Two, 8-cyl. 4 S.C.S.A. (256 × 310mm) 8 MDZC type oil engines manufactured by Anglo-Belgian Corp., B. V., Gent, geared to twin stern-mounted directional propellers. 4,800 bhp. Thwartship thrust propellers forward.
Fire-fighting polution control tug.

23.4.1993: Keel laid by S. A. Balenciaga, Zumaya (Yard No. 359), for BP Exploration Ltd. (Targe Towing Ltd., managers). 14.12.1993: Launched. 12.5.1994: Completed for BP Shipping Ltd, thence to Robert Fleming Leasing Ltd. (same managers).

BT. 455. HOPETOUN (1997–)

O.N. 730116. 947g. 184n. 43.50 × 14.20 × 6.040 metres.
Two, 16-cyl. 4 S.C.S.A. (250 × 30mm) Normo KVMB-16 oil engines manufactured by Ulstein Bergen A/S, Bergen, geared to twin stern-mounted directional propellers. 9,696bhp. Thwartship thrust controllable-pitch propellers forward.
Fire-fighting polution control tug.

27.2.1996: Keel laid by Const. Navale Santodomingo S. A., Vigo (Yard No. 610) for BP Shipping Ltd. 26.9.1996: Launched. 14.2.1997: Completed (Targe Towing Ltd., managers). 1999: Owners restyled as BP Amoco Shipping Ltd. 2001: Owners restyled as BP Shipping Ltd. 2003: Lloyd's Register amended owners to Targe Towing Ltd.

BT. 456. BRITISH STRENGTH (3) (1998)

see ship No. BT. 441 above.

Hopetoun. (Tom Woolley – Targe Towing Ltd)

Cancellations

MITSUBISHI cancellations. 2.1976.

Yard No. 1767–**BRITISH REALM** Very large crude carrier (VLCC) & 1768–**BRITISH RESTRAINT** Very large crude carrier (VLCC) both contracts re-negotiated by Airlease International as four multi-purpose cargo vessels for charter to Blue Funnel Line.

MENELAUS (1977–1980)

BARBER MENELAUS (1980–1984)

MENELAUS (1984–1989)

O.N. 378032. 16,031g. 8,666n.
164.62 × 26.04 × 10.624 metres.
7-cyl. 2 S.C.S. A. (760 × 1,550mm) Sulzer 7RND76M type motor engine manufactured by the shipbuilder, at Kobe. 16,800 bhp. 18 kts. Thwartship thrust controllable-pitch propeller forward.
Multi-purpose dry cargo & container vessel.

16.4.1977: Launched by Mitsubishi Heavy Industries Ltd., Nagasaki (Yard No. 1806), for Airlease International Nominees (Moorgate) Ltd. (on behalf of British Petroleum) London. 7.1977: Completed for lease to Ocean Transport & Trading Ltd., and management by Ocean Fleets Ltd. 14.12.1980: Renamed BARBER MENELAUS. 1982: Transferred to Barber Menelaus Shipping Corporation (same managers), Panama. 1984: Transferred to Airlease International Nominees (Moorgate) Ltd. (same managers), and renamed MENELAUS, under Liverpool registry. 8.2.1985: Ocean Marine Ltd., appointed as managers. 1988: Transferred to Isle of Man registry, Ocean Fleets Ltd., appointed as managers. 4.1989: Sold to Trade Green Shipping Corporation, Panama, and renamed TRADE GREEN. 12.1989: Registry transferred to St. Vincent and the Grenadines (Worlder Shipping Ltd., appointed as managers). 7.1995: Sold to Georgian Maritime Corporation (Chartworld Shipping Corporation, managers), St. Vincent and the Grenadines, and renamed NORTH SEA. 9.1995: Renamed MSC NICOLE. 4.1997: Renamed NORTH SEA. 15.1.1998: Arrived at Eleusis and laid up. 8.10.1999: Still in port. 2000: Returned to trading. 14.1.2001: Arrived at Alang for demolition.

MEMNON (1977–1980)

BARBER MEMNON (1980–1984)

MEMNON (1984)

LLOYD SAN FRANCISCO (1984 -1985)

MEMNON (1985–1989)

O.N. 378037. 16,031g. 8,666n.
164.62 × 26.07 × 10.630 metres.
7-cyl. 2 S.C.S. A. (760 × 1,550mm) Sulzer 7RND76M type motor engine manufactured by the shipbuilder, at Kobe. 16,800 bhp. 18 kts. Thwartship thrust controllable-pitch propeller forward.
Multi-purpose dry cargo & container vessel.

28.5.1977: Launched by Mitsubishi Heavy Industries Ltd., Nagasaki (Yard No. 1807), for Airlease International Nominees (Moorgate) Ltd. (on behalf of British Petroleum) London. 8.1977: Completed for lease to Ocean Transport & Trading Ltd., and management by Ocean Fleets Ltd. 14.12.1980: Renamed BARBER MEMNON. 1982: Transferred to Barber Menelaus Shipping Corporation (same managers), Panama. 1984: Transferred to Airlease International Nominees (Moorgate) Ltd. (same managers), and renamed MEMNON, under Liverpool registry. 1984: Renamed LLOYD SAN FRANCISCO. 8.2.1985: Ocean Marine Ltd., appointed as managers. 1986: Renamed MEMNON. 1987: Transferred to Isle of Man registry. 1988: Ocean Fleets Ltd., appointed as managers. 4.1989: Sold to Pacific International Lines (Private) Ltd., Panama, and renamed HAI XIONG. 1990: Sold to Hai Xiong Shipping Inc. (Pacific International Lines (Private) Ltd., managers), Singapore. 2000: Transferred to Panamanian flag. 21.12.2001: Arrived at Mumbai for demolition.

MELAMPUS (1977–1989)

O.N. 378039. 16,031g. 8,666n.
164.62 × 26.07 × 10.624 metres.
Post 1995: 17,146g. 9,381n.
7-cyl. 2 S.C.S. A. (760 × 1,550mm) Sulzer 7RND76M type motor engine manufactured by the shipbuilder, at Kobe. 16,800 bhp. 18 kts. Thwartship thrust controllable-pitch propeller forward.
Multi-purpose dry cargo & container vessel.

9.7.1977: Launched by Mitsubishi Heavy Industries Ltd., Nagasaki (Yard No. 1808), for Airlease International Nominees (Moorgate) Ltd. (on behalf of British Petroleum) London. 11.1977: Completed for lease to Ocean Transport & Trading Ltd., and management by Ocean Fleets Ltd. 8.2.1985: Ocean Marine Ltd., appointed as managers. 1987: Transferred to Isle of Man registry. 1988: Ocean Fleets Ltd., appointed as managers. 3.1989: Sold to N.V. CMB S. A., Belgium, and renamed CMB EBONY, retaining British registry. 1990: Sold to Bresso Ltd. (Anglo-Eastern Ship Management Ltd., managers), Hong Kong. 1997: Sold to Pamir Shipping Company Ltd. (Techomar Shipping Inc., managers), Cyprus. 4.2000: Renamed EBONY. 8.2001: Renamed DELMAS BANDIA. 2002: renamed EBONY. 3.10.2002: Arrived at Alang for demolition. 10.10.2002: Beached and Ispat Pvt.Ltd., commenced work.

MENESTHEUS (1977–1980)

BARBER MENESTHEUS (1980–1984)

MENESTHEUS (1984)

LLOYD PARANA (1984 -1985)

MENESTHEUS (1985–1986)

APAPA PALM (1986–1988)

O.N. 378040. 16,031g. 8,666n.
164.62 × 26.04 × 10.602 metres.
Post 1995: 17,146g. 9,381n.
7-cyl. 2 S.C.S. A. (760 × 1,550mm) Sulzer 7RND76M type motor engine manufactured by the shipbuilder, at Kobe. 16,800 bhp. 18 kts. Thwartship thrust controllable-pitch propeller forward.
Multi-purpose dry cargo & container vessel.

27.8.1977: Launched by Mitsubishi Heavy Industries Ltd., Nagasaki (Yard No. 1809), for Airlease International Nominees (Moorgate) Ltd. (on behalf of British Petroleum) London. 12.1977: Completed for lease to Ocean Transport & Trading Ltd., and management by Ocean Fleets Ltd. 4.11.1980: Renamed BARBER MENESTHEUS. 5.1.1982: Transferred to Barber Menelaus Shipping Corporation (same managers), Panama. 28.12.1983: Transferred to Airlease International Nominees (Moorgate) Ltd. (same managers). 1984: renamed MENESTHEUS, under Liverpool registry. 18.4.1984: Renamed LLOYD PARANA. 29.1.1985: Renamed MENESTHEUS. 8.2.1985: Ocean Marine Ltd., appointed as managers. 2.1986: Renamed APAPA PALM. 1987: Transferred to Isle of Man registry. 1988: Sold to N.V. CMB S. A., Belgium, and renamed CMB ESPRIT. 1990: Transferred to CMB Transport (Luxembourg) S. A. (Aemas Luxembourg S. A., managers), Luxembourg. 12.1992: Sold to Irvona Ltd. (Coldwell Ship Management (Agency) Ltd., Hong Kong, and renamed WOERMANN EXPERT. 1995: Anglo-Eastern Ship Management Ltd., appointed as managers. 1997: Sold to Twinsea Shipping Company Ltd. (Primera Maritime (Hellas) Ltd., managers), Cyprus. 6.2000: Renamed EXPERT. 9.2001: Renamed DELMAS SYCAMORE. Still listed in Lloyd's Register 2004/05.

4.10.1991: A letter of intent was issued by BP Shipping Ltd., to Mitsubishi Heavy Industries Ltd., Kobe, for the construction of a 20,000g. 33,000d. tanker.
12.1992: This letter proposal was cancelled.

Section Two

Managed

By The British Tanker Company, and their successors.

The British Tanker Company Ltd.
1955–Restyled as
The BP Tanker Company Ltd.
1981- Restyled as
BP Shipping Ltd.
1999- Restyled as
BP Amoco Shipping Ltd.
2001–Restyled as
BP Shipping Ltd.

M. 1. BRITISH LIGHT (1) (1917–1937)

O.N. 140499. 6,470g. 3,899n. 419.7 × 54.3 × 32.4 feet.
T.3-cyl. (28″, 46″ & 76″ × 51″) engine manufactured by the shipbuilder. 2,930 hp.
Ocean-going tanker.

12.1917: Completed by Palmer's Shipbuilding & Iron Company Ltd., Newcastle (Yard No. 878), for the Shipping Controller (The British Tanker Company Ltd., managers). 1919: Transferred to the Admiralty (same managers). 1937: Renamed OLWEN and removed from management. 1949: Sold to Gulf Steam Ships Ltd., Karachi, and renamed MUSHTARI. 1960: Sold to the Sindh Steel Corporation, Karachi, for demolition. 11.9.1960: Work commenced.

British Light. (World Ship Society Photograph Library)

M. 2. BRITISH STAR (1) (1917–1937)

O.N. 142377. 6,888g. 4,080n. 430.0 × 57.0 × 33.0 feet.
T.3-cyl. (27″, 45″ & 74″ × 54″) engine manufactured by the shipbuilder. 3,100 hp.
Ocean-going tanker.

3.1918: Completed by Swan, Hunter & Wigham, Richardson Ltd., Newcastle (Yard No. 1040), for the Shipping Controller (The British Tanker Company Ltd., managers). 1919: Transferred to the Admiralty (same managers). 1937: Renamed OLYNTHUS and removed from management. 1949: Sold to Ditta Luigi Pittaluga Vapori, Italy, and renamed PENSILVANIA. 1959: Sold for demolition in Italy.

M. 3. ARAS (1917–1918)

O.N. 101829. 3,210g. 2,088n. 325.0 × 42.7 × 21.0 feet.
T.3-cyl. (24″, 40½″ & 64″ × 42″) engine manufactured by the shipbuilder. 1,475 hp.
Ocean-going tanker.

30.3.1893: Launched by Palmer's Shipbuilding & Iron Company Ltd., Newcastle (Yard No. 672), for Bessler, Waechter & Company, London (Stephens & Mawson, managers). 6.1893: Completed. 1894: Transferred to the Aras Steam Ship Company Ltd. (Bessler, Waechter & Company, London) (Stephens & Mawson, managers). 1901: On dissolution of partnership, managers restyled as Stephens, Sutton & Stephens. 16.11.1917: The British Tanker Company Ltd., appointed as managers. 25.10.1918: Sold to Petroleum Steam Ship Company Ltd. 1930: Sold to Tito Campanella Societa di Nav., Italy, and renamed LINA CAMPANELLA. 5.1945: Taken as a prize by Yugoslavia in the Adriatic and allocated as a depot ship to the Yugoslavian navy. No further details located.

M. 4. KURA (1917–1918)

see ship No. BT. 34 in main fleet.

M. 5. RION (1917–1918)

O.N. 96150. 2,186g. 1,419n. 279.0 × 37.7 × 19.1 feet.
T.3-cyl. (22″, 35″ & 58″ × 39″) engine manufactured by the shipbuilder. 1,080 hp.
Ocean-going tanker.

17.6.1889: Launched by Palmer's Shipbuilding & Iron Company Ltd., Jarrow (Yard No. 629), for Rion Steam Ship Company Ltd. (Bessler, Waechter & Company, London). 1890: Stephens & Mawson, appointed as managers. 8.1889: Completed. 1901: On dissolution of partnership, managers restyled as Stephens, Sutton & Stephens. 16.11.1917: The British Tanker Company Ltd., appointed as managers. 25.10.1918: Sold to Petroleum Steamship Company Ltd. 8.4.1920: Sold to the Rion Steam Ship Company Ltd. (S. & J. Thompson, managers). 1923: Sold to Societa Armatrice Italiana, Italy, and renamed ITALIANO. 1925: Sold to F. Garolla, Italy, and renamed FEDERICO GAROLLA. 19.4.1930: Whilst on a voyage from Fiume to Novorossisk suffered an explosion and fire at a position off Zante and sank.

M. 6. SURAM (1917–1918)

O.N. 101828. 3,629g. 2,338n. 325.0 × 42.6 × 21.2 feet.
T.3-cyl. (25 3/16″, 40″ & 64″ × 42″) engine manufactured by George Clark Ltd., Sunderland. 1,435 hp.
Ocean-going tanker.

18.4.1893: Launched by James Laing, Sunderland (Yard No. 527), for the Suram Steam Ship Company Ltd. (Bessler, Waechter & Company, London) (Stephens & Mawson, managers). 5.1893: Completed. 1901: On

Aras. (World Ship Society Photograph Library)

dissolution of partnership, managers restyled as Stephens, Sutton & Stephens. 16.11.1917: Purchased by Aras Steam Ship Company Ltd. (The British Tanker Company Ltd., managers), London. 25.10.1918: Sold to Petroleum Steamship Company Ltd. 13.1.1920: Sold to the Anglo-Saxon Petroleum Company Ltd., London, and renamed BITHINA. 5.1931: Sold to Japanese shipbreakers.

M. 7. BRITISH LANTERN (1) (1918–1937)

O.N. 142604. 6,897g. 4,067n. 430.1 × 57.0 × 33.0 feet.
T.3-cyl. (27″, 45″ & 75″ × 54″) engine manufactured by the shipbuilder. 3,170 hp.
Ocean-going tanker.

8.1918: Completed by Workman, Clark & Company Ltd., Belfast (Yard No. 424), for the Shipping Controller (The British Tanker Company Ltd., managers). 1919: Transferred to the Admiralty (same managers). 1937: Renamed OLIGARCH and removed from management. 1.7.1943: Damaged by a torpedo from the German submarine U-453, at a position 40 miles NW of Derna. 14.4.1946: Scuttled with obsolete ammunition in the Red Sea.

M. 8. BRITISH BEACON (1) (1918–1937)163

O.N. 142670. 6,891g. 4,065n. 430.1 × 57.0 × 33.0 feet.
T.3-cyl. (27″, 45″ & 75″ × 54″) engine manufactured by the shipbuilder. 3,170 hp.
Ocean-going tanker.

10.1918: Completed by Workman, Clark & Company Ltd., Belfast (Yard No. 428), for the Shipping Controller (The British Tanker Company Ltd., managers). 1919: Transferred to the Admiralty (same managers). 1937: Renamed OLCADES and removed from management. 1948: Hulked. 18.4.1953: Arrived in tow at Blyth for demolition by Hughes, Bolckow Shipbreaking Company Ltd.

M. 9. EMIL GEORG VON STRAUSS (1918–1922)

O.N. 145188. 5,311g. 3,229n. 390.9 × 53.0 × 29.2 feet.
T.3-cyl. (24″, $39\frac{3}{4}$″ & $66\frac{1}{8}$″ × $47\frac{1}{4}$″) engine manufactured by Bremer-Vulkan, Vegesak. 1,910 hp.
Ocean-going tanker.

1914: Laid down as OLEX by Nordseewerke, Emden (Yard No. 52), for the Deutsche Petroleum Gesellschaft, Germany. 1917: Launched as EMIL GEORG VON STRAUSS.

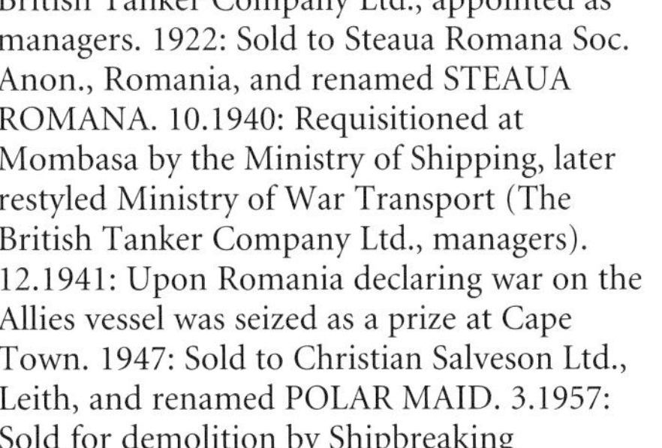

1918: Surrendered to British authorities (The British Tanker Company Ltd., appointed as managers. 1922: Sold to Steaua Romana Soc. Anon., Romania, and renamed STEAUA ROMANA. 10.1940: Requisitioned at Mombasa by the Ministry of Shipping, later restyled Ministry of War Transport (The British Tanker Company Ltd., managers). 12.1941: Upon Romania declaring war on the Allies vessel was seized as a prize at Cape Town. 1947: Sold to Christian Salveson Ltd., Leith, and renamed POLAR MAID. 3.1957: Sold for demolition by Shipbreaking Industries Ltd., Rosyth.

M. 10. WAR NIZAM (1918–1921)

O.N. 142691. 5,605g. 3,450n. 400.0 × 52.3 × 28.4 feet.
T.3-cyl. (27″, 44″ & 73″ × 48″) engine manufactured by the shipbuilder. 2,585 hp.
Ocean-going tanker.

8.1918: Launched by Palmers Shipbuilding & Iron Company Ltd., Newcastle (Yard No. 889), for the Shipping Controller (The British Tanker Company Ltd., managers). 10.1918: Completed. 1921: Transferred to the Admiralty. 1947: Sold to the Basinghall Shipping Company Ltd. (P. Bauer, manager), London, and renamed BASINGHALL. 1949: Sold to R. de Corle, 25, Rue Charles Rogieu, Antwerp, for demolition. 16.7.1949: Delivered at Antwerp.

M. 11. WAR RAJAH (1918–1920)

see ship No. BT. 35 in main fleet.

M. 12. WAR RAJPUT (1918–1920)

O.N. 142613. 5,562g. 3,472n. 400.0 × 52.4 × 28.4 feet.
T.3-cyl. (27″, 44″ & 73″ × 48″) engine manufactured by R. & W. Hawthorn, Leslie & Company Ltd., Newcastle. 2,585 hp.
Ocean-going tanker.

8.1918: Completed by Armstrong, Whitworth & Company Ltd., Newcastle (Yard No. 947), for the Shipping Controller (The British Tanker Company Ltd., managers). 13.1.1920: Sold to the Anglo-Saxon Petroleum Company Ltd. 1922: Renamed CONIA. 1924: Sold to British Molasses Ltd., and renamed ATHELBEACH. 1931: Sold to G. Ronneberg & F. Geltung, Norway, and renamed REALF. 1936: Sold to United Molasses Ltd., Liverpool, and renamed ATHELMERE. 1951: Sold to Mageolia Naviera S. A., Panama, and renamed ALEXANDROS. 15.3.1964: Arrived at Split for demolition.

Suram. (World Ship Society Photograph Library)

M. 13. WAR RANEE (1918–1920)

O.N. 142456. 5,559g. 3,447n. 400.0 × 52.3 × 28.4 feet.
T.3-cyl. (27″, 44″ & 73″ × 48″) engine manufactured by the shipbuilder. 2,585 hp.
Ocean-going tanker.

6.1918: Completed by Swan, Hunter & Wigham, Richardson Ltd., Newcastle (Yard No. 1052), for the Shipping Controller (The British Tanker Company Ltd., managers). 18.2.1920: Sold to the Anglo-Saxon Petroleum Company Ltd. 1922: Renamed CORBIS. 1928: Sold to F. Mowinckel, Norway, and renamed GRANLUND. 1931: Sold to H. R. Aass, Norway, and renamed SOLNA. 1939: Sold to the Hellenic Navy, Greece, and renamed ARGO. 1962: Entry removed from Lloyd's Register.

M. 14. WAR PARSEE (1919–1920)

Proposed: 5,559g. 3,447n. 400.0 × 52.3 × 28.4 feet.
As built: 4,697g. 2,894n. 384.8 × 52.0 × 26.7 feet.
T.3-cyl. (27″, 45″ & 74″ × 51″) engine manufactured by Rankin & Blackmore Ltd., Greenock. 2,585 hp.
Proposed as an ocean going tanker.

1919: Laid down as a tanker by Russell & Company Ltd.*, Port Glasgow (Yard No. 724), for the Shipping Controller (The British Tanker Company Ltd., managers). Subsequently sold and removed from management. 20.5.1920: Launched as BOGSTAD (dry cargo), for DS AS Aker, Norway. 30.7.1920: Completed by builders restyled Lithgows Ltd. 1921: Sold to AS Glittre (Fernley & Eger, managers), Norway. 1924: Sold to Kurohime Kisen Goshi Kaisha (Itaya Shosen K. K., managers), Japan, and renamed KUROHIME MARU. 30.3.1943: Whilst at position 00.22S., 147.46E., was sunk by the US submarine TUNA.

* Lloyd's Register 1923/24 quotes Lithgows Ltd as builders.

M. 15. WAR PESHWA (1919–1920)

Proposed: 5,559g. 3,447n. 400.0 × 52.3 × 28.4 feet.
As built: 4,818g. 2,875n. 384.7 × 52.0 × 26.7 feet.
T.3-cyl. (27″, 44″ & 73″ × 48″) engine manufactured by Rankin & Blackmore Ltd., Greenock. 2,585 hp.
Proposed as an ocean going tanker.

1919: Laid down as a tanker by Russell & Company Ltd., Port Glasgow (Yard No. 725), for the Shipping Controller (The British Tanker Company Ltd., managers). Subsequently sold whilst still under construction and removed from management. 30.7.1920: Launched as MAUDIE (whale oil refinery), for A/S Hvalen (N. Bugge), Norway. 9.1920: Completed by builders restyled Lithgows Ltd. 1937: Sold to B. Krogius, Finland, and renamed ANGRA. 1942: Sold to Finland-America Line, Finland, and renamed MERCATOR. 1943: Seized by German forces. 16.4.1945: Damaged by aircraft bombing at Hela in the Baltic Sea. 5.1945: Seized by British Authorities at Copenhagen, allocated to the Ministry of War Transport, and renamed EMPIRE CROUCH. 1946: Chartered to the Government of Finland and reverted to MERCATOR. 1948: Returned to Finland-America Line. 1951: Owners restyled as Finska Line. 1956: Sold to J. Nurminen, Finland, and renamed RUTH NURMINEN. 1959: Sold for demolition at Yokohama. 5.1959: Work commenced.

M. 16. WAR NAWAB (1919–1921)

O.N. 143383. 5,605g. 3,450n. 400.0 × 52.3 × 28.4 feet. T.3-cyl. (27″, 44″ & 73″ × 48″) engine manufactured by the shipbuilder. 2,585 hp.
Ocean-going tanker.

13.6.1919: Launched by Palmers Shipbuilding & Iron Company Ltd., Newcastle (Yard No. 886), for the Shipping Controller (The British Tanker Company Ltd., managers). 8.1919: Completed. 1921: Transferred to the Admiralty. 11.1946: Converted into an oil hulk. 26.7.1958: Arrived at Troon for demolition by West of Scotland Shipbreaking Company Ltd.

M. 17. WAR BEGUM (1919–1920)

O.N. 143358. 5,578g. 3,428n. 400.2 × 52.4 × 28.4 feet. T.3-cyl. (27″, 44″ & 73″ × 48″) engine manufactured by the shipbuilder. 2,585 hp.
Ocean-going tanker.

5.6.1919: Launched by Palmers Shipbuilding & Iron Company Ltd., Hebburn (Yard No. 890), for the Shipping Controller (The British Tanker Company Ltd., managers). 8.1919: Completed. 13.1.1920: Sold to the Anglo-Saxon Petroleum Company Ltd., 1922: Renamed CONUS. 1928: Sold to Sigurd Herlofsen, Norway, and renamed HERBORG. 1930: Sold to T. O. Tonnevald, Norway, and renamed THELMA. 1937: Sold to Kitagawa Sangyo Kaiun K. K., Japan, and renamed HOKKI MARU. 27.9.1944: Whilst at position 15.50N., 117.41E., was sunk by the US submarine LAPON.

M. 18. WAR BHARATA (1920–1921)

O.N. 144311. 5,826g. 3,424n. 400.2 × 52.4 × 28.4 feet. T.3-cyl. (27″, 44″ & 73″ × 48″) engine manufactured by the shipbuilder. 2,585 hp.
Ocean-going tanker.

24.11.1919: Launched by Palmers Shipbuilding & Iron Company Ltd., Newcastle (Yard No. 895), for the Shipping Controller (The British Tanker Company Ltd., managers). 30.3.1920: Completed. 1921: Transferred to the Admiralty. 1948: Sold to Verano Steamship Company Ltd. (Fred V. Andlaw, manager), London, and renamed WOLF ROCK. 5.1953: Arrived at Troon for demolition by West of Scotland Shipbreaking Company Ltd.

M. 19. WAR SUDRA (1920–1921)

O.N. 144527. 5,627g. 3,413n. 400.2 × 52.4 × 28.4 feet. T.3-cyl. (27″, 44″ & 73″ × 48″) engine manufactured by the shipbuilder. 2,585 hp.
Ocean-going tanker.

18.3.1920: Launched by Palmers Shipbuilding & Iron Company Ltd., Newcastle (Yard No. 893), for the Shipping Controller (The British Tanker Company Ltd., managers). 5,1920: Completed. 1921: Transferred to the Admiralty. 1948: Sold to the Oak Shipping Company Ltd. (Union Maritime & Shipping Company Ltd., managers), London. 1951: Renamed GERMAINE. 23.7.1954: Arrived at Pernis, from Constantza, and following discharge was laid up for sale. 11.11.1954: Sold to N. V. Frank Rijsdijk's Ond Ind. for demolition. 12.1954: Arrived at Hendrik Ido Ambacht for demolition.

M. 20. SCOTTISH BARD (1920–1923)

O.N. 142731. 5,549g. 3,480n. 400.0 × 52.4 × 28.5 feet. T.3-cyl. (27″, 44″ & 73″ × 48″) engine manufactured by Palmer's Shipbuilding & Iron Company Ltd., Newcastle. 2,585 hp.
Ocean-going tanker.

2.10.1918: Launched as WAR PUNDIT by Sir James Laing, Sunderland (Yard No. 673), for the Shipping Controller. 12.1918: Completed. 1.1920: Sold to Scottish American Oil & Transport Company Ltd., London, and renamed SCOTTISH BARD. 1920: Owners restyled as Tankers Ltd. (The British Tanker Company Ltd., appointed as managers). 1923: Management ceased. 1930: Sold to Corrado Soc. Anon. Di Nav., Italy, and renamed BACININ PADRE. 1940: Interned at Porto Cabello, Venezuela. 1941: Seized and allocated to Cia.Anonima Venezuelana de Navegacion, and renamed MANZANARES. 12.1941: Taken over by the United States War Shipping Administration, and renamed SWIVEL. 1943: Renamed SAINT MARY. 3.1944: Renamed CLYDE. 11.1945: Reverted to SWIVEL. 1948: Offered back to her Italian owners but was declined. 1950: Reported as abandoned in a damaged condition.

M. 21. SCOTTISH AMERICAN (1920–1923)

O.N. 144695. 6,981g. 4,420n. 425.0 × 57.0 × 33.1 feet. T.3-cyl. (27″, 45″ & 74″ × 54″) engine manufactured by G. Clark Ltd., Sunderland. 2,010 hp.
Ocean-going tanker.

29.6.1920: Launched by James Laing & Sons Ltd., Sunderland (Yard No. 667), for Scottish American Oil & Transport Company Ltd., London. 1920: Completed. 1920: Owners restyled as Tankers Ltd. (The British Tanker Company Ltd., appointed as managers). 1923: Management ceased. 27.4.1940: Whilst at position 58.41N. 04.40W., was damaged by a submarine torpedo. 1940: Reported as taken over by Admiralty. 1948: Re entered Lloyd's Register. 1949: Sold to Cia. Atlantica y Pacifica S. A., Panama, and renamed FAIRWATER. 8.2.1954: Societa Industriale Demolizioni Riparajioni Marittime, commenced demolition at Trieste.

M. 22. PANDO (1) (1921–1924)

see ship No. AP. 23 in APOC section.

M. 23. PERSO (1) (1921–1924)

see ship No. AP. 24 in APOC section.

M. 24. PETRO (1)/PHERO (1921–1924)

see ship No. AP. 25 in APOC section.

M. 25. PHILO (1921–1924)

see ship No. AP. 26 in APOC section.

M. 26. POILO (1) (1921–1924)

see ship No. AP. 27 in APOC section.

M. 27. SCOTTISH STANDARD (1921–1923)

O.N. 146137. 6,999g. 4,044n. 425.0 × 57.0 × 33.2 feet. Two, 6-cyl. 4 S.C.S.A. (24½″ × 39″) oil engines manufactured by the shipbuilder. 5,620 bhp
Ocean-going tanker.

8.5.1921: Launched by Vickers Ltd., Barrow in Furness (Yard No. 580), for Tankers Ltd. (the British Tanker Company Ltd., managers). 10.1921: Completed. 1923: Management ceased. 21.2.1941: Whilst at position 59.09N., 16.18W., was attacked by aircraft. 21.2.1941: Whilst at position 59.20N., 16.12W., was sunk by a torpedo from a German submarine.

M. 28. SCOTTISH MAIDEN (1921–1923)

O.N. 146198. 6,993g. 4,036n. 425.0 × 57.0 × 33.2 feet. Two, 6-cyl. 4 S.C.S.A. (24½″ × 39″) oil engines manufactured by the shipbuilder. 2,810 hp.
Ocean-going tanker.

7.7.1921: Launched by Vickers Ltd., Barrow in Furness (Yard No. 581), for Tankers Ltd. (The British Tanker Company Ltd., managers). 30.11.1921: Completed. 1923: Management ceased. 5.11.1940: Whilst at position 54.36N., 14.23W., was sunk by a torpedo from a German submarine.

M. 29. ST. PATRICE (1) (1922)

see ship No. BT. 45 in main fleet above.

M. 30. SCOTTISH MINSTREL (1922–1923)

O.N. 146531. 6,998g. 4,026n. 425.3 × 57.0 × 33.2 feet. Two, 6-cyl. 4 S.C.S.A. (24½″ × 39″) oil engines manufactured by the shipbuilder. 5,620 bhp.
Ocean-going tanker.

15.11.1921: Launched by Vickers Ltd., Barrow in Furness (Yard No. 582), for Tankers Ltd. (The British Tanker Company Ltd., managers). 3.1922: Completed. 1923: Management ceased. 16.7.1940: Whilst at position 56.10N., 10.20W., was damaged by a torpedo from a German submarine. 17.7.1940: Sank.

M. 31. SCOTTISH MUSICIAN (1922–1923)

O.N. 146597. 6,998g. 4,019n. 425.3 × 57.0 × 33.2 feet. Two, 6-cyl. 4 S.C.S.A. (24½″ × 39″) oil engines manufactured by the shipbuilder. 5,620 bhp.
Post 1946: Two, 5-cyl. 2 S.C.S.A. (19″ × 35″) B&W type oil engines manufactured by J. G. Kincaid & Company Ltd., Greenock. 3,956 bhp.

Scottish Bard. (World Ship Society Photograph Library)

Ocean-going tanker.
14.2.1922: Launched by Vickers Ltd., Barrow in Furness (Yard No. 583), for Tankers Ltd. (The British Tanker Company Ltd., managers). 7.1922: Completed. 1923: Management ceased. 1946: Re-engined. 1951: Sold to Mar de Sur Cia. Naviera S. A., Costa Rica., and renamed ASTER. 1954: Sold to General Shipping Finance Corp., Costa Rica, and renamed DARNEL. 1956: Transferred to Greek registry and renamed PINDOS. 1960: Sold for demolition.

M. 32. SCOTTISH STRATH (1922–1923)

O.N. 146586. 7,417g. 4,600. 440.8 × 57.4 × 34.0 feet.
T.3-cyl. (27″, 46″ & 77″ × 51″) oil engine manufactured by the shipbuilder. 2,120 hp.
Ocean-going tanker.
14.2.1922: Launched by Armstrong, Whitworth & Company Ltd., Newcastle (Yard No. 978), for Tankers Ltd. (The British Tanker Company Ltd., managers). 1922: Completed. 1923: Management ceased. 1938: Sold to A/S Jensens Rederi II (Jorgen P. Jensen, manager), Norway, and renamed MARIT II. 18.9.1946: Broke in two and sank 100 miles east of Cape Hatteras N.C., in a position 35.9N., 73.34W. 21.9.1946: Search for 11 missing persons called off.

M. 33. SCOTTISH CASTLE (1922–1923)

O.N. 146674. 7,417g. 4,524. 440.0 × 57.5 × 34.1 feet.
T.3-cyl. (27″, 46″ & 77″ × 51″) oil engine manufactured by the shipbuilder. 2,120 hp.
Ocean-going tanker.
14.2.1922: Launched by Armstrong, Whitworth & Company Ltd., Newcastle (Yard No. 979), for Tankers Ltd. (The British Tanker Company Ltd., managers). 1922: Completed. 1923: Management ceased. 1938: Sold to A/S Jensens Rederi II (Jorgen P. Jensen, manager), Norway, and renamed PETTER II. 28.11.1954: Arrived at Blyth from lay-up at Arendal, for demolition by Hughes, Bolckow Ltd.

M. 34. SCOTTISH BORDERER (1923)

O.N. 147498. 6,996g. 4,111n. 426.5 × 56.9 × 33.4 feet.
Two, 4-cyl. 2 S.C.S.A. ($23\frac{1}{2}$″ × $41\frac{3}{4}$″) oil engines manufactured by the shipbuilder. 1,935 bhp.
Ocean-going tanker.
19.4.1923: Launched by Wm. Denny & Bros. Ltd., Dumbarton (Yard No. 1139), for Tankers Ltd. (The British Tanker Company Ltd., managers). 1923: Completed. 1923: Management ceased. 1938: Sold to Braathens Rederi (L. G. Braathen, manager), Norway, and renamed BRARENA. 22.7.1941: Sunk by German aircraft at Naples.

Phenix. (World Ship Society Photograph Library)

M. 35. SCOTTISH HIGHLANDS (1923)

Proposed: 7,520g. 4,600n. 440.0 × 57.5 × 34.1 feet.
Two, 4-cyl. 2 S.C.S.A. ($23\frac{3}{8}$″ × $41\frac{7}{10}$″) oil engines manufactured by the shipbuilder. 1,935 bhp.
Ocean-going tanker.
1923: Laid down by Armstrong, Whitworth & Company Ltd., Newcastle (Yard No. 981), for Tankers Ltd. (The British Tanker Company Ltd., managers). 1923: Work suspended, management ceased and subsequently sold. 16.7.1924: Launched as LUBRAFOL. 9.1924: Completed for Soc. Anon d'Armement d'Industri et de Commerce, Belgium. 1933: Sold to Belgian Gulf Oil Company S. A. Belgium, same name. 1941: Transferred to the Gulf Oil Corporation, Panama, same name. 9.5.1942: Whilst on a voyage from Aruba to New York, was struck by a torpedo from the German submarine U-564, at position 26.26N., 80.00W, set ablaze and abandoned. 11.5.1942: 04:40hrs – reported as burning and drifting and subsequently sank.

M. 36. MELPOMENE (1940–1942)

O.N. 174215. 7,011g. 3,989n. 426.9 × 56.7 × 32.6 feet.
T.3-cyl. ($27\frac{9}{10}$″, $46\frac{1}{10}$″ & 76″ × $51\frac{9}{10}$″) engine manufactured by Societe Provincale de Construcione Navale, La Ciotat. 2,080 hp.
Ocean-going tanker.
1923: Completed by Chantiers et Ateliers de La Gironde, Bordeaux, for Compagnie Auxiliare de Navigation, France. 1940: Taken over by the Ministry of Shipping, later restyled Ministry of War Transport (The British Tanker Company Ltd., managers). 5.3.1942: Whilst on a voyage from Falmouth to Baton Rouge, via Belfast, was sunk by a torpedo from the Italian submarine FINZI, at position 23.35N., 62.39W.

M. 37. PHENIX (1940–1941)

O.N. 174206. 5,907g. 3,337n. 400.5 × 51.2 × 30.8 feet.
T.3-cyl. (27″, 44″ & 73″ × 48″) engine manufactured by D. Rowan & Company Ltd., Glasgow. 2,585 hp.
Ocean-going tanker.
10.1920: Completed as ORIFLAMME by Lithgows Ltd., Port Glasgow (Yard No. 740), for Oriflame Steam Ship Company Ltd. (Lane & MacAndrew Ltd., managers). 1921: Davies & Newman Ltd., appointed as managers. 1926: Sold to Cie. Havraise de Magasinage et de Transport, France, and renamed HENRI DESMARAIS. 1935: Sold to Courtage & Transports S. A., France, converted into a depot ship, and renamed PHENIX. 1940: Requisitioned by the Ministry of Shipping (The British Tanker Company Ltd., managers), and registered at Aden. 24.12.1941: Exploded a mine and sank in Haifa Harbour.

M. 38. EMPIRE OIL (1940–1941)

O.N. 165991. 8,145g. 47,43n. 463.2 × 61.2 × 33.1 feet.
6-cyl. 4 S.C.S.A. ($19\frac{1}{8}$″ × $59\frac{1}{16}$″) B&W type oil engine manufactured by J. G. Kincaid & Company Ltd., Greenock. 2,450 bhp.
Ocean-going tanker.
15.11.1940: Launched by Blythswood Shipbuilding Company Ltd., Glasgow (Yard No. 61), for the Ministry of Shipping (The British Tanker Company Ltd., appointed as managers). 2.1941: Completed, as DARKDALE, for the Admiralty and removed from management. 22.10.1941: Sunk by a torpedo from the German submarine U-68 whilst anchored off St. Helena, S. Atlantic.

M. 39. ROXANE (1940–1945)

O.N. 174213. 7,813g. 4,185n. 445.4 × 62.1 × 34.2 feet.
Two, 6-cyl. 4 S.C.S.A. ($21\frac{11}{16}$″ × $59\frac{1}{16}$″) oil engine manufactured by Burmeister & Wains Maskin og Shipsbyggeri, Copenhagen. 2,660 bhp.
Ocean-going tanker.
1929: Completed by Ateliers et Chantiers du Sud Ouest, Bordeaux (Yard No. 22), for Compagnie Auxiliare de Navigation, France. 1940: Taken over by the Ministry of Shipping, later restyled as Ministry of War Transport (The British Tanker Company Ltd., managers). 1945: Returned to owners. 30.10.1953: Arrived at Port de Bouc from

Scottish Musician in original funnel markings. (World Ship Society Photograph Library)

Oltenia. (World Ship Society Photograph Library)

Tripoli and laid up. 1954: Sold to Societe Anon Cantieri Navali Santa-Maria, Genoa, for demolition.

M. 40. EMPIRE DIPLOMAT (1940–1944)

see ship No. BT. 79 in main fleet.

M. 41. STEAUA ROMANA (1941–1947)

see ship No. M. 9 above.

M. 42. OLTENIA/OLTENIA II (1941–1943)

O.N. 159351. 6,394g. 3,845n. 423.7 × 55.3 × 32.4 feet.
Q.4-cyl. ($25^1/_2$", $36^1/_2$" $52^1/_4$" & 75" × 48") engine manufactured by the Wallsend Slipway Company Ltd. 2,665 hp.
Ocean-going tanker.

6.3.1928: Launched as OLTENIA by Armstrong, Whitworth & Company Ltd., Newcastle (Yard No. 1031), for Steaua Romana Soc. Anon., Romania. 4.1928: Completed. 1940: Taken over by the Ministry of Shipping, later restyled Ministry of War Transport (The British Tanker Company Ltd., managers). 1941: Renamed OLTENIA II and transferred to the Kenya Registry. 29.3.1942: Damaged by aircraft bombing at position 18.36N., 85.33E. 8.1.1943: Whilst on a voyage in Convoy TM 1 from Trinidad to E. Africa was sunk with two torpedoes by the German submarine U-436, at position 27.59 N., 28.50W.

M. 43. EMPIRE GEM (1941–1942)

O.N. 168691. 8,139g. 7,234n. 463.2 × 61.2 × 33.1 feet.
8-cyl. 4 S.C.S.A. ($25^9/_{16}$" × $55^1/_8$") B&W type oil engine manufactured by the shipbuilder. 2,510 bhp.
Ocean-going tanker.

29.5.1941: Launched by Harland & Wolff Ltd., Glasgow (Yard No. 1045 G), for the Ministry of War Transport (The British Tanker Company Ltd., managers). 9.1941: Completed. 24.1.1942: Broke in two when torpedoed by the German submarine U-66, at position 35.06N., 74.58W., off the Virginia Capes, U.S.A. The after part sank and the forepart remained afloat for some time before eventually sinking at position 35.02N., 75.33W.

M. 44. EMPIRE SAPPHIRE (1941–1942)

O.N. 164847. 8,031g. 4,693n. 463.5 × 61.2 × 33.0 feet.
T.3-cyl. (27", 44" & 76" × 51") engine manufactured by Richardsons, Westgarth & Company Ltd., Hartlepool. 3,370 hp.
Ocean-going tanker.

9.8.1940: Keel laid by Furness Shipbuilding Company Ltd., Haverton Hill on Tees (Yard No. 329), for the Ministry of War Transport (The British Tanker Company Ltd., managers). 27.5.1941: Launched. 7.1941: Completed. 1942: Anglo-American Oil Company Ltd., appointed as managers. 1943: The British Tanker Company Ltd., re-appointed as managers. 1945: Anglo-American Oil Company Ltd., re-appointed as managers. 1946: Sold to the Anglo-American Oil Company Ltd. (R. A. Carder, manager), London, and renamed ESSO SARANAC. 23.9.1947: Suffered a boiler explosion whilst in a position 36.20N., 71.25W. during a voyage from Corpus Christi to Hull. Towed to Norfolk, USA for repairs and boiler re-tubing. 31.10.1947: Departed Norfolk following repairs. 1951: Sold to the Esso Petroleum Company Ltd. (Esso Transportation Company Ltd., managers), London. 1958: Laid up at Fawley. 25.1.1959: Arrived at Antwerp for demolition by Scrappingco S. A.

M. 45. EMPIRE TROPHY (1941–1944)

O.N. 162277. 5,211g. 2,875n. 416.7 × 51.2 × 28.3 feet.
Two, T.3-cyl. ($23^3/_5$", $38^3/_5$" & $63^4/_5$" × $35^2/_5$") engines manufactured by the shipbuilder. 2,420 hp
Ocean-going tanker.

1916: Completed as GIOVE by Cantieri Navali Riuniti, Palermo, for Italian State Railways. 1941: Taken as a prize by the Royal Navy and allocated to the Ministry of War Transport (The British Tanker Company Ltd., managers), and renamed EMPIRE TROPHY. 2.9.1944: Laid-up at Bombay. 21.3.1947: Sold to local Bombay shipbreakers.

M. 46. EMPIRE PERI (1941–1946)

O.N. 168224. 4,769g. 2,861n. 392.2 × 47.1 × 31.3 feet.
Two, T.3-cyl. ($22^3/_5$", $36^2/_5$" & $60^3/_5$" × $39^3/_8$") engines manufactured by the shipbuilder. 2,300 hp.
Ocean-going tanker.

1905: Completed as BRONTE by Fratelli Orlando, Leghorn, for the Italian Navy. 25.8.1941: Whilst at Bandar Shapur was taken as a prize by the Royal Navy, allocated to the Ministry of War Transport (The British Tanker Company Ltd., managers), and renamed EMPIRE PERI. 1946: Laid up in use as a water supply vessel at Bombay. 1947: Demolished by local Bombay shipbreakers.

M. 47. EMPIRE PRIZE (1941–1943)

O.N. 149881. 3,245g. 2,0255n. 292.3 × 47.2 × 26.9 feet.
Two, 4-cyl. 2 S.C.S.A. (20 $^1/_2$" × 29 $^1/_2$") oil engines manufactured by J. & C. G. Bollinger Company Ltd., Skarham. 286 nhp.
Post 1927: Two, T.3-cyl. (18", $26^1/_2$" & 42" × 27") engines manufactured in 1913 by the London & Glasgow Engineering & Iron Shipbuilding Company Ltd., Glasgow. 1,490 hp.
Ocean-going tanker.

1917: Completed as HOLDEN EVANS by the Baltimore Shipbuilding Corp., Baltimore (Yard No. 76), for the Holden Evans Steamship Company, U.S.A. 1926: Sold to European Shipping Company Ltd. (A. A. Rapp, manager), London, and renamed OLVIGORE. 1927: Re-engined and renamed OILVIGOR. 1930: Sold to Titi Campanella fu Pietro, Italy, and renamed CLELIA CAMPANELLA. 8.4.1941: Whilst at Massowah, was scuttled alongside to avoid capture by British forces. Subsequently salvaged by Royal Naval personnel, declared a prize, allocated to the Ministry of War Transport (The British Tanker Company Ltd., managers), and renamed EMPIRE PRIZE. 1943: Anglo-Saxon Petroleum Company Ltd., appointed as managers. 1946: Purchased by the Anglo-Saxon Petroleum Company Ltd., and renamed BANKIVIA. 10.1949: Demolished at Hong Kong.

M. 48. EMPIRE TAJ (1941–1948)

O.N. 168225. 3,065g. 1,825n. 313.0 × 43.7 × 25.1 feet.
T.3-cyl. ($21^1/_{16}$", $34^1/_2$" & 57" × 42") engine manufactured by the shipbuilder. 1,375 hp.
Ocean-going tanker.

1912: Completed as L. V. STODDARD by Toledo Shipbuilding Corp., Toledo (Yard No. 125), for the Boston Virginia Transportation Corp. 1914: Sold to Sinclair Gulf Corp., U.S.A., and renamed WALTER HARDCASTLE. 1917: Owners restyled as Sinclair Navigation Corp., and vessel renamed W. L. CONNELLY. 1937: Sold to Enrico Insom, Italy, and renamed BARBARA. 25.8.1941: Whilst at Bandar Shapur, was taken as a prize by the Royal Navy, towed to Karachi, allocated to the Ministry of War Transport (The British Tanker Company Ltd., managers), and renamed EMPIRE TAJ. 1948: Laid up at Abadan. 10.1949: Sold to the Pakistan Navy for employment as a fuel hulk at Karachi, and renamed ATTOCK. Subsequently demolished.

M. 49. EMPIRE ONYX (1941–1942)

O.N. 168703. 8,220g. 4,768n. 465.6 × 59.5 × 33.8 feet.
8-cyl. 4 S.C.S.A. ($25^9/_{16}$" × $55^1/_8$") B&W type oil engine manufactured by the shipbuilder. 2,510 bhp.
Ocean-going tanker.

21.8.1941: Launched by Harland & Wolff Ltd., Glasgow (Yard No. 1083 G), for the Ministry of War Transport (The British Tanker Company Ltd., managers). 25.12.1941: Completed. 1942: Transferred to the Government of Norway and renamed NORTIND. 20.6.1942: Damaged by a torpedo from the German submarine U-67, whilst in the Gulf of Mexico, at position 28.41N., 89.34W. Returned to New Orleans thence Mobile for repairs. 26.1.1943: Whilst straggling from Convoy HX 223 (Curacao – New York – Liverpool), was sunk by a torpedo from the German submarine U-358, at position 58.40N., 33.10W., east of Cape Farewell, Greenland.

M. 50. EMPIRE JET (1941–1942)

O.N. 168683. 8,134g 4,821n. 463.2 × 61.2 × 33.0 feet.
6-cyl. 4 S.C.S.A. ($29^1/_8$" × $59^1/_{16}$") B&W type oil engine manufactured by J. G. Kincaid & Company Ltd., Glasgow. 2,450 bhp.

Ocean-going tanker.
27.5.1941: Launched by Blythswood Shipbuilding Company Ltd., Glasgow (Yard No. 63), for the Ministry of War Transport (The British Tanker Company Ltd., managers). 8.1941: Completed. 1942: C. T. Bowring & Company Ltd., appointed as managers. 1946: Purchased by the Bowring Steamship Company Ltd. (same managers), and renamed REGENT JAGUAR. 2.6.1958: Arrived at Briton Ferry for demolition by T. W. Ward Ltd., Sheffield.

M. 51. EMPIRE PICT (1941–1942)

O.N. 168700. 8,145g. 4,761n. 463.2 × 61.2 × 33.0 feet.
6-cyl. 4 S.C.S.A. (29 1/8″ × 59 1/16″) B&W type oil engine manufactured by J. G. Kincaid & Company Ltd., Greenock. 2,450 bhp.
Ocean-going tanker.
11.9.1941: Launched by Blythswood Shipbuilding Company Ltd., Glasgow (Yard No. 64), for the Ministry of Shipping (The British Tanker Company Ltd., appointed as managers). 11.1941: Completed. 1942: Transferred to the Government of Norway (Norwegian Shipping and Trade Mission, managers), Norway, and renamed NORLAND. 20.5.1942: Whilst on a ballast voyage from Clyde to Corpus Christi, in Convoy ON93 was sunk by a torpedo from the German submarine U-108, at position 31.29N., 55.37W.

M. 52. EMPIRE DIAMOND (1941–1942)

O.N. 168507. 8,236g. 4,794n. 465.6 × 59.5 × 34.0 feet.
8-cyl. 4 S.C.S.A. (25 9/16″ × 55 1/8″) B&W type motor engine manufactured by the shipbuilder. 2,510 bhp
Ocean-going tanker.
10.7.1941: Launched by Harland & Wolff Ltd., Belfast (Yard No. 1053), for the Ministry of Shipping (The British Tanker Company Ltd., appointed as managers). 11.1941: Completed. 1942: Transferred to the Government of Norway, and renamed NORSOL. 1946: Sold to A/S Kollbjorg (Odd Berg, manager), Norway, and renamed KOLLBJORG. 1956: Sold to Rederi Norland (Oddmark and Anderssen, managers), Sweden, and renamed STORO. 20.11.1959: Delivered at Hong Kong for demolition.

M. 53. EMPIRE CHAPMAN (1942–1946)

see ship No. BT. 164 in main fleet.

M. 54. EMPIRE CORPORAL (1942)

see ship No. BT. 48 in main fleet.

M. 55. JOSEFINA THORDEN (1942–1943)

O.N. 165827. 6,620g. 3,809n. 408.1 × 55.2 × 32.4 feet.
Two, 6-cyl. 4 S.C.S.A. (21 5/8″ × 39 3/8″) oil engines manufactured by the shipbuilder. 2,714 bhp.
Ocean-going tanker.
1932: Completed by Eriksbergs Mek. Verksted AB, Gothenburg (Yard No. 246), for Suomi Tankers AB (G. Thorden, manager), Finland. 1942: Taken over by The Ministry of War Transport (The British Tanker Company Ltd., appointed as managers). 6.4.1943: Whilst on a voyage from Curacao to Shellhaven, exploded a mine at a position near Sunk Head Buoy, Thames Estuary, beached to prevent sinking but later became a total loss.

M. 56. EMPIRE METAL (1942–1943)

O.N. 168730. 8,201g. 4,768n. 465.6 × 59.5 × 33.8 feet.
8-cyl. 4 S.C.S.A. (25 9/16″ × 55 1/8″) B&W type oil engine manufactured by the shipbuilder. 2,510 bhp.
Ocean-going tanker.
30.6.1942: Launched by Harland & Wolff Ltd., Glasgow (Yard No. 1160 G), for the Ministry of War Transport (The British Tanker Company Ltd., managers). 24.9. 1942: Completed. 2.1.1943: Sunk by aircraft bombing at Bone Harbour, Algeria. 8.1949: Raised and broke into two pieces. 5.1950: Afterpart removed and demolished on the beach at Grenouilliere. 29.8.1950: Forepart arrived at Savona for demolition. Machinery removed and shipped to Canada for re-conditioning. 1954: Machinery fitted to CAPTAIN C. D. SECORD (6,943g./1900).

M. 57. EMPIRE SAPPHIRE (1943–1945)

see ship No. M. 44 above.

M. 58. EMPIRE MACCABE (1943–1946)

see ship No. BT. 166 in main fleet.

M. 59. EMPIRE MACKAY (1943–1946)

see ship No. BT. 169 in main fleet.

M. 60. EMPIRE MACCOLL (1943–1946)

see ship No. BT. 167 in main fleet.

M. 61. EMPIRE ALLIANCE (1944–1945)

see ship No. BT. 155 in main fleet.

M. 62. EMPIRE CAVALIER (1944–1946)

see ship No. BT. 153 in main fleet.

M. 63. EMPIRE GARRICK (1944–1945)

see ship No. BT. 156 in main fleet.

M. 64. EMPIRE WORDSWORTH (1944–1945)

see ship No. BT. 154 in main fleet.

M. 65. EMPIRE MARS (1944–1946)

O.N. 180153. 8,199g. 4,644n. 473.0 × 64.1 × 35.6 feet.
Two, steam turbines manufactured by Metropolitan Vickers Electric Company Ltd., Manchester, geared to a single screw shaft. (6,180 shp).
Ocean-going tanker.
16.11.1944: Launched by Sir James Laing & Sons Ltd., Sunderland (Yard No. 755), for The Ministry of War Transport (The British Tanker Company Ltd., managers). 4.1945: Completed. 1946: Owners restyled The Ministry of Transport (Hadley Shipping Company Ltd., London, appointed as managers). 1946: Renamed WAVE DUKE. 1947: Transferred to the Admiralty, and removed from management. 1964: Owners restyled as The Secretary of State for Defence (Naval Department), Royal Fleet Auxiliary service appointed as managers/operators. 25.12.1969: Arrived in tow at Bilbao, from Plymouth to be demolished.

M. 66. EMPIRE JUPITER (1944–1946)

O.N. 169429. 8,217g. 4,773n. 465.6 × 59.5 × 33.8 feet.
6-cyl. 4 S.C.S.A. (29 1/8″ × 59 1/16″) B&W type oil engine manufactured by the shipbuilder. 3,200 bhp.
Ocean-going tanker.
21.9.1944: Launched by Harland & Wolff Ltd., Glasgow (Yard No. 1243 G), for the Ministry of War Transport (The British Tanker Company Ltd., managers), London. 29.12.1944: Completed. 1946: Sold to the Government of France (Ministere de la Marine Marchande) (Soc. Anon Les Petroles d'Outre-Mer, appointed as managers), and renamed SAINT GAUDENS. 1948: Sold to Soc. Anon Les Petroles d'Outre-Mer, France, and renamed SEVANE. 1958: Sold to Jugoslavenska Tankerska Plovidba, Yugoslavia, and renamed PROGRES. 9.11.1970: Arrived at Split for demolition by Brodospas.

M. 67. EMPIRE ENSIGN (1944–1946)

see ship No. BT. 165 in main fleet.

M. 68. EMPIRE BOMBARDIER (1944–1946)

see ship No. BT. 162 in main fleet.

M. 69. EMPIRE MILNER (1945–1946)

O.N. 169143. 8,135g. 4,634n. 473.8 × 64.3 × 35.4 feet.
Two steam turbines manufactured by Richardsons, Westgarth & Company Ltd., Hartlepool, geared to a single screw shaft. (6,050 shp).
Ocean-going tanker.
1.3.1943: Keel laid by the Furness Shipbuilding Company Ltd., Haverton Hill on Tees (Yard No. 358), for The Ministry of War Transport (Anglo-Saxon Petroleum Company Ltd., managers). 9.2.1944: Launched. 6.1944: Completed. 1945: The British Tanker Company Ltd., appointed as managers. 1946: Owners restyled Ministry of Transport (Hadley Shipping Company Ltd., London, appointed as managers). 1946: Renamed WAVE LIBERATOR. 1947: Transferred to the Admiralty, and removed from management. 1958: Sustained collision damage and was laid-up at Bombay. 5.4.1959: Departed Bombay, in tow of GOLDEN CAPE (525g./42). 2.5.1959: Arrived at Hong Kong. 4.5.1959: The Hong Kong Salvage & Towage Company Ltd., commenced demolition.

M. 70. TARASCON (1945–1946)

O.N. 180617. 3,235g. 2,041n. 309.2 × 48.4 × 21.9 feet.
Post 1963: 3,930g. 2,381n. 382′ 2″ × 48′ 5″ × 18′ 11 1/4″
6-cyl. 2 S.C.S.A. (18″ × 25″) oil engine manufactured by Nordberg Manufacturing Corp., Milwaukee. 1,400 bhp.
Ocean-going tanker.
7.1945: Completed by the Todd Houston Shipbuilding Corporation, Houston (Yard No. 209), for the United States War Shipping Administration, chartered to the Ministry of War Transport (The British Tanker Company Ltd., managers). 1946: Released from charter. 1947: Sold to N. V. Standard Vacuum Tankvaart Maatschappij, Netherlands, and renamed TALANG AKAR. 1948: Renamed STANVAC TALANG AKAR. 1950s: Sold to Panama Transport Corp., Panama. 1962: Sold to Esso Transport Company Inc., Panama, and renamed ESSO TALANG AKAR. 1963: Lengthened, converted into a partial liquified gas carrier and renamed ESSO ADVANCE. 1972: Sold to Luzon Stevedoring Corp., Philippines, and renamed LSCO PEGASUS. 28.4.1973: Tai Kien Industry Company Ltd., commenced demolition at Kaohsiung.

M. 71. TARANTELLA (1945–1946)

O.N. 180618. 3,235g. 2,041n. 309.2 × 48.4 × 21.9 feet.

6-cyl. 2 S.C.S.A. (18″ × 25″) oil engine manufactured by Nordberg Manufacturing Corp., Milwaukee. 1,400 bhp. Ocean-going tanker.

8.1945: Completed by the Todd Houston Shipbuilding Corporation, Houston (Yard No. 210), for the United States War Shipping Administration, chartered to the Ministry of War Transport, London (The British Tanker Company Ltd., managers). 1946: Released from charter. 1947: Sold to Nederlandsche Kol Tankvaart Maatschappij, Netherlands, and renamed DJIRAK. 1948: Sold to Standard Vacuum Oil Company Ltd., Panama, and renamed STANVAC DJIRAK. 1957: Sold to N.V. Standard Vacuum Tankvaart Maatschappij, Netherlands,. 1958: Sold to the Petroleum Shipping Company Ltd., Panama. 1963: Sold to the Petroleum Shipping Services Company Inc., Panama, and renamed REGULUS. 1972: Renamed ESSO REGULUS. 15.1.1976: Grounded on Mengalum Island. 17.1.1976: Refloated and declared as beyond economical repair. 3.3.1976: Arrived at Hong Kong for demolition by Loy Kee Shipbreaker and Transportation Company. 5.4.1976: Work commenced.

M. 72. TARAUCA (1945)

**O.N. 180630. 3,235g. 2,041n. 309.2 × 48.4 × 21.9 feet.
Post 1962: 4,596g. 2,968n. 382′ 3″ × 48′ 4″ × 19′ 10¾″
6-cyl. 2 S.C.S.A. (18″ × 25″) oil engine manufactured by Nordberg Manufacturing Corp., Milwaukee. 1,400 bhp.**

8.1945: Completed by the Todd Houston Shipbuilding Corporation, Houston (Yard No. 211), for the United States War Shipping Administration, chartered to the Ministry of War Transport, London (The British Tanker Company Ltd., managers). 1945: Released from charter. 1945: Renamed MONTEBELLO. 1947: Sold to Cia. De Petroleo Lago, Venezuela, and renamed ESSO VENEZUELA. 1962: Sold to Esso Transport Company Inc., Panama, lengthened and converted into a LPG carrier by A. G. 'Weser', Bremerhaven, and renamed ESSO CENTRO AMERICA. 11.1962: Old midship section scrapped at Hamburg. 1969: Sold to Mundogas (Storage) Inc., Panama. 12.6.1969: Arrived in tow at Zeebrugge for conversion into a storage vessel. Subsequently renamed MONOMER VENTURE and towed to Porsgrunn. 1984: Sold to Gulf Gas S. A., Panama, and renamed GAS VENTURE. 1992: Sold for demolition.

M. 73. EMPIRE ARROW (1945–1946)

see ship No. BT. 163 in main fleet.

M. 74. TARCOOLA (1945)

**O.N. 180629. 3,235g. 2,041n. 309.2 × 48.4 × 21.9 feet.
6-cyl. 2 S.C.S.A. (18″ × 25″) oil engine manufactured by Nordberg Manufacturing Corp., Milwaukee. 1,400 bhp. Ocean-going tanker.**

9.1945: Completed by the Todd Houston Shipbuilding Corporation, Houston (Yard No. 212), for the United States War Shipping Administration, chartered to the Ministry of War Transport, London (The British Tanker Company Ltd., managers). 1945: Released from charter and renamed BELRIDGE. 1950: NODAWAY (AOG 78) United States Navy Reserve. No further details.

M. 75. TARLAND (1945–1946)

**O.N. 180619. 3,235g. 2,041n. 309.2 × 48.4 × 21.9 feet.
6-cyl. 2 S.C.S.A. (18″ × 25″) oil engine manufactured by Nordberg Manufacturing Corp., Milwaukee. 1,400 bhp. Ocean-going tanker.**

10.1945: Completed by the Todd Houston Shipbuilding Corporation, Houston (Yard No. 213), for the United States War Shipping Administration, chartered to the Ministry of War Transport, London (The British Tanker Company Ltd., managers). 1946: Released from charter. 1950: Renamed RINCON (AOG 77) United States Navy Reserve. No further details.

M. 76. TARLETON (1945)

**O.N. 180620. 3,235g. 2,041n. 309.2 × 48.4 × 21.9 feet.
6-cyl. 2 S.C.S.A. (18″ × 25″) oil engine manufactured by Nordberg Manufacturing Corp., Milwaukee. 1,400 bhp. Ocean-going tanker.**

10.1945: Completed by the Todd Houston Shipbuilding Corporation, Houston (Yard No. 214), for the United States War Shipping Administration, chartered to the Ministry of War Transport, London (The British Tanker Company Ltd., managers). 1945: Released from charter and renamed KONAWA. 1947: Sold to Argentine Government (Yacimientos Petroliferos Fiscales), and renamed SAN CLEMENTE. 1982: Sold for demolition.

M. 77. TAROGLE (1945)

**O.N. 180621. 3,235g. 2,041n. 309.2 × 48.4 × 21.9 feet.
6-cyl. 2 S.C.S.A. (18″ × 25″) oil engine manufactured by Nordberg Manufacturing Corp., Milwaukee. 1,400 bhp. Ocean-going tanker.**

10.1945: Completed by the Todd Houston Shipbuilding Corporation, Houston (Yard No. 215), for the United States War Shipping Administration, chartered to the Ministry of War Transport, London (The British Tanker Company Ltd., managers). 1945: Released from charter and renamed TINSLEY. 1948: Sold to Tide Water Associated Oil Company, U.S.A., and renamed TYDOL FLYING A. 1959: Transferred to Tidewater Oil Company, U.S.A., and renamed PROVIDENCE GETTY. Subsequently sold to Getty Oil Company, U.S.A. 1974: Transferred to Getty Oil (Eastern Operations) Inc., U.S.A. 1978: Transferred to Getty Refining and Marketing Company. 1980: Sold to Ecuanave C. A., Ecuador, and renamed CRISTINA E.

M. 78. TARLAC (1945)

**O.N. 180622. 3,235g. 2,041n. 309.2 × 48.4 × 21.9 feet.
6-cyl. 2 S.C.S.A. (18″ × 25″) oil engine manufactured by Nordberg Manufacturing Corp., Milwaukee. 1,400 bhp. Ocean-going tanker.**

10.1945: Completed by the Todd Houston Shipbuilding Corporation, Houston (Yard No. 216), for the United States War Shipping Administration, chartered to the Ministry of War Transport, London (The British Tanker Company Ltd., managers). 1945: Released from charter and renamed LANCE CREEK. 1947: Sold to N. V. Standard Vacuum Tankvaart Maatschappij, Netherlands, and renamed STANVAC PENDOPO. 1958: Sold to Petroleum Shipping Company Ltd., Panama. 1963: Transferred to Petroleum Shipping services Company Inc., Panama, and renamed CANOPUS. 1972: Transferred to Petroleum Tankship Company Inc., Panama. 1978: Sold for demolition.

M. 79. TARVES (1945)

**O.N. 180625. 3,235g. 2,041n. 309.2 × 48.4 × 21.9 feet.
6-cyl. 2 S.C.S.A. (18″ × 25″) oil engine manufactured by Nordberg Manufacturing Corp., Milwaukee. 1,400 bhp. Ocean-going tanker.**

10.1945: Completed by the Todd Houston Shipbuilding Corporation, Houston (Yard No. 217), for the United States War Shipping Administration, chartered to the Ministry of War Transport, London (The British Tanker Company Ltd., managers). 1945: Released from charter and renamed HEWITT 1946: Sold to Esso Standard Oil (Central America) S. A., Panama, and renamed ESSO GUATEMALA. 1958: Transferred to Esso Standard Oil S. A., Panama. 1965: Sold to Mustang Island Inc., Panama, and renamed MUSTANG ISLAND. 1968: Sold to Societe Petromer, France, and renamed GARONNE. 1970: Sold to Cie. Europeene d'Armement, France. 2.1973: Ferrobirques commenced demolition at Bilbao.

M. 80. EMPIRE FITZROY (1945–1946)

**O.N. 169450. 890g. 379n. 193.0 × 32.0 × 14.5 feet.
4-cyl. 2 S.C.S.A. (13⅜″ × 22⁷⁄₁₆″) Polar type oil engine manufactured by British Polar Engines Ltd., Glasgow. 1,250 bhp.
Coastal refined products tanker.**

12.6.1945: Launched by A. & J. Inglis Ltd., Glasgow (Yard No. 1301p), for The Ministry of War Transport (The British Tanker Company Ltd., managers). 9.10.1945: Completed. 1946: Owners restyled as The Ministry of Transport (The Anglo-Saxon Petroleum Company Ltd., managers). 1950: Coastal Tankers Ltd., appointed as managers. 1952: Sold to Everard Shipping Company Ltd., London, and renamed ALIGNITY. 18.11.1971: Hughes, Bolckow Ltd., commenced demolition at Blyth.

Empire Fitzroy. (World Ship Society Photograph Library)

M. 81. TARTARY (1945)

O.N. 180624. 3,235g. 2,041n. 309.2 × 48.4 × 21.9 feet.
6-cyl. 2 S.C.S.A. (18″ × 25″) oil engine manufactured by Nordberg Manufacturing Corp., Milwaukee. 1,400 bhp.
Ocean-going tanker.

11.1945: Completed by the Todd Houston Shipbuilding Corporation, Houston (Yard No. 218), for the United States War Shipping Administration, chartered to the Ministry of War Transport, London (The British Tanker Company Ltd., managers). 1945: Released from charter and renamed SEGNO. 1947: Sold to N. V. Standard Vacuum Tankvaart Maatschappij, Netherlands, and renamed STANVAC BENEKAT. 1958: Sold to Petroleum Shipping Company Ltd., Panama. 1963: PROCYON.

M. 82. EMPIRE GRENADA (1945–1946)

see ship No. BT. 168 in main fleet.

M. 83. EMPIRE MALDON (1945–1946)

O.N. 181129. 3,734g. 1,982n. 343.5 × 48.3 × 26.5 feet.
3-cyl. 2 S.C.S.A. (23 5/16″ × 91 5/16″) oil engine manufactured by Wm. Doxford & Sons Ltd., Sunderland. 2,670 bhp.
Ocean-going tanker.

19.11.1945: Launched by Sir James Laing & Sons Ltd., Sunderland (Yard No. 766), for the Ministry of War Transport (The British Tanker Company Ltd., appointed as managers). 4.1946: Completed. 1946: Sold to Imperial Oil Ltd. (Marine Dept.), Canada. 1946: Transferred to Imperial Oil Company Ltd., Canada, and renamed IMPERIAL HALIFAX. 1970: Sold to Johnston Shipping Ltd., Canada, and renamed CONGAR. 11.1977: Demolished at Hamilton, Ontario.

M. 84. EMPIRE TESELLA (1946–1951)

see ship No. BT. 2578 in main fleet.

M. 85. SHWEDAGON (1947–1953)

O.N. 129306. 3,391g. 1,999n. 300.4 × 44.1 × 31.3 feet.
T.3-cyl. (19″, 31″ & 51″ × 36″) engine manufactured by the Wallsend Slipway Company Ltd., Wallsend.
Ocean-going tanker.

5.1912: Completed by Sir W. G. Armstrong, Whitworth & Company Ltd., Newcastle (Yard No. 843), for the Indo-Burma Petroleum Company Ltd., Calcutta. 1947: The British Tanker Company Ltd., appointed as managers. 1953: Demolished at Sunderland by T. Young Ltd.

M. 86. BRITISH NORNESS (1973–1988) Charter/lease

O.N. 360834. 132,942g. 108,735n. 260,905d. 338.34(BB) × 53.62 × 20.657 metres.
Two, steam turbines manufactured by the Nagasaki Shipbuilding and Engineering Works, double reduction geared to screw shaft. 30,000 shp.
Very large crude carrier (VLCC)

1971: Ordered as BRITISH ROVER by Mitsubishi Heavy Industries Ltd., Nagasaki (Yard No. 1705), for BP Medway Tanker Company Ltd. Contract sold and 15.6.1973: Launched as BRITISH NORNESS for Norcape Shipping Company (Bermuda) Ltd., London, for a 15-year demise charter to the BP Tanker Company Ltd. (operators and managers). 9.1973: Completed. 1981: Managers restyled as BP Shipping Ltd. 1982: Sold to Lombard Finance Ltd. (same managers), London. 1986: Transferred to Gibraltar registry. 1988: Renamed HAPPY NORNESS (same managers). 1989: Sold to K/S Happy Norness (Norman International A/S, managers). 1991: Sold to K/S Thorness (A/S Thor Dahl Shipping, managers), Norway (NIS), and renamed THORNESS. 1993: Sold to Symi Shipping Company, Greece, and renamed SYMI. 1997: Sold to E. M. E. Symi Ltd. (Aeolos Management S. A., managers), Greece. 23.2.2000: Arrived at Alang for demolition.

M. 87. BRITISH RESPECT (2) (1974–1990)

see ship No. BT. 440 in main fleet.

M. 88. BRITISH TRIDENT (1974–1989) Charter/lease.

O.N. 363290. 133,035g. 108,854n. 270,983d. 338.34(BB) × 53.68 × 20.714 metres.
Two, steam turbines manufactured by the shipbuilder, double reduction geared to screw shaft. 30,000 shp.
Very large crude carrier (VLCC)

30.1.1974: Launched by Mitsubishi Heavy Industries Ltd., Nagasaki (Yard No. 1706), for Airlease International Nominees Ltd. (Leased to Charter Shipping Ltd,/ P. & O. Bulk Shipping Division, managers), London. 4.6.1974: Completed for a 15-year demise charter to and operation by BP Tanker Company Ltd. 1981: Charterers restyled as BP Shipping Ltd. 31.5.1983 until 9.7.1986: Laid up at Brunei Bay. 1989: Renamed EASTERN TRUST (same managers). 1990: World-Wide Shipping Agency Ltd., appointed as managers. 1991: Sold to Ritara Ltd. (same managers). 1992: Sold to Blue Wave Maritime S. A., Panama, and renamed ASSOS BAY. 11.11.1995: Repossessed by United States Trust Company, as Mortgagees. 3.3.1996: Renamed FORTUNE QUEEN under United Arab Emirates flag. 1.4.1996: Arrived at Gadani Beach for demolition.

M. 89. BRITISH RESOURCE (3) (1975–1976)

see ship No. BT. 426 in main fleet.

M. 90. BRITISH RELIANCE (3) (1975–1985)

see ship No. BT. 435 in main fleet.

M. 91. BRITISH RANGER (2) (1976–1990)

see ship No. BT. 442 in main fleet.

M. 92. BORDER CASTLE (1976–1979)

see ship No. BT. 427 in main fleet.

M. 93. BORDER CHIEFTAIN (1976–1979)

see ship No. BT. 431 in main fleet.

M. 94. BORDER FALCON (1976–1979)

see ship No. BT. 428 in main fleet.

M. 95. BORDER PELE (1976–1979)

see ship No. BT. 429 in main fleet.

M. 96. BORDER SHEPHERD (1976–1979)

see ship No. BT. 430 in main fleet.

M. 97. SULAIR (1979–1989)

see ship No. DEV 2 in BP Developm't.

M. 98. FASGADAIR (1980–1988)

see ship No. DEV 3 in BP Developm't.

M. 99. GAS ENTERPRISE (1980–1992)

O.N. 390816. 43,733g. 28,724n. 53,500d. 231.12(BB) × ? × 13.552 metres.
Two,10-cyl. 4 S.C.S.A. (570 × 620mm) Pielstick 10PC4-2V-570 vee type oil engines manufactured by Chantiers de l'Atlantique, St.Nazaire, reduction geared to single screw shaft. 30,000 bhp.
Liquified gas carrier.

18.12.1976: Launched as RAZI by Chantier Navales de La Ciotat, La Ciotat (Yard No. 313), for IRANOCEAN (Gazocean Armement, managers), Iran. 1977: Completed. 1980: Sold to Barclays Mercantile Industrial Finance Ltd. (BP Shipping Ltd., managers), and renamed GAS ENTERPRISE. 1992: Sold to Furness Withy (Shipping) Ltd., and renamed DARWIN. 1999: Sold to Furness Withy & Company Ltd. 2000: Sold to Andrean Gas S. A. (Benelux Overseas Inc., managers), Bahamas, and renamed ANDEAN GAS Still listed in Lloyd's Register 2004/05.

M. 100. SEAGAIR (1982–1988)

see ship No. DEV 4 in BP Development.

M. 101. IOLAIR (1982 –)

see ship No. DEV 10 in BP Development.

M. 102. COLTAIR (1982–1986)

see ship No. DEV 7 in BP Development.

M. 103. BP VIGOUR (1985–1988) Charter/Lease.
TEEKAY VIGOUR (1988 – 1989)

O.N. 375885. 44,572g. 33,237n. 87,271d. 245.37(BB) × 38.99 × 13.552 metres.
Post 1994: 48,999g. 30,884n. 87,271d.
7-cyl. 2 S.C.S.A. (900 × 1550mm) Sulzer type oil engine manufactured by Ishikawajima Harima Heavy Industries (I.H.I.), Aioi. 20,300 bhp.

12.6.1975: Keel laid as PROSPERITY QUEEN by Koyo Dockyard Company Ltd., Mihara (Yard No. 668), for Cosmos Navigation Inc., Singapore. 7.9.1975: Launched 20.12.1975: Completed. 1983: Sold to Camellia Tankship

Gas Enterprise. (World Ship Society Photograph Library)

Ltd., Liberia (O.N. 7530). 1985: Sold to Lea Marine Ltd. (BP Shipping Ltd., managers), Bahamas, and renamed BP VIGOUR. 1988: Renamed TEEKAY VIGOUR. 1989: Teekay Shipping Company Inc., appointed as managers). 1990: Teekay Norbulk Ltd. appointed as managers. 1992: Sold to BP International Shipping Ltd. (Teekay Shipping (Japan) Ltd., managers). 8.1993: Sold to Glasgow Shipping Ltd., Malta, and renamed VIGOUR. 1995: Dynacom Tankers Management Ltd., appointed as managers. 8.1998: Sold to Bishop Shipping Ltd. (same managers), Malta, and renamed HALCYON. 11.10.1999: Arrived at Chittagong for demolition.

M. 104. BP VISION (1985–1988) Charter/Lease.

O.N. 356873. 45,001g. 35,988n. 89,735d.
241.59(BB) × 40.06 × 14.183 metres.
Post 1994: 46,389g. 33,902n. 89,735d.
7-cyl. 2 S.C.S.A. (900 × 1550mm) Sulzer type oil engine manufactured by Sumitomo Heavy Industries Ltd., Tamashima. 20,300 bhp.
Tanker.

15.11.1974: Keel laid as HELLESPONT GLORY by Oshima Shipbuilding Company, Nagasaki (Yard No. 001), for Canes Shipping Ltd., Singapore. 28.2.1975: Launched. 20.6.1975: Completed (Sanko Steamship Company Lyd., managers). 1978: Papachristidis Maritime Inc., appointed as managers. 1980: Sold to Satyr Overseas Navigation Inc. (same managers), Singapore. 1984: Sanko Steamship Company Lyd. (Sanko Kisen K. K.), appointed as managers. 1985: Sold to Stort Marine Ltd. (BP Shipping Ltd., managers), Bahamas, and renamed BP VISION. 1988: Sold to BP International Shipping Ltd (Teekay Shipping (Japan) Ltd., managers), and renamed TEEKAY VISION. 9.1993: Sold to Maritime Wanderer Ltd., Cyprus (Greenwich Brokerage Naviera S.A., managers), and renamed ARAB WANDERER (O.N. 709976). 1998: World Tankers Management Private Ltd., appointed as managers. 24.12.1999: Arrived at Gadani Beach, Pakistan, for demolition.

M. 105. BALBLAIR (1985–1993)

O.N. 701174. 2,501g. 756n. 2,500d.
81.08 × 18.04 × 4.323 metres.
Two, 6-cyl. 4 S.C.S.A. (320 × 420mm) MaK 6M453Ak type oil engines manufactured by MaK Maschinenbau GmbH, Kiel, geared to twin shafts with controllable-pitch propellers. Twin controllable-pitch propeller thwartship thrusters forward and aft. 4,800 bhp.
Deck-cargo, pipe-carrier, supply ship.

28.9.1979: Launched as TENDER CHAMPION by Ulstein Hatlo A/S, Ulsteinvik (Yard No. 164), for Partrederiet Wilhelmsen Offshore Services (Wilh. Wilhelmsen, managers), Norway. 5.11.1979: Completed. 11.2.1985: Sold to Baltersan Offshore Ltd. (BP Shipping Ltd., managers), Aberdeen, and renamed BALBLAIR. 1988: BP Shipping Ltd. (Offshore Group), appointed as managers. 1993: Sold to Gulf Offshore North Sea Ltd., Aberdeen, and renamed HIGHLAND CHAMPION. Still listed in Lloyd's Register 2004/05.

M. 106. NORTHAM OSPREY (1987–)

see ship No. TR 11 in BP Trading section.

Stout Truck. (World Ship Society Photograph Library)

M. 107. STOUT TRUCK (1987–1991)

O.N. 709262. 499g. 198n. 1,420d.
59.49 × 14.51 × 6.119 metres
1,010g. 329n. 2,100d. × 5.130 metres
Two, 8-cyl. 4 S.C.S.A. (280 × 320mm) Alpha 8SL28L-VO type oil engines manufactured by B&W Alpha Diesel Div. of B&W Diesel A/S, Frederikshavn, geared to twin shafts with controllable-pitch propellers. Thwartship thrust propeller aft and two with controllable-pitch propellers forward. 4,300 bhp.
Deck-cargo supply ship.

26.3.1982: Keel laid by Schiffs.u.Masch. Paul Lindenau GmbH & Company K. G., Kiel (Yard No. 197), for K/S Sea Truck Trading A/S & Company (I/S Larsen and Hagen Shipping, managers), Norway. 12.6.1982: Launched. 10.9.1982: Completed. 1985: Transferred to Sea Truck Shipping A/S, and removed from management. 1987: Transferred to Sea Truck Supply Ltd. (BP Shipping Ltd. (Offshore Group), managers), Aberdeen. 1991: Sold to Parktor Shipping N. V. (O.I.L. Ltd., managers), Netherlands Antilles and Aruba, and renamed OIL ONYX. 1994: Sold to O.I.L.Ltd., London. 1998: Sold to Parktor Shipping N.V. (Tidewater Marine (North Sea) Ltd., managers). 1999: Sold to Tidewater Marine (North Sea) Ltd. 2001: Sold to TT Boat Corp. (Tidewater Maritime, managers). Still listed in Lloyd's Register 2004/05.

M. 108. SEAWAY JURA (1987–1990)

O.N. 377915. 1,329g. 398n. 844d.
63.58 × 13.01 × 5.100 metres.
Two, 6-cyl. 4 S.C.S.A. (320 × 420mm) MaK 6M453AK type oil engines manufactured by MaK. Maschinenbau G.m.b.H., Kiel, geared to twin shafts with controllable-pitch propellers. Thwartship thrust propeller forward and aft. 4,200 bhp.
Ice-strengthened, fire-fighting, stand-by safety, pollution control vessel for offshore installations.

20.1.1976: Launched by Kaarbos M/V A/S, Harstad (Yard No. 82), for K/S Seaway Supply & Support Ships A/S & Company (Stolt-Nielsens R/A, managers), Norway. 17.6.1976: Completed. 1979: Managers restyled as Stolt-Nielsens Rederi A/S. 1980: Converted from a tug/deck-cargo supply ship and transferred to Stolt-Nielsens Offshore (U.K.) Ltd. (Harrisons (Clyde) Ltd., appointed as managers), Aberdeen. 1987: Sold to Seaway Technology Ltd. (BP Shipping Ltd. (Offshore Group), managers). 1990: Sold to Sea Truck Supply Ltd. (same managers), and renamed SAFE TRUCK. 1993: Gulf Offshore North Sea Ltd., appointed as managers. 1995: Sold to Putford Enterprises Ltd., Lowestoft, and renamed PUTFORD TRADER. 2003: Sold to Boston Putford Offshore Safety Ltd. (Seacor Marine (International) Southern North Sea Ltd. (Seacor(SNS), managers). Still listed in Lloyd's Register 2004/05.

M. 109. BP ENERGY (1987–1990)

see ship No. BT. 437 in main fleet.

M. 110. BP ADVOCATE (1988–1993) charter/lease.

O.N. 715271. 25,368g. 10,927n. 39,538d.
182.30(BB) × 31.42 × 10.950 metres.
6-cyl. 2 S.C.S.A. (500 × 1910mm) B&W 6S50MC type oil engine manufactured by Mitsui Engineering & Shipbuilding Company Ltd., Tamano, reverse reduction geared to screw shaft. 10,680 bhp.
Ocean-going refined products tanker.

30.1.1988: Keel laid as ONOMICHI SPIRIT by Onomichi Zosen K. K., Onomichi, Nagasaki (Yard No. 327), for Nakata Maritime Corp., Japan (Teekay Shipping (Canada) Ltd., managers), Bahamas registry. 21.3.1988: Launched. 10.8.1988: Completed as BP ADVOCATE. 7.1993: Sold to Primar Shipping Ltd. (Stelmar Tankers (Management) Ltd., managers), Greece, and renamed PRIMAR. Still listed in Lloyd's Register 2004/05.

M. 111. BP ARCHITECT (1988–1993) charter/lease.

O.N. 715272. 25,368g. 10,927n. 39,538d.
182.30(BB) × 31.42 × 10.950 metres.
6-cyl. 2 S.C.S.A. (500 × 1910mm) B&W 6S50MC type oil engine manufactured by Mitsui Engineering & Shipbuilding Company Ltd., Tamano, reverse reduction geared to screw shaft. 10,680 bhp.
Ocean-going refined products tanker.

21.3.1988: Keel laid as NAKATA SPIRIT, by Onomichi Zosen K. K., Onomichi, Nagasaki (Yard No. 328), for Nakata Gumi Company, Japan (Teekay Shipping (Canada) Ltd., managers), Bahamas registry. 29.5.1988: Launched. 17.10.1988: Completed as BP ARCHITECT. 1993: Sold to Plow World Maritime S. A. (Korea Tanker Company Ltd., managers), Panama, and renamed KOREA VENUS. 1994: Hoyu Tanker Company Ltd., appointed as managers. 1999: Sold to Lg-Caltex Oil Corp, and transferred to Korea registry. 2000: Sangji Shipping Company Ltd., appointed as managers. Still listed in Lloyd's Register 2004/05.

M. 112. SEA TRUCK (1988–1993)

O.N. 714146. 2,652g. 795n. 2,495d.
81.26 × 18.34 × 4.301 metres.
Two, 12-cyl. 4 S.C.S.A. (250 × 300mm) Polar F212V-D vee type oil engines manufactured by AB Bofors Nohab, Trollhattan, geared to twin shafts with controllable-pitch propellers. Twin thwartship thrust propellers forward and aft. 4,600 bhp.
Fire-fighting, deck-cargo supply ship, pipe-layer, cable-layer.

4.2.1979: Launched as FLEXSERVICE 2 by Ankerlokken Verft Floro A/S, Floro (Yard No. 111), for K/S Staholm Supply A/S (Helmer Staubo & Company, managers), Norway. 1979: Completed. 1985: Managers restyled as Helmer Staubo & Company Management A/S. 1986: Renamed EDDA SEA. 1988: Renamed NOR TRUCK. 1988: Sold to Sea Truck (U.K.) Ltd. (BP Shipping Ltd. (Offshore Group), managers), Aberdeen, and renamed SEA TRUCK. 1993: Gulf Offshore North Sea Ltd., appointed as managers. 1999: Transferred to Norway register and Sea Truck Shipping A/S., appointed as managers. 9.200: Sold to Seatruck (UK) Ltd. (Gulf Offshore Norge AS, managers, and renamed ZACHARIAS, under Norway NIS register. 2.2004: Renamed SENTINEL. Still listed in Lloyd's Register 2004/05.

M. 113. HAPPY NORNESS (1988–1989)

see ship No. M. 86 above.

M. 114. EASTERN TRUST (1989–1990)

see ship No. M. 86 above.

M. 115. STRATHFARRAR (1989–1994)

O.N. 714152. 1,670g. 821n. 2,500d.
81.08 × 18.04 × 4.301 metres.
Two, 12-cyl. 4 S.C.S.A. (250 × 300mm) Polar F212V-B vee type oil engines manufactured by Ab Bofors Nohab, Trollhattan, geared to twin shafts with controllable-pitch propellers. Twin thwartship thrust propellers forward and one aft. 4,600 bhp.
Deck-cargo, supply ship, diving-support ship with moonpool.

11.4.1978: Keel laid as STAD TROLL by Molde Verft AS, Hjelset (Yard No. 162), for PR Stad Troll (AS Ivarans Rederi, managers), Norway. 30.3.1979: Launched 12.5.1979: Completed. 1987: Sold to Offshore Support Services AS (same managers). 1988: Transferred to Bahamian registry and removed from management. 1989: Sold to Strath Shipping Company Ltd. (BP Shipping Ltd. (Offshore Group), managers), Aberdeen, and renamed STRATHFARRAR. 1990: Sold to AS Ivarans Rederi (same managers). 1994: Sold to Strath Shipping Company Ltd. (Gulf Offshore North Sea Ltd., managers). 1996: Sold to Toisa Ltd. 1996: Sold to Boa Ltd. (Taubatkompaniet AS., managers), and renamed BOA TRADER, under Cayman Islands register. 1998: Sold to Havila Supply ships AS. (Havila Supply ASA, managers), and renamed HAVILA TRADER, under Bahamas register. 9.2003: Sold to Borboun Ships AS. (Borboun Offshore Norway AS, managers), and renamed BORBOUN TRADER. Still listed in Lloyd's Register 2004/05.

M. 116. NORTHERN FORTRESS (1989–1993)

O.N. 714162. 1,566g. 791n. 2,500d.
77.91(BB) × ? × 5.004 metres.
Post 1987: 2,567g. 770n. 3,200d.
Two, 12-cyl. 4 S.C.S.A.(200 × 300mm) Normo KVMB-12 vee type oil engines manufactured by AS Bergens NV, Bergen, geared to twin shafts with controllable-pitch propellers. Twin controllable-pitch propeller thwartship thrusters forward and aft. 6,120 bhp.
Deck-cargo supply ship with accommodation for 12 berthed passengers.

15.6.1981: Keel laid as NORTHERN FORTRESS by Ulstein Halto AS, Ulsteinvik (Yard No. 178), for KS Stobakk & Volle AS (Noralf Stobakk & Saebtorn Volle, managers), Norway. 13.2.1982: Launched. 14.5.1982: Completed. 1989: Sold to Sunship 1 Ltd. (BP Shipping Ltd. (Offshore Group), managers), Aberdeen. 1991: Sold to BP Shipping Ltd. (same managers). 1993: Sold to Gulf Offshore N. S. Ltd., and renamed HIGHLAND FORTRESS. 2000: Sold to Seaworks International Ltd., and renamed SEARANGER, under Vanuatu register. Still listed in Lloyd's Register 2004/05.

M. 117. NORTH PRINCE (1989–1993)

O.N. 714160 . 2,342g. 702n. 2,250d.
78.87 × 15.24 × 6.447 metres.
Two, 6-cyl. 4 S.C.S.A. (370 × 400mm) Deutz RSBV6M540 type oil engines manufactured by Kloeckner-Humboldt-Deutz, Koeln, geared to twin screw shafts. 6,000 bhp.
Ice-strengthened, fire-fighting, deck-cargo supply ship.

1978: Completed as FALDERNTOR by Hermann Suerken Gmbh & Company K G, Papenburg (Yard No. 295), for VTG-Vereingte Tanklager u. Transportmittel GmbH, W. Germany. 1981: Transferred to Partenreederei m.s. 'Falderntor' (VTG-Versorgungsschiffahrt, managers). 1988: Transferred to VTG-Vereingte Tanklager u. Transportmittel GmbH (VTG Offshore, managers). 1989: Sold to Eide Shipping Ltd. (Eide Shipping AS, managers), Aberdeen, and renamed SUN PRINCE. 1989: Sold to North Prince Ltd. (BP Shipping Ltd. (Offshore Group), managers), and renamed NORTH PRINCE. 1993: Gulf Offshore North Sea Ltd., appointed as managers. 1996: Sold to Brovig Offshore ASA (same managers). 1998: Sold to Gulf Offshore N.S.Ltd. Still listed in Lloyd's Register 2004/05.

M. 118. SEILLEAN (1990–1996)

see ship No. DEV 11 in BP Development

M. 119. SAFE TRUCK (1990–1993)

see M. 108 above.

M. 120. NORTHWEST SHEARWATER (1991–)

see I.G.T.C. section.

M. 121. WELSH VENTURE (1993–1997)

151,127g. 84,409n. 280,000d.
330.00(BB) × 59.40 × 20.850 metres.
7-cyl. 2 S.C.S.A. (900 × 2916mm) B&W 7L90MC type oil engine manufactured by Mitsui Engineering & Shipbuilding Company Ltd., Tamano. 21,127bhp. 14.2kts.
Very large crude carrier (VLCC)

14.2.1991: Keel laid by Sasebo Heavy Industries Company Ltd., Sasebo Yard, Sasebo (Yard No. 382), for Probe Shipping S. A. (Mitsui O. S. K. Lines Ltd., managers), under Panamanian registry. 5.9.1991: Launched. 26.12.1991: Completed. 1993: Sold to Perennial Transport Inc. (BP Shipping Ltd., appointed as managers). 1997: Sold to Probe Shipping S. A. (MOL Tankship Management Ltd., appointed as managers). Still listed in Lloyd's Register 2004/05.

M. 122. ORIENTAL VENTURE (1993–1997)

154,071g. 84,637n. 281,018d.
330.00(BB) × 59.40 × 20.932 metres.
7-cyl. 2 S.C.S.A. (800 × 3056mm) B&W 7S80MC type oil engine manufactured by the shipbuilder at Tamano. 21,700bhp. 14.2kts.
Very large crude carrier (VLCC)

13.5.1991: Keel laid by Mitsui Engineering & Shipbuilding Company Ltd., Chiba (Yard No. 1362), for Star Express Inc. (Mitsui O. S. K. Lines Ltd., managers), under Panamanian registry. 22.11.1991: Launched. 26.2.1992: Completed. 1993: BP Shipping Ltd., appointed as managers. 1997: International Energy Transport Company Ltd., appointed as managers. 1997: Sold to Star Express Inc. (MOL Tankships Management Ltd., managers). Still listed in Lloyd's Register 2004/05.

M. 124. BRITISH VIGILANCE (3) (1997–2002)

O.N. DR-0037. 158,475g. 95,332n. 210,575d.
343.71(BB) × 56.44 × 21,575 metres.

BP Advocate at Singapore 11 November 1992. (World Ship Society Photograph Library)

British Vigilance. (World Ship Society Photograph Library)

8-cyl. 2 S.C.S.A. (750 × 2800mm) Mitsubishi 8UEC75LS11 type oil engine manufactured by Mitsubishi Heavy Industries Ltd., Kobe. 31,995bhp. 14kts.
Very large crude carrier (VLCC)

12.2.1993: Keel laid as EMMA MAERSK by Odense Staalskibsvaerft AS, Lindo (Yard No. 143), for AS DS Svendborg & DS af 1912 AS, Denmark. 2.7.1993: Launched. 1.9.1993: Completed. 1997: Renamed BRITISH VIGILANCE (BP Shipping Ltd., appointed as managers). 1999: Managers restyled as BP Amoco Shipping Ltd. 2001: Managers restyled as BP Shipping Ltd. 7.2002: Released from charter and renamed EUGEN MAERSK. 25.3. – 17.7.2003: Undergoing unspecified casualty repairs. Still listed in Lloyd's Register 2003/04.

M. 123. BRITISH VALOUR (3) (1997–2002)

O.N. DR-0036. 158,475g. 95,332n. 210,575d. 343.71(BB) × 56.44 × 21,575 metres.
8-cyl. 2 S.C.S.A. (750 × 2800mm) Mitsubishi 8UEC75LS11 type oil engine manufactured by Mitsubishi Heavy Industries Ltd., Kobe. 31,995bhp. 14 kts.
Very large crude carrier (VLCC)

10.11.1992: Keel laid as ELIZABETH MAERSK by Odense Staalskibsvaerft AS, Lindo (Yard No. 142), for AS DS Svendborg & DS af 1912 AS, Denmark. 12.3.1993: Launched. 10.5.1993: Completed. 1997: Renamed BRITISH VALOUR (BP Shipping Ltd., appointed as managers). 1999: Managers restyled as BP Amoco Shipping Ltd. 2001: Managers restyled as BP Shipping Ltd. 2002: Renamed EHM MAERSK. 10.2003: Sold to Seacoast Shipping Company, Panama, and renamed LA ESPERANZA. Still listed in Lloyd's Register 2004/05.

M. 125. BRITISH HARRIER (1997–)

O.N. 727419. 80,187g. 48,050n. 151,459d. 274.10(BB) × 46.04 × 17.00 metres.
7-cyl. 2 S.C.S.A. (700 × 2674mm) B&W 6S70MC type oil engine manufactured by the shipbuilder at Changwon. 20,685bhp. 14.5 kts.
Double hulled, crude oil tanker.

18.2.1997: Keel laid by Samsung Heavy Industries Company Ltd., Koje (Yard No. 1191), for North American Tanker Shipping Ltd. (BP Amoco Shipping Ltd., managers), Bermuda. 22.4.1997: Launched. 2.8.1997: Completed. 2001: Managers restyled as BP Shipping Ltd. Still listed in Lloyd's Register 2004/05.

M. 126. BRITISH HAWK (1997–)

O.N. 727420. 80,187g. 48,050n. 151,475d. 274.05(BB) × 46.04 × 15.85 metres.
7-cyl. 2 S.C.S.A. (700 × 2674mm) B&W 6S70MC type oil engine manufactured by the shipbuilder at Changwon. 20,685bhp. 14.5 kts.
Double hulled, crude oil tanker.

10.3.1997: Keel laid by Samsung Heavy Industries Company Ltd., Koje (Yard No. 1192), for North American Tanker Shipping Ltd. (BP Amoco Shipping Ltd., managers), Bermuda. 5.7.1997: Launched. 4.10.1997: Completed. 2001: Managers restyled as BP Shipping Ltd. Still listed in Lloyd's Register 2004/05.

M. 127. BRITISH HUNTER (1997–)

O.N. 727421. 80,187g. 48,050n. 151,401d. 274.10(BB) × 46.04 × 17.00 metres.
7-cyl. 2 S.C.S.A. (700 × 2674mm) B&W 6S70MC type oil engine manufactured by the shipbuilder at Changwon. 20,685bhp. 14.5 kts.
Double hulled, crude oil tanker.

20.5.1997: Keel laid by Samsung Heavy Industries Company Ltd., Koje (Yard No. 1193), for North American Tanker Shipping Ltd. (BP Amoco Shipping Ltd., managers), Bermuda. 29.9.1997: Launched. 23.12.1997: Completed. 2001: Managers restyled as BP Shipping Ltd. Still listed in Lloyd's Register 2004/05.

M. 128. LOCH RANNOCH (1998–)

O.N. 901255. 75,526g. 36,352n. 130,031d. 269.73 (BB) × 46.03 × 15.632 metres.
Two, 7-cyl. 2 S.C.S.A. (500 × 1910mm) B&W 7S50MC type oil engine manufactured by Korea Heavy Industries & Construction Company Ltd., Changwon, driving twin controllable-pitch propellers. 27,136 bhp. 14kts. Twin thwartship thrust controllable-pitch propellers forward and aft.
Double hulled, crude oil tanker.

15.12.1997: Keel laid by Daewoo Heavy Industries Ltd., Okpo (Yard No. 5109), for The Maersk Company Ltd., London (BP Shipping Ltd., managers). 14.3.1998: Launched. 17.8.1998: Completed. 1999: Managers restyled as BP Amoco Shipping Ltd. 2001: Managers restyled as BP Shipping Ltd. Still listed in Lloyd's Register 2004/05.

M. 129. BRITISH SKILL (2) (1999–2002)

see ship No. BT. 432 in main fleet.

M. 130. BRITISH SPIRIT (1999–2002)

see ship No. BT. 433 in main fleet.

M. 131. BRITISH STRENGTH (3) (1999–2003)

see ship No. BT. 441 in main fleet.

M. 132. BRITISH SUCCESS (2) (1999–2002)

see ship No. BT. 434 in main fleet.

M. 133. BRITISH PIONEER (3) (1999–)

O.N. 732637. 160,216g. 105,889n. 306,397d. 334.00(BB) × 58.04 × 22.520 metres.
7-cyl. 2 S.C.S.A. (800 × 3056mm) B&W 7S80MC type oil engine manufactured by the shipbuilder at Changwon. 34,624bhp. 15 kts.
Very large crude carrier (VLCC)

12.4.1999: Keel laid by Samsung Heavy Industries Company Ltd., Koje (Yard No. 1241), for Abbey National December Leasing (2) Ltd. (BP Amoco Shipping Ltd., managers), London. 25.7.1999: Launched. 2.12.1999: Completed. 2001: Managers restyled as BP Shipping Ltd. Still listed in Lloyd's Register 2004/05.

M. 134. BRITISH PROGRESS (4) (2000–)

O.N. 732638. 160,216g. 105,889n. 306,397d. 333.96(BB) × 58.04 × 22.250 metres.
7-cyl. 2 S.C.S.A. (800 × 3056mm) B&W 7S80MC type oil engine manufactured by the shipbuilder at Changwon. 34,624bhp. 15 kts.
Very large crude carrier (VLCC)

8.11.1999: Keel laid by Samsung Heavy Industries Company Ltd., Koje (Yard No. 1242), for Abbey National December Leasing (2) Ltd. (BP Amoco Shipping Ltd., managers), London. 3.1.2000: Launched. 19.6.2000: Completed. 2001: Managers restyled as BP Shipping Ltd. Still listed in Lloyd's Register 2004/05.

British Progress. (World Ship Society Photograph Library)

M. 135. BRITISH PURPOSE (3) (2000–)

O.N. 732639. 160,216g. 105,889n. 306,307d. 333.96(BB) × 58.04 × 22.520 metres.
7-cyl. 2 S.C.S.A. (800 × 3056mm) B&W 7S80MC type oil engine manufactured by the shipbuilder at Changwon. 34,624bhp. 15 kts.
Very large crude carrier (VLCC)

31.1.2000: Keel laid by Samsung Heavy Industries Company Ltd., Koje (Yard No. 1243), for Abbey National June Leasing (2) Ltd. (BP Amoco Shipping Ltd., managers), London. 16.4.2000: Launched. 10.8.2000: Completed. 2001: Managers restyled as BP Shipping Ltd. Still listed in Lloyd's Register 2004/05.

British Hawthorn in the Bosphorus. (World Ship Society Photograph Library)

M. 136. BRITISH PRIDE (3) (2000–)

O.N. 732640. 160,216g. 105,889n. 305,994d. 334.00(BB) × 58.04 × 22.520 metres.
7-cyl. 2 S.C.S.A. (800 × 3056mm) B&W 7S80MC type oil engine manufactured by the shipbuilder at Changwon. 34,624bhp. 15 kts.
Very large crude carrier (VLCC)

29.5.2000: Keel laid by Samsung Heavy Industries Company Ltd., Koje (Yard No. 1244), for Abbey National June Leasing (2) Ltd. (BP Amoco Shipping Ltd., managers), London. 3.9.2000: Launched. 16.11.2000: Completed. 2001: Managers restyled as BP Shipping Ltd. Still listed in Lloyd's Register 2004/05.

M. 137. BRITISH ENERGY (3) (2001–)

O.N. 904083. 23,682g. 8,834n. 35,858d. 183.00 (BB) × ? × 11.017 metres.
6-cyl. 2 S.C.S.A. (480 × 2000mm) Sulzer 6RTA48T type oil engine manufactured by Hyundai Heavy Industries Company Ltd., Ulsan. 11,257bhp. 14.2 kts.
Double hulled; molasses /chemical/oil products tanker.

12.6.2000: Keel laid by Daedong Shipbuilding Company Ltd., Chinhae (Yard No. 1053), for Indico Star Shipping Ltd., BVI (BP Amoco Shipping Ltd., managers), London. 11.11.2000: Launched. 11.1.2001: Completed. 2001: Managers restyled as BP Shipping Ltd. Still listed in Lloyd's Register 2004/05.

M. 138. BRITISH ENTERPRISE (3) (2001–)

O.N. 904084. 23,682g. 8,834n. 35,858d. 183.00 (BB) × 27.3 × 11.017 metres.
6-cyl. 2 S.C.S.A. (480 × 2000mm) Sulzer 6RTA48T type oil engine manufactured by Hyundai Heavy Industries Company Ltd., Ulsan. 11,257bhp. 14.2 kts.
Double hulled; molasses /chemical/oil products tanker.

25.9.2000: Keel laid by Daedong Shipbuilding Company Ltd., Chinhae (Yard No. 1054), for New Star Shipping Ltd. (BP Amoco Shipping Ltd., managers), London. 30.12.2000: Launched. 28.2.2001: Completed. 2001: Managers restyled as BP Shipping Ltd. Still listed in Lloyd's Register 2004/05.

9242479

M. 139. BRITISH ENDEAVOUR (3) (2002–)

O.N. 905850. 23,235g. 10,129n. 37224d. 182.55 × 27.4 × 16.7 metres.
6-cyl. 2 S.C.S.A. (500 × 2000 mm) B&W 6S50MC-C type oil engine manufactured by Hyundai Heavy Industries Company Ltd., Ulsan. 12,870 bhp. 15 kts.
Double hulled; molasses /chemical/oil products tanker.

14.12.2001: Keel laid by Hyundai Mipo Dockyard Company Ltd, Ulsan (Yard No. 025), for Artemis Shipping Company Ltd., St. Helier, Jersey (Seaworld Management & Trading) (BP Shipping Ltd., managers), under the London register. 16.3.2002: Launched. 19.6.2002: Completed. Still listed in Lloyd's Register 2004/05.

9242481

M. 140. BRITISH ENDURANCE (2) (2002–)

O.N. 905853. 23,235g. 10129n. 37296d. 182.55 × 27.4 × 16.7 metres.
6-cyl. 2 S.C.S.A. (500 × 2000 mm) B&W 6S50MC-C type oil engine manufactured by Hyundai Heavy Industries Company Ltd., Ulsan. 10,940 bhp. 14.5 kts.
Double hulled; molasses /chemical/oil products tanker.

18.3.2002: Keel laid by Hyundai Mipo Dockyard, Ulsan (Yard No. 026), for Aphrodite Shipping Company Ltd., Hemel Hempstead (BP Shipping Ltd., managers), under the London register. 12.6.2002: Launched. 13.9.2002: Completed. Still listed in Lloyd's Register 2004/05.

9251810

M. 141. BRITISH LAUREL (2) (2002–)

O.N. 734782. 57,567g. 32,118n. 106,500d. 240.5 (BB) × 42.03 × 21.2 metres.
6-cyl. 2 S.C.S.A. (600 × 2290 mm) B&W 6S50MC type oil engine manufactured by Mitsui Engineering & Shipbuilding Company Ltd. 16,642 bhp. 15 kts.
Double hulled crude oil tanker.

25.4.2002: Keel laid by Tsuneishi Shipbuilding, Tadotsu (Yard No. 1239), for Ithaki Shipping Company Ltd, Hemel Hempstead (BP Shipping Ltd., managers), Isle of Man registry. 5.8.2002: Launched. 12.11.2002: Completed. Still listed in Lloyd's Register 2004/05.

9238038

M. 142. BRITISH TRADER (3) (2002–)

O.N. 734759. 93,498g. 28,049n. 75,109d. 278.88 (BB) × 42.63 × 26.00 metres.
Kawasaki UA-400 type steam turbine, manufactured by 'Uljanik'-Strojogradjna d.d. 39,469hp. 19.5 kts. Thwartship thrust controllable-pitch propeller forward.
Liquid natural gas (LNG) tanker.

3.9.2001: Keel laid by Samsung Heavy Industries, Koje Island (Yard No. 1380), for Sea Breeze Leasing Ltd, Hemel Hempstead (BP Shipping Ltd., managers), Isle of Man registry. 9.12.2001: Launched. 13.11.2002: Completed. Still listed in Lloyd's Register 2004/05.

9247780

M. 143. BRITISH HAWTHORN (2) (2003–)

O.N. 734784. 57,567g. 32,118n. 106,500d. 240.5 (BB) × 42.03 × 21.2 metres.
6-cyl. 2 S.C.S.A. (600 × 2290 mm) B&W 6S50MC type oil engine manufactured by Mitsui Engineering & Shipbuilding Company Ltd. 16,642 bhp. 15 kts.
Double hulled crude oil tanker.

17.6.2002: Keel laid by Tsuneishi Shipbuilding, Tadotsu (Yard No. 1236), for Antonios Shipping Company Ltd, Hemel Hempstead (BP Shipping Ltd., managers). 30.9.2002: Launched. 10.1.2003: Completed. Still listed in Lloyd's Register 2004/05.

9251561

M. 144. BRITISH EXPLORER (3) (2003–)

O.N. 906644. 23,235g. 10,129n. 37,321d. 182.55 × 27.4 × 16.7 metres.

British Enterprise. (World Ship Society Photograph Library)

6-cyl. 2 S.C.S.A. (500 × 2000 mm) B&W 6S50MC-C type oil engine manufactured by Hyundai Heavy Industries Company Ltd., Ulsan. 10,940 bhp. 14.5 kts.
Double hulled; molasses /chemical/oil products tanker.
14.6.2002: Keel laid by Hyundai Mipo Dockyard Company Ltd., Ulsan (Yard No. 0105), for Athina Shipping Company Ltd, Hemel Hempstead (BP Shipping Ltd., managers). 16.9.2002: Launched. 15.1.2003: Completed. Still listed in Lloyd's Register 2004/05.

9260017
M. 145. BALTIC COMMODORE (2003)

O.N. 736393. 23,235g. 10129n. 37296d.
182.55 × 27.4 × 16.7 metres.
6-cyl. 2 S.C.S.A. (500 × 2000 mm) B&W 6S50MC-C type oil engine manufactured by Hyundai Heavy Industries Company Ltd., Ulsan. 10,940 bhp. 14.5 kts.
Double hulled; molasses /chemical/oil products tanker.
5.32.2003: Keel laid by Hyundai Mipo Dockyard Company Ltd., Ulsan (Yard No. 0129), for First Base Shipping, Cyprus (BP Shipping Ltd., managers). 23.4.2003: Launched. 26.6.2003: Completed (Interorient Navigation Company Ltd., managers), Isle of Man. Still listed in Lloyd's Register 2004/05.

9260029
M. 146. BALTIC CHAMPION (2003)

O.N. 736403. 23,235g. 10129n. 37296d.
182.55 × 27.4 × 16.7 metres.
6-cyl. 2 S.C.S.A. (500 × 2000 mm) B&W 6S50MC-C type oil engine manufactured by Hyundai Heavy Industries Company Ltd., Ulsan. 10,940 bhp. 14.5 kts.
Double hulled; molasses /chemical/oil products tanker.
13.3.2003: Keel laid by Hyundai Mipo Dockyard Company Ltd., Ulsan (Yard No. 0130), for Flame Creek Shipping Company Ltd., Cyprus (BP Shipping Ltd., managers). 30.5.2003: Launched. 31.7.2003: Completed (Interorient Navigation Company Ltd., managers), Isle of Man. Still listed in Lloyd's Register 2004/05.

9251822
M. 147. BRITISH WILLOW (2) (2003)

O.N. 734785 . 57,567g. 32,118n. 106,000d.
240.5 (BB) × 42.03 × 21.2 metres.
6-cyl. 2 S.C.S.A. (600 × 2290 mm) B&W 6S60MC type oil engine manufactured by Mitsui Engineering & Shipbuilding Company Ltd. 16,642 bhp. 15 kts.
Double hulled crude oil tanker.
25.6.2002: Keel laid by Tsuneishi Shipbuilding, Tadotsu (Yard No.1240), for Sieg Shipping Co. Ltd, Singapore (Executive Shipping Management) (BP Shipping Ltd., managers). 19.11.2002: Launched. 25.2.2003: Completed (Executive Ship Management (Private) Ltd., managers), Isle of Man registry. Still listed in Lloyd's Register 2004/05.

9251573
M. 148. BRITISH ESTEEM (2003–)

O.N. 906807. 23,235g. 10,129n. 37,220d.
182.55 × 27.4 × 16.7 metres.
6-cyl. 2 S.C.S.A. (500 × 2000 mm) B&W 6S50MC-C type oil engine manufactured by Hyundai Heavy Industries Company Ltd., Ulsan. 12,870 bhp. 15 kts.
Double hulled; molasses /chemical/oil products tanker.
14.6.2002: Keel laid by Hyundai Mipo Dockyard Company Ltd., Ulsan (Yard No. 0106), for Eleni Ltd, Hemel Hempstead (BP Shipping Ltd., managers). 9.12.2002: Launched. 10.3.2003: Completed. Still listed in Lloyd's Register 2004/05.

9238040
M. 149. BRITISH INNOVATOR (2003–)

O.N. 734760. 93,409g. 28,049n. 67,850d.
278.88 (BB) × 42.63 × 26.00 metres.
Kawasaki UA-400 type steam turbine, manufactured by " Kawasaki Heavy Industries Ltd., Japan 39,469hp. 19.5 kts. Thwartship thrust controllable-pitch propeller forward.
Liquified natural gas (LNG) tanker.
10.12.2001: Keel laid by Samsung Heavy Industries, Koje Island (Yard No.1381), for unspecified owners (BP Shipping Ltd., managers). 16.3.2002: Launched. 29.3.2003: Completed. Still listed in Lloyd's Register 2004/05.

9247792
M. 150. BRITISH OAK (2) (2003)

O.N. 734786. 57,567g. 32,188n. 106,000d.
240.5(BB) × 42.03 × 14.878 metres.
6-cyl. 2 S.C.S.A. (600 × 2292mm) B&W 6S60-MC type oil engine manufactured by Mitsui Engineering & Shipbuilding Company Ltd., Tamano. 16,640bhp. 15.2 kts.
Double hulled crude oil tanker.
25.6.2002: Keel laid by Tsuneishi Shipbuilding, Tadotsu (Yard No. 1237), for Caesar Shipping Company Ltd., Singapore (Executive Ship Management) (BP Shipping Ltd., managers). 15.1.2003: Launched. 16.4.2003: Completed (Executive Ship Management (Private) Ltd., managers), Isle of Man registry. Still listed in Lloyd's Register 2004/05.

9258868
M. 151. BRITISH SWIFT (2) (2003–)

O.N. 736381. 63,661g. 34,210n. 114,809d.
251.56(BB) × 43.84 × 15.023 metres.
7-cyl. 2 S.C.S.A. (600 × 2400mm) B&W 7S60MC-C type oil engine manufactured by Hyundai Heavy Industries Company Ltd., Ulsan. 21,509bhp.
Double hulled crude oil tanker.
5.11.2002: Keel laid by Samsung Heavy Industries, Koje Island (Yard No. 1430), for Maisie Ltd., Hemel Hempstead (BP Shipping Ltd., managers). 4.1.2003: Launched. 15.5.2003: Completed. Still listed in Lloyd's Register 2004/05.

9250191
M. 152. BRITISH MERCHANT (3) (2003–)

O.N. 734761. 93,409g. 28,049n. 67,850d.
278.80 (BB) × 42.63 × 11.3 metres.
Kawasaki UA-400 type steam turbine, manufactured by Kawasaki Heavy Industries Ltd., Japan 39,472shp. 19.5 kts. Thwartship thrust controllable-pitch propeller forward.
Liquified natural gas (LNG) tanker.
19.3.2002: Keel laid by Samsung Heavy Industries, Koje Island (Yard No. 1416), for unspecified owners (BP Shipping Ltd., managers). 29.6.2003: Launched. 1.7.2003: Completed. Still listed in Lloyd's Register 2004/05.

9258870
M. 153. BRITISH MERLIN (2) (2003)

O.N. 736382. 63,661g. 34,210n. 114,809d.
250.500(BB) × 43.84 × 13.6 metres.
7-cyl. 2 S.C.S.A. (600 × 2400mm) B&W 7S60MC-C type oil engine manufactured by Hyundai Heavy Industries Company Ltd., Ulsan. 21,509bhp. 15.7 kts.
Double hulled crude oil tanker.
13.1.2003: Keel laid by Samsung Heavy Industries, Koje Island (Yard No. 1431), for Mandolin Ltd, Sunbury on Thames (BP Shipping Ltd., managers). 8.3.2003: Launched. 23.7.2003: Completed (Executive Ship Management (Private) Ltd., managers), Isle of Man registry.

9266841
M. 154. BRITISH BEECH (2) (2003)

O.N. 736410. 57,567g. 32,188n. 106,138d.
240.5(BB) × 42.03 × 14.850 metres.
6-cyl. 2 S.C.S.A. (600 × 2292mm) B&W 6S60-MC type oil engine manufactured by Mitsui Engineering & Shipbuilding Company Ltd., Tamano. 16,640bhp. 15.2 kts.
Double hulled crude oil tanker.
26.3.2003: Keel laid by Tsuneishi Shipbuilders, Tadotsu (Yard No. 1254), for Millerfield Ltd, Sunbury on Thames (BP Shipping Ltd., managers). 19.7.2003: Launched. 4.11.2003: Completed (Executive Ship Management (Private) Ltd., managers), Isle of Man registry.

9258882
M. 155. BRITISH OSPREY (2) (2003–)

O.N. 736383. 63,661g. 34,210n. 101,760d.
250.0(BB) × 43.84 × 13.6 metres.
7-cyl. 2 S.C.S.A. (600 × 2400mm) B&W 7S60MC-C type oil engine manufactured by Hyundai Heavy Industries Company Ltd., Ulsan. 21,509bhp. 15.7 kts.
Double hulled crude oil tanker.
12.5.2003: Keel laid by Samsung Heavy Industries, Koje Island (Yard No. 1432), for Statuette Ltd., Sunbury on Thames, (BP Shipping Ltd., managers). 10.7.2003: Launched. 17.12.2003: Completed. Still listed in Lloyd's Register 2004/05.

9266853
M. 156. BRITISH HAZEL (2) (2004)

O.N. 736412. 58,070g. 32,118n. 106,085d.
240.5(BB) × 42.03 × 14.878 metres.
6-cyl. 2 S.C.S.A. (600 × 2292mm) B&W 6S60-MC type oil engine manufactured by Mitsui Engineering & Shipbuilding Company Ltd., Tamano. 16,642bhp. 14.5 kts.
Double hulled crude oil tanker.
27.5.2003: Keel laid by Tsuneishi Shipbuilders,

British Esteem. (World Ship Society Photograph Library)

Tadotsu (Yard No. 1255), for Patriot Sky Ltd., Sunbury on Thames (BP Shipping Ltd., managers). 20.9.2003: Launched. 4.1.2004: Completed (Executive Ship Management (Private) Ltd., Singapore, appointed as managers). Isle of Man registry.

9258894
M. 157. BRITISH CURLEW (2) (2004–)

O.N. 736384. 63,661g. 34,210n. 114,761d. 252.50(BB) × 43.82 × 15.0 metres.
7-cyl. 2 S.C.S.A. (600 × 2400mm) B&W 7S60MC-C type oil engine manufactured by Hyundai Heavy Industries Company Ltd., Ulsan. 21,509bhp. 15.7 kts.
Double hulled, crude oil tanker.
25.7.2003: Keel laid by Samsung Heavy Industries, Koji Island (Yard No.1433), for Winter Jasmine Ltd., Sunbury on Thames (BP Shipping Ltd., managers). 8.10.2003: Launched. 9.1.2004: Completed.

9266865
M. 158. BRITISH HOLLY (4) (2004)

O.N. 736412. 58,070g. 32,118n. 106,070d. 240.5(BB) × 42.03 × 14.878 metres.
6-cyl. 2 S.C.S.A. (600 × 2292mm) B&W 6S60-MC type oil engine manufactured by Mitsui Engineering & Shipbuilding Company Ltd., Tamano. 16,642bhp. 14.5 kts.
Double hulled, crude oil tanker.
24.7.2003: Keel laid by Tsuneishi Shipbuilders, Tadotsu (Yard No. 1256), for Silver Rock Ltd. (BP Shipping Ltd., Sunbury on Thames, managers). 10.11.2003: Launched. 22.3.2004: Completed, Executive Ship Management (Private) Ltd., Singapore, appointed as managers). Isle of Man registry.

9266877
M. 159. BRITISH VINE (3) (2004–)

O.N. 736413. 58,070g. 32,118n. 106,070d. 240.5(BB) × 42.03 × 14.878 metres.
6-cyl. 2 S.C.S.A. (600 × 2292mm) B&W 6S60-MC type oil engine manufactured by Mitsui Engineering & Shipbuilding Company Ltd., Tamano. 16,642bhp. 14.5 kts.
Double hulled, crude oil tanker.
25.9.2003: Keel laid by Tsuneishi Shipbuilders, Tadotsu (Yard No. 1257), for Veronesse Shipping, Sunbury on Thames, (BP Shipping Ltd., managers). 6.1.2004: Launched. 2.4.2004: Completed.

9285706
M. 160. BRITISH TENACITY (3) (2004–)

O.N. 737103. 29,335g. 11,917n. 46,803d. 183.0 × 32.22 × 12.2 metres.
6-cyl. 2 S.C.S.A. (500 × 2000 mm) B&W 6S50MC-C type oil engine manufactured by Hyundai Heavy Industries Company Ltd., Ulsan. 12,870bhp.
Double hulled, molasses, chemical/oil products tanker.
1.12.2003: Keel laid by Hyundai Mipo Dockyard Company Ltd., Ulsan (Yard No. 0217), for unspecified owners (BP Shipping Ltd., Sunbury on Thames, managers). 12.2.2004: Launched. 14.4.2004: Completed.

9285718
M. 161. BRITISH SECURITY (4) (2004–)

O.N. 737104. 29,335g. 11,917n. 46,803d. 183.0 × 32.22 × 12.2 metres.
6-cyl. 2 S.C.S.A. (500 × 2000 mm) B&W 6S50MC-C type oil engine manufactured by Hyundai Heavy Industries Company Ltd., Ulsan. 12,870bhp.
Double hulled, molasses, chemical/oil products tanker.
13.2.2004: Keel laid by Hyundai Mipo Dockyard Company Ltd., Ulsan (Yard No. 0218), for unspecified owners (BP Shipping Ltd., Sunbury on Thames, managers). 20.4.2004: Launched. 17.6.2004: Completed.

British Loyalty. (Andrew Mackinnon, Port Phillip Bay)

9285720
M. 162. BRITISH LOYALTY (4) (2004–)

O.N. 737105. 29,335g. 11,917n. 46,803d. 183.0 × 32.22 × 12.2 metres.
6-cyl. 2 S.C.S.A. (500 × 2000 mm) B&W 6S50MC-C type oil engine manufactured by Hyundai Heavy Industries Company Ltd., Ulsan. 12,870bhp.
Double hulled, molasses, chemical/oil products tanker.
15.12.2003: Keel laid by Hyundai Mipo Dockyard Company Ltd., Ulsan (Yard No. 0219), for Magpie Shipping Company Ltd. (BP Shipping Ltd., Sunbury on Thames, managers). 20.5.2004: Launched. 12.7.2004: Completed.

9285732
M. 163. BRITISH UNITY (3) (2004–)

O.N. . 29,335g. 11,917n. 46,803d. 183.0 × 32.22 × 12.2 metres.
6-cyl. 2 S.C.S.A. (500 × 2000 mm) B&W 6S50MC-C type oil engine manufactured by Hyundai Heavy Industries Company Ltd., Ulsan. 12,870bhp.
Double hulled, molasses, chemical/oil products tanker.
21.4.2004: Keel laid by Hyundai Mipo Dockyard Company Ltd., Ulsan (Yard No. 0220), for Pipton Ltd. (BP Shipping Ltd., Sunbury on Thames, managers). 26.6.2004: Launched. 27.8.2004: Completed.

9285744
M. 164. BRITISH FIDELITY (3) (2004–)

O.N. 737433. 29,335g. 11,917n. 46,803d. 183.0 × 32.22 × 12.2 metres.
6-cyl. 2 S.C.S.A. (500 × 2000 mm) B&W 6S50MC-C type oil engine manufactured by Hyundai Heavy Industries Company Ltd., Ulsan. 12,870bhp.
Double hulled, molasses, chemical/oil products tanker.
21.4.2004: Keel laid by Hyundai Mipo Dockyard Company Ltd., Ulsan (Yard No. 0221), for Speed Shipping Company Ltd. (BP Shipping Ltd., managers). 26.6.2004: Launched. 2.9.2004: Completed.

9285756
M. 165. BRITISH LIBERTY (4) (2004–)

O.N. . 29,335g. 11,917n. 46,803d. 183.0 × 32.22 × 12.2 metres.
6-cyl. 2 S.C.S.A. (500 × 2000 mm) B&W 6S50MC-C type oil engine manufactured by Hyundai Heavy Industries Company Ltd., Ulsan. 12,870bhp.
Double hulled, molasses, chemical/oil products tanker.
28.6.2004: Keel laid by Hyundai Mipo Dockyard Company Ltd., Ulsan (Yard No. 0222 – later changed to 0330), for St. James Shipping Company Ltd. (BP Shipping Ltd., Sunbury on Thames, managers). 11.9.2004: Launched. 5.11.2004: Completed.

9288758
M. 166. BRITISH INTEGRITY (2) (2004–)

O.N. 737106. 29,335g. 11,917n. 46,803d. 183.0 × 32.22 × 12.2 metres.
6-cyl. 2 S.C.S.A. (500 × 2000 mm) B&W 6S50MC-C type oil engine manufactured by Hyundai Heavy Industries Company Ltd., Ulsan. 12,870bhp.
Double hulled, molasses, chemical/oil products tanker.
28.6.2004: Keel laid by Hyundai Mipo Dockyard Company Ltd., Ulsan (Yard No. 0223 – later changed to 0331), for Blackcomb Ltd. (BP Shipping Ltd., managers). 11.9.2004: Launched. 11.11.2004: Completed.

9282479
M. 167. BRITISH MALLARD (2) (2004–)

O.N. 737109 . 63,661g. 34,210n. 114,809d. 250.0 × 43.836 × 15.0 metres.
7-cyl. 2 S.C.S.A. (600 × 2400 mm) B&W 7S60MC-C type oil engine manufactured by HSD Engine Company Ltd., Changwan. 21,483bhp. 15.7 kts.
Double hulled, crude oil tanker.
26.7.2004: Keel laid Samsung Heavy Industries, Koje Island (Yard No. 1480), for

British Unity. (World Ship Society Photograph Library)

Jalousie Ltd. (BP Shipping Ltd., managers). 19.9.2004: Launched. 12.1.2005: Completed.

9288760
M. 168. BRITISH CHIVALRY (3) (2005–)

O.N. 737114. 29,335g. 11,917n. 46,000d. 183.0 × 32.22 × 12.2 metres.
6-cyl. 2 S.C.S.A. (500 × 2000 mm) B&W 6S50MC-C type oil engine manufactured by Hyundai Heavy Industries Company Ltd., Ulsan. 12,870bhp.
Double hulled, molasses, chemical/oil products tanker.
13.9.2004: Keel laid by Hyundai Mipo Dockyard Company Ltd., Ulsan (Yard No. 0224 – later changed to 0332), for Kelso Ltd. (BP Shipping Ltd., managers). 24.11.2004: Launched. 24.1.2005: Completed.

9282481
M. 169. BRITISH GANNET(2) (2005–)

O.N. . 63,661g. 34,210n. 114,760d. 250.0 × 43.836 × 15.0 metres.
7-cyl. 2 S.C.S.A. (600 × 2400 mm) B&W 7S60MC-C type oil engine manufactured by HSD Engine Company Ltd., Changwan. 21,483bhp. 15.7 kts.
Double hulled, crude oil tanker.
20.9.2004: Keel laid by Samsung Heavy Industries, Koje Island (Yard No. 1481), for Kimlee Ltd. (BP Shipping Ltd., managers). 6.11.2004: Launched. 27.2.2005: Completed.

Vessels On Order Or Under Construction In March 2005.

9288813
BRITISH HARMONY (2) (2005–)

29,335g. 11,917n. 46,803d. 183.0 × 32.22 × 12.2 metres.
6-cyl. 2 S.C.S.A. (500 × 2000 mm) B&W 6S50MC-C type oil engine manufactured by Hyundai Heavy Industries Company Ltd., Ulsan. 12,870bhp.
Double hulled, molasses, chemical/oil products tanker.
28.12.2004: Keel laid by Hyundai Mipo Dockyard Company Ltd., Ulsan (Yard No. 0246 = later changed to 0333), for unspecified owners (BP Shipping Ltd., managers).

9288825
BRITISH COURTESY (2005–)

29,335g. 11,917n. 46,803d. 183.0 × 32.22 × 12.2 metres.
6-cyl. 2 S.C.S.A. (500 × 2000 mm) B&W 6S50MC-C type oil engine manufactured by Hyundai Heavy Industries Company Ltd., Ulsan. 12,870bhp.
Double hulled, molasses, chemical/oil products tanker.
2005: due to be completed by Hyundai Mipo Dockyard Company Ltd., Ulsan (Yard No. 0247 – later changed to 0334), for unspecified owners (BP Shipping Ltd., managers).

9288837
BRITISH SERENITY (2005–)

29,335g. 11,917n. 46,803d. 183.0 × 32.22 × 12.2 metres.
6-cyl. 2 S.C.S.A. (500 × 2000 mm) B&W 6S50MC-C type oil engine manufactured by Hyundai Heavy Industries Company Ltd., Ulsan. 12,870bhp.
Double hulled, molasses, chemical/oil products tanker.
2005: due to be completed by Hyundai Mipo Dockyard Company Ltd., Ulsan (Yard No. 0248 – later changed to 0335), for unspecified owners (BP Shipping Ltd., managers).

9288849
BRITISH TRANQUILITY (2005–)

29,335g. 11,917n. 46,803d. 183.0 × 32.22 × 12.2 metres.
6-cyl. 2 S.C.S.A. (500 × 2000 mm) B&W 6S50MC-C type oil engine manufactured by Hyundai Heavy Industries Company Ltd., Ulsan. 12,870bhp.
Double hulled, molasses, chemical/oil products tanker.
2005: due to be completed by Hyundai Mipo Dockyard Company Ltd., Ulsan (Yard No. 0249 – later changed to 0336), for unspecified owners (BP Shipping Ltd., managers).

9282493
BRITISH CORMORANT(2) (2005–)

63,661g. 34,210n. 113,120d. 250.0 × 43.836 × 15.0 metres.
7-cyl. 2 S.C.S.A. (600 × 2400 mm) B&W 7S60MC-C type oil engine manufactured by HSD Engine Company Ltd., Changwan. 21,483bhp.
Double hulled, crude oil tanker.
8.11.2004: Keel laid by Samsung Heavy Industries, Koje Island (Yard No. 1482), for Kooper Ltd. (BP Shipping Ltd., managers). 6.2005: due to be completed.

9282508
BRITISH ROBIN (2) (2005–)

63,661g. 34,210n. 114,760d. 250.0 × 43.836 × 15.0 metres.
7-cyl. 2 S.C.S.A. (600 × 2400 mm) B&W 7S60MC-C type oil engine manufactured by HSD Engine Company Ltd., Changwan. 21,483bhp.
Double hulled, crude oil tanker.
2005: due to be completed by Samsung Heavy Industries, Koje Island (Yard No. 1483), for unspecified owners (BP Shipping Ltd., managers).

9297345
BRITISH CYGNET (2) (2005–)

63,661g. 34,210n. 114,760d. 250.0 × 43.836 × 15.0 metres.
7-cyl. 2 S.C.S.A. (600 × 2400 mm) B&W 7S60MC-C type oil engine manufactured by HSD Engine Company Ltd., Changwan. 21,483bhp.
Double hulled, crude oil tanker.
2005: due to be completed by Samsung Heavy Industries, Koje Island (Yard No. 1530), for unspecified owners (BP Shipping Ltd., managers).

9297357
BRITISH KESTREL (2) (2006–)

63,661g. 34,210n. 114,760d. 250.0 × 43.836 × 15.0 metres.
7-cyl. 2 S.C.S.A. (600 × 2400 mm) B&W 7S60MC-C type oil engine manufactured by HSD Engine Company Ltd., Changwan. 21,483bhp.
Double hulled, crude oil tanker.
2006: due to be completed by Samsung Heavy Industries, Koje Island (Yard No. 1531), for unspecified owners (BP Shipping Ltd., managers).

9297369
BRITISH FALCON (2006–)

63,661g. 34,210n. 114,760d. 250.0 × 43.836 × 15.0 metres.
7-cyl. 2 S.C.S.A. (600 × 2400 mm) B&W 7S60MC-C type oil engine manufactured by HSD Engine Company Ltd., Changwan. 21,483bhp.
Double hulled, crude oil tanker.
2006: due to be completed by Samsung Heavy Industries, Koje Island (Yard No. 1532), for unspecified owners (BP Shipping Ltd., managers).

9297371
BRITISH EAGLE (2006–)

63,661g. 34,210n. 114,760d. 250.0 × 43.836 × 15.0 metres.
7-cyl. 2 S.C.S.A. (600 × 2400 mm) B&W 7S60MC-C type oil engine manufactured by HSD Engine Company Ltd., Changwan. 21,483bhp.
Double hulled, crude oil tanker.
2006: due to be completed by Samsung Heavy Industries, Koje Island (Yard No. 1533), for unspecified owners (BP Shipping Ltd., managers).

9307736
BRITISH CONFIDENCE (3) (2006–)

47,000g. ?n. 51,000d. 230.0 × ? × 11.15 metres.
7-cyl. 2 S.C.S.A. (600 × 2400 mm) MAN-B&W 7S60MC-C type oil engine manufactured by Kawasaki Heavy Industries Ltd., Japan 21,483bhp.
Liquefied petroleum gas (LPG) tanker.
2006: due to be completed by Mitsubishi Heavy Industries, Nagasaki (Yard No. 2202), for Abbie Shipping Ltd. (BP Shipping Ltd., managers).

9307748
BRITISH COURAGE (3) (2006–)

47,000g. ?n. 51,000d. 230.0 × ? × 11.15 metres.
7-cyl. 2 S.C.S.A. (600 × 2400 mm) MAN-B&W 7S60MC-C type oil engine manufactured by Kawasaki Heavy Industries Ltd., Japan 21,483bhp.
Liquefied petroleum gas (LPG) tanker.
2006: due to be completed by Mitsubishi Heavy Industries, Nagasaki (Yard No. 2203), for Charlotte Shipping Ltd. (BP Shipping Ltd., managers).

9307750
BRITISH COMMERCE (4) (2006–)

47,000g. ?n. 51,000d. 230.0 × ? × 11.15 metres.
7-cyl. 2 S.C.S.A. (600 × 2400 mm) MAN-B&W 7S60MC-C type oil engine manufactured by Kawasaki Heavy Industries Ltd., Japan 21,483bhp.
Liquefied petroleum gas (LPG) tanker.
2007: due to be completed by Mitsubishi Heavy Industries, Nagasaki (Yard No. 2209), for Hazel Ltd. (BP Shipping Ltd., managers).

BRITISH COUNCILLOR (3) (2007–)

47,000g. ?n. 51,000d. 230.0 × ? × 11.15 metres.
7-cyl. 2 S.C.S.A. (600 × 2400 mm) MAN-B&W 7S60MC-C type oil engine manufactured by Kawasaki Heavy Industries Ltd., Japan 21,483bhp.
Liquefied petroleum gas (LPG) tanker.
2007: due to be completed by Mitsubishi Heavy Industries, Nagasaki (Yard No. 2204), for Sophie Ltd. (BP Shipping Ltd., managers).

9333591
BRITISH ( ) (2007–)

98,100g. ? n. ? d. ? × ? × ? metres.
? bhp. ? kts.
Liquified Natural Gas Carrier
2007: due to be completed by Hyundai Heavy Industries, Ulsan (Yard No. 1777), for unspecified owners (BP Shipping Ltd., managers).

9333606
BRITISH ( ) (2008–)

98,100g. ? n. ? d. ? × ? × ? metres.
? bhp. ? kts.
Liquified Natural Gas Carrier
2008: due to be completed by Hyundai Heavy Industries, Ulsan (Yard No. 1778), for unspecified owners (BP Shipping Ltd., managers).

9333618
BRITISH ( ) (2008–)

98,100g. ? n. ? d. ? × ? × ? metres.
? bhp. ? kts.
Liquified Natural Gas Carrier

2008: due to be completed by Hyundai Heavy Industries, Ulsan (Yard No. 1779), for unspecified owners (BP Shipping Ltd., managers).

9333620
BRITISH ( ) (2008–)

120,000g. ? n. ? d. ? × ? × ? metres.
? bhp. ? kts.
Liquified Natural Gas Carrier
2008: due to be completed by Hyundai Heavy Industries, Samho (Yard No. 5296), for unspecified owners (BP Shipping Ltd., managers).

9333632
BRITISH ( ) (2008–)

91,800g. ? n. ? d. ? × ? × ? metres.
? bhp. ? kts.
Liquified Natural Gas Carrier
2008: due to be completed by Hyundai Heavy Industries, Samho (Yard No. 5297), for unspecified owners (BP Shipping Ltd., managers).

Jubilee Shipping Group – As Bareboat Charterers To BP

It was announced to the press in 2003 that the Jubilee Shipping Group would construct a series of approximately 12 product/chemical tankers of between 1,500 – 5,000 tons dwt, for operation by or bareboat charter to BP. These would be registered under various flags and companies with only some directly managed by BP Shipping Ltd.

Darwin Shipping Company

9287833
J.1. BORDER HEATHER (2004–)

2,159g. 824n. 3,185d. 75.0 × 14.168 × 5.75 metres.
8-cyl. 4 S.C.S.A. (255 × 400 mm) MaK 8M25 type oil engine manufactured by Caterpillar Motoren GmbH & Co. K.G., Kiel. 2,400 bhp.
Double hulled, chemical/oil products tanker.
2003: Ordered from Damen, Bergum (Yard No. 1035 later 9357), by Jubilee Shipping Ltd., on behalf of charterer BP Oil Shipping Ltd. 6.8.2003: Keel laid. 2004: Transferred to Darwin Shipping Ltd., Nassau. 8.4.2004: Launched. 10.9.2004: Completed

9287819
J.2. BORDER THISTLE (2004–)

737434. 3,248g. 1,278n. 4,500d. 80.0 × ? × 6.3 metres.
8-cyl. 4 S.C.S.A. (255 × 400 mm) MaK 8M25 type oil engine manufactured by Caterpillar Motoren GmbH & Co. K.G., Kiel. 2,400 bhp.
Double hulled, chemical/oil products tanker.
2003: Ordered from Damen, Bergum (Yard No. 1036 later 9355), by Jubilee Shipping Ltd., on behalf of charterer BP Oil Shipping Ltd. 1.10.2003: Keel laid. 2004: Transferred to Darwin Shipping Ltd., Nassau. 16.7.2004: Launched. 29.11.2004: Completed.

9287821
J.3. BORDER TARTAN (2005–)

3,248g. 1,273n. 4,500d. 79.9 × ? × 6.3 metres.
8-cyl. 4 S.C.S.A. (255 × 400 mm) MaK 8M25 type oil engine manufactured by Caterpillar Motoren GmbH & Co. K.G., Kiel. 2,400 bhp.
Double hulled, chemical/oil products tanker.
2003: Ordered from Damen, Bergum (Yard No. 1037 later 9356), by Jubilee Shipping Ltd., on behalf of charterer BP Oil Shipping Ltd. 1.10.2003: Keel laid. 2004: Transferred to Darwin Shipping Ltd., Nassau. 26.8.2004: Launched.

Gordian Shipping Company

9301639
J.4. ALIOS ATHENA (2004–)

2,192g. 657n. 1,952d. 80.0 × 13.818 × 4.512 metres.
6-cyl. 4 S.C.S.A. (260 × 380 mm) 6DKM26L type oil engine manufactured by Daihatsu Diesel Manufacturing Company Ltd., Japan. 2,600bhp.
Double hulled, chemical/oil products tanker.
2003: Ordered from K. K. Miura Zosensho, Saiki (Yard No. 1275), by Jubilee Shipping Ltd., on behalf of charterer BP Oil Shipping Ltd. 14.4.2004: Keel laid. 2004: Transferred to Gordian Shipping Ltd., London (BP Shipping Ltd., managers). 7.6.2004: Launched. 19.8.2004: Completed.

9301641
J.5. ALIOS APOLLO (2004–)

2,191g. 657n. 1,952d. 80.0 × 13.824 × 4.5 metres.
6-cyl. 4 S.C.S.A. (260 × 380 mm) 6DKM26L type oil engine manufactured by Daihatsu Diesel Manufacturing Company Ltd., Japan. 2,600bhp.
Double hulled, chemical/oil products tanker.
2003: Ordered from K. K. Miura Zosensho, Saiki (Yard No. 1276), by Jubilee Shipping Ltd., on behalf of charterer BP Oil Shipping Ltd. 26.5.2004: Keel laid. 2004: Transferred to Gordian Shipping Ltd., London. (BP Shipping Ltd., managers). 24.7.2004: Launched. 19.10.2004: Completed.

Border Heather. (Internet source)

Donald Line Ltd.

9301615
J.6. ALIOS HERMES (2004–)

2,097g. 629n. 1,504d. 80.0 × 14.72 × 5.5 metres.
6-cyl. 4 S.C.S.A. (260 × 380 mm) 6DKM26L type oil engine manufactured by Daihatsu Diesel Manufacturing Company Ltd., Japan. 2,600bhp.
Double hulled, chemical/oil products tanker.
2003: Ordered from K. K. Miura Zosensho, Saiki (Yard No. 1272), by Jubilee Shipping Ltd., on behalf of charterer BP Oil Shipping Ltd. 13.1.2004: Keel laid. 18.3.2004: Launched. 2004: Transferred to Gordian Shipping Ltd., London. (Ceres Hellas Maritime Company, Piraeus, managers). 28.5.2004: Completed. 2004: Transferred to Donald Line Ltd. (same managers).

9301627
J.7. ALIOS HERA (2004–)

2,097g. 629n. 1,504d. 80.0 × 14.72 × 3.412 metres.
6-cyl. 4 S.C.S.A. (260 × 380 mm) 6DKM26L type oil engine manufactured by Daihatsu Diesel Manufacturing Company Ltd., Japan. 2,600bhp.
Double hulled, chemical/oil products tanker.
2003: Ordered from K. K. Miura Zosensho, Saiki (Yard No. 1273), by Jubilee Shipping Ltd., on behalf of charterer BP Oil Shipping Ltd. 3.3.2004: Keel laid. 21.4.2004: Launched for Goodeal Tanker Company Ltd., Sunbury on Thames (BP Shipping Ltd., managers). 15.7.2004: Completed for Donald Line Ltd.

Goodeal Tanker Company Ltd.

9301653
J.8. ALIOS ARTEMIS (2004–)

2,192g. 1,520n. 3,500d. 80.0 × 13.818 × 4.6 metres.
6-cyl. 4 S.C.S.A. (260 × 380 mm) 6DKM26L type oil engine manufactured by Daihatsu Diesel Manufacturing Company Ltd., Japan. 2,600bhp.
Double hulled, chemical/oil products tanker.
2003: Ordered from K. K. Miura Zosensho, Saiki (Yard No. 1277), by Jubilee Shipping Ltd., on behalf of charterer BP Oil Shipping Ltd. 2004: Transferred to Gordian Shipping Ltd., London. 20.9.2004: Keel laid. 1.12.2004: Launched for Goodeal Tanker Company Ltd., Sunbury on Thames (Ceres Hellas Maritime Company, Piraeus, managers), under Panamanian flag.

9301677
J.9. ALIOS POSEIDON (2004–)

2,192g. 1,520n. 3,500d. 80.0 × 13.818 × 4.6 metres.
6-cyl. 4 S.C.S.A. (260 × 380 mm) 6DKM26L type oil engine manufactured by Daihatsu Diesel Manufacturing Company Ltd., Japan. 2,600bhp.
Double hulled, chemical/oil products tanker.
2003: Ordered from K. K. Miura Zosensho, Saiki (Yard No. 1280), by Jubilee Shipping Ltd., on behalf of charterer BP Oil Shipping Ltd. 2004: Transferred to Goodeal Tanker Company Ltd., Sunbury on Thames (Ceres Hellas Maritime Company, Piraeus, managers), under Panamanian flag.

9301665
J.10. ANATOLIA SEA (2004–)

2,150g. 1,100n. 1,950d. 80.0 × 13.818 × 4.6 metres.
6-cyl. 4 S.C.S.A. (280 × 380 mm) 6DKM28L type oil engine manufactured by Daihatsu Diesel Manufacturing Company Ltd., Japan. 2,600bhp.
Double hulled, chemical/oil products tanker.
2003: Ordered from K. K. Miura Zosensho, Saiki (Yard No. 1278), by Jubilee Shipping

Ltd., on behalf of charterer BP Oil Shipping Ltd. 15.11.2004: Keel laid for Goodeal Tanker Company Ltd., Sunbury on Thames (Ceres Hellas Maritime Company, Piraeus, managers), under Panamanian flag.

Anatolian Shipping Company

9301689

J.11. ANATOLIA SUN

2,980g. ? n. ? d. ? × ? × ? metres.
-cyl. S.C.S.A. (? × ? mm) type oil engine manufactured by ? bhp. ? kts.
Double hulled, chemical/oil products tanker.

2003: Ordered from K. K. Miura Zosensho, Saiki (Yard No. 1281), by Jubilee Shipping Ltd., on behalf of charterer BP Oil Shipping Ltd.

9301691

J.12. ANATOLIA STAR

2,980g. ? n. ? d. ? × ? × ? metres.
-cyl. S.C.S.A. (? × ? mm) type oil engine manufactured by ?.
? bhp. ? kts.
Double hulled, chemical/oil products tanker.

2003: Ordered from K. K. Miura Zosensho, Saiki (Yard No. 1282), by Jubilee Shipping Ltd., on behalf of charterer BP Oil Shipping Ltd.

Subsidary and Associate Companies

Section Three

The Petroleum Steam Ship Company Ltd.
Formed 1906:
Managed by Lane, & MacAndrew
11.2.1907: Acquired first vessels.
1916: Manager restyled as Lane, & MacAndrew Ltd.
25.10.1917: Acquired by Anglo-Persian Oil Company (British Tanker Company Ltd.)
Vessels listed in *ITALIC* type were not acquired but have been included for completeness of the fleet details.

1957: Restyled as
The BP Clyde Tanker Company Ltd.

PS. 1. TEREK (1907–1917)

O.N. 110150. 3,710g. 2,352n. 335.5 × 45.0 × 28.1 feet.
T.3-cyl. (24[13]/16″, 40″ & 66″ × 45″) engine manufactured by G. Clark Ltd., Sunderland. 1,630 hp.
Ocean-going tanker.

24.5.1899: Launched by J. Laing & Company, Sunderland (Yard No. 569), for the Caucasian Steam Ship Company Ltd. (Lane & MacAndrew, managers). 6.1899: Completed. 11.2.1907: Transferred to the Petroleum Steam Ship Company Ltd. (same managers). 1916: Managers restyled as a limited company. 6.1917: Owners purchased by the British Tanker Company Ltd., and vessel renamed BRITISH DUKE. 1930: Sold to Societa Anonima di Navigazione Corrado, Italy, and renamed LAURA CORRADO. 30.3.1941: Torpedoed and sunk in the Mediterranean.

PS. 2. BALAKANI (1907–1915)

O.N. 110185. 3,696g. 2,367n. 335.0 × 45.0 × 28.0 feet.
T.3-cyl. (24$^1/_2$″, 40″ & 66″ × 45″) engine manufactured by G. Clark Ltd., Sunderland. 1,630 hp.
Ocean-going tanker.

9.1899: Completed by J. Laing & Company, Sunderland (Yard No. 570), for the Caucasian Steam Ship Company Ltd. (Lane & MacAndrew, managers). 11.2.1907: Transferred to the Petroleum Steam Ship Company Ltd. (same managers). 9.9.1915: Whilst on a voyage from Port Arthur to London with fuel oil, exploded a mine, laid by the German submarine UC 1, at position 51.31N., 1.20E., $^1/_2$ mile S. W. by S. from the Long Sand Buoy, Thames Estuary, and sank.

PS. 3. CAUCASIAN (1907–1915)

O.N. 112645. 4,657g. 3,003n. 365.3 × 49.8 × 28.0 feet.
T.3-cyl. (25$^1/_2$″, 42″ & 69″ × 45″) engine manufactured by G. Clark Ltd., Sunderland. 1,845 hp.
Ocean-going tanker.

12.1899: Completed by J. Laing & Company, Sunderland (Yard No. 571), for the Caucasian Steam Ship Company Ltd. (Lane & MacAndrew, managers). 11.2.1907: Transferred to the Petroleum Steam Ship Company Ltd. (same managers). 1.7.1915: Whilst on a voyage from London to New Orleans with creosote, was sunk by a torpedo from the German submarine U-39, at a position 60 miles S. W. of the Lizard.

PS. 4. EUPLECTELA (1907)

O.N. 102844. 3,918g. 2,507n. 340.0 × 44.0 × 22.9 feet.
T.3-cyl. (25″, 41″ & 67″ × 48″) engine manufactured by the Wallsend Slipway Company Ltd., Wallsend. 1,625 hp.
Ocean-going tanker.

2.1894: Completed by Sir W. G. Armstrong, Mitchell & Company Ltd., Newcastle (Yard No. 603), for Shell Transport & Trading Company Ltd. (M. Samuel & Company, managers), London. 21.9.1906: Sold to Lane & MacAndrew. 11.2.1907: Transferred to the Petroleum Steam Ship Company Ltd. (Lane & MacAndrew, managers). 9.7.1907: Sold to the Asiatic Petroleum Company Ltd. 5.1921: Became a depot ship at Barcelona. 1927: Sold to Societa Anonima di Navigazione Danubio, Italy, and renamed PERSEUS. 1928: Renamed CENTAURUS. 9.1933: Sold for demolition at Savona.

PS. 5. TURBO (1907–1908)

O.N. 101951. 4,134g. 2,659n. 347.5 × 45.7 × 27.3 feet.
T.3-cyl. (26″, 42$^1/_2$″ & 69″ × 45″) engine manufactured by G. Clark Ltd., Sunderland. 1,705 hp.
Ocean-going tanker.

12.1892: Completed by J. Laing & Company, Sunderland (Yard No. 635), for Shell Transport & Trading Company Ltd. (M. Samuel & Company, managers), London. 1.11.1906: Sold to Lane & MacAndrew. 11.2.1907: Transferred to the Petroleum Steam Ship Company Ltd. (Lane & MacAndrew, managers). 6.1.1908: Whilst on a voyage from Batum to Hamburg, wrecked at Nieuwe Diep.

PS. 6. ROCK LIGHT (1907–1917)

see ship No. BT. 12 in main fleet.

PS. 7. PINNA (1907–1917)

O.N. 112311. 6,288g. 4,100n. 420.8 × 52.1 × 32.2 feet.
T.3-cyl. (27$^1/_2$″, 46″ & 77″ × 48″) engine manufactured by the North Eastern Marine Engineering Company Ltd., Newcastle. 2,780 hp.
Ocean-going tanker.

8.12.1900: Launched by Armstrong, Whitworth & Company Ltd., Newcastle (Yard No. 705), for Shell Transport & Trading Company Ltd. (M. Samuel & Company, managers), London. 3.1901: Completed. 12.11.1906: Sold to Lane & MacAndrew. 11.2.1907: Transferred to the Petroleum Steam Ship Company Ltd. (Lane & MacAndrew, managers). 1916: Managers restyled as a limited company. 6.1917: Owners purchased by the British Tanker Company Ltd., and vessel renamed BRITISH EARL. 1929: Sold to Tankschiff Rederi Julius Schindler G.m.b.H., Germany, and renamed TANKSCHINDLER. 1931: Sold to Societa Anonima Impresse Navale et Affini, Italy, and renamed TROTTIERA. 1938: Sold to Societa Anonima Transporti Marghera, Italy. 10.6.1940: Interned at Puerto Cabello, Venezuela. 31.3.1941: Scuttled by her crew. Subsequently taken over by the Venezuela Government. 1943: Sold to, and raised by the United States Navy, refurbished and renamed ORISSA. 1948: Sold to the Asia Development Corp, China. 1950: Entry deleted from Lloyd's Register.

PS. 8. SERVIAN (1908–1917)

O.N. 125685. 4,997g. 3,134n. 385.0 × 51.0 × 27.7 feet.
T.3-cyl. (26$^1/_2$″, 44″ & 72″ × 48″) engine manufactured by J. Dickinson & Sons Ltd., Sunderland. 2,180 hp.
Ocean-going tanker.

5.1908: Completed by J. Laing & Company, Sunderland (Yard No. 628), for the Petroleum Steam Ship Company Ltd. (Lane & MacAndrew, managers). 1916: Managers restyled as a limited company. 6.1917: Owners purchased by the British Tanker Company Ltd., and vessel renamed BRITISH MARQUIS. 1930: Sold to Societa Anonima Impresse Navale et Affini, Italy, and renamed CONTE DI MISURATA. 1934: Sold to Imprese Navale Commercial Societa Anonima (I.N.C.S.A.), Italy. 9.11.1941: War loss.

PS. 9. CARPATHIAN (1908–1917)

O.N. 125715. 4,900g. 3,087n. 385.0 × 51.0 × 33.7 feet.
T.3-cyl. (26$^1/_2$″, 44″ & 72″ × 48″) engine manufactured by the Wallsend Slipway Company Ltd., Newcastle. 2,125 hp.

20.5.1908: Launched by Armstrong, Whitworth & Company Ltd., Newcastle (Yard No. 802), for the Petroleum Steam Ship Company Ltd. (Lane & MacAndrew, managers). 7.1908: Completed. 1916: Managers restyled as a limited company. 6.1917: Owners purchased by the British Tanker Company Ltd., and vessel renamed BRITISH PEER. 1930: Sold to Imprese Navale Commercial Societa Anonima (I.N.C.S.A.), Italy, and renamed TAMPICOMPANY 11.1941: Seriously damaged by a torpedo in the Mediterranean. 1947: Demolished.

PS. 10. ROUMANIAN (1908–1917)

O.N. 125723. 4,906g. 3,089n. 385.0 × 51.0 × 27.6 feet.
T.3-cyl. (26$^1/_2$″, 44″ & 72″ × 48″) engine manufactured by the Wallsend Slipway Company Ltd., Newcastle. 2,125 hp.
Ocean-going tanker.

27.7.1908: Launched by Armstrong, Whitworth & Company Ltd., Newcastle (Yard No. 803), for the Petroleum Steam Ship Company Ltd. (Lane & MacAndrew, managers). 9.1908: Completed. 1916: Managers restyled as a limited company. 6.1917: Owners purchased by the British Tanker Company Ltd., and vessel renamed BRITISH BARON. 17.4.1925: Sold to K. Kuhnle, Norway, and renamed NORNE. 1928: Sold to Soc. Anon. Industrie Marinare, Italy, and renamed VINCAS. 1932: Sold to the Pacific Oil Company Ltd., London. 1935: Sold for demolition.

PS. 11. DANUBIAN (1909–1917)

O.N. 125769. 5,064g. 3,166n. 387.2 × 51.8 × 27.9 feet.
T.3-cyl. (27″, 45″ & 74″ × 48″) engine manufactured by the Wallsend Slipway Company Ltd., Newcastle. 2,235 hp.
Ocean-going tanker.

21.1.1909: Launched by Swan, Hunter & Wigham, Richardson Ltd., Newcastle (Yard No. 823), for the Petroleum Steam Ship Company Ltd. (Lane & MacAndrew, managers). 3.1909: Completed. 1916: Managers restyled as a limited company. 6.1917: Owners purchased by the British Tanker Company Ltd., and vessel renamed BRITISH KNIGHT. 1929: Sold to Skibs Ranvik (Anders Jahre, manager), Norway, and renamed RANVIK. 1938: Sold to Leonardo Arrivabene, Italy, and renamed C. ARRIVABENE. 5.1.1940: Whilst on a voyage from Augusta to Venezuela, was wrecked at a position 2 miles south of Fedahal, Morocco.

PS. 12. SAXONIAN (1914–1917)

O.N. 136690. 4,855g. 2,978n. 373.5 × 57.4 × 27.7 feet.
T.3-cyl. (27″, 44″ & 73″ × 48″) engine manufactured by Dunsmuir & Jackson Ltd., Glasgow. 2,160 hp.
Ocean-going tanker.

6.1914: Completed by Greenock & Grangemouth Dockyard Company Ltd., Greenock (Yard No. ?), for the Petroleum Steamship Company Ltd. (Lane & MacAndrew, managers). 1916: Managers restyled as a limited company. 7.2.1917: Whilst on a voyage from Port Arthur to Dartmouth with paraffin, was sunk by a German warship at position 320 miles S. W. of Fastnet.

PS. 13. TEUTONIAN (1914–1916)

O.N. 136657. 4,824g. 2,874n. 374.0 × 50.8 × 27.6 feet.
T.3-cyl. (26″, 44″ & 72″ × 48″) engine manufactured by J. Dickinson & Sons Ltd., Sunderland. 2,240 hp.
Ocean-going tanker.

7.1914: Completed by Sir. J. Laing & Sons, Sunderland (Yard No. 646), for the Petroleum Steamship Company Ltd. (Lane & MacAndrew, managers) 4.3.1916: Whilst on a voyage from Sabine to Avonmouth with refined oil was sunk by a German warship at position 50.55N., 10.20W.

1917
At this juncture the ANGLO-PERSIAN OIL COMPANY acquired control.
(British Tanker Company Ltd., operating managers),

PS. 14. BRITISH BARON (1) (1917–1925)

see ship No. PS. 10 above.

PS. 15. BRITISH DUKE (1) (1917–1930)

see ship No. PS. 1 above.

PS. 16. BRITISH EARL (1) (1917–1929)

see ship No. PS. 7 above.

PS. 17. BRITISH KNIGHT (1) (1917–1929)

see ship No. PS. 11 above.

PS. 18. BRITISH MARQUIS (1) (1917–1930)

see ship No. PS. 8 above.

PS. 19. BRITISH PEER (1) (1917–1930)

see ship No. PS. 9 above.

PS. 20. BRITISH VISCOUNT (1) (1917–1918)

see ship No. PS. 6 above.

PS. 21. BAGHDAD (1) (1917–1939)

O.N. 166329. 19g. 12n. 42.0 × 12.0 × 5.0 feet.
3 bhp, oil engine
Wooden hull launch.

1917: Completed by unspecified builder for the Petroleum Steamship Company Ltd. 1939: Transferred to the Rafadain Oil Company Ltd. 25.6.1946: Burnt at Busreh.

PS. 22. ARAS (1918–1930)

see ship No. M. 3 in the Brit. Tkr. managed section.

PS. 23. KURA (1918–1920)

see ship No. BT. 34 in main fleet.

PS. 24. RION (1918–1920)

see ship No. M. 5 in the Brit. Tkr. managed section.

PS. 25. SURAM (1918–1920)

see ship No. M. 6 in the Brit. Tkr. managed section.

PS. 26. BETWAND (1921–1951)

O.N. 147631. 117g. 59n. 100.0 × 20.0 × 7.5 feet.
C.2-cyl. (10″ & 20″ × 14″) engine manufactured by the shipbuilder. 17 nhp.
Water barge.

1914: Completed as NYAUNGBIN by Dalla Dockyard, Dalla, for the Irrawaddy Flotilla Company, Rangoon. 1916: Requisitioned by the Royal Indian Marine as SB 1. 1920: Sold to the Burmah Oil Company Ltd., and renamed BETWAND. 1921: Sold to the Petroleum Steam Ship Company Ltd. 1934: Converted to a water barge. 1951: Seized by the Iranian Government. No further details located. (A faint possibility exists that this vessel may have been sister-ship SHABIN originally.)

PS. 27. NAFTAK (1921–1947)

see ship No. AP.6 in A. P. O. C. section

PS. 28. DEHLURAN (1921–1927)

O.N. 136206. 224g. 192n. 132.1 × 32.0 × 5.3 feet.
C.2-cyl. horizontal (15″ & 27″ × 54″) engine manufactured by the shipbuilder. 32 hp.
Stern 1/4 paddle steamer.

1914: Completed, as SIKKIM*, by Yarrow Shipbuilders, Scotstoun (Yard No. 1408 ?), for the Irrawaddy Flotilla Company, Rangoon. 1915: Requisitioned by the War Office, Inland Waterway Transport Department, London, as a hospital sternwheeler and renamed HS.1, for Mesopotamian service. 1918: Re-designated as an ambulance sternwheeler SA 5. 1919: Reverted to HS 1. 1920: Sold to the Anglo-Persian Oil Company Ltd., and renamed DEHLURAN. 1921: Transferred to the Petroleum Steamship Company Ltd. 22.7.1927: Burnt at Ahwaz, machinery removed for stock and damaged hull sold for demolition.

* another source states SICCIM.

PS. 29. NAFTUN (1921–)

see ship No. AP. 4 in A. P. O. C. section.

PS. 30. Unknown (1) (1921–1927)

see ship No. AP. 7 in A. P. O. C. section.

PS. 31. DIYALA (1921–1951)

see ship No. AP. 8 in A. P. O. C. section.

PS. 32. CHARDINE (1921–1937)

see ship No. AP. 9 in A. P. O. C. section.

PS. 33. AMINIYEH (1921–1951)

see ship No. AP. 10 in A. P. O. C. section.

PS. 34. EUPHRATES (1921–1951)

see ship No. AP. 11 in A. P. O. C. section.

PS. 35. MAMATAIN (1921–1932)

see ship No. AP. 12 in A. P. O. C. section.

PS. 36. TIB (1921–1951)

see ship No. AP. 13 in A. P. O. C. section.

PS. 37. TIGRIS (1921–1951)

see ship No. AP. 14 in A. P. O. C. section.

PS. 38. Unknown (2) (1921–)

see ship No. AP. 15 in A. P. O. C. section.

PS. 39. LADY CURZON (1921–1953)

see ship No. BT. 2 in main fleet.

PS. 40. THEGON (1922–1951)

see ship No. AP. 5 in A. P. O. C. section.

PS. 41. FERRARA (1922–1923)

see ship No. BT. 4 in main fleet.

PS. 42. FRIESLAND (1922–)

see ship No. BT. 3 in main fleet.

PS. 43. HERALD (1922–1953)

see ship No. BT. 23 in main fleet.

PS. 44. SHABTAB (1923–1937)

O.N. 160532. 97g. 37n. 120.0 × 20.3 × 4.6 feet.
Originally steam powered.
Post 1928: 4-cyl. 4 S.C.S.A. engine manufactured in 1918 by Bergius Company, Glasgow. (possibly refitted from m/launch TANOOMAH). 60 bhp.
Fire float – formerly a 'Fly' class river gunboat.

1915: Completed as either CADDISFLY (F12) or WATERFLY (F. 4) by Yarrow, Scotstoun, for the Admiralty. 1916: Re-erected at Abadan. 1918: Transferred to the War Office as F.4 and F.12 respectively. 17.2.1923: Both vessels sold to the Petroleum Steamship Company Ltd., one being renamed SHABTAB. 1928: Motorised and converted to a firefloat for Abadan. 1938: Dismantled – hull demolished and machinery transferred to a muhailla (local sailing craft) hull.

PS. 45. Unknown (3) (1923–19)

O.N. . 97g. 37n. 120.0 × 20.3 × 4.6 feet.
Originally steam powered.
Fire float – formerly a 'Fly' class river gunboat.

1915: Completed as either CADDISFLY (F.12) or WATERFLY (F. 4) by Yarrow, Scotstoun (Yard No.), for the Admiralty. 1916: Re-erected at Abadan. 1918: Transferred to the War Office as F.4 and 12 respectively. 17.2.1923: Both vessels sold to the Petroleum Steamship Company Ltd. WATERFLY at Basrah. No other details located.

PS. 46. BIBIAN (1923–1951)

see ship No. AP. 20 in A. P. O. C. section.

PS. 47. KALGAH (1924–1942)

see ship No. AP. 21 in A. P. O. C. section.

PS. 48. ST. ATHAN (1924–1948)

O.N. 143447. 427g. 135.0 × 29.1 × 13.7 feet.
T.3-cyl. (18¼″, 28½″ & 48¼″ × 28″) engine manufactured by the shipbuilder. 1,040 hp.
Tug.

11.1919: Completed by Day, Summers & Company Ltd., Southampton (Yard No. 175), for the Admiralty, pennant No. W 40. 17.11.1924: Purchased by the Petroleum Steam Ship Company Ltd., London. 1948: Sold to Loucas Matsas & Sons, Piraeus, and renamed MARIGO MATSAS III. 1967: Placed in lay-up. 1968: Sold for demolition in Greece.

PS. 49. ST. EWE (1926–1927)

O.N. 143183. 441g. 4n 135.4 × 29.0 × 13.6 feet.
Post 1926: 432g. 5n.
T.3-cyl. (18¼″, 28½″ & 48¼″ × 28″) engine manufactured by Ross & Duncan Ltd., Glasgow. 116 nhp 1,200 ihp.
Tug.

1.4.1919: Launched by Murdoch & Murray Ltd., Port Glasgow (Yard No. 288), for the Admiralty. 6.1919: Completed. 1926: Sold to Harry G. Page, London. 1926: Purchased by the Petroleum Steam Ship Company Ltd. 24.11.1926: Transferred to the British Tanker Company Ltd., converted to a pilot vessel and renamed ALARM. 1927: Sold to the Basra Port Director and Director General of Navigation, Iraq, Owners subsequently restyled as Iraq Government (Directorate General of Navigation). 1963: Owners restyled Government of Iraq (Directorate General of Ports and Navigation). 1966: Renamed SHU'ALAH. 1975: Owners restyled as Government of Iraq (Iraqi Ports Administration). 1976: Owners restyled as State Organisation of Iraqi Ports. 1978: Owners restyled as Government of Iraq (State Organisation of Iraqi Ports). 1979: Owners restyled as Government of the Republic of Iraq (State Organisation of Iraqi Ports). 1998: Lloyd's Register deleted entry – 'Reported to be in a non-seagoing condition at Basrah'.

PS. 50. KHUZISTAN (1924–1953)

O.N. 147673. 871g. 374n. 176.0 × 32.7 × 13.8 feet.
T.3-cyl. (14″, 23″ & 38″ × 27″) engine manufactured by Wm. Beardmore & Company Ltd., Glasgow. 510 hp.
Cased petrol carrier.

22.4.1924: Launched by the Amble Shipbuilding Company Ltd., Amble (Yard No. 36), for the Petroleum Steam Ship Company Ltd. 21.6.1924: Completed. 20.10.1953: Sold to Ambassador Steam Ship Ltd. (F. Collis & Company, managers), Bombay, and renamed EFFIGYNY. 1962: Sold for demolition.

PS. 51. TEMBI (1924–1938)

65g. ?n. × ? × ? feet.
Oil engine .
Wooden hulled.

1924: Built for the Petroleum Steamship Company Ltd. 1938: Dismantled at Abadan.

PS. 52. KUMAKI (1928–1953)

O.N. 143062. 434g. 135.5 × 29.0 × 13.6 feet.
Post 1953 370g. 13n.
T.3-cyl. (18¼″, 28½″ & 48¼″ × 28″) engine manufactured by Earle's Shipbuilding & Engineering Company Ltd., Hull. 1,040 hp.
Tug.

3.1919: Completed as ST. BOTOLPH, by Livingstone, Cooper Ltd., Hessle (Yard No. 185), for the Admiralty, pennant No. W 34. 29.12.1926: Sold to G. Maclean. 1.1.1928: Purchased by the Petroleum Steam Ship Company Ltd., and renamed KUMAKI. 4.4.1928: Sailed from Leith. 7.5.1928: Arrived at Abadan. 1953: Sold to Nicolas E. Vernicos Shipping Company Ltd., Greece, and renamed VERNICOS NICOLAOS. 1968: Demolished.

PS. 53. TARAQQI (1930–1955)

O.N. 162493. 388g. 134n. 140.6 × 29.1 × 7.8 feet
Two, C.2-cyl. (11″ & 22″ × 14″) engines manufactured by McKie & Baxter Ltd., Glasgow. 470ihp.
Twin screw general cargo vessel.

1930: Launched by G. Brown & Company, Greenock (Yard No.176), for the Petroleum Steam Ship Company Ltd. 10.1930: Completed. 26.10.1930: Sailed from Swansea en route to Abadan. 30.5.1955: Sold to Yusif A. Alghanim, Kuwait. 1967: Sold to Al Rashid Industrial & Contracting Company, Kuwait. 1973: Sold to A. Salem & J. Ghanim, Kuwait, and renamed TARAQI. 1998: Lloyd's Register deleted entry – 'Continued existence in doubt'.

PS. 54. PESHIN (1931–)

see ship No. BT 105 above.

PS. 55. PAHRA (1931–)

see ship No. BT 104 above.

PS. 56. KASHAN (1932–1951)

O.N. 162674. 308g. 160.0 × 25.0 × 7.7 feet.
Dumb tank barge.

3.1932: Completed by Henry Robb Ltd., Leith, for the Petroleum Steam Ship Company Ltd. 1932: Re-erected at Abadan. 1951: Seized by the Iranian Government. *Due to small size and type of this vessel no further details have been recorded by the authors.*

PS. 57. KAZVIN (1932–1951)

O.N. 162692. 309g. 160.0 × 25.2 × 7.7 feet.
Dumb tank barge.

3.1932: Completed by Henry Robb Ltd., Leith, for the Petroleum Steam Ship Company Ltd. 1932: Re-erected at Abadan. 1951: Seized by the Iranian Government. *Due to small size and type of this vessel no further details have been recorded by the authors.*

PS. 58. ONGER (1935)

2,371g. 1,033n. 286.8 x 47.2 x 19.9 feet.
Two, T.3-cyl. (18", 28" & 48" x 27") engines manufactured by the shipbuilder. 2,114 hp
Twin screw suction hopper dredger.

4.1935: Completed by W. Simons & Company Ltd., Renfrew (Yard No. 705), for the Petroleum Steamship Company Ltd. 5.1935: Sold to the Iraq Government (Directorate General of Navigation). 1963: Owners restyled Government of Iraq (Directorate General of Ports and Navigation). 1958: Renamed SULAIMANIYAH. 1975: Owners restyled as Government of Iraq (Iraqi Ports Administration). 1976: Owners restyled as State Organisation of Iraqi Ports. 1978: Owners restyled as Government of Iraq (State Organisation of Iraqi Ports). 1979: Owners restyled as Government of the Republic of Iraq (State Organisation of Iraqi Ports). Still listed in Lloyd's Register 2003/04.

PS. 59. SHIRAZ (1937–1951)

O.N. 166339. 80g. 43n. 81.6 × 17.6 × 4.2 feet.
Two, 4-cyl. 2 S.C.S.A. (9″ × 11″) oil engines manufactured by Norris, Henty & Gardner Ltd., Manchester. 192 bhp.
Tug.

1936: Ordered by the Anglo-Iranian Oil Company Ltd., from Ferguson Bros. Ltd., Port Glasgow (Yard No. 315), for the Petroleum Steamship Company Ltd. 1937: Completed and dismantled for shipment. 1937: Re-erected at Abadan. 1951: Seized by the Iranian Government. *Due to small size and type of this vessel no further details have been recorded by the authors.*

PS. 60. SHAHABAD (1937–1951)

O.N. 166341. 80g. 43n. 81.6 × 17.6 × 4.2 feet.
Two, 4-cyl. 2 S.C.S.A. (9″ × 11″) oil engines manufactured by Norris, Henty & Gardner Ltd., Manchester. 192 bhp.
Tug.

1936: Ordered by the Anglo-Iranian Oil Company Ltd., from Ferguson Bros. Ltd., Port Glasgow (Yard No. 316), for the Petroleum Steamship Company Ltd. 1937: Completed and dismantled for shipment. 1937: Re-erected at Abadan. 1951: Seized by the Iranian

Khuzistan – cased oil carrier. (World Ship Society Photograph Library)

Government. *Due to small size and type of this vessel no further details have been recorded by the authors.*

PS. 61. SHIMRAN (1937–1951)

O.N. 166340. 80g. 43n. 81.6 × 17.6 × 4.2 feet.
Two, 4-cyl. 2 S.C.S.A. (9″ × 11″) oil engines manufactured by Norris, Henty & Gardner Ltd., Manchester. 192 bhp.
Tug.
1936: Ordered by the Anglo-Iranian Oil Company Ltd., from Ferguson Bros. Ltd., Port Glasgow (Yard No. 317), for the Petroleum Steamship Company Ltd. 1937: Completed and dismantled for shipment. 1937: Re-erected at Abadan. 1951: Seized by the Iranian Government. *Due to small size and type of this vessel no further details have been recorded by the authors.*

PS. 62. SHUSTAR (1937–1951)

O.N. 166342. 80g. 34n. 81.6 × 17.6 × 4.2 feet.
Two, 4-cyl. 2 S.C.S.A. (9″ × 11″) oil engines manufactured by Norris, Henty & Gardner Ltd., Manchester. 192 bhp.
Tug.
1936: Ordered by the Anglo-Iranian Oil Company Ltd., from Ferguson Bros. Ltd., Port Glasgow (Yard No. 318), for the Petroleum Steamship Company Ltd. 1937: Completed and dismantled for shipment. 1937: Re-erected at Abadan. 1951: Seized by the Iranian Government. *Due to small size and type of this vessel no further details have been recorded by the authors.*

PS. 63. BASRA (1937)

2,547g. 1,075n. 286.8 × 50.2 × 20.0 feet.
Two, T.3-cyl. (18″, 28″ & 48″ × 27″) engines manufactured by the shipbuilder. 1,057 hp.
Twin screw suction hopper dredger.
1936: Ordered by the Anglo–Iranian Oil Company Ltd., from W. Simons & Company Ltd., Renfrew (Yard No. 711), for the Petroleum Steam Ship Company Ltd. 9.1937: Completed for the Iraq Government (Directorate General of Navigation). 1963: Owners restyled Government of Iraq (Directorate General of Ports and Navigation). 1975: Owners restyled as Government of Iraq (Iraqi Ports Administration). 1976: Owners restyled as State Organisation of Iraqi Ports. 1978: Owners restyled as Government of Iraq (State Organisation of Iraqi Ports). 1979: Owners restyled as Government of the Republic of Iraq (State Organisation of Iraqi Ports).

PS. 64. ATLASI (1937–??)

O.N. 162789. 56g. 34n. 70.0 × 14.5 × 8.4 feet.
Two, 6-cyl. 4 S.C.S.A. (4¼″ × 6″) oil engines manufactured by Gardner Engines Ltd., Patricroft.
Wooden hulled yacht.
1933: Completed as BRINMARIC by Camper & Nicholson Ltd., Gosport, for Eric S. Fox, Portsmouth. 1937: Lloyd's Confidential Index states purchased by the Petroleum Steamship Company Ltd., and renamed ATLASI. Yacht register retains entry until 1955 whereupon it states sold to USA. No further details located.

PS. 65. SINJAR (1938)

O.N. 167148. 37g. 23n. 60.2 × 12.6 × 4.1 feet
4-cyl. 2 S.C.S.A. (9″ × 11″) oil engine manufactured by Gardner & Sons, Manchester. 96 bhp.
Tug.
1937: Ordered by the Anglo-Iranian Oil Company Ltd., from G. Brown & Company (Marine) Ltd., Greenock (Yard No. 205), for the Petroleum Steamship Company Ltd. 2.4.1938: Launched. 1938: Completed, and subsequently transferred to the Rafidain Oil Company Ltd. 1952: Owners sold to Iraqi Authorities. No further details located.

PS. 66. SULAF (1938)

O.N. 167149. 37g. 23n. 60.2 × 12.6 × 4.1 feet
4-cyl. 2 S.C.S.A. (9″ × 11″) oil engine manufactured by Gardner & Sons, Manchester. 96 bhp.
Tug.
1937: Ordered by the Anglo-Iranian Oil Company Ltd., from G. Brown & Company (Marine) Ltd., Greenock (Yard No. 206), for the Petroleum Steamship Company Ltd. 2.4.1938: Launched. 1938: Completed, and subsequently transferred to the Rafidain Oil Company Ltd. 1952: Owners sold to Iraqi Authorities. No further details located.

PS. 67. UN-NAMED (1) (1938–1951)

80.0 × 25.0 × 5.0 feet.
Dumb tank barge
1937: Ordered by the Anglo-Iranian Oil Company Ltd., from Ferguson Bros. Ltd., Port Glasgow (Yard No. 327), for the Petroleum Steamship Company Ltd. 1937: Completed and dismantled for shipment. 1938: Re-erected at Abadan. 1951: Seized by the Iranian Government. *Due to small size and type of this vessel no further details have been recorded by the authors.*

PS. 68. UN-NAMED (2) (1938–1951)

80.0 × 25.0 × 5.0 feet.
Dumb tank barge
1937: Ordered by the Anglo-Iranian Oil Company Ltd., from Ferguson Bros. Ltd., Port Glasgow (Yard No. 328), for the Petroleum Steamship Company Ltd. 1937: Completed and dismantled for shipment. 1938: Re-erected at Abadan. 1951: Seized by the Iranian Government. *Due to small size and type of this vessel no further details have been recorded by the authors.*

PS. 69. SIVAND (1938–1951)

O.N. 166538. 81g. 34n. 81.7 × 17.5 × 4.2 feet.
Two, 4-cyl. 2 S.C.S.A. (9″ × 11″) oil engines manufactured by Gardner & Sons, Manchester. 192 bhp.
Twin screw tunnel tug.
1937: Ordered by the Anglo-Iranian Oil Company Ltd., from Ferguson Bros. Ltd., Port Glasgow (Yard No. 329), for the Petroleum Steamship Company Ltd. 1938: Completed and dismantled for shipment. 1938: Re-erected at Abadan. 1951: Seized by the Iranian Government. *Due to small size and type of this vessel no further details have been recorded by the authors.*

PS. 70. SAMNAN (1938–1951)

O.N. 166561. 81g. 34n. 81.7 × 17.5 × 4.2 feet.
Two, 4-cyl. 2 S.C.S.A. (9″ × 11″) oil engines manufactured by Gardner & Sons, Manchester. 192 bhp.
Twin screw tunnel tug.
1937: Ordered by the Anglo-Iranian Oil Company Ltd., from Ferguson Bros.Ltd., Port Glasgow (Yard No. 330), for the Petroleum Steamship Company Ltd. 1937: Completed and dismantled for shipment. 1938: Re-erected at Abadan. 1951: Seized by the Iranian Government. *Due to small size and type of this vessel no further details have been recorded by the authors.*

PS. 71. SURUK (1938–1951)

O.N. 166562. 81g. 34n. 81.7 × 17.5 × 4.2 feet.
Two, 4-cyl. 2 S.C.S.A. (9″ × 11″) oil engines manufactured by Gardner & Sons, Manchester. 192 bhp.
Twin screw tunnel tug.
1937: Ordered by the Anglo-Iranian Oil Company Ltd., from Ferguson Bros. Ltd., Port Glasgow (Yard No. 331), for the Petroleum Steamship Company Ltd. 1938: Completed and dismantled for shipment. 1938: Re-erected at Abadan. 1951: Seized by the Iranian Government. *Due to small size and type of this vessel no further details have been recorded by the authors.*

PS. 72. SHAMIL (1938–1951)

O.N. 166595. 81g. 34n. 81.7 × 17.5 × 4.2 feet.
Two, 4-cyl. 2 S.C.S.A. (9″ × 11″) oil engines manufactured by Gardner & Sons, Manchester. 192 bhp.
Twin screw tunnel tug.
1937: Ordered by the Anglo-Iranian Oil Company Ltd., from Ferguson Bros. Ltd., Port Glasgow (Yard No. 332), for the Petroleum Steamship Company Ltd. 1937: Completed and dismantled for shipment. 1938: Re-erected at Abadan. 1951: Seized by the Iranian Government. *Due to small size and type of this vessel no further details have been recorded by the authors.*

PS. 73. SHAHVEH (1938–1951)

O.N. 166596. 81g. 34n. 81.7 × 17.5 × 4.2 feet.
Two, 4-cyl. 2 S.C.S.A. (9″ × 11″) oil engines manufactured by Gardner & Sons, Manchester. 192 bhp.
Twin screw tunnel tug.
1937: Ordered by the Anglo-Iranian Oil Company Ltd., from Ferguson Bros. Ltd., Port Glasgow (Yard No. 333), for the Petroleum Steamship Company Ltd. 1937: Completed and dismantled for shipment. 1938: Re-erected at Abadan. 1951: Seized by the Iranian Government. *Due to small size and type of this vessel no further details have been recorded by the authors.*

PS. 74. SOODMARD (1938–1951)

O.N. 164515. 39g. 11n. 58.0 × 15.0 × 6.8 feet.
5-cyl. 2 S.C.S.A. (180 × 300mm) Polar type oil engine manufactured by British Auxiliaries Ltd., Glasgow. 180bhp. 9.5 kts
Tug.
15.8.1935: Completed as CONSUTA by Philip & Son Ltd., Dartmouth (Yard No. 827), for the Suez Canal Lighterage Company, London. 1938: Sold to the Petroleum Steamship Company Ltd., and renamed SOODMARD. 1951: Seized by the Iranian Government. *Due to small size and type of this vessel no further details have been recorded by the authors.*

PS. 75. MIHRABAD (1938–1951)

O.N. 166609. 79g. 19n. 73.4 × 15.6 × 5.9 feet.
Two 5-cyl. 2 S.C.S.A. (230 × 300mm) oil engine manufactured by W. H. Allen, Sons & Company, Bedford, geared to twin screw shafts. 260 bhp.
Twin screw tug.
27.10.1938: Launched by Clelands (Successors) Ltd., Newcastle (Yard No. 48), for the Petroleum Steamship Company Ltd. 11.1938: Completed. 1951: Seized by the Iranian Government. *Due to small size and type of this vessel no further details have been recorded by the authors.*

PS. 76. PUDAR (1938–)

O.N. 166355. 360g. 332n. 165.8 × 26.1 × 7.8 feet.

Dumb tank barge.
28.2.1938: Launched by Scott & Sons, Bowling (Yard No. 346), for the Petroleum Steam Ship Company Ltd. 2.1938: Completed. *Due to small size and type of this vessel no further details have been recorded by the authors.*

PS. 77. ZURMAND (1) (1938–1955)

see ship No. BT. 288 in main fleet.

PS. 78. KARIND (1938–1951)

O.N. 166539. 309g. 160.0 × 25.2 × 7.7 feet.
Dumb tank barge.
26.8.1938: Launched by Henry Robb Ltd., Leith (Yard No. 275), for the Petroleum Steam Ship Company Ltd. 8.1938: Completed. 1938: Re-erected at Abadan. 1951: Seized by the Iranian Government. 1955: Transferred to the National Iranian Oil Company Ltd., Iran. *Due to small size and type of this vessel no further details have been recorded by the authors.*

PS. 79. KANGAN (1938–1951)

O.N. 166540. 309g. 160.0 × 25.2 × 7.7 feet.
Dumb tank barge.
25.8.1938: Launched by Henry Robb Ltd., Leith (Yard No. 274), for the Petroleum Steam Ship Company Ltd. 8.1938: Completed. 1938: Re-erected at Abadan. 1951: Seized by the Iranian Government. 1955: Transferred to the National Iranian Oil Company Ltd., Iran. *Due to small size and type of this vessel no further details have been recorded by the authors.*

PS. 80. ZERANG (1) (1938–1954)

O.N. 166542. 361g. ? n. 120.5 × 31.1 × 13.0 feet.
As built T.3-cyl. (16½″, 27″ & 46″ × 30″) engine manufactured by Plenty & Son Ltd., Newbury. 870 hp.
Post 1962: 6-cyl. 4 S.C.S.A. (15″ × 18″) National KSSDM-6 type oil engine manufactured by Mirrlees, Bickerton & Day Ltd., Stockport. 1,250bhp. 10 kts.
Tug.
31.5.1938: Launched by Scott & Sons, Bowling (Yard No. 348), for the Petroleum Steam Ship Company Ltd. 8.1938: Completed. 23.8.1938: Sailed from Glasgow. 24.10.1938: Arrived at Busreh. 1939 until 7.1944: Admiralty service in the Persian Gulf and Bay of Bengal. 1954: Transferred to BP (Kwinana) Pty Ltd., Australia. 2.11.1954: Arrived at Fremantle from Djakarta. 10.1.1955: Registered at Fremantle as COCKBURN. 8.12.1959: Sold to J. Fenwick & Company Pty Ltd., Sydney. 1.6.1960: Registered at Sydney. 9.5.1961: Renamed MANLY COVE. 1960–2: Rebuilt and re-engined by Sydney Slipway & Engineering Company Pty Ltd., Mort's Bay. 31.7.1974: Sold to J. F. Causing Inc, Cebu, Philippines. 1975: Sold to Atlas Consolidated Mining & Development Corporation, Toledo City, Philippines, and renamed MARIA AURORA II. 1976: Sold to United Salvage & Towage Inc., Manila, and renamed CHINA SEA. 1978: Renamed PHILIPPINE SEA. Still listed in Lloyd's Register 2003/04.

PS. 81. NAIN (1938–1951)

O.N. 166620. 86g. 32n. 84.9 × 17.5 × 4.1 feet.
Two, 5-cyl. 2 S.C.S.A. (9″ × 12″) oil engines manufactured by W. H. Allen, Sons & Company, Bedford. 260 bhp.
Twin screw tug.
1938: Ordered by the Anglo-Iranian Oil Company Ltd., from Ferguson Bros. Ltd., Port Glasgow (Yard No. 334), for the Petroleum Steamship Company Ltd. 1938: Completed and dismantled for shipment. 1938: Re-erected at Abadan. 1951: Seized by the Iranian Government. *Due to small size and type of this vessel no further details have been recorded by the authors.*

Zurmand on the R. Medway. (World Ship Society Photograph Library)

PS. 82. NATANZ (1938–1951)

O.N. 167163. 86g. 32n. 84.9 × 17.5 × 4.1 feet.
Two, 5-cyl. 2 S.C.S.A. (9″ × 12″) oil engines manufactured by W. H. Allen, Sons & Company, Bedford. 260 bhp.
Twin screw tug.
1938: Ordered by the Anglo-Iranian Oil Company Ltd., from Ferguson Bros. Ltd., Port Glasgow (Yard No. 335), for the Petroleum Steamship Company Ltd. 1938: Completed. 1951: Seized by the Iranian Government. *Due to small size and type of this vessel no further details have been recorded by the authors.*

PS. 83. NABAND (1938–1951)

O.N. 167190. 83g. 32n. 84.9 × 17.5 × 4.1 feet.
Two, 5-cyl. 2 S.C.S.A. (9″ × 12″) oil engines manufactured by W. H. Allen, Sons & Company, Bedford. 260 bhp.
Twin screw tug.
1938: Ordered by the Anglo-Iranian Oil Company Ltd., from Ferguson Bros. Ltd., Port Glasgow (Yard No. 336), for the Petroleum Steamship Company Ltd. 1938: Completed. 1951: Seized by the Iranian Government. *Due to small size and type of this vessel no further details have been recorded by the authors.*

PS. 84. ANBAR (1938–1951)

O.N. 167270. 177g. 86n. 105.1 × 22.1 × 7.4 feet.
Two, 4-cyl. 2 S.C.S.A. (9″ × 11″) oil engines manufactured by L. Gardner & Sons Ltd., Manchester.
Stores barge.
1938: Completed. by Clelands (Successors) Ltd., Willington Quay on Tyne, for the Petroleum Steam Ship Company Ltd. Subsequently dismantled for transportation and 1939: Re-erected at Abadan. 1951: Seized by the Iranian Government. *Due to small size and type of this vessel no further details have been recorded by the authors.*

PS. 85. DELAVAR (1) (1939–1954)

O.N. 167174. 361g. 4n. 120.5 × 31.1 × 13.0 feet.
As built T.3-cyl. (16½″, 27″ & 46″ × 30″) engine manufactured by Plenty & Son Ltd., Newbury. 870 hp.
Post 1962: 6-cyl. 4 S.C.S.A. (15″ × 18″) National KSSDM-6 type oil engine manufactured by Mirrlees, Bickerton & Day Ltd., Stockport. 1,250bhp. 10kts.
Tug.
8.12.1938: Launched by Scott & Sons, Bowling (Yard No. 350), for the Petroleum Steam Ship Company Ltd. 2.1939: Completed. 25.2.1939: Sailed from Leith with barges in tow. 27.4.1939: Arrived at Abadan. 1954: Transferred to BP (Kwinana) Pty Ltd., Australia. 2.11.1954: Arrived at Fremantle from Djakarta. 11.2.1955: Registered at Fremantle as PARMELIA. 8.12.1959: Sold to J. Fenwick & Company Pty Ltd., Sydney. 1.6.1960: Registered at Sydney. 9.5.1961: Renamed FARM COVE. 1960 – 1962: Rebuilt and re-engined by S. G. White Pty Ltd., East Balmain. 6.1976: Sold to China Pacific

Zerang. (Courtesy B J Brown)

Intermodal Ltd (Transpac Marine S.A., Panama, and renamed TITAN then TITAN 1. 3.7.1976: Departed Sydney for the Philippines. 1989: Lloyd's Register removed entry as no trace since 1987 – 'continued existence in doubt'.

PS. 86. KAVAR (1939–1951)

O.N. 167178. 309g. 160.0 × 25.2 × 7.7 feet.
Dumb tank barge.

8.2.1939: Launched by Henry Robb Ltd., Leith (Yard No. 285), for the Petroleum Steam Ship Company Ltd. 2.1939: Completed. 25.2.1939: Sailed from Leith in tow of DELAVAR. 27.4.1939: Arrived at Abadan. 1951: Seized by the Iranian Government. *Due to small size and type of this vessel no further details have been recorded by the authors.*

PS. 87. KHAMIR (1939–1951)

O.N. 167179. 309g. 160.0 × 25.2 × 7.7 feet.
Dumb tank barge.

7.2.1939: Launched by Henry Robb Ltd., Leith (Yard No. 284), for the Petroleum Steam Ship Company Ltd. 2.1939: Completed. 25.2.1939: Sailed from Leith in tow of DELAVAR. 27.4.1939: Arrived at Abadan. 1951: Seized by the Iranian Government. *Due to small size and type of this vessel no further details have been recorded by the authors.*

PS. 88. TAVANA (1939–1958)

see ship No. BT. 309 in main fleet.

PS. 89. KHUMAIN (1939–1951)

O.N. 167184. 309g. 160.0 × 25.2 × 7.7 feet.
Dumb tank barge.

23.2.1939: Launched by Henry Robb Ltd., Leith (Yard No. 287), for the Petroleum Steam Ship Company Ltd. 3.1939: Completed. 4.3.1939: Sailed from Leith in tow of TAVANA. 29.4.1939: Arrived at Abadan. 1951: Seized by the Iranian Government. *Due to small size and type of this vessel no further details have been recorded by the authors.*

PS. 90. KHUNSAR (1939–1951)

O.N. 167185. 309g. 160.0 × 25.2 × 7.7 feet.
Dumb tank barge.

23.2.1939: Launched by Henry Robb Ltd., Leith (Yard No. 286), for the Petroleum Steam Ship Company Ltd. 3.1939: Completed. 4.3.1939: Sailed from Leith in tow of TAVANA. 29.4.1939: Arrived at Abadan. 1951: Seized by the Iranian Government. *Due to small size and type of this vessel no further details have been recorded by the authors.*

PS. 91. KHARGUN (1939–19)

O.N. 167219. 309g. 160.0 × 25.2 × 7.7 feet.
Dumb tank barge.

1.4.1939: Launched by Henry Robb Ltd., Leith (Yard No. 288), for the Petroleum Steam Ship Company Ltd. 4.1939: Completed. 1951: Seized by the Iranian Government. 1955: Transferred to the National Iranian Oil Company Ltd., Iran. *Due to small size and type of this vessel no further details have been recorded by the authors.*

PS. 92. NIKA (1939–1951)

O.N. 167194. 86g. 32n. 84.9 × 17.5 × 4.1 feet.
Two, 5-cyl. 2 S.C.S.A. (9″ × 11″) oil engines manufactured by Norris, Henty & Gardner Ltd., Manchester. 240 bhp.
Twin screw tug.

1938: Ordered by the Anglo-Iranian Oil Company Ltd., from Ferguson Bros. Ltd., Port Glasgow (Yard No. 337), for the Petroleum Steamship Company Ltd. 1939: Completed. 1951: Seized by the Iranian Government. *Due to small size and type of this vessel no further details have been recorded by the authors.*

PS. 93. NIGAR (1939–1951)

O.N. 167207. 86g. 32n. 84.9 × 17.5 × 4.1 feet.
Two, 5-cyl. 2 S.C.S.A. (9″ × 11″) oil engines manufactured by Norris, Henty & Gardner Ltd., Manchester. 240 bhp.
Twin screw tug.

1938: Ordered by the Anglo-Iranian Oil Company Ltd., from Ferguson Bros. Ltd., Port Glasgow (Yard No. 338), for the Petroleum Steamship Company Ltd. 1939: Completed. 1951: Seized by the Iranian Government. *Due to small size and type of this vessel no further details have been recorded by the authors.*

PS. 94. NIRIZ (1939–1951)

O.N. 167209. 86g. 32n. 84.9 × 17.5 × 4.1 feet.
Two, 5-cyl. 2 S.C.S.A. (9″ × 11″) oil engines manufactured by Norris, Henty & Gardner Ltd., Manchester. 240 bhp.
Twin screw tug.

1938: Ordered by the Anglo-Iranian Oil Company Ltd., from Ferguson Bros. Ltd., Port Glasgow (Yard No. 339), for the Petroleum Steamship Company Ltd. 23.3.1939: Launched. 1939: Completed. 1951: Seized by the Iranian Government. *Due to small size and type of this vessel no further details have been recorded by the authors.*

PS. 95. BAMRUD (1939–)

232g. 150.0 × 27.0 × 6.5 feet.
Dumb tank barge.

3.1939: Completed by Mazagon Dock Ltd., Bombay (Yard No. 253 b), for the Petroleum Steam Ship Company Ltd. *Due to small size and type of this vessel no further details have been recorded by the authors.*

PS. 96. BASTAK (1939–)

232g. 150.0 × 27.0 × 6.5 feet.
Dumb tank barge.

3.1939: Completed by Mazagon Dock Ltd., Bombay (Yard No. 253 a), for the Petroleum Steam Ship Company Ltd. *Due to small size and type of this vessel no further details have been recorded by the authors.*

PS. 97. BAGHDAD (2) (1939)

2,790g. 1,85n. 296.4 × 54.2 × 19.9 feet.
Two, T.3-cyl. (18″, 28″ & 48″ × 27″) engines manufactured by the shipbuilder. 1,057 hp.
Twin screw suction hopper dredger.

1939: Ordered by the Anglo-Iranian Oil Company Ltd., from W. Simons & Company Ltd., Renfrew (Yard No. 726), for the Petroleum Steam Ship Company Ltd. 12.12.1939: Launched for the Iraq Government (Directorate General of Navigation). 2.1940: Completed. 1963: Owners restyled Government of Iraq (Directorate General of Ports and Navigation). 1975: Owners restyled as Government of Iraq (Iraqi Ports Administration). 1976: Owners restyled as State Organisation of Iraqi Ports. 1978: Owners restyled as Government of Iraq (State Organisation of Iraqi Ports). 1979: Owners restyled as Government of the Republic of Iraq (State Organisation of Iraqi Ports). Still listed in Lloyd's Register 2003/04.

PS. 98. NIRUMAND (1946–1955)

see ship No. BT. 291 in main fleet.

PS. 99. EMPIRE SALLY/ DANESHMAND (1946–1958)

see ship No. BT. 307 in main fleet.

PS. 100. TANUMAND (1946–1958)

see ship No. BT. 308 in main fleet.

PS. 101. HADHAR (1946–1951)

O.N. 180982. 176g. 10n. 109.5 × 22.1 × 10.8 feet.
8-cyl. 4 S.C.S.A. (10½″ × 13½″) oil engine manufactured by Crossley Bros. Ltd., Manchester.
Wooden hulled tug.

1941: Completed as M.M.S. 29 by Camper, Nicholson Ltd., Southampton, for the Admiralty. 1946: Sold to Petroleum Steamship Company Ltd., converted from a minesweeper, and renamed HADHAR. 1951: Purchased by the Kuwait Oil Company Ltd. 1954: Sold for demolition.

PS. 102. MISHDAKH / HAKIM (1946–1951)

O.N. 181599. 174g. 10n. 109.5 × 22.1 × 10.8 feet.
8-cyl. 4 S.C.S.A. (10½″ × 13½″) oil engine manufactured by Crossley Bros. Ltd., Manchester.
Wooden hulled tug.

1941: Completed as M.M.S. 60 by J. G. Forbes, Fraserburgh, for the Admiralty. 1946: Sold to Petroleum Steamship Company Ltd., converted from a minesweeper, and renamed MISHDAKH. 1947: Renamed HAKIM. 1951: Sold to the Kuwait Oil Company Ltd. 1954: Sold for demolition.

PS. 103. LALI (1947–1951)

O.N. 181510. 145g. 52n. 95.4 × 22.1 × 4.3 feet.
7-cyl. 4 S.C.S.A. (9 1/16″ × 11 13/16″) oil engine manufactured by W. H. Allen, Sons & Company, Bedford, geared to a Voith type directional propeller. 215 bhp.
Double deck tug/passenger vessel.

1939: Ordered by the Anglo-Iranian Oil Company Ltd., from Ferguson Bros. Ltd., Port Glasgow (Yard No. 342), for the Petroleum Steamship Company Ltd. Work suspended upon the outbreak of War. 13.8.1946: Launched. 11.1946: Completed and dismantled. 5.1948: Re-erected at Abadan. 1951: Seized by the Iranian Government. *Due to small size and type of this vessel no further details have been recorded by the authors.*

PS. 104. EMPIRE DORIS / BAHRAMAND (1947–1958)

see ship No. BT. 306 in main fleet.

PS. 105. KHANABAD (1947–1951)

O.N. 181542. 299g. 160.1 × 25.2 × 7.8 feet.
Dumb tank barge.

1.1947: Completed by J. Bolson & Son Ltd., Poole (Yard No. ?), for the Petroleum Steam Ship Company Ltd. 1951: Seized by the Iranian Government. *Due to small size and type of this vessel no further details have been recorded by the authors.*

PS. 106. KHALAFABAD (1947–1951)

O.N. 181543. 299g. 160.1 × 25.2 × 7.7 feet.
Dumb tank barge.

2.1947: Completed by J. Bolson & Son Ltd., Poole (for the Petroleum Steam Ship Company Ltd. 1951: Seized by the Iranian Government. 1955: Transferred to the National Iranian Oil Company Ltd., Iran, and renamed KARPAN. *Due to small size and type of this vessel no further details have been recorded by the authors.*

PS. 107. KAZERUN (1947–1951)

O.N. 181742. 307g. 159.6 × 26.1 × 7.7 feet.
Dumb tank barge.
1947: Completed by the Lagan Construction Company Ltd., Belfast, for the Petroleum Steam Ship Company Ltd. 1951: Seized by the Iranian Government. *Due to small size and type of this vessel no further details have been recorded by the authors.*

PS. 108. KHURASAN (1947–1951)

O.N. 181853. 307g. 159.6 × 26.1 × 7.7 feet.
Dumb tank barge.
1947: Completed by the Lagan Construction Company Ltd., Belfast, for the Petroleum Steam Ship Company Ltd. 1951: Seized by the Iranian Government and renamed KOHISTAK. *Due to small size and type of this vessel no further details have been recorded by the authors.*

PS. 109. TABAS (1948–1951)

O.N. 181942. 209g. 11n. 104.4 × 23.2 × 8.4 feet.
Two, C.2-cyl. (11″ & 22″ × 16″) engines manufactured by Plenty & Son Ltd., Newbury. 54 nhp, 400 ihp.
Twin screw tug.
12.5.1948: Launched by Scott & Sons, Bowling (Yard No. 383), for the Petroleum Steam Ship Company Ltd. 8.1948: Completed. 1951: Seized by the Iranian Government. 1955: Transferred to the National Iranian Oil Company Ltd., Iran, and renamed TORSHIZ. 1963: Sold to Yusef Shalomi & Son. 1998: Lloyd's Register deleted entry – 'Continued existence in doubt'.

PS. 110. TAFTAN (1948–1951)

O.N. 181977. 209g. 11n. 104.4 × 23.2 × 8.4 feet.
Two, C.2-cyl. (11″ & 22″ × 16″) engines manufactured by Plenty & Son Ltd., Newbury. 54 nhp, 400 ihp.
Twin screw tug.
24.5.1948: Launched by Scott & Sons, Bowling (Yard No. 384), for the Petroleum Steam Ship Company Ltd. 8.1948: Completed. 1951: Seized by the Iranian Government. 1955: Transferred to the National Iranian Oil Company Ltd., Iran, and renamed TORBAT.1998: Lloyd's Register deleted entry – 'Continued existence in doubt'.

PS. 111. ANGLIRAN 16 (1948–1949)

see ship No. BT. 223 in main fleet

PS. 112. TAFT (1949–1960)

see ship No. BT. 215 in main fleet.

PS. 113. TANB (1949)

see ship No. BT. 216 in main fleet.

PS. 114. KUNG (1949–1955)

O.N. 182904. 299g. 160.1 × 25.0 × 7.8 feet.
Dumb tank barge.
1.1949: Completed by J. Bolson & Son Ltd., Poole, for the Petroleum Steam Ship Company Ltd. 1955: Sold to the National Iranian Oil Company. *Due to small size and type of this vessel no further details have been recorded by the authors.*

PS. 115. KAND (1949–1955)

O.N. 182905. 299g. 160.1 × 25.0 × 7.8 feet.
Dumb tank barge.
4.12.1948: Launched by J. Bolson & Son Ltd., Poole (Yard No.423), for the Petroleum Steam Ship Company Ltd. 1.1949: Completed. 1955: Sold to the National Iranian Oil Company. *Due to small size and type of this vessel no further details have been recorded by the authors.*

PS. 116. P. U. B. 1 (1949–)

15g. 67.7 × 22.0 × 6.0 feet.
4-cyl. 4 S.C.S.A. (5″ × 6¼″) oil engine manufactured by Crossley Bros. Ltd., Manchester, single reduction geared to screw shaft.
Steel pick-up boat.
16.2.1949: Launched by Philips & Son Ltd., Dartmouth (Yard No. 1185), for Petroleum Steam Ship Company Ltd. 4.1949: Completed. 21.4.1949: Departed in tow from Dartmouth, for London. *Due to small size and type of this vessel no further details have been recorded by the authors.*

PETROLEUM STEAM SHIP COMPANY LTD., on 16 OCTOBER 1957 was restyled as BP CLYDE TANKER COMPANY LTD.

And re-entered tanker operations with vessels transferred from the main fleet.

PS. 117. CLYDE SCIENTIST (1957–1963)

see ship No. BT. 199 in main fleet.

PS. 118. CLYDE RANGER (1957–1963)

see ship No. BT. 202 in main fleet.

PS. 119. CLYDE INVENTOR (1957–1963)

see ship No. BT. 232 in main fleet.

PS. 120. CLYDE EXPLORER (1957–1964)

see ship No. BT. 234 in main fleet.

PS. 121. CLYDE CRUSADER (1957–1964)

see ship No. BT. 275 in main fleet.

PS. 122. CLYDE PIONEER (1958–1965)

see ship No. BT. 261 in main fleet.

PS. 123. CLYDE CHIVALRY (1958–1963)

see ship No. BT. 208 in main fleet.

PS. 124. CLYDE PROSPECTOR (1958–1964)

see ship No. BT. 240 in main fleet.

PS. 125. CLYDE GUARDIAN (1958–1963)

see ship No. BT. 272 in main fleet.

Clyde Scientist. (World Ship Society Photograph Library)

Clyde Inventor. (World Ship Society Photograph Library)

Clyde Explorer. (World Ship Society Photograph Library)

Clyde Crusader. (World Ship Society Photograph Library)

Clyde Pioneer. (World Ship Society Photograph Library)

Clyde Guardian. (World Ship Society Photograph Library)

Clyde Gunner. (World Ship Society Photograph Library)

PS. 126. CLYDE ENVOY (1958–1963)

scc ship No. BT. 273 in main fleet.

PS. 127. CLYDE CORPORAL (1960–1964)

see ship No. BT. 279 in main fleet.

PS. 128. CLYDE SURVEYOR (1961–1964)

see ship No. BT. 244 in main fleet.

PS. 129. CLYDE GUNNER (1961–1964)

see ship No. BT. 277 in main fleet.

PS. 130. CLYDE CHANCELLOR (1961–1964)

see ship No. BT. 281 in main fleet.

PS. 131. CLYDE SERGEANT (1961–1963)

see ship No. BT. 282 in main fleet.

PS. 132. ZABARDAST (1965–1975)

O.N. 307780. 367g. 44n. 131′ 1″ × 33′ 2″ × 12′ 4½″ .
8-cyl. 2 S.C.S.A. (14½″ × 19″) oil engine manufactured by Crossley Bros. Ltd., Manchester, double reduction geared with flexible couplings.
Tug.

15.2.1965: Launched by Appledore Shipbuilders Ltd., Appledore (Yard No. A. S. 7), for BP Clyde Tanker Company Ltd. 6.1965: Completed. 1975: Sold to the National Iranian Oil Company Ltd., Iran. 2.3.1975: Whilst fire-fighting at Ipaq Well No.7 in the Darius Oil Field, Persian Gulf, sank at position 29.10.27N., 50.14.51E., as a result of a collision. At 02:25hrs she was struck on her port side by the Iranian tug MINA (192g/64) which proceeded to collide with a fixed structure and sink at position 29.10.84N., 50.14.27E.

PS. 133. ZURMAND (3) (1966–1975)

O.N. 308072. 367g. 44n. 131′ 1″ × 33′ 2″ × 12′ 4½″ .
8-cyl. 2 S.C.S.A. (14½″ × 19″) oil engine manufactured by Crossley Bros Ltd., Manchester, double reduction geared with flexible couplings.
Fire-fighting tug.

23.11.1965: Launched by Appledore Shipbuilders Ltd., Appledore (Yard No. A. S. 13), for BP Clyde Tanker Company Ltd. 4.1966: Completed. 1975: Sold to the National Iranian Oil Company Ltd., Iran. 1990: Owners restyled as NIOC Tug Boat Services. Still listed in Lloyd's Register 2003/04

PS. 134. SEA QUEST (1966–)

g. n. Tri-angular platform 342′ 8″ each side.
Three Paxman 12YLCW type oil engines powering electric generators. 1,640 bhp
Semi-submersible drilling rig.

6.1966: Completed by Harland & Wolff Ltd., Belfast, for BP Clyde Tanker Company Ltd. (BP Petroleum Development Ltd., operator/managers). *Due to type of this vessel no further details have been recorded by the authors.*

PS. 135. HOOSHMAND (1966–1975)

O.N. 308209. 373g. 59n. 133′ 5″ × 33′ 2″ × 12′ 4½″ .
8-cyl. 2 S.C.S.A. (14½″ × 19″) oil engine manufactured by Crossley Bros., Ltd., Manchester, single reverse reduction geared with flexible couplings.
Fire-fighting tug.

11.3.1966: Launched by C. D. Holmes & Company Ltd., Beverley (Yard No. 1001), for

Clyde Chancellor. (World Ship Society Photograph Library)

Clyde Sergeant. (World Ship Society Photograph Library)

Kheradmand. (Courtesy Alan Hughes)

BP Clyde Tanker Company Ltd. 6.1966: Completed. 1975: Sold to the National Iranian Oil Company Ltd., Iran. 1990: Owners restyled as NIOC Tug Boat Services. Still listed in Lloyd's Register 2003/04

PS. 136. KHERADMAND (1966–1975)

O.N. 309705. 373g. 59n. 133′ 5″ × 33′ 2″ × 12′ 4½″ .
8-cyl. 2 S.C.S.A. (14½″ × 19″) oil engine manufactured by Crossley Bros., Ltd., Manchester, single reverse reduction geared with flexible couplings.
Fire-fighting tug.

Hooshmand. (Courtesy Alan Hughes)

6.6.1966: Launched by C. D. Holmes & Company Ltd., Beverley (Yard No. 1002), for BP Clyde Tanker Company Ltd. 10.1966: Completed. 1975: Sold to the National Iranian Oil Company Ltd., Iran. 1990: Owners restyled as NIOC Tug Boat Services. Still listed in Lloyd's Register 2003/04

PS. 137. TAHAMTAN (1971–1975)

O.N. 341438. 377g. 126′ 9″ × 33′ 10″ × ?.
Two, 12-cyl. 4 S.C.S.A. (215 × 260mm) vee type oil engines manufactured by Stork Werkspoor B. V., Amsterdam, geared to twin directional propellers.
Fire-fighting tug.

2.1.1971: Launched by C. D. Holmes & Company Ltd., Beverley (Yard No. 1030), for the BP Clyde Tanker Company Ltd. 7.1971: Completed. 1974: Sold to the National Iranian Oil Company Ltd., Iran, and renamed PILTAN. 1990: Owners restyled as NIOC Tug Boat Services. Still listed in Lloyd's Register 2003/04

PS. 138. ROUINTAN (1971–1975)

O.N. 342924. 377g. 126′ 9″ × 33′ 10″ × ?.
Two, 12-cyl. 4 S.C.S.A. (215 × 260mm) vee type oil engines manufactured by Stork Werkspoor B. V., Amsterdam, geared to twin directional propellers.
Fire-fighting tug.

9.3.1971: Launched by C. D. Holmes & Company Ltd., Beverley (Yard No.1031), for the BP Clyde Tanker Company Ltd. 10.1971: Completed. 1975: Sold to the National Iranian Oil Company Ltd., Iran. 1990: Owners restyled as NIOC Tug Boat Services. Still listed in Lloyd's Register 2003/04

PS. 139. BP GUARD (1972–1975)

see ship No. BT. 238 in main fleet list.

PS. 140. BP WARDEN (1972–1975)

see ship No. BT. 248 in main fleet list.

PS. 141. ZERANG (2) (1972–1975)

see ship No. BT. 319 in main fleet list.

PS. 142. DELAVAR (2) (1972–1975)

see ship No. BT. 317 in main fleet list.

The 1976 constructed National Iranian Tanker Company tug *Behzad* wearing BP funnel markings. (Courtesy Alan Hughes)

In 1975 the tug fleet in Iranian waters was transferred to the National Iranian Oil Company as part of the establishment of the Anglo-Iranian Shipping Company by both partners. The new Iranian tugs wore the BP funnel marking for some time.

Association Petroliere
Founded 1921
19 and 21 Rue de la Bienfaisance, Paris 8.

12.1954: Restyled as
Societe Maritime Des Petroles BP

Kobad. (World Ship Society Photograph Library)

F. 1. ST. PATRICE (1) (1921–1922)

see ship No. BT. 44 in main fleet.

F. 2. PECHELBRONN (1922–1928)

4,825g. 2,975n. 386.0 × 52.5 × 28.5 feet.
Q.4-cyl. (19¾″, 28″, 41″ & 59″ × 41⅜″) engine manufactured by the shipbuilder. 224 nhp.

1914: Completed by Howaldtswerke A.G., Kiel (Yard No. 564), for Deutsche Erdol Aktien Geselschaft, Hamburg. 1921: Purchased by Societe Navale De L'Ouest, France. 1922: Transferred to Association Petroliere. (It was proposed to be renamed ST. ADRIEN). 1928: Renamed ARDESHIR. 19.7.1936: Sustained severe fire damage. 20.7.1936: Fire extinguished, vessel declared a total loss and sold to Italian shipbreakers.

F. 3. ST. JEROME (1922–1928)

see ship No. BT. 52 in main fleet.

F. 4. ST. BONIFACE (1922–1928)

7,787g. 4,100n. 452.0 × 57.0 × 35.0 feet.
Three, steam turbines manufactured by Ateliers et Chantiers de la Loire, St. Nazaire, double reduction geared to a single screw shaft. 569 nhp.

29.4.1922: Launched by Chantier Navale Francaise, Caen (Yard No. 21), for Societe Navale de L' Ouest. 10.1922: Completed for Association Petroliere. 1928: Renamed BAHRAM. 1953: Sold to P. Atychides, Greece, and renamed EVANTHIA. 1954: Sold to Sudatlantica Cia. Nav. S.A., Panama. 1956: Renamed LOEX. 1956: Sold to Neptune Transportation S.A., Costa Rica, and renamed NORMA. 4.6.1958: Laid up at Port de Bouc. 1959: Sold to A.R.D.E.N., for demolition at Savona.

F. 5. FIRUZ (1928–1942)

7,454g. 4,201n. 446.8 × 56.8 × 33.3 feet.
T.3-cyl. (26″, 44″ & 74″ × 51″) engine manufactured by North Eastern Marine Engineering Company Ltd., Wallsend. 391 nhp.

7.11.1928: Launched by Chantier Navale Francaise, Caen (Yard No. 84), for Association Petroliere. 1928: Completed. 27.11.1942: Siezed by German invasion forces at Toulon and renamed FRIEDRIKE. 5.1943: Allocated to the Kriegsmarine Black Sea fleet. 11.5.1944: Damaged by a torpedo from a Russian submarine, and towed into Constantza for repairs. 20.8.1944: Sunk by German forces as a blockship at Constantza. Subsequently salvaged by the Russian Authorities, repaired and renamed VOLGANEFT. 1958: Reported as sold for demolition.

F. 6. ARDESHIR (1) (1928–1936)

see ship No. F. 2 above.

F. 7. SHAPUR (1) (1928–1939)

see ship No. F. 3 above.

F. 8. BAHRAM (1928–1953)

see ship No. F. 4 above.

F. 9. KOBAD (1929–1963)

7,454g. 4,142n. 446.8 × 56.8 × 34.1 feet.
T.3-cyl. (26″, 44″ & 74″ × 51″) engine manufactured by North Eastern Marine Engineering Company Ltd., Wallsend. 391 nhp.

1929: Completed by Chantier Navale Francaise, Caen (Yard No. 89), for Association Petroliere. 12.1954: Owners restyled as Societe Maritime des Petroles BP. 12.3.1963: Arrived at Split for demolition by Brodospas.

F. 10. ATAR (1935–1952)

332g. 166n. 115.4 × 25.7 × 12.0 feet.
2-cyl 2 S.C.S.A. (16¾″ × 19″) engine manufactured by J. & C. Bolinders Company Ltd., Skarhamn. 96 nhp, 400bhp.
Post 1945: 8-cyl. 4 S.C.S.A. (240 x 300mm) oil engine manufactured by Mot. Baudoun, Marseilles.

1922: Completed by Chantiers Navale du Midi, Martique, for Societe Generale des Huiles de Petrole (Association Petroliere, managers). 1935: Transferred to Association Petroliere. 1952: Reverted to Societe Generale des Huiles de Petrole. 1954: Transferred to Societe Francaise des Petroles BP., and renamed BP MARSEILLES. 1962: Sold to Estrine et Cie., Marseilles. 1965: Renamed CINNA. 1969: Sold to Societe Maritime S.A., France, and renamed MARITIMA 5. *Due to small size and type of this vessel no further details have been recorded by the authors.*

F. 11. CYRUS (1935–1943)

435g. 210n. 150.7 × 25.7 × 12.3 feet.
T.3-cyl. (9¾″, 15¾″ & 26″ × 18″) engine manufactured by Cooper & Greig Ltd., Dundee. 270 ihp.

1922: Completed by Chantiers Navale Francaise, Blainville (Yard No. 25), for Societe Generale des Huiles de Petrole (Association Petroliere, managers). 1935: Transferred to Association Petroliere. 1943: Sold to the Government of Turkey thence Denizcilik Bankasi T. A. O., Turkey, and renamed BEYKOZ. 1961: Liman Isletmesi, appointed as managers. *Due to small size and type of this vessel no further details have been recorded by the authors.*

F. 12. ARTABAZE (1935–1952)

435g. 198n. 649d. 150.7 × 25.7 × 12.3 feet.
T.3-cyl. (9¾″, 15¾″ & 26″ × 18″) engine manufactured by Cooper & Greig Ltd., Dundee. 245ihp.

1922: Completed by Chantiers Navale Francaise, Blainville (Yard No. 27), for Societe Generale des Huiles de Petrole (Association Petroliere, managers). 1935: Transferred to Association Petroliere. 1952: Reverted to Societe Generale Des Huiles de Petrole. 1954: Owners restyled as Societe Francaise Des Petroles BP., and renamed BP LAVERA. 1958: Sold to Ottavio Novella, Genoa, and renamed SORI. *Due to small size and type of this vessel no further details have been recorded by the authors.*

F. 13. TOMYRIS (1935–1952)

435g. 210n. 150.7 × 25.7 × 12.3 feet.
T.3-cyl. (9¾″, 15¾″ & 26″ × 18″) engine manufactured by Cooper & Greig Ltd., Dundee. 245ihp.

1923: Completed by Chantiers Navale Francaise, Blainville (Yard No. 26), for Societe Generale des Huiles de Petrole (Association Petroliere, managers). 1935: Transferred to Association Petroliere. During WW2 vessel was damaged whilst in the River Gironde, and was still there in 1949. 1952: Transferred to Societe des Petroles (BP) d'Algerie.
1955: Renamed BP ORAN. 1972: Condemned.

Fernand-Gilabert. (World Ship Society Photograph Library)

F. 14. FERNAND-GILABERT (1948–1959)

10,448g. 6,301n. 504.0 × 68.2 × 39.2 feet.
Steam turbine manufactured by General Electric Corp., Lynn, U.S.A., connected to an electric motor driving screw shaft.

1944: Completed as COULEE DAM by Kaiser Company Inc., Portland, Oregon (Yard No. 62), for the United States War Shipping Administration, later U. S. Maritime Commission. 1946: Sold to the Government of France (Ministiere de la Marine Marchands) (Association Petroliere, managers), and renamed SHAPUR. 1948: Sold to Association Petroliere, and renamed FERNAND-GILABERT. 13.9.1958: Sustained collision and fire damage off the Oman Coast following a collision with the Liberian tanker MELIKA (20,551g./54). 20.9.1958: Arrived in tow at Karachi, for inspection. Declared a constructive total loss. 8.1959: Arrived at Bombay for demolition.

F. 15. ARDESHIR (2) (1948–1954)

As built: 10,448g. 6,301n. 504.0 × 68.2 × 39.2 feet.
Post 1962: 14,130g. 592′ × 75′ ×.
Steam turbine manufactured by General Electric Corp., Lynn, U.S.A., connected to an electric motor driving screw shaft.

1944: Completed as RAINIER by Kaiser Company Inc., Portland, Oregon (Yard No. 54), for the United States War Shipping Administration, later U. S. Maritime Commission. 1948: Sold to the Government of France (Ministiere de la Marine Marchands) (Association Petroliere, managers), and renamed ARDESHIR. 1948: Sold to Association Petroliere. 1954: Renamed LANGEAIS. 1959: Sold to Caribbean Maritime Enterprises Inc., Liberia, and renamed CARIBBEAN WAVE . 1962: Converted into a bulk carrier, and renamed PAPADIAMANDIS. 22.12.1965: Whilst on a voyage from New Orleans to Hamburg with grain and soya beans, in heavy weather, stranded 1/2 mile south from Faja Grande Lighthouse, Flores Island, Azores. 27.12.1965: Broke into three pieces and subsequently sank.

F. 16. ST. PATRICE (2) (1952–1954)

11,087g. 6,074n. 522.2 × 70.1 × 33.4 feet.
8-cyl. 2 S.C.S.A. (29 1/8″ × 55 1/8″) oil engine manufactured by Schneider, Le Creusot.

1952: Completed by Ateliers and Chantiers de la Seine Maritime, Worms et Compagnie, Le Trait, for Association Petroliere. 1954: Renamed LUYNES. 1966: Sold to Societe des Entrepots de Liquides Industriels de Djibouti, France, and renamed THORONET. 1968: Sold to Gem Shipping Company, Somalia, and renamed TREFONTAINE. . 12.1.1973: Whilst on passage from Mina Al Ahmadi, suffered hull damage. 12.2.1973: Arrived at Singapore Roads and was subsequently sold for demolition. 30.6.1973: Arrived at Kaohsiung for demolition by Long Jung Industry Company Ltd.

F. 17. GABIAN (1952–1954)

As built: 640g. 231n. 186.6 × 31.0 × 13.1 feet.
Post 1954: 728g. 343n. 890d.
221′ 7″ × 29′ 5″ × 13′ 0″ overall.
Two, 7-cyl. 2 S.C.S.A. (11 7/8″ × 19 11/16″) oil engine manufactured by Const.Mec. Sulzer, St. Denis, geared to twin screw shafts.

1946: Completed by Chantier Navale Francaise, Blainville S/Orne, for the Government of France (Ministiere de la Marine Marchands) (Association Petroliere, managers). 1952: Transferred to Association Petroliere. 1954: Sold to Entreprise Herve Nader, France, converted into a bulk wine tanker, and renamed ST. JOSEPH. 1962: Owner restyled as Herve Nader (Compagnie Celte de Gerance et d'Armement, managers). 1966: Sold to Fortuna Soc. Anon., Greece, and renamed AGHIOS IOSIF. 1969: Sold to Ergantinank Shipping Company Ltd., Cyprus, and name corrected to AGIOS IOSIF. 1971: Demolished.

F. 18. LANGEAIS (1) (1954–1959)

see ship No. F. 15 above.

F. 19. LUYNES (1954–1966)

see ship No. F. 16 above.

F. 20. BRISSAC (1) (1955–1959)

see ship No. BT. 184 in main fleet.

F. 21. MONTSOREAU (1) (1955–1961)

see ship No. BT. 189 in main fleet.

F. 22. VILLANDRY (1955–1961)

see ship No. BT. 191 in main fleet.

F. 23. CHAMBORD (1) (1955–1973)

21,432g. 12,490n. 667′ 0″ × 86′ 4″ × 35′ 6″.
Two, steam turbines manufactured by Chantiers et Ateliers de St. Nazaire (Penhoet), St. Nazaire, double reduction geared to screw shaft.

11.1.1955: Launched by Ateliers et Chantiers de France, Dunkirk (Yard No. 213), for Societe Maritime des Petroles BP, France. 1955: Completed. 1973: Sold to Bayazi Shipping & Contracting Company S.A., Panama, and converted into a non-propelled crane barge by the Viktor Lenac Shipyard, Rijeka. No further details located.

F. 24. CHENONCEAUX (1) (1955–1975)

21,432g. 12,490n. 668′ 2″ × 86′ 4″ × 35′ 6″.
Two, steam turbines manufactured by Chantiers et Ateliers de St. Nazaire (Penhoet), St. Nazaire, double reduction geared to screw shaft.

28.3.1955: Launched by Ateliers et Chantiers de France, Dunkirk (Yard No. 214), for Societe Maritime des Petroles BP, France. 1955: Completed. 27.10.1974: Laid up at Brest. 15.4.1975: Arrived in tow at Bilbao for demolition. 18.4.1975: Revalorizacion de Materiales S. A. commenced work.

F. 25. CHEVERNY (1) (1956–1976)

21,430g. 12,491n. 668′ 2″ × 86′ 6″ × 35′ 6″.
Two, Parsons type steam turbines manufactured by Compagnie de Fives-Lille, Lille, double reduction geared to screw shaft.

9.6.1956: Launched by Ateliers et Chantiers de France, Dunkirk (Yard No. 217), for Societe Maritime des Petroles BP, France. 1956: Completed. 12.5.1976: Laid up at Brest. 9.6.1976: Departed Brest, in tow bound to Castellon for demolition. 23.6.1976: Arrived. 26.6.1976: I. Varela Davalillo, commenced work.

Montsoreau at Cape Town. (World Ship Society Photograph Library)

Chenonceaux. (World Ship Society Photograph Library)

Chenverny. (World Ship Society Photograph Library)

29.3.1968: Launched by Ateliers et Chantiers de Dunkerque et Bordeaux (France-Gironde), Dunkirk (Yard No. 259), for Societe Maritime des Petroles BP, France. 1968: Completed. 1976: Sold to Navieros Oceanicos S.A., Greece, and renamed TRADE JUSTICE. 5.3.1978: Laid up at Piraeus. 1978: Sold to Trade Bulkers Inc., Greece. 1978: Sold to Conoco Petroleum. 5.3.1978: Arrived at Piraeus for conversion as a storage barge. 1978: Sold to Dubai Petroleum Company, Liberia, and renamed AL WASEL. 11.1978: Conversion being undertaken at Kynosoura. 8.6.1979: Suffered severe explosion and fire damage, during conversion. 1979: Transferred to Chantiers Navales de la Ciotat, France for repair and completion of conversion. No further information located.

Chaumont. (World Ship Society Photograph Library)

F. 26. CHAUMONT (1) (1958–1975)

21,083g. 12,588n. 668′ 2″ × 86′ 9″ × 35′ 6¼″.
Two, Parsons type steam turbines manufactured by Compagnie de Fives-Lille, Lille, double reduction geared to screw shaft.

8.2.1958: Launched by Ateliers et Chantiers de France, Dunkirk (Yard No. 225), for Societe Maritime des Petroles BP, France. 8.5.1958: Completed. 18.8.1975: Laid up at Brest. 5.9.1976: Arrived in tow at Valencia for demolition by Hierros Ardes S. A.

F. 27. AMBOISE (1961–1977)

31,971g. 17,226n. 747′ 11″ × 99′ 8″ × 39′ 5¾″.
Two, steam turbines manufactured by Ateliers et Chantiers de Bretagne, Nantes, double reduction geared to screw shaft.

22.10.1960: Launched by Ateliers et Chantiers de Dunkerque et Bordeaux (France-Gironde), Dunkirk (Yard No. 232), for Societe Maritime des Petroles BP, France. 25.2.1961: Completed. 3.8.1977: Laid up at Brest. 22.10.1977: Departed Brest in tow for Valencia for demolition. 27.10.1977: Arrived. 3.11.1977: Industrial y Comercial de Levante S.A., commenced work.

F. 28. AZAY LE RIDEAU (1964–1978)

31,959g. 17,215n. 746′ 5″ × 100′ 10″ × 38′ 6″.
Two, steam turbines manufactured by Ateliers et Chantiers de Bretagne, Nantes, double reduction geared to screw shaft.

1964: Completed by Ateliers et Chantiers de Dunkerque et Bordeaux (France-Gironde), Dunkirk (Yard No. 237), for Societe Maritime des Petroles BP, France. 1978: Sold to Conoco Shipping Company, Liberia, and renamed VENTURE LOUISIANA. 26.5.1982: Arrived at Kaohsiung for demolition.

F. 29. MONTSOREAU (2) (1968–1976)

67,280g. 46,829n. 124,082d. 900.0(BB) × ? × 50′ 10″.
Two, steam turbines manufactured by Ateliers et Chantiers l'Atlantique, St Nazaire, double reduction geared to screw shaft. 24,000shp. 16 kts.

Montsoreau. (World Ship Society Photograph Library)

F. 30. LANGEAIS (2) (1971–1981)

O.N. 9090. 41,570g. 23,524n. 76,066d. 779′ 11″ × 121′ 2″ × 41′ 11¾″.
9-cyl. 2 S.C.S.A. (840 × 1800mm) B&W type oil engine manufactured by Mitsui Zosen, Tamano. 20,700 bhp.

2.11.1964: Launched as THORSHEIMER by Mitsui Shipbuilding & Engineering Company Ltd., Tamano (Yard No.705), for Thor Dahl's Hualfangselskap AS & AS Oram, Norway. 1965: Completed. 1971: Purchased by Societe Maritime des Petroles BP, France, and renamed LANGEAIS. 1981: Sold to Trident Tankers S.A., Greece, and renamed TRIDENT. 1985: Renamed IDEA. 1986: Sold to Goldenlane Shipping Ltd. (Styga Compania Naviera S.A., managers), Cyprus, and renamed PAPANIKOLIS. 1986: Sold to New Age Maritime Enterprises Ltd., Malta, and renamed TENACITY. 1990: Sold to Toledo Shipping Company S.A. (Kalypso Star Oil Carriers S.A., managers), and renamed

Langeais. (World Ship Society Photograph Library)

UNITED SPIRIT under Honduran registry. 1991: Renamed JASMINITO. 1992: Sold for demolition.

F. 31. BLOIS (1970–1981)

118,414g. 86,016n. 239,708d. 1,084′ 10″ × 160′ 0″ × 66′ 9″.
Two, Stal-Laval type steam turbines, manufactured by Chantiers de l'Atlantique, St. Nazaire, double reduction geared to screw shaft. 32,400 shp.
6.4.1970: Launched by Chantiers Naval de La Ciotat, La Ciotat (Yard No. 264), for Societe Maritime des Petroles BP, France. 1970: Completed. 1981: Sold to Um Denizcilik ve Ticaret AS, Turkey, and renamed ZAFER. 1983: Renamed ZAFER M. 1986: Reported as sold to unspecified buyers and proposed to be renamed TARZAN under British registry. 19.4.1986: Arrived at Kaohsiung as ZAFER M., for demolition. 17.5.1986: Shieng Yek Steel Corporation commenced work.

F. 32. BEAUGENCY (1973–1981)

118,460g. 86,078n. 239,604d. 1,085′ 0″ × 159′ 10″ × 66′ 8½″.
Two, Stal-Laval type steam turbines, manufactured by Chantiers de l'Atlantique, St. Nazaire, double reduction geared to screw shaft. 32,400 shp.
22.7.1972: Launched by Chantiers Navals de La Ciotat, La Ciotat (Yard No. 288), for Societe Maritime des Petroles BP, France. 3.3.1973: Completed. 1981: Transferred to Societe Francaise des Petrolieres BP (Societe Maritime des Petroles BP, managers), France. 1982: Sold to Navy First Compania Naviera S .A., Cyprus, and renamed POLYS. 7.12.1985: At 18:45hrs GMT, whilst part loaded at a position 56 miles south of Kharg Island was damaged near the bow by an Iraqi missile. Subsequently repaired at Dubai. 1986: Renamed POLIKON. 24.2.1986: Struck aft by an Iraqi missile whilst anchored in ballast off Kharg Island. Towed to Sirri Island. Damage extent not reported. 2.3.1986: Arrived in tow at Dubai for repairs. 11.5.1986: Returned to service. 28.7.1986: Struck in No.1 port tank by an Iraqi missile whilst anchored off Kharg Island, sustaining a 4-foot diameter hole. Fire extinguished and vessel taken to Bahrain for repair. 5.4.1987: At 06:43hrs GMT, whilst on a ballast voyage from Larak Island to Kharg Island, was struck aft by an Iraqi Exocet missile at position 28.22N., 50.56E., sustaining fire damage to engine room and accommodation. Towed to Larak Island for inspection, and subsequently towed to and laid up at Hormuz Terminal prior to 1.1.1988. 1990: Owners deleted from Lloyd's Register. 1991: Sold to unspecified United Arab Emirates owners and renamed MICKY under Cyprus registry. 22.12.1991: Arrived at Gadani Beach for demolition.

F. 33. CHEVERNY (2) (1974–proposed)

133,255g. 117,868n. 338.64(BB) × 53.62 × 20.397 metres.
Two, steam turbines manufactured by the shipbuilder, double reduction geared to screw shaft. 34,000 shp.
12.2.1971: Ordered from Mitsubishi Heavy Industries Ltd., Nagasaki (Yard No. 1707), by Societe Maritime des Petroles BP, France. 14.5.1974: Keel laid as CHEVERNY but the contract was sold to the Compagnie Navale des Petroles, France. 27.9.1974: Launched as ONYX. 21.1.1975: Completed. 1980: Sold to Total Compagnie Francaise Navigation (T.C.F.N.), France. 1986: Sold to Elfilikon Inc (Ceres Hellenic Shipping Enterprise Ltd., managers), Greece, and renamed FAROSHIP L. 1994: Sold for demolition.

Chaumont. (World Ship Society Photograph Library)

F. 34. CHAMBORD (2) (1974)

131,628g. 114,335n. 274,075d. 338.34 × 53.62 × 20.397 metres.
Two, steam turbines manufactured by the shipbuilder, double reduction geared to screw shaft. 34,000 shp.
14.6.1974: Launched by Mitsubishi Heavy Industries Ltd., Nagasaki (Yard No. 1736), for Societe Maritime des Petroles BP, France. 3.10.1974: Completed for Societe de Developpement de Transport Petrolier (Societe Maritime des Petroles BP, managers), France. 1985: Sold to Societe Maritime des Petroles BP et Cie., France. 1986: Transferred to Societe Francaise des Petroles BP (Societe Maritime des Petroles BP et Cie., managers), France. 1987: Sold to Compagnie de Gestion et D'Exploitation Ltd. (Societe D'Exploitation Maritime Ltd., managers), Gibraltar, and renamd AMBOR. 1988: Sold to Clavering Shipping Inc. (Fred Olsen & Company., managers), and renamed KNOCK MORE, under Liberia registry. 1993: Red Band AS, appointed as managers. 1994: Sold to More Shipping Ltd. (same managers). 1995: Sold to Davieship Inc., & Davieship II Inc. (same managers). 1999: Sold for demolition.

F. 35. CHINON (1974)

131,654g. 112,807n. 269,709d. 338.34 × 52.62 × 20.397 metres.
Two, steam turbines manufactured by the shipbuilder, double reduction geared to screw shaft. 34,000 shp.
3.9.1974: Launched by Mitsubishi Heavy Industries Ltd., Nagasaki (Yard No. 1737), for Societe Maritime des Petroles BP, France. 10.12.1974: Completed for Societe de Developpement de Transport Petrolier (Societe Maritime des Petroles BP et Cie, managers), France. 1984: Sold to Elfilikon Inc (Ceres Hellenic Shipping Enterprise Ltd., managers), Greece, and renamed FAIRSHIP L. 4.2.1985: Whilst on a ballast voyage from Ulsan to Kharg Island was struck in the engine room aft by an Iraqi missile at position 28.24N., 50.26E., 60 miles south of Kharg Island. 8.2.1985: Arrived in tow at Dubai for examination and was subsequently sold to Taiwan breakers.

F. 36. BRISSAC (2) (1976–1981)

118,460g. 86,078n. 239,604d. 334.12(BB) × 48.75 × 20.340 metres.
Two, Stal-Laval type steam turbines, manufactured by Chantiers de l'Atlantique, St. Nazaire, double reduction geared to screw shaft. 32,400 shp.
12.6.1975: Launched by Chantiers Navals de La Ciotat, La Ciotat (Yard No. 303), for Societe Maritime des Petroles BP, France. 9.3.1976: Completed. 1981: Transferred to Societe Francaise des Petrolieres BP (Societe Maritime des Petroles BP, managers), France. 3.4.1986: Departed from Ras Tanura bound to Europort. 6.4.1986: Attacked by Iranian forces whilst off Qatar. Damage was not reported. 13.9.1986: At 03:10hrs GMT, whilst on a voyage from Fos to Kuwait was attacked by Iranian helicopter launched missiles at position 25.12N., 54.23E., 55 miles S.W. of Abu Musa. Both missiles failed to explode and were defused at Dubai. One missile struck the accommodation area and the other the engine room causing minor damage. 1987: Transferred to the Vanuatu register, and renamed BRISK. 1988: Sold to National Iranian Tanker Company, Iran, and renamed KOOHE ZAGROS. 24.10.1994: Arrived at Gadani Beach for demolition.

F. 37. CHAUMONT (2) (1976–1981)

129,233g. 108,048n. 269,713d. 338.62 × 52.62 × 20.704 metres.
Two, steam turbines manufactured by the shipbuilder, geared to screw shaft. 34,000 shp.
11.5.1976: Launched by Mitsubishi Heavy Industries Ltd., Nagasaki (Yard No. 1758), for Societe Maritime des Petroles BP, France. 28.9.1976: Completed. 1981: Transferred to Societe de Developpement de Transport Petrolier (Societe Maritime des Petroles BP et Cie., managers), France. 5.3.1986: At 13:58hrs GMT, whilst on a ballast voyage from Fos to Ras Tanura was attacked by Iranian aircraft at position 25.57N., 52.43E., 70 miles off Doha, diverted to Dubai thence continued her voyage. Sustained a hole on the starboard side of engine room. 18.3.1986: Departed from Ras Tanura. 1987: BP France appointed as managers. 1992: Transferred to BP France (Maritime BP, managers). 1994: Sold to Sycamore Maritime Inc. (Societe Nouvelle de Transports Petroliers (S.N.T.P.), managers), France. 1997: Sold to Kerivor S. A. (France Shipmanagement S.A. (FRANSHIP), appointed as managers). *c*2000: Demolished.

Vessels Managed by Association Petrolieres For Their Subsidiaries

Societe Generale des Huiles de Petrole,
subsequently restyled as
Societe Francaise Des Petroles BP.
16, Rue Colbert
Marseilles
(Estrine et Cie., & Association Petrolieres)
1987 Restyled as **BP France**

FM. 1. FELIX (1922–1929)

197g. 167n. ? × ? × ? feet.

1903: Built in Belgium. 1922: Purchased by Societe Generale Des Huiles, and rebuilt. 1929: Lost. No further details located.

FM. 2. PAULY (1922–1929)

201g. 170n. ? × ? × ? feet.

1909: Built in Belgium. 1922: Purchased by Societe Generale Des Huiles, and rebuilt. 1929: Lost. No further details located.

FM. 3. ATAR (1922–1935)

see ship No. F. 10 above.

FM. 4. CYRUS (1922–1935)

see ship No. F. 11 above.

FM. 5. ARTABAZE (1922–1935)

see ship No. F. 12 above.

FM. 6. TOMYRIS (1922–1935)

see ship No. F. 13 above.

FM. 7. NICATOR (1923–1928)

435g. 198n. 150.7 × 25.7 × 12.3 feet.
T.3-cyl. (9¾″, 15¾″ & 26″ × 18″) 29 nhp engine manufactured by Cooper & Greig Ltd., Dundee.

1923: Completed by Chantier Navale Francaise, Caen (Yard No. 28), for Societe Generale des Huiles de Petrole (Association Petroliere, managers). 19.10.1928: Whilst on a ballast voyage from Blage to Donges, was wrecked on Le Pilier Rocks, R. Loire.

FM. 8. XERXES (1926–)

100g. ? n. ? × ? × ? feet.

1926: Built in France for Societe Generale Des Huiles. No further details located.

FM. 9. STYX (1924–)

7g. 5n. ? × ? × ? feet.
Launch ex pilot vessel.

1914: Built in Belgium. 1924: Sold to Compagnie Occidentale de Produits de Petrole (Association Petroliere, managers). No further details located.

FM. 10. BOUVREUIL (1925–1934)

122g. 8n. 92.0 × 17.8 × 11.6 feet.
T.3-cyl. (10¾″, 17″ & 28¾″ × 20″) engine manufactured by the shipbuilders. 36 nhp.
Tug converted from a whaler.

1908: Completed as FUNDING by Nylands Vaerksted, Oslo (Yard No. 191), for A. Monsen, Faroe Islands. 1925: Sold to Societe Generale Des Huiles de Petrole. 1928: Sold to Compagnie Occidentale de Produits de Petrole (Association Petroliere, managers). 1934: Sold for demolition.

FM. 11. ENERGIC I (1926–)

240d. ? × ? × ? feet.

1926: Completed for Societe Generale Des Huiles De Petrole. No further details located.

FM. 12. ENERGIC II (1926–)

240d. ? × ? × ? feet.

1926: Completed for Societe Generale Des Huiles De Petrole. No further details located.

FM. 13. ENERGIC III (1926–)

240d. ? × ? × ? feet.

1926: Completed for Societe Generale Des Huiles De Petrole. No further details located.

FM. 14. ENERGIC IV (1926–)

240d. ? × ? × ? feet.

1926: Completed for Societe Generale Des Huiles De Petrole. No further details located.

FM. 15. ENERGIC V (1926–)

240d. ? × ? × ? feet.

1926: Completed for Societe Generale Des Huiles De Petrole. No further details located.

FM. 16. ENERGIC VI (1927–)

240d. ? × ? × ? feet.

1927: Completed for Societe Generale Des Huiles De Petrole. No further details located.

FM. 17. ENERGIC VII (1927–)

240d. ? × ? × ? feet.

1927: Completed for Societe Generale Des Huiles De Petrole. No further details located.

FM. 18. NAPTHA CYCLE I (1927–)

240d. ? × ? × ? feet.

1927: Completed for Societe Generale Des Huiles De Petrole. No further details located.

FM. 19. NAPTHA CYCLE II (1927–)

240d. ? × ? × ? feet.

1927: Completed for Societe Generale Des Huiles De Petrole. No further details located.

FM. 20. OUFI (1927–1934)

17g. ? n. ? × ? × ? feet.
Launch.

1916: Built at an unspecified location. 1927: Purchased by Societe Generale Des Huiles De Petrole. 1934: Demolished. No further details located.

FM. 21. GABIAN (1946–1952)

see ship No. F. 17 above.

FM. 22. SHAPUR (2) (1946–1948)

see ship No. F. 14 above.

FM. 23. ARDESHIR (2) (1948–1954)

see ship No. F. 15 above.

FM. 24. ANAHITA (1951–1954)

5g. 5n. ? × ? × ? feet.
Towing launch

Oil engine.

19 : Built as HAM for unspecified owners. 1951: Sold to Societe Generale Des Huiles De Petrole, and renamed ANAHITA. 1954: Sold for demolition. No further details located.

FM. 25. BP MARSEILLES (1954–1962)

see ship No. FM. 3 above.

FM. 26. BP LAVERA (1954–1958)

see ship No. FM. 5 above.

FM. 27. BP ORAN (1955–1972)

see ship No. FM. 6 above.

FM. 28. CHAMBORD (2) (1974–1985)

see ship No. F. 34 above.

FM. 29. CHINON (1974–1984)

see ship No. F. 35 above.

FM. 30. CHENONCEAUX (2) (1976–1987)

129,849g. 107,998n. 269,713d.
338.62 × 52.62 × 20.704 metres.
Two, steam turbines manufactured by the shipbuilder, geared to screw shaft. 34,000 shp.

27.2.1976: Launched by Mitsubishi Heavy Industries Ltd., Nagasaki (Yard No. 1757), for Societe d'Investissement de Transports Petroliers (BP France, managers), France. 1976: Completed. 1987: Transferred to Vanuatu registry, and renamed ONCE. 1987: BP France appointed as managers. 1992: Transferred to BP France (Maritime BP, managers). 1994: Sold to Hull Navigation Ltd., French Antarctic Territories registry. (Societe Nouvelle de Transports Petroliers (S.N.T.P.), managers), France. 1997: Sold to Kerivor S.A. (France Shipmanagement S.A. (FRANSHIP), appointed as managers). 2001: Sold to Euronav Luxembourg S.A. (same managers). 2001: Reported as having been demolished.

FM. 31. BEAUGENCY (1981–1982)

see ship No. F.32 above.

FM. 32. BRISSAC (2) (1981–1987)

see ship No. F.36 above.

FM. 33. CHAUMONT (2) (1981–1994)

see ship No. F.37 above.

FM. 34. CHAMBORD (2) (1986–1987)

see ship No. F. 34 above.

FM. 35. BRISK (1987–1988)

see ship No. F. 36 above.

FM. 36. ONCE (1987–1994)

see ship No. FM. 30 above.

British Tankers Australia Pty. Ltd.

BP (Kwinana) Pty. Ltd.
founded 1954.

K. 0. K L 1 (1954–)

7g. 10.06 × ? × ? metres.
Oil engine manufactured by L. Gardner & Sons Ltd., Manchester. 65 bhp.
Line-running launch.
1953: Completed by unspecified Australian builders for British Tankers Australia Pty. Ltd. 1954: Transferred to BP (Kwinana) Pty. Ltd., Australia. No other details located.

K. 1. K L 2 (1954–1965)

7g. 10.06 × ? × ? metres.
Oil engine manufactured by L. Gardner & Sons Ltd., Manchester. 65 bhp.
Line-running launch.
1953: Completed by unspecified Australian builders for British Tankers Australia Pty. Ltd. 1954: Transferred to BP (Kwinana) Pty. Ltd., Australia. 1965: Transferred to BP Oil Supplies Pty. Ltd. 1970: Transferred to BP Australia Ltd. 23.7.1975: Sold to P&O Australia Ltd. (Kwinana Towage Services, managers). 1984: Sold to unspecified buyers. No further details located.

K. 2. K L 3 (1954–1965)

7g. 10.06 × ? × ? metres.
Oil engine manufactured by L. Gardner & Sons Ltd., Manchester. 65 bhp.
Line-running launch.
1953: Completed by unspecified Australian builders for British Tankers Australia Pty. Ltd. 1954: Transferred to BP (Kwinana) Pty. Ltd., Australia. 1965: Transferred to BP Oil Supplies Pty. Ltd. 1970: Transferred to BP Australia Ltd. 23.7.1975: Sold to P&O Australia Ltd. (Kwinana Towage Services, managers). 10.1981: Sold to unspecified buyers. No further details located.

K. 3. ZERANG (1)/COCKBURN (1954–1959)

see ship No. PS. 80 in Pet. SS section.

K. 4. DELAVAR (1) /PARMELIA (1954–1959)

see ship No. PS. 85 in Pet. SS section.

K. 5. BIARA (1954–1965)

7g. 6.1 × ? × ? metres.
Oil engine manufactured by L. Gardner & Sons Ltd., Manchester. 25 bhp.
1954: Completed by unspecified Australian builders for British Tankers Australia Pty. Ltd. 1954: Transferred to BP (Kwinana) Pty. Ltd., Australia. 1965: Transferred to BP Oil Supplies Pty. Ltd. 1970: Transferred to BP Australia Ltd. 23.7.1975: Sold to P&O Australia Ltd. (Kwinana Towage Services, managers). 1985: Sold to unspecified buyers. No further details located.

Parmelia. (Courtesy of B. J. Brown)

K. 6. GOBUL (1954–1965)

7g. 6.1 × ? × ? metres.
Oil engine manufactured by L. Gardner & Sons Ltd., Manchester. 25 bhp.
1954: Completed by unspecified Australian builders for British Tankers Australia Pty. Ltd. 1954: Transferred to BP (Kwinana) Pty. Ltd., Australia. 1965: Transferred to BP Oil Supplies Pty. Ltd. 1970: Transferred to BP Australia Ltd. 23.7.1975: Sold to P&O Australia Ltd. (Kwinana Towage Services, managers). 1985: Sold to unspecified buyers. No further details located.

K. 7. NERIMBA (1956–1965)

32g. 16.76 × 4.27 × 2.74 metres.
Two oil engines manufactured by Caterpillar Diesels.
1956: Completed by unspecified Australian builders for BP (Kwinana) Pty. Ltd., Australia. 1965: Transferred to BP Oil Supplies Pty. Ltd. 1970: Transferred to BP Australia Ltd. 23.7.1975: Sold to P&O Australia Ltd. (Kwinana Towage Services, managers). 1985: Sold to unspecified buyers. No further details located.

K. 8. BP COCKBURN (1959–1965)

O.N. 196904. 419g. 118n. 42.40 × 9.96 × 4.42 metres.
8-cyl. 2 S.C.S.A. (368 × 483mm) CGL8 type oil engine manufactured by Crossley Bros. Ltd., Manchester.
Tug.
2.9.1959: Launched by Evans Deakin & Company Pty. Ltd., Brisbane (Yard No. 40), for BP (Kwinana) Pty. Ltd., Australia. 9.11.1959: Completed. 1965: Transferred to BP Oil Supplies Pty. Ltd. 19.1.1970: Transferred to BP Australia Ltd. 18.7.1975: Sold to P&O Australia Ltd. (Kwinana Towage Services, managers). 14.10.1975: Renamed COCKBURN. 4.10.1982: Sold to Lease Industrial Finance Ltd. and Phipson Nominees Pty. Ltd. (Charter Craft & Marine Services Pty. Ltd., managers). 12.11.1985: Owners restyled as Sanwa Australia Leasing Ltd. 26.10.1983: Renamed TASMAN HAULER. 6.7.1988: During a storm broke her moorings at Twofold Bay, and grounded. 9.7.1988: Refloated by the tugs WEELA (232g./68) and WOOTAKARRA (95g./66). Upon inspection was declared as a constructive total loss. 8.1988: Stripped and prepared for disposal. 1.10.1988: Scuttled off Twofold Bay, NSW. 24.1.1989: Register closed.

K. 9. BP PARMELIA (1959–1965)

O.N. 196905. 419g. 118n. 42.37 × 9.96 × 4.45 metres.
8-cyl. 2 S.C.S.A. (368 × 483mm) CGL8 type oil engine manufactured by Crossley Bros.Ltd., Manchester.
Tug.
3.10.1959: Launched by Evans Deakin & Company Pty. Ltd., Brisbane (Yard No. 41), for BP (Kwinana) Pty. Ltd., Australia. 22.12.1959: Completed. 1965: Transferred to BP Oil Supplies Pty. Ltd. 19.1.1970: Transferred to BP Australia Ltd. 18.7.1975: Sold to P&O Australia Ltd. (Kwinana Towage Services, managers) 14.10.1975: Renamed PARMELIA. 23.9.1985: Sold to Maritime Hire (Pty) Ltd., Australia. 13.6.1986: Renamed CLARENCE BEACH. 6.8.1987: Sold to Louise Christine Mitchell and Betty Jean Mitchell (Aquatic Timeshare Pty. Ltd., managers), Australia. 15.7.1988: Sold to Fobipe Pty Ltd. (S. Llewellyn & Company, Maclean, NSW.), and converted at Yamba NSW and Brisbane for fishing. 7.8.1991: Sold by mortgagees Household Financial Services Pty Ltd., to Lakeside Developments Pty Ltd., Fremantle. 24.7.1992: Offered for sale by auction, at Townsville, by the Supreme Court of Queensland. 19.2.1993: Renamed PROVINCIAL TRADER. 22.4.1993: Departed Townsville en route for Cairns. (reported as renamed SUSAN B) 28.4.1994: Reported as disabled. 1.5.1994: Whilst under tow to Eden, sank in Twofold Bay, NSW. 11.1994: Salvage attempts failed. 3.1995: Raised by barge and scuttled offshore.

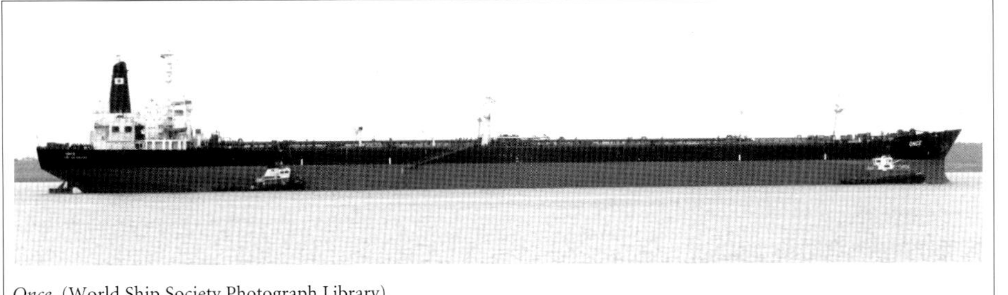
Once. (World Ship Society Photograph Library)

BP (Aden) Ltd.

AD. 1. BP ADEN (1954–)

O.N. 186083. 311g. 279n. 125′ 4″ × 28′ 6″ × 10′ 6″.
Dumb tank barge.

6.1954: Completed by Clelands (Successors) Ltd., Wallsend (Yard No. 190), for BP (Aden) Ltd. *Due to small size and type of this vessel no further details have been recorded by the authors.*

AD. 2. BP TAWAHI (1954–)

O.N. 186116. 114g. 76n. 150d. 80′ 7″ × 23′ 2″ × 5′ 0″.
Dumb tank barge.

18.8.1954: Launched by Clelands (Successors) Ltd., Wallsend (Yard No. 200), for BP (Aden) Ltd. 9.1954: Completed. *Due to small size and type of this vessel no further details have been recorded by the authors.*

AD. 3. BP HEDJUFF (1954–)

O.N. 186117. 75g. 50n. 80′ 7″ × 19′ 0″ × 4′ 6″.
Dumb tank barge.

28.8.1954: Launched by Clelands (Successors) Ltd., Wallsend (Yard No. 201), for BP (Aden) Ltd. 9.1954: Completed. *Due to small size and type of this vessel no further details have been recorded by the authors.*

AD. 4. BP MAALA (1956–)

see ship No. AP. 22 in A. P. O. C. section.

AD. 5. BP 31 (1957–)

see ship No. AP. 55 in A. P. O. C. section.

AD. 6. BP 32 (1) (1957–)

see ship No. AP. 56 in A. P. O. C. section.

AD. 7. BP 37 (1) (1959–)

70g. 61′ 1″ × 23′ 11″ × 4′ 0″.
Dumb tank barge.

1959: Launched by Clelands (Successors) Ltd., Wallsend (Yard No. 240), for British Petroleum Company Ltd. 3.1959: Completed for BP (Aden) Ltd. *Due to small size and type of this vessel no further details have been recorded by the authors.*

AD. 8. BP 38 (1959–)

70g. 61′ 1″ × 23′ 11″ × 4′ 0″.
Dumb tank barge.

1959: Launched by Clelands (Successors) Ltd., Wallsend (Yard No.241), for British Petroleum Company Ltd. 3.1959: Completed for BP (Aden) Ltd. *Due to small size and type of this vessel no further details have been recorded by the authors.*

AD. 9. BP AL-RODHA (1960–)

O.N. 301077. 47g. 24n. 73′ 6″ × 15′ 0″ × 5′ 0″.
6-cyl. 4 S.C.S.A. (5 1/2″ × 7 3/4″) oil engine manufactured by L. Gardner & Sons Ltd., Manchester, reverse geared to screw shaft. 106 bhp.
Powered tank barge.

3.1960: Completed by J. Bolson & Son Ltd., Poole (Yard No. 534), for BP (Aden) Ltd. *Due to small size and type of this vessel no further details have been recorded by the authors.*

AD. 10. BP 21 (1960–)

see ship No. AP. 45 in A. P. O. C. section.

BP Aden. (World Ship Society Photograph Library)

AD. 11. BP 24 (1960–1961)

see ship No. AP. 46 in A. P. O. C. section.

AD. 12. BP 27 (1) (1960–)

see ship No. AP. 47 in A. P. O. C. section.

AD. 13. BP 28 (1) (1960–)

see ship No. AP. 48 in A. P. O. C. section.

AD. 14. BP 29 (1960–)

see ship No. AP. 49 in A. P. O. C. section.

AD. 15. BP 30 (1960–)

see ship No. AP. 50 in A. P. O. C. section.

AD. 16. BP 106 (1961–)

see ship No. AD. 11 above.

BP Trading Ltd.

founded 1953.
1981: Restyled as
BP International Ltd.

TR. 1. BP GHENT (1953–)

O.N. 301209. 144g. 94n. 285d. 122.6 × 16.6 × ? feet.
2-cyl. 2 S.C.S.A. (242 × 320mm) oil engine manufactured by Anglo-Belgian Company, Ghent. 90 bhp
Powered tank barge.

1950: Completed as BP VI by Chantiers Navales de Rupelmonde, Antwerp (Yard No.), for unspecified Belgian owners. 1953: Transferred to BP Trading Ltd., London, and renamed BP GHENT. *Due to small size and type of this vessel no further details have been recorded by the authors.*

TR. 2. BP ANTWERP (1955–1960)

see ship No. AP. 39 in A. P. O. C. section.

TR. 3. BP ELBE (1955–1960)

see ship No. AP. 40 in A. P. O. C. section.

TR. 4. BP ROTTERDAM (1955–1962)

see ship No. AP. 41 in A. P. O. C. section.

TR. 5. LADY DUFF (1953–)

O.N. 183603. 12g. 7n. 40.0 × 8.75 × 5.0 feet.
Post 1948: Two, 6-cyl. 4 S.C.S.A. (4 3/8″ × 5″) Perkins type oil engines. 18 bhp
Wooden launch.

1944: Completed by Brooke Marine Ltd., Lowestoft for F. C. Pollard, Southampton. 1948: Motorised. 1953: Purchased by AIOC/BP Trading Ltd., on behalf of George Wimpey & Company Ltd., for use at Aden.

TR. 6. PHANTOM (1953–1957)

O.N. 185875. 10g. 8n. 39.2 × 9.0 × 4.7 feet.
100bhp. oil engine.
Wooden launch.

19 ?: Built at Cowes (Yard No.)
1953: Purchased by AIOC/BP Trading Ltd.
1957: Lost.
Due to small size and type of this vessel no further details have been located by the authors.

TR. 7. SINIBIR (1955–)

Due to small size and type of this vessel no further details have been located by the authors.

TR. 8. IERLAND (1955–)

see ship No. AP. 53 in A. P. O. C. section.

TR. 9. BP SHIPBUILDER (1956–1961)

see ship No. AP. 42 in A. P. O. C. section.

TR. 10. BP BRUGES (1956–)

Due to small size and type of this vessel no further details have been located by the authors.

BP Elbe. (World Ship Society Photograph Library)

BP Dormangen. (World Ship Society Photograph Library)

Northam Osprey. (World Ship Society Photograph Library)

TR. 11. BP DORMANGEN (1956–)

Due to small size and type of this vessel no further details have been located by the authors.

TR. 12. NORTHAM OSPREY (1982–1996)

O.N. 700318. 155g. 45n. 103d. 28.45 × 7.42 × 1.907 metres.
Two, 6-cyl. 4 S.C.S.A. (127 × 140mm) Lister JW6M type oil engines manufactured by Lister Marine, R. A. Lister & Company Ltd., Marine Division, Dursley, geared to twin directional propellers. 450 bhp.
Training ship for pollution control.

3.2.1981: Keel laid by New Holland Shipyard Ltd., New Holland (Yard No.Y10), for BP International Ltd. 27.3.1982: Launched. 18.5.1982: Completed. 1987: BP Shipping Ltd., appointed as managers. 1996: Sold to Dolphin Offshore (Consolidated Projects, managers), and renamed DOLPHIN WORKER under St. Vincent and The Grenadines register. Still listed in Lloyd's Register 2003/04.

TR. 13. BP TWEED (1985–1986)

see ship No. TH. 9 above

TR. 14. BP HUMBER (1985–1991)

see ship No. BT. 423 above

Kent Oil Refinery Ltd.
Isle of Grain

KOR. 1. SIDNEY BERNARD (1955–)

O.N. 184674. 27g. 13n. 47.4 × 12.9 × 6.0 feet.
106bhp oil engine
Launch type wooden C. P. & tug.

1952: Built at Brightlingsea for unspecified owners. 1955: Purchased by Anglo-Iranian Oil Company, for use on the River Medway. *Due to small size and type of this vessel no further details have been recorded by the authors.*

D'Arcy Exploration Company Ltd.
founded 1955.

1957: Restyled as
BP Exploration Company Ltd.

EX. 1. GOWERA (1957–1965)

O.N. 187676. 250g. 63n. 110′ 0″ × 26′ 8″ × 4′ 11″.
Two, 8-cyl. 4 S.C.S.A. (5 1/2″ × 7 3/4″) oil engines manufactured by Gardner & Sons Ltd., Manchester. 288 bhp.
Beach Landing Craft.

6.1957: Launched by Clelands (Successors) Ltd., Wallsend (Yard No. 231), for the company. 8.1957: Completed for BP Exploration Company Ltd. Towed from Tyne to Zanzibar. 1965: Sold to Gray McKenzie & Company, London. *Due to small size and type of this vessel no further details have been recorded by the authors.*

EX. 2. KARIMAH (1957–1958)

O.N. 187640. 88g. 51n. 71.4 × 20.5 × 7.3 feet.
286bhp oil engine.
Steel workboat.

9.1957: Completed at Brightlingsea for BP Exploration Company Ltd. 1958: Transferred to Abu Dhabi Marine Areas Ltd. *Due to small size and type of this vessel no further details have been recorded by the authors.*

EX. 3. WRANGLER (1957–1966)

see ship No. AP. 54 in A. P. O. C. section.

EX. 4. AZIZAH (1957–1958)

O.N. 187654. 88g. 51n. 71.4 × 20.5 × 7.3 feet.
286bhp oil engine.
Steel workboat.

10.1957: Completed at Brightlingsea for BP Exploration Company Ltd. 1958: Transferred to Abu Dhabi Marine Areas Ltd. *Due to small size and type of this vessel no further details have been recorded by the authors.*

EX. 5. SARIFAH (1957–1958)

O.N. 187707. 88g. 51n. 71.4 × 20.5 × 7.3 feet.
286bhp oil engine.
Steel workboat.

12.1957: Completed at Brightlingsea for BP Exploration Company Ltd. 1958: Transferred to Abu Dhabi Marine Areas Ltd. *Due to small size and type of this vessel no further details have been recorded by the authors.*

BP Benzin Und Petroleum A. G.

1956: Founded.
1975 : Restyled
Deutsche BP A.G.

BEN. 1. BP OLEX 35 (1958–1964)

102g. 54n. 1549d. 101′ 3″ × 17′ 2″ × ?.
8-cyl. 4 S.C.S.A. (140 × 180mm) oil engine manufactured by Motorenwerke Mannheim (MWM), Mannheim, coupled to a directional propeller. 170 bhp.
Powered tank barge.

1958: Completed by Scheel and Johnk, Hamburg (Yard No. 401), for BP Benzin Und Petroleum A. G. 1964: Renamed BP 35. *Due to small size and type of this vessel no further details have been recorded by the authors.*

BEN. 2. BP OLEX 36 (1958–1964)

102g. 54n. 159d. 101′ 3″ × 17′ 2″ × ?.
8-cyl. 4 S.C.S.A. (140 × 180mm) oil engine manufactured by Suddtsch. Bremsen A.G., Munich, coupled to a directional propeller. 210 bhp.
Powered tank barge.

1958: Completed by Scheel & Johnk, Hamburg (Yard No. 402), for BP Benzin Und Petroleum A. G.
1964: Renamed BP 36. *Due to small size and type of this vessel no further details have been recorded by the authors.*

BP Humber, Piraeus Roads 29 May 1988 (World Ship Society Photograph Library)

BEN. 3. BP OLEX 39 (1961–1964)

150g. 83n. 257d. 115′ 4″ × 19′ 2″ × ?.
6-cyl. 4 S.C.S.A. (215 × 300mm) oil engine manufactured by Motorenwerke Mannheim (MWM), Mannheim, coupled to a directional propeller. 235 bhp.
Powered tank barge.

1961: Completed by Scheel & Johnk, Hamburg (Yard No. 424), for BP Benzin Und Petroleum A. G. 1964: Renamed BP 39. *Due to small size and type of this vessel no further details have been recorded by the authors.*

BEN. 4. BP KIEL (1961–)

694g. 320n. 183′ 9″ × 30′ 3″ × ?.
6-cyl. 4 S.C.S.A. (320 × 480mm) oil engine manufactured by Motorenwerke Mannheim (MWM), Mannheim.
Powered tank barge.

16.2.1961: Launched by J. G. Hizler, Lauenburg (Yard No. 654), for BP Benzin Und Petroleum A. G. 1961: Completed. *Due to small size and type of this vessel no further details have been recorded by the authors.*

BEN. 5. BP OLEX 37 (1963–1964)

100g. 53n. 147d. 99′ 11″ × 18′ 5″ × ?.
8-cyl. 4 S.C.S.A. (140 × 180mm) oil engine manufactured by Motorenwerke Mannheim (MWM), Mannheim, coupled to a directional propeller. 200 bhp.
Powered tank barge.

1963: Completed by Ernst Menzer Werft, Geesthacht, for BP Benzin Und Petroleum A.G. 1964: Renamed BP 37. *Due to small size and type of this vessel no further details have been recorded by the authors.*

BEN. 6. BP OLEX 46 (1963–1964)

O.N. 10492. 101g. 53n. 147d. 99′ 11″ × 18′ 5″ × ?.
8-cyl. 4 S.C.S.A. (140 × 180mm) oil engine manufactured by Motorenwerke Mannheim (MWM), Mannheim, coupled to a directional propeller. 200 bhp.
Powered tank barge.

1963: Completed by Ernst Menzer Werft, Geesthacht (Yard No. 473), for BP Benzin Und Petroleum A.G. 1964: Renamed BP 46. *Due to small size and type of this vessel no further details have been recorded by the authors.*

BEN. 7. BP OLEX 32 (1963–1964)

O.N. 19530. 174g. 97n. 292d. 133′ 11″ × 20′ 8″ × ?.
6-cyl. 4 S.C.S.A. (250 × 350mm) oil engine manufactured by Motorenwerke Mannheim (MWM), Mannheim, coupled to a directional propeller. 280 bhp.
Powered tank barge.

1963: Completed by Scheel & Johnk, Hamburg (Yard No. 440), for BP Benzin Und Petroleum A. G. 1964: Renamed BP 32. *Due to small size and type of this vessel no further details have been recorded by the authors.*

BEN. 8. BP 32 (2) (1964–)

see ship No. BEN. 7 above.

BEN. 9. BP 35 (2) (1964–)

see ship No. BEN. 1 above.

BEN. 10. BP 36 (1964–)

see ship No. BEN. 2 above.

BEN. 11. BP 37 (2) (1964–)

see ship No. BEN. 5 above.

BEN. 12. BP 39 (1964–)

see ship No. BEN. 3 above.

BEN. 13. BP 46 (1964–)

see ship No. BEN. 6 above.

BEN. 14. BP 96 (1971–)

O.N. 3581. 139g. 79n. 111′ 0″ × 21′ 0″ × 7′ 0″ .
6-cyl. 4 S.C.S.A. (215 × 300mm) oil engine manufactured by Motorenwerk Mannheim (MWM), Mannheim. 225 bhp.
Powered tank barge.

1966: Completed as HELGA WALLENSTEIN by Scheel & Johnk, Hamburg, for Karl Tiedtke, W. Germany. 1971: Renamed BP 96. *Due to small size and type of this vessel no further details have been recorded by the authors.*

Tankskibsrederiet AS.

1959: Founded Denmark
1967: restyled as
BP Tankskibsrederiet AS.
1988: restyled as
BP Gastankers AS.
1989: restyled as
BP Danmark AS.

D. 1. BP NETTE (1959–1977)

289g. 138n. 148′ 10″ × 26′ 0″ × 8′ 4¼″.
Two, 6-cyl. 4 S.C.S.A. (130 × 170mm) oil engines manufactured by Kloeckner Humboldt Deutz, Koeln, driving generators powering five electric motors coupled to screw shaft.
Post 1965: 6-cyl. 4 S.C.S.A. (120 × 140mm) oil engine manufactured by Ab Volvo-Penta, Gothenburg, fitted as replacement for port side engine.
Post 1969: 6-cyl. 4 S.C.S.A. (120 × 140mm) oil engine manufactured by Ab Volvo-Penta, Gothenburg, fitted as replacement for starboard side engine.
Powered tank barge.

3.2.1958: Launched by Schiffswerf W. Holst, Hamburg (Yard No. 223), for AS Tankskibsrederiet. 8.1959: Completed. 5.1965: Part re-engined. 1967: Owners restyled as BP Tankskibsredereit AS. 8.1969: Part re-engined. 1977: Renamed BUNKER NETTE. 1980: Sold to Educom Oil A.G., Switzerland, and renamed LORD JOHN. 1983: Sold to Langeberg Shipping B.V., Amsterdam, and renamed MICHAEL LANGEBERG. 1997: Sold to Kruijff Bunker Services (KSB), Den Helder, and renamed MICHAEL 2002: Sold to Gulf Oil Nederland B.V. 2004: Renamed KRUIJFF. Still listed in Lloyd's Register 2004/05.

D. 2. BP ESTRED (1960–1969)

As built: 99g. 36n. 110d. 92′ 0″ × 19′ 5″ × 8′ 6″.
Post 1963: 115g. 48n. 150d. 104′ 3″ × 19′ 6″ × 8′ 6″.
3-cyl. 2 S.C.S.A.(230 × 400mm) Alpha type oil engine manufactured by Frederikshavns Jernst & Msk., Frederikshavn. 200 bhp.
Powered tank barge.

1939: Completed as ESTRED by Svendborg Skibsverf, Svendborg, for unspecified owners. 1960: Purchased and renamed BP ESTRED. 1963: Lengthened. 1967: Owners restyled as BP Tankskibsredereit AS. 1969: Sold to M.H. Sorensen Partenrederi, Denmark, and renamed PIA. *Due to small size and type of this vessel no further details have been recorded by the authors.*

D. 3. BP VERA (1964–1986)

69g. 27n. 66′ 0″ × 19′ 9″ × ?.
6-cyl. 4 S.C.S.A. (5½″ × 6″) oil engine manufactured by Rolls Royce Ltd., Shrewsbury. 170 bhp.
Powered tank barge.

8.1964: Completed by Bolsones Verft, Molde, for AS Tankskibsrederiet. 1967: Owners restyled as BP Tankskibsredereit AS. 1986: Sold to Kuwait Petroleum (Danmark) Ltd., and removed from Lloyd's Register as being below 100g. for harbour use only. *Due to small size and type of this vessel no further details have been recorded by the authors.*

D. 4. BP DIANA (1969–)

150g. 54n. 276d. 115′ 6″ × 26′ 4″ × 9′ 1¾″.
As built 8-cyl. 4 S.C.S.A. (130 × 152mm) oil engine manufactured by Rolls Royce Ltd., Shrewsbury. 380 bhp.
Post 1971 6-cyl. 4 S.C.S.A. (5½″ × 6½″) oil engine manufactured by Caterpillar Tractor Company, Peoria, Illinois. 365 bhp.
Powered tank barge.

3.1969: Completed by AS Svendborg Skibsverf, Svendborg for BP Tankskibsrederiet AS. 1974: Removed from Lloyd's Register – for river service only. *Due to small size and type of this vessel no further details have been recorded by the authors.*

D. 5. DANISH ARROW (1976–2002)

499g. 344n. 625d. 66.53 × 10.67 × 3.322 metres.
8-cyl. 4 S.C.S.A. (225 × 300mm) oil engine manufactured by Alpha Diesel AS, Frederikshavn. 1,160 bhp.
Liquefied gas carrier.

6.8.1975: Keel laid by AS Svendborg Skibsverk, Svendborg (Yard No. 151) for BP Tankskibsrederiet AS. 17.1.1976: Launched. 3.6.1976: Completed. 10.2002: Sold to Soltin Marine AS (Soltin Shipment AS, Aarhus, managers), Denmark, and renamed ARROW. Still listed in Lloyd's Register 2004/05.

D. 6. DANISH DART (1976–2002)

499g. 344n. 625d. 66.53 × 10.67 × 3.322 metres.
8-cyl. 4 S.C.S.A. (225 × 300mm) oil engine manufactured by Alpha Diesel AS, Frederikshavn. 1,160 bhp.
Liquefied gas carrier.

4.3.1976: Keel laid by AS Svendborg Skibsverk,

BP Estred. (World Ship Society Photograph Library)

Svendborg (Yard No. 152) for BP Tankskibsrederiet AS. 8.5.1976: Launched. 11.9.1976: Completed. 10.2002: Sold to Soltin Marine AS (Soltin Shipment AS, Aarhus, managers), Denmark, and renamed DART. Still listed in Lloyd's Register 2004/05.

BUNKER NETTE (1977–1980)

see ship No. D.1 above.

BP Oil Supplies Pty. Ltd.

OS. 1. BP COCKBURN (1965–1970)

see ship No. K. 8 in BP Kwinana Pty. Ltd.

OS. 2. BP PARMELIA (1965–1970)

see ship No. K. 9 in BP Kwinana Pty. Ltd.

OS. 3. K L 2 (1965–1970)

see ship No. K. 1 in BP Kwinana Pty. Ltd.

OS. 4. K L 3 (1965–1970)

see ship No. K. 2 in BP Kwinana Pty. Ltd.

OS. 5. BIARA (1965–1970)

see ship No. K. 5 in BP Kwinana Pty. Ltd.

OS. 6. GOBUL (1965–1970)

see ship No. K. 6 in BP Kwinana Pty. Ltd.

OS. 7. NERIMBA (1965–1970)

see ship No. K. 7 in BP Kwinana Pty. Ltd.

British Petroleum Australia Ltd.
(including British Tankers Australia Pty. Ltd)

AU. 1. BP SYDNEY (1) (1960–1977)

450g. n. 600d. 121′ 5″ × 31′ 5″ × 10′ 9″.
Dumb oil barge.

30.12.1959: Launched by Chadwick Engineering Pty. Ltd., Sydney (Yard No. 2), for British Petroleum Australia Ltd. 1960: Completed. 1977: Renamed BP NEWCASTLE. *Due to small size and type of this vessel no further details have been recorded by the authors.*

AU. 2. BP COCKBURN (1970–1975)

see ship No. K. 8 in BP Kwinana Pty. Ltd.

AU. 3. BP PARMELIA (1970–1975)

see ship No. K. 9 in BP Kwinana Pty. Ltd.

AU. 4. BIARA (1970–1975)

see ship No. K. 5 in BP Kwinana Pty. Ltd.

AU. 5. GOBUL (1970–1975)

see ship No. K. 6 in BP Kwinana Pty. Ltd.

AU. 6. K L 2 (1970–1975)

see ship No. K. 1 in BP Kwinana Pty. Ltd.

AU. 7. K L 3 (1970–1975)

see ship No. K. 2 in BP Kwinana Pty. Ltd.

AU. 8. BP NEWCASTLE (1977–)

see ship AU 1 above.

BP Sydney in November 1977. (World Ship Society Photograph Library)

AU. 8. BP SYDNEY (2) (1977–)

O.N. 374400. 896g. 395n. 1,700d. 54.01 × 13.90 × 3,785 metres.
Two, 12-cyl. 4 S.C.S.A.(140 × 152mm) vee type oil engines manufactured by Cummins Engine Company, Columbus, geared to twin screw shafts. 800 bhp
Powered tank barge.

1977: Completed by Hornibrooks Northern Group, Brisbane (Yard No. ES20), for BP Australia Ltd. *Due to small size and type of this vessel no further details have been recorded by the authors.*

BP Refinery (Llandarcy) Ltd.

BP FIREMASTER (1960–)

O.N. 168599. 88g. 88n. 60′ 0″ × 38′ 0″ × ?.
Two, 6-cyl. 4 S.C.S.A. (140 × 160mm) oil engines manufactured by W. H. Dorman & Company Ltd., Stafford. (Removeable propelling and steering units).
Twin hulled fire-float.

31.12.1959: Pontoons launched by J. S. Watson (Gainsboro) Ltd., Gainsborough (Yard No. 1764). 1.1961: Lengthened and completed by R. S. Hayes (Pembroke Dock) Ltd., Pembroke Dock (Yard No. 507), for BP Refinery (Llandarcy) Ltd. *Due to small size and type of this vessel no further details have been recorded by the authors.*

BP Handel Maatschappij Nederland B.V.

Both vessels for inland waterway use and in 1985/86 Lloyd's Register.

BP HOLLAND 27 (1961–)

O.N. 2005817. ?g. ?n. 1,310d. 84.64 × 9.50 × ? metres.
Two, 5-cyl. 2 S.C.S.A. (190 × 350mm) engines manufactured by 'Bolnes' Motorenfabriek B.V., Krimpen aan den Lek, reverse reduction geared to twin screw shafts. 500bhp. Thwartship thrust propeller forward.

1961: Completed by N.V. Scheepswerv 'Piet Hein' v/h W. Schram & Zonen, Papendrecht (Yard No. 676), for unspecified owners. Inland waterway use – no further details located.

BP HOLLAND 33 (1964–)

?g. ?n. ?d. 80.02 × 9.0 × ? metres.
Two, 6-cyl. 2 S.C.S.A. (190 × 350mm) engines manufactured by 'Bolnes' Motorenfabriek B.V., Krimpen aan den Lek, reverse reduction geared to twin screw shafts 600bhp. Thwartship thrust propeller forward.

1964: Completed by N.V. Scheepswerv 'Piet Hein' v/h W. Schram & Zonen, Papendrecht (Yard No. 712), for unspecified owners. Inland waterway use – no further details located.

BP Thames Tanker Company Ltd.

TH. 1. BRITISH BEECH (1) (1964–1975)

see ship No. BT. 425 in main fleet.

TH. 2. BRITISH HOLLY (3) (1965–1983)

see ship No. BT. 369 in main fleet.

TH. 3. BRITISH WILLOW (1965–1975)

see ship No. BT. 371 in main fleet.

TH. 4. BRITISH AVON (1972–1985)

O.N. 343240. 15,540g. 9,551n. 25,215d. 562′ 6″ (BB) × 82′ 2″. 31′ 5¼″.
6-cyl. 2 S.C.S.A. (760 × 1550mm) Sulzer 6RND76 type oil engine manufactured by Scotts' Engineering Company (1969) Ltd., Greenock. 9,000 bhp.
Ocean-going refined products tanker.

28.3.1972: Launched by Scotts' Shipbuilding Company (1969) Ltd., Greenock (Yard No. 724), for BP Thames Tanker Company Ltd. 11.1972: Completed. 1985: Sold to Misano di

British Avon on 10 June 1982. (World Ship Society Photograph Library)

Navigazione S.p.A., Italy, and renamed MARE DI KARA. 1986: Sold to Transporti Marittima Riuniti S.p.A., Palermo. 1987: Sold to Venezia Tankers Srl., Venice, and renamed CARNIA. 1988: Sold to Starlauro S.p.A. (Rivergas S.p.a., managers), Naples, and renamed LAUROTANK CARNIA. 1989: Reverted to CARNIA. 1990: Sold to Feldene Shipping Corp., Panama. 1993: Sold to Lefkaritis Brothers Marine Ltd., Limassol, Cyprus. 1997: Columbia Shipmanagement (Netherlands) B.V., appointed as managers. 8.4.2000: Arrived at Alang for demolition.

TH. 5. BRITISH TAMAR (1973–1990)

O.N. 358940. 15,642g. 9,650n. 25,094d.
562′ 7″ (BB) × 82′ 2″ . 31′ 6″.
6-cyl. 2 S.C.S.A. (740 × 1600mm) B&W 6K74EF type oil engine manufactured by S. A. Cockerill-Ougree-Providence, Seraing. Thwartship thrust propeller forward. 9,000 bhp.
Ocean-going refined products tanker.

4.12.1972: Launched by N. V. Boelwerf S. A., Tamise/Temse (Yard No. 1469), for BP Thames Tanker Company Ltd. 5.1973: Completed. 1990: Transferred to BP Shipping Ltd., Bermuda registry (O.N.358940). 1999: Owners restyled as BP Amoco Shipping Ltd. 2000: Sold to Xinhui Ship Breaking Iron & Steel Company, China, for demolition. 2.12.2000: Departed from Singapore en route to breakers yard. 8.12.2000: Work commenced at Xinhui.

British Tamar. (J K Byass)

TH. 6. BRITISH KENNET (1973–1986)

O.N. 360540. 15,538g. 9,539n. 25,127d.
562′ 6″ (BB) × 82′ 2″ × 31′ 5½″.
6-cyl. 2 S.C.S.A. (760 × 1550mm) Sulzer 6RND76 type oil engine manufactured by Scotts' Engineering Company (1969) Ltd., Greenock. 9,000 bhp.
Ocean-going refined products tanker.

11.12.1972: Launched by Scotts' Shipbuilding Company (1969) Ltd., Greenock (Yard No. 725), for BP Thames Tanker Company Ltd. 5.1973: Completed. 1986: Sold to the National Iranian Tanker Company Ltd., and renamed MINAB 2. 5.4.2002: Arrived at Alang for demolition.

British Kennet. (World Ship Society Photograph Library)

TH. 7. BRITISH ESK (1973–1990)

O.N. 360799. 15,644g. 9,664n. 25,178d.
562′ 7″ (BB) × 82′ 2″ × 31′ 6″.
6-cyl. 2 S.C.S.A. (740 × 1600mm) B&W 6K74EF type oil engine manufactured by S. A. Cockerill-Ougree-Providence, Seraing. Thwartship thrust propeller forward. 9,000 bhp.
Ocean-going refined products tanker.

6.3.1973: Launched by N. V. Boelwerf S. A., Tamise/Temse (Yard No. 1470), for BP Thames Tanker Company Ltd. 9.1973: Completed. 1990: Transferred to BP Shipping Ltd., Bermuda registry (O.N.360799). 1999: Owners restyled as BP Amoco Shipping Ltd. 2001: Owners restyled as BP Shipping Ltd. 3.4.2001: Demolition commenced at an unspecified location.

British Esk. (World Ship Society Photograph Library)

TH. 8. BRITISH PRIDE (2) (1973–1976)

O.N. 360825. 111,980g. 91,543n. 218,467d.
329.62 × 48.21 × 19.406 metres.
Two, Stal-Laval type steam turbines manufactured by the shipbuilder, double reduction and triple geared to screw shaft. 32,400 shp.
Very Large crude carrier (VLCC).

16.6.1973: Launched by Chantiers del'Atlantique, St. Nazaire (Yard No. C. 25), for BP Thames Tanker Company Ltd. 10.1973: Completed. 1976: Sold to the National Iranian Tanker Company, Iran, and renamed SUSANGIRD. 9.12.1987: At 22:00hrs GMT attacked by Iraqi aircraft at position 28.10N., 51.03E., and was disabled by fire. 10.12.1987: At 02:00hrs GMT attacked again at position 28.05N., 51.07E. 21 crew killed. 14.4.1988: Arrived at Singapore for repairs. 15.2.1995: Beached at Alang for demolition.

British Pride. (J K Byass)

British Tweed. (J K Byass)

British Progress. (World Ship Society Photograph Library)

British Forth. (World Ship Society Photograph Library)

British Promise. (World Ship Society Photograph Library)

TH. 9. BRITISH TWEED (1973–1985)

O.N. 360815. 15,538g. 9,539n. 25,559d.
562′ 6″ (BB) × 82′ 2″ × 31′ 5$^{1}/_{4}$″.
6-cyl. 2 S.C.S.A. (760 × 1550mm) Sulzer 6RND76 type oil engine manufactured by Scotts' Engineering Company Ltd., Greenock. 9,000 bhp.
Ocean-going refined products tanker.

29.3.1973: Launched by Scotts' Shipbuilding Company Ltd., Greenock (Yard No. 726), for BP Thames Tanker Company Ltd. 10.1973: Completed. 1985: Transferred to BP International Ltd., Bahamas (BP Shipping Ltd., managers), and renamed BP TWEED. 1986: Sold to the National Iranian Tanker Company Ltd., and renamed AZNA. 1997: Renamed MINAB 1. 14.12.2003: Sailed from Fujairah anchorage en route to Gadani Beach for demolition.

TH. 10. BRITISH PROGRESS (3) (1973–1985)

O.N. 360787. 117,536g. 96,350n. 224,989d.
330.01(BB) × 48.75 × 19.902 metres.
Two, GEC type steam turbines manufactured by Verolme Maschinefabrik, Isselmonde, double reduction geared to screw shaft. 32,000 shp.
Very Large crude carrier (VLCC).

24.2.1973: Afterpart (Yard No. 845), launched by Nederlandsche Dok & Scheepswerf, Amsterdam.
12.5.1973: Forepart (Yard No. 845), launched by Nederlandsche Dok & Scheepswerf, Amsterdam. 10.1973: Completed for BP Thames Tanker Company Ltd. 5.3.1985: Arrived at Kaohsiung for demolition.

TH. 11. BRITISH FORTH (1973–1990)

O.N. 360944. 15,540g. 9,551n. 25,551d.
562′ 6″ (BB) × 82′ 2″ . 31′ 5$^{1}/_{4}$″.
6-cyl. 2 S.C.S.A. (760 × 1550mm) Sulzer 6RND76 type oil engine manufactured by the shipbuilder. 9,000 bhp.
Ocean-going refined products tanker.

1.6.1973: Launched by Scotts' Shipbuilding Company Ltd., Greenock (Yard No. 727), for BP Thames Tanker Company Ltd. 12.1973: Completed. 1990: Transferred to BP Shipping Ltd. 1993: Sold to Camargue Shipping Company Ltd. (Arminter S. A. M., managers), Malta, and renamed CAMARGUE. 2000: Sold to Therissos Shipping Company S.A. (Avin International S.A., managers), Greece, and renamed CHRYSSI 6.2003: Sold to Palm Hellenic Navigation S.A., Panama, and renamed BEDOUR 2003. Still in Lloyd's Register 2004/5.

TH. 12. BRITISH PROMISE (2) (1974–1976)

O.N. 360973. 131,402g. 110,693n. 253,839d.
344.41(BB) × 51.87 × 19.952 metres.
Two, GEC type steam turbines manufactured by General Electric Company, Lynn, Mass., double reduction geared to screw shaft. 32,000 shp.
Very Large crude carrier (VLCC).

11.8.1973: Launched by Verolme Dok & Scheepswerf, Rosenburg (Yard No. 850), for BP Thames Tanker Company Ltd. 1.1974: Completed. 1976: Sold to the National Iranian Tanker Company, Iran, and renamed SANANDAJ. 30.8.1987: Attacked by Iraqi aircraft whilst loading at Kharg Island. 19.3.1988: Attacked by Iraqi aircraft whilst lying at Kharg Island and was seriously damaged aft by fire. 26 killed. 4 rescued.

TH. 13. BRITISH PURPOSE (2) (1974–1985)

O.N. 360974. 117,536g. 96,294n. 228,600d.
330.01(BB) × 48.75 × 19.898 metres.
Two, GEC type steam turbines manufactured by Verolme Machinefabrik, Ijsselmonde, double reduction geared to screw shaft. 31,550 shp.
Very Large crude carrier (VLCC).

11.8.1973: Afterpart (Yard No. 846), launched by Nederlandsche Dok and Scheepswerf, Amsterdam. 13.10.1973: Forepart (Yard No. 846), launched by Nederlandsche Dok and Scheepswerf, Amsterdam. 3.1974: Completed for BP Thames Tanker Company Ltd. 19.2.1985: Arrived at Kaohsiung for demolition.

British Purpose. (World Ship Society Photograph Library)

British Spey. (World Ship Society Photograph Library)

TH. 14. BRITISH SPEY (1974–1985)

**O.N. 363288. 15,590g. 9,443n. 25,590d.
562′ 6″ (BB) × 82′ 2″ × 31′ 5″.
6-cyl. 2 S.C.S.A. (740 × 1600mm) B&W 6K74EF type oil engine manufactured by J. G. Kincaid & Company Ltd., Greenock. 9,000 bhp.
Ocean-going refined products tanker.**

15.10.1973: Launched by Lithgows Ltd., Port Glasgow (Yard No. 1187), for BP Thames Tanker Company Ltd. 5.1974: Completed. 31.7.1985: Reported as having been attacked with a missile in the Gulf area. No other details given. 1985: Sold to Sprint Performance Inc., Panama, and renamed TANK PROGRESS. 4.1996: Sold to Fort Shipping Ltd., Malta, and renamed PROGRESO. 1.2003: Sold to unspecified N. Korean owners, and renamed PROGRESS. 22.1.2003: Demolition commenced at an unspecified location.

TH. 15. BRITISH PATIENCE (2) (1974–1982)

**O.N. 360787. 117,536g. 96,350n. 253,839d.
330.01(BB) × 48.75 × 19.902 metres.
Two, GEC steam turbines manufactured by Verolme Maschinefabrik, Isselmonde, double reduction geared to screw shaft. 32,000 shp.
Very Large crude carrier (VLCC).**

22.12.1973: Launched by Verolme Dok & Scheepswerf, Rozenburg (Yard No. 851), for BP Thames Tanker Company Ltd. 5.1974: Completed. 27.10.1982: Arrived at Ulsan for demolition.

TH. 16. BRITISH SPIRIT (1983)

see ship No. BT. 433 in main fleet.

TH. 17. BRITISH SKILL (2) (1983)

see ship No. BT. 432 in main fleet.

TH. 19. BP ACHIEVER (1983–1991)

see ship No. BT. 441 in main fleet.

TH. 20. BRITISH SUCCESS (2) (1983–1984)

see ship No. BT. 434 in main fleet.

TH. 21. BRITISH RENOWN (3) (1985–1990)

see ship No. BT. 443 in main fleet.

TH. 22. BRITISH RESOLUTION (2) (1985–1990)

see ship No. BT. 444 in main fleet.

TH. 23. BRITISH TENACITY (2) (1985–1989)

see ship No. BT. 391 in main fleet.

BP Tyne Tanker Company Ltd.

TY. 1. BRITISH COMMERCE (3) (1965–1983)

see ship No. BT. 372 in main fleet.

TY. 2. BRITISH ADMIRAL (3) (1967–1976)

see ship No. BT. 374 in main fleet.

TY. 3. BRITISH SECURITY (3) (1976–1989)

see ship No. BT. 390 in main fleet.

TY. 4. BRITISH TENACITY (2) (1976–1985)

see ship No. BT. 391 in main fleet.

BP Singapore Pte. Ltd.

BP MARINE 70 (1970–1985)

**O.N. 333218. 466g. 377n. 754d. 149′ 11″ × 34′ 6″ × 9′ 6″.
Two, 6-cyl. 4 S.C.S.A. (5 1/8″ × 6″) oil engines manufactured by Rolls Royce Ltd., Shrewsbury, geared to twin screw shafts. 490 bhp.
Powered tank barge.**

4.1970: Completed by Jurong Shipyard Ltd., Singapore (Yard No. 66), for BP Singapore Pte. Ltd. 1985: Sold to Ocean Tankers (Pte.) Ltd., Singapore, and renamed MARINE EXPRESS. Subsequently to Xin Guang Shipping Pte Ltd., Singapore. *Due to small size and type of this vessel no further details have been recorded by the authors.*

BP Medway Tanker Company Ltd.

MT. 1 BRITISH EXPLORER (2) (1970–1981)

**O.N. 339034. 108,530g. 82,576n. 215,603d.
1,069′ 7″ (BB) × 160′ 0″ × 62′ 0″.
Two, Westinghouse type steam turbines manufactured by the shipbuilder, double reduction geared to screw shaft. 30,000 shp.
Very Large crude carrier (VLCC).**

16.11.1969: Launched by Mitsubishi Heavy Industries, Nagasaki (Yard No. 1162), for the BP Medway Tanker Company Ltd. 3.1970: Completed. 1976: Irano-British Ship Service Company Ltd., appointed as managers. 1981: Sold for demolition at Kaohsiung.

MT. 2. BRITISH INVENTOR (2) (1970–1981)

**O.N. 339160. 108,530g. 82,576n. 215,523d.
1,069′ 7″ (BB) × 160′ 0″ × 62′ 4″.
Two, Westinghouse type steam turbines manufactured by the shipbuilder, double reduction geared to screw shaft. 30,000 shp.
Very Large crude carrier (VLCC).**

15.1.1970: Launched by Mitsubishi Heavy Industries, Nagasaki (Yard No. 1163), for the BP Medway Tanker Company Ltd. 6.1970: Completed. 1976: Irano-British Ship Service Company Ltd., appointed as managers. 7.7.1981: Arrived at Kaohsiung for demolition.

MT. 3. BRITISH PIONEER (2) (1971–1981)

**O.N. 341429. 108,500g. 82,995n. 226,137d.
1,063′ 8″ (BB) × 160′ 2″ × 64′ 5″.
Two, Westinghouse type steam turbines manufactured by Mitsubishi Heavy Industries, Nagasaki, double reduction geared to screw shaft. 30,000 shp.
Very Large crude carrier (VLCC).**

30.3.1971: Launched by Mitsui Shipbuilding & Engineering, Chiba (Yard No. 847), for the BP Medway Tanker Company Ltd. 6.1971: Completed. 1976: Irano-British Ship Service Company Ltd., appointed as managers. 1981: Sold to Tishpion Navigation Ltd., Greece, and

British Patience. (World Ship Society Photograph Library)

British Explorer. (Internet source)

British Pioneer. (Internet source)

renamed TISHPION. 1981: Sold to Cerrahogullari Umumi Nakliyat Vapourculuk ve Ticaret T. A. S., Turkey, and renamed M. CEYHAN. 12.7.1985: At 06:15hrs local time, whilst on a voyage from Kharg Island to Sirri Island with 200,000 tons crude oil was struck by Iraqi missiles at position 27.46N., 51.11E., 100 miles south of Kharg Island and set ablaze. 14.7.1985: Fire extinguished. Engine room and accommodation both extensively damage by fire and engine room flooded. 16.7.1985: Arrived in tow off Sirri Island, and anchored at position 25.59N., 54.38E. Subsequently declared as a war constructive total loss and sold to Taiwan breakers.

MT. 4. BRITISH NAVIGATOR (2) (1971–1976)

O.N. 341428. 108,531g. 82,576n. 215,139d.
1,069′ 7″ (BB) × 160′ 0″ × 62′ 4″ .
Two, Westinghouse type steam turbines manufactured by the shipbuilder, double reduction geared to screw shaft. 30,000 shp.
Very Large crude carrier (VLCC).

7.3.1971: Launched by Mitsubishi Heavy Industries, Nagasaki (Yard No. 1674), for the BP Medway Tanker Company Ltd. 6.1971: Completed. 1976: Sold to the National Iranian Tanker Company, Iran, and renamed SIVAND. 12.10.1984: At 13:30hrs local time, struck by a missile whilst off Kharg Island sustaining minor unreported damage. 15.10.1984: Whilst on a loaded voyage from Kharg Island to Sirri Island was attacked by Iraqi aircraft and set ablaze. Fire extinguished and vessel towed to Sirri Island for discharge and inspection. Laid up at Sirri Island. 7.5.1986: Arrived under tow at Kaohsiung for demolition.

MT. 5. BRITISH SCIENTIST (2) (1971)

O.N. 342923. 108,635g. 82,772n. 219,994d.
1,063′ 0″ (BB) × 159′ 11″ × 63′ 3″ .
Two, Westinghouse type steam turbines manufactured by the shipbuilder, double reduction geared to screw shaft. 30,000 shp.
Very Large crude carrier (VLCC).

12.7.1971: Launched by Kawasaki Dockyard, Kobe (Yard No. 1133), for the Clyde Charter Company Ltd. 10.1971: Completed for BP Medway Tanker Company Ltd. 1971: Transferred to the Clyde Charter Company Ltd. 1981: Sold for demolition at Kaohsiung.

MT. 6. BRITISH PROSPECTOR (2) (1971–1979)

O.N. 342959. 108,531g. 82,519n. 218,814d.
1,068′ 2″ (BB) × 160′ 0″ × 62′ 7¼″ .
Two, steam turbines manufactured by the shipbuilder, double reduction geared to screw shaft. 30,000 shp.
Very Large crude carrier (VLCC).

8.7.1971: Launched by Mitsubishi Heavy Industries Ltd., Nagasaki (Yard No. 1675), for BP Medway Tanker Company Ltd. 11.1971: Completed. 1979: Sold to South Foundation Shipping Inc., Liberia., and renamed SOUTH

British Prospector. (World Ship Society Photograph Library)

British Scientist. (World Ship Society Photograph Library)

FOUNDATION. 1.2.1983: Demolition commenced at Ulsan.

MT. 7. BRITISH SURVEYOR (2) (1972–1976)

O.N. 343072. 112,742g. 82,811n. 222,745d. 1,063′ 8″ (BB) × 160′ 2″ × 64′ 4½″. Two, steam turbines manufactured by Mitsubishi Heavy Industries Ltd., Nagasaki, double reduction geared to screw shaft. 30,000 shp. Very Large crude carrier (VLCC).

22.12.1971: Launched by Mitsui Shipbuilding & Engineering, Ichihara (Yard No. 872), for BP Medway Tanker Company Ltd. 3.1972: Completed. 1976: Sold to the National Iranian Tanker Company, Iran, and renamed SHOUSH. 29.8.1987: Struck in the port side hull near the engine room by an Iraqi missile at position 27.36N., 50.39E. Damage not reported. 31.8.1987: Whilst en route to Dubai for repair, was attacked by Iraqi aircraft. Subsequently anchored off Dubai for repair to unspecified damage. 4.6.1988: Attacked by Iraqi aircraft off Kharg Island. Damage not reported.

MT. 8. BRITISH RENOWN (3) (1974–1985)

see ship No. BT. 443 in main fleet.

MT. 9. BRITISH RESOLUTION (2) (1974–1985)

see ship No. BT. 444 in main fleet.

1985: Company wound up upon transfer of the last two vessels above.

BP Oil Development Ltd.

BP Petroleum Development Ltd.

DEV. 1. FORTIES KIWI (1976–1982)

see ship No. BT. 334 in main fleet.

DEV. 2. SULAIR (1979–1989)

O.N. 386277. 1,939g. 928n. 2,560d. 87.94 × 18.32 × 4.301 metres. Post 1996 3,969g. 1,190n. 2,560d. Two, 12-cyl. 4 S.C.S.A. (250 × 300mm) Polar F212V-D vee type oil engines manufactured by Ab Bofors Nohab, Trollhattan, geared to twin shafts with controllable-pitch propellers. 4,600 bhp. Three thwartship thrust propellers forward and one aft. Deck-cargo supply ship, Diving support with moonpool.

1979: Completed by G. Eides & Sonner AS, Hoylandsbygd (Yard No. 105), for BP Oil Development Ltd. (BP Shipping Ltd. (Offshore Group), managers). 1989: Sold to Tamar Charterers Ltd. (TNT Sealion Ltd., managers), and renamed TNT PUMA. 1990: Sold to Toisa Ltd. (same managers), and renamed TOISA PUMA. 1995: Sold to Coastal Cable Company Inc. (Transoceanic Cable Ship Company Inc., managers), and renamed COASTAL CONNECTOR, under Marshall Islands flag. 1996: Sold to Transoceanic Cable Ship Company Inc. (DOCKWISE N.V., Netherlands, managers). 1998: Sold to Coastal Cable Company Inc. (Acomarit (UK) Ltd., managers). Still in Lloyd's Register 2003/04.

DEV. 3. FASGADAIR (1980–1988)

O.N. 376457. 1,226g. 629n. 76.99 × 13.09 × 2.845 metres. Two, 16-cyl. 4 S.C.S.A. (159 × 203mm) oil engines manufactured by Caterpillar Tractor Company, Peoria, Illinois. 2,280 bhp. Thwartship thrust propeller forward. Oil pollution recovery vessel with bow door.

1969: Completed as BRUNNECK by T. Van Duijvendijks Scheepswerf, Lekkekerk (Yard No. Z85), for D. D. G.Hansa, W. Germany. 1980: Sold to BP Oil Development Ltd., and renamed FASGADAIR. 1981: Converted from a RoRo vessel and transferred to BP Petroleum Development Ltd. 1982: BP Shipping Ltd. (Offshore Group), assumed management. 1988: Sold to Briggs Marine Ltd., and renamed FORTH EXPLORER. 1998: Sold to IOSL Explorer Liberia Inc. (IOSL Marine Services Ltd., managers), and renamed IOSL EXPLORER, under Panamanian flag. Still in Lloyd's Register 2003/04.

DEV. 4. SEAGAIR (1982–1988)

O.N. 399388. 2,826g. 945n. 2,996d. 94.32 × 19.82 × 4.674 metres. Four, 16-cyl. 4 S.C.S.A. (250 × 300mm) Polar type oil engines manufactured by British Polar Engines Ltd., Glasgow, each 3,200 bhp., driving a generator connected to two 2,535 shp electric motors geared to twin screw shafts with controllable-pitch propellers. Two thwartship thrust controllable-pitch propellers forward and aft. Fire-fighting, stand-by safety, pollution control vessel for offshore installations.

7.1982: Completed by Richards (Shipbuilders) Ltd., Lowestoft (Yard No. 550), for BP Petroleum Development Ltd. (BP Shipping Ltd (Offshore Group) managers). 1988: Sold to Tamar Charterers Ltd. (TNT Sealion Ltd., managers), and renamed TNT SENTINEL. 1990: Sold to Toisa Ltd. (same managers), and renamed TOISA SENTINEL. Still in Lloyd's Register 2003/04.

DEV.5. BUCHAN A (1983–)

10,189g. 7,335n. Pentagonal – 33′ 11½″ × 348′ 10½″ × 116′ 8½″. Floating Production Unit – North Sea.

1972: Ordered by unspecified owners as PENTAGONE 83 from Cie, Francaise d'Enterprieses Metalligues, Le Havre. 1973: Completed as the mobile drilling rig DRILL MASTER, for AS Norsedrill & Company, Oslo. 1979: Sold to unspecified buyers, and renamed PENTAGONE. 1980: Commenced conversion into an F.P.U. for the Buchan Oilfield by Lewis Offshore, Stornoway. 1983: Sold to BP Petroleum Development Ltd., and renamed BUCHAN A. *Due to type of this vessel no further details have been recorded by the authors.*

DEV.6. SEA CONQUEST (1979–1982)

O.N. 376547. 8,397g. 4,710n. 355 × 221 × 120 feet. Engines manufactured by Ruston Paxman Diesels Ltd., Lincoln, driving electric generators, powering four electric motors connected in pairs to twin screws. 10,560bhp total. 8 kts. Self-propelled, semi-submersible oil rig.

1974: Ordered as ATLANTIC 3 from Rauma Repola Oy, Pori, Finland for Atlantic Drilling Company (Reardon Smith Exploration Ltd., managers), Cardiff. 1976: Completed as SEA CONQUEST for Celtic Drilling Company (Reardon Smith Exploration Ltd., managers), for bare-boat charter to British Petroleum Company Ltd., London. 1.1979: Sold to BP Petroleum Development Ltd., London. 7.1982: Sold to Ben Line Group, Leith, and renamed OCEAN BENLOYAL. *Due to type of this vessel no further details have been recorded by the authors.*

DEV.7. COLTAIR (1982–1986)

see DEV.1. above.

DEV.8. SEA EXPLORER (1983–)

9,086g. 5,765n. 300.0 × 249.0 × 130.0 metres. Transit draught 20.0 metres. Three, 12-cyl. 4 S.C.S.A. Ruston 12RKCZ type oil engines manufactured by Ruston Diesels Ltd., Newton Le Willows (9,960 bhp total), powering three electric generators (each 2,892Kw), driving four 1,600 bhp Pleuger type azimuthing propeller units. Sedco 700 type semi-submersible drilling rig.

1983: Completed by Scott Lithgow Ltd. (Yard No. 2001), for BP Petroleum Development Ltd., and commenced a major upgrading programme before entering service to meet a change to her planned activity. 2.1985: Delivered. *Due to type of this vessel no further details have been recorded by the authors.*

DEV.9. SEDCO/BP 471 (1986 –)

7,538g. 3,839n. 470′ 1″ × 71′ 2½″ × 32′ 0″. Five 16-cylinder 4 S.C.S.A. EMD16E9 type oil engines (14,375 bhp total) and two 16-cylinder 4 S.C.S.A. EMD16E8 type oil engines (3,900 bhp total), manufactured by General Motors Corporation, powering five electric generators (each 2,100 kw), connected to twelve motors geared to twin screw shafts. 14 kts. Self-propelled drilling ship.

1978: Completed by Hawker Siddeley Ltd., Halifax Shipyards Division, Halifax NS (Yard No. H68), for Overseas Drilling Ltd. 1986: Transferred to BP Petroleum Development Ltd. *Due to type of this vessel no further details have been recorded by the authors.*

DEV.10. IOLAIR (1990–)

O.N. 376461. 11,019g. 5,513n. Rectangular platform 334′ 8″ × 194′ 5″ × 105′ 11¾″. Service draught 50′ 1″ with 19,362 tons displacement. Six, 18-cyl. 4 S.C.S.A. (250 × 300mm) M.A.N. 18ASV 25/30

Forties Kiwi. (J K Byass)

Seillean. (World Ship Society Photograph Library)

type oil engines (each 4,800 bhp), manufactured by Harland & Wolff Ltd., Belfast, each driving a generator connected to four electric motors (each 3,000 shp) geared to twin screw shafts, and four positioning thrusters (each 2,000 shp).
Self-propelled semi-submersible fire-fighting, diving support vessel.

23.4.1979: Keel laid by Lithgows Ltd., Port Glasgow (Yard No. 1200), for BP Oil Development Ltd. 6.4.1981: Launched. 6.1982: Completed. 12.8.1982: Delivered to BP Oil Development Ltd & British National Oil Corporation (BP Shipping Ltd., managers). 1990: BP Shipping Ltd. (Offshore Group), assumed management. 1990: Transferred to BP Exploration Operation Company Ltd. (BP Shipping Ltd., managers). *Due to type of this vessel no further details have been recorded by the authors.*

DEV.11 . SEILLEAN (1990–1996)

O.N. 149505. 50,928g. 15,278n. 79,608d.
249.70 × 37.63 × 11.540 metres.
Three, 8-cyl. 4 S.C.S.A. (400 × 450mm) M.A.N. 8L40/50 type oil engines (each 9,900bhp) manufactured by the shipbuilder, each driving a generator connected to a 4,079 shp electric motor and three gas turbines manufactured by Ruston Diesels Ltd., Newton Le Willows, geared to twin shaft with directional propellers. Thwartship thrust propeller and two retractable directional thrust propellers forward.
Diesel-electric and gas-turbine powered processing and storage vessel for offshore installations.

18.9.1986: Keel laid by Harland & Wolff Ltd., Belfast (Yard No. 1726), for BP Petroleum Development Ltd. (BP Shipping Ltd., managers). 17.6.1988: Launched. 4.4.1990: Completed by builders restyled as Harland & Wolff Shipbuilding and Heavy Industries Ltd. 8.1996: Sold to Reading & Bates Development Company (Reading & Bates (UK) Ltd., managers), and transferred to Panamanian registry. 1997: Sold to RB FBSO L. P. (same managers). 1998: R&B Falcon Ltd., appointed as managers. 2001: Transocean Brasil Ltda., appointed as managers. Still in Lloyd's Register 2003/04.

BP Oil Development Ltd & British National Oil Corporation

DEV. 12. IOLAIR (1982–1990)

see ship No. Dev. 10 above.

BP Petroleum Development Ltd & North American Exploration Shipping Inc.

DEV. 13. SEDCO/BP 711 (1978 – 1986)

see ship No. Dev. 9 above.

DEV. 14. SEDCO/BP 471 (1982 – 1986)

7,889g. 5,768n. 295′ 2″ × 249′ 2″ × 130′ 0″ .
Three, 16-cyl. 4 S.C.S.A. EMD-645-E9B type oil engines manufactured by General Motors Corporation (9,210 bhp total), powering three electric generators (each 2,220Kw), driving four Pleuger type azimuthing propeller units (each 1,600 bhp).
Sedco 700 type semi-submersible drilling rig.

1982: Completed by Hyundai Heavy Industries Company Ltd., Ulsan (Yard No. 711), for BP Petroleum Development Ltd & North American Exploration Shipping Inc. 1986: Transferred to BP Petroleum Development Ltd. *Due to small size and type of this vessel no further details have been recorded by the authors.*

Anglo-Iranian Oil Company (China) Ltd.

Originally founded in 1947.
1952: Restyled as
BP (China) Ltd.

1968: Restyled as
BP Refineries Ltd.
1971: Restyled as
BP Oil Ltd.
1989: Restyled as
BP Oil UK Ltd.

OIL. 1. PRONTO/BP ALERT (1975–1983)

see ship No. SMBP. 90.

OIL. 2. INVERNESS/BP BATTLER (1975–1997)

see ship No. SMBP. 96.

OIL. 3. SWANSEA/BP JOUSTER (1975–1997)

see ship No. SMBP. 102.

OIL. 4. SHEPPEY/BP RAPID (1975–1986)

see ship No. SMBP. 104.

OIL. 6. DUBLIN/BP SPRINGER (1975–1997)

see ship No. SMBP. 99.

OIL. 7. TORKSEY/BP SPRITE (1975–1984)

see ship No. SMBP. 85.

OIL.5. KILLINGHOLME/BP SCORCHER (1975–1983)

see ship No. SMBP. 83.

OIL. 8. ST. LEONARDS/BP STURDY (1975–1981)

see ship No. SMBP. 84.

BP Alert. (World Ship Society Photograph Library)

BP Battler (J K Byass)

BP Jouster (J K Byass)

BP Scorcher. (World Ship Society Photograph Library)

BP Sprite. (J K Byass)

OIL. 9. GRANGEMOUTH/BP WARRIOR (1975–1997)

see ship No. SMBP. 98.

OIL. 10. BEN HAROLD SMITH/BP ZEST (1975–1980)

see ship No. SMBP. 75.

OIL. 11. BP ADVANCE (1979–1989)

O.N. 388244. ? g. ? n. ? d. ? × 8.72 × ? metres.
Post 1979: 561g. 398n. 1,032d. 68.10 × 8.72 × 2.485 metres.
10-cyl. 2 S.C.S.A. (190 × 350mm) vee type oil engine manufactured by 'Bolnes' Motorenfabriek N. V., Krimpen aan den Lek. 600 bhp.
Powered tank barge.

1963: Completed as SHELL 43 by N.V. Scheeps v.d. Werf, Deest, for unspecified owners. 1974: Sold to unspecified owners and renamed RICY III. 1979: Sold to BP Oil Ltd., London, shortened, and renamed BP ADVANCE. 1989: Owners restyled as BP Oil UK Ltd. 1989: Sold to unspecified owners, entry deleted from Lloyd's Register, for inland waterway use only.

OIL. 12. BP HARRIER (1980–1991)

O.N. 388356. 1,595g. 1,052n. 3,120d. 82.02(BB) × 15.04 × 5.755 metres.
16-cyl. 4 S.C.S.A.(250 × 300mm) Polar F216V-B vee type oil engine manufactured by British Polar Engines Ltd., Glasgow, geared to a controllable-pitch propeller. 2,940 bhp. Thwartship thrust propeller forward.
Coastal oil products tanker.

16.5.1979: Keel laid by Appledore Shipbuilders Ltd., Appledore (Yard No. 127), for BP Oil Ltd. 5.1.1980: Launched. 7.5.1980: Completed. 1989: Owners restyled as BP Oil UK Ltd. 1991: Sold to Coe Metcalf Shipping Ltd., Liverpool, and renamed DAVID M. 1995: Owners restyled as James Fisher & Sons (Liverpool) Ltd. (James Fisher (Shipping Services) Ltd., managers). 1999: Renamed WEAR FISHER. 2000: Owners restyled as James Fisher (Shipping Services) Ltd. Still in Lloyd's Register 2003/04.

BP Warrior. (J K Byass)

OIL. 13. BP HUNTER (1980–1991)

O.N. 388508. 1,595g. 1,052n. 3,120d. 82.00(BB) × 15.04 × 5.755 metres.
16-cyl. 4 S.C.S.A.(250 × 300mm) Polar F216V-B vee type oil engine manufactured by British Polar Engines Ltd., Glasgow, geared to a controllable-pitch propeller. 2,940 bhp. Thwartship thrust propeller forward.
Coastal oil products tanker.

17.7.1979: Keel laid by Appledore Shipbuilders Ltd., Appledore (Yard No. 128), for BP Oil Ltd. 14.3.1980: Launched. 23.7.1980: Completed. 1989: Owners restyled as BP Oil UK Ltd. 1991: Sold to Coe Metcalf Shipping Ltd., Liverpool, and renamed MICHAEL M. 1995: Owners restyled as James Fisher & Sons (Liverpool) Ltd. (James Fisher (Shipping Services) Ltd., managers). 1999: Renamed TEES FISHER. 2000: Owners restyled as James Fisher (Shipping Services) Ltd. Still in Lloyd's Register 2003/04.

OIL. 14 BORDER BATTLER (1997–)

see ship No. OIL. 2 above.

OIL. 15 BORDER WARRIOR (1997–2004)

see ship No. OIL. 9 above.

OIL. 16 BORDER SPRINGER (1997–2004)

see ship No. OIL. 6 above.

OIL. 17 BORDER JOUSTER (1997–)

see ship No. OIL. 3 above.

BP International Shipping Ltd.

BPIS. 1. TEEKAY VISION (1988 – 1993)

see ship No. M.104 above.

BPIS. 2. TEEKAY VIGOUR (1992 – 1993)

see ship No. M.103 above.

BP Harrier (J K Byass)

BP Hunter (World Ship Society Photograph Library)

Border Battler (World Ship Society Photograph Library)

Border Springer (World Ship Society Photograph Library)

Al Khaznah Inc.
Crew only supplied by BP Shipping Ltd

AL KHAZNAH (1994–)

110,895g. 33,269n. 71,543d.
293 00(BB) × 45.84 × 11.250 metres.
Two steam turbines manufactured by Kawasaki Heavy Industries Ltd, Kobe, geared to screw shaft. 35,116shp. 19.5 kts.
Liquified Gas Tanker.

27.2.1992: Keel laid by Mitsui Engineering & Shipbuilding Company Ltd., Chiba (Yard No. 1390), for Al Khaznah Inc., Liberia (crewed by BP Shipping Ltd.) (National Gas Shipping Company Ltd., Abu Dhabi, operating managers), under Liberia registry. 8.5.1993: Launched. 2.6.1994: Completed. Still in Lloyd's Register 2003/04.

Shahamah Inc.
Crew only supplied by BP Shipping Ltd

SHAHAMAH (1994–)

110,895g. 33,269n. 71,543d.
293 00(BB) × 45.84 × 10.950 metres.
Two steam turbines manufactured by Kawasaki Heavy Industries Ltd, Kobe, geared to screw shaft. 39,030shp. 19.5 kts.
Liquified Gas Tanker.

22.3.1993: Keel laid by Kawasaki Heavy Industries Industries Ltd., Sakaide (Yard No. 1438), as sub contract for Mitsui Eng. & S.B. Company Ltd. 30.7.1993: Launched. 3.10.1994: Completed by Mitsui Engineering & Shipbuilding Company Ltd., Chiba (Yard No. 1391), for Shahamah Inc., Liberia (crewed by BP Shipping Ltd.) (National Gas Shipping Company Ltd., Abu Dhabi, operating managers), under Liberia registry. Still in Lloyd's Register 2003/04.

Ish Inc.
Crew only supplied by BP Shipping Ltd

ISH (1995–)

110,895g. 33,269n. 71,593d.
293 00(BB) × 45.84 × 11.270 metres.
Two steam turbines manufactured by Kawasaki Heavy Industries Ltd, Kobe, geared to screw shaft. 35,116shp. 19.5 kts.
Liquified Gas Tanker.

26.3.1994: Keel laid by Mitsubishi Heavy Industries Ltd., Nagasaki (Yard No. 2067), as sub contract for Mitsui Eng. & S.B. Company Ltd. 23.9.1994: Launched. 11.10.1995: Completed by Mitsui Engineering & Shipbuilding Company Ltd., Chiba (Yard No. 1393), for Ish Inc., Liberia (crewed by BP Shipping Ltd.) (National Gas Shipping Company Ltd., Abu Dhabi, operating managers), under Liberia registry. Still in Lloyd's Register 2003/04.

Ghaghas Inc.
Crew only supplied by BP Shipping Ltd

GHASHA (1995–)

110,895g. 33,269n. 71,593d.
293 00(BB) × 45.84 × 11.270 metres.
Two steam turbines manufactured by Kawasaki Heavy Industries Ltd, Kobe, geared to screw shaft. 35,116shp. 19? kts.
Liquified Gas Tanker.

28.10.1992: Keel laid by Mitsui Engineering & Shipbuilding Company Ltd., Chiba (Yard No. 1392), for Ghaghas Inc., Liberia (crewed by BP Shipping Ltd.) (National Gas Shipping Company Ltd., Abu Dhabi, operating managers), under Liberia registry. 5.2.1994: Launched. 1.6.1995: Completed. Still in Lloyd's Register 2003/04.

BP Oil Shipping Company.
Founded 1999

ATLANTA BAY (1999–)

O.N. 646348. 272g. 185n. 419d. ? × ? × 5.941 metres.
Two 16-cyl. 4 S.C.S.A. (230 × 254mm) 16-645-E7B vee type oil engines manufactured by General Motors Corporation, Electro-motive Division, La Grange, geared to a controllable-pitch propeller. 5,800 bhp. 7.75 kts.
Pusher tug operating with the tank barge VIRGINIA BAY q.v. below.

Border Jouster. (World Ship Society Photograph Library)

Ish. (P Harrington)

12.6.1981: Keel laid as AMOCO ATLANTA by Mc Dermott Shipyard, Morgan City, Louisiana (Yard No. 262), for Coastwise Trading Company Inc., Wilmington. 17.12.1981: Launched. 12.4.1982: Completed. 1986: Renamed ATLANTA BAY. 1999: Sold to BP Oil Shipping Company (Keystone Barge Services Inc, managers). Still in Lloyd's Register 2004/05.

COLUMBIA BAY (1999–)

O.N. 648470. 272g. 185n. 419d. ? × ? × 5.941 metres.
Two 16-cyl. 4 S.C.S.A. (230 × 254mm) 16-645-E7B vee type oil engines manufactured by General Motors Corporation, Electro-motive Division, La Grange, geared to a controllable-pitch propeller. 5,800bhp. 7.75 kts.
Pusher tug operating with the tank barge SOUTH CAROLINA BAY q.v. below.

13,11.1981: Keel laid as AMOCO COLUMBIA by Mc Dermott Shipyard, Morgan City, Louisiana (Yard No. 266), for Coastwise Trading Company Inc., Wilmington. 9.3.1982: Launched. 17.8.1982: Completed. 1986: Renamed COLUMBIA BAY. 1999: Sold to BP Oil Shipping Company (Keystone Barge Services Inc, managers). Still in Lloyd's Register 2004/05.

TALLAHASSEE BAY (1999–)

O.N. 640635. 272g. 185n. 419d. ? × ? × 5.941 metres.
Two 16-cyl. 4 S.C.S.A. (230 × 254mm) 16-645-E7B vee type oil engines manufactured by General Motors Corporation, Electro-motive Division, La Grange, geared to a controllable-pitch propeller. 7.75 kts.
Pusher tug operating with the tank barge FLORIDA BAY q.v. below.

6.5.1981: Keel laid as AMOCO TALLAHASSEE by Mc Dermott Shipyard, Morgan City, Louisiana (Yard No. 260), for Coastwise Trading Company Inc., Wilmington. 1.7.1981: Launched. 22.9.1981: Completed. 1986: Renamed TALLAHASSEE BAY. 1999: Sold to BP Oil Shipping Company (Keystone Barge Services Inc, managers). Still in Lloyd's Register 2004/05.

8645026
FLORIDA BAY (1999–)

O.N. 640014. 11,295g.
Pusher tank barge powered by tug TALLAHASSEE BAY q.v. above

19.11.1980: Keel laid as AMOCO FLORIDA by the General Dynamics Corporation (Yard No. 73), for Coastwise Trading Company Inc., Wilmington. 12.8.1981: Launched. 3.9.1981: Completed. 1986: Renamed FLORIDA BAY. 1999: Sold to BP Oil Shipping Company (Keystone Barge Services Inc, managers). Still in Lloyd's Register 2004/05.

8645038
SOUTH CAROLINA BAY (1999–)

O.N. 645759. 11,321g.
Pusher tank barge powered by tug COLUMBIA BAY q.v. above

26.5.1981: Keel laid as AMOCO SOUTH CAROLINA by the General Dynamics Corporation (Yard No. 74), for Coastwise Trading Company Inc., Wilmington. 26.2.1982: Launched. 5.3.1982: Completed. 1986: Renamed SOUTH CAROLINA BAY. 1999: Sold to BP Oil Shipping Company (Keystone Barge Services Inc, managers). Still in Lloyd's Register 2004/05.

8645040
VIRGINIA BAY (1999–)

O.N. 642492. 11,295g.
Pusher tank barge powered by tug ATLANTA BAY q.v. above

3.2.1981: Keel laid as AMOCO VIRGINIA by the General Dynamics Corporation (Yard No. 75), for Coastwise Trading Company Inc., Wilmington. 30.10.1981: Launched. 20.10.1982: Completed. 1986: Renamed VIRGINIA BAY. 1999: Sold to BP Oil Shipping Company (Keystone Barge Services Inc, managers). Still in Lloyd's Register 2004/05.

Alaska Tanker Company (ATC)

Created by BP Oil Shipping Company, to operate the following 4 new vessels.

9244659
ATC.1. ALASKAN PIONEER (2004)

110,693g. n. 185,000d. 287.0 × 50.0 × 18.75 metres, approximately.
Four, ? -cyl. S.C.S.A. (? × ?), MAN B&W type oil engines, manufactured by ?, powering electric motors, driving twin screw shafts. Bhp. 15.3kts.

20.1.2003: Keel laid by National Steel Shipbuilders (Yard No. 484), for BP Oil Shipping Company (BP Amoco Corp managers – Chicago). 5.11.2003: Launched as ALASKAN PIONEER. 14.6.2004: Renamed ALASKAN FRONTIER. 11.2004: Completed.

ATC.2. ALASKAN FRONTIER (2004–)

see ship No. ATC.1 above.

Tallahassee Bay notched into the stern of *Florida Bay*. (Courtesy of Paul Andow)

9244661
ATC.3. ALASKAN EXPLORER (2004–)

? g. ? n. 185,000d. 287.0 × 50.0 × 18.75 metres, approximately.
Four, ?-cyl. S.C.S.A. (? × ?), MAN B&W type oil engines, manufactured by ?, powering electric motors, driving twin screw shafts. Bhp. 15.3kts.
Double hulled crude oil carrier.
6.11.2003: Keel laid by National Steel Shipbuilders, San Diego (Yard No. 485), for BP Oil Shipping Company (BP Amoco Corp managers – Chicago). 12.7.2004: Launched.

9244673
ATC.4. ALASKAN NAVIGATOR (2005–)

? g. ? n. 185,000d. 287.0 × 50.0 × 18.75 metres, approximately.
Four, ?-cyl. S.C.S.A. (? × ?), MAN B&W type oil engines, manufactured by ?, powering electric motors, driving twin screw shafts. Bhp. 15.3kts.
Double hulled crude oil carrier.
13.7.2004: Keel laid by National Steel Shipbuilders, San Diego (Yard No. 486), for BP Oil Shipping Company (BP Amoco Corp managers – Chicago). 2005: Due for completion.

9271432
ATC.5. ALASKAN LEGEND (2006–)

? g. ? n. 185,000d. 287.0 × 50.0 × 18.75 metres, approximately.
Four, ?-cyl. S.C.S.A. (? × ?), MAN B&W type oil engines, manufactured by ?, powering electric motors, driving twin screw shafts. Bhp. 15.3kts
Double hulled crude oil carrier.
2006: Due for completion by National Steel Shipbuilders, San Diego (Yard No. 487), for BP Oil Shipping Company (BP Amoco Corp managers – Chicago).

Burmah Oil Company Ltd.

Founded 1899:
175, West George Street, Glasgow.

Early vessels registered at Rangoon. Lloyds Confidential Index First entry September 1917 edition also states to "also see index of Colonial steamers".

C1920: Additional address at Britannic House, Gt. Winchester St. London.

Lloyds Confidential Index states in June 1928 edition
"Associated with Anglo-Persian Oil Company Ltd"

Finlay & Fleming Company Ltd., Rangoon, managers and agents.

BUR. 1. SYRIAM (1899–1924)

O.N. 95935. 1,426g. 891n. 235.0 × 32.6 × 15.9 feet.
T.3-cyl. (19″ 31″ & 51″ × 36″) engine manufactured by Hutson & Son Ltd., Glasgow. 165 nhp.
Tanker.
10.1899: Completed by Grangemouth Dockyard Company Ltd., Grangemouth (Yard No. 201), for the Burmah Oil Company Ltd. 1902: Transferred to The Burmah Oil Company (1902) Ltd. 1924: Sold to Soc. Nazional Oil I Minerali, Genoa, and renamed ROMAGNA. 1927: Sold to Azienda Generale Italiana Petroli. 1929: Sold to Soc. Maritima Fratelli Narizzano, Genoa. 1934: Sold to Navigazione Commercio Soc. Anon, Italiana, Genoa. 8.1943: Reported as a war loss.

BUR. 2. KOKINE (1899–1900)

O.N. 95936. 1,426g. 891n. 235.0 × 32.6 × 15.9 feet.
T.3-cyl. (19″ 31″ & 51″ × 36″) engine manufactured by Hutson & Son Ltd., Glasgow. 165 nhp.
Tanker.
12.1899: Completed by Grangemouth Dockyard Company Ltd., Grangemouth (Yard No. 202), for the Burmah Oil Company Ltd. 25.2.1900: Whilst on a voyage from Suez to Penang and Singapore was burnt out at Rangoon.

BUR. 3. KHODAUNG (1) (1900–1924)

O.N. 95937. 1,457g. 913n. 235.0 × 34.2 × 15.6 feet.
T.3-cyl. (19″ 31″ & 51″ × 36″) engine manufactured by the Wallsend Slipway Company Ltd., Wallsend. 174 nhp.
Tanker.
12.1900: Completed by Armstrong, Whitworth & Company Ltd., Newcastle (Yard No. 707), for the Burmah Oil Company Ltd. 1902: Transferred to The Burmah Oil Company (1902) Ltd. 1914 until 1918: Admiralty oiler No. 93. 1924: Sold to Anglo-Saxon Petroleum Company Ltd., London. 1931: Sold to Japanese shipbreakers.

BUR. 4. TWINGONE (1902–1913)

O.N. 95938. 1,771g. 1,120n. 250.0 × 36.5 × 16.8 feet.
T.3-cyl. (20″ 33″ & 54″ × 36″) engine manufactured by the Wallsend Slipway Company Ltd., Wallsend. 198 nhp.
Tanker.
8.1902: Completed by Armstrong, Whitworth & Company Ltd., Newcastle (Yard No.), for the Burmah Oil Company Ltd. 4.11.1913: Burnt at Tuticorn. and register closed. 1914: Wreck sold to Anglo-Saxon Petroleum Company Ltd., repaired, renamed UNIO, and re-registered. 1923: Sold to Nederland Indische Tankstoomboot Maatschappij. 1931: Sold to Safta Societe Italiana del Petrolio ed Affini, Italy. 1943: Renamed CASSALIA. 2.12.1943: Sunk by aircraft at Bari. 1952: Raised and scrapped.

BUR. 5. GOLD MEHUR (1903–1931)

O.N. 129313. 42g. 1n. 68.3 xx 13.1 × 7.2 feet.
24 hp. engine
Towing launch.
1903: Built at Rangoon for The Burmah Oil Company Ltd. 1931: Sold to Khan Dahadur Wali Mahomed. *Due to small size and type of this vessel no further details have been recorded by the authors.*

BUR. 6. ORIENTAL (1903–1939)

O.N. 129311. 55g. 3n. 80.2 × 13.9 × 8.4 feet.
Towing launch.
1903: Built at Rangoon for The Burmah Oil Company Ltd. 1939: Transferred to The Burmah Oil Company (Burmah Trading) Ltd. 7.3.1942: Scuttled at Rangoon. Declared as a 'war loss'.

BUR. 7. SINGU (1) (1903–1931)

O.N. 95939. 3,037g. 1,912n. 309.5 × 41.5 × 20.5 feet.
T.3-cyl. (22″ 37″ & 61″ × 42″) engine manufactured by the Wallsend Slipway Company Ltd., Wallsend. 265 nhp.
Tanker.
12.1903: Completed by Armstrong, Whitworth & Company Ltd., Newcastle (Yard No. 742), for the Burmah Oil Company Ltd. 1931: Sold to Dah Fung Shipping Company, China, and renamed DAH FUNG. 1933: Demolished.

BUR. 8. BEME (1) (1904–1932)

O.N. 95940. 3,037g. 1,912n. 309.5 × 41.5 × 20.5 feet.
T.3-cyl. (22″ 37″ & 61″ × 42″) engine manufactured by the Wallsend Slipway Company Ltd., Wallsend. 265 nhp.
Tanker.
5.1904: Completed by Armstrong, Whitworth & Company Ltd., Newcastle (Yard No. 749), for the Burmah Oil Company Ltd. 1932: Sold to Anglo-Persian Shipping & Trading Company (S. Gatsell & Company, managers). 1936: Sold to P. Diacon Zadeh, Panama. 1940: Reported as a 'war loss'.

BUR. 9. ZERO (1904–1938)

O.N. 129309. 112g. 50n. 96.3 × 20.6 × 6.1 feet.
Two, C.2-cyl. (11¼″ & 20?″ × 15″) engines manufactured by the shipbuilder. 18 rhp.
Creek steamer.
31.11898: Shipped by Denny Bros., Dumbarton (Yard No. 612), for the Irrawadi Flotilla Company Ltd. 12.1898: Machinery shipped. 1899: Completed. 1904: Purchased by the Burmah Oil Company Ltd. 1938: Sold to the Irrawadi Flotilla Company Ltd. 7.3.1942: Scuttled above Mandalay. Declared as a 'war loss'.

BUR. 10. PAGODA (1907–1939)

O.N. 129310. 55g. 3n. 80.2 × 13.9 × 8.4 feet.
33 hp. engine
Towing launch.
1907: Built at Rangoon for The Burmah Oil Company Ltd. 1939: Transferred to The Burmah Oil Company (Burmah Trading) Ltd. 7.3.1942: Scuttled at Rangoon. Declared as a 'war loss'.

BUR. 11. MINBU (1907–1939)

O.N. 129317. 139g. 93n. 96.1 × 21.2 × 6.3 feet.
Two, C.2-cyl. (11¼″ & 20½″ × 15″) engines manufactured by the shipbuilder. 27 nhp.
Creek steamer.
1907: Completed by Denny Bros., Dumbarton (Yard No.), for the Burmah Oil Company Ltd. 1939: Transferred to The Burmah Oil Company (Burmah Concessions) Ltd. 7.3.1942: Scuttled at Katha. Declared as a 'war loss'.

BUR. 12. NYOUNGHIA (1909–1939)

O.N. 124984. 382g. 132n. 160.0 × 31.1 × 8.1 feet.
Two, T.3-cyl. (9″, 14½″ & 24″ × 15″) engines manufactured by Baird Bros., N. Shields. 58 nhp.
Powered tank barge.
1909: Completed by Armstrong, Whitworth & Company Ltd., Newcastle (Yard No. 815), for the Burmah Oil Company Ltd. 1939: Transferred to The Burmah Oil Company (Burmah Trading) Ltd. 7.3.1942: Scuttled at Rangoon. Declared as a 'war loss'.

BUR. 13. MINHLA (1909–1929)

O.N. 124981. 1,300g. 630n. 200.0 × 34.0 × 17.5 feet.
T.3-cyl. (17″, 28″ & 46″ × 30″) engine manufactured by the Wallsend Slipway Company Ltd., Wallsend. 136 nhp.
Tanker.
3.1909: Completed by Armstrong, Whitworth & Company Ltd., Newcastle (Yard No. 813), for the Burmah Oil Company Ltd. 1916: Purchased by Burmah Oil Company Ltd. 1929: Sold to R Dunderdale. 1932: Sold to Levant Oil Transport Company Ltd., London. 1934: Sold to Lotco Shipping Company Ltd.,

London. 1937: Sold to Navigazione e Commercia Soc. Anon Italiano, Genoa, and renamed LINA. 3.1944: Reported as a 'war loss'.

BUR. 14. MAGIVE (1909–)

O.N. 124982. 382g. 132n. 160.0 × 31.1 × 8.1 feet.
Two, T.3-cyl. (9″, 14½″ & 24″ × 15″) engines manufactured by Baird Bros., N. Shields. 29 nhp.
Powered tank barge.
1909: Completed by Armstrong, Whitworth & Company Ltd., Newcastle (Yard No. 817), for the Burmah Oil Company Ltd. *Due to small size and type of this vessel no further details have been recorded by the authors.*

BUR. 15. PAUNGLIN (1910–)

O.N. 129316. 175g. 98n. 115.9 × 24.3 × 7.0 feet.
Two, T.3-cyl. (8½″, 14″ & 23″ × 12″) engines manufactured by McKie & Baxter, Glasgow. 54 rhp.
Tanker.
1910: Completed by the Irrawadi Flotilla Company Ltd., Rangoon for the Burmah Oil Company Ltd. *Due to small size and type of this vessel no further details have been recorded by the authors.*

BUR. 16. YOMAH (1913–1924)

O.N. 134983. 536g. 339n. 185.0 × 25.7 × 10.3 feet.
T.3-cyl. (12½″, 20″ & 33¾″ × 21″) engine manufactured by Maatschappij de Maas, Rotterdam. 64 nhp.
Tanker.
10.1897: Completed as BABALAN by Rjikee & Company, Rotterdam, for Kon. Nederlandsche tot Exploitatie v Petroleum Bronnen in Nederlands Indie, Rotterdam. 1913: Sold to the Burmah Oil Company Ltd., and renamed YOMAH. 1924: Sold to Societa Nationali Olli Mineralli, Italy, and renamed ABRUZZI. 1927: Sold to Azienda Generale Italiana Petroli, Italy. 4.1945: Following cessation of hostilities, vessel found sunk at Spezia. Subsequently raised. 1.1948: Demolition commenced by Bartoli & Cavalletti at Savona.

BUR. 17. WATER LILY (1915–1939)

O.N. 129318. 52g. 36n. 87.3 × 15.0 × 5.8 feet.
15 hp engine.
Towing launch.
1915: Built at Glasgow for the Burmah Oil Company Ltd. 1916: Re-erected at Rangoon. 1939: Transferred to The Burmah Oil Company (Pipe Lines) Ltd. 25–30.4.1942: Scuttled at R. Irrawaddy. Declared as a 'war loss'.

BUR. 18. THEGON (1915–1920)

see ship No. AP. 5 in the A. P. O. C. section.

BUR. 19. AUNGBAN (1) (1917–1937)

O.N. 133591. 5,125g. 3,006n. 350.4 × 50.1 × 34.5 feet.
T.3-cyl. (25″, 41″ & 67″ × 45″) engine manufactured by the shipbuilder. 446 nhp.
Ocean-going tanker.
2.1917: Completed by Palmers Ship Building & Iron Company Ltd., Newcastle (Yard No.845), for the Burmah Oil Company Ltd. 11.1937: Delivered to Japanese ship breakers. 1938: Resold to Okada Gumi K.K., Japan, and renamed TOEN MARU. 2.3.1943: Sunk by an American submarine at position 3.29S., 117.17E.

BUR. 20. AYUTHIA (1917–1918)

O.N. 118394. 1,135g. 694n. 231.4 × 34.1 × 13.6 feet.
T.3-cyl. (17″, 28½″ & 46″ × 33″) engine manufactured by Cooper & Greig, Dundee. 154 nhp.
Tanker.
2.1904: Completed by the Grangemouth & Greenock Dockyard Company, Grangemouth (Yard No.249), for the Borneo Company Ltd. 1910: Sold to the Bengal Coal Company Ltd., thence the Assam Steam Ship Company Ltd., thence to the consortium Bengal-Assam Steam Ship Company Ltd. (A.Yule & Company, managers), Rangoon. 5.11.1917: Purchased by the Burmah Oil Company Ltd. 7.2.1918: Burnt out whilst loading at Rangoon.

BUR. 21. CHAUK (1918–1939)

419g. 394n. × ? × ? feet.
Steam engine.
Sternwheeler.
1918: Built in Canada for The Burmah Oil Company Ltd. 1919: Re-erected at Rangoon. 1939: Transferred to The Burmah Oil Company (Burmah Trading) Ltd. 7.3.1942: Scuttled at Rangoon. Declared as a 'war loss'.

BUR. 22. ALLISON (1919–1939)

O.N. 151527. 266g. 181n. 135.0 × 24.5 × 6.5 feet.
Two, T.3-cyl. (9″, 14½″ & 24″ × 15″) engine manufactured by South Shipbuilding & Engineering Company, Glasgow. 92 hp.
Towing launch.
1919: Completed by Wm. Denny & Bros Ltd., Dumbarton (Yard No.1109), for the Burmah Oil Company Ltd. 1920: Re-erected at Rangoon. 1939: Transferred to The Burmah Oil Company (Burmah Trading) Ltd. 1950: Sold to the Government of Burma. *Due to small size and type of this vessel no further details have been recorded by the authors.*

BUR. 23. SADAING (1919–1939)

O.N. 151528. 266g. 181n. 135.0 × 24.5 × 6.5 feet.
Two, T.3-cyl. (9″, 14½″ & 24″ × 15″) engine manufactured by South Shipbuilding & Engineering Company, Glasgow. 92 hp.
Towing launch.
1919: Completed by Wm. Denny & Bros Ltd., Dumbarton (Yard No. 1108), for The Burmah Oil Company Ltd. 1920: Re-erected at Rangoon. 1939: Transferred to The Burmah Oil Company (Burmah Concessions) Ltd. 1942: Declared as a 'war loss'.

BUR. 23A. BETWAND (1920–1921)

see ship No. PS. 26 above

BUR. 24. YAW (1) (1920–1939)

O.N. 151526. 97g. 11n. 100.4 × 17.5 × 8.0 feet.
450 ihp engine.
Towing launch.
1920: Built at Newcastle for The Burmah Oil Company Ltd. 1921: Re-erected at Rangoon. 1939: Transferred to The Burmah Oil Company (Burmah Trading) Ltd. 7.3.1942: Scuttled at Rangoon. Declared as a 'war loss'.

BUR. 25. MON (1) (1921–1939)

O.N. 151525. 97g. 11n. 100.4 × 17.5 × 8.0 feet.
450 ihp engine.
Towing launch.
1921: Built at Newcastle for The Burmah Oil Company Ltd. 1921: Re-erected at Rangoon. 1939: Transferred to The Burmah Oil Company (Burmah Trading) Ltd. 7.3.1942: Scuttled at Rangoon. Declared as a 'war loss'.

BUR. 26. SALIN (1921–1939)

O.N. 151530. 102g. 46n. 100.0 × 17.5 × 9.6 feet.
T.3-cyl. (10½″, 16½″ & 28″ × 16″) engine manufactured by the shipbuilder. 63 hp.
Towing launch.
1921: Completed by Fleming & Ferguson Ltd., Paisley (Yard No.472), for the Burmah Oil Company Ltd. 1921: Re-erected at Rangoon. 1939: Transferred to The Burmah Oil Company (Burmah Concessions) Ltd. 1940: Transferred to The Burmah Oil Company (Burmah Trading) Ltd. 7.3.1942: Scuttled at Rangoon. Declared as a 'war loss'.

BUR. 27. BADARPUR (1922–1939)

O.N. 151783. 8,079g. 4,949n. 400.0 × 57.1 × 38.9 feet.
T.3-cyl. (30″, 50″ & 80″ × 54″) engine manufactured by the shipbuilder. 715 nhp.
Tanker.
6.1922: Completed by Hawthorn, Leslie & Company Ltd., Newcastle (Yard No.528), for the Burmah Oil Company Ltd. 1939: Transferred to The Burmah Oil Company (Tankers) Ltd. 1958: Demolished.

BUR. 28. MU (1922–1930)

O.N. ?. ?g. ?n. ? × ? × ? feet.
Steam engine.
Towing launch.
1922: Built in Holland for The Burmah Oil Company Ltd. 1923: Re-erected in India. 1930: Transferred to The Burmah-Shell Oil Storage & Distribution Company of India Ltd. *Due to small size and type of this vessel no further details have been recorded by the authors.*

BUR. 29. CHUKKER (1924–1930)

111g. 10n. ? × ? × ? feet.
Steam engine.
Towing launch.
1924: Built at Rangoon for The Burmah Oil Company Ltd. 1930: Transferred to The Burmah-Shell Oil Storage & Distribution Company of India Ltd. 10.5.1930: Whilst on a voyage from Mormugao to Cochin, capsized and sank off Cannanore.

BUR. 30. MASIMPUR (1927–1939)

O.N. 148357. 5,556g. 3,201n. 389.7 × 54.3 × 32.7 feet.
T.3-cyl. (27½″, 46½″ & 79″ × 54″) engine manufactured by G. Clark Ltd., Sunderland. 658 nhp.
Tanker.
12.1927: Completed by J. Laing & Sons Ltd., Sunderland (Yard No.698), for the Burmah Oil Company Ltd. 1939: Transferred to The Burmah Oil Company (Tankers) Ltd. 1952: Sold to Mageolia Naviera S.A., Panama, and renamed GEORGIA. 1958: Sold to Myrrenella Nav. S.A. 1964: Demolished.

BUR. 31. MEGOHM (1927–1939)

O.N. 153469. 124g. 56n. 86.0 × 24.0 × 6.1 feet.
C.2-cyl. (10″ & 21″ × 12″) engine manufactured by the shipbuilder. 30 rhp.
Suction dredger.
1927: Completed by Fleming & Ferguson Ltd., Paisley (Yard No.490), for the Burmah Oil Company Ltd. 1927: Re-erected at Rangoon. 1939: Transferred to The Burmah Oil Company (Burmah Concessions) Ltd. 18.4.1942: Exploded in the River Irrawaddy. Declared as a 'war loss'.

BUR. 32. MERGUI (1928–1938)

O.N. ?. ?g. ?n. ? × ? × ? feet.
? . ?-cyl. ( ) engine manufactured by ?.
1928: Built at Rangoon for The Burmah Oil Company Ltd. 1.5.1938: Sunk following a

collision off Akyab. No other details were located.

BUR. 33. SINGU (2) (1931–1939)

O.N. 161563. 4,927g. 2,740n. 381.5 × 55.3 × 29.4 feet.
T.3-cyl. (26½″, 45¼″ & 76″ × 51″) engine manufactured by the Wallsend Slipway Company Ltd. Wallsend. 677 nhp.
Tanker.
12.1931: Completed by Swan, Hunter & Wigham, Richardson Ltd., Newcastle (Yard No.1469), for the Burmah Oil Company Ltd. 1939: Transferred to The Burmah Oil Company (Tankers) Ltd. 1953: Demolished.

BUR. 34. BALBUS (1934–)

550g. ? n. 164.0 × 41.0 × 10.0 feet.
Non-propelled dredger for river service.
1934: Completed by Wm. Simons & Company Ltd., Renfrew, for the Burmah Oil Company Ltd. 8.1934: Re-erected at Rangoon. *Due to small size and type of this vessel no further details have been recorded by the authors.*

BUR. 35. KHODAUNG (2) (1934–1939)

O.N. 157579. 254g. 154n. 146.7 × 26.0 × 7.7 feet.
Two, 4-cyl. 4 S.C.S.A. (10″ × 14½″) oil engines manufactured by Petters Ltd., Yeovil. 140 nhp.
1934: Completed by the Irrawadi Flotilla Company Ltd., Rangoon (Yard No.), for the Burmah Oil Company Ltd. 1939: Transferred to The Burmah Oil Company (Burmah Trading) Ltd. 4–6.1942: Burnt at Katha on the R. Irrawaddy. Declared as a 'war loss'.

BUR. 36. YENANGAUNG (1937–1939)

O.N. 161608. 5,447g. 3,031n. 387.6 × 54.2 31.1 feet.
4-cyl. 2 S.C.S.A. (23⅝″ × 91³⁄₁₆″) oil engine manufactured by Wm. Doxford & Sons Ltd., Sunderland. 687 nhp.
Tanker.
8.1937: Completed by Swan, Hunter & Wigham, Richardson Ltd., Newcastle (Yard No.1531), for the Burmah Oil Company Ltd. 1939: Transferred to The Burmah Oil Company (Tankers) Ltd. 1960: Demolished.

BUR. 37. MINHLA II (1938–1939)

O.N. 171467. 13g. 8n. 47.4 × 10.0 × 4.4 feet.
38bhp oil engine.
Launch.
1938: Completed by Richard Dunston Ltd., Thorne, for the Burmah Oil Company Ltd. 1939: Transferred to The Burmah Oil Company (Burmah Trading) Ltd. 25–30.4.1942: Scuttled in the R. Irrawaddy. Declared as a 'war loss'.

1939:
With the outbreak of WW2 the structure of the Company was altered and broken down into several operational sectors as below:-

Burmah Oil Company (Burmah Trading) Ltd.

a. ORIENTAL (1939–1942)

see ship No. BUR. 6 above.

b. PAGODA (1939–1942)

see ship No. BUR. 10 above.

c. NYOUNGHIA (1939–1942)

see ship No. BUR. 12 above.

d. KHODAUNG (2) (1939–1942)

see ship No. BUR. 35 above.

e. CHAUK (1939–1942)

see ship No. BUR. 21 above.

f. ALLISON (1939–1950)

see ship No. BUR. 22 above.

g. YAW (1) (1939–1942)

see ship No. BUR. 24 above.

h. MON (1) (1939–1942)

see ship No. BUR. 25 above.

i. MINHLA II (1939–1942)

see ship No. BUR. 37 above.

j. SALIN (1940–1942)

see ship No. BUR. 26 above.

BUR. 38. B.No.1 (1946–)

40g. 91.1 × 19.7 × 8.0 feet.
Dumb tank barge.
1946: Built in kit form by Clelands (Successors) Ltd., Wallsend (Yard No. 100), for Burmah Oil Company (Burmah Trading) Ltd. Subsequently re-erected in Burma. *Due to small size and type of this vessel no further details have been recorded by the authors.*

BUR. 39. B.No.2 (1946–)

40g. 91.1 × 19.7 × 8.0 feet.
Dumb tank barge.
1946: Built in kit form by Clelands (Successors) Ltd., Wallsend (Yard No. 101), for Burmah Oil Company (Burmah Trading) Ltd. Subsequently re-erected in Burma. *Due to small size and type of this vessel no further details have been recorded by the authors.*

BUR. 40. B.No.3 (1946–)

40g. 91.1 × 19.7 × 8.0 feet.
Dumb tank barge.
1946: Built in kit form by Clelands (Successors) Ltd., Wallsend (Yard No. 102), for Burmah Oil Company (Burmah Trading) Ltd. Subsequently re-erected in Burma. *Due to small size and type of this vessel no further details have been recorded by the authors.*

BUR. 41. B.No.4 (1946–)

40g. 91.1 × 19.7 × 8.0 feet.
Dumb tank barge.
1946: Built in kit form by Clelands (Successors) Ltd., Wallsend (Yard No. 103), for Burmah Oil Company (Burmah Trading) Ltd. Subsequently re-erected in Burma. *Due to small size and type of this vessel no further details have been recorded by the authors.*

BUR. 42. B.No.5 (1946–)

40g. 91.1 × 19.7 × 8.0 feet.
Dumb tank barge.
1946: Built in kit form by Clelands (Successors) Ltd., Wallsend (Yard No. 104), for Burmah Oil Company (Burmah Trading) Ltd. Subsequently re-erected in Burma. *Due to small size and type of this vessel no further details have been recorded by the authors.*

BUR. 43. B.No.6 (1946–)

40g. 91.1 × 19.7 × 8.0 feet.
Dumb tank barge.
1946: Built in kit form by Clelands (Successors) Ltd., Wallsend (Yard No. 105), for Burmah Oil Company (Burmah Trading) Ltd. Subsequently re-erected in Burma. *Due to small size and type of this vessel no further details have been recorded by the authors.*

BUR. 44. B. O. C. No. 38 (1946–)

40g. 58.5 × 14.2 × 6.2 feet.
6-cyl. 4 S.C.S.A. (5″ × 6¼″) oil engine manufactured by Crossley Bros. Ltd., Manchester, double reduction geared to screw shaft.
Powered tank barge.
1946: Built by Clelands (Successors) Ltd., Wallsend (Yard No. 140), for The Burmah Oil Company (Burma Trading) Ltd. *Due to small size and type of this vessel no further details have been recorded by the authors.*

BUR. 45. B. O. C. No. 39 (1946–)

40g. 58.5 × 14.2 × 6.2 feet.
6-cyl. 4 S.C.S.A. (5″ × 6¼″) oil engine manufactured by Crossley Bros. Ltd., Manchester, double reduction geared to screw shaft.
Powered tank barge.
1946: Built by Clelands (Successors) Ltd., Wallsend (Yard No. 141) for The Burmah Oil Company (Burma Trading) Ltd. *Due to small size and type of this vessel no further details have been recorded by the authors.*

BUR. 46. B. O. C. No. 40 (1946–)

40g. 58.5 × 14.2 × 6.2 feet.
6-cyl. 4 S.C.S.A. (5″ × 6¼″) oil engine manufactured by Crossley Bros. Ltd., Manchester, double reduction geared to screw shaft.
Powered tank barge.
1946: Built by Clelands (Successors) Ltd., Wallsend (Yard No. 142), for The Burmah Oil Company (Burma Trading) Ltd. *Due to small size and type of this vessel no further details have been recorded by the authors.*

BUR. 47. B. O. C. No. 41 (1946–)

40g. 58.5 × 14.2 × 6.2 feet.
6-cyl. 4 S.C.S.A. (5″ × 6¼″) oil engine manufactured by Crossley Bros. Ltd., Manchester, double reduction geared to screw shaft.
Powered tank barge.
1946: Built by Clelands (Successors) Ltd., Wallsend (Yard No. 143), for The Burmah Oil Company (Burma Trading) Ltd. *Due to small size and type of this vessel no further details have been recorded by the authors.*

BUR. 48. B. O. C. No. 42 (1946–)

40g. 58.5 × 14.2 × 6.2 feet.
6-cyl. 4 S.C.S.A. (5″ × 6¼″) oil engine manufactured by Crossley Bros. Ltd., Manchester, double reduction geared to screw shaft.
Powered tank barge.
1946: Built by Clelands (Successors) Ltd., Wallsend (Yard No. 144), for The Burmah Oil Company (Burma Trading) Ltd. *Due to small size and type of this vessel no further details have been recorded by the authors.*

BUR. 49. B. O. C. No. 71 (1946–)

163d. 92.4 × 20.1 × 6.8 feet.
Dumb tank barge.
1946: Launched by Clelands (Successors) Ltd., Wallsend (Yard No. 99), for The Burmah Oil Company (Burma Trading) Ltd. 10.1947: Re-erected and registered at Rangoon. *Due to*

small size and type of this vessel no further details have been recorded by the authors.

BUR. 50. B. O. C. No. 72 (1946–)

163d. 92.4 × 20.1 × 6.8 feet.
Dumb tank barge.

1946: Launched by Clelands (Successors) Ltd., Wallsend (Yard No. 100), for The Burmah Oil Company (Burma Trading) Ltd. 9.1947: Re-erected and registered at Rangoon. *Due to small size and type of this vessel no further details have been recorded by the authors.*

BUR. 51. B. O. C. No. 73 (1946–)

163d. 92.4 × 20.1 × 6.8 feet.
Dumb tank barge.

1946: Launched by Clelands (Successors) Ltd., Wallsend (Yard No. 101), for The Burmah Oil Company (Burma Trading) Ltd. 9.1947: Re-erected and registered at Rangoon. *Due to small size and type of this vessel no further details have been recorded by the authors.*

BUR. 52. B. O. C. No. 74 (1946–)

163d. 92.4 × 20.1 × 6.8 feet.
Dumb tank barge.

1946: Launched by Clelands (Successors) Ltd., Wallsend (Yard No. 102), for The Burmah Oil Company (Burma Trading) Ltd. 10.1947: Re-erected and registered at Rangoon. *Due to small size and type of this vessel no further details have been recorded by the authors.*

BUR. 53. B. O. C. No. 75 (1946–)

163d. 92.4 × 20.1 × 6.8 feet.
Dumb tank barge.

1946: Launched by Clelands (Successors) Ltd., Wallsend (Yard No. 103), for The Burmah Oil Company (Burma Trading) Ltd. 10.1948: Re-erected and registered at Rangoon. *Due to small size and type of this vessel no further details have been recorded by the authors.*

BUR. 54. B. O. C. No. 76 (1946–)

163d. 92.4 × 20.1 × 6.8 feet.
Dumb tank barge.

1946: Launched by Clelands (Successors) Ltd., Wallsend (Yard No. 104), for The Burmah Oil Company (Burma Trading) Ltd. 8.1948: Re-erected and registered at Rangoon. *Due to small size and type of this vessel no further details have been recorded by the authors.*

BUR. 55. BEME (2) (1948–1963)

O.N. 1692 . 975g. 341n. 193.5 × 34.2 × 14.7 feet.
T.3-cyl. (13½″, 22¾″ & 38″ × 27″) engine manufactured by the North Eastern Marine Engineering Company (1938) Ltd., Wallsend.
Coastal products tanker.

22.10.1945: Launched as EMPIRE TESDALE by Swan, Hunter & Wigham, Richardson Ltd., Newcastle (Yard No.1844), for the Ministry of War Transport (Anglo-Saxon Petroleum Company Ltd., managers). 5.1946: Completed for the Ministry of Transport (same managers). 1946: Purchased by Burmah Oil Company (Tankers) Ltd., and renamed BEME. 1948: Transferred to The Burmah Oil Company (Burmah Trading) Ltd. 1963: Sold to The People's Oil Industry, Burma. 1964: Transferred to The Government of Burma (Rangoon Port Corporation, managers), and renamed YENAN. 1980: Sold for local demolition.

Burmah Oil Company (Burma Concessions) Ltd.

a. MINBU (1939–1942)

see ship No. BUR. 11 above.

b. SADAING (1939–1942)

see ship No. BUR. 23 above.

c. SALIN (1939–1940)

see ship No. BUR. 26 above.

d. MEGOHM (1939–1942)

see ship No. BUR. 31 above.

BUR. 56. B.C. 1 (1946–)

Unspecified details.

1946: Built in kit form by Clelands (Successors) Ltd., Wallsend (Yard No. 84), for The Burmah Oil Company (Burma Concessions) Ltd. Re-erected and registered at Rangoon. *Due to small size and type of this vessel no further details have been recorded by the authors.*

BUR. 57 . B.C. 2 (1946–)

Unspecified details.

1946: Built in kit form by Clelands (Successors) Ltd., Wallsend (Yard No. 85), for The Burmah Oil Company (Burma Concessions) Ltd. Re-erected and registered at Rangoon. *Due to small size and type of this vessel no further details have been recorded by the authors.*

BUR. 58. B.C. 3 (1946–)

Unspecified details.

1946: Built in kit form by Clelands (Successors) Ltd., Wallsend (Yard No. 86), for The Burmah Oil Company (Burma Concessions) Ltd. Re-erected and registered at Rangoon. *Due to small size and type of this vessel no further details have been recorded by the authors.*

BUR. 59. MON (2) (1947–)

Unspecified details.

18.9.1946: Launched by Clelands (Successors) Ltd., Wallsend (Yard No. 106), for The Burmah Oil Company (Burma Concessions) Ltd. Re-erected and registered at Rangoon. *Due to small size and type of this vessel no further details have been recorded by the authors.*

BUR. 60. YAW (2) (1947–)

Unspecified details.

30.9.1946: Launched by Clelands (Successors) Ltd., Wallsend (Yard No. 107), for The Burmah Oil Company (Burma Concessions) Ltd. Re-erected and registered at Rangoon. *Due to small size and type of this vessel no further details have been recorded by the authors.*

BUR. 61. CHINDIT (1949–1952)

150g. ? n. ? × ? × ? feet.
Unspecified details.

20.4.1948: Launched by Clelands (Successors) Ltd., Wallsend (Yard No. 111), for The Burmah Oil Company (Burma Concessions) Ltd. 1952: Sold to the Government of Thailand, for naval use. *Due to small size and type of this vessel no further details have been recorded by the authors.*

Burmah Oil Company (Pipe Lines) Ltd.

a. WATER LILY (1939–1942)

see ship No. BUR. 16 above.

BUR. 62. PLUTO (1948–)

72g. ? n. ? × ? × ? feet.
Unspecified details.

1948: Built by an unspecified UK yard for The Burmah Oil Company (Pipe Lines) Ltd. 1953: Still lying unused in the UK waiting a buyer. *Due to small size and type of this vessel no further details have been recorded by the authors.*

Burmah Oil Company (Tankers) Ltd.

a. BADARPUR (1939–1958)

see ship No. BUR. 27 above.

b. SINGU (2) (1939–1953)

see ship No. BUR. 33 above.

c. MASIMPUR (1939–1952)

see ship No. BUR. 30 above.

d. YENANGAUNG (1939–1960)

see ship No. BUR. 36 above.

BUR. 63. BEME (2) (1946–1948)

see ship No. BUR. 55 above.

BUR. 64. BURMAH EMERALD (1952–1963)

O.N. 184721. 6,250g. 3,356n. 8,400d.
434′ 4″ × 56′ 2″ × 25′ 1¾″ .
5-cyl. 2 S.C.S.A. (720 × 1250mm) Sulzer type oil engine manufactured by Sulzer Bros. Ltd., Winterthur.
Tanker.

11.1952: Completed by Cammell, Laird & Company Ltd., Birkenhead (Yard No. 1224), for The Burmah Oil Company (Tankers) Ltd. 1963: Sold to Republik Indonesia (Perusahaan Negara Pertambangan Minjak Nasional, managers), Indonesia, and renamed PERMINA 101. 1980: Owners restyled as P. N. Perusahaan Pertambangan Minyak & Gas Bumi Negara (PERTAMINA). 1982: Demolished.

BUR. 65. BURMAH SAPPHIRE (1953–1961)

O.N. 185941. 6,231g. 3,345n. 8,400d.
434′ 2″ × 56′ 2″ × 25′ 2¼″ .
4-cyl. 2 S.C.S.A. (600 × 2320mm) oil engine manufactured by the Wallsend Slipway Company Ltd, Wallsend.
Tanker.

8.1953: Completed by Swan, Hunter & Wigham, Richardson Ltd., Wallsend (Yard No. 1821), for The Burmah Oil Company (Tankers) Ltd. 10.9.1961: Whilst on a voyage from Calcutta to Abadan, collided with BALARI in the River Hooghly, and sustained major damage. 7.11.1961: Arrived at Hong Kong. 12.1961: Four Seas Enterprises commenced demolition.

Burmah Sapphire. (World Ship Society Photograph Library)

BUR. 66. BURMAH STAR (1953–1962)

O.N. 185940. 6,250g. 3,356n. 8,400d. 434′ 4″ × 56′ 2″ × 25′ $1^3/_4$″.
5-cyl. 2 S.C.S.A. (720 × 1250mm) Sulzer type oil engine manufactured by Sulzer Bros. Ltd., Winterthur. Tanker.

8.1953: Completed by Cammell, Laird & Company Ltd., Birkenhead (Yard No. 1240), for The Burmah Oil Company (Tankers) Ltd. 1962: Sold to Cia. De Transporte Edna S.A., Panama and renamed RUBY STAR. 1963: Sold to Republik Indonesia (Perusahaan Negara Pertambangan Minjak Nasional, managers), Indonesia, and renamed PERMINA 102. 1980: Owners restyled as P. N. Perusahaan Pertambangan Minyak & Gas Bumi Negara (PERTAMINA). 1984: Reported as having been demolished.

Burmah Oil Trading Ltd.

BurOT.1. EL LOBO (1966–1976)

O.N. 300890. 12,078g. 6,784n. 16,600d. 547′ 4″ × 72′ 9″ × 29′ $6^1/_4$″ oa.
6-cyl. 2 S.C.S.A. (670 × 2320mm) Doxford type oil engine manufactured by the Wallsend Slipway & Engineering Company Ltd., Wallsend. 6,250bhp. 14 kts. Tanker.

5.1959: Completed by Swan, Hunter & Wigham Richardson Ltd., Wallsend (Yard No. ?), for Lobitos Oilfields Ltd., London (C. T. Bowring & Company Ltd., managers). 1966: Sold to Burmah Oil Trading Ltd. (same managers). 1967: Managers restyled as Bowring Steamship Company Ltd. 23.7.1976: Lloyd's Register classification deleted – 'Vessel demolished'.

Burmah Oil Tankers Ltd.

Formed 1970 – New York & London

Apart from owning their own vessels, this company operated vessels under lease and also owned under single ship companies controlled by their American arm. These have all been placed under this heading.

BOTL. 1. BURMAH JADE (1971–1975)

10,203g. 5,913n. 16,570d. 160.15 × 19.56 × 9.056 metres.
7-cyl. 2 S.C.S.A. (740 × 1600mm) oil engine manufactured by Burmeister & Wains Maskin-og-Skibsbyggeri, Copenhagen. 6,500bhp. 14 kts.

16.6.1950: Keel laid as BITTERNCOURT SAMPAIO by Uddevallavarvet Ab., Uddavalla (Yard No. 120), for Frota Nacional de Petroles, Rio de Janiero. 28.4.1951: Launched. 13.10.1951: Completed. 1953: Renamed FNP BITTERNCOURT SAMPAIO. 1954: Reverted to BITTERNCOURT SAMPAIO. 1970: Sold to Lyra Shipping Corp., Liberia. 1971: Sold to Burmah Oil Tankers Ltd., London, and renamed BURMAH JADE. 1975: Sold to Harp Shipping Corp., Greece. 11.1.1975: Reported as arriving Karachi for demolition. 31.5.1975: Placed into lay-up at Trincomalee. 11.11.1975: Arrived at Kaohsiung for demolition by Li Chong Steel & Iron Company Ltd.

BOTL. 2. BURMAH LAPIS (1971–1979)

21,576g. 14,590n. 40,984d. 673′ 0″ × 92′ 4″ × 34′ $7^3/_4$″.
Two steam turbines manufactured in 1944 by General Electric Corp Lyn, Massachussets, double reduction geared to screw shaft. 17,600shp. 16 kts.

1953: Completed as PETROEMPEROR by National Bulk Carriers Inc. (Kure Shipyard Division), Kure (Yard No. 32), for Universe Tankships Inc. (J. Ludwig's National Carriers Group), Liberia. 1967: Sold to Gorgona

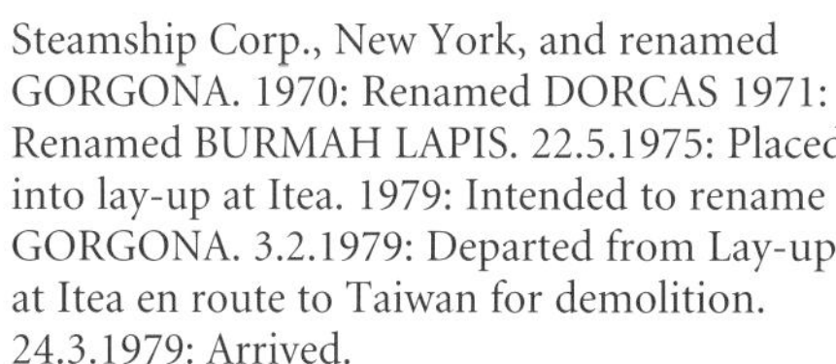

Steamship Corp., New York, and renamed GORGONA. 1970: Renamed DORCAS 1971: Renamed BURMAH LAPIS. 22.5.1975: Placed into lay-up at Itea. 1979: Intended to rename GORGONA. 3.2.1979: Departed from Lay-up at Itea en route to Taiwan for demolition. 24.3.1979: Arrived.

BOTL. 3. BURMAH TOPAZ (1972–1976)

17,116g. 12,586n. 28,209d. 597′ 6″ × 84′ 6″ × 32′ $8^1/_4$″.
Steam turbine (7,240shp) manufactured by General Electric Corp., Lynn, Massachussets, driving driving an electric generator powering a motor connected to the screw shaft. 6,000shp.

1952: Forward and cargo sections completed as part of WANETA by Bethlehem Steel Company, Quincy, for Brilliant Transportation Company S. A., Panama. 1956: Sold to Mobil Tankers Company S.A., Panama. 1963: Sold to Iberian Tankers Co. S. A., Panama. 1964: Renamed SANTA SUZANA. 1967: Joined with a new after machinery section.
1943: Aft machinery section completed as part of FORT HENRY by Kaiser Company Inc., Swan Island, for the United States War Shipping Administration. 1948: Sold to Harcon Steamship Company Inc., Wilmington USA, and renamed PONCA CITY. 1967: Joined with a new forward cargo section, and the resultant "new" vessel was renamed SEAFARER by Ocean Messengers Inc. 1972: Sold to Topaz Shipping Company, New York, and renamed BURMAH TOPAZ. 1975: Transferred to Panamanian registry. 5.1975: Placed in lay-up at Itea. 5.7.1976: Arrived at Split for demolition by Brodospas.

BOTL. 4. BURMAH OPAL (1972–1978)

O.N. 357498. 35,351g. 22,837n. 62,553d. 775′ 0″ × 105′ 10″ × 41′ $5^3/_4$″.
Post 1977: 34,921g. 22,837n. 62,553d.
10-cyl. 2 S.C.S.A. (840 × 1600mm) MAN type oil engine manufactured by the shipbuilder. 19,000bhp. 16.5 kts.

1964: Completed as JONWI by Kockums Mekaniska Verksteder Ab, Malmo (Yard No. 489), for KS Harwi (Rederi Aktie. R. Wigands managers), Norway 1972: Sold to William Brandts (Seventh Leasing) Ltd., Glasgow, and renamed BURMAH OPAL. 1977: Sold to Burmah Oil Tankers Ltd. (Denholm Ship Management Ltd., managers), London. 1978: Sold to Gamma Maritime Inc., Greece, and renamed COSMAS. 1982: A. & C. Anastassiou Shipmanagement Ltd., appointed as managers. 1983: Sold to Sapphire Bay Shipping Co. Ltd., under Panamanian flag. 1983: Demolished.

BOTL. 5. BURMAH AGATE (1973–1979)

32,285g. 20,514n. 61,674d. 771′ 8″ × 105′ 10″ × 41′ $6^3/_4$″.
9-cyl. 2 S.C.S.A. (850 × 1700mm) oil engine manufactured by Ab Gotaverken, Gothenburg. 18,900bhp. 16.5 kts.

12.1963: Completed as DANALAND by Nederlandsche Droogdok & Scheepswerf, Amsterdam (Yard No. 514), for Rederi Ab Motortank, Sweden. 1973: Sold to Central Transport Company Inc. New York, and renamed BURMAH AGATE, under Liberian registry. 1976: Sold to Allseas Maritime S. A., Liberia. 1977: Sold to Burmah Oil Tankers Ltd. (Broom Marine Ltd., managers), London. 1978: Sold to Allseas Maritime S. A., Liberia. 1.11.1979: Whilst anchored at the entrance to Galveston Bay, was rammed by the bulk

Burmah Star. (World Ship Society Photograph Library)

carrier MIMOSA (19,654g./72), broke in two and one part sank. 5.11.1979: The remaining section drifted ashore 29.17N., 94.37W., and continued to burn and explode throughout the month. 14.2.1980: Refloated and towed to Brownsville, Texas for demolition. 7.1980: Brownsville Steel & Salvage commenced work.

BOTL. 6. BURMAH BERYL (1973–1978)

As built 31,044g. 17,564n. 48,035d. 740′ 0″ × 102′ 4″ × 37′ 8¼″.
Post 1963: 48,585d. × 38′ 0¼″.
Post 1967: 37,753g. 27,638n. 73,216d. 854′ 0″ × 102′ 4″ × 44. 6½″.
Two, steam turbines manufactured by the shipbuilder, double reduction gearted to screw shaft. 19,000 shp. 15.5 kts.

1959: Completed as HADRIAN by A. G. Weser, Bremerhaven (Yard No. 1364), for Hilmar Reksen, Bergen. 1967: Lengthened (mid-body section) by Mitsubishi Heavy Industries Ltd., Nagasaki. 1972: Sold to Rederi Aktie. Diocletian (H. Reksten, manager), Norway, and renamed ARRIAN. 1973: Sold to Rosignol Development Corp., and renamed BURMAH BERYL, under Liberian registry. 12.2.1975: Placed into lay-up at Pylos. 1977: Broom Marine Ltd., appointed as managers. 2.5.1978: Departed Pylos en route for demolition at Barcelona. 18.5.1978: Arrived. 2.7.1978: Desgauces Condal S. A., commenced work.

BOTL. 7. BURMAH GARNET (1973–1978)

36,136g. 23,374n. 60,617d. 775′ 0″ × 106′ 0″ × 41′ 2½″.
9-cyl. 2 S.C.S.A. (850 × 1700mm) Gotaverken type oil engine manufactured by the shipbuilder. 19,000bhp. 16 kts.

1964: Completed as the tanker VARDEFJELL by Kieler Howaldtswerke A. G., Kiel (Yard No.1170), for AS Flakefjell & AS Dovrefjell (Olsen & Ugelstad, managers), Norway. 1968: Converted into an oil/ore carrier. 1973: Sold to Hoccus Poccus Ltd., London, and renamed BURMAH GARNET. 1974: Sold to Wm. Brandts (Eighth Leasing) Ltd., under Glasgow registry. 1977: Sold to Burmah Oil Tankers Ltd. (Denholm Ship Management Ltd., managers), London. 2.5.1978: Demolition commenced.

BOTL. 8. BURMAH PEARL (1973–1985)

O.N. 356280. 75,049g. 51,959n. 140,512d. 887′ 5″ (BB) × 144′ 6″ × 55′ 9″.
10-cyl. 2 S.C.S.A. (840 × 1800mm) B&W type oil engine manufactured by the shipbuilder. 25,000 bhp. 16 kts.

3.8.1973: Launched by Mutsui Shipbuilding & Engineering Company Ltd., Tamano (Yard No. 967), for Burmah Oil Company Ltd. 11.1973: Completed. 1974: Sold to Airlease International Nominees (Fenchurch) Ltd. (Denholm Ship Management Ltd., managers), under Bermuda registry. 1977: Broom Marine Ltd., appointed as managers. 1979: Sold to Sold to Airlease International Nominees (Fenchurch) Ltd. (same managers). 1985: Sold to Chisbury Maritime Corp., Liberia, and renamed NOTOS. 1991: Sold to Kythira Shipping Company Ltd., and renamed KYTHIRA. 1993: Owner restyled E.N.E.Kythira Ltd. (Aeolos Shipmanagement S.A., managers). c2000: Demolished.

BOTL. 9. BURMAH AMBER (1973–1974)

28,687g. 18,646n. 54,950d. 740′ 1″ × 102′ 2″ × 40′ 7¾″.
Two steam turbines manufactured by the shipbuilder, double reduction geared to screw shaft. 17,300 shp. 15.5 kts.

1962: Completed as JAGARDA by Kieler Howaldtswerke A.G., Kiel (Yard No. 1125), for AS Kosmos (Anders Jahre, manager), Norway. 1972: Sold to Immingham Shipping Company Ltd., Piraeus, and renamed IMMINGHAM. 1973: Sold to F. R. H. M., Liberia, and renamed ASTERIX. 1973: Sold to Aire Shipping Company Ltd., London, and renamed BURMAH AMBER. 1974: Renamed PERMINA SAMUDRA XI. 1979: Demolished.

BOTL. 10. BURMAH PERIDOT (1974–1985)

O.N. 356287. 75,049g. 51,959n. 140,512d. 887′ 5″ (BB) × 144′ 6″ × 55′ 9″.
10-cyl. 2 S.C.S.A. (840 × 1800mm) B&W type oil engine manufactured by the shipbuilder. 25,000 bhp. 16 kts.

2.11.1973: Launched by Mitsui Shipbuilding & Engineering Company Ltd., Tamano (Yard No. 968), for Burmah Oil Company Ltd. 2.1974: Completed. 1974: Sold to Airlease International Nominees (Fenchurch) Ltd. (Denholm Ship Management Ltd., managers), under Bermuda registry. 1977: Broom Marine Ltd., appointed as managers. 7.4.1975: Arrived at Dumai for employment as a storage vessel. 11.1.1976: Arrived at Sungei for employment as a storage vessel. Sold to Airlease International Nominees (Fenchurch) Ltd. (same managers). 1981: Burmah Oil Tankers Ltd., appointed as managers. 1985: Sold to Vourkoti Maritime Corp., Liberia, and renamed SKYRON. 1991: Sold to Kerkyra Shipping Company Ltd., and renamed KERKYRA. 1993: Owner restyled E. N. E. Kythira Ltd. (Aeolos Shipmanagement S.A., managers). *c*2000: Demolished.

BOTL. 11. BURMAH CORAL (1974–1977)

40,468g. 26,036n. 70,383d. 848′ 0″ × 108′ 4″ × 42′ 10½″.
Two steam turbines manufactured by the shipbuilder at Hamburg, geared to screw shaft. 21,480 shp. 16.25 kts.

1960: Completed as NAESS SPIRIT by Kieler Howaldtswerke A. G., Kiel, for Norcape Shipping Company (Bermuda) Ltd. (Naess, Denholm & Company Ltd., managers), subsequently Norcape (Liberia) Inc. (same managers). 1974: Sold to Libmar One Inc., Liberia, and renamed BURMAH CORAL. 11.2.1975: Placed into lay-up at Pylos. 1977: Sold to Dover Navigation Company Ltd., and renamed CORAL I 6.1977: Sold from lay-up to Taiwan shipbreakers.

BOTL. 12. BURMAH JET (1974–1977)

54,489g. 37,737n. 96,916d. 874′ 10″ × 122′ 6″ × 49′ 11⅞″.
Two steam turbines manufactured by the shipbuilder, geared to screw shaft. 24,000 shp. 17.25 kts.

1962: Completed as NAESS CHAMPION by Mitsubishi Zosen, Nagasaki, Sovereign Shipping Company Ltd. (Naess, Denholm & Company Ltd., managers). 1974: Sold to Allocean Tankers Inc., and renamed BURMAH JET. 2.6.1975: Placed in Lay-up at Stylis. 1977: Broom Marine Ltd., appointed as managers. 22.6.1977: Arrived at Barcelona for demolition by Desgauces Condal S.A. 14.7.1977: Work commenced.

BOTL. 13. BURMAH CAMEO (1974–1977)

30,731g. 19,415n. 51,908d. 740′ 9″ × 103′ 11″ × 37′ 11¾″.
Two Parsons type steam turbines manufactured by the shipbuilder, geared to screw shaft. 19,250 shp. 17.25 kts.

1960: Completed as NAESS ENDEAVOUR by Nederlandsche Dok & Scheepswerf, Amsterdam, for Sovereign Shipping Company Ltd. (Naess, Denholm & Company Ltd., managers). 1974: Sold to Arbeit Tankers Inc., and renamed BURMAH CAMEO. 3.2.1975: Placed into lay-up at Pylos. 1977: Broom Marine Ltd., appointed as managers. 5.5.1977: Departed Pylos en route for demolition at Barcelona. 12.5.1977: Arrived. 23.5.1977: Desgauces Condal S. A., commenced work.

BOTL. 14. BURMAH ONYX (1974–1977)

40,468g. 26,036n. 70,383d. 848′ 0″ × 108′ 4″ × 44′ 6½″.
Two steam turbines manufactured by the shipbuilder at Hamburg, geared to screw shaft. 21,480 shp. 16.25 kts.

1962: Completed as NAESS PRIDE by Kieler Howaldtswerke A. G., Kiel, for Norcape Shipping Company (Bermuda) Ltd. (Naess, Denholm & Company Ltd., managers), subsequently Norcape (Liberia) Inc. (same managers). 1974: Sold to Libmar Two Inc., Liberia, and renamed BURMAH ONYX. 10.1975: Placed into lay-up at Stylis. 1977: Sold to Dover Navigation Company Ltd., and renamed ONYX 6.1977: Sold from lay-up to Taiwan shipbreakers.

BOTL. 15. BURMAH ZIRCON (1974–1977)

54,466g. 36,995n. 96,750d. 874′ 10″ × 122′ 6″ × 48′ 1½″.
Two steam turbines manufactured by the shipbuilder, geared to screw shaft. 24,000 shp. 16.25 kts.

1961: Completed as NAESS SOVEREIGN by Mitsubishi Zosen, Nagasaki, for Sovereign Shipping Company Ltd. (Naess, Denholm & Company Ltd., managers). 1974: Sold to Sealane Tankers Inc., and renamed BURMAH ZIRCON. 2.6.1975: Placed in lay-up at Itea. 1977: Broom Marine Ltd., appointed as managers. 12.6.1977: Arrived at Barcelona for demolition by Desgauces Condal. 12.7.1977: Work commenced.

BOTL. 16. BURMAH GEM (1974–1976)

As built: 33,642g. 23,766n. 59,797d. 734′ 0″ × 109′ 8″ × 40′ 0½″.
Post 1976: 34,048g. 21,898n. 59,797d.
9-cyl. 2 S.C.S.A. (860 × 1600mm) MAN type oil engine manufactured by Verolme Maschinenfabriek, Ijsselmonde. 18,000bhp. 15.5 kts.

1964: Completed as MOSLI by Verolme Dok & Scheepsbouw, Rosenburg (Yard No. 668), for AS Mosvold Shipping Company, Norway. 1975: Sold to Choral Ltd., Bermuda, and renamed BURMAH GEM. 1975: Sold to Gem Maritime Company Inc., Liberia. 1976: Sold to Fatherco Cia. Nav. S. A., Greece, and renamed PANOCEANIC FAME. 15.5.1983: Whilst on a voyage from Lavan Island to Bandar Khomeini with a cargo of gasoil was struck by two Iraqi missiles – one in the engine room and one in the amidship accommodation, at the entrance to the Khor Musa Channel. Set ablaze and abandoned by 35 crew and subsequently sank.

BOTL. 17. BURMAH SPAR (1974–1982)

38,690g. 28,234n. 75,543d. 785′ 0″ × 121′ 0″ × 41′ 9½″.
9-cyl. 2 S.C.S.A. (850 × 1700mm) oil engine manufactured

by the shipbuilder at Gothenburg. 19,800bhp. 16.5 kts.
1965: Completed as SAGA SKY by Ab Gotaverken, Arendal (Yard No. 787), for IS Saga Sky, Sweden. 1974: Sold to Ritz Shipping Inc., New York, and renamed BURMAH SPAR, under Liberia registry. 5.6.1982: Arrived at Gadani Beach for demolition. 9.6.1982: Zulfiqar Metal Industries, commenced work.

BOTL. 18. BURMAH LEGACY (1979–1985)

As built: 65,062g. 49,496n. 128,255d.
263.71 (BB) × 40.85 × 16.746 metres.
Post 1985: 60,250g. 50,004n. 128,255d.
7-cyl 2 S.C.S.A. (900 × 1800mm) B&W type oil engine manufactured by the shipbuilder. 23,900bhp. 16.25 kts.
1974: Completed as FAGERFJELL by Uddevallavarvet Ab., Uddevalla (Yard No. 284), for AS Fagerfjell (Olsen & Ugelstad, managers), Norway. 1979: Sold to Wynn Shipping Ltd., London, and renamed BURMAH LEGACY. 1979: Sold to Burtank Ltd., Liberia. 1982: Burmah Oil Tankers Ltd., appointed as managers. . 1983: Sold to P. S. & S. (Shipping) Ltd., Bermuda. 27.9.1984: Whilst on a voyage from Sullom Voe to Philadelphia, suffered flooding of the engine room and was taken in tow. 7.10.1984: Arrived at Halifax N.S., for repair. 1985: Sold to Lavandara Maritime Corp., Liberia, and renamed LAVANDARA. 1991: Sold to Kalamos Shipping Company Ltd., and renamed KALAMOS. 1993: Owner restyled E.N.E.Kalamos Ltd. (Aeolos Shipmanagement S.A., managers). c2000: Demolished.

Burmah Oil Tankers Ltd.
Managed vessels

BOTLM. 1. BURMAH EXCELSIOR (1980–1985)

38,974g. 20,641n. 57,692d. 228.61 × ? × 11.923 metres.
6-cyl. 2 S.C.S.A. (760 × 1550mm) Sulzer type oil engine manufactured by Ishikawajima Harima Heavy Industries (I.H.I.), Aioi. 13,680bhp. 14.5 kts.
1980: Completed by Koyo Dockyard Company Ltd., Japan (Yard No. 877), for Starfield Shipping Company Ltd. (Burmah Oil Tankers Ltd., managers). under Japanese registry. 1985: Sold to Seiriki One (Panama) S.A., and renamed LUNAMAR II. 1995: Renamed GRAND BANKS, V Ships USA Inc., appointed as managers. 1997: Sold to Gecrone Shipping Company S.A. (Roxana Shipping S.A., managers), Panama, and renamed PROVIDENCE. Still in Lloyd's Register 2003/04.

BOTLM. 2. BURMAH BAHAMAS (1980–1985)

38,975g. 20,644n. 57,708d. 228.61 × ? × 11.900 metres.
6-cyl. 2 S.C.S.A. (760 × 1550mm) Sulzer type oil engine manufactured by Ishikawajima Harima Heavy Industries (I.H.I.), Aioi. 13,680bhp. 14.5 kts.
1980: Completed by Koyo Dockyard Company Ltd., Japan (Yard No. 878), for Starfield Shipping Company Ltd. (Burmah Oil Tankers Ltd., managers), under Japanese registry. 1985: Sold Seiriki Three (Panama) S.A., and renamed MIRAMAR. 1995: Renamed BIMINI and V Ships USA Inc., appointed as managers. 1997: Sold to Gecrone Shipping Company S.A. (Roxana Shipping S.A., managers), Panama, and renamed SANTA PANAGIA. 2000: Sold to Santa Panagia Shipping Company Ltd. (same managers) and to Maltese flag. 2002: Avin International S.A., appointed as managers. Still in Lloyd's Register 2003/04.

BOTLM. 3. BURMAH PERIDOT (1981–1985)

see ship No. BOTL. 10 above.

BOTLM. 4. BURMAH PEARL (1981–1985)

see ship No. BOTL. 8 above.

BOTLM. 5. BURMAH LEGACY (1982–1985)

see ship No. BOTL. 18 above.

BOTLM. 6. BURMAH ENTERPRISE (1983–1988)

231,629g. 183,336n. 457,927d.
378.42(BB) × 68.05 × 25.04 metres.
Two, steam turbines manufactured by Ishikawajima Harima Heavy Industries (I.H.I.), Tokyo, double reduction geared to screw shaft. 45,000 shp. 15.25 kts.
Ultra large crude carrier (U.L.C.C.).
1973: Ordered as BURMAH ENTERPRISE from China Shipbuilding Corp., Kaohsiung (Yard No. 2), by Marine Transport Lines (Oswego), Liberia. 31.1.1978: Launched for Burmah Enterprise Ltd. (Denholm Ship Management Ltd., managers), London. 1978: Completed. 1983: Burmah Oil Tankers Ltd., appointed as managers. 1986: Transferred to Bermuda flag. 22.12.1987: Whilst berthed at Larak Island suffered minor damage, inflicted by Iraqi aircraft. 1988: Chartered with option to purchase by Stena Bulk Ab, and renamed STENA KING. 1990: Option taken and transferred to Royal Blue Shipping Ltd. (Northern Marine Management Ltd., managers). 2002: Sold to Oceanic Trans Shipping, Saudi Arabia (same managers), and renamed FOLK II. 1.6.2003: Reported departing Barbados bound to mainland China shipbreakers.

BOTLM. 7. BURMAH ENDEAVOUR (1983–1988)

O.N. 379622. 231,629g. 183,336n.
457,927d. 378.42(BB) × 68.05 × 25.04 metres.
Two, steam turbines manufactured by Ishikawajima Harima Heavy Industries (I.H.I.) Tokyo, double reduction geared to screw shaft. 45,000shp. 15.25 kts.
Ultra large crude carrier (U.L.C.C.).
1973: Ordered as BURMAH ENDEAVOUR from China Shipbuilding Corp., Kaohsiung (Yard No. 1), by Marine Transport Lines (Oswego), Liberia. 3.6.1977: Launched for Burmah Endeavour Ltd. (Denholm Ship Management Ltd., managers), London. 1977: Completed. 1983: Burmah Oil Tankers Ltd., appointed as managers. 1986: Transferred to Bermuda flag. 14.5.1988: Whilst being used as a storage vessel at Hormuz Terminal, Larak Island, was attacked by Iraqi aircraft and set on fire. Fire was quickly extinguished and vessel sustained only minor damage. 1988: Chartered with option to purchase by Stena Bulk Ab, and renamed STENA QUEEN. 1990: Option taken and transferred to Royal Sky Shipping Ltd. (Northern Marine Management Ltd., managers). 2002: Sold to Oceanic Trans Shipping, Saudi Arabia (same managers), and renamed FOLK I. 9.4.2003: Reported departing Kakinada bound to mainland China shipbreakers.

BOTLM. 8. STENA KING (1988–1990)

see ship No. BOTL. 6 above.

BOTLM. 9. STENA QUEEN (1988–1990)

see ship No. BOTL. 7 above.

Norsk Braendselolje A/S.
Formed 1926 in Oslo and established BP in Norway
As parent of subsidiaries as listed below.

NB. 1. MIL (2) (1948–1949)

61g. 23n. 69.3 × 15.9 × 8.2 feet.
Two, 8-cyl. 4 S.C.S.A. (6″ × 7″) oil engine manufactured by Gleniffer Engines Ltd., Glasgow.
Wooden hulled.
194?: Built in the U.K. for unspecified owners, believed Military. 1948: Sold to Norsk Brandselolje A/S, Oslo, converted into a tanker and renamed MIL. 1949: Transferred to Norsk Tankanlaeg A/S, Oslo. 1955: Renamed BP. *Due to small size and type of this vessel no further details have been recorded by the authors.*

Norsk Tankanlaeg AS.
Formed 1923 in Oslo

NOR. 1. MIL (1) (1923–1944)

244g. 114n. 113.7 × 22.6 × 10.1 feet.
Post 1930: 4-cyl. 2 S.C.S.A. (13″ × 13 3/8″) oil engine manufactured by Ab Atlas Diesel, Skarhamn.
Powered tank barge.
1923: Completed by Trosviks Mekaniska Verksteder, Brevik for Norsk Tankanlaeg AS, Oslo. 1940: Seized by the German Kreigsmarine. 25.1.1944: Whilst on a voyage from Vando to Kirkenes, exploded a mine in the Varanger Fjord and sank with the loss of six lives.

NOR. 2. MIL 40/ BP 40 (1937–)

273g. 132n. 129. 6 × 22. 8 × 10.4 feet.
4-cyl. 2 S.C.S.A. (380 × 400mm) oil engine manufactured by M. Haldorsen & Son, Rubbestadneset. 158nhp.
Powered tank barge.
1937: Completed as MIL 40 by Nylands Verksted, Oslo (Yard No. 331), for Norsk Tankanlaeg AS, Oslo. 1955: Renamed BP 40. *Due to small size and type of this vessel no further details have been recorded by the authors.*

NOR. 3. MIL 30/ BP 30 (1946–)

195g. 68n. 106. 6 × 20. 1 × 8.9 feet.
5-cyl. 2 S.C.S.A. (91 13/16″ × 23 5/8″) oil engine manufactured by Nydqvist & Holm Ab., Trollhattan,
Powered tank barge.
1946: Completed, as MIL 30, by Drammen Slip & Verks, Drammen (Yard No. 22), for Norsk Tankanlaeg AS, Oslo. 1955: Renamed BP 30. *Due to small size and type of this vessel no further details have been recorded by the authors.*

NOR. 4. MIL 10/ BP 10 (1947–1963)

195g. 67n. 106.8 × 20.1 × 9.0 feet.
5-cyl. 2 S.C.S.A. (250 × 420mm) oil engine manufactured by Nydqvist & Holm Ab, Trollhattan.
Powered tank barge.
1947: Completed as MIL 10 by Drammen Slip & Verks, Drammen (Yard No. 24), for Norsk Tankanlaeg AS, Oslo. 1955: Renamed BP 10. 1963: Sold to Martin Nielsen Partenrederi,

Mil 20. (World Ship Society Photograph Library)

Denmark, and renamed OSTRIC. *Due to small size and type of this vessel no further details have been recorded by the authors.*

NOR. 5. MIL 20/ BP 20 (1947–)

337g. 182n. 136.3 × 24.8 × 9.6 feet.
4-cyl. 4 S.C.S.A. (285 × 420mm) oil engine manufactured by Maschinenbau Augsburg-Nurnberg, A.G. Augsburg. 49nhp.
Coastal products tanker.

1936: Completed, as BELT, by Nobiskrug Werft, Rendsburg (Yard No. 445), for John T. Essberger, Hamburg. 1947: Sold to Norsk Tankanlaeg AS, Oslo, and renamed MIL 20. 1955: Renamed BP 20. *Due to small size and type of this vessel no further details have been recorded by the authors.*

NOR. 6. MIL 50 (1946–1955)

288g. 111n. 136. 4 × 21. 6 × 8.5 feet.
6-cyl. 2 S.C.S.A. (10 1/2″ × 18 1/2″) oil engine manufactured by Crossley Bros Ltd., Manchester. 116mn.
Powered tank barge.

11.12.1943: Launched as EMPIRE ALDERNEY by J. Harker Ltd., Knottingley (Yard No. 166), for the Ministry of War Transport (T. J. Metcalf, London, managers), London. 1946: Sold to Norsk Tankanlaeg AS, Oslo, and renamed MIL 50. 1955: Sold to Partenreederei Max S (Max Sotje, manager), Germany, and renamed MAX S. 1958: Sold to Marina Mercante Nicaraguense (Mamenic Lines, managers), Nicaragua. 1959: Sold to Cia. Maritima Mundial, Nicaragua. 1980: Sold to Trafford Holdings Ltd., Cayman Islands. *Due to small size and type of this vessel no further details have been recorded by the authors.*

NOR. 7. MIL 51 (1946–1955)

486g. 333n. 179.9 × 38.1 × 6.7 feet.
Two, 6-cyl. 4 S.C.S.A. (7″ × 7 3/4″) oil engine manufactured by Davey, Paxman & Company Ltd., Colchester.
Coastal products tanker.

1944: Built by unspecified shipyard in the UK. 1946: Sold to Norsk Tankanlaeg AS, Oslo, converted into a tanker, and renamed MIL 50. 1955: Sold to unspecified buyers. *Due to small size and type of this vessel no further details have been recorded by the authors.*

NOR. 8. MIL 52/BP 52 (1946–1959)

430g. 175n. 147′ 7″ × 27′ 1″ × 9′ 0″ .
4-cyl. 2 S.C.S.A. (265 × 345mm) 4HRL type oil engine manufactured by Crossley Bros Ltd., Manchester.
Coastal products tanker.

2.1944: Launched, as CHANT 1, by Henry Scarr Ltd., Hessle (Yard No. 435), for the Ministry of War Transport, London (C. Rowbotham & Sons, appointed as managers). 3.1944: Completed, (Bulk Oil Steam Ship Company Ltd (J.W. Cook & Company Ltd., managers), appointed as managers). 1946: Sold to Norsk Tankanlaeg AS, Norway (BP Group), and renamed MIL 52. 1955: Renamed BP 52. 1959: Sold to Ottavio Novella, Italy, and renamed CENISIO. 1975: Sold to Ciane-Anapo Compagnia di Navigazione & Bunkeraggi, Italy. 15.1.1985: Fercomit S.p.A., commenced demolition at Brindisi.

NOR. 9. MIL 1/ BP 1 (1949–1963)

473g. 183n. 159.5 × 25.8 × 6.9 feet.
6-cyl. 4 S.C.S.A. (14 1/2″ × 21 11/16″) oil engine manufactured by Motorenwerke Mannheim A.G., Mannheim.
Coastal products tanker.

1948: Completed as KLOVERNES by Pusnaes MV, Arendal (Yard No. 65), for unspecified Norwegian owners. 1949: Sold to Norsk Tankanlaeg AS, Oslo, and renamed MIL 1. 1955: Renamed BP 1. 1963: Sold to Egidio Baradel & Company, Italy, and renamed S. EGIDIO. *Due to small size and type of this vessel no further details have been recorded by the authors.*

NOR. 10. MIL/BP (1949–)

see ship NB 1 above.

NOR. 10a. BP 35 (1) (1953–)

247g. 90n. 110.2 × 22′ 5″ × 9″ 7 1/4″ .
6-cyl. 4 S.C.S.A. (270 × 360mm) oil engine manufactured by Kloeckner-Humboldt-Deutz, Koeln.
Powered tank barge.

1952: Completed, as BINDAL, by Paul Lindenau Schiffs, Kiel (Yard No. S90), for unspecified owners. 1953: Sold to Erling Sannes, Norway, and renamed MIL 35. 1955: Renamed BP 35. *Due to small size and type of this vessel no further details have been recorded by the authors.*

NOR. 11. MIL 25 (1953 – 1955)

387g. 134n. 154′ 3″ × 26′ 5″ × 10′ 6″ .
8-cyl. 4 S.C.S.A. (290 × 420mm) oil engine manufactured by Maschinenbau Kiel A.G., Kiel.
Coastal products tanker.

1953: Completed, as MIL 25, by D.W. Kremer, Sohn, Elmshorn (Yard No. 1020), for Norsk Tankanlaeg AS, Oslo. 1955: Transferred to Norsk Braendselolje AS, Svolvaer, Norway, and renamed BP 25. Subsequently sold to Michel Basile Yamanis, Panama. 1985: Sold to Commercial Air Transport Sales Ltd. *Due to small size and type of this vessel no further details have been recorded by the authors.*

NOR. 12. MIL 26 (1953 – 1955)

387g. 126n. 154′ 3″ × 26′ 5″ × 10′ 6″ .
8-cyl. 4 S.C.S.A. (290 × 420mm) oil engine manufactured by Maschinenbau Kiel A.G., Kiel.
Coastal products tanker.

1953: Completed, as MIL 26, by Ottensener Eisenwerke A.G. (Yard No. 471), for Norsk Tankanlaeg AS, Oslo. 1955: Transferred to Norsk Braendselolje AS, Svolvaer, Norway, and renamed BP 26. *Due to small size and type of this vessel no further details have been recorded by the authors.*

NOR. 13. BP 28 (2) (1958 –1968)

As built: 499g. 177n. 740d. 186′ 3″ × 28′ 5″ × 12′ 2 1/2″ .
Post 1971: 568g. 232n. 905d. 258′ 0″ × 28′ 5″ × 13′ 5″ .
6-cyl. 4 S.C.S.A. (385 × 580mm) oil engine manufactured by Maschinenbau Kiel A.G., Kiel. 750 bhp.
Coastal products tanker.

1958: Completed by Glommens Mek.Verksted AS, Frederikstad (Yard No. 159), for Norsk Braendselolje AS. Svolvaer. 1968: Tranferred to Norsk Tankanlaeg AS. 1971: Lengthened. *Due to small size and type of this vessel no further details have been recorded by the authors.*

Norsk Braendselolje Svolvaer AS.
Formed 1953 in Svolvaer

NBS. 1. BP 25 (1955 – 19)

see ship No. NOR 11 above.

NBS. 2. BP 26 (1955–19)

see ship No. NOR 12 above.

NBS. 3. BP 27 (2) (1958–)

As built 499g. 177n. 740d. 186′ 3″ × 28′ 5″ × 12′ 2 1/4″ .
Post 1971: 568g. 232n. 905d. 258′0″ × 28′5″ × 13′5″ .
6-cyl. 4 S.C.S.A. (385 × 580mm) oil engine manufactured by Maschinenbau Kiel A.G., Kiel. 750 bhp.
Coastal products tanker.

1958: Completed by Glommens Mek.Verksted AS, Frederikstad (Yard No. 158), for Norsk Braendselolje Svolvaer A/S. 1971: Lengthened. *Due to small size and type of this vessel no further details have been recorded by the authors.*

NBS. 4. BP 28 (2) (1968–)

see ship No. NOR 13 above.

MIL Tankrederi AS.
Formed 1957 in Oslo

MIL. 11. NORSK JARL (1957 – 1960)

As built: 8,129g. 4,631n. 465.9 × 59.4 × 33.8 feet.
Post 1947: 7,934g. 4,463n.
As built. T.3-cyl. (26 1/2″, 44″ & 73″ × 48″) engine manufactured by the shipbuilder. 629nhp.
Post 1947: 8-cyl. 2 S.C.S.A. (680 × 1200mm) MAN type oil engine manufactured by N.V. Wilton-Fijenoord, Fijenoord.
Ocean-going tanker.

2.12.1941: Launched as EMPIRE SAXON by Swan, Hunter & Wigham Richardson Ltd., Newcastle (Yard No. 1706), for the Ministry of War Transport, London. 2.1942: Completed as NORFJELL for the Norwegian Government (The Norwegian Shipping & Trade Mission, managers), Oslo. 1946: Sold to Skibsrederi AS Ringfonn (Sigval Bergesen, Oslo, manager), Norway, and renamed NORDFONN. 1947: Fitted with an oil engine. 1957: Sold to MIL

Tankrederi AS (Norsk Braendselolje AS., managers), and renamed NORSK JARL. 27.6.1960: Arrived at Bo'ness for demolition by P. & W. McLellan Ltd.

MIL. 2. NORSK SKALD (1960 – 1964)

11,117g. 6,430n. 514.2 × 67.4 × 37.2 feet.
4-cyl. 2 S.C.S.A. (29½″ × 98 7/16″) Doxford type engine manufactured by Barclay, Curle & Company Ltd., Glasgow. 1,052mn.
Ocean-going tanker.

1951: Completed as CASTOR by C. Connell & Company Ltd., Glasgow (Yard No. 469), for Det Bergenske Dampsskibsselskabologet, Norway. 1960: Sold to MIL Tankrederi AS (Norsk Braendselolje AS., managers), and renamed NORSK SKALD. 1964: Sold to A/S Selvaagbygg (Th. Brovig, manager), Norway, and renamed GEZINA BROVIG. 3.1.1970: Whilst on a voyage from Aruba to Bucksport, sank following a main engine explosion which shot a piston through the side of the ship in position 22.46N., 68.48W., about 300 miles N. E. of San Juan P.R.

MIL. 3. NORSK DROT (1961 – 1968)

18,483g. 11,306n. 29,247d. 643′ 9″ × 80′ 11″ × 34′ 6¼″ .
7-cyl. 2 S.C.S.A. (750 × 1500mm) B&W type oil engine manufactured by the shipbuilder. 11,600 bhp. 15 kts.
Ocean-going tanker.

20.12.1960: Launched by Harland & Wolff Ltd., Govan (Yard No. 1603G) for Norsk Braendselolje AS., Norway. 28.4.1961: Completed for MIL Tankrederi AS (Norsk Braendselolje AS., managers). 1968: Sold to Botapa Shipping Company Ltd., Greece, and renamed GALAXIAS. 10.1974: Reported as in port damaged. 1983: Sold for demolition.

MIL. 4. NORSK VIKING (1963–1969)

11,142g. 6,408n. 17,260d. 550′ 0″ × 66′ 2″ × 30′ 3¾″.
5-cyl. 2 S.C.S.A. (750 × 1500mm) B&W 5-74VTBF – 150/50 type oil engine manufactured by the shipbuilder. 7,300 bhp. 15 kts.
Ocean-going tanker.

1958: Completed as FARMAND by AS Akers Mekaniska Verksted, Oslo (Yard No. 514), for AS Antarctic (Anton Von der Lippe, manager), Norway. 1963: Sold to MIL Tankrederi AS (Norsk Braendselolje AS., managers), and renamed NORSK VIKING. 1969: Renamed PET (Svend Fyn Bruun, appointed as manager). 1970: Sold to China Ocean Shipping Company, PRC, and renamed DA QING 37. 1992: Entry removed from Lloyd's Register.

MIL. 5. NORSK BARDE (1965–1969)

12,962g. 7,844n. 19,552d. 560′ 1″ × 71′ 11″ × 31′ 1″.
7-cyl. 2 S.C.S.A. (760 × 1550mm) Sulzer type oil engine manufactured by Uraga Diesel Kyogo, Tamashima.
Ocean-going tanker.

1958: Completed as LEIKANGER by Nagoya Zosen, Nagoya (Yard No. 135), for Westfal Larsen & Company AS, Norway. 1965: Sold to MIL Tankrederi AS (Norsk Braendselolje AS., managers), and renamed NORSK BARDE. 1969: Renamed PETUNIA (Svend Fyn Bruun, appointed as manager). By 1975: No longer listed in Lloyd's Register.

MIL. 6. PETUNIA (1969 – pre 1975)

see ship No. MIL. 5. above.

MIL. 7. PET (1969–1970)

see ship No. MIL. 4. above.

—— • ——

Khanaqin Oil Company Ltd.
1933 restyled as
Rafidain Oil Company Ltd.
1952 transferred into Iraqi ownership.

RAF. 1. SAFIYEH (1931–1951)

O.N. 162636. 176g. 73n. 138.0 × 26.6 × 4.8 feet.
Two, 4-cyl. 2 S.C.S.A. (9″ × 11″) oil engines manufactured by L. Gardner & Sons Ltd., Manchester.
Powered tank barge.

6.1931: Completed by G. Brown & Company, Greenock (Yard No. 177), for the Khanaqin Oil Company Ltd. 1931: Re-erected at Abadan. 1933: Owners restyled as Rafidain Oil Company Ltd. *Due to small size and type of this vessel no further details have been recorded by the authors.*

RAF. 2. SALIMEH (1932–1952)

O.N. 162659. 176g. 73n. 138.0 × 26.6 × 4.8 feet.
Two, 4-cyl. 2 S.C.S.A. (9″ × 11″) oil engines manufactured by L. Gardner & Sons Ltd., Manchester.
Powered tank barge.

3.1932: Completed by G. Brown & Company, Greenock (Yard No. 178), for the Khanaqin Oil Company Ltd. 1932: Re-erected at Abadan. 1933: Owners restyled as Rafidain Oil Company Ltd. *Due to small size and type of this vessel no further details have been recorded by the authors.*

RAF. 3. ROC 1 (1937–1952)

O.N. 165581. 18g. 9n. 46.8 × 10.0 × 4.9 feet.
66bhp., oil engine manufactured by W. H. Allen, Bedford.
Powered tank launch.

8.1937: Launched by James Pollock, Son & Company Ltd., Faversham (Yard No. 1631), for Rafidain Oil Company Ltd. 10.1937: Completed. *Due to small size and type of this vessel no further details have been recorded by the authors.*

BP 28. (World Ship Society Photograph Library)

RAF. 4. ROC 2 (1937–1952)

O.N. 165599. 18g. 9n. 46.8 × 10.0 × 4.9 feet.
66bhp. oil engine manufactured by W. H. Allen, Bedford.
Powered tank launch.

9.1937: Launched by James Pollock, Son & Company Ltd., Faversham (Yard No. 1632), for Rafidain Oil Company Ltd. 12.1937: Completed. 195 : Transferred to the Anglo-Iranian Oil Company Ltd. *Due to small size and type of this vessel no further details have been recorded by the authors.*

RAF. 5. ROC 3 (1937–WW2)

O.N. 165619. 18g. 9n. 46.8 × 10.0 × 4.9 feet.
66bhp. oil engine manufactured by W. H. Allen, Bedford.
Powered tank launch.

10.1937: Launched by James Pollock, Son & Company Ltd., Faversham (Yard No. 1633), for Rafidain Oil Company Ltd. 12.1937: Completed. WW2: Captured in Norway and trace lost. 7.7.1955: Re-located and sold to Norwegian interests. *Due to small size and type of this vessel no further details have been recorded by the authors.*

RAF. 6. ROC 4 (1939–1952)

O.N.166379. 15g. 9n. 46.7 × 10.0 × 4.6 feet.
66bhp. oil engine manufactured by W. H. Allen, Bedford.
Powered tank launch.

1939: Completed by Rowhedge Iron Works Ltd., Rowhedge, for Rafidain Oil Company Ltd. *Due to small size and type of this vessel no further details have been recorded by the authors.*

RAF. 7. ROC 5 (1939–1952)

O.N. 167410. 20g. 9n. 49.5 × 10.3 × 4.9 feet.
16hp. oil engine.
Powered tank launch.

1937: Completed by W. J. Yarwood & Sons Ltd., Northwich, for Rafidain Oil Company Ltd. *Due to small size and type of this vessel no further details have been recorded by the authors.*

RAF. 8. SINJAR (1938–1952)

O.N. 167148. 37g. 23n 60.2 × 12.6 × 4.1 feet.
4-cyl. 2 S.C.S.A. (9″ × 11″) oil engine manufactured by L. Gardner & Sons Ltd., Manchester. 30bhp.
Tug.

1938: Completed by G. Brown & Company (Marine) Ltd., Greenock, for the Petroleum Steamship Company Ltd, thence to the Rafidain Oil Company Ltd. *Due to small size and type of this vessel no further details have been recorded by the authors.*

RAF. 9. SULAF (1938–1952)

O.N. 167149. 37g. 23n. 60.2 × 12.6 × 4.1 feet.
4-cyl. 2 S.C.S.A. (9″ × 11″) oil engine manufactured by L. Gardner & Sons Ltd., Manchester. 30bhp.
Tug.

1938: Completed by G. Brown & Company (Marine) Ltd., Greenock, for the Petroleum Steamship Company Ltd., thence to the Rafidain Oil Company Ltd. *Due to small size and type of this vessel no further details have been recorded by the authors.*

RAF. 10. BAGHDAD (1939–1946)

see ship No. PS. 21 in Petroleum Steam Ship section.

Shell-Mex & BP Ltd.

1932:- British Petroleum Company Ltd. (1) q.v., was restyled as an associate company following an amalgamation and change of shareholdings.

Shell Petroleum Company Ltd., and Eagle Tankers Ltd. jointly 50 per cent
and
Anglo-Persian Oil Company Ltd. 50 per cent
1975: Partnership dissolved and fleet divided between Shell UK Ltd and BP Oil Ltd.

Poilo. (World Ship Society Photograph Library)

SMBP. 1. BRITISH BEAGLE (1932–)

see ship No. BP. 20 in BP section.

SMBP. 2. BRITISH BOY (1932–)

see ship No. BP. 22 in BP section.

SMBP. 2a. BRITISH FLAME (1932–1956)

see ship No. BP. 15 in BP section.

SMBP. 3. BRITISH GIRL (1932–)

see ship No. BP. 23 in BP section.

SMBP. 4. BRITISH LUSTRE (1932–1950)

see ship No. BP. 16 in BP section.

SMBP. 5. BRITISH MAIDEN (1932–)

see ship No. BP. 21 in BP section.

SMBP. 6. BRITISH SPARK (1932–1935)

see ship No. BP. 17 in BP section.

SMBP. 7. BRITISH SPINNER (1932–1933)

see ship No. BP. 14 in BP section.

SMBP. 8. BRITISH TOILER (1932–1975)

see ship No. BP. 6 in BP section.

SMBP. 9. BRITISH TORCH (1932–1935)

see ship No. BP. 18 in BP section.

SMBP. 10. BRITISH YOUTH (1932–1956)

see ship No. BP. 24 in BP section.

SMBP. 11. HOME LIGHT (1932–1933)

see ship No. BP. 4 in BP section.

SMBP. 12. ROYAL STANDARD (1932–)

see ship No. BP. 5 in BP section.

SMBP. 13. WHITE MAY (1932–1936)

see ship No. BP. 3 in BP section.

SMBP. 14. PANDO (1) (1932–1967)

see ship No. AP. 23 in APOC section.

SMBP. 15. PERSO (1) (1932–1967)

see ship No. AP. 24 in APOC section.

SMBP. 16. PHERO (1932–1967)

see ship No. AP. 25 in APOC section.

SMBP. 17. PHILO (1932–1967)

see ship No. AP. 26 in APOC section.

SMBP. 18. POILO (1) (1932–1967)

see ship No. AP. 27 in APOC section.

SMBP. 19. SHELL-MEX 6 (1932–1948)

O.N. 148671. 103g. 46n. ? d. 91.2 × 18.3 × 6.1 feet.
2-cyl. 2 S.C.S.A. ($12\frac{7}{8}'' \times 13\frac{3}{4}''$) oil engine manufactured by Kromhout Motorenfabriek, Amsterdam. 29 nhp.
Powered tank barge.

1925: Completed by N. V. Scheepswerf van P. Smit junior, Rotterdam, for Shell-Mex Ltd., London. 1932: Sold to Shell-Mex & BP Ltd. 1948: Sold to Risdon, Beazley Ltd. (R. A. Beazley, manager), Southampton. *Due to small size and type of this vessel no further details have been recorded by the authors.*

SMBP. 20. SHELL-MEX 7 (1932–)

O.N. 149893. 132g. 111n. ? d. 100.0 × 20.0 × 8.5 feet.
Dumb tank barge.

1.9.1927: Launched by Charles Hill & Sons Ltd., Bristol, for Shell-Mex Ltd., London. 9.1927: Completed. 1932: Sold to Shell-Mex & BP Ltd. *Due to small size and type of this vessel no further details have been recorded by the authors.*

SMBP. 21. SHELL-MEX 8 (1932–1936)

O.N. 160497. 349g. 238n. ? d. 136.0 × 24.0 × 10.0 feet.
4-cyl. 2 S.C.S.A. ($16\frac{1}{2}'' \times 18\frac{7}{8}''$) oil engine manufactured by N. V. Kromhaut Motorenfabriek, Amsterdam. 100 bhp.
Post 1950: 4-cyl. 2 S.C.S.A. (250 × 420mm) oil engine manufactured by British Polar Diesels Ltd., Glasgow.
Coastal oil products tanker.

7.5.1928: Launched by Charles Hill & Sons Ltd., Bristol, for Shell-Mex Ltd., London. 6.1928: Completed. 12.1932: Sold to Shell-Mex & BP Ltd. 1936: Renamed SHELBRIT 4. 1943: Anglo-Saxon Petroleum Company Ltd., appointed as managers. 4.1950: Re-engined. 5.1952: Renamed SHELL DRIVER. 9.1956: Sold to Channel Shipping Ltd., and converted into a dry cargo vessel. 3.1957: Renamed GOREY. 7.1963: Sold to W. J. Sutton and R. L. Morrish, Hull, and renamed CHARGER. 1.1966: Sold to Overseas and General Brokerage and Finance Company Ltd., London. 12.1976: Sold for demolition in U. K.

SMBP. 22. SHELLFEN (1932–)

O.N. 167221. 11g. 7n. 42.8 × 8.9 × 3.2 feet.
21 bhp., oil engine.
Unspecified vessel type.

Year unknown: Built as PROGRESS for unspecified owner. 1932: Purchased by Shell-Mex & BP Ltd., and renamed SHELLFEN, for inland waterway use. *Due to small size and type of this vessel no further details have been recorded by the authors.*

SMBP. 23. SHELL-MEX 3 (1932–1968)

O.N. 145266. 123g. 111n. ? d. 105.8 × 21.1 × 7.4 feet.
2-cyl. 2 S.C.S.A. ($9'' \times 9\frac{1}{2}''$) oil engine manufactured by J. Pollock, Sons & Company Ltd., Faversham. 29 nhp.
Post 1957: 5-cyl. 4 S.C.S.A. ($5\frac{3}{8}'' \times 8''$) oil engine manufactured by Ruston & Hornsby Ltd., 5 kts.
Powered tank barge.

1916: Completed by W. Dobson & Company, Newcastle, for Shell-Mex Ltd., London. 1932: Sold to Shell-Mex & BP Ltd. 1957: re-engined. 1968: Sold to Pounds Shipowners & Shipbreakers Ltd., Portsmouth. 1971: Sold to N. W. Woods, and converted into a dredger. 6.5.1974: Sank off Hayling Island. 7.5.1974:

Shell-Mex 6. (World Ship Society Photograph Library)

Shelbrit. (World Ship Society Photograph Library)

Shelbrit 2. (World Ship Society Photograph Library)

Shelbrit 3. (World Ship Society Photograph Library)

Refloated and laid up at Portsmouth pending a decision on her future. No further details located.

SMBP. 23a. MEXTRENT (1932 – 19)

O.N. 145150. 110g. ? × ? × ? feet.
Dumb tank barge.
1920: Built at Portsmouth Shell-Mex Ltd., London. 1932: Sold to Shell-Mex & BP Ltd. *Due to small size and type of this vessel no further details have been recorded by the authors.*

SMBP. 23b. MEXDEE (1932 – 19)

O.N. 136251. 44g. ? × ? × ? feet.
Dumb tank barge.
1910: Built at Hessle as LEEDS STARS for unspecified owners. 1920: Sold to Shell-Mex Ltd., London, and renamed MEXDEE. 1932: Sold to Shell-Mex & BP Ltd. *Due to small size and type of this vessel no further details have been recorded by the authors.*

SMBP. 24. SHELBRIT (1934–1937)

O.N. 163445. 460g. 193 n. ? d. 157.4 × 27.1 × 12.0 feet.
8-cyl. 2 S.C.S.A. ($11^{1}/_{2}''$ × $13^{1}/_{2}''$) oil engine manufactured by H. Widdop & Company Ltd., Keighley. 186 nhp.
Powered tank barge.
18.12.1933: Launched by G. Brown & Company Ltd., Greenock (Yard No. 186), for Shell-Mex & BP Ltd. 3.1934: Completed. 1937: Renamed SHELBRIT 3. 1954: Sold to Loucos Matsas & Sons, Greece, and renamed VICTORIA. 7.9.1963: Whilst on passage from Pireaus to Antilochia, sank off Derveni, Gulf of Corinth.

SMBP. 25. ENERGIE (1936–1952)

O.N. 160692. 501g. 313n. 150.2 × 27.6 × 10.2 feet.
Two, 4-cyl. 4 S.C.S.A. ($11''$ × $17^{11}/_{16}''$) oil engines manufactured by Motorenfabrik 'Deutz' A. G., Koln-Deutz, geared to twin screw shafts. 47 nhp.
Coastal oil products tanker.
18.7.1928: Launched by I. J. Abdela & Mitchell (1925) Ltd., Queensferry (Yard No. 535), for Medway Oil & Storage Company Ltd., Rochester. 9.1928: Completed. 4.1936: Purchased by Shell-Mex & BP Ltd. 1952: Renamed SHELL WELDER. 1954: Demolished.

SMBP. 26. THRIFTIE * (1936)

see ship No. BT. 101 in main fleet.

SMBP. 27. SHELBRIT 1 * (1936–1940)

see ship No. BT. 99 in main fleet.

SMBP. 28. SHELBRIT 2 * (1936–1943)

see ship No. SMBP. 26 above.

N.B. * = Operated by Shell-Mex & BP Ltd., but remained owned by the British Tanker Company Ltd.

SMBP. 29. SHELBRIT 4 (1936–1952)

see ship No. SMBP. 21 above.

SMBP. 30. SHELBRIT 3 (1937–1954)

see ship No. SMBP. 24 above.

SMBP. 31. MEXSHELL (1937–1939)

O.N. ?. ? g. ? n. ? × ? × ? feet.
Oil engine.
Powered tank launch for Southampton water use.
1937: Built for Shell-Mex & BP Ltd. 1939: Burnt. *Due to small size and type of this vessel no further details have been located by the authors.*

SMBP. 32. MEXSHELL 2 (1937–1960)

O.N. ? . ? g. ?n. 46.0 × 10.0 × 5.0 feet.
36bhp., oil engine manufactured by H. Widdop & Company Ltd., Keighley.
Powered tank launch for Southampton water use.
12.1939: Launched by James Pollock, Son & Company Ltd., Faversham (Yard No. 1756), for for Shell-Mex & BP Ltd. 1.1940: Completed. 1960: Sold to Southern Salvage & Demolition Company Ltd., Southampton, for demolition.

Shelbrit 6. (World Ship Society Photograph Library)

SMBP. 33. SHELBRIT 5 (1946–1952)

O.N. 169403. 814g. 332n. ? d. 193.0 × 30.7 × 13.8 feet.
T.3-cyl. (15″, 25½″ & 41″ × 30″) engine manufactured by Aitchison, Blair Ltd., Clydebank.
Coastal oil products tanker.

10.11.1943: Launched as EMPIRE HARVEST by A. & J. Inglis Ltd., Glasgow (Yard No. 1225p), for the Ministry of War Transport (F. T. Everard & Sons Ltd., managers), London. 12.1943: Completed. 4.1946: Owners restyled as the Ministry of Transport. 5.1946: Sold to Shell-Mex & BP Ltd., and renamed SHELBRIT 5. 1952: Renamed BP ENGINEER. 5.1965: Sold to Scrappingco S. A., Brussels, for demolition. 25.5.1965: Passed Antwerp en route to Bruges. 31.5.1965: Work commenced.

SMBP. 34. SHELBRIT 6 (1947–1952)

O.N. 180360. 797g. 380 n. ? d. 193.0 × 30.7 × 14.1 feet.
T.3-cyl. (15″, 25½″ & 41″ × 30″) engine manufactured by D. Rowan & Company Ltd., Glasgow.
Coastal oil products tanker.

7.10.1944: Launched as EMPIRE DRURY by the Grangemouth Dockyard Company Ltd., Grangemouth (Yard No.460), for the Ministry of War Transport (F. T. Everard & Sons Ltd., managers). 12.1944: Completed. 1945: Anglo-Saxon Petroleum Company Ltd., appointed as managers. 4.1946: Owners restyled as Ministry of Transport. 1947: Sold to Shell-Mex & BP Ltd., and renamed SHELBRIT 6. 1952: Renamed BP REFINER. 1964: Sold to Compagnia Siciliana Navigazione Cisterna S. p. A., Italy, and renamed COSINA. 6.1973: Sold to V. Ferrara et C., Palermo, for demolition. 25.6.1973: Work commenced.

SMBP. 35. SHELBRIT 7 (1948–1952)

O.N. 168754. 814g. 322 n. ? d. 193.0 × 30.7 × 13.8 feet.
T.3-cyl. (15″, 25½″ & 41″ × 30″) engine manufactured by D. Rowan & Company Ltd., Glasgow.
Coastal oil products tanker.

26.12.1942: Launched as EMPIRE FAY by A. & J. Inglis Ltd., Glasgow (Yard No. 1184p), for the Ministry of War Transport (Hemsley, Bell Ltd., managers), London. 4.1943: Completed. 1945: Anglo-Saxon Petroleum Company Ltd., appointed as managers. 4.1946: Owners restyled as Ministry of Transport. 1946: Sold to Anglo-Saxon Petroleum Company Ltd., and renamed KLEINELLA. 1947: Transferred to Shell Company of East Africa Ltd. 1948: Sold to Shell-Mex & BP Ltd., and renamed SHELBRIT 7. 1952: Renamed BP MARKETER. 1964: Sold to Augusta Garolla thence Sarda Bunkers SpA, Italy, and renamed SARROCH. 9.1983: Sold for demolition.

SMBP. 36. SHELBRIT 8 (1948–1952)

O.N. 169208. 980g. 341 n. ? d. 193.5 × 34.2 × 14.7 feet.
Post 1954: 1,157g. 240.6 × 34.2 × ? feet.
T.3-cyl. (13½″, 22¾″ & 38″ × 27″) engine manufactured by the North Eastern Marine Engineering Company (1938) Ltd., Newcastle.
Coastal oil products tanker.

5.10.1945: Launched as EMPIRE TESLIN by Swan, Hunter & Wigham, Richardson Ltd., Newcastle (Yard No. 1842), for the Ministry of War Transport (Anglo-Saxon Petroleum Company Ltd., managers). 4.1946: Completed for a restyled Ministry of Transport. 1946: Sold to Anglo-Saxon Petroleum Company Ltd., and renamed FRAGUM. 1948: Sold to Shell-Mex & BP Ltd., and renamed SHELBRIT 8. 1952: Renamed SHELL SUPPLIER. 1954: Lengthened. 1967: Sold to Marine Water Supply Company (N. E. Vernicos Shipping Company Ltd., managers), Greece, and renamed SOFIA. 5.1971: Demolished at Perama.

SMBP. 37. SHELBRIT 9 (1948–1952)

O.N. 169449. 979g. 341 n. ? d. 193.5 × 34.2 × 14.7 feet.
T.3-cyl. (13½″, 22¾″ & 38″ × 27″) engine manufactured by J. Dickinson & Sons Ltd., Sunderland.
Coastal oil products tanker.

31.7.1945: Launched as EMPIRE TESLAND by Harland & Wolff Ltd., Glasgow (Yard No. 1315 G), for the Ministry of War Transport (Anglo-Saxon Petroleum Company Ltd., managers). 9.1945: Completed. 4.1946: Owners restyled Ministry of Transport. 1946: Sold to Anglo-Saxon Petroleum Company Ltd., and renamed FULGUR. 1948: Sold to Shell-Mex & BP Ltd., and renamed SHELBRIT 9. 1952: Renamed BP MANAGER. 1956: Lengthened. 6.1967: Sold for demolition at Antwerp.

SMBP. 38. SHELBRIT 10 (1948–1952)

O.N. 169208. 980g. 341 n. ? d. 193.5 × 34.2 × 14.7 feet.
4-cyl. 2 S.C.S.A. (13⅜″ × 22⁷⁄₁₆″) oil engine manufactured by British Polar Diesels Ltd., Glasgow.
Coastal oil products tanker.

30.11.1945: Launched as EMPIRE TEDPORT by A. & J. Inglis Ltd., Glasgow (Yard No. 1312p), for the Ministry of War Transport (Anglo-Saxon Petroleum Company Ltd., managers). 3.1946: Completed. 4.1946: Owners restyled Ministry of Transport. 1947: Sold to Anglo-Saxon Petroleum Company Ltd., and renamed FELIPES. 1948: Sold to Shell-Mex & BP Ltd., and renamed SHELBRIT 10. 1952: Renamed SHELL DIRECTOR. 18.8.1966: Arrived at Bo'ness for demolition by P. & W. MacLellan Ltd.

SMBP. 39. BP DISTRIBUTOR (1952–1965)

O.N. 180356. 797g. 380n. 193.0 × 30.7 × 14.1 feet.
T.3-cyl. (15″, 25½″ & 41″ × 30″) engine manufactured by D. Rowan & Company Ltd., Glasgow.
Coastal oil products tanker.

22.9.1944: Launched as EMPIRE TROTWOOD by the Grangemouth Dockyard Company Ltd., Grangemouth (Yard No. 455), for the Ministry of War Transport (F. T. Everard & Sons Ltd., managers). 5.1944: Completed. 1946: Anglo-Saxon Petroleum Company Ltd., appointed as managers. 1947: Sold to the Kuwait Oil Company Ltd., and renamed AMIR. 1952: Sold to Shell-Mex & BP Ltd., and renamed BP DISTRIBUTOR. 5.1965: Sold for demolition at Willebroek. 31.5.1965: Scrappingco S. A., commenced work.

SMBP. 40. BP MANAGER (1952–1967)

see ship No. SMBP. 37 above.

Shelbrit 7. (World Ship Society Photograph Library)

BP Distributor. (World Ship Society Photograph Library)

BP Manager. (World Ship Society Photograph Library)

SMBP. 41. BP MARKETER (1952–1964)

see ship No. SMBP. 35 above.

SMBP. 42. BP ENGINEER (1952–1965)

see ship No. SMBP. 33 above.

SMBP. 43. BP REFINER (1952–1964)

see ship No. SMBP. 34 above.

SMBP. 44. SHELL DIRECTOR (1) (1952–1966)

see ship No. SMBP. 38 above.

SMBP. 45. SHELL DRIVER (1952–1956)

see ship No. SMBP. 21 above.

SMBP. 46. SHELL LOADER (1952–1961)

see ship No. SMBP. 26 above.

SMBP. 47. SHELL SUPPLIER (1952–1967)

see ship No. SMBP. 36 above.

SMBP. 48. SHELL WELDER (1) (1952–1954)

see ship No. SMBP. 25 above.

SMBP. 49. BP TRANSPORTER (1952–1965)

O.N. 169436. 813g. 334n. 193.0 × 30.7 × 13.8 feet.
T.3-cyl. (15″, $25^{1}/_{2}$″ & 41″ × 30″) engine manufactured by Rankin and Blackmore Ltd., Glasgow.
Coastal oil products tanker.

19.1.1945: Launched as EMPIRE SHETLAND by A. & J. Inglis Ltd., Glasgow (Yard No. 1288p), for The Ministry of War Transport (The Anglo-Saxon Petroleum Company Ltd., managers). 11.4.1945: Completed. 1945: Coastal Tankers Ltd., appointed as managers. 1946: Owners restyled The Ministry of Transport. 1947: Sold to The Kuwait Oil Company Ltd., London, and renamed ADIB. 1952: Sold to Shell-Mex & BP Ltd., London, and renamed BP TRANSPORTER. 18.6.1965: Scrappingco S. A., Brussels, commenced demolition at Antwerp.

SMBP. 50. SHELL DRILLER (1952–1966)

O.N. 181122. 969g. 415n. 1,043d. 193.5 × 34.2 × 14.7 feet.
4-cyl. 2 S.C.S.A. ($13^{3}/_{8}$″ × $22^{7}/_{16}$″) oil engine manufactured by British Polar Diesels Ltd., Glasgow.
Coastal oil products tanker.

25.9.1945: Launched as EMPIRE TEDILLA by Sir J. Laing & Sons Ltd., Sunderland (Yard No. 773), for the Ministry of War Transport (Anglo-Saxon Petroleum Company Ltd., managers). 2.1946: Completed. 4.1946: Owners restyled Ministry of Transport. 1947: Sold to Anglo-Saxon Petroleum Company Ltd., and renamed FORSKALIA. 11.1949: Sold to J. Harker (Coasters) Ltd., Knottingley, and renamed DANESDALE H. 1952: Sold to Shell-Mex & BP Ltd., and renamed SHELL DRILLER. 23.8.1966: Arrived at Faslane for demolition.

BP Marketer. (World Ship Society Photograph Library)

BP Engineer. (World Ship Society Photograph Library)

BP Refiner. (J K Byass)

SMBP. 51. SHELL FITTER (1952–1964)

O.N. 168764. 813g. 339n. 193.0 × 30.7 × 13.8 feet.
T.3-cyl. (15″, $25\frac{1}{2}$″ & 41″ × 30″) engine manufactured by D. Rowan & Company Ltd., Glasgow.
Coastal oil products tanker.

27.3.1943: Launched as EMPIRE COPPICE by A. & J. Inglis Ltd., Glasgow (Yard No.1190p), for The Ministry of War Transport (Coastal Tankers Ltd., managers), London. 22.6.1943: Completed. 1946: Owners restyled Ministry of Transport. 1947: Sold to Coastal Tankers Ltd. 1948: Sold to The Kuwait Oil Company Ltd., London, and renamed AMIN. 1952: Purchased by Shell-Mex & BP Ltd., and renamed SHELL FITTER. 1964: Sold to Dionyssios I. Philippopoulos, Greece, and renamed ALIKI. 1967: Sold to Naftiki Idrotiki (C. Vernicos, manager), Greece. 1968: Sold to Marine Water Supply Company Ltd., Greece. 10.9.1969: Kavership commenced demolition at Perama.

Shell Director (World Ship Society Photograph Library)

SMBP. 52. BP SUPERVISOR (1953–1966)

O.N. 181269. 860g. 392n. 1,073d. 193.5 × 34.2 × 14.7 feet.
4-cyl. 2 S.C.S.A. ($13\frac{3}{8}$″ × $22\frac{7}{16}$″) oil engine manufactured by British Polar Diesels Ltd., Glasgow.
Coastal oil products tanker.

4.2.1946: Launched as EMPIRE TEDBURGH by Short Bros Ltd., Sunderland (Yard No. 491), for the Ministry of War Transport (Anglo-Saxon Petroleum Company Ltd., managers). 7.1946: Completed for a restyled Ministry of Transport. 7.1946: Sold to J. Harker (Coasters) Ltd., Knottingley, and renamed DOVEDALE H. 1953: Sold to Shell-Mex & BP Ltd., and renamed BP SUPERVISOR. 1966: Sold to Antonia Shipping Company Ltd. (J. Livanos & Sons Ltd., managers), Greece, and renamed RAINBOW. 1967: Sold to Ionian Tank Shipping S. A. (G. Kalogeratos & Company, managers), Greece. 6.11.1977: Caught fire and sank in Eleusis Bay, Greece. Subsequently declared a total loss, sold, raised and 9.1978: Demolished at Piraeus.

N.B. One source referred to declares vessel as being completed as DOVEDALE H. whereas several others including Harker records state completed as EMPIRE TEDBURGH and purchased within days of completion.

Shell Driver. (World Ship Society Photograph Library)

SMBP. 53. JORIE (1953–)

O.N. 148379. 80g. 55n. 85′ 7″ × 18′ 1″ × 6′ 0″ .
Post 1938: 130g. 97n. 116′ 2″ × 18′ 1″ × ?.
Post 1928: Two, -unspecified type oil engines, ? bhp.
Post 1938: Two, 6-cyl. 4 S.C.S.A. ($5\frac{11}{16}$″ × $7\frac{1}{16}$″) oil engines manufactured by W. H. Allen, Sons & Company Ltd., Bedford.
Post 1948: Two, 6-cyl. 4 S.C.S.A. (125 × 160mm) oil engines manufactured in 1945 by Crossley Bros Ltd., Manchester.
Post 1963: Two, 6-cyl 4 S.C.S.A. ($5\frac{1}{4}$″ × $7\frac{3}{4}$″) oil engines manufactured by in 1948 by Norris, Henty & Gardner Ltd., Manchester.
Powered tank barge.

1925: Completed by N. V. Scheepsbouw Baanhoek, Sliedrecht, for unspecified owners. 1928: Sold to the Medway Oil & Storage Company Ltd., Rochester. 1928: Motorised. 1938: Lengthened. 1948: Re-engined. 1953: Sold to Shell-Mex & BP Ltd. 1963: Re-engined. *Due to small size and type of this vessel no further details have been recorded by the authors.*

Shell Loader. (World Ship Society Photograph Library)

SMBP. 54. FEALTIE (1953–1966)

O.N. 160703. 351g. 271n. 152.7 × 24.2 × 8.9 feet.
3-cyl. 4 S.C.S.A. (280 × 450mm) oil engine manufactured by Motorenfabrik Deutz, Koln-Deutz.
Powered tank barge.

1928: Completed by Industrie Maatschappij De Noord, Alblasserdam (Yard No. ?), for the Medway Oil & Storage Company Ltd. 1953: Sold to Shell-Mex & BP Ltd. 1966: Sold to J. P. Knight (London) Ltd., and renamed KINGSABBEY. *Due to small size and type of this vessel no further details have been recorded by the authors.*

SMBP. 55. TEMERITIE (1953–1956)

O.N. 164998. 38g. 5n. 64.0 × 14.5 × 4.8 feet.
Unspecified oil engine.
Towing launch.

1937: Completed by Richard Dunston Ltd., Thorne (Yard No. ?), for Medway Oil & Storage Company Ltd., Rochester. 1953: Sold to Shell-Mex & BP Ltd., London. 1956: Sold to Dashwood & Partners Ltd. *Due to small size and type of this vessel no further details have been recorded by the authors.*

SMBP. 56. BP HAULIER (1955–1975)

O.N. 186960. 315g. 173n. ? d. 148′ 0″ × 29′ 1″ × ?.
6-cyl. 4 S.C.S.A. (222 × 292mm) oil engine manufactured by Blackstone & Company Ltd., Stamford, geared to a directional propeller.
Powered tank barge.

22.4.1955: Launched by J. Pollock, Sons & Company Ltd., Faversham (Yard No. 2060), for Shell-Mex & BP Ltd. 8.1955: Completed. 1975: Sold to A. Cornish. *Due to small size and type of this vessel no further details have been recorded by the authors.*

1SMBP. 57. SHELLDRAKE (1955–)

33g. ? n. ? × ? × ?.
Unspecified oil engine.
Towing launch.

6.1955: Completed by unspecified builders, for Shell-Mex & BP Ltd. *Due to small size and type of this vessel no further details have been recorded by the authors.*

SMBP. 58. SHELL WELDER (2) (1955–1973)

O.N. 186210. 569g. 202 n. ? d. 170′ 11″ × 29′8″ × 10′ 5⅝″.
6-cyl. 2 S.C.S.A. (265 × 345mm) oil engine manufactured by Crossley Bros Ltd., Manchester. 570 bhp.
Coastal oil products tanker.

12.11.1954: Launched by Clelands (Successors) Ltd., Wallsend (Yard No.193), for Shell-Mex & BP Ltd. 17.3.1955: Completed. 1973: Sold to Pounds Shipowners and Shipbreakers Ltd., Portsmouth. 1973: Sold to Northwood (Fareham) Ltd, converted into a dredger and renamed STEEL WELDER. 1993: Reported by Lloyd's Register as having been demolished.

SMBP. 59. SHELL FARMER (1955–1975)

O.N. 186308. 313g. 174n. 450d. 145′4″ × 29′4″ × ?.
6-cyl. 4 S.C.S.A. (222 × 292mm) oil engine manufactured by Blackstone & Company Ltd., Stamford, geared to a directional propeller.
Coastal oil products tanker.

8.7.1955: Launched by Cook, Welton & Gemmell, Ltd., Beverley (Yard No. 887), for Shell-Mex & BP Ltd. 21.10.1955: Completed. 1975: Sold to A. Cornish, and renamed COAST FARMER. 1976: Converted into a dredger. *Due to small size and type of this vessel*

Shell Supplier. (World Ship Society Photograph Library)

Shell Welder (1). (World Ship Society Photograph Library)

Shell Driller. (World Ship Society Photograph Library)

Shell Fitter. (World Ship Society Photograph Library)

BP Supervisor. (World Ship Society Photograph Library)

BP Haulier. (World Ship Society Photograph Library)

Shell Welder (2) (World Ship Society Photograph Library)

Shell Farmer. (World Ship Society Photograph Library)

no further details have been recorded by the authors.

SMBP. 60. FIDELITIE (1956–)

O.N. 165672. 140g. 110n. 109.2 × 17.4 × 4.7 feet.
Post 1939: Unspecified oil engine fitted.
Powered tank barge.

1929: Built for Medway Oil & Storage Company Ltd., Rochester. 1939: Motorised. 1955: Transferred to Power Petroleum Ltd. 1956: Sold to Shell-Mex & BP Ltd. *Due to small size and type of this vessel no further details have been recorded by the authors.*

SMBP. 61. UNITIE (1956–)

O.N. 164977. 84g. 63n. ? × ? × ? feet.
Post 1948: Unspecified oil engine fitted.
Powered tank barge.

24.11.1936: Launched by Henry Scarr, Hessle (Yard No. 382), for Medway Oil & Storage Company Ltd., Rochester. 1948: Motorised. 1955: Transferred to Power Petroleum Ltd. 1956: Sold to Shell-Mex & BP Ltd. *Due to small size and type of this vessel no further details have been recorded by the authors.*

SMBP. 62. ALACRITIE (1956–)

O.N. 164978. 84g. 63n. × ? × ? feet.
Post 1948: Unspecified oil engine fitted.
Powered tank barge.

2.12.1936: Launched by H. Scarr, Hessle (Yard No. 383), for Medway Oil & Storage Company Ltd., Rochester. 1948: Motorised. 1955: Transferred to Power Petroleum Ltd. 1956: Sold to Shell-Mex & BP Ltd. *Due to small size and type of this vessel no further details have been recorded by the authors.*

SMBP. 63. MOBILITIE (1956–1962)

O.N. 165741. 63g. 50n. 61.1 × 15.5 × 7.5 feet.
50 bhp. oil engine.
Powered tank barge.

24.10.1938: Launched by Richard Dunstan Ltd., Thorne (Yard No. 332), for Medway Oil & Storage Company Ltd., Rochester. 1955: Transferred to Power Petroleum Ltd. 1956: Sold to Shell-Mex & BP Ltd. 1962: Sold to Collinson's Waterboats Ltd., Hull. *Due to small size and type of this vessel no further details have been recorded by the authors.*

SMBP. 64. TENACITIE (1956–1960)

O.N. 165742. 63g. 50n. 61.1 × 15.5 × 7.5 feet.
50 bhp. oil engine.
Powered tank barge.

14.12.1938: Launched by Richard Dunston Ltd., Thorne (Yard No. 333), for Medway Oil & Storage Company Ltd., Rochester. 1955: Transferred to Power Petroleum Ltd. 1956: Sold to Shell-Mex & BP Ltd. 1960: Sold to Hull Waterboats Company Ltd., and R. C. Collinson, Hull, and renamed WATERBOAT No. 3. *Due to small size and type of this vessel no further details have been recorded by the authors.*

SMBP. 65. SHELL ROADBUILDER (1956–1971)

O.N. 187400. 301g. 171n. 450d.
139′ 3″ × 21′ 10 × 10′ 5½″.
6-cyl. 4 S.C.S.A. (222 × 292mm) oil engine manufactured by Blackstone & Company Ltd., Stamford, geared to a directional propeller. 324 bhp.
Coastal oil products tanker.

9.12.1955: Launched by Clelands (Successors) Ltd., Wallsend (Yard No. 205), for Shell-Mex & BP Ltd. 25.5.1956: Completed. 1971: Sold to Southern Tanker & Bunkering Company Ltd., and renamed SOUTHERNSTAN. 1975: Sold to Bowker & King Ltd., London, and renamed BURLESDON. 1981: Sold to Gillyot & Scott Ltd., Hull. 1986: Sold for demolition. 8.1987: Demolition at Southampton, completed.

SMBP. 66. SHELL STEELMAKER (1956–1969)

O.N. 187363. 303g. 189 n. ? d. 139′ 3″ × 21′ 9″ × 10′ 5½″.
6-cyl. 4 S.C.S.A. (222 × 292mm) oil engine manufactured by Blackstone & Company Ltd., Stamford, geared to a directional propeller. 324bhp.
Coastal oil products tanker.

5.12.1955: Launched by Cook, Welton & Gemmell, Ltd., Beverley (Yard No. 911), for

Shell Roadbuilder. (World Ship Society Photograph Library)

Shell Steelmaker. (World Ship Society Photograph Library)

BP Manufacturer. (World Ship Society Photograph Library)

BP Miller. (World Ship Society Photograph Library)

BP Explorer. (World Ship Society Photograph Library)

Shell-Mex & BP Ltd. 28.2.1956: Completed. 1969: Sold to J. P. Knight (London) Ltd., and renamed KINGSCLERE. 1983: Sold to Henderson-Morez Ltd., for demolition at Northfleet. 5.1993: Work commenced.

SMBP. 67. BP MANUFACTURER (1956–1968)

O.N. 187438. 303g. 188n. 460d.
139′ 6″ × 21′ 10″ × 10′ 5¼″.
6-cyl. 4 S.C.S.A. (222 × 292mm) oil engine manufactured by Blackstone & Company Ltd., Stamford, geared to a directional propeller.
Coastal oil products tanker.

20.12.1955: Launched by W. J. Yarwood & Sons Ltd., Northwich (Yard No. 899), for Shell-Mex & BP Ltd. 20.7.1956: Completed. 1968: Sold to J. P. Knight (London) Ltd., and renamed KINGSTHORPE. *Due to small size and type of this vessel no further details have been recorded by the authors.*

SMBP. 68. BP MILLER (1956–1969)

O.N. 187368. 301g. 173n. ? d. 139′ 3″ × 21′ 10″ × 10′ 6″.
6-cyl. 4 S.C.S.A. (222 × 292mm) oil engine manufactured by Blackstone & Company Ltd., Stamford, geared to a directional propeller.
Coastal oil products tanker.

5.10.1955: Launched by Clelands (Successors) Ltd., Wallsend (Yard No. 204), for Shell-Mex & BP Ltd. 1.3.1956: Completed. 1969: Sold to Celtic Coasters Ltd., Eire. 1971: Renamed CELTIC III. 1974: Sold for demolition.

SMBP. 69. BP EXPLORER (1) (1957–1961)

O.N. 187368. 303g. 188n. 460d. 139′ 6″ × 21′ 10″ × 10′ 5″.
6-cyl. 4 S.C.S.A. (222 × 292mm) oil engine manufactured by Blackstone & Company Ltd., Dursley, geared to a directional propeller.
Coastal oil products tanker.

28.9.1956: Launched by W. J. Yarwood & Sons Ltd., Northwich (Yard No. 900), for Shell-Mex & BP Ltd. 31.12.1956: Completed. 3.1.1957: Delivered. 17.2.1961: Whilst on a voyage from Swansea to Gloucester, capsized at Berkeley, R. Severn. Drifted upriver and grounded on Northern Bank, Lydney. Refloated and towed in her inverted state to Sharpness. 20.4.1961: Righted, subsequently refurbished, and renamed BP DRIVER. *Due to small size and type of this vessel no further details have been recorded by the authors.*

SMBP. 70. SHELL GLASSMAKER (1957–1969)

O.N. 187629. 303g. 188n. 460d.
139′ 6″ × 21′ 10″ × 10′ 5¾″.
6-cyl. 4 S.C.S.A. (222 × 292mm) oil engine manufactured by Blackstone & Company Ltd., Stamford, geared to a directional propeller.
Coastal oil products tanker.

7.5.1957: Launched by W. J. Yarwood & Sons Ltd., Northwich (Yard No. 902), for Shell-Mex & BP Ltd. 28.8.1957: Completed. 1969: Sold to Celtic Coasters Ltd., Eire, and renamed CELTIC II. 1971: Sold to Haulbowline Industries Ltd. Passage West, Cork, for demolition.

SMBP. 71. SHELL TRAVELLER (1958–1969)

O.N. 187716. 303g. 189n. 460d. 139′ 3″ × 21′ 9″ × 10′ 5½″.
6-cyl. 4 S.C.S.A. (222 × 292mm) oil engine manufactured by Blackstone & Company Ltd., Stamford, geared to a directional propeller. 324bhp.
Coastal oil products tanker.

21.10.1957: Launched by Cook, Welton & Gemmell Ltd., Beverley (Yard No. 911a), for Shell-Mex & BP Ltd. 27.1.1958: Completed. 1969: Sold to Celtic Coasters Ltd., Eire, and renamed CELTIC I. 3.1972: Haulbowline Industries Ltd. commenced demolition at Passage West, Cork.

SMBP. 72. BEN BATES (1959–1972)

O.N. 187507. 489g. 212n. 500d. 159′ 9″ × 27′ 10″ × 12′ 0¼″. Post 1961: 522g. 246n. 696d. 181′ 0″ × 27′ 7″ × 11′ 7″. 6-cyl. 2 S.C.S.A. (250 × 420mm) oil engine manufactured by British Polar Engines Ltd., Glasgow. 560 bhp. Coastal oil products tanker.

6.9.1956: Launched by Rowhedge Ironworks Company Ltd., Rowhedge (Yard No. 840), for National Benzole Company Ltd., London. 17.12.1956: Completed. 1959: Sold to Shell-Mex & BP Ltd. 1961: Lengthened. 1972: Sold to Woodward's Oil Ltd., Goose Bay, Labrador, retaining London registry. 1973: Renamed TANA WOODWARD. 1976: Sold to Coastal Shipping Ltd., St Johns NF. 6.1986: Laid-up with surveys overdue. 1987: Sold for demolition.

SMBP. 73. BEN HEBDEN (1959–1965)

O.N. 181777. 410g. 184n. 390d. 145′ 0″ × 25′ 0″ × 11′ 5″. 6-cyl. 2 S.C.S.A. (245 × 420mm) oil engine manufactured by British Polar Engines Ltd., Glasgow. Coastal oil products tanker.

11.1947: Completed by Rowhedge Ironworks Company Ltd., Rowhedge (Yard No. 675), for National Benzole Company Ltd. 1959: Sold to Shell-Mex & BP Ltd. 1965: Sold to Penfolds Builders Merchants Ltd., converted into a gravel dredger, and renamed PEN ITCHEN. 1966: Sold to Seaborne Aggregate Company Ltd. 1968: Sold to Fleetwood Sand & Fravel Company. 1975: Sold to Kingston Minerals Ltd. 1976: Demolition commenced at Fleetwood by Mayer, Newman & Company Ltd.

SMBP. 74. BEN HITTINGER (1959–1972)

O.N. 184473. 446g. 197n. 510d. 160′ 0″ × 27′ 7″ × 11′ 10″. Post 1961: 522g. 246n. 696d. 181′ 0″ × 27′ 7″ × 11′ 7″. 6-cyl. 2 S.C.S.A. (250 × 420mm) oil engines manufactured by British Polar Engines Ltd., Glasgow. 560 bhp. Coastal oil products tanker.

21.5.1951: Launched by Charles Hill & Sons Ltd., Bristol (Yard No. 373), for National Benzole Company Ltd. 7.1951: Completed. 1959: Sold to Shell-Mex & BP Ltd. 1961: Lengthened. 1972: Sold to Ball & Plumb Shipping Company Ltd., Gravesend, and renamed SPIRIT CARRIER II. 1975: Sold to E. W. Tankers Ltd., Gravesend. 1976: Sold to J. P. Knight (London) Ltd., and renamed KINGSTHORPE. for use as a mooring hulk. 1986: Sold for demolition.

SMBP. 75. BEN HAROLD SMITH (1959–1975)

O.N. 184701. 325g. 162n. 322d. 136′ 0″ × 26′ 1″ × 7′ 6¾″. 4-cyl. 2 S.C.S.A. (250 × 420mm) M441 type oil engine manufactured by British Polar Engines Ltd., Glasgow. 310 bhp. Coastal oil products tanker.

22.5.1952: Launched by Rowhedge Ironworks Company Ltd., Rowhedge (Yard No. 742), for National Benzole Company Ltd., London. 4.9.1952: Completed. 1959: Sold to Shell-Mex & BP Ltd., London. 1975: Transferred to BP Oil Ltd. 1976: Renamed BP ZEST. 1980: Sold

Shell Glassmaker. (World Ship Society Photograph Library)

Shell Traveller. (World Ship Society Photograph Library)

Ben Bates. (J K Byass)

Ben Hebden with National Benzole funnel. (World Ship Society Photograph Library)

Ben Hittinger. (World Ship Society Photograph Library)

Ben Harold Smith with National Benzole markings. (World Ship Society Photograph Library)

to Gamma Navigation Company, Greece, and renamed GAMMA. 1982: Renamed DOXA. 1989: Vera Shipping Company Ltd., appointed as managers. 1994: Owners deleted. 1996: Sold to Thalassopouli Maritime Company, Piraeus, and renamed VASOULA. Still listed in Lloyd's Register 2003/04.

SMBP. 76. BEN HENSHAW (1959–1959)

O.N. 163694. 377g. 168n. 350d. 142′ 0″ × 25′ 1″ × 11′ 6″. Two, 5-cyl. 2 S.C.S.A. (280 × 335mm) oil engines manufactured by L. Gardner & Sons Ltd., Manchester. Coastal oil products tanker.

10.1933: Completed by Rowhedge Ironworks Company Ltd., Rowhedge (Yard No. 5484), for National Benzole Company Ltd. 1959: Sold to Shell-Mex & BP Ltd. thence for demolition.

SMBP. 77. BEN JOHNSON (1959–1964)

O.N. 166438. 228g. 100n. 240d. 118′ 0″ × 22′ 8″ × 9′ 3½″. 7-cyl. 2 S.C.S.A. (180 × 300mm) Polar type oil engine manufactured by British Auxiliaries Ltd., Glasgow. Powered tank barge.

4.1938: Completed by Rowhedge Ironworks Company Ltd., Rowhedge (Yard No. 561), for National Benzole Company Ltd. 1959: Sold to Shell-Mex & BP Ltd. 1964: Sold to John P. Katsoulakos, Greece, and renamed VARKIZA. *Due to small size and type of this vessel no further details have been recorded by the authors.*

SMBP. 78. BEN OLLIVER (1959–)

O.N. 164497. 147g. 48n. 140d. 95′ 0″ × 19′ 1″ × 8′ 6″. 5-cyl. 2 S.C.S.A. (180 × 300mm) Polar type oil engine manufactured by British Auxiliaries Ltd., Glasgow. Powered tank barge.

7.1935: Completed by Rowhedge Ironworks Company Ltd., Rowhedge (Yard No. 509), for National Benzole Company Ltd. 1959: Sold to Shell-Mex & BP Ltd. *Due to small size and type of this vessel no further details have been recorded by the authors.*

SMBP. 79. BEN SADLER (1959)

O.N. 162656. 289g. 161n. 320d. 136′ 6″ × 25′ 0″ × 7′ 9½″. 5-cyl. 2 S.C.S.A. (280 × 335mm) oil engine manufactured by Norris, Henty & Gardner Ltd., Manchester. Powered tank barge.

11.1931: Completed by Rowhedge Ironworks Company Ltd., Rowhedge, for National Benzole Company Ltd. 1959: Sold to Shell-Mex & BP Ltd. 1959: Sold for demolition.

SMBP. 80. SHELL-MEX 4 (1960)

O.N. 146194. 423g. 227n. 140.5 × 27.6 × 10.9 feet. C.2-cyl. (15½″ & 32″ × 24″) engine manufactured by I. J. Abdela & Mitchell Ltd., Brimscombe. 58 rhp. Powered tank barge.

12.1921: Completed by I. J. Abdela & Mitchell Ltd., Queensferry (Yard No. 462), for Eagle Oil & Shipping Company Ltd., London. 22.5.1960: Transferred to Shell-Mex & BP Ltd. 1.6.1960: Arrived at Preston for demolition

SMBP. 80a. BP DRIVER (1961–)

see ship No. SMBP.69 above.

SMPB. 80b. SHELL-MEX 5 (1963–1966)

O.N. 145296. 423g. 227n. 140.5 × 27.6 × 10.9 feet. C.2-cyl. (15½″ & 32″ × 24″) engine manufactured by I. J. Abdela & Mitchell Ltd., Brimscombe. 58 rhp. Powered tank barge.

4.1921: Completed by I. J. Abdela & Mitchell Ltd., Queensferry (Yard No. 460) for Eagle Oil & Shipping Company Ltd., London. 1959: Transferred to Cork and Irish Registry (O.N. 400161). 1963: Transferred to Shell-Mex & BP Ltd. 31.12.1966: Delivered to Irish Shipbreakers Ltd., Ballinacurra, County Cork for demolition.

Shell-Mex 5. (World Ship Society Photograph Library)

Shell-Mex 4. (World Ship Society Photograph Library)

Shell Dispenser. (J K Byass)

SMBP. 81. SHELL DISPENSER (1963–1975)

O.N. 304728. 239g. 119n. 254d. 133′ 0″ × 27′ 1″ × ?. 6-cyl. 4 S.C.S.A. (8¾″ × 11½″) oil engine manufactured by Lister Blackstone Marine Ltd., Dursley. 337 bhp Powered tank barge.

23.7.1963: Launched by J. W. Cook &

Company (Wivenhoe) Ltd., Wivenhoe (Yard No. 1252), for Shell-Mex & BP Ltd. 4.11.1963: Completed. 1975: Transferred to Shell UK Ltd. 1978: Sold to Ostrakon Maritime Company S. A., Greece, and renamed BYRON. 1994: Deleted from Lloyd's Register as 'for harbour use only'.

SMBP. 82. HAMBLE (1964–1975)

O.N. 305976. 1,182g. 530n. 1,424d.
214′ 10″ × 37′ 3″ × 14′ 0½″.
Post 1982: 1,657g. 1,026n. 1,511d.
83.67 × 11.36 × 4.280 metres.
6-cyl. 2 S.C.S.A. (340 × 570mm) MN16S type oil engine manufactured by British Polar Engines Ltd., Glasgow. 1,230 bhp.
Coastal oil products tanker.

14.2.1964: Launched by Henry Robb Ltd., Leith (Yard No. 486), for Shell-Mex & BP Ltd. 24.4.1964: Completed. 1975: Transferred to Shell UK Ltd. 1979: Renamed SHELL REFINER. 1981: Sold to Shediac Bulk Shipping Company Ltd., Canada, and renamed METRO STAR. 1982: Lengthened by Marystown Shipyard Ltd. 31.10.1982: Whilst on a loaded voyage from Halifax N.S. to Havre St. Pierre, touched bottom, holed and was beached in St Augustin Bay at position 51.10.18N., 58.31.42W. with a flooding engine room. 4.11.1982: Refloated, and although declared a constructive total loss was repaired, including lengthening and deepening. 1984: Sold to Laurentide Financial Corporation Ltd. (Shediac Tanker Corporation, managers), Canada. 1987: Sold to Coastal Shipping Ltd., Canada, and renamed ERIN T. 1992: Sold to Specialize Shipping Chartering Inc., Panama, and renamed MARINE SUPPLIER. 1995: Sold to unspecified Nigerian flag buyers for employment as a bunkering vessel. Still listed without owners in Lloyd's Register 2003/04.

SMBP. 83. KILLINGHOLME (1964–1975)

O.N. 306044. 1,182g. 530n. 1,424d.
214′ 10″ × 37′ 3″ × 14′ 0½″.
6-cyl. 2 S.C.S.A. (340 × 570mm) MN16S type oil engine manufactured by British Polar Engines Ltd., Glasgow. 1,230 bhp.
Coastal oil products tanker.

14.5.1964: Launched by Henry Robb Ltd., Leith (Yard No. 487), for Shell-Mex & BP Ltd., London. 14.7.1964: Completed. 1975: Transferred to BP Oil Ltd. 1976: Renamed BP SCORCHER. 1983: Sold to Ferrea Shipping Corp., Liberia, and renamed NIGERIAN STAR (Honduran registry). 1995: Owners deleted. Still listed without owners in Lloyd's Register 2003/04.

Falmouth with Shell funnel–after the 1975 separation. (J K Byass)

SMBP. 84. ST. LEONARDS (1964–1975)

O.N. 306096. 215g. 114n. 300d. 117′ 0″ × 26′ 7″ × ?.
6-cyl. 4 S.C.S.A. (8¾″ × 11½″) ER6 type oil engine manufactured by Blackstone & Company Ltd., Stamford. 337 bhp.
Powered tank barge.

13.5.1964: Launched by R. Dunston (Hessle) Ltd., Hessle (Yard No. S813), for Shell-Mex & BP Ltd. 1.10.1964: Completed. 1968: Sold to J. R. L. Moore, London (Shell-Mex & BP Ltd., operator managers), London. 1975: Transferred to BP Oil Ltd. 1976: Renamed BP STURDY. 1981: Sold to Bullas Tankcraft Company Ltd., Southfleet, and renamed CHRISTIAN B. 5.1985: Medway Metals Ltd., commenced demolition at Bloors Wharf, Rainham.

SMBP. 85. TORKSEY (1964–1975)

O.N. 306174. 215g. 114n. 300d. 117′ 0″ × 26′ 7″ × ?.
6-cyl. 4 S.C.S.A. (8¾″ × 11½″) ER6 type oil engine manufactured by Blackstone & Company Ltd., Stamford. 337 bhp.
Powered tank barge.

3.9.1964: Launched by R. Dunston (Hessle) Ltd., Hessle (Yard No. S814), for Shell-Mex & BP Ltd., London. 8.12.1964: Completed. 1975: Transferred to BP Oil Ltd. 1976: Renamed BP SPRITE. 1984: Sold to Exnor Craggs Ltd., Immingham, and renamed GOOD HAND. 1993: Sold to General Port Services, London, and renamed GOODHAND. 1993: Sold to Southern Bunkering Ltd. (General Port Services managers), Isle of Wight. Still listed in Lloyd's Register 2003/04.

SMBP. 86. FALMOUTH (1965–1975)

O.N. 307930. 982g. 394n. 1,094d.
201′ 7″ × 34′ 5″ × 13′ 10″.
6-cyl. 2 S.C.S.A. (340 × 570mm) MN16 type oil engine manufactured by British Polar Engines Ltd., Glasgow. 1,120 bhp.
Coastal oil products tanker.

18.3.1965: Launched by Grangemouth Dockyard Company Ltd., Grangemouth (Yard No. 534), for Shell-Mex & BP Ltd., London. 22.4.1965: Suffered extensive fire damage whilst fitting out. 30.4.1965: Arrived under tow at Smith's Dock Company Ltd., N. Shields yard for repair. 21.9.1965: Completed. 1975: Transferred to Shell UK Ltd. 1980: Renamed SHELL MARINER. 1982: Sold to Coastal Shipping Ltd., Canada and renamed JENNIE W, retaining London registry. 1996: Sold to Agencia Commercial Maritima Gavino Reyes S. A., Panama. 1999: Sold to Nadine Investments S. A., Panama, and renamed ORFEO. 2000: Sold to unspecified Mexico flag operators. Still listed without owners in Lloyd's Register 2003/04.

SMBP. 87. PARTINGTON (1965–1975)

O.N. 307998. 982g. 394n. 1,094d.
201′ 7″ × 34′ 5″ × 13′ 10″.
6-cyl. 2 S.C.S.A. (340 × 570mm) MN16 type oil engine manufactured by British Polar Engines Ltd., Glasgow. 1,120 bhp.
Coastal oil products tanker.

30.6.1965: Launched by Grangemouth Dockyard Company Ltd., Grangemouth (Yard No. 535), for Shell-Mex & BP Ltd., London. 15.12.1965: Completed. 1975: Transferred to Shell UK Ltd. 1979: Renamed SHELL SCIENTIST. 1981: Sold to Metro Oil Company Ltd., Canada and renamed METRO SUN. 1982: Sold to Shediac Coastal Carrier Corporation, Canada. 1984: Sold to Laurentide Financial Corporation Ltd. (Shediac Tanker Corporation, managers), Canada. 1985: Sold to ULS International Inc., Canada and renamed HAMILTON ENERGY. 1985: Sold to Provmar Fuels Inc., Canada. 1993: ULS Corporation appointed as managers. Still listed in Lloyd's Register 2003/04.

SMBP. 88. TEESPORT (1966–1975)

O.N. 309763. 1,177g. 525n. 1,414d.
215′ 0″ × 37′ 3″ × 14′ 1″.
6-cyl. 2 S.C.S.A. (340 × 570mm) MN16S type oil engine manufactured by British Polar Engines Ltd., Glasgow. 1,230 bhp.
Coastal oil products tanker.

17.8.1965: Ordered as ESK BANK from Grangemouth Dockyard Company Ltd.,

Killingholme. (World Ship Society Photograph Library)

Partington. (J K Byass)

Teesport. (J K Byass)

Grangemouth (Yard No. 537), by Shell-Mex & BP Ltd., London. 16.8.1966: Launched as TEESPORT. 13.10.1966: Completed. 1975: Transferred to Shell UK Ltd. 1979: Renamed SHELL TRADER. 1990: Sold to Gozo Maritime Ltd. (North Africa-Middle East Shipping Company Ltd (NAMESCO), managers), Malta, and renamed GOZO TRADER. 1992: Sold to Challenge Navigation Ltd. (same managers), Malta, and renamed STAR I. 1993: Renamed STAR ONE. 1995: Sold to Olympus Navigation Ltd. (Island Oil Ltd., managers), Malta, and renamed VERONICA. Still listed in Lloyd's Register 2003/04.

SMBP. 89. DINGLE BANK (1966–1975)

O.N. 308211. 1,177g. 525n. 1,414d. 215′ 0″ × 37′ 3″ × 14′ 1″.
6-cyl. 2 S.C.S.A. (340 × 570mm) MN16S type oil engine manufactured by British Polar Engines Ltd., Glasgow. 1,230 bhp.
Coastal oil products tanker.

17.8.1965: Ordered from Grangemouth Dockyard Company Ltd., Grangemouth (Yard No. 536), by Shell-Mex & BP Ltd., London. 21.4.1966: Launched. 27.6.1966: Completed. 1975: Transferred to Shell UK Ltd. 1979: Renamed SHELL ENGINEER. 1990: Sold to Gozo Maritime Ltd. (North Africa-Middle East Shipping Company Ltd (NAMESCO), managers), Malta, and renamed GOZO ENGINEER. 1994: Sold to West Coast Shipping Line Ltd., Nigeria, and renamed BEL-AIR. 1998: Sold to Hensmor Nigeria Ltd., and renamed HENSMOR AGRO ALLIDE. Still listed in Lloyd's Register 2003/04.

SMBP. 90. PRONTO (1967–1975)

O.N. 309916. 588g. 243n. 811d. 172′ 3″ × 35′ 1″ × 9′ 3″.
Post 1970: 652g. 310n. 1,008d. 193′ 3″ × 35′ 1″ × 9′ 0″.
6-cyl. 4 S.C.S.A. (9¾″ × 12½″) oil engine manufactured by Mirrlees National Ltd., Stockport. 708 bhp.
Powered tank barge.

16.9.1966: Launched by Cochrane & Sons Ltd., Selby (Yard No. 1508), for Shell-Mex & BP Ltd. 20.6.1967: Completed. 1970: Lengthened. 1975: Transferred to BP Oil Ltd. 1976: Renamed BP ALERT. 1983: Sold to Songhai Petroleum Company Ltd., Nigeria, and renamed SONGHAI No.1. 1988: Entry removed from Lloyd's Register – for river service only.

SMBP. 91. PERFECTO (1967–1975)

O.N. 334609. 588g. 243n. 811d. 172′ 3″ × 35′ 1″ × 9′ 3″.
Post 1969: 652g. 310n. 1,008d. 193′ 3″ × 35′ 1″ × 9′ 0″.
6-cyl. 4 S.C.S.A. (9¾″ × 12½″) oil engine manufactured by Mirrlees National Ltd., Stockport. 708 bhp.
Post 1975: 8-cyl. 4 S.C.S.A. (260 × 450mm) Alpha type oil engine manufactured by Alpha Diesel AS, Frederickshavn, geared to a controllable-pitch propeller. 582bhp.
Powered tank barge.

28.1.1967: Launched by Cochrane & Sons Ltd., Selby (Yard No.1509), for Shell-Mex & BP Ltd. 24.8.1967: Completed. 1969: Lengthened. 1975: Transferred to Shell UK Ltd. 9.1975: Re-engined. 1979: Renamed SHELL DRIVER. 1989: Sold to C. Crawley Ltd., Gravesend, and reverted to PERFECTO. 1999: Sold to Nortech (Scotland) Ltd. 2000: Solf to Petrostar Nigeria Ltd., and renamed FECTO, under Sao Tome and Principe flag. Still listed in Lloyd's Register 2003/04

Pronto. (World Ship Society Photograph Library)

Dingle Bank with Shell funnel–after the 1975 separation. (J K Byass)

Perfecto (above J K Byass) below in later life with her wheelhouse moved further aft. (World Ship Society Photograph Library)

Poilo. (J K Byass)

SMBP. 92. POILO (2) (1967–1976)

O.N. 334662. 581g. 238n. 811d. 171′ 3″ × 35′ 1″ × 9′ 3″.
Post 1969: 652g. 310n. 1,008d. 193′ 3″ × 35′ 1″ × 9′ 0″.
6-cyl. 4 S.C.S.A. (8″ × 10¾″) Ruston 6AP2 type oil engine manufactured by Ruston & Hornsby Ltd., Lincoln. 755 bhp.
Powered tank barge.

25.7.1967: Launched by Appledore Shipbuilders Ltd., Appledore (Yard No. A.S.36), for Shell-Mex & BP Ltd. 11.10.1967: Completed. 1969: Lengthened. 1975: Transferred to Shell UK Ltd. 1979: Renamed SHELL TRANSPORTER. 1984: Sold to John H. Whitaker (Tankers) Ltd., Hull, and renamed HUMBER TRANSPORTER. 1987: Sold to Whitfleet Ltd. (John H. Whitaker (Holdings) Ltd., managers) Hull. 1993: Sold to John H. Whitaker (Tankers) Ltd. 1998: Sold to Delta Marine, and renamed DELMAR EAGLE under the Nigeria flag. Still listed in Lloyd's Register 2003/04.

SMBP. 93. PERSO (2) (1967–1975)

O.N. 334693. 581g. 238n. 811d. 171′ 3″ × 35′ 1″ × 9′ 3″.
Post 1969: 647g. 311n. 1,056d. 193′ 3″ × 35′ 1″ × 9′ 0″.
6-cyl. 4 S.C.S.A. (8″ × 10¾″) Ruston 6AP2 type oil engine manufactured by Ruston & Hornsby Ltd., Lincoln. 755 bhp.
Powered tank barge.

3.10.1967: Launched by Appledore Shipbuilders Ltd., Appledore (Yard No. A.S.37), for Shell-Mex & BP Ltd. 21.11.1967: Completed. 1969: Lengthened. 1975: Transferred to Shell UK Ltd. 1980: Sold to Agencia Maritima Challaco S.r.L., Argentina, and renamed ESTRELLA DEL ALBA. 1995: Sold to Jorge Rodolfo Ibargoyen, under Panamanian flag. Entry removed from Lloyd's Register 2003/04.

SMBP. 94. POINT LAW (1967–197)

O.N. 334704. 1,529g. 762n. 2,221d. 249′ 2″ × 40′ 11″ × 15′ 6″.
6-cyl. 2 S.C.S.A.(340 × 570mm) MN16S type oil engine manufactured by British Polar Engines Ltd., Glasgow. 1,280 bhp.
Coastal oil products tanker.

20.9.1967: Launched by Hall, Russell & Company Ltd., Aberdeen (Yard No. 935), for Shell-Mex & BP Ltd., London. 18.12.1967: Completed. 15.7.1975: Whilst on a ballast voyage from St. Sampson, Guernsey, to the Isle of Grain, grounded S. W. of Alderney, Channel Islands, was abandoned and later broke up.

SMBP. 95. PANDO (2) (1968–1975)

O.N. 334743. 581g. 238n. 811d. 171′ 3″ × 35′ 1″ × 9′ 3″.
Post 1969: 647g. 311n. 1,056d. 193′ 3″ × 35′ 1″ × 9′ 0″.
6-cyl. 4 S.C.S.A. (8″ × 10¾″) 6AP2 type oil engine manufactured by Ruston & Hornsby Ltd., Lincoln. 755 bhp.
Powered tank barge.

31.10.1967: Launched by Appledore Shipbuilders Ltd., Appledore (Yard No. A.S.38), for Shell-Mex & BP Ltd. 10.1.1968: Completed. 1969: Lengthened. 1975: Transferred to Shell UK Ltd. 1977: Sold to Bowker & King Ltd., London and renamed BEBINGTON. 1983: Sold to Ormara Navigation Company Ltd., Cyprus, and renamed VERMION. 1984: Sold to Dean and Dyball Shipping Ltd., Poole, converted into an effluent tanker, and renamed JAMES RAYEL. 1988: Sold to John H. Whitaker (Tankers) Ltd., Hull, re-converted into a tank barge and renamed SOLENT RAIDER.1998: Sold to

Point Law. (World Ship Society Photograph Library)

Pando. (World Ship Society Photograph Library)

Inverness leaving Gt. Yarmouth. (J K Byass)

Ardrossan with Shell funnel – after the 1975 separation. (J K Byass)

Island Petroleum Mariner Ltd. (Petronav Ship Management Ltd., managers), and renamed ISLAND MARINER under the Cypriot flag. Still listed in Lloyd's Register 2003/04.

SMBP. 96. INVERNESS (1968–1975)

O.N. 334765. 1,529g. 762n. 2,228d.
249′ 2″ × 40′ 11″ × 15′ 6″.
As built: 6-cyl. 2 S.C.S.A. (340 × 670mm) oil engine manufactured by British Polar Engines Ltd., Glasgow, geared to a controllable-pitch propeller. 1,280 bhp.
Post 1987: 8-cyl. 4 S.C.S.A. (225 × 300mm) Alpha 8L23/30KV type oil engine manufactured by MAN-B&W Diesel AS Frederikshavn. 1,468 bhp.
Coastal oil products tanker.

16.12.1967: Launched by Hall, Russell & Company Ltd., Aberdeen (Yard No.936), for Shell-Mex & BP Ltd., London. 16.2.1968: Completed. 6.1970: Fitted with a new double bottom. 1975: Transferred to BP Oil Ltd. 1976: Renamed BP BATTLER. 11.1987: Re-engined by Wear Dockyard Ltd., Sunderland. 1989: Owners restyled as BP Oil UK Ltd. 1997: Renamed BORDER BATTLER (BP Amoco Shipping Ltd., managers). Still listed in Lloyd's Register 2003/04

SMBP. 97. ARDROSSAN (1968–1975)

O.N. 335716. 1,529g. 762n. 2,221d.
249′ 2″ × 40′ 11″ × 15′ 3¾″.
Post 1991: 1,580g. 974n. 2,654d.
84.33 × 12.84 × 4.668 metres.
12-cyl. 4 S.C.S.A.(250 × 300mm) Polar vee type oil engine manufactured by Nydqvist & Holm Ab., Trollhattan. 1,350 bhp.
Post 1991: 6-cyl. 4 S.C.S.A. (280 × 320mm) Alpha 6S28LU type oil engine manufactured in 1974 by B&W-Alpha Diesel AS, Frederikshavn. 1,591 bhp. 14.5 kts.
Coastal oil products tanker.

29.2.1968: Launched by Hall, Russell & Company Ltd., Aberdeen (Yard No. 937), for Shell-Mex & BP Ltd., London. 3.5.1968: Completed. 1975: Transferred to Shell UK Ltd. 1979: Renamed SHELL CRAFTSMAN. 1989: Shell U.K. Oil Ltd., appointed as managers. 1991: Lengthened and re-engined by Wear Dockyard Ltd. 1993: Renamed ACHATINA. 1999: Sold to F. T. Everard & Sons Management Ltd., London, and renamed APTITY. 2001: Sold to Fairseas Explorer Shipping Ltd. (EDT Towage & Salvage Company Ltd., managers), and renamed BONNIE, under the Cyprus flag. Still listed in Lloyd's Register 2003/04

SMBP. 98. GRANGEMOUTH (1968–1975)

O.N. 335821. 1,529g. 762n. 2,221d.
249′ 2″ × 40′ 11″ × 15′ 6″.
As built: 12-cyl. 4 S.C.S.A. (250 × 300mm) Polar vee type oil engine manufactured by Nydqvist & Holm Ab, Trollhattan, geared to a controllable-pitch propeller. 1,250 bhp.
Post 1987: 8-cyl. 4 S.C.S.A. (225 × 300mm) Alpha 8L23/30KV type oil engine manufactured by MAN-B&W Diesel A/S Frederikshavn. 1,468 bhp.
Coastal oil products tanker.

25.4.1968: Launched by Hall, Russel & Company Ltd., Aberdeen (Yard No. 938), for Shell-Mex & BP Ltd., London. 2.7.1968: Completed. 1975: Transferred to BP Oil Ltd. 1976: Renamed BP. WARRIOR. 11.1987: Re-engined by Wear Dockyard Ltd., Sunderland. 1989: Owners restyled as BP Oil UK Ltd. 1997: Renamed BORDER WARRIOR (BP Amoco Shipping Ltd., managers). 22.8.2004: Arrived at Santander for demolition.

SMBP. 99. DUBLIN (1969–1975)

O.N. 337105. 1,077g. 493n. 1,537d.
214′ 9″ × 37′ 2″ × 14′ 7¼″.
As built: 8-cyl. 4 S.C.S.A. (250 × 300mm) MN16S type oil engine manufactured by British Polar Engines Ltd., Glasgow. 1,200 bhp.
Post 1974: 6-cyl. 4 S.C.S.A. (280 × 320) B&W type oil engine manufactured by Holeby Diesel Motor Fabrik, Holeby, geared to a controllable-pitch propeller. 1,590 bhp.
Post 1988: 8-cyl. 4 S.C.S.A. (225 × 300mm) Alpha 8L23/30 type oil engine manufactured by MAN-B&W Diesel A/S Frederikshavn. 1,468 bhp.
Coastal oil products tanker.

4.12.1968: Launched by Hall, Russell & Company Ltd., Aberdeen (Yard No. 944), for Shell-Mex & BP Ltd., London. 27.3.1969: Completed. 4.4.1969: Delivered. 1974: Re-engined. 1975: Transferred to BP Oil Ltd. 1976: Renamed BP SPRINGER. 11.1988: Re-engined by Wear Dockyard Ltd., Sunderland. 1989: Owners restyled as BP Oil UK Ltd. 1997: Renamed BORDER SPRINGER (BP Amoco Shipping Ltd., managers). 11.2004: Arrived at Santander for demolition.

SMBP. 100. CAERNARVON (1972–1975)

O.N. 358523. 1,210g. 574n. 1,300d.
217′ 2″ × 37′ 9″ × 14′ 4″.
8-cyl. 4 S.C.S.A. (250 × 300mm) Nohab F28V vee type oil engine manufactured by British Polar Engines Ltd., Glasgow. 1,200 bhp. 11 kts.
Coastal oil products tanker.

24.6.1972: Launched by Appledore Shipbuilders Ltd., Appledore (Yard No. A.S.88), for Shell-Mex & BP Ltd. 17.7.1972: Completed. 1975: Transferred to Shell UK Ltd. 1979: Renamed SHELL DIRECTOR. 1989: Shell U.K. Oil Ltd., appointed as managers.

Grangemouth. (J K Byass)

Dublin. (J K Byass)

Caernarvon. (J K Byass)

Plymouth with Shell funnel – after the 1975 separation. (World Ship Society Photograph Library)

Swansea. (J K Byass)

1993: Sold to C. Crawley Ltd., Gravesend, and renamed FRANK C. 1994: Sold to John H. Whitaker (Tankers) Ltd., and renamed WHITHAVEN. Still listed in Lloyd's Register 2003/04

SMBP. 101. PLYMOUTH (1972–1975)

O.N. 358618. 1,210g. 574n. 1,300d.
217′ 2″ × 37′ 9″ × 14′ 4″.
8-cyl. 4 S.C.S.A. (250 × 300mm) Nohab F28V vee type oil engine manufactured by British Polar Engines Ltd., Glasgow. 1,200 bhp.
Coastal oil products tanker.

22.8.1972: Launched by Appledore Shipbuilders Ltd., Appledore (Yard No. A.S.89), for Shell-Mex & BP Ltd. 11.9.1972: Completed. 1975: Transferred to Shell UK Ltd. 1979: Renamed SHELL SUPPLIER. 1989: Shell U.K. Oil Ltd., appointed as managers. 1992: Sold to Koumasi maritime Company Ltd. (Teodo Shipping Agency Ltd., managers), Malta, and renamed MODERN SUPPLIER. 1998: Sold to Universe Maritime Company, and renamed KONSTANTINA under Greek flag. Still listed in Lloyd's Register 2003/04

SMBP. 102. SWANSEA (1972–1975)

O.N. 358682. 1,598g. 771n. 2,305d.
259′ 0″ × 41′ 3″ × 15′ 6½″.
As built: 14-cyl. 4 S.C.S.A. (225 × 300mm) Alpha 14V23HU vee type oil engine manufactured by Alpha Diesel A/S, Frederikshavn, geared to a controllable-pitch propeller. 1,890 bhp.
Post 1977: 12-cyl. 4 S.C.S.A. (225 × 300mm) Alpha type oil engine manufactured by Alpha-Diesel A/S., Frederikshavn. 1,860 bhp.
Coastal oil products tanker.

11.10.1972: Launched by Appledore Shipbuilders Ltd., Appledore (Yard No. A.S.90), for Shell-Mex & BP Ltd., London. 24.11.1972: Completed. 1975: Transferred to BP Oil Ltd. 1976: Renamed BP JOUSTER. 5.1977: Re-engined. 1989: Owners restyled as BP Oil UK Ltd. 1997: Renamed BORDER JOUSTER (BP Amoco Shipping Ltd., managers). Still listed in Lloyd's Register 2003/04

SMBP. 103. DUNDEE (1972–1975)

O.N. 358762. 1,598g. 771n. 2,305d.
259′ 0″ × 41′ 3″ × 15′ 6½″.
14-cyl. 4 S.C.S.A. (225 × 300mm) Alpha 14V23HU vee type oil engine manufactured by Alpha-Diesel A/S, Frederikshavn, geared to a controllable-pitch propeller. 1,890 bhp.
Coastal oil products tanker.

25.11.1972: Launched by Appledore Shipbuilders Ltd., Appledore (Yard No. A.S.91), for Shell-Mex & BP Ltd. 14.12.1972: Completed. 1975: Transferred to Shell UK Ltd. 6.1977: Engine received major overhaul. 1979: Renamed SHELL EXPLORER. 1989: Shell U.K. Oil Ltd., appointed as managers. 1993: Sold to S.H. Supply S. A. (HCH Suez, managers), Panama, and renamed AL KARNAK III. Still listed in Lloyd's Register 2003/04

SMBP. 104. SHEPPEY (1974–1975)

O.N. 363490. 589g. 286n. 704d.
58.91 × 10.27 × 2.490 metres.
8-cyl. 2 S.C.S.A. (260 × 400) B&W 408-26VO type oil engine manufactured by Alpha-Diesel A/S, Frederikshavn, geared to a controllable-pitch propeller. 880 bhp.
Powered tank barge.

27.9.1974: Launched by Appledore Shipbuilders Ltd., Appledore (Yard No. A.S.102), for Shell-Mex & BP Ltd., London.

Dundee with Shell funnel – after the 1975 separation. (World Ship Society Photograph Library)

21.10.1974: Completed. 1975: Transferred to BP Oil Ltd. 1976: Renamed BP RAPID. 1986: Sold to Bullas Tankcraft Company Ltd., Rochester, and renamed RAPID. 1986: Renamed THAMES RAPID. 1994: Deleted from Lloyd's Register as 'for harbour use only'.

SMBP. 105. HARTY (1974–1975)

O.N. 363530. 589g. 286n. 704d. 59.14 × 10.04 × 2.490 metres.
8-cyl. 2 S.C.S.A. (260 × 400) B&W 408-26VO type oil engine manufactured by Alpha-Diesel A/S, Frederikshavn, geared to a controllable-pitch propeller. 880 bhp.
Powered tank barge.

16.11.1974: Launched by Appledore Shipbuilders Ltd., Appledore (Yard No. A.S.103), for Shell-Mex & BP Ltd., London. 26.11.1974: Completed. 1975: Transferred to Shell UK Ltd. 1979: Renamed SHELL DISTRIBUTOR. 1989: Shell U.K. Oil Ltd., appointed as managers. 1991: Sold to Port of Pembroke Ltd., Pembroke, converted into a bunkering tanker, and renamed G. D. DISTRIBUTOR. 11.1997: Laid-up with surveys overdue. 1998: Sold to Milford Dock Company. 1999: Sold to Tomini Shipping Company Ltd., Bolivia, and renamed M. C. BUTOR. .11.12.1999: Lloyd's Register class suspended upon vessel sailing from lay-up at Pembroke Dock. 2000: Lloyd's Register entry deleted – 'vessel no longer sea-going'.

Long-term Chartered From The Union Lighterage Company Ltd.

16, Philpot Lane
London

Vessels constructed for operation on long-term charter to Shell-Mex & BP Ltd.

UL. 1. SHELL SPIRIT 1 (1938–1972)

O.N. 167151. 440g. 234n. 157.5 × 32.1 × 8.9 feet.
8-cyl. 4 S.C.S.A. (11″ × 17¾″) oil engines manufactured by Humboldt Deutzmotoren A. G., Koeln-Deutz. 94 nhp.
Post 1974: 8-cyl. 4 S.C.S.A. (222 × 292mm) ER8 type oil engine manufactured in 1957 by Blackstone & Company Ltd., Stamford. 450 bhp. 8.5 kts.
Powered tank barge.

29.8.1938: Launched by L. Smit & Zoon, Kinderdijk (Yard No. 890), for Union Lighterage Company Ltd., London. 12.1938: Completed. 1966: Sold to Beagle Shipping Ltd. (Union Lighterage Company Ltd., managers), London. 1971: Sold by Spirit Shipping Ltd. (Wharf Holding Ltd., managers), London. 1972: Sold to Bowker & King Ltd., London, and renamed BOREHAM.1974: Re-engined. 1977: Sold to Mossad Shilbaya, Egypt. Still listed in Lloyd's Register 2003/04

UL .2. SHELL SPIRIT 2 (1939–1972)

O.N. 167162. 440g. 234n. 157.5 × 32.1 × 8.9 feet.
8-cyl. 4 S.C.S.A. (11″ × 17¾″) oil engines manufactured by Humboldt Deutzmotoren A. G., Koeln-Deutz. 94 nhp.
Powered tank barge.

29.9.1938: Launched by L. Smit & Zoon, Kinderdijk (Yard No. 891), for Union Lighterage Company Ltd., London. 1.1939: Completed. 1966: Sold to Beagle Shipping Ltd. (Union Lighterage Company Ltd., managers), London. 1971: Sold by Spirit Shipping Ltd. (Wharf Holding Ltd., managers), London. 1972: Sold to Bowker & King Ltd., London, and renamed BERMONDSEY. 1979: Sold for demolition.

UL. 3. PETRO (2) (1939–1972)

O.N. 167275. 444g. 228n. 157.7 × 32.1 × 8.9 feet.
8-cyl. 4 S.C.S.A. (11″ × 17¾″) oil engines manufactured by Humboldt Deutzmotoren A. G., Koeln-Deutz. 94 nhp.
Powered tank barge.

6.1939: Completed by Ferguson Bros. (Port Glasgow) Ltd., Port Glasgow (Yard No. 341), for Union Lighterage Company Ltd., London. 1972: Sold to Rea Ltd., Liverpool, converted from a tanker into a dry cargo barge and renamed PICKEREL. *Due to small size and type of this vessel no further details have been recorded by the authors.*

UL. 4. BP SPIRIT (1939–1972)

O.N. 167206. 440g. 234n. 157.5 × 32.1 × 8.9 feet.
8-cyl. 4 S.C.S.A. (11″ × 17¾″) oil engines manufactured by Humboldt Deutzmotoren A. G., Koeln-Deutz. 94 nhp.
Powered tank barge.

12.1.1939: Launched by L. Smit & Zoon, Kinderdijk (Yard No. 892), for Union

Shell Spirit 1. (World Ship Society Photograph Library)

Shell Spirit 2. (World Ship Society Photograph Library)

Petro. (World Ship Society Photograph Library)

BP Spirit. (World Ship Society Photograph Library)

Lighterage Company Ltd., London. 3.1939: Completed. 1966: Sold to Beagle Shipping Ltd. (Union Lighterage Company Ltd., managers), London. 1970: Sold to Lambert Barge & Hire Company Ltd. 1971: Sold to Spirit Shipping Ltd. (Wharf Holding Ltd., managers), London. 1972: Sold to Bowker & King Ltd., London, and renamed BREEDER. 17.3.1981: Delivered to S. Evans & Sons, Widnes for demolition.

Medway Oil & Storage Company Ltd.
C/O Power Petroleum Company Ltd., 76–88 Strand, London.

founded in 1928
'Associated' with Anglo-Persian Oil Company from 1935.
'Associated' with Shell-Mex & BP Ltd., from 1942.

MED. 1. ENERGIE (1928–1936)

see ship No. SMBP. 25 above.

MED. 2. JORIE (1928–1953)

see ship No. SMBP. 53 above.

MED. 3. LOYALTIE (1928)

O.N. 160686. 83g. 62n. × ? × ? feet.
Post 1949: Unspecified oil engine fitted .
Powered tank barge.

1928: Launched as LOYALTIE by Industrie Maatschappij De Noord, Alblasserdam, for the Medway Oil & Storage Company Ltd., Rochester. 1928: Completed as SEVERN VENTURER for the Severn Canal Carrying Company Ltd., Birmingham. 1949: Purchased by Medway Oil & Storage Company Ltd., Rochester, motorised, and renamed VEROCITIE. 1955: Sold to Hull Waterboat Company Ltd. & Collinson's Waterboat Company, Hull. *Due to small size and type of this vessel no further details have been recorded by the authors.*

MED. 4. TRUSTIE (1929–1949)

O.N. 160697. 24g. 3n. 52.1 × 12.0 × 5.9 feet.
C. 2-cyl. (9″ & 18″ × 12″) engine manufactured by the shipbuilder. 14 hp.
Tug.

1929: Completed by Abdela & Mitchell, Shipbuilders & Engineers, Briscombe, Gloucester (Yard No.1749), for Medway Oil & Storage Company Ltd., Rochester. 1949: Sold to J. E. Fisher. *Due to small size and type of this vessel no further details have been recorded by the authors.*

MED. 5. AUDACITIE (1929–1949)

O.N. 160699. 24g. 3n. 52.1 × 12.0 × 5.9 feet.
C. 2-cyl. (9″ & 18″ × 12″) engine manufactured by the shipbuilder. 14 hp.
Tug.

1929: Completed by Abdela & Mitchell, Shipbuilders & Engineers, Briscombe, Gloucester (Yard No.1750), for Medway Oil & Storage Company Ltd., Rochester. 1949: Sold to J. E. Fisher. *Due to small size and type of this vessel no further details have been recorded by the authors.*

MED. 6. FIDELITIE (1929–1955)

see ship No. SMBP. 60 above.

MED. 7. FEALTIE (1931–1953)

see ship No. SMBP. 54 above.

Fealtie. (World Ship Society Photograph Library)

Audacitie. (World Ship Society Photograph Library)

Energie at Shoreham 1935. (World Ship Society Photograph Library)

Tenacitie. (World Ship Society Photograph Library)

MED. 8. ALACRITIE (1936–1955)

see ship No. SMBP. 62 above.

MED. 9. UNITIE (1936–1955)

see ship No. SMBP. 61 above.

MED. 10. TEMERITIE (1937–1953)

see ship No. SMBP. 55 above.

MED. 11. MOBILITIE (1938–1955)

see ship No. SMBP. 63 above.

MED. 12. TENACITIE (1938–1955)

see ship No. SMBP. 64 above.

MED. 13. VEROCITIE (1949–1955)

see ship No. MED. 3 above.

THRIFTIE was owned by British Tanker Company Ltd but operated by MOSCO Ltd

The Kuwait Oil Company Ltd.
1, Great Cumberland Place, London & Britannic House.

Founded 1946 on a 50:50 basis by
British Petroleum Company Ltd.
Gulf Oil Corporation, U.S.A.

1951: With upheaval in the Gulf region many changes were undertaken:-

Kuwait Oil Company (London) Ltd.,
a non-shipowning arm of the parent was restyled as
D'Arcy Kuwait Company Ltd.
1, Gt. Cumberland Place, London.
Partner–**Gulf Oil Corp**. created a new subsidiary **Gulf Kuwait Company Ltd.**
The two new companies then created a **new KUWAIT OIL COMPANY LTD.,** which acquired the assets of the **old KUWAIT OIL COMPANY LTD.,** which was then wound up.

1955:
D'Arcy Kuwait Company Ltd.,
restyled as
BP Kuwait Company Ltd.

KU. 1. HALVA (1946–1948)

O.N. 181586. 408g. 217n. 179.7 × 38.1 × 6.7 feet.
Two, 12-cyl. 4 S.C.S.A. oil engines manufactured by Davey Paxman & Company (Colchester) Ltd., Colchester.

1942: Completed as LCT 1216 by Stockton Construction Company Ltd., Stockton, for the Admiralty. 1946: Purchased by the Kuwait Oil Company Ltd., and renamed HALVA. 1948: Renamed AFRI. 1951: Sold to Petroleum Development (Qatar) Ltd. (Iraq Petroleum Company Ltd., managers). 1954: Sold to Qatar Petroleum Company Ltd., and entry removed from Lloyd's Register.

KU. 2. KADHAMAH (1946–)

O.N. 180880. 309g. 309n. 160.0 × 25.1 × 7.6 feet.
Dumb tank barge.
16.5.1946: Launched by Clelands (Successors) Ltd., Willington Quay on Tyne (Yard No. 82), for the Kuwait Oil Company Ltd. 6.1946: Completed. *Due to small size and type of this vessel no further details have been recorded by the authors.*

KU. 3. KAWAIKIH (1946–)

O.N. 180881. 309g. 309n. 160.0 × 25.1 × 7.6 feet.
Dumb tank barge.
30.11.1946: Launched by Clelands (Successors) Ltd., Willington Quay on Tyne (Yard No. 83), for the Kuwait Oil Company Ltd. 6.1946: Completed. *Due to small size and type of this vessel no further details have been recorded by the authors.*

KU. 4. ADIB (1947–1952)

see ship No. SMBP. 49 above.

KU. 5. AMIR (1947–1952)

see ship No. SMBP. 39 above.

KU. 6. FRISKY/HASAN (1947–1964)

O.N. 181802. 601g. 3n. 146.7 × 33.2 × 15.2 feet.
T.3-cyl. (17″ 28″ & 46″ × 33″) engine manufactured by C. D. Holmes & Company Ltd., Hull. 222 nhp.
Tug.
27.5.1941: Launched as FRISKY by Cochrane & Sons Ltd., Selby (Yard No.1232), for the Admiralty. 10.1941: Completed. 29.12.1947: Sold to the Kuwait Oil Company Ltd. 1.1948: Renamed HASAN. 5.1960; Laid up with surveys overdue. 1961: Sold to Nicolas E. Vernicos Shipping Company Ltd., Greece, and renamed VERNICOS MARINA. 1972: Demolished.

KU. 7. AMIN (1948–1952)

see ship No. SMBP. 51 above.

KU. 8. ANIS (1948–1954)

O.N. 168779. 861g. 362n. 1,057d. 188.7 × 31.3 × 14.0 feet.
Post 1956: 983g. 466n. 1,057d. 210.4 × 31.3 × 14.0 feet.
T.3-cyl. (15″ 25″ & 42″ × 27″) engine manufactured by Amos & Smith Ltd., Hull. 750ihp.
Coastal oil products tanker.
22.11.1941: Launched as EMPIRE HARP, by Goole Shipbuilding and Repairing Company Ltd., Goole (Yard No.371), for The Ministry of War Transport (Coastal Tanker Ltd., managers), London. 3.1942: Completed. 1946: Owner restyled The Ministry of Transport (The Anglo-Saxon Petroleum Company Ltd., managers). 1946: Coastal Tankers Ltd., London, appointed as managers. 1948: Sold to The Kuwait Oil Company Ltd., London, and renamed ANIS. 1954: Sold to F. T. Everard & Sons Ltd., London, and renamed AUTHENTICITY. 1956: Lengthened.1966: Sold to Margarita Shipping & Trading Corp. (John S.Latsis, manager), Greece, and renamed PETROLA 1. 1969: Sold to Spyros J.Latsis (same manager). 1977: Sold to Maritime & Commercial Company Argonaftis S.A. (same manager), Greece. 1984: Bilinder Marine Corp. S.A., became managers. 9.1984: Halivdeboeiki E.P.E., commenced demolition, at Aspropyrgos, Greece.

KU. 9. HAYAT (1948–1961)

see ship No. AP.24 above.

KU. 10. HAMMAL (1948–1965)

O.N. 181954. 363g. 13n. 120.5 × 31.3 × 13.0 feet.
T.3-cyl. (16½″ 27″ & 46″ × 30″) engine manufactured by Plenty & Son Ltd., Newbury. 1000 ihp.
Tug.

Amin. (World Ship Society Photograph Library)

28.1.1948: Launched by Scott & Sons, Bowling (Yard No. 382), for the Kuwait Oil Company Ltd. 8.1948: Completed. 1965: Sold to Philipp Holzmann A.G., W. Germany, and renamed GEIER. 1968: Sold to Kuwait Maritime Transport Company, Trucial States, and renamed KHALDOON. 21.1.1972: Lloyd's Register classification cancelled. 1976: Sold to Kuwait Coast Line Company W.L.L., and renamed SAHIL-6. Entry removed from Lloyd's Register 2002/03 – 'continued existence in doubt'.

KU. 11. MEGAN (1948–)

O.N. 181529. 55g. 19n. 69.0 × 15.5 × 7.8 feet.
Unspecified type oil engine. 300 bhp.
Tug.
8.1948: Completed by unspecified builders, for the Kuwait Oil Company Ltd. *Due to small size and type of this vessel no further details have been recorded by the authors.*

KU. 12. MADAD (1948–)

O.N. 182910. 54g. 22n. 72.3 × 15.6 × 7.9 feet.
Wooden hull.
1942: Completed, as M.L.1043, by unspecified builders for the Admiralty. 1944: Renamed H.D.M.L.1043. 1948: Sold to the Kuwait Oil Company Ltd., and renamed MADAD. *Due to small size and type of this vessel no further details have been recorded by the authors.*

KU. 13. TARU/HALIF (1948–1960)

O.N. 182871. 209g. 11n. 104.4 × 23.2 × 8.4 feet.
Two, C.2-cyl. (11″ & 22″ × 16″) engines manufactured by Plenty & Son Ltd., Newbury.
Twin screw tug.
1947: Ordered as TARU by Petroleum Steamship Company Ltd., from Scott & Sons, Bowling (Yard No. 385). 6.9.1948: Launched for the Kuwait Oil Company Ltd. 10.1948: Completed as HALIF. 1960: Sold to Abdul Rezzak Mohamed Al-Saleh, Iraq, and renamed RYAD. Still listed in Lloyd's Register 2003/04.

KU. 14. HIDAYAH (1948-1964)

O.N. 182911. 209g. 11n. 104.4 × 23.2 × 8.4 feet.
Two, C.2-cyl. (11″ & 22″ × 16″) engines manufactured by Plenty & Son Ltd., Newbury.
Twin screw tug.
1947: Ordered as TARHAN by Petroleum Steamship Company Ltd., from Scott & Sons, Bowling (Yard No.386). 22.9.1948: Launched as HIDAYAH for the Kuwait Oil Company Ltd. 4.1949: Completed. 1964: Sold to Al-Rasheed Industrial & Contracting Company, Kuwait, and renamed SAMIR. Entry removed from Lloyd's Register 2002/03 – 'continued existence in doubt'.

KU. 15. AFRI (1948–1951)

see ship No. KU. 1 above.

KU. 16. AKHAWI (1948–1954)

O.N. 139134. 1,173g. 576n. 210.1 × 34.8 × 15.6 feet.
T.3-cyl. (16″, 26″ & 43″ × 27″) engine manufactured by the North Eastern Marine Engineering Company Ltd., Newcastle.
Coastal oil products tanker.
7.1916: Completed as DISTOL by W. Dobson & Company, Newcastle, for the Admiralty. 1946: Transferred to the Ministry of Transport. 1948: Sold to the Kuwait Oil Company Ltd., and renamed AKHAWI. 1954: Demolished.

Himma in later years when owned in New Zealand. (World Ship Society Photograph Library)

KU. 17. HIMMA (1949–1950)

O.N. 168788. 274g. 105.2 × 26.6 × 12.2 feet.
T.3-cyl. (15″, 25″ & 42″ × 27″) engine manufactured by Amos & Smith Ltd., Hull.
Tug.
3.5.1942: Launched as EMPIRE PAT by Cochrane & Sons Ltd., Selby (Yard No.1249), for the Ministry of War Transport. 24.8.1942: Completed. 1946: Owners restyled as the Ministry of Transport. 9.10.1946: Chartered to the Anglo-Iranian Oil Company Ltd. 1949: Sold to the Kuwait Oil Company Ltd., and renamed HIMMA. 1950: Sold to J. Fenwick & Company Pty. Ltd., Australia. 1972: Sold to Pimco Shipping Pty. Ltd., New Guinea. 1974: Sold to W. J. Byers, New Guinea. 1977: Scuttled as an artificial fish reef off the coast of New South Wales.

KU. 18. HAIL (1950–1969)

O.N. 183284. 462g. 14n. 126.4 × 33.1 × 13.5 feet.
T.3-cyl. (17″ 28″ & 46″ × 33″) engine manufactured by Plenty & Son Ltd., Newbury.
Tug.
4.4.1950: Launched by Scott & Sons, Bowling (Yard No.391), for the Kuwait Oil Company Ltd. 7.1950: Completed. 1969: Sold to Saeed Al-Rifaie (Al-Rifaie Trading Establishment, Towage & Salvage, managers), Kuwait, and renamed SAEED 1. 1972: Sold to Pent-Ocean Steamships Pvt. Ltd., India, and renamed NANDI. 1980: Demolished.

KU. 19. FORRERIA (1950–1952)

O.N. 181134. 933g. 382n. 193.0 × 34.1 × 14.7 feet.
4-cyl. 2 S.C.S.A. ($13^3/_8$″ × $22^7/_{16}$″) Polar type oil engine manufactured by British Polar Engines Ltd., Glasgow.
Coastal oil products tanker.
18.1.1946: Launched, as EMPIRE TEDLORA, by Short Brothers Ltd., Sunderland (Yard No.490), for The Ministry of War Transport (Anglo-Saxon Petroleum Company Ltd., managers). 5.1946: Completed for the Ministry of Transport. 1.1947: Sold to the Anglo-Saxon Petroleum Company Ltd., and renamed FORRERIA. 1948: Sold to the Sheikh of Kuwait (Kuwait Oil Company Ltd., managers). 12.1950: Transferred to the Kuwait Oil Company Ltd. 3.1951: Sold to Everard Shipping Company Ltd., London, and renamed AUSTILITY. 1.1969: Sold to G.Kalogeratos, Greece, and renamed PIRAEUS IV. 1971: Sold to Naftiliaki E.P.E., Greece, and renamed ASPROPYRGOS. 1983: Converted into a non-propelled barge. No further details located.

KU. 20. FISCHERIA (1950–1951)

O.N. 169460. 891g. 381n. 193.0 × 32.0 × 14.5 feet.
4-cyl. 2 S.C.S.A. ($13^3/_8$″ × $22^7/_{16}$″) Polar type oil engine manufactured by British Polar Engines Ltd., Glasgow.
Coastal oil products tanker.
20.10.1945: Launched, as EMPIRE TEDSHIP, by A. & J. Inglis Ltd., Glasgow (Yard No.1311p), for The Ministry of War Transport (Anglo-Saxon Petroleum Company Ltd., managers). 4.2.1946: Completed. 4.1946: Owners restyled as Ministry of Transport. 1.1947: Sold to the Anglo-Saxon Petroleum Company Ltd., and renamed FISCHERIA. 1948: Sold to the Sheikh of Kuwait (Kuwait Oil Company Ltd., managers). 12.1950: Transferred to the Kuwait Oil Company Ltd. 3.1951: Sold to Everard Shipping Company Ltd., London, and renamed ACUITY. 10.1967: Sold to Bettamar Carriers Ltd., Somalia, and renamed VITTORIOSA. 1969: Sold to 'Campania' di Davide Russo & Cie. S.a.S.,

Fischeria wearing Everard funnel markings. (World Ship Society Photograph Library)

Italy, and renamed NEPTUNIA TERZA. 21.4.1975: S. Ricardi commenced demolition at Vado Ligure, Italy.

KU. 21. HADHAR (1951–1954)

see ship No. PS. 101 in Petroleum SS section.

KU. 22. HAKIM (1951–1954)

see ship No. PS. 102 in Petroleum SS section.

KU. 23. HUDA (1954–1965)

O.N. 169180. 479g. n. 136.0 30.1 × 15.3 feet.
T.3-cyl. ($16^1/_2$", 27" & 46" × 30") engine manufactured by George Clark (1938) Ltd., Sunderland. 1,250 ihp.
Tug.

27.11.1943: Launched as EMPIRE AID by Clelands (Successors) Ltd., Willington Quay on Tyne. (Yard No. 69), for the Ministry of War Transport. (Overseas Towage & Salvage Company Ltd., managers). 17.4.1944: Completed. 4.1946: Owners restyled as Ministry of Transport. 1952: Sold to Overseas Towage & Salvage Company Ltd., and renamed MARINIA. 1954: Sold to the Kuwait Oil Company Ltd., and renamed HUDA. 1965: Sold to Hussain Hassan Deeb, Kuwait. 1967: Reported as having been towed to Basrah, Iraq, minus her boiler, engine, auxiliary deckhouse and funnel and as such was considered by Lloyd's Register to have been dismantled.

KU. 24. HAZIM (1) (1954)

462g. 14n. 135′ 1" × 34′ 6" × 13′ 6" .
T.3-cyl. (17", 28" & 46" × 33") engine manufactured by Plenty & Son Ltd., Newbury. 1,350ihp. 12.5 kts.
Tug.

6.1954: Completed by Scott & Sons, Bowling (Yard No. 401), for the Kuwait Oil Company Ltd. 1954: Transferred to Government of Iraq (Directorate of Ports). 1963: Owners restyled Government of Iraq (Directorate General of Ports and Navigation). 1966: Renamed FURAT. 1975: Owners restyled as Government of Iraq (Iraqi Ports Administration). 1976: Owners restyled as State Organisation of Iraqi Ports. 1978: Owners restyled as Government of Iraq (State Organisation of Iraqi Ports). 1979: Owners restyled as Government of the Republic of Iraq (State Organisation of Iraqi Ports). Still listed in Lloyd's Register 2003/04.

KU. 25. HASHIM (1957)

462g. 14n. 135′ 1" × 34′ 6" × 13′ 6" .
T.3-cyl. (17", 28" & 46" × 33") engine manufactured by Plenty & Son Ltd., Newbury. 1,350ihp. 12.5 kts.
Tug.

10.1957: Completed by Scott & Sons, Bowling (Yard No. 416), for the Kuwait Oil Company Ltd. 1957: Transferred to Government of Iraq (Directorate of Ports). 1963: Owners restyled Government of Iraq (Directorate General of Ports and Navigation). 1966: Renamed DIJLAH. 1975: Owners restyled as Government of Iraq (Iraqi Ports Administration). 1976: Owners restyled as State Organisation of Iraqi Ports. 1978: Owners restyled as Government of Iraq (State Organisation of Iraqi Ports). 1979: Owners restyled as Government of the Republic of Iraq (State Organisation of Iraqi Ports). Entry removed from Lloyd's Register 2000/01 – 'continued existence in doubt'.

KU. 26. HABAB (1959–1974)

O.N. 300884. 387g. 131′ 2" × 32′ 5" × 13′ 6" .
8-cyl. 2 S.C.S.A. ($14^1/_2$" × 19") CGL8 type oil engine manufactured by Crossley Bros.Ltd., Manchester, single reverse reduction geared to screw shaft. 1,500 bhp.
Tug.

9.2.1959: Launched by Clelands (Successors) Ltd., Willington Quay on Tyne (Yard No.234), for the Kuwait Oil Company Ltd. 12.5.1959: Completed. 1974: Transferred to BP Clyde Tanker Company Ltd. 1978: Sold to the Aden Refinery Company, Peoples Democratic Republic of Yemen. Entry removed from Lloyd's Register 2000/01 – 'continued existence in doubt'.

KU. 27. HAMASAH (1959–1974)

O.N. 300927. 387g. 131′ 2" × 32′ 5" × 13′ 6" .
8-cyl. 2 S.C.S.A. ($14^1/_2$" × 19") CGL8 type oil engine manufactured by Crossley Bros.Ltd., Manchester, single reverse reduction geared to screw shaft. 1,500 bhp.
Tug.

26.3.1959: Launched by Clelands (Successors) Ltd., Willington Quay on Tyne (Yard No.235), for the Kuwait Oil Company Ltd. 31.7.1959: Completed. 1974: Transferred to BP Clyde Tanker Company Ltd. 1978: Sold to the Aden Refinery Company, Peoples Democratic Republic of Yemen. Entry removed from Lloyd's Register 2000/01 – 'continued existence in doubt'.

KU. 28. HILAL (1963–1974)

O.N. 304501. 393g. 122n. 132′ 0" × 33′ 1" × 13′ $11^1/_2$" .
8-cyl. 2 S.C.S.A. ($14^1/_2$" × 19") CGL8 type oil engine manufactured by Crossley Bros.Ltd., Manchester, single reverse reduction geared to screw shaft. 1,500 bhp.
Tug.

14.12.1962: Launched by Scott & Sons (Bowling) Ltd., Bowling (Yard No. 428), for the Kuwait Oil Company Ltd. 4.1963: Completed. 1974: All interests held by BP were transferred to the Kuwait Government and vessel transferred to Kuwait Registry. 1989: Sold to Bulk Traders International, and renamed TAREK under Lebanon flag. Owners deleted from Lloyd's Register 2002/03.
Still listed without owners in Lloyd's Register 2003/04.

KU. 29. HADI (1964–1974)

O.N. 306006. 411g. 122n. 132′ 0" × 33′ 1" × 13′ $11^1/_2$" .
8-cyl. 2 S.C.S.A. ($14^1/_2$" × 19") CGL8 type oil engine manufactured by Crossley Bros.Ltd., Manchester, single reverse reduction geared to screw shaft. 1,500bhp.
Tug.

17.3.1964: Launched by Scott & Sons (Bowling) Ltd., Bowling (Yard No.430), for the Kuwait Oil Company Ltd. 6.1964: Completed. 1974: All interests held by BP were transferred to the Kuwait Government and vessel transferred to Kuwait Registry. 2.1989: Laid-up with surveys overdue. 1990: Sold to Blue Gulf Trading Company W.L.L., Kuwait. 1992: Sold to Al Modather General Trading LLC, and renamed DUBAI under Tonga flag, then DUBAI I.

KU. 30. HAZIM (2) (1968–1974)

O.N. 336908. 334g. 195n. 133′ 5" × 33′ 1" × 12′ $4^3/_4$" .
9-cyl. 4 S.C.S.A. ($12^1/_2$" × $14^1/_2$") 9ATCM type oil engine manufactured by Ruston & Hornsby, Lincoln, reverse reduction geared to screw shaft. 2,260 bhp.
Tug.

30.4.1968: Launched by Charles D. Holmes & Company Ltd., Beverley (Yard No. 1011), for the Kuwait Oil Company Ltd. 2.10.1968: Completed. 1974: All interests held by BP were transferred to the Kuwait Government and vessel transferred to Kuwait Registry. 1975: Renamed HASSAN. 1984: Sold to Whitesea Shipping & Supply Company, United Arab Emirates. 1991: Sold to Abdul Saheb Mohammed Al Ali, Iran, and renamed GOL. 1996: Sold to unspecified buyers and renamed SS-1. Still listed, without owners or nationality in Lloyd's Register 2003/04.

KU. 31. HUMAM (1968–1974)

O.N. 336956. 334g. 195n. 133′ 5" × 33′ 1" × 12′ $4^3/_4$" .
9-cyl. 4 S.C.S.A. ($12^1/_2$" × $14^1/_2$") 9ATCM type oil engine manufactured by Ruston & Hornsby, Lincoln, reverse reduction geared to screw shaft. 2,260bhp.
Tug.

14.6.1968: Launched by Charles D.Holmes & Company Ltd., Beverley (Yard No. 1012), for the Kuwait Oil Company Ltd. 13.11.1968: Completed. 1974: All interests held by BP were transferred to the Kuwait Government and vessel to Kuwait registry. 1975: Vessel transferred to the Government Of The State of Kuwait (Shuwaikh Port Authority), 9.11.1984: Lloyd's Register class withdrawn – reported defects. 1985: Sold to Whitesea Shipping & Supply Company, United Arab Emirates. 1988: Demolished.

In the latter part of 1974 60 per cent of the interests held in the Kuwait Oil Company Ltd., by BP /Gulf were taken over by the Kuwait Government and the other 40 per cent in 1975, the company title continued under Kuwaiti control subsequently re-styling as Kuwait Oil Company KSC.

Oddities:-

LCM 2 ex LCM 152 4.10.1948: Sank at moorings at Fahaheel. Later raised and beached CTL.

Anglo-Bahamian Petroleum Company Ltd.

1946: Formed.
1948: All vessels disposed of. (Not all names located).

ABP. 1. BAHAMAS EXPLORER (1946–1948)

O.N. 180930. 502g. 204n. 153.0 × 23.5 × 7.5 feet.
Unspecified type oil engine. 101bhp.
Survey vessel, former landing craft.

1943: Completed as Q.492 by unspecified builder at Quincy, Massachussets, for the U. S. Navy. 1946: Purchased, converted and renamed BAHAMAS EXPLORER. 1948: Sold to Middle East Pipelines Ltd., and renamed LEVANT EXPLORER. 1950: Sold to Abdul Rakim Makkawi Bey, Egypt. *Due to small size and type of this vessel no further details have been recorded by the authors.*

ABP. 2. BLACKBIRD (1947–1948)

see ship No. BT. 196 in main fleet section.

ABP. 3. BAHAMAS CROTON (1947–1948)

O.N. 178614. 44g. 29n. 72.0 × 15.5 × 6.3 feet.
Unspecified type oil engine. 290bhp.
Wooden hulled.

1943: Built as HDML 1232 in the UK (Yard No.), for unspecified owners. 1947: Purchased. 1948: Sold. *Due to small size and type of this vessel no further details have been recorded by the authors.*

ABP. 4. AMARYLLIS (1947–1948)

O.N. 176994. 48g. 33n. 64.9 × 16.5 × 6.7 feet.
Unspecified type oil engine. 230bhp.
Wooden hulled.

Unspecified construction and previous ownerships. 1947: Purchased. 1948: Sold to Paradise Beach & Transportation Company Ltd., Nassau. *Due to small size and type of this vessel no further details have been recorded by the authors.*

Border Keep. (World Ship Society Photograph Library)

The Lowland Tanker Company Ltd.

c1949: Planned.
14 April 1951 : Founded, jointly by British Tanker Company Ltd; (50 per cent) Matheson & Company Ltd., Hong Kong (25 per cent)
Common Bros. Ltd.(25 per cent)

1976: BP Company Ltd., took over management of fleet.
1979: BP Company Ltd., purchased the 50 per cent held jointly by Common Bros. Ltd., and Matheson & Company Ltd., making it a wholly owned subsidiary.

Border Lass. (World Ship Society Photograph Library)

LT. 1. BORDER REGIMENT (1953–1969)

O.N. 169243. 11,311g. 6,400n. 525.5 × 69.8 × 37.5 feet.
6-cyl. 2 S.C.S.A. (26³/₈″ × 91⁵/₁₆″) Doxford type oil engine manufactured by the shipbuilder.
Ocean-going oil products tanker.

4.11.1952: Launched by Scotts' Shipbuilding & Engineering Company Ltd., Greenock (Yard No. 660), for the Lowland Tanker Company Ltd. (Common Bros. Ltd., managers), Newcastle. 24.3.1953: Completed. 4.3.1969: Sold to Fortuity Cia. Nav. S. A. (Southern Shipping & Finance Company Ltd., London, managers), Liberia, and renamed FORTUITY. 20.2.1975: Korea Iron & Steel Company, S. Korea commenced demolition at Masan. 15.4.1975: Work completed.

LT. 2. BORDER KEEP (1953–1970)

O.N. 169253. 11,321g. 6,408n. 525.0 × 69.8 × 37.5 feet.
6-cyl. 2 S.C.S.A. (26³/₈″ × 91⁵/₁₆″) Doxford type oil engine manufactured by D. Rowan & Company Ltd., Glasgow.
Ocean-going oil products tanker.

12.8.1953: Launched by Blythswood Shipbuilding Company Ltd., Glasgow (Yard No. 105), for the Lowland Tanker Company Ltd. (Common Bros. Ltd., managers), Newcastle. 19.11.1953: Completed. 2.2.1970: Arrived at Kaohsiung for demolition. 4.2.1970: Delivered to Yung Tai Steel & Iron Works Ltd.

LT. 3. BORDER LASS (1954–1970)

O.N. 169255. 11,344g. 6,328n. 525.5 × 69.7 × 37.5 feet.
6-cyl. 2 S.C.S.A. (26³/₈″ × 91⁵/₁₆″) oil engine manufactured by the shipbuilder.
Ocean-going oil products tanker.

8.12.1953: Launched by Wm. Doxford & Sons Ltd., Sunderland (Yard No. 800), for the Lowland Tanker Company Ltd. (Common Bros. Ltd., managers), Newcastle. 7.4.1954: Completed. 24.4.1970: Sold to Eretria Development Corp. S. A. (N. & J. Vlassopulos Ltd., London, managers), Greece, and renamed MIKRASIATIS. 1974: Renamed JUANITA H. 29.8.1974: Arrived at Split for demolition by Brodospas. 3.1975: Work commenced.

Border Regiment. (World Ship Society Photograph Library)

LT. 4. BORDER HUNTER (1954–1970)

O.N. 169256. 11,301g. 6,247n. 525.5 × 69.8 × 37.5 feet.
6-cyl. 2 S.C.S.A. (26³/₈″ × 91⁵/₁₆″) Doxford type oil engine manufactured by the shipbuilder.
Ocean-going oil products tanker.

22.12.1953: Launched by Scotts' Shipbuilding & Engineering Company Ltd., Greenock (Yard No. 661), for the Lowland Tanker Company Ltd. (Common Bros. Ltd., managers), Newcastle. 21.4.1954: Completed. 6.4.1970: Sold to Nereide Shipping Corporation (Southern Shipping & Finance Company Ltd., London, managers), Liberia, and renamed NEREIDE. 11.4.1975: Arrived at Bilbao for demolition by Alfonso Garcia. 5.1975: Work commenced.

LT. 5. BORDER FUSILIER (1954–1970)

O.N. 169258. 11,330g. 6,335n. 525.5 × 69.8 × 37.5 feet.
6-cyl. 2 S.C.S.A. (26³/₈″ × 91⁵/₁₆″) Doxford type oil engine manufactured by the shipbuilder.
Ocean-going oil products tanker.

19.1.1954: Launched by R. & W. Hawthorn, Leslie & Company Ltd., Hebburn (Yard No. 717), for the Lowland Tanker Company Ltd. (Common Bros. Ltd., managers), Newcastle. 11.6.1954: Completed. 136.4.1970: Sold to Nemeo Shipping Corporation (Southern Shipping & Finance Company Ltd., London,

Border Hunter. (World Ship Society Photograph Library)

Border Fusilier. (World Ship Society Photograph Library)

Border Minstrel at Cape Town. (World Ship Society Photograph Library)

Border Reiver. (World Ship Society Photograph Library)

managers), Liberia, and renamed NEMEO. 12.7.1975: Arrived at Gadani Beach for demolition by Dada Steel Mill. 8.1975: Work commenced.

LT. 6. BORDER MINSTREL (1954–1972)

O.N. 186837. 11,339g. 6,289n. 525.5 × 69.8 × 37.5 feet.
6-cyl. 2 S.C.S.A. ($26^{3}/_{8}''$ × $91^{5}/_{16}''$) Doxford type oil engine manufactured by D. Rowan & Company Ltd., Glasgow.
Ocean-going oil products tanker.

31.8.1954: Launched by Blythswood Shipbuilding Company Ltd., Glasgow (Yard No. 108), for the Lowland Tanker Company Ltd. (Common Bros. Ltd., managers), Newcastle. 15.12.1954: Completed. 1970: Common Bros. (Management) Ltd., appointed as managers. 1.5.1972: Arrived at Bilbao for demolition. 3.5.1972: Delivered to Revalorizacion de Materiales S. A. (REMASA). 6.1972: Work commenced.

LT. 7. BORDER REIVER (1955–1971)

O.N. 186846. 11,356g. 6,331n. 525.5 × 69.8 × 37.5 feet.
6-cyl. 2 S.C.S.A. ($26^{3}/_{8}''$ × $91^{5}/_{16}''$) oil engine manufactured by Wm. Doxford & Sons Ltd., Sunderland.
Ocean-going oil products tanker.

20.5.1955: Launched by Sir James Laing & Sons.Ltd., Sunderland (Yard No. 805), for the Lowland Tanker Company Ltd. (Common Bros. Ltd., managers), Newcastle. 30.10.1955: Completed. 1970: Common Bros. (Management) Ltd., appointed as managers. 14.12.1971: Sold to Nicea Shipping Corporation (Southern Shipping & Finance Company Ltd., London, managers), Liberia, and renamed NICEA. 1976: Sold to Desguaces Aviles, Spain for demolition. 20.4.1976: Work commenced at San Esteban de Pravia. 14.8.1976: Work completed.

LT. 8. BORDER SENTINEL (1955–1970)

O.N. 186849. 11,335g. 6,334n. 525.5 × 69.8 × 37.5 feet.
6-cyl. 2 S.C.S.A. ($26^{3}/_{8}''$ × $91^{5}/_{16}''$) Doxford type oil engine manufactured by the shipbuilder.
Ocean-going oil products tanker.

19.7.1955: Launched by Swan, Hunter & Wigham, Richardson Ltd., Newcastle (Yard No. 1904), for the Lowland Tanker Company Ltd. (Common Bros. Ltd., managers), Newcastle. 4.11.1955: Completed. 23.3.1970: Sold to Nettuno Shipping Corporation (Southern Shipping & Finance Company Ltd., London, managers), Liberia, and renamed NETTUNO. 4.2.1976: Arrived at Gadani Beach for demolition.

LT. 9. BORDER LAIRD (1955–1972)

O.N. 186848. 11,366g. 6,289n. 525.5 × 69.8 × 37.5 feet.
6-cyl. 2 S.C.S.A. ($26^{3}/_{8}''$ × $91^{5}/_{16}''$) Doxford type oil engine manufactured by the Fairfield Shipbuilding & Engineering Company Ltd., Glasgow.
Ocean-going oil products tanker.

1.7.1955: Launched (delayed from 27.6.1955), by Lithgows Ltd., Port Glasgow (Yard No. 1111), for the Lowland Tanker Company Ltd. (Common Bros. Ltd., managers), Newcastle. 17.11.1955: Completed. 1970: Common Bros. (Management) Ltd., appointed as managers. 27.6.1972: Departed from Singapore Roads. 5.7.1972: Arrived at Kaohsiung for demolition. 1.9.1972: Yung Tai Steel and Iron Works commenced work.

LT. 10. BORDER TERRIER (1956–1972)

O.N. 186856. 11,347g. 6,323n. 525.5 × 69.8 × 37.5 feet.
6-cyl. 2 S.C.S.A. ($26^{3}/_{8}''$ × $91^{5}/_{16}''$) Doxford type oil engine manufactured by R. & W. Hawthorn, Leslie & Company Ltd., Newcastle.
Ocean-going oil products tanker.

29.12.1955: Launched by J. L. Thompson & Sons Ltd., Sunderland (Yard No. 685), for the Lowland Tanker Company Ltd. (Common Bros. Ltd., managers), Newcastle. 26.4.1956:

Border Sentinel. (J K Byass)

Border Laird. (World Ship Society Photograph Library)

Border Terrier. (World Ship Society Photograph Library)

Border Shepherd. (J K Byass)

Border Falcon. (World Ship Society Photograph Library)

Completed. 1970: Common Bros. (Management) Ltd., appointed as managers. 27.9.1972: Departed from Hong Kong for demolition at Whampoa. 7.10.1972: Handed over to China National Machinery Import & Export Corp.

LT. 11. BORDER SHEPHERD (1960–1979)

see ship No. BT. 430 in main fleet.

LT. 12. BORDER FALCON (1961–1979)

see ship No. BT. 428 in main fleet.

LT. 13. BORDER CASTLE (1961–1979)

see ship No. BT. 427 in main fleet.

LT. 14. BORDER PELE (1961–1979)

see ship No. BT. 429 in main list.

LT. 15. BORDER CHIEFTAIN (1962–1979)

see ship No. BT. 431 in main fleet.

Shell-D'Arcy Petroleum Development Company of Nigeria Ltd.

Founded 1953;
Restyled 1960 as:-

Shell-BP Petroleum Development Company of Nigeria Ltd.

SDN. 1. ALBERT HUMPHRIES (1953–)

O.N. 196678. 278g. 193n. 100′ 0″ × 30′ 8″ × 4′ 6″.
Two, 6-cyl. 4 S.C.S.A. (115 × 125mm) oil engines manufactured by General Motors Corp., Detroit, geared to twin screws.
Beach landing craft.

1953: Completed by Werf I. S. Figee N. V., Vlaardingen, Netherlands, for Shell D'Arcy Petroleum Development Company of Nigeria Ltd. 1960: Owners restyled as Shell-BP Petroleum Development Company of Nigeria Ltd. *Due to small size and type of this vessel no further details have been recorded by the authors.*

SDN. 2. DB 1 (1957–)

O.N. 315474. 1,431g. 1,168n. 1,460d.
158′ 11″ × 80′ 10″ × 7′ 0 1/2″.
Drilling barge.

9.1957: Completed by N. V. Werf Gusto, Slikkerveer, Netherlands (Yard No. 132) for Shell D'Arcy Petroleum Development Company of Nigeria Ltd. 1960: Owners restyled as Shell-BP Petroleum Development Company of Nigeria Ltd. *Due to small size and type of this vessel no further details have been recorded by the authors.*

SDN. 3. DB 2 (1959–)

O.N. 315475. 1,431g. 1,172n. 1,460d.
158′ 11″ × 80′ 10″ × 7′ 0 3/4″.
Drilling barge.

1.1959: Completed by N. V. Werf Gusto, Slikkerveer, Netherlands (Yard No. 154) for Shell D'Arcy Petroleum Development Company of Nigeria Ltd. 1960: Owners restyled as Shell-BP Petroleum Development Company of Nigeria Ltd. *Due to small size and type of this vessel no further details have been recorded by the authors.*

Border Castle. (World Ship Society Photograph Library)

Border Pele. (J K Byass)

Border Cheiftain. (J K Byass)

SDN. 4. SB 1 (1959–)

O.N. 315476. 436g. 353n. 114′ 6″ × 55′ 9″ × ?.
Drilling platform.
2.1959: Completed by Bouw and Montagebedrijf, Zwijndrecht, Netherlands for Shell D'Arcy Petroleum Development Company of Nigeria Ltd. 1960: Owners restyled as Shell-BP Petroleum Development Company of Nigeria Ltd. *Due to small size and type of this vessel no further details have been recorded by the authors.*

SDN. 5. EKOLE CREEK (1959–)

O.N. 300987. 158g. 11n. 102′ 0″ × 28′ 9″ × 9′ $9\frac{1}{2}$″.
Two, 8-cyl. 2 S.C.S.A. (7″ × 9″) oil engines manufactured by Crossley Bros. Ltd., Manchester, geared to twin screw shafts.
Tug for river service.
9.1959: Completed by P. K. Harris & Sons Ltd., Appledore (Yard No. 121), for Shell D'Arcy Petroleum Development Company of Nigeria Ltd. 1960: Owners restyled as Shell-BP Petroleum Development Company of Nigeria Ltd. *Due to small size and type of this vessel no further details have been recorded by the authors.*

SDN. 6. ELELE CREEK (1959–)

O.N. 315507. 106g. 5n. 82′ 9″ × 20′ 7″ × 7′ $6\frac{3}{4}$″.
Two, 6-cyl. 2 S.C.S.A. (7″ × 9″) oil engines manufactured by Crossley Bros. Ltd., Manchester, geared to twin screw shafts.
Tug for river service.
1.1959: Completed by Richard Dunston Ltd., Thorne (Yard No. T998), for Shell D'Arcy Petroleum Development Company of Nigeria Ltd. 1960: Owners restyled as Shell-BP Petroleum Development Company of Nigeria Ltd. *Due to small size and type of this vessel no further details have been recorded by the authors.*

SDN. 6A. NANA LAGOON (1959–)

270g. unspecified type vessel.
24.12.1958: Launched by Clelands (Successors) Ltd., Willington Quay on Tyne (Yard No. 236), for Shell D'Arcy Petroleum Development Company of Nigeria Ltd. 10.2.1959: Completed. 1960: Owners restyled as Shell-BP Petroleum Development Company of Nigeria Ltd. *Due to small size and type of this vessel no further details have been recorded by the authors.*

SDN. 7. NZAM CREEK (1960–)

O.N. 301140. 184g. 31n. 105′ 5″ × 23′ 2″ × 4′ 8″.
Two, 12-cyl. 4 S.C.S.A. (7″ × $7\frac{3}{4}$″) oil engines manufactured by Davey, Paxman & Company Ltd., Colchester, geared to twin screw shafts.
Tug for river service.
2.1960: Completed by Yarrow & Company Ltd., Glasgow (Yard No. 2187), for Shell D'Arcy Petroleum Development Company of Nigeria Ltd. 1960: Owners restyled as Shell-BP Petroleum Development Company of Nigeria Ltd. *Due to small size and type of this vessel no further details have been recorded by the authors.*

SDN. 8. OSIMIRI I (1960–)

O.N. 301019. 419g. 434n. 138′ 5″ × 34′ 10″ × 8′ $3\frac{3}{4}$″.
Two, 8-cyl. 2 S.C.S.A.(7″ × 9″) oil engines manufactured by Crossley Bros.Ltd., Manchester, geared to twin screw shafts.
Supply ship.
3.1960: Completed by Clelands Shipbuilding Company Ltd., Wallsend (Yard No. 242), for Shell D'Arcy Petroleum Development Company of Nigeria Ltd. 1960: Owners restyled as Shell-BP Petroleum Development Company of Nigeria Ltd. *Due to small size and type of this vessel no further details have been recorded by the authors.*

SDN. 9. NNOM RIVER (1960–)

O.N. 301150. 447g. 123n. 152′ 2″ × 35′ 1″ × 6′ $9\frac{1}{2}$″.
Two, 8-cyl. 2 S.C.S.A. (7″ × 9″) oil engines manufactured by Crossley Bros.Ltd., Manchester, geared to twin screw shafts.
Beach Landing Craft.
7.1960: Completed by Bouw & Montagebedrijf, Zwijndrecht, Netherlands, for Shell D'Arcy Petroleum Development Company of Nigeria Ltd. 1960: Owners restyled as Shell-BP Petroleum Development Company of Nigeria Ltd. *Due to small size and type of this vessel no further details have been recorded by the authors.*

D'Arcy–Shell Petroleum Company of Tangyanika Ltd.

Founded 1955:
1956 restyled as
BP–Shell Petroleum Company of Tangyanika Ltd.

DS. 1. WRANGLER (1955–1957)

see ship No. AP. 42 in A. P. O. C. section.

Abu Dhabi Marine Areas Ltd.
London
1955: Founded.

ABU. 1. ADMA I (1955–)

O.N. 187393. 1,169g. 585n. 225′ 0″ × 38′ 0″ × ?
Four, 12-cyl. 4 S.C.S.A. (7″ × 7 3/4″) oil engines manufactured by Davey, Paxman & Company Ltd., Colchester, geared in pairs to twin screw shafts.

1945: Completed as LCT 4148 by Warrenpoint Shipyards Ltd., Warrenpoint, for the Admiralty. 1955: Sold to Abu Dhabi Marine Areas Ltd. and renamed ADMA 1. 5.6.1956: Sailed from Avonmouth bound to Bahrain. 4.8.1956: Arrived. Subsequently sold to Zaid Bin Sultan, Trucial States. *Due to small size and type of this vessel no further details have been recorded by the authors.*

ABU. 2. BURGAN (1956–1957)

see ship No. BT. 274 in main fleet.

ABU. 3. ADMA ENTERPRISE (1957–)

3,005g. 2,961n. 223′ 0″ × 106′ 0″ × ?
Drilling rig.

1957: Completed by Gutehoffnungshutte Sterkrade A. G., Dusseldorf, for Abu Dhabi Marine Areas Ltd. *Due to small size and type of this vessel no further details have been recorded by the authors.*

ABU. 4. BADIYA (1957–)

O.N. 187605. 79g. 76n. 100d. 80′ 0″ × 18′ 8″ × ?
Dumb tank barge.

6.1957: Completed by J. W. Cook & Company (Wivenhoe) Ltd., Wivenhoe, for Abu Dhabi Marine Areas Ltd. Still registered in 1975. *Due to small size and type of this vessel no further details have been recorded by the authors.*

ABU. 5. BATEEN (1957–)

O.N. 187607. 79g. 76n. 100d. 80′ 0″ × 18′ 8″ × ?
Dumb tank barge.

7.1957: Completed by J. W. Cook & Company (Wivenhoe) Ltd., Wivenhoe, for Abu Dhabi Marine Areas Ltd. Still registered in 1975. *Due to small size and type of this vessel no further details have been recorded by the authors.*

ABU. 6. BARRADA (1957–)

O.N. 187606. 81g. 75n. 100d. 75′ 0″ × 18′ 8″ × ?
Barge.

8.1957: Completed by J. W. Cook & Company (Wivenhoe) Ltd., Wivenhoe, for Abu Dhabi Marine Areas Ltd. Still registered in 1975. *Due to small size and type of this vessel no further details have been recorded by the authors.*

ABU. 7. BURAIMI (1957–)

O.N. 187626. 84g. 80n. 121d. 81′ 9″ × 18′ 2″ × 6′ 4 3/4″.
Barge.

8.1957: Completed by Clelands (Successors) Ltd., Wallsend (Yard No. 227), for Abu Dhabi Marine Areas Ltd. Still registered in 1975. *Due to small size and type of this vessel no further details have been recorded by the authors.*

ABU. 8. BAZAM (1957–)

O.N. 187628. 84g. 80n. 121d. 81′ 9″ × 18′ 2″ × 6′ 4 3/4″.
Barge.

8.1957: Completed by Clelands (Successors) Ltd., Wallsend (Yard No. 228), for Abu Dhabi Marine Areas Ltd. Still registered in 1975. *Due to small size and type of this vessel no further details have been recorded by the authors.*

ABU. 9. BASHUBAR (1957–)

O.N. 187627. 84g. 80n. 121d. 81′ 9″ × 18′ 2″ × 6′ 4 3/4″.
Barge.

8.1957: Completed by Clelands (Successors) Ltd., Wallsend (Yard No. 229), for Abu Dhabi Marine Areas Ltd. Still registered in 1975. *Due to small size and type of this vessel no further details have been recorded by the authors.*

ABU. 10. KARIMAH (1958–)

see ship No. EX.2 in BP Exploration section.

ABU. 11. AZIZAH (1958–)

see ship No. EX.4 in BP Exploration section.

ABU. 12. SARIFAH (1958–)

see ship No. EX.5 in BP Exploration section.

ABU. 13. MUTHMIRAH (1960–1977)

O.N. 301185. 677g. 247n. 822d. 180′ 3″ × 35′ 5″ × 10′ 6″.
8-cyl. 4 S.C.S.A. (8 3/4″ × 11 1/2″) Blackstone ERS8M type oil engine manufactured by Lister, Blackstone Marine Ltd., Dursley. 660 bhp. 9 kts.
Tanker/production testing vessel

5.1960: Launched by Clelands Shipbuilding Company Ltd., Wallsend (Yard No. 244), for Abu Dhabi Marine Areas Ltd. 7.1960: Completed. 1977: Sold to Abu Dhabi National Oil Company & Abu Dhabi Marine Areas Ltd., and registered at Abu Dhabi. 1980: Sold to Unimar Company, Egypt, later restyled as United Navigation & Marine Service Company (UNIMAR), Egypt. 1988: Sold to International Investment & Navigation Company, and renamed ENJI 1. 1990: Sold to Demetrios & Panteleimon Theodosiou & Polyxemi Georgadji, Greece, converted into a pure tanker, and renamed INJI 1. Still listed in Lloyd's Register 2003/04.

ABU. 14. ARIDHAH (1960–)

O.N. 301222. 98g. 97n. 169d. 81′ 5″ × 26′ 5″ × 4′ 6″.
Drilling Pontoon.

8.1960: Completed by Clelands Shipbuilding Company Ltd., Wallsend (Yard No. 252), for Abu Dhabi Marine Areas Ltd. *Due to small size and type of this vessel no further details have been recorded by the authors.*

ABU. 15. ADMA CONSTRUCTOR (1961–)

2,845g. 2,845n. 221′ 1″ × 90′ 1″ × ?
Drilling rig.

1961: Completed by Swan, Hunter & Wigham, Richardson Ltd., Wallsend (Yard No. ?), for Abu Dhabi Marine Areas Ltd. *Due to the type of this vessel no further details have been recorded by the authors.*

ABU. 16. ARZANAH (1961–1977)

O.N. 302889. 359g. 47n. 131′ 11″ × 33′ 1″ × 12′ 6 3/4″.
8-cyl. 2 S.C.S.A. (14 1/2″ × 19″) oil engine manufactured by Crossley Bros. Ltd., Manchester. 1,500 bhp.
Tug.

11.1961: Completed by Ferguson Bros (Port Glasgow) Ltd., Port Glasgow (Yard No. 433), for Abu Dhabi Marine Areas Ltd. 19.11.1961: Sailed from Greenock. 2.2.1962: Arrived at Ras Tanura. 1977: Sold to Abu Dhabi Marine Operating Company (ADMA-OPCO), Ocean Inchcape Ltd. (OIL Ltd), appointed as managers). 1984: Sold to Adil Trading Establishment, Abu Dhabi. 1987: Sold to Juma Obaid Mubarak (Mubarak Shipping Company, managers, Dubai. 1988: Sold to Fal Bunkering Company Ltd., Saudi Arabia. 1989: Renamed VOYAGER, and sold for demolition.

ABU. 17. DALMAH (1962–1977)

O.N. 302889. 371g. 47n. 131′ 5″ × 33′ 1″ × 13′ 5″.
8-cyl. 2 S.C.S.A. (14 1/2″ × 19″) oi! engine manufactured by Crossley Bros. Ltd., Manchester. 1,500 bhp.
Tug.

2.1962: Completed by Scott & Sons (Bowling) Ltd., Bowling (Yard No. 427), for Abu Dhabi Marine Areas Ltd. 1977: Sold to Abu Dhabi Marine Operating Company (ADMA-OPCO), Ocean Inchcape Ltd. (OIL Ltd) appointed as managers). 1984: Sold to Adil Trading Establishment, Abu Dhabi. 1986: Renamed SAAD 2. 1987: Sold for demolition.

ABU. 18. RASHIDAH (1962 – 1975)

O.N. 304346. 351g. 105 n. ? d. 126′ 0″ × 33′ 1″ × 9′ 6 1/2″.
Two, 6-cyl. 4 S.C.S.A. (7″ × 7 3/4″) oil engines manufactured by Davey, Paxman & Company Ltd., Colchester. 674 bhp.
Buoy ship.

9.1962: Completed by J. Bolson & Son Ltd., Poole (Yard No. 540), for Abu Dhabi Marine Areas Ltd. 1975: Sold to The Scrap Company, retaining London registry. *Due to small size and type of this vessel no further details have been recorded by the authors.*

ABU. 19. HAMILAH (1962–1977)

O.N. 304386. 222g. 217n. 279d. 111′ 5″ × 37′ 5″ × ?
Pontoon.

11.1962: Completed by Clelands Shipbuilding Company Ltd., Wallsend (Yard No. 263), for Abu Dhabi Marine Areas Ltd. 1977: Sold to

Dalmah. (Courtesy of Alan Hughes)

Rashidah. (World Ship Society Photograph Library)

Abu Dhabi Marine Operating Company (ADMA-OPCO). 1987: Sold to Abu Dhabi Petroleum Operating Co. (ADPPOC). *Due to small size and type of this vessel no further details have been recorded by the authors.*

ABU. 20. SIYANAH (1963–1976)

O.N. 304613. 216g. 59 n. ? d. 98′ 10″ × 24′ 7″ × 8′ 3¼″.
Two, 4-cyl. 4 S.C.S.A. (7″ × 7¾″) vee type oil engines manufactured by Davey, Paxman & Company Ltd., Colchester. 396 bhp.
Buoy ship.

7.1963: Completed by J. Bolson & Son Ltd., Poole (Yard No. 542), for Abu Dhabi Marine Areas Ltd. 1975: Sold to Al-Zaabi Transport & General Contracting Company, Saudi Arabia. *Due to small size and type of this vessel no further details have been recorded by the authors.*

ABU. 21. ZAAEDAH (1966–)

O.N. 309693. 352g. 316n. 406d. 35.49 × 11.10 × ? metres.
Barge.

8.1966: Completed by Appledore Shipbuilders Ltd., Appledore (Yard No. AS21), for Abu Dhabi Marine Areas Ltd. *Due to small size and type of this vessel no further details have been recorded by the authors.*

ABU. 22. AL GAFFAY (1968–1977)

O.N. 334750. 368g. 47n. 133′ 5″ × 33′ 2″ × 13′ 5″.
9-cyl. 4 S.C.S.A. (318 × 368mm) 9ATC type oil engine manufactured by Ruston & Hornsby Ltd., Lincoln. 2,459bhp. 11.5 kts.
Tug.

2.1968: Completed by Charles D. Holmes & Company Ltd., Beverley (Yard No. 1007), for Abu Dhabi Marine Areas Ltd. 1977: Sold to Abu Dhabi Marine Operating Company (ADMA-OPCO). 1986: Sold to Almighty Shipping Corporation, Abu Dhabi, and renamed HADI, under Panamanian flag. 1990: Sold to Almighty Shipping Company Ltd., under St Vincent and The Grenadines flag (Almighty Shipping Corp., Abu Dhabi, managers). 1992: Sold to Iran Marine Services Company (Al Ramah Marine Services, managers), and renamed PORKAR. 1999: Sold to unspecified buyers and renamed BLUE BIRD. Still listed, without owners, in Lloyd's Register 2003/04.

Abu Dhabi Marine Operating Company Ltd. (ADMA-OPCO)

1977:
Abu Dhabi National Oil Company & BP group

ADOP.1. HAMILAH (1977–1987)

see ship No. ABU. 19 above.

ADOP.2. AL GAFFAY (1977–1986)

see ship No. ABU. 22 above.

ADOP.3. ARZANAH (1977–1984)

see ship No. ABU. 16 above.

ADOP.4. DALMAH (1977–1984)

see ship No. ABU. 17 above.

ADOP.5. AL-ZABBOUT (1978–1987)

777g. 0n. 558d. 48.01 × 12.17 × 5.106 metres.
Two 12-cyl. 4 S.C.S.A. (280 × 320mm) Niigata 12V28BX type oil engines manufactured by Niigata Engine Company Ltd., Ota, geared to controllable-pitch propellers. 12.5 kts. Thwartship thrust propeller forward.
Fire-fighting, salvage tug.

1977: Hull completed by Kanrei Zosen K. K., Tokoshima (Yard No. 251), as subcontract for Mitsui Ocean Development & Engineering Co. Ltd., Japan. 1.1978: Completed (Yard No. S-123), for Abu Dhabi Marine Operating Company (ADMA-OPCO), United Arab Emirates. 1987: Sold to Abu Dhabi Petroleum Operating Co. (ADPPOC). Still listed in Lloyd's Register 2003/04.

ADOP.6. AL-HYLEH (1981–)

6,590 tons displacement.
62 × 33.01 × 7.01 metres transit draught.
Self-elevating maintenance platform.

3.1981: Completed by Hitachi Zosen, Osaka Works, Sakai (Yard No. K1022), for Abu Dhabi Marine Operating Company (ADMA-OPCO), United Arab Emirates. *Due to the type of this vessel no further details have been recorded by the authors.*

Australasian Petroleum Company Pty. Ltd.

52, Pitt Street, Sydney.
founded 1947.
1955: Associated with BP and Vacuum Oil Corp.

AUS. 1. PAPUAN EXPLORER (1955–1960)

O.N. 196126. 507g. 300n. 190.3 × 30.5 × 8.6 feet.
6-cyl. 2 S.C.S.A. (14½″ × 19″) oil engine manufactured by Crossley Brothers Ltd., Manchester. 114 bhp.

1952: Completed, as HANNE SVEN, by N.V. Scheepswerf 'Gideon' v/h/ J. Koster, Hoogezand, for Rederi AS af 1944 (P. B. P. Svendsen, manager), Copenhagen. 1955: Purchased and renamed PAPUAN EXPLORER. 1960: Sold to A. H. Basse, Denmark. *Due to small size and type of this vessel no further details have been recorded by the authors.*

AUS. 2. KIBULI (1955–)

O.N. 174117. 50g. 40n. 51.2 × 16.0 × 4.2 feet.
Unspecified oil engine. 150 bhp.

1945: Built at Sydney NSW for unspecified owners. *Due to small size and type of this vessel no further details have been recorded by the authors.*

AUS. 3. KIBENE (1955–)

O.N. 179925. 40g. 33n. 52.8 × 16.1 × 4.1 feet.
Unspecified oil engine. 150 bhp.

1945: Built at Sydney NSW for unspecified owners. *Due to small size and type of this vessel no further details have been recorded by the authors.*

AUS. 4. DAVARA (1955–1959)

O.N. 174175. 145g. 81n. 95′ 0″ × 21′ 11″ × 7′ 6″ .
6-cyl. 4 S.C.S.A. (230 × 305mm) oil engine manufactured by National Supply Company, New York.
Wood.

1947: Completed by Lars Halvorsen Sons Pty. Ltd., Ryde N, for the company. 1959: Sold to Kimberley, King Island Trading Pty. Ltd. *Due to small size and type of this vessel no further details have been recorded by the authors.*

AUS. 5. DAREGA (1955–1959)

O.N. 179913. 204g. 120n. 123′ 6″ × 24′ 0″ × 7′ 5″ .
Unspecified oil engine.
Post 1959: Two, 8-cyl. 4 S.C.S.A. (5½″ × 7¾″) oil engines manufactured in 1955 by L. Gardner & Sons Ltd., Manchester. (From sunken GEBOSO q.v.)

1945: Completed by Tullochs Pty. Ltd., for unspecified owners. 1949: Acquired. 1959: Sold to R. H. Houfe & Company, and re-engined. *Due to small size and type of this vessel no further details have been recorded by the authors.*

AUS. 6. DOBIRI (1955–1958)

O.N. 196125. 135g. 66n. 82.7 × 22.0 × 6.9 feet.
8-cyl. 4 S.C.S.A. (140 × 195mm) oil engine manufactured by L. Gardner & Sons Ltd., Manchester.
Wood hull.

1941: Completed by E. Mercer, Noumea, for unspecified owners. 1955: Acquired. 1958: Sold to H. Williams. *Due to small size and type of this vessel no further details have been recorded by the authors.*

AUS. 7. POTRERO (1955–1956)

**O.N. 155932. 78g. 46n. 64.0 × 18.0 × 6.5 feet.
Unspecified type oil engine. 144bhp.
Wooden.**

1938: Completed for Island Export Company Pty. Ltd., Papua. 1947: Acquired. 17.1.1956: Grounded at Vari Vari Island near Port Moresby. *Due to small size and type of this vessel no further details have been recorded by the authors.*

AUS. 8. GOGO (1955–1957)

**40g. ? n. ? × ? × ? feet.
Two, 8-cyl. 4 S.C.S.A. (5¹/₂″ × 7³/₄″) oil engines manufactured by L.Gardner & Sons Ltd., Manchester.
Beach landing craft.**

1954: Completed by Clelands (Successors) Ltd., Wallsend (Yard No. 206), for the Company. 6.8.1957: Broke moorings on the Kikori River, Papua, and sank. *Due to small size and type of this vessel no further details have been recorded by the authors.*

AUS. 9. GIMADA (1955–1960)

**O.N. 196130. 210g. 63n. 110′ 0″ × 26′ 8″ × 4′ 11¹/₂″.
Two, 8-cyl. 4 S.C.S.A. (5¹/₂″ × 7³/₄″) oil engines manufactured by L.Gardner & Sons Ltd., Manchester.
Beach Landing craft.**

25.5.1955: Launched by Clelands (Successors) Ltd., Wallsend (Yard No. 207), for the company. 18.8.1955: Departed Tyne bound in tow to Port Moresby. 19.11.1955: Arrived. 1960: Sold to Pacific Island Timbers Ltd. *Due to small size and type of this vessel no further details have been recorded by the authors.*

AUS. 10. GEBOSO (1955–1956)

**O.N. 196129. 210g. 63n. 110′ 0″ × 26′ 8″ × 4′ 11¹/₂″.
Two, 8-cyl. 4 S.C.S.A. (5¹/₂″ × 7³/₄″) oil engines manufactured by L. Gardner & Sons Ltd., Manchester.
Beach Landing Craft.**

6.1955: Launched by Clelands (Successors) Ltd., Wallsend (Yard No. 209), for the company. 18.8.1955: Departed Tyne bound in tow to Port Moresby. 19.11.1955: Arrived. 2.4.1956: Capsized 8.10S., 140.53E., and sank. Engines transferred to DAREGA q.v.

AUS. 11. GURUBI (1956–)

**O.N. 196133. 210g. 63n. 110′ 0″ × 26′ 8″ × 4′ 11¹/₂″.
Two, 8-cyl. 4 S.C.S.A. (5¹/₂″ × 7³/₄″) oil engines manufactured by L. Gardner & Sons Ltd., Manchester.
Beach landing craft.**

11.1955: Launched by Clelands (Successors) Ltd., Wallsend (Yard No. 213), for the company. 23.2.1956: Departed Tyne bound in tow to Port Moresby. *Due to small size and type of this vessel no further details have been recorded by the authors.*

AUS. 12. G'AGOMA (1957–)

**O.N. 196137. 210g. 63n. 110′ 0″ × 26′ 8″ × 4′ 11¹/₂″.
Two, 8-cyl. 4 S.C.S.A. (5¹/₂″ × 7³/₄″) oil engines manufactured by L. Gardner & Sons Ltd., Manchester.
Beach landing craft.**

1957: Completed by Clelands (Successors) Ltd., Wallsend (Yard No. 230), for the company. *Due to small size and type of this vessel no further details have been recorded by the authors.*

AUS. 13. GOWERA (1957)

**O.N. 187676. 210g. 63n. 110′ 0″ × 26′ 8″ × 4′ 11¹/₂″.
Two, 8-cyl. 4 S.C.S.A. (5¹/₂″ × 7³/₄″) oil engines manufactured by L. Gardner & Sons Ltd., Manchester.
Beach landing craft.**

6.1957: Launched by Clelands (Successors) Ltd., Wallsend (Yard No. 231), for the company. 1957: Completed and transferred to BP Exploration Company Ltd. Towed from Tyne to Zanzibar. *Due to small size and type of this vessel no further details have been recorded by the authors.*

The Tanker Charter Company Ltd.

TC. 1. BRITISH INDUSTRY (3) (1957–1972)

see ship No. BT. 399 in main fleet.

TC. 2. BRITISH RENOWN (2) (1957–1970)

see ship No. BT. 293 in main fleet.

TC. 3. BRITISH VIGILANCE (2) (1957–1973)

see ship No. BT. 294 in main fleet.

TC. 4. BRITISH GLORY (2) (1957–1973)

see ship No. BT. 295 in main fleet.

TC. 5. BRITISH VALOUR (2) (1957–1973)

see ship No. BT. 296 in main fleet.

TC. 6. BRITISH TRADER (2) (1957–1973)

see ship No. BT. 297 in main fleet.

TC. 7. BRITISH COURAGE (2) (1957–1973)

see ship No. BT. 298 in main fleet.

TC. 8. BRITISH JUSTICE (2) (1958–1972)

see ship No. BT. 311 in main fleet.

TC. 9. BRITISH HONOUR (2) (1958–1973)

see ship No. BT. 312 in main fleet.

TC. 10. BRITISH FAITH (2) (1958–1972)

see ship No. BT. 406 in main fleet.

TC. 11. BRITISH ARCHITECT (2) (1958–1972)

see ship No. BT. 313 in main fleet.

TC. 12. BRITISH ENERGY (2) (1958–1972)

see ship No. BT. 314 in main fleet.

TC. 13. BRITISH AVIATOR (2) (1958–1972)

see ship No. BT. 315 in main fleet.

TC. 14. BRITISH DUCHESS (2) (1958–1972)

see ship No. BT. 316 in main fleet.

TC. 15. BRITISH STATESMAN (2) (1959–1972)

see ship No. BT. 321 in main fleet.

TC. 16. BRITISH JUDGE (2) (1959–1972)

see ship No. BT. 322 in main fleet.

TC. 17. BRITISH QUEEN (1959–1972)

see ship No. BT. 330 in main fleet.

TC. 18. BRITISH CONFIDENCE (2) (1965–1972)

**O.N. 307875. 38,119g. 24,090n. 67,944d.
815′ 8″ × 108′ 3″ × 42′ 4″.
Two, steam turbines manufactured by the shipbuilder, double reduction geared to screw shaft. 18,000 shp.
Ocean-going tanker.**

17.2.1965: Launched by J. Brown & Company (Clydebank) Ltd., Clydebank (Yard No. 716), for the BP Tanker Company Ltd. 8.1965: Completed for the Tanker Charter Company Ltd. 1972: Transferred to the BP Tanker Company Ltd. 22.12.1975: Laid up at Singapore Roads. 21.2.1976: Sold to Kanematsu-Goshi (Belgium) S. A., for demolition. 24.2.1976: Departed from Singapore. 1.3.1976: Arrived at Kaohsiung. Resold and 9.4.1976: Nan Yung Steel & Iron Company Ltd., commenced work.

TC. 19. BRITISH CAPTAIN (3) (1966–1967) & (1972–1976)

see ship No. BT. 382 in main fleet.

TC. 20. BRITISH CENTAUR (1966–1967) & (1972–1983)

see ship No. BT. 381 in main fleet.

TC. 21. BRITISH COMMODORE (2) (1975–1982)

see ship No. BT. 380 in main fleet.

Nordic Tankships A/S

Denmark.

Founded by A/S Det Ostasiatiske Kompagni.(EAC) to take over the contracts from, and operate the ships on guaranteed contract to the BP Tanker Company Ltd.

NT. 1. NORDIC HAWK (1959–1970)

**22,622g. 12,374n. 37,252d. 683′ 0″ × 86′ 5″ × 37′ 11¹/₂″.
Two, steam turbines manufactured by the shipbuilder, double reduction geared to screw shaft. 15,500 shp.
Ocean-going oil products tanker.**

3.1956: Ordered by BP Tanker Company Ltd., from Fairfield Shipbuilding & Engineering Company Ltd., Glasgow (Yard No. 783). 30.6.1958: Launched for Nordic Tankships I/S (A/S Det Ostasiatiske Kompagni, managers), Denmark. 13.1.1959: Completed. 1970: Sold to Thiressia Nav.Ltd., Liberia, and renamed THIRESSIA VENIZELOS. 1.2.1975: Laid up at Piraeus. 28.1.1977: Departed under tow from Piraeus. 24.4.1977: Arrived at Kaohsiung for demolition by Shyeh Sheng Huat Steel & Iron Works Company Ltd.

NT. 2. NORDIC HERON (1959–1970)

**22,638g. 12,459n. 37,356d. 683′ 4″ × 86′ 5″ × 37′ 11¹/₂″.
Two, steam turbines manufactured by the Parsons Marine Steam Turbine Company, Wallsend, double reduction geared to screw shaft. 15,500 shp.
Ocean-going oil products tanker.**

3.1956: Ordered by BP Tanker Company Ltd., from J. L. Thompson & Sons Ltd., Sunderland (Yard No. 692). 9.12.1958: Launched for

Nordic Hawk. (World Ship Society Photograph Library)

Nordic Heron. (World Ship Society Photograph Library)

Nordic Tankships I/S (A/S Det Ostasiatiske Kompagni, managers), Denmark. 17.4.1959: Completed. 1970: Sold to Hariclia Nav. Ltd., Liberia, and renamed HARICLIA VENIZELOS. 15.10.1974: Laid up at Piraeus. 29.1.1977: Departed under tow from Piraeus. 26.4.1977: Arrived at Kaohsiung for demolition by Shyeh Sheng Huat Steel & Iron Works Company Ltd. 14.7.1977: Work commenced.

The Clyde Charter Company Ltd.

CC. 1. BRITISH TRUST (3) (1959–1972)

see ship No. BT. 325 in main fleet.

CC. 2. BRITISH SWIFT (1) (1959–1972)

see ship No. BT. 326 in main fleet.

CC. 3. BRITISH GANNET (1) (1959–1972)

see ship No. BT. 328 in main fleet.

CC. 4. BRITISH FULMAR (1959–1972)

see ship No. BT. 412 in main fleet.

CC. 5. BRITISH POWER (2) (1959–1972)

see ship No. BT. 327 in main fleet.

CC. 6. BRITISH DESTINY (2) (1959–1972)

see ship No. BT. 329 in main fleet.

CC. 7. BRITISH BEACON (2) (1960–1972)

see ship No. BT. 323 in main fleet.

CC. 8. BRITISH CURLEW (1) (1960–1972)

see ship No. BT. 336 in main fleet.

CC. 9. BRITISH MALLARD (1) (1960–1972)

see ship No. BT. 335 in main fleet.

CC. 10. BRITISH GULL (1960–1972)

see ship No. BT. 334 in main fleet.

CC. 11. BRITISH ROBIN (1) (1960–1972)

see ship No. BT. 332 in main fleet.

CC. 12. BRITISH KIWI (1960–1972)

see ship No. BT. 331 in main fleet.

CC. 13. BRITISH SCIENTIST (2) (1971–1976)

see ship No. MT. 5 in BP Medway Tkr.

Warwick Tanker Company Ltd.

Founded by Houlder Bros. & Company Ltd., to take over the contracts from, and operate the ships on guaranteed contract to the BP Tanker Company Ltd.

WT. 1. BRANDON PRIORY (1960–1975)

O.N. 301101. 22,735g. 12,582n. 35,703d. 683′ 0″ × 86′ 5″ × 37′ 8½″.
Two, steam turbines manufactured by Hawthorn, Leslie (Engineering) Ltd., Newcastle, double reduction geared to screw shaft. 15,500 shp.
Ocean-going oil products tanker.

5.10.1959: Launched by Hawthorn, Leslie (Shipbuilders) Ltd., Newcastle (Yard No. 741), for Warwick Tanker Company Ltd. (Houlder Bros & Company Ltd., managers), London. 5.1960: Completed. 9.6.1975: Arrived at Castellon for demolition.

WT. 2. BIDFORD PRIORY (1960–1975)

O.N. 301242. 22,748g. 12,596n. 37,148d. 683′ 2″ × 86′ 5″ × 38′ 11½″.
Two, steam turbines manufactured by the shipbuilder, double reduction geared to screw shaft. 15,500 shp.
Ocean-going oil products tanker.

27.4.1960: Launched by Cammell, Laird

Brandon Priory. (World Ship Society Photograph Library)

Brandon Priory. (World Ship Society Photograph Library)

Northwest Shearwater. at Zeebrugge (World Ship Society Photograph Library)

(Shipbuilders and Engineers) Ltd., Birkenhead (Yard No. 1280), for Warwick Tanker Company Ltd. (Houlder Bros & Company Ltd., managers), London. 10.1960: Completed. 29.10.1975: Arrived at Faslane for demolition by Shipbreaking Industries Ltd.

International Gas Transportation Company Ltd. (I.G.T.C.)
Bermuda.
1986: Formed by:-
Chevron LNG Company Ltd.
BHP Petroleum (LNG Ships) Pty. Ltd.
BP Australia Ltd.
Shell Development(Australia)Pty. Ltd.
Woodside Mid-Eastern Oil Ltd.
Woodside Petroleum Development Pty. Ltd.
Japan–Australia LNG (MIMI) Pty. Ltd.
(participants of the last named company, above:-
Kawasaki Kisen Kaisha Ltd; Nippon Yusen Kaisha;
Mitsui O.S.K.Lines Ltd; Navix Line Ltd., & Showa Line Ltd.)

IGT. 1. NORTHWEST SWALLOW (1989–)

O.N. 128756. 106,717g. 32,015n. 62,510d. 272.00(BB) × 47.24 × 10.951 metres.
Two, steam turbines manufactured by Mitsubishi Heavy Industries Ltd., Nagasaki, double reduction geared to a single screw shaft. 23,301 shp.
Liquified Gas Tanker.

4.12.1987: Keel laid by Mitsui Engineering & Shipbuilding Company Ltd., Chiba Works, Ichihara (Yard No. 1351), for Kawasaki Kisen Kaisha Ltd., Nippon Yusen Kaisha, Mitsui O.S.K.Lines Ltd., Navix Line Ltd., & Showa Line Ltd., Japan registry. 4.10.1988: Launched. 30.11.1989: Completed. Still listed in Lloyd's Register 2003/04.

IGT. 2. NORTHWEST SWIFT (1989–)

O.N. 131162. 107,146g. 32,143n. 67,024d. 272.00(BB) × 47.28 × 11.400 metres.
Two, steam turbines manufactured by the shipbuilder, double reduction geared to a single screw shaft. 23,302 shp. Thwartship thrust controllable-pitch propeller forward.
Liquified Gas Tanker.

14.4.1988: Keel laid by Mitsubishi Heavy Industries Ltd., Nagasaki (Yard No. 2000), for Kawasaki Kisen Kaisha Ltd., Nippon Yusen Kaisha, Mitsui O.S.K. Lines Ltd., Navix Line Ltd., & Showa Line Ltd., Japan registry. 8.10.1988: Launched. 1.9.1989: Completed. Still listed in Lloyd's Register 2003/04.

IGT. 3. NORTHWEST SANDERLING (1989–)

O.N. 853416. 105,010g. 31,503n. 66,6810. 272.00(BB) × 47.28 × 11.395 metres.
Two, steam turbines manufactured by the shipbuilder, double reduction geared to a single screw shaft. 23,302 shp.
Liquified Gas Tanker.

26.12.1987: Keel laid by Mitsubishi Heavy Industries Ltd., Nagasaki (Yard No. 1996), for I.G.T.C. (Australian LNG Ship Operating Company Pty. Ltd. (ALSOC), managers), Australian registry. 29.4.1988: Launched. 30.6.1989: Completed. Still listed in Lloyd's Register 2003/04.

IGT. 4. NORTHWEST SNIPE (1990–)

O.N. 853794. 105,010g. 31,503n. 66,695d. 272.00(BB) × 47.28 × 11.375 metres.
Two, steam turbines manufactured by Mitsubishi Heavy Industries Ltd., Nagasaki, double reduction geared to a single screw shaft. 23,302 shp.
Liquified Gas Tanker.

28.10.1988: Keel laid by Mitsui Engineering & Shipbuilding Company Ltd., Chiba Works, Ichihara (Yard No.1352), for I.G.T.C. (Australian LNG Ship Operating Company Pty. Ltd. (ALSOC), managers), Australia registry. 23.6.1989: Launched. 28.9.1990: Completed. Still listed in Lloyd's Register 2003/04.

IGT. 5. NORTHWEST SHEARWATER (1991–)

O.N. 716311. 106,283g. 31,884n. 66,802d. 272.00(BB) × 47.28 × 11.374 metres.
Two, steam turbines manufactured by Mitsubishi Heavy Industries Ltd., Nagasaki, double reduction geared to a single screw shaft. 23,302 shp.
Liquified Gas Tanker.

30.11.1989: Keel laid by Kawasaki Heavy Industries Ltd., Sakaide (Yard No. 1410), for I.G.T.C. (BP Shipping Ltd., managers), Bermuda. 1999: Managers restyled as BP Amoco Shipping Ltd. 2001: Managers restyled as BP Shipping Ltd. 14.12.1990: Launched. 24.9.1991: Completed. Still listed in Lloyd's Register 2003/04.

IGT. 6. NORTHWEST SEAEAGLE (1992–)

O.N. 716332. 106,283g. 31,884n. 62,510d. 272.00(BB) × 47.28 × 11.370 metres.
Two, steam turbines manufactured by the shipbuilder, double reduction geared to a single screw shaft. 23,302 shp.
Liquified Gas Tanker.

12.10.1991: Keel laid by Mitsubishi Heavy Industries Ltd., Nagasaki (Yard No. 2043), for I.G.T.C. (Shell Tankers (U.K.) Ltd., managers), Bermuda. 29.2.1992: Launched. 30.11.1992: Completed. Still listed in Lloyd's Register 2003/04.

IGT. 7. NORTHWEST SANDPIPER (1993–)

O.N. 853795. 105,010g. 31,503n. 66,768d. 272.00(BB) × 47.28 × 11.374 metres.
Two, steam turbines manufactured by Mitsubishi Heavy Industries Ltd., Nagasaki, double eduction geared to a single screw shaft. 23,302 shp.
Liquified Gas Tanker.

8.11.1990: Keel laid by Mitsui Engineering & Shipbuilding Company Ltd., Chiba Works, Ichihara (Yard No.1370), for I.G.T.C. (Australian LNG Ship Operating Company Pty. Ltd. (ALSOC), managers), Australia registry. 10.4.1992: Launched. 26.2.1993: Completed. Still listed in Lloyd's Register 2003/04.

BP Exploration Operating Company Ltd., & Others.
Britoil Plc
Shell U.K. Ltd.
Amerada Hess Ltd.
Statoil U. K. Ltd.
Murphy Petroleum Ltd.
OMV (U.K.) Ltd.

Exp. 1. SCHIEHALLION (1998–)

85,000g. 42,000n. 152,630d. 244.81 × ? × 20.030 metres.
Unspecified type diesel-electric propulsion units.
Processing tanker/storage vessel for offshore installations.

5.6.1996: Keel laid by Harland & Wolff Shipbuilding & Heavy Industries Ltd., Belfast (Yard No. 1737), for BP Exploration Operating Company Ltd., Britoil Plc., Shell U.K. Ltd., Amerada Hess Ltd., Statoil U. K. Ltd., Murphy Petroleum Ltd., OMV (U.K.) Ltd. (BP Exploration Operating Company Ltd., managers), London. 10.1.1997: Launched. 22.1.1998: Completed.

Petra Tugs.
Douglas, Isle Of Man
(Associated with Trinity Finance)

9316397

STANFORD (2005–)

381g. 115n. 260d. 32.5 × ? × 5.0 metres.
Two, 6-cyl. 4 S.C.S.A. (? × ? mm) MaK 6M25 type oil engines manufactured by Caterpillar Motoren GmbH & Company KG, Kiel, geared to twin stern-mounted azimuthing propeller units. 3,960 bhp.

2004: Ordered from B. V. Scheepswerf Damen Gorinchem (Yard No. 511210) by Petra Tugs, Douglas Isle of Man. 24.5.2004: Keel laid. 31.1.2005: Launched, and Targe Towing Ltd., Montrose, appointed as managers.

9316402

CASTLE POINT (2005–)

381g. 115n. 260d. 32.5 × ? × 5.0 metres.
Two, 6-cyl. 4 S.C.S.A. (? × ? mm) MaK 6M25 type oil engines manufactured by Caterpillar Motoren GmbH & Company KG, Kiel, geared to twin stern-mounted azimuthing propeller units. 3,960 bhp.

2004: Ordered from Damen Gorinchem (Yard No. 511211) by Petra Tugs, Douglas Isle of Man. 24.3.2004: Keel laid. 24.10.2004: Launched. 1.2005: Targe Towing Ltd., Montrose, appointed as managers.

Schiehallion. (Internet source)

9316414

CORRINGHAM (2005–)

381g. 115n. 260d. 32.5 × ? × 5.0 metres.
Two, 6-cyl. 4 S.C.S.A. (? × ? mm) MaK 6M25 type oil engines manufactured by Caterpillar Motoren GmbH & Company KG, Kiel, geared to twin stern-mounted azimuthing propeller units. 3,960 bhp.

2004: Ordered from Damen Gorinchem (Yard No. 511212) by Petra Tugs, Douglas Isle of Man. 3.8.2004: Keel laid. 1.2005: Targe Towing Ltd., appointed as managers.

Stanford. (Internet source)

Bibliography

PART ONE

Beck, G E, *Navigation Systems* (1971).
Bes, J, *Tanker Shipping* (1963).
Corkhill, M, *The Tonnage Measurement of Ships* (1980).
Dewar, Commander M D, *Collisions at Sea – How?* (1989).
Dunn, L, *The World's Tankers* (1956).
Ffookes, R, *Natural Gas by Sea* (1979: 1993).
Gavin, A G, *Double-Hulled Tankers* (1995).
Hogg, R S, *Naval Architecture and Ship Construction,* (1948: 1959).
Hysing, T, and Torset, O, *Reduction of Oil Outflow at Collisions and Groundings* (1993).
International Maritime Organisation (IMO), *Crude Oil Washing Systems* (1981).
IMO, *MARPOL 73/78 Consolidated Edition* (1992).
ISGOTT Manual (1996)
King, Commodore G A B, *Tanker Practice* (1956; 1965).
Lavery, Captain H I, *Shipboard Operations* (1984: 1990).
Magelssen, D, *Double-Hull – A Political Reality – For and Against* (1993).
Murray, J M, *A New Approach to Longitudinal Strength* (1961/2).
Solly, Dr R J, *Supertankers: Anatomy and Operation* (2001).
Tanker Structure Co-Operative Forum, *Guidance Manual for Tanker Structures* (1992).

Various Editions of the following Magazines:

Fairplay; *Lloyd's List*; *The Motor Ship*; *Seafarer*; *Seatrade*; *Shipping*; *Shipping and Transport*; *Syren and Shipping*; *Shipping World and Shipbuilder*; *Tanker Operator*; *Tanker Times*; *Tanker and Bulk Carrier.*

PART TWO

Colledge, J, *Ships Of The Royal Navy Vol. 1 & 2* (1987, 1989 respectively).
Harvey, W J, *Cory Towage – A Group Fleet History* (2000).
__________, *Hadley – History of the Warwick & Esplen Group of Companies* (1997).
__________, and Telford, P J, *Clyde Shipping Company 1815 – 2000* (2002).
Lingwood, J, *The Trades Increase – The History of Common Brothers* (1993).
Nicholson, T, *Taking The Strain – The History of the Alexandra Towing Company* (1990).
Sawyer, L A, and Mitchell, W H, *The Empire Ships* (2nd Edition, 1990).
__________________________, *Standard Ships of World War One* (1968).
__________________________, *Victory Ships & Tankers* (1974).
Thomas, P N, *British Steam Tugs* (1983).
World Ship Society, *Marine News – Monthly Journal.*
World Ship Society, *War Loss Records.*
Yergin, Daniel, *The Prize* (Date unknown).

Sources of Reference

Board of Trade – Mercantile Navy Lists.
Lloyd's Register Of Shipping – Register books for the relevant period.
Lloyd's Register Of Shipping – Casualty Returns.
Lloyd's Register Of Shipping – List Of Shipowners.
Lloyd's Register Of Shipping – Register of International Shipowning Groups.
Lloyd's Register Of Shipping – Shipbuilding Records.
Lloyd's Register Of Shipping – Wreck Books.
Lloyd's Register Of Shipping – Yacht Registers.
Lloyd's of London Collection – Guildhall Library, London.
Lloyd's of London – Confidential Indices.
Lloyd's of London – Shipping Indices.

Index

Part I
General Index

Part I
Ship Index

Part II
Ship Index

Names in UPPER-CASE were those carried during BP Group involvement. Lower-case and those marked with an asterisk were carried before or afterward.